Environmental Law

ASPEN CASEBOOK SERIES

Environmental Law
A Conceptual and Pragmatic Approach
Third Edition

David M. Driesen
University Professor
Syracuse University College of Law

Robert W. Adler
Jefferson B. and Rita E. Fordham Dean and
University Distinguished Professor of Law
University of Utah, S.J. Quinney College of Law

Kirsten H. Engel
Charles E. Ares Professor of Law
University of Arizona

Wolters Kluwer

Published by Wolters Kluwer in New York.

Wolters Kluwer Legal & Regulatory Solutions U.S. serves customers worldwide with CCH, Aspen Publishers, and Kluwer Law International products. (www.WKLegaledu.com)

To contact Customer Service, e-mail customer.service@wolterskluwer.com, call 1-800-234-1660, fax 1-800-901-9075, or mail correspondence to:

Wolters Kluwer
Attn: Order Department
PO Box 990
Frederick, MD 21705

Printed in the United States of America.

2 3 4 5 6 7 8 9 0

ISBN 978-1-4548-7001-2

Library of Congress Cataloging-in-Publication Data

Names: Driesen, David M., author. | Adler, Robert W., 1955- author. | Engel, Kirsten, author.
Title: Environmental law : a conceptual and pragmatic approach / David M. Driesen, University Professor, Syracuse University College of Law; Robert W. Adler, Jefferson B. and Rita E. Fordham Dean and University Distinguished Professor of Law, University of Utah, S.J. Quinney College of Law; Kirsten H. Engel, Charles E. Ares Professor of Law University of Arizona.
Description: Third edition. | New York : Wolters Kluwer, 2016.
Identifiers: LCCN 2015043384 | ISBN 9781454870012
Subjects: LCSH: Environmental law—United States. | Environmental protection—United States. | Liability for environmental damages—United States. | LCGFT: Casebooks.
Classification: LCC KF3775 .D75 2016 | DDC 344.7304/6—dc23
LC record available at http://lccn.loc.gov/2015043384

About Wolters Kluwer Legal & Regulatory Solutions U.S.

Wolters Kluwer Legal & Regulatory Solutions U.S. delivers expert content and solutions in the areas of law, corporate compliance, health compliance, reimbursement, and legal education. Its practical solutions help customers successfully navigate the demands of a changing environment to drive their daily activities, enhance decision quality and inspire confident outcomes.

Serving customers worldwide, its legal and regulatory solutions portfolio includes products under the Aspen Publishers, CCH Incorporated, Kluwer Law International, ftwilliam.com and MediRegs names. They are regarded as exceptional and trusted resources for general legal and practice-specific knowledge, compliance and risk management, dynamic workflow solutions, and expert commentary.

To our parents, George and Sue Driesen, the late David and Juanita Adler, and John Ronald and Joan Gibb Engel

Summary of Contents

Contents

3 *From Common Law to Administrative Law* 59

PART III
Allocation of Responsibility   407

PART IV
Compliance and Enforcement

14   Detecting Violations: Permitting, Monitoring, Record Keeping, and Reporting

15   Government Enforcement

Preface

This third edition teaches the principal concepts that underlie environmental law. The book's structure reflects this emphasis, as it offers chapters on key concepts, such as technology-based standard setting, economic incentives, and citizen enforcement. This approach takes advantage of some of the commonalities that bind environmental law together in order to provide a coherent introduction to environmental law.

While we weave detailed information about particular environmental statutes into the text and summarize statutory schemes where needed to put cases in context, we single out for special emphasis details that help illustrate key concepts. This approach recognizes that it is not possible to teach all of environmental law, or even all of one of the more comprehensive statutes, in a single introductory environmental law course. This means that textbooks must reflect some selection principle or risk presenting environmental law as an incoherent mass of meaningless detail. We have employed a principle of choosing the materials that best illustrate the concepts most central to environmental policy and practice.

We also employ problems to give students practice in applying the law illustrating key concepts to concrete facts. The problems focus on climate disruption—perhaps the defining environmental issue of our time—and its many environmental ramifications and potential legal and policy responses. By using this example in many different chapters, we help students see how many statutes and concepts can often address a single problem. Also, by using a common problem throughout the book, we hope to increase the depth of students' understanding and free them to devote most of their energy to learning the law.

No environmental law course can hope to teach practitioners all of the law they might need to know. But such a course can orient students, so that they know important aspects of the law and are well prepared to deeply understand new material, even material that is not part of the law today. We hope this book provides a coherent introduction to this complex field.

January 2016

David M. Driesen
Robert W. Adler
Kirsten H. Engel

Acknowledgments

The authors want to express their great appreciation to Aspen's Richard Mixter, who supported this book from the time it was a mere possibility, and Eric Holt, our editor. We benefitted from thoughtful comments from Douglas Kysar, Amy Sinden, Amy Wildermuth, and anonymous reviewers of the text.

David Driesen would also like to thank George Aposporos for getting his book writing off to a great start by providing wonderful companionship and a great setting to get underway. Syracuse University colleague Robin Malloy helped him see the potential scholarly value of a textbook. He's grateful to former Syracuse University College of Law (SUCOL) Dean Hannah Arterian for a research leave and other crucial support for the book. SUCOL and University of Michigan library staffs provided wonderful help in assembling materials, and Wendy Scott and Josh Gillette helped out with copyright permissions. He also thanks Meredith Lee-Clarke, Daniel Salstein, Sarah Treptow, Amy Gilbert, and Gabriela Girona for research assistance and Christy Ramsdell for editorial assistance with respect to the second and third editions. Finally, his students have made many helpful suggestions over the years.

Bob Adler also wants to thank Sandra Fatt and Laura Skousen for editorial and other assistance, and Kirsten Uchitel, Mason Baker and Megan Osswald for research assistance. The students in his Fall 2005 Environmental Law class served as guinea pigs by studying from the first draft of the first edition of the book, and his Fall 2010 class from the second edition. Several of those students provided useful comments about everything from typos to improvements to questions and problems to case selection. The staff of the S.J. Quinney Law Library at the University of Utah provided their usual high level of service, and the College of Law's IT staff helped to solve a number of technical problems.

Kirsten Engel would like to thank the Law College Association of the University of Arizona for financial assistance during the summer of 2010 during which she made her contributions to the Second Edition of the book and also during the summer of 2015 during which she worked on the third edition. Finally, she wishes to thank her co-authors, who have made working on this edition such an enlightening and collegial experience.

The authors would like to acknowledge the permission of the authors, publishers, and copyright holders of the following publications for permission to reproduce excerpts herein:

Bruce A. Ackerman & Richard B. Stewart, Comment: Reforming Environmental Law, Stanford Law Review, 37, 1334-47 Copyright © 1986 by Stanford Law Review. Reproduced with permission of Stanford Law Review in the format, Textbook via Copyright Clearance Center.

From *Restoring Colorado River Ecosystems* by Robert W. Adler. Copyright © 2007 Robert W. Adler. Reproduced by permission of Island Press, Washington, D.C.

Garrett Hardin, The Tragedy of the Commons, Science December 13, 1968. Copyright © 1968. Reprinted with permission from AAAS.

James A. Harris, Richard J. Hobbs, Eric Higgs & James Aronson, Ecological Restoration and Global Climate Change, 14 Restoration Ecology 170, 171-73 (2006). Reprinted by permission of John Wiley & Sons.

Krier, James E., The Irrational National Air Quality Standards: Macro- and Micro-Mistakes, 22 UCLA Law Review 323-26. Copyright © 1974-1975. Reprinted by permission.

Richard J. Lazarus, Restoring What's Environmental about Environmental Law in the Supreme Court, UCLA Law Review 47, 703. Copyright © 2000. Reprinted by permission.

Arnold W. Reitze, Jr., Air Quality Protection Using State Implementation Plans: Thirty-Seven Years of Increasing Complexity, Villanova Law Review 15, 209. Copyright © 2004. Reprinted by permission.

From *Environmental Law Reporter Update* by Byron Swift. Copyright © 2001 by Environmental Law Institute. Reproduced with permission of Environmental Law Institute in the formats Text and Other Book via Copyright Clearance Center.

Environmental Law

Introduction

This book offers a conceptual and pragmatic approach to environmental law. It reflects a conviction that a set of core concepts lies behind the mass of details found in environmental statutes, cases, and regulations, and that learning these concepts prepares students to master and make sense of the details they will encounter in practice. Mastery of these concepts also prepares students, including students who will not practice environmental law, to participate in the formulation of environmental policy as citizens. Accordingly, this book employs a conceptual organization, with sections of the book devoted to studying criteria for setting standards, the means of meeting environmental goals, the distribution of authority and responsibility among actors, and the means of enforcing standards. We hope that this conceptual organization will make it easier for you to grasp the meaning of the materials that you study, rather than to think of environmental law as simply a mass of meaningless detail.

This book does, however, provide a lot of information about individual statutes and how they operate, including trail guides to summarize key statutes and describe how they operate. Because the field has become too vast to offer a comprehensive introduction to natural resources law and pollution control law in one course, we include materials on the major pollution control statutes and the two statutes in other areas most often included in general environmental law courses, the Endangered Species Act and the National Environmental Policy Act, as well as one major statute governing resource extraction: the Surface Mining Control and Reclamation Act. This book includes the materials that best emphasize the major policy issues and concepts that animate environmental law. We orient students to the core concepts at the beginning of Part II with some foreshadowing in the first three introductory statutes (on environmental law, common law, and administrative law). Subsequent chapters provide practice in mastering some of the complexities in these statutes, but focus on those details that help them make sense of core concepts that they should master.

We present edited cases to illustrate the core concepts without leaving out important contextual information. We then use notes and questions to further

1

develop students' understanding of the core concepts and how lawyers and agency officials use them in practice. Most chapters include a problem designed to allow students to integrate the concepts taught. Some of these problems also provide practice in applying detailed statutory and regulatory provisions to complex questions, a skill students must master to practice in the field.

The book begins with three chapters devoted to providing basic background. The first of these chapters presents an overview of environmental problems to help students appreciate the challenges confronting environmental law. The second of these introductory chapters provides an overview of the common law, asking why policy makers turned to statutory solutions in the 1970s. The third introductory chapter discusses the idea of statutory schemes, the role of administrative agencies and judicial review.

The book's second part addresses environmental standard setting. After an introduction to many of the concepts in the book, it discusses criteria that govern the stringency of regulations that often determine how much clean-up is accomplished. It includes chapters on the criteria that most frequently govern decisions about the stringency of regulatory standards, namely effects-based (or health- and environment-based), technology-based, and cost-benefit-based criteria.

The second part continues with a section addressesing the means of environmental protection. This part's first chapter (Chapter 7) addresses traditional regulation, which some commentators refer to as command-and-control regulation. The second chapter (Chapter 8) discusses market-based alternatives. The third chapter (Chapter 9) discusses information-based approaches, including the role of the National Environmental Policy Act and the Toxic Substances Control Act in generating information. The fourth chapter (Chapter 10) discusses pollution prevention and recycling. We provide material on the Resource Conservation and Recovery Act here, because policy regarding recycling has played such an important role in that statute. The fifth chapter (Chapter 11) addresses environmental restoration, involving efforts to clean up contaminated sites or restore the function of damaged ecosystems.

The book's third part addresses the problem of distributing responsibility, both for clean-up and for making the decisions designed to spur clean-up. It begins with a chapter (Chapter 12) on the distribution of responsibility for clean-up under the Superfund statute. The next chapter (Chapter 13) addresses the distribution of responsibilities among governmental units. Both chapters show how Congress has used the concepts that we highlight in this book to create statutory schemes.

The book closes with an enforcement part. After a general introduction to enforcement philosophy, it addresses both government and citizen enforcement of environmental statutes.

We believe that this book offers a coherent education in environmental law that will provide a solid foundation for subsequent work. It requires attention to detail, but offers a framework for understanding what this area of law is about.

I

The Nature and Evolution of Environmental Law

What *is* environmental law? How does it differ from other kinds of law, and why? To some, it is simply a vast, somewhat disjointed collection of relatively recent environmental statutes, regulations, policies, cases, and other documents written to address an array of threats to human health and environmental quality caused by our modern economy and lifestyle. This view, although accurate as far as it goes, misses a lot, and makes the field hard to study. It misses the much longer history of common law and other approaches to environmental protection that pre-dated, and, to some degree, informed the era of environmental statutes and regulations. By approaching environmental law merely as a collection of separate statutes, regulations, and interpretive cases, the field becomes just another application of general administrative law. More importantly, approaching environmental law as a series of discrete statutes obscures the cohesion that becomes evident by taking a more holistic view, in which broader themes become apparent.

Under the narrow view, environmental law is a very new field. Of course, this is true in the sense that we only began to adopt comprehensive statutory approaches to environmental protection in the 1960s. Efforts to protect people and property from environmental harm, however, date back to the early days of English common law. *See, e.g.*, A.S. WISDOM, THE LAW ON THE POLLUTION OF WATERS 3 (1956).

To the extent that "environmental" issues involve efforts to allocate various resources among competing users—including public, shared resources, such as clean air, as well as more traditional "natural resources" like coal or water—environmental law has roots in property law. Likewise, if environmental issues involve efforts to prevent one person's activity from causing inappropriate harm to other people or environmental resources, or to compensate for that harm, environmental law has precedents in the law of torts. Some of those themes also persist in modern environmental statutes. Other somewhat more obscure common law doctrines have been resurrected over the past several decades to protect environmental values. For example, under the public trust doctrine, the government holds certain lands—such as the beds and banks of navigable waters and lands submerged by the tides—in trust for the public at large, and must preserve those resources for common purposes such as navigation, commerce, and fishing. *See, e.g.*, Joseph Sax, *The Public Trust Doctrine in Natural Resource Law: Effective Judicial Intervention*, 68 MICH. L. REV. 471 (1970) (arguing for resurrection and expansion of public trust doctrine to protect environmental resources); National Audubon Society v. Superior Court, 658 P.2d 709 (Cal. 1983) (applying public trust doctrine to protect the ecosystem of Mono Lake and associated wildlife resources from water depletions).

The very fact that we now have so many complex environmental statutes indicates that Congress and others believed that common law approaches did not adequately address modern environmental problems. *See, e.g.*, RACHEL CARSON, SILENT SPRING (1962) (urging increased attention to the problem of contamination by pesticides and other toxic pollutants, and leading eventually to passage of remedial federal legislation). In some of these laws, Congress borrowed principles from existing common law approaches, or modified them to fit new circumstances and the contours of an administrative regulatory system. In others, Congress adopted entirely new approaches to environmental protection.

In this opening part of the book, our goal is to orient you to a conceptual approach to environmental law by addressing three questions. First, what is the nature of environmental problems, and what particular challenges do they pose for the law? Second, how did the common law respond to those challenges, and to what degree and in what ways did those approaches succeed or fail? Third, in what major ways does the modern statutory and regulatory system complement, supplement, or supplant common law approaches, and why? These questions are addressed in the first three chapters of this book, respectively.

1

The Nature of Environmental Problems

What are the problems with which environmental law must wrestle? Billows of black smoke emanating from factory smokestacks? Torrents of noxious brew spewing from pipes into our otherwise pristine rivers? Rusty barrels of hazardous waste laying half buried in abandoned lots, leaking into groundwater and causing clusters of cancer cases in adjacent communities? Certainly these kinds of problems remain, in some places and to some degree. Much more varied, often subtle, and frequently complex forms of environmental degradation also present key challenges for environmental law. We have addressed some of the most obvious forms of pollution through common law or statutory remedies. Others remain, but linkages between ongoing pollution and the kinds of harm for which legal solutions are appropriate may be less clear. Big players, such as petrochemical plants and public sewage treatment facilities, continue to pose problems, but the range of "polluters" is much larger. Indeed, all of us pollute in some ways. Significant issues of chemical contamination continue unabated, but environmental harm is caused by a litany of less obvious activities as well, from residential development to seemingly "green" golf courses. *See Golf Contaminates Environment*, Golf Course News, March 2003.

This chapter has two basic purposes. First, we provide a brief summary of the kinds of environmental problems that modern environmental law addresses. Any effort to "summarize" the nature of environmental problems is necessarily incomplete, as many volumes have been written even about individual kinds of environmental harm. Rather, our goal is to provide enough information to give you a feel for the range, complexity, and severity of various forms of environmental harm so that you can understand why this field is so important, and the basic nature of the challenges addressed by environmental law.

Second, we want to use this information as a platform from which to explore the various ways in which environmental problems present particular kinds of legal challenges. These are the issues that largely characterize environmental law, as distinct from other kinds of issues and disputes with which lawyers must grapple. This will guide our journey through the maze of laws, regulations, and cases, and help you to understand what some of the theories and methods that underpin environmental law seek to accomplish, and how.

5

A note about nomenclature and distinctions is in order before we begin. In this chapter, we use the term "environmental problems" somewhat broadly, to encompass pollution, overuse of natural resources, and ecosystem degradation. These issues are often closely related. The more resources we use, for example, the more waste we are likely to generate. Similarly, when we pollute more, and when we disturb land through various kinds of development, we will likely cause more significant changes to natural ecosystems. Regardless of the breadth of a particular course, it is useful to explore all three general categories of environmental harm briefly before we begin to evaluate various legal responses and solutions to those problems.

As you read the following information, take note of the characteristics of environmental problems that pose particular challenges for the law. What is "unique" or different about these issues, compared to those addressed by other areas of law? Likewise, what issues seem similar to those addressed by other areas of law you may have studied, such that principles from those other legal fields might be borrowed or modified to resolve environmental issues?

A. POLLUTION

When we extract resources, and use them to make things, we often produce either products or by-products that contain substances that may harm human health or the environment. Harmful substances may be released into the air, water, or onto the land because we no longer want or need them, and because discarding them is cheaper or easier than reducing or eliminating the pollution. We categorize all of these issues in the general category of "pollution."[1]

1. Air Pollution

The following is based in part on a summary of data and analysis of air pollution trends produced by the U.S. Environmental Protection Agency (EPA) over a period of nearly 40 years.[2] According to these estimates, the air pollution "glass" is half empty and half full.

The bad news is that EPA estimates that about 123 million tons of air pollutants are emitted into the atmosphere in the United States every year. The good news is that significant progress has been made in the four decades since Congress passed the 1970 Clean Air Act (CAA). During that time, total emissions of the six

---

1. The Clean Water Act includes an even more comprehensive definition of "pollution" as "the man-made or man-induced, alteration of the chemical, physical, biological, and radiological integrity of water." 33 U.S.C. §1362(19).

2. These data are from EPA, Our Nation's Air—Status and Trends Through 2010, http://www.epa.gov/airtrends/2011/report/airpollution.pdf/; EPA, Air Emissions Trends—Continued Progress Through 2007, http://www.epa.gov/airtrends/. Information on trends in emissions of particular pollutants is also available at this site.

major air pollutants have declined by 59 percent. To put those improvements in further perspective, EPA notes that during the same period gross domestic product increased by 65 percent, total vehicle miles traveled increased 40 percent, energy consumption increased 15 percent, and the U.S. population grew by 24 percent. Thus, total air emissions decreased markedly (59 percent) in spite of the fact that there are more of us, and that most of us travel more and consume more of the goods and resources that contribute to air pollution. On the other hand, during this period emissions of carbon dioxide in the United States increased by 8 percent. Carbon dioxide is a "greenhouse gas" that contributes to climate disruption, often called "climate change" or "global warming."

As with almost all environmental data, some caution is in order when evaluating these statistics. It is not easy to estimate total air emissions accurately on a nationwide basis, given the large diversity of air pollution sources. Those sources include major "stationary sources" such as factories, power plants, and incinerators. Even for this fixed, relatively easy to identify category of sources, emissions estimates can be challenging because old facilities are retired and new ones built, production levels and other factors vary over time, and technical limitations prevent reliable monitoring of some of their emissions. However, air pollution also comes from a wide range and much larger number of smaller but cumulatively significant sources, called "area sources," such as auto paint shops and dry cleaners. Significant air pollution is emitted from the hundreds of millions of fossil-fuel–powered vehicles ("mobile sources") that most of us drive, both on- and off-road. One of the major challenges in air pollution law and policy is how to address pollution from such a substantial and diverse number of emissions sources. Emissions estimates are also complicated by changes over time in the emissions we "count" as part of the analysis, and in the methods of analysis.[3] One key skill for environmental lawyers is to think critically about sources of information, and more importantly, the likely limitations in that information.

EPA has issued national air quality standards for six ubiquitous air pollutants, known as "criteria pollutants": particulate matter, carbon monoxide, nitrogen oxides, sulfur dioxide, lead, and ozone (which is formed in the lower atmosphere by the interaction of various "precursor" pollutants and sunlight).[4] These pollutants cause a wide range of adverse health and environmental effects, as shown in Table 1-1.

---

3. EPA has changed its methods for estimating various emissions several times, for different pollutants. This makes it somewhat challenging to compare EPA's estimates over the decades. Likewise, during various periods EPA either counted, or did not count, certain sources of emissions, such as nitrous oxide emissions from fires.

4. *See* http://www.epa.gov/air/urbanair/6poll.html for more information about each of these pollutants and their effects.

TABLE 1-1
Effects of Criteria Air Pollutants

Pollutant and Key Sources	Effects
• Particulate matter • Fuel combustion • Agriculture; plowing and burning fields • Unpaved roads	Associated with tens of thousands of annual deaths. Coughing and painful or difficult breathing. Increased risk of respiratory infections. Causes or exacerbates respiratory illnesses such as asthma and chronic bronchitis, and can make heart attacks and strokes more likely. Reduces visibility, adds excess nutrients to water bodies and soil, acidifies lakes and streams, and causes damage to forests and crops.
Lead • Metal industry; smelters • Leaded gasoline combustion in piston aircraft • Waste incinerators • Battery manufacturing	Causes harm to various parts of the body, including the kidneys, liver, brain, and the nervous, cardiovascular, reproductive, and developmental systems. Brain and central nervous system impacts include lower IQ, reduced attention spans and other behavioral disorders, and effects on growth, language abilities, and learning. Lead in the environment can also harm fish and wildlife.
Ozone • Chemical reaction of volatile organic compounds and nitrogen oxide in the presence of sunlight.	Irritates and inflames the lungs, causing wheezing, coughing, and painful and difficult breathing. Can lead to permanent lung damage, exacerbation of other respiratory conditions such as asthma, higher rates of pneumonia, and bronchitis. Harms crops and other plants.
Carbon monoxide • Fuel combustion (especially vehicles).	Causes chest pain and adverse cardiovascular effects, especially to persons with existing heart conditions. It also harms the central nervous system, with effects on vision, attention span, and impaired learning and manual dexterity.
Nitrous oxides • Fuel combustion; electric utilities, industrial boilers, and vehicles • Wood burning	Contribute to ozone formation, and to acid rain that impairs lakes, streams, and forests, and damages cars and buildings. Nitric acid in the atmosphere can impair breathing and cause lung damage, reduce visibility, and add excess nutrients to large water bodies. Recent scientific evidence demonstrates short-term nitrous oxides exposure (30 minutes to 24 hours) can have adverse respiratory effects on healthy people, while increasing respiratory symptoms in people with asthma.
Sulfur dioxides • Fuel combustion (especially high-sulfur coal) • Electric utilities • Natural sources; volcanoes	Impair breathing, especially for those with asthma, other forms of respiratory illness, and heart disease. They also reduce visibility, contribute to acid rain, and damage plants and buildings.

In addition to these large volume pollutants, toxic air pollutants emitted in smaller quantities can cause cancer, reproductive problems, birth defects, and other adverse health and environmental effects. *See* 42 U.S.C. §7412(b)(1) (long list of hazardous air pollutants identified by Congress).

Despite the apparent improvements noted above, air pollution in the United States continues to contribute to significant human health and other problems. According to EPA, thousands in the United States suffer daily from air-pollution–related health effects, including premature deaths, as well as illnesses from diseases such as asthma, emphysema, upper respiratory infections, and other pulmonary disorders. Air pollution also damages property, such as buildings and crops, and environmental resources, such as forests and lakes.

Finally, some air pollutants have more global impacts, contributing to depletion of the stratospheric ozone layer that protects us from solar radiation,[5] and to climate disruption. We return to the problem of climate disruption at the end of this chapter, and use it throughout the book to illustrate the main concepts in environmental law.

2. Water Pollution

Water pollution similarly results from a surprisingly wide range and large number of sources. The stereotypical water polluter is a large factory spewing a noxious brew of chemicals into an otherwise pristine river. And while industrial pollution remains a problem for U.S. waterways, pollutants find their way into rivers, lakes, and other waters from many other sources that are more closely connected with the everyday lives of most citizens. Most obviously, every time we flush the toilet or wash household chemicals down the drain we send wastes into the public sewer system. Safe collection, treatment, and disposal of municipal sewage is one of our largest, and most expensive, water pollution challenges.

Perhaps less obvious is the pollution that reaches our waterways from virtually every human activity that changes the character of land. Because this form of pollution usually stems from precipitation and runoff from large areas, rather than discrete pipes or ditches, it is known as "nonpoint source pollution," or more descriptively, as polluted runoff. Soil tilled on farms is exposed to wind and rain, and can erode in large quantities into adjacent waters. (This both wastes valuable soil as a natural resource and pollutes waterways.) Fertilizers and pesticides used to grow crops add to the broad scope of agricultural pollution. But while agricultural runoff is the largest single source of polluted runoff, virtually every land-altering activity adds its own mix of pollutants. Land disturbed by construction, grazing, logging, and mining contributes sediment and other pollutants, particularly after intensive rainfall. An even wider range of pollutants runs off of built and paved surfaces (roads, buildings, parking lots), because of the wide range of chemicals and other pollutants that collect there. These pollutants include oil and other fluids from motor vehicles; metals, paints, and other materials that wear off of structures; stored or spilled industrial or construction chemicals; and organic waste from a

---

5. Ozone is a deleterious pollutant at lower levels (the "troposphere") where it is a respiratory irritant, but is an important part of our protective atmosphere at much higher elevations.

wide variety of sources (including pet wastes). Much like mobile and area source air pollution, nonpoint source water pollution poses a serious challenge due to the sheer volume and diversity of sources.

As with the air pollution picture, U.S. water pollution control efforts over the past several decades involve a mixture of success and failure. Although major problems remain, available evidence shows significant progress in reducing discharges of pollutants to U.S. waters over the past 30 years, in large part due to requirements imposed in the Clean Water Act (CWA).

In 1972, despite decades of significant federal, state, and local investment in public sewage treatment infrastructure, domestic sewage remained one of the major unaddressed sources of water pollution. By 1996, modern public sewage treatment plants served approximately 73 percent of the U.S. population. Lest this fact lull us into complacency, however, we have still not solved this aspect of water pollution control. According to EPA's most recent analysis, the nation faces estimated public sewerage needs of over $298 billion "for up to a 20-year period" starting as of January 1, 2008, for publicly owned wastewater pipes and treatment facilities; combined sewer overflow correction; and stormwater management.[6] Similarly, from 1972 through the early 1990s, U.S. industry invested over $57 billion in water pollution control. This resulted in reductions of millions of tons of conventional pollutants and over a billion pounds of toxic pollutants[7] per year. As is true for municipal sewage, however, significant releases of industrial pollutants into U.S. waterways continue. In 2007, for example, U.S. industries reported releases of almost 246 million pounds of toxic pollutants to surface waters.[8]

Despite progress in reducing the discharge of pollutants from municipal and industrial point sources, trends in ambient water quality remain ambiguous and inconsistent. This is due in part to the ongoing releases of point source pollutants discussed above, and in large part to the runoff of pollutants from nonpoint sources. Large numbers of urban watersheds remain chemically impaired due to pathogens, phosphorus, insecticides, herbicides, and toxics from municipal and industrial sources; and many rural watersheds remain chemically impaired due to nutrients, sediment, and agricultural chemicals.[9] Long-term water quality trends can be difficult to assess due to gaps in data, differences in methods of data collection and analysis, and other factors, although methods and information have improved in recent years.[10] Available evidence, however, indicates that the nationwide reduction in releases of pollutants from point sources has not translated

6. U.S. Environmental Protection Agency, Clean Watersheds Needs Survey: 2008 Report to Congress, available at http://water.epa.gov/scitech/datait/databases/cwns/upload/cwns2008rtc.pdf (visited Sept. 4, 2014).

7. "Conventional" pollutants include biological oxygen demand, suspended solids, fecal coliform, and pH. 33 U.S.C. §1314(a)(4). The toxic "priority pollutants" were identified in a 1976 Consent Decree between EPA and national environmental groups, which was later ratified by Congress. See 33 U.S.C. §1311(b)(2)(C).

8. U.S. Environmental Protection Agency, TRI 2007 Data Release, available at http://www.epa.gov/tri/tridata/tri07/index.htm (released March 19, 2009).

9. See U.S. Department of the Interior, U.S. Geological Survey, Selected Findings and Current Perspectives on Urban and Agricultural Water Quality by the National Water-Quality Assessment Program (USGS Fact Sheet FS-047-01, April 2001).

10. See Richard B. Alexander et al., Data from Selected U.S. Geological Survey National Stream Water Quality Monitoring Networks, 34 Water Res. 2401 (1998).

universally to improved ambient water quality. Where consistent, long-term water quality data are available, more often than not they show *no clear trends* in ambient water quality. Improvements are evident largely in areas where pollution comes predominantly from point sources, but water quality has remained steady or declined in areas where nonpoint sources predominate.

The evidence of ongoing impairment of chemical water quality in some areas, in turn, translates to documented harm to human health and aquatic ecosystems. Nearly half (44 percent) of the nation's rivers and nearly two-thirds (64 percent) of its lakes do not have sufficiently high water quality to protect uses such as drinking water, swimming, and fishing, in whole or in part, due to a combination of chemical pollution and other factors.[11] For example, the states and EPA issued over 2,800 fish and wildlife consumption advisories in 2000, and more than 3,200 in the year 2004, due to toxics and other contaminants in waterways (mercury, PCBs, chlordane, dioxins, DDT residues), reflecting a steady increase since 1993. The 2004 fish advisories issued covered over 35 percent of the nation's lakes and 24 percent of the nation's river miles. (The apparent increasing trend may be due in part to better monitoring and reporting. The majority of new fish advisories are due to mercury, and U.S. mercury emissions have decreased by 45 percent since 1990.)[12] Similarly, states and localities issued at least 20,000 beach closings or advisory days in 2008, some due to heavy rainfall but most due to pathogens and other contaminants, marking the fourth consecutive year that closing and advisory days reached 20,000.[13]

3. Solid and Hazardous Wastes

In the business of modern life we produce a lot of garbage, especially in the United States. U.S. citizens, businesses, and institutions generated over 251 million tons of "municipal solid waste" in 2012, an average of 4.38 pounds per person per day (up significantly from an estimated 2.7 pounds in 1960).[14] While not as dangerous in small amounts as the "hazardous waste" discussed below, municipal waste still poses serious environmental problems if it is not handled safely. In the past, we sent much of our municipal garbage to open dumps, which contaminated land and water and posed public health hazards from pathogens. Other waste we burned in unregulated incinerators, causing air pollution, and still more

11. U.S. Environmental Protection Agency, National Water Quality Inventory, 2004 Report to Congress (EPA-841-R-08-001, January 2009) (2004 National Water Quality Inventory).

12. *See* U.S. Environmental Protection Agency, National Water Quality Inventory, 1998 Report to Congress 191-221 (EPA-841-R-00-001, June 2002) (1998 National Water Quality Inventory); 2004 National Water Quality Inventory, *supra* note 11, at ES-4. *See also* U.S. Environmental Protection Agency, National Listing of Fish and Wildlife Consumption Advisories, http://www.epa.gov/ost/fish; and U.S. Environmental Protection Agency, Fact Sheet: National Listing of Fish and Wildlife Advisories, EPA-820-F-13-058 (December 2013).

13. *See* Natural Resources Defense Council, Testing the Waters 2009: A Guide to Water Quality at Vacation Beaches, available at http://www.nrdc.org/water/oceans/ttw/ttw2009.pdf.

14. This information is available at http://www.epa.gov/epawaste/nonhaz/index.htm; EPA, Municipal Solid Waste Generation, Recycling, and Disposal in the United States: Facts and Figures 2012, http://www.epa.gov/osw/nonhaz/municipal/pubs/2012_msw_fs.pdf.

we simply dumped into the ocean or other large water bodies. Moreover, not all of our household waste is ordinary "garbage." Household hazardous waste includes a wide range of chemicals that can be every bit as toxic as industrial "hazardous wastes." For example, hazardous ingredients are commonly found in oven cleaners, toilet cleaners, laundry bleach, lawn insecticides, indoor pesticides, mouse and rat poisons, paint thinners, turpentine, oil and enamel-based paints, wood stains and finishes, fluorescent light bulbs, batteries and several automotive products.[15] While each of us may generate only a small amount of this waste, collectively we produce over one and a half million tons of household hazardous waste a year.

Under federal law, we have taken several steps to handle this huge solid waste burden more carefully. First, by encouraging material reuse and recycling, we try to reduce the amount of waste material that must be disposed of. (At the same time, by reusing and recycling these materials, we reduce the amount of virgin natural resources used for new products.) We recycled and composted 86.6 million tons of municipal solid waste in the United States in 2012, double the amount recycled just a decade and a half earlier, and more than a ten-fold increase from 1960. Second, we have prohibited unsafe open dumping of garbage, and require states to regulate the design and operation of landfills and incinerators, to reduce adverse environmental impacts from those practices. Nonetheless, the safe disposal of the remaining 70 percent of municipal solid waste every year presents a huge ongoing challenge. Properly designed and operated sanitary landfills require a considerable amount of space, which is particularly problematic in crowded urban areas. Moreover, both landfills and incinerators now must meet strict siting requirements, further limiting the number of available locations for these activities. Landfills, for example, cannot be placed in wetlands or flood plains where groundwater contamination is likely, and incinerators must be situated where they will not cause or exacerbate air pollution health problems.

The amount of waste we each generate to sustain our modern lifestyle is not limited to the bags of garbage we take to the curb every week. Virtually everything we produce creates industrial waste, only some of which is released as air and water pollution. The rest is treated as solid waste, *i.e.*, disposed of on land, in storage pits or lagoons, injected into underground wells, or incinerated. Ironically, the pollution control methods developed to stem air and water pollution concentrated many of those wastes into municipal and industrial sludge or other forms of solid waste that now must be addressed in some other way to prevent environmental harm. As with municipal waste, federal law encourages material reuse and recycling to reduce our industrial waste burden as much as possible. Nevertheless, the United States produces huge volumes of industrial wastes every year.[16]

Some industrial waste is no more dangerous than municipal waste, and can be disposed of safely in well-designed and located landfills. Other kinds of industrial

15. *See* http://www.epa.gov/msw/hhw-list.htm for further information on household hazardous waste items, and http://www.epa.gov/msw/hhw.htm for further information on disposal issues and figures related to household hazardous waste.

16. In 2006, EPA estimated that 7.6 billion tons of industrial solid waste were generated and disposed of in the United States per year. EPA, Office of Solid Waste and Emergency Response, http://www.epa.gov/waste/nonhaz/industrial/guide.htm.

waste are generated in smaller volumes but have far greater potential for harm due to their inherent toxicity and other properties. According to data reported to EPA,[17] over 16,000 facilities generated at least 34 million tons of legally defined hazardous waste in the United States in 2011.[18] These wastes cannot safely be disposed of through methods used for other kinds of solid waste without prior treatment, unless more carefully constructed and operated facilities are used.

The nation awoke with a start to the legacy of our past inattention to hazardous waste disposal as hazardous waste nightmares surfaced in the 1960s and 1970s. The most notorious example was the "Love Canal" site in Tonawanda, New York, in which huge volumes of highly toxic wastes had been dumped for many years in an area later developed as a typical American suburb (complete with homes, schools, and playgrounds later found to be contaminated). *See* ADELIN GORDON LEVINE, LOVE CANAL: SCIENCE, POLITICS AND PEOPLE (1982). In this and in many other locations around the country, controversy continues about how many people were exposed to what kinds of wastes, and how much increased health and environmental risk resulted from that exposure. In some cases, evidence exists of "cancer clusters" and other concentrations of illness in the vicinity of hazardous waste sites. But a range of contaminants from other sources, routine chemical use and exposure (addressed in the following subsection), smoking and diet, and a wide range of other variables complicate our ability to determine clear cause-and-effect relationships.

Nevertheless, the problem of haphazard past hazardous waste disposal practices remains a major national problem now addressed by the federal Superfund program, which establishes a system of identifying and ranking large hazardous waste sites, cleaning them up or minimizing their risks, and allocating responsibility for cleanup among responsible parties (if they can be located or even still exist). As of November 12, 2013, the list of Superfund sites around the country[19] included 1,739 active sites, with 51 more proposed. (This list does not include the thousands of other hazardous waste disposal sites around the country that do not meet the criteria for the Superfund program.) On EPA's website, you can locate listed Superfund sites in your state.[20] While EPA, state agencies, and private parties have taken actions to reduce risks or to clean up many sites,[21] the problem of solving past improper waste disposal practices remains serious.

---

17. EPA, THE NATIONAL BIENNIAL RCRA HAZARDOUS WASTE REPORT (BASED ON 2011 DATA) (EPA 530-R-03-007, July 2003), http://www.epa.gov/epawaste/inforesources/data/br11/national11.pdf.

18. This statistic is conservative for several reasons. First, the legal definition of what "solid waste" is also "hazardous waste" is complex and often uncertain. Second, the data reported above includes only "large quantity generators," typically only those facilities that generate more than 1,000 kg (1.1 tons) of hazardous waste in any one month. Small quantity generators (generators who produce more than 100 kg but less than 1,000 kg of hazardous waste in any month), taken together, may add significantly to this amount.

19. *See* http://www.epa.gov/superfund/sites/query/queryhtm/npltotal.htm.

20. http://www.epa.gov/superfund/sites/index.htm.

21. EPA reports that over 6,400 actions have been taken to reduce public health and environmental risks at Superfund sites, and that cleanups have been completed at 757 sites. *See* http://www.epa.gov/superfund/action/20years/preface.htm.

4. Toxic Chemicals

Not all of the chemicals and other materials that pose hazards to human health and to the environment are "pollutants" or "wastes," although they can become so if stored, used, or transported improperly. Depending on the substances, some chemicals can pose human health and environmental risks even when used as intended, due to their toxicity, persistence in the environment or in our bodies, combinations with other chemicals, and other factors.

The growth of chemicals used in modern life has been astonishing.[22] As of 1976, an estimated 60,000 chemicals were used in the United States, most of which were developed and manufactured absent any testing or other regulatory requirements to determine potential harm to human users or to the environment. Moreover, an estimated 1,000 new chemicals enter the market every year. The sheer volume of chemicals used has grown rapidly as well. Between 1966 and 1994, the production of synthetic organic chemicals alone grew from 40 to 149 million tons per year. Agricultural pesticide use in the United States increased as well, from about 400 million pounds a year in the mid-1960s to over 800 million pounds annually by 1985.[23] When we tally all uses of insecticides, herbicides, and fungicides, for activities ranging from water disinfection to crop protection to lawn and garden maintenance, more than one billion pounds of pesticide products are used annually in the United States.[24]

Determining what health and environmental risks this huge array of chemicals may present is a daunting and uncertain task. If a human subpopulation experiences an increase in cancer, or if birds in a local lake begin to develop abnormalities or have trouble reproducing, how do we know where to fix blame, given the wide range of potential causes? Even if one or more chemicals appears to be implicated, how can we determine what levels of exposure pose what degree of risk? We do know that many chemicals, including some that provide useful services to society, can cause cancer or other health risks, including birth defects and other developmental harm to fetuses and infants, and genetic changes that may affect future generations. More recent evidence suggests that many chemicals affect our endocrine (hormone) systems, with changes in reproductive health and other impacts on our children. *See* THEO COLBORN, DIANNE DUMANOSKI & JOHN PETERSON MYERS, OUR STOLEN FUTURE (1996). Certain chemicals persist for long times within the global ecosystem, posing similar risks to fish and wildlife populations worldwide. Even in the remote arctic, we find persistent toxic chemicals in the fat of seals and polar bears.[25]

As you might imagine, regulation of environmental risks from chemicals that otherwise provide useful services to society presents somewhat different challenges from those discussed above with respect to pollutants and waste products. We can

---

22. Data in this section are taken from Lynn R. Goldman, *Toxic Chemicals and Pesticides, in* STUMBLING TOWARD SUSTAINABILITY (John Dernbach ed., 2002).

23. Nonagricultural use of pesticides, on the other hand, decreased by a third between 1970 and 1990.

24. U.S. ENVIRONMENTAL PROTECTION AGENCY, 2006-2007 PESTICIDE MARKET ESTIMATES: USAGE, available at http://www.epa.gov/opp00001/pestsales/07pestsales/usage2007.htm.

25. *See* WORLD WILDLIFE FUND, THE TIP OF THE ICEBERG: CHEMICAL CONTAMINATION IN THE ARCTIC (2005).

reduce risks from production process wastes (known as "residuals") without necessarily forgoing the good or service produced, by changing production methods or materials, by installing pollution controls at the end of the process, or both. We neither want nor need the residual itself, but rather the good or service provided. A different set of choices is suggested when a risk is inherent in the useful product itself. We can simply decide that the benefits from the product outweigh its risks, or vice versa. We can determine whether those risks can be reduced to acceptable levels by changing the way in which we use that product (safe handling requirements, quantity restrictions, place restrictions, etc.). Or, we can phase out the use of a particularly dangerous chemical if viable substitutes are found.

B. OVERUSE OF NATURAL RESOURCES

By virtually any measure, we Americans are profligate in our use of resources. *See* CONFRONTING CONSUMPTION (Thomas Princen, Michael F. Maniates & Ken Conca eds., 2002); ALAN DURNING, HOW MUCH IS ENOUGH: THE CONSUMER SOCIETY AND THE FUTURE OF THE EARTH (1992). As of 1990, it took over 50 kilograms (110 pounds) of raw materials per person per day (not including water) to support the lifestyle of the average American, and that amount increased by another 10 percent by the turn of the century.[26] Over the course of the twentieth century, raw material extraction and use in the United States increased at an astonishing rate, from less than 100 million metric tons to nearly 3 billion metric tons, growing more than twice as fast as population over the same period.

Natural resource use is the flip side of pollution, because the more resources we use, the more waste and other forms of pollution we are likely to generate. Moreover, we cause additional environmental harm when we extract (dig, drill, mine) resources, transport them to where they will be used, and convert them into usable products. Finally, with respect to some resources, our current rate of use exceeds sustainable levels. This trend is particularly troubling for materials and other resources that are not renewable, *i.e.*, whose supplies are not continuously regenerated by natural processes, including fossil fuels (such as coal and oil). Even renewable resources, such as trees, however, are depleted if we use them faster than they are naturally or artificially replaced.

Americans are especially notorious for our use of energy, particularly non-renewable fossil fuels, emissions from which also contribute significantly to the threat of climate disruption. Recent trends in energy use are not encouraging. Total energy use in the United States jumped 20 percent from 1992 to 2000, and energy-related emissions of carbon dioxide (the major gas contributing to climate disruption) increased by 10 percent during the same period.[27] Increased

---

26. Statistics in this paragraph come from Amit Kapur & Thomas E. Graedel, *Production and Consumption of Materials, in* STUMBLING TOWARD SUSTAINABILITY, *supra* note 22, at 63.

27. Lynn Price & Mark D. Levine, *Production and Consumption of Energy, in* STUMBLING TOWARD SUSTAINABILITY, *supra* note 22, at 79, 86.

energy use stems both from our increasing population and from our love affairs with energy-consuming devices, from cars to computers, and our desire that these products themselves become more powerful. This persistent growth in energy demand, in turn, prompts proposals to drill for more oil and gas (in places like the Arctic National Wildlife Refuge in Alaska and other wilderness areas in the West), dig more coal, build more dams, or seek alternative sources of energy or ways to use existing energy more efficiently. Recently, policy makers have showed renewed interest in nuclear power, which currently generates about 20 percent of our electric power, but which has seen no new plant construction for over a quarter century.

Water is perhaps our most basic natural resource. Total water supplies in the United States are abundant, especially relative to many other countries. But we do not always have clean, fresh water where and when we want it. Some regions of the United States have abundant supplies, while others are more arid. In some areas, water is plentiful during wet seasons of the year but not others, or in wet periods but not during droughts.[28] Americans also *use* considerably more water than do people in most other countries. Per capita water use in the United States is higher, in most cases significantly, than in all but five relatively small countries.[29]

Many areas of the country, historically in the West but increasingly in the eastern states as well, face serious periodic water shortages during times of drought, especially given rapid urban growth and competition with agriculture and other traditional water users. In most western states, surface water resources are already fully allocated to specified uses, but population growth continues.[30] In some regions, such as the Ogalalla aquifer in the high plains region, fresh water is being withdrawn from groundwater at rates significantly higher than the rate of natural renewal. Obviously, this practice of "mining" groundwater cannot be sustained indefinitely.[31] On a more positive note, however, while U.S. water use grew steadily throughout most of the twentieth century, on both an absolute and per capita basis, both total water withdrawals and per capita consumptive use have actually declined since 1980,[32] reflecting some improvements in water use efficiency.

Dwindling agricultural and other productive land resources are also a concern in many parts of the country. According to the National Resources Inventory[33] prepared by the Natural Resources Conservation Service, a branch of the U.S. Department of Agriculture, between 1982 and 2001 about 34 million acres—roughly the size of Illinois—was converted to development. Almost half

---

28. Information in this paragraph is taken from Robert W. Adler, *Fresh Water, in* STUMBLING TOWARD SUSTAINABILITY, *supra* note 22, at 215-16.

29. PETER H. GLEICK, THE WORLD'S WATER 2000-2001, 205-11 (2000).

30. *See* WESTERN WATER POLICY REVIEW ADVISORY COMMISSION, WATER IN THE WEST: THE CHALLENGE FOR THE NEXT CENTURY 3-6 (1998).

31. *See* ROBERT GLENNON, WATER FOLLIES (2002).

32. *See* WAYNE SOLLEY ET AL., ESTIMATED WATER USE IN THE UNITED STATES 1995, 1 (U.S. Geological Survey Circular No. 1200). Offstream water use continued to grow between 1950 and 1980; that same use dropped between 1980 and 1985 and has remained approximately level since then, despite continuing growth in the U.S. population. *Id.* at 63.

33. These data are reported as follows: Development: http://www.nrcs.usda.gov/technical/land/nri01/nri01dev.html. Erosion: http://www.nrcs.usda.gov/technical/land/nri01/nri01eros.html. Land use: http://www.nrcs.usda.gov/technical/land/nri01/nri01lu.html.

of this land was formerly forested, about a fifth was crop land, and another 16 percent was pasture. Increasingly, lands identified as "prime farmland" are the targets of this development. Thus, during this period the nation lost about 12 percent of its total crop land. Americans also continue to cut forests at a rapid pace, although reforestation efforts have increased, and reliable information on the health of our forest base is scarce.[34] According to the National Report on Forest Resources prepared by the U.S. Forest Service,[35] while the amount of forested land in the United States has dropped by more than 20 percent since the time of European settlement, total forested acreage has remained relatively constant since about 1920 (between 700-800 million acres). That statistic about net acreage is somewhat misleading, however, because considerable amounts of old growth forest have been cut and replaced with newer forests. We cut timber on about 10 million acres of that land each year, about 38 percent by clear cutting.

C. ECOSYSTEM DEGRADATION

Very often the law of pollution, with its attention to toxic and other chemicals, focuses heavily on human health issues. Much environmental law, however, also addresses the destruction, alteration, or degradation of the ecosystems on which human and other life depends. To some extent, humans have always altered the natural world—at least since the beginning of recorded history, and probably long before then.[36] In the modern industrial world, we accelerated such changes with unprecedented magnitude and speed. This degree of change presents a different kind of challenge for environmental law.

Aquatic ecosystems present one of the most dramatic examples of the degree to which humans have changed the natural world at the expense of ecosystem health. Waterfront areas were among the first to be developed in the Old World, because proximity to water served a multitude of purposes, including navigation, irrigation, industry, defense, and culinary uses. Relatively flat, fertile floodplain lands were easier to build on and more productive to farm. Similarly, from the earliest days of the American Republic, waterways were critical for transportation and trade, settlement, fishing, farming, and defense.[37]

To promote these uses, America's waters have been dammed, channelized, dewatered, levied, and riprapped, and farms and communities have been developed right up to the water's edge, at the expense of natural floodplain, wetland, and riparian habitats. These changes caused severe accompanying degradation of our

---

34. *See* Robert L. Fischman, *Forestry, in* STUMBLING TOWARD SUSTAINABILITY, *supra* note 22, at 327, 329.

35. W. BRAD SMITH ET AL., FOREST RESOURCES OF THE UNITED STATES 2002 (U.S. Forest Service, General Technical Report NC-241, 2004).

36. *See, e.g.,* DONALD WORSTER, RIVERS OF EMPIRE, WATER, ARIDITY AND THE GROWTH OF THE AMERICAN WEST (1985) (describing ecosystem-altering deforestation by American Indians many centuries ago).

37. *See* Charles F. Wilkinson, *The Headwaters of the Public Trust: Some Thoughts on the Sources and Scope of the Traditional Doctrine,* 19 ENVTL. L. 425, 431-35 (1989) (describing the importance of waterways in the early United States).

aquatic resources.[38] According to the Federal Emergency Management Agency, floodplain development has destroyed about one-half of the natural woody riparian habitat in the contiguous states. Dams have caused the inundation of over 600,000 stream miles, and diversions from those structures seriously alter natural stream flows and habitats. The U.S. Fish and Wildlife Service reports that over one-half of the wetlands in the coterminous states have been lost; and while the rate of wetlands destruction has slowed, we continue to lose smaller amounts of some wetlands types every year, but have achieved recent gains in other kinds of wetlands.[39] This is significant because functioning wetlands serve as natural filters for pollutants, greatly reduce the potential impacts of flooding, and provide invaluable habitat for plants, fish, and wildlife.[40]

This development on or near waterways led to a serious decline in freshwater aquatic biodiversity in the United States. According to a comprehensive national survey conducted by The Nature Conservancy, "animals that depend on freshwater habitat—mussels, crayfishes, fishes, and amphibians—are in the worst condition overall."[41] Approximately 10 percent of bird, mammal, and reptile species are threatened or endangered, compared to about 30 percent for amphibians and fishes, and an alarming 60 to 70 percent for freshwater crayfishes and mussels. The World Wildlife Fund–U.S. concluded that sufficient numbers of aquatic species are affected that entire "faunal assemblages are in a precarious state." Likewise, an assessment of riparian area health published by a committee of the National Research Council[42] reported widespread impairment of riparian habitats, along with accompanying impacts to water quality and aquatic ecosystem health.

Aquatic ecosystems are not alone in this regard. The U.S. Fish and Wildlife Service and the National Marine Fisheries Service have listed over 2,100 species as threatened or endangered (or some combination, depending on location) under the Endangered Species Act (ESA).[43] But most experts agree that these agencies have formally listed only a fraction of imperiled species under the ESA. As with aquatic ecosystems, most of this lost biodiversity stems from extensive habitat loss and degradation. Over the past two centuries, we plowed most of the extensive grassland prairies that once covered large portions of the continent. Likewise, while raw acreage of land covered by forests has remained relatively constant since the 1930s (following the initial decline from pre-Colonial times), most of the natural, planted substitutes have replaced ecologically rich old growth forest. These planted forests generally consist of much less diverse and less healthy monocultures. In the West, grazing lands once covered with a diverse assemblage of resilient natural

---

38. *See* Robin A. Bell et al., Freshwater Ecoregions of North America: A Conservation Assessment (2000); Robert W. Adler, *The Two Lost Books in the Water Quality Trilogy: The Elusive Objectives of Physical and Biological Integrity*, 33 Envtl. L. 29, 71 (2003) (evidence from state bioassessment programs that stressors other than pollutants are responsible for more damage to aquatic ecosystem integrity).

39. T.E. Dahl, Status and Trends of Wetlands in the Coterminous United States 2004 to 2009 (U.S. Department of the Interior, Fish and Wildlife Service 2011).

40. EPA, Functions and Values of Wetlands (EPA-843-F-01-002c, September 2001).

41. Bruce A. Stein & Stephanie R. Flack, 1997 Species Report Card: The State of U.S. Plants and Animals.

42. National Research Council, Riparian Areas: Functions and Strategies for Management 8-13 (2002).

43. 16 U.S.C. §§1531 *et seq. See* http://ecos.fws.gov/tess_public/pub/boxScore.jsp.

grasses and shrubs have either been denuded, or replaced with vast swaths of cheat grass and other exotic or invasive species.[44]

Exotic (non-native, or "alien") species, in fact, are one of our most pervasive, potentially destructive, and least appreciated forms of ecosystem alteration.[45] Invasive plants infest an estimated 100 million acres in the United States, and are spreading to another three million acres a year. According to the National Invasive Species Information Center, human action is the primary culprit in the proliferation of non-native species in the United States.[46] Exotic species sometimes are introduced intentionally (for example, as ornamental plants) but spread well beyond their intended domesticated areas. In other cases, they are introduced accidentally, for example, in the ballast water or cargo holds of ships.

Exotic species can cause fundamental ecosystem changes. The giant reed (*Arundo donax*) now clogs rivers in southern California, and the leafy spurge (*Euphorbia esula*) covers over 2.5 million acres of range across the Great Plains. Cheat grass has accelerated the fire cycle in the West by a factor of 20. In a sense, this form of environmental change is more insidious than clear cut forests or dense urban smog, which are readily apparent to the untrained eye (or nose). And the problem of invasive plants continues to grow. The Biota of North America Program at the University of North Carolina, Chapel Hill, adds about 300 species per year to the list of the nation's flora, and only about 10 percent of those are natives. But the precise scope of the problem is not well known. Total estimates of non-native species introduced to the United States range from 5,000 to 50,000.

Invasive animal species pose similar threats to ecosystem health. The Asian long-horned beetle destroys city trees. The nutria, a South American rodent, is devastating wetland ecosystems. Other obvious examples include the West Nile virus, red fire ants, and the notorious zebra mussel. Introduced to the Great Lakes during the 1980s via discharged ballast water from ships, by 1999 zebra mussels had spread throughout much of the Mississippi River basin and northward into Canada. Collectively, exotic species cause severe ecological and economic harm. Almost half of all listed endangered species in the United States are adversely affected by invasive species. The National Invasive Species Council identified the problem as one of the most serious environmental threats of the twenty-first century. One group of researchers at Cornell University estimated that invasive species impose an economic cost in the United States of $137 billion per year.

Ecosystem alteration, with its serious implications for human society and other species, is not just a domestic problem. In 2005, a group of over 1,300 scientists in 95 countries prepared a comprehensive inventory and assessment of the Earth's ecosystems.[47] The conclusions are sobering. According to these scientists, virtually all of the Earth's ecosystems have been significantly transformed by human activity. Large groups of species are in danger of extinction on an unprecedented scale,

---

44. With respect to the grazing issue, see DEBORA L. DONAHUE, THE WESTERN RANGE REVISITED, REMOVING LIVESTOCK FROM PUBLIC LANDS TO CONSERVE BIODIVERSITY (1999).

45. NATIONAL INVASIVE SPECIES COUNCIL, MEETING THE INVASIVE SPECIES CHALLENGE, MANAGEMENT PLAN (2001).

46. *See* http://www.invasivespeciesinfo.gov/whatis.shtml.

47. MILLENNIUM ECOSYSTEM ASSESSMENT SYNTHESIS REPORT, A REPORT OF THE MILLENNIUM ECOSYSTEM ASSESSMENT (Prepublication Final Draft Mar. 23, 2005).

with between 10 and 50 percent of species at risk, depending on the categories of species studied. Prominent experts like Paul Ehrlich and Edward O. Wilson believe that up to a quarter of all species that currently exist will be extinct by the middle of the twenty-first century, especially if tropical deforestation continues at current levels. *See* YVONNE BASKIN, THE WORK OF NATURE, HOW THE DIVERSITY OF LIFE SUSTAINS US 10 (1997). In the oceans, the total mass of commercially used species has plummeted by 90 percent throughout much of the world. On land, over half of our grasslands and forests have been converted to farms, and that has changed dramatically the use and release of soil, sediment, and nutrients such as nitrogen and phosphorus in the terrestrial and aquatic environments. Water withdrawals from rivers and lakes doubled between 1960 and 2000, and groundwater use has skyrocketed in many areas as well. In addition to our ethical obligation to preserve and protect other species and their habitats, as recognized in laws such as the Endangered Species Act, many scientists and economists are increasingly taking note of the "ecosystem services" that are lost when species become extinct and other ecosystem resources are lost. *See* NATURE'S SERVICES, SOCIETAL DEPENDENCE ON NATURAL ECOSYSTEMS (Gretchen C. Daily ed., 1997).

D. IMPLICATIONS FOR ENVIRONMENTAL LAW

In previous sections of the article from which the following is excerpted, Professor Richard Lazarus evaluated the environmental decisions of the U.S. Supreme Court (and of individual Supreme Court Justices), and concluded that the Supreme Court has improperly failed to view environmental law as anything more than a subset of general administrative law. In short, it has failed to appreciate the particular characteristics that define and distinguish environmental law. In the following part of the article, Professor Lazarus sets forth his view of what those characteristics are, and their implications.

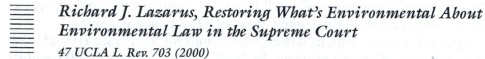

Richard J. Lazarus, Restoring What's Environmental About Environmental Law in the Supreme Court
47 UCLA L. Rev. 703 (2000)

A. What Is Environmental About Environmental Law—The Nature of
    Environmental Injury

What makes environmental law distinctive is largely traceable to the nature of the injury that environmental protection law seeks to reduce, minimize, or sometimes prevent altogether. Environmental law is concerned, in the first instance, with impacts on the natural environment. Hence, although some environmental laws are concerned about human health effects, as are many other types of laws (e.g., food and drug, worker safety, Medicare, and food stamp programs), environmental law is concerned only about human health effects resulting from impacts on the natural environment. And, of course, many environmental laws are concerned only with those impacts and not with possible human health effects at all.

A common denominator, therefore, for environmental law is the ecological injury that serves as the law's threshold and often exclusive focus. That common denominator is also the primary source of the special challenges environmental law presents for lawmaking. Ecological injury has several recurring features that render its redress through law especially difficult. These pertain to both the "cause" and the "effect" of such injury, each of which inevitably becomes a regulatory touchstone in any legal regime for environmental protection. Some of the more obvious features are discussed below.

1. *Irreversible, Catastrophic, and Continuing Injury.* Environmental law is often concerned about the avoidance of irreversible, catastrophic results. The destruction of an aquifer upon which a community depends for drinking water, the erosion of soil necessary for farming that required centuries to develop, and the destruction of the ozone layer are not possibilities to be lightly taken. Such potential downsides render enormously costly any errors in decision making. Yet, while errors are costly, so too can be delays in decision making. Even the best resolution is worth little if it is developed too late to prevent a chain of events inexorably leading to ecological disaster.

Finally, a closely related trait of some environmental injury is its continuing nature. Environmental law must address harm that increases over time. The harm is dynamic and not static in character. An oil spill addressed quickly may be confined to manageable dimensions. But conversely, if not quickly addressed, it may rapidly and exponentially increase in scope to overwhelming dimensions. Legal regimes that are inherently cautious and slow to react do not readily lend themselves to the quick action often necessary in the ecological context.

2. *Physically Distant Injury.* Ecological injury is often not physically confineable. Actions in one location may have substantial adverse effects in very distant locations. This may be because the pollutants actually travel from one place to another. Or it may be as the result of the adverse impacts of activities in one locale on a global commons, upon the viability of which many regions are dependent.

Long-range transportation of airborne pollutants is an example of the former. The ozone layer in the upper atmosphere exemplifies the transboundary implications of degradation of a commons resource, as the destruction of the ozone layer by activities in one part of the world can have serious environmental and human health effects in other parts of the world. Global warming presents a similar physical dimension.

For each, the associated challenges for the establishment of any legal regime are great, especially because the costs of control are imposed in one area and the benefits are enjoyed in a very different area. Such a distributional mismatch renders the adoption, implementation, and enforcement of the necessary transboundary legal rules very difficult. This is certainly true in the international arenas, but even far more localized spreadings of causes and effects between states and counties resist ready political resolutions.

3. Temporally Distant Injury: Much of the injury environmental law seeks to address is not imminent. Sometimes actions now may trigger the injury, but the injury itself will be realized only in the distant future. Sometimes the injury will be realized now and will increase, inexorably, over time. To the extent that the latter is occurring, this temporal character to some environmental injury may become, as a practical matter, irreversible and thus collapse into the first feature of ecological injury described above.

This temporal feature of ecological injuries poses challenges to legal doctrine and lawmaking analogous to those presented by the "physically distant" characteristic discussed above. The same distributional mismatch is presented but even more problematically, because the benefits to be enjoyed will generally inure only to future generations lacking any representation in current lawmaking fora. Such intergenerational effects raise issues regarding the propriety of "discounting" the value of future benefits (including human lives) in selecting environmental controls today. Even more fundamentally, however, the intergenerational dimension to ecological injury raises basic questions regarding the moral responsibilities that current generations have to safeguard the interests of future generations.

4. Uncertainty and Risk: There is much uncertainty associated with environmental injury, which poses even further challenges for lawmaking. The primary source of this uncertainty is the sheer complexity of the natural environment and, accordingly, how much is still unknown about it. This uncertainty expresses itself in our inability to know beforehand the environmental impact of certain actions. It equally undermines our ability to apprehend, after the fact, what precisely caused certain environmental impacts.

The inevitable upshot is that environmental laws that seek to prevent harm are directed to risk rather than to actual impact. It similarly means that environmental laws that seek to assign responsibility for harm that has already occurred are limited in their ability to do so.

Because, moreover, environmental law is concerned with risk, there is an inherently psychological dimension to the injury being redressed. The injury is not confined to that which occurs if the risk is itself realized. There is often psychological harm resulting from the risk itself, whether or not ever realized. For this same reason, by failing to address that mental dimension, one can increase the associated injury even if the numerical probability of the risk's physical realization remains the same.

5. Multiple Causes: Ecological injuries are rarely the product of a single action at an isolated moment of time. Putting aside the pervasive uncertainty issues, environmental harms are more typically the cumulative and synergistic result of multiple actions, often spread over significant time and space. This is primarily traceable to the sharing inherent in any common natural resource base, which is the object of so many simultaneous and sporadic actions over time and space.

6. *Noneconomic, Nonhuman Character*: Many of the ecological injuries resulting from environmental degradation are not readily susceptible to monetary valuation and have a distinctively nonhuman character. There is simply no readily available market analogue. The nonexclusive nature of the natural resources at stake is often one factor prompting resistance of valuation. Even more generally, the decision to protect the ecological interest in question may have been deliberately made notwithstanding any notion of economic value. It could, of course, be ultimately rooted in notions of uncertainty and concerns about adverse human health effects—e.g., the after-the-fact discovery that the DNA of a subspecies of fly would have cured the common cold. But it may instead be, and often is, based on the deeper notion that there are certain results—such as species extinction or resource destruction—that humankind should strive to avoid because they fall beyond its legitimate authority.

Other kinds of injury that resist ready monetary valuation are the adverse human health effects that can result from environmental degradation, although these valuation issues are shared by all laws designed to safeguard human health. For some economists, all human health effects of this kind must be susceptible to such valuation for the simple reason that tradeoffs are inevitably made in any allocation of limited societal resources. Nothing has infinite value, and each decision has opportunity costs related to opportunities thereby foregone. But some environmental laws reflect a very different philosophy, which posits that there are some adverse human health effects that are presumptively out of bounds for policymakers. For those who share that policy view, economic valuation and tradeoffs are therefore not legitimate topics for policy discussion.

Perhaps, moreover, it is this normative dimension of ecological injury that is ultimately the most telling. The environmental dimension of environmental law teaches that the nonhuman, nonmonetizable dimensions of ecological injury not only exist but are worth protecting. They reflect positive values that are entitled to weight in the balancing in which members of the executive, legislative, and judicial branches are ultimately engaged as part of their respective lawmaking and policymaking responsibilities.

B. Challenges for Law and Lawmaking

Because of these varied features of ecological injuries, the challenges of constructing a legal regime for environmental protection are considerable. Some of the challenges affect substantive areas of law. Others pertain more to the process of lawmaking and the related institutions than to any distinct area of law. In certain circumstances, a full appreciation of the associated challenges may well justify a modification of current law or the functioning of certain lawmaking institutions, but confined to the environmental context. In other circumstances, however, the lessons to be learned from environmental law may have more far-reaching import. They may suggest that an entire area of law, or the ways in which particular lawmaking institutions operate, should be rethought . . . .

NOTES AND QUESTIONS ON LAZARUS ARTICLE

1. *Other characteristics?* Would you add anything to Professor Lazarus' list? Would you change or delete anything?

2. *Possible legal solutions?* For each of the six characteristics identified by Professor Lazarus, identify a set of possible legal solutions, perhaps drawing from approaches to similar issues you have learned in other courses. This is a good way to scope out the possible key concepts of environmental law in advance.

A CONTINUING CASE STUDY—CLIMATE DISRUPTION

Working through a problem is a good way to understand how the various concepts we discuss in this book might apply to a real-world situation. We have chosen to use a single, very current, and very difficult real-world situation as the basis for most of the problems throughout this book.

That problem is global climate disruption, perhaps the defining environmental problem of our generation and for those of generations to come. We use the term "climate disruption" rather than the conventional "climate change" or "global warming" because we believe it is the most accurate term. The impacts of the global buildup of greenhouse gases will, in a possibly abrupt fashion, profoundly alter the world's ecosystems and many aspects of human experience on earth. In the words of John P. Holdren, the White House's top science policy adviser, " 'global warming' is a misnomer because it implies something gradual, uniform, and benign, none of which is true." *Presentation to the Board Chairman, American Ass'n for the Advancement of Science*, John F. Kennedy School of Government (Nov. 6, 2007). The same is true of the term "climate change," a label that could as easily refer to purely natural alterations in the climate system as to those driven by human activities.

Included below is some background information on climate disruption together with an excerpt from a recent scientific report. As you read these, consider whether, and to what extent, climate disruption exemplifies the characteristics of environmental injury highlighted by Richard Lazarus in his article, "What Is Environmental About Environmental Injury"?

Climate disruption results from the buildup of greenhouse gases in the troposphere, much of which originates from gases emitted by human activities. A primary source of such gases is the combustion of fossil fuels such as the coal, oil, and natural gas used to generate electricity, power transportation vehicles, and operate factories and other industrial facilities. A secondary source of greenhouse gases is the release of the carbon stored in trees and terrestrial biota when forests are cut down or land is converted from open space to commercial or residential development.

Greenhouse gases are so named because, in rough analogy to a greenhouse, they warm the earth's surface. Greenhouse gases allow visible sunlight to pass through the atmosphere, but tend to trap the infrared radiation (heat) that would otherwise be radiated back into space. This "greenhouse effect" results in the net warming of the earth's surface. Three main greenhouse gases that are increasing in the atmosphere because of increased emissions from human activities are carbon dioxide, methane, and nitrous oxide. In addition, some synthetic chemicals, including sulfur hexafluoride and several hydrofluorocarbons and perfluorocarbons, are strong greenhouse gases whose emissions are growing rapidly because they are substitutes for ozone-depleting chemicals being phased out under an international treaty, the Montreal Protocol. Each of these chemicals has different heat-trapping capability and lasts different amounts of time in the atmosphere. These two characteristics, heat-trapping capacity and atmospheric lifetime, can be combined into a single measurement known as the gas's "global warming potential." Carbon dioxide is used as a reference and thus is defined to have a global warming potential of 1 over a 100-year time horizon. By comparison, sulfur hexafluoride, perhaps the most potent and long-lived anthropogenic greenhouse gas, has a greenhouse gas potential of 22,800. INTERGOVERNMENTAL PANEL ON CLIMATE CHANGE, FOURTH ASSESSMENT REPORT (2007).

We rely upon some measure of greenhouse gas emissions to warm the earth to habitable levels and much of these emissions come from natural processes, such as water evaporation. However, it is the addition of human-caused emissions to natural emissions that today threatens to effect major changes to the earth's climate and ecosystems. Over the course of the past century, the concentration of greenhouse gases in the atmosphere has skyrocketed. For 10,000 years prior to the industrial revolution, levels of carbon dioxide in the atmosphere hovered between 260 and 280 parts per million (ppm). Between 1750 and the present, however, levels of greenhouse gases increased dramatically—by 40 percent to reach 391 ppm in 2011. INTERGOVERNMENTAL PANEL ON CLIMATE CHANGE (IPCC), FIFTH ASSESSMENT REPORT, SUMMARY FOR POLICYMAKERS (2013). As reported in the most recent summary from the IPCC:

> [A]tmospheric concentrations of carbon dioxide, methane, and nitrous oxide have increased to levels unprecedented in at least the last 800,000 years. Carbon dioxide concentrations have increased by 40 percent since pre-industrial times, primarily from fossil fuel emissions and secondarily from net land use change emissions. The ocean has absorbed about 30 percent of the emitted anthropogenic carbon dioxide, causing ocean acidification.

Id. at 11.

As discussed in the excerpt below, scientists fault human activities for most of this growth.

Efforts to slow or reverse climate disruption are complicated by the fact that it is a global phenomenon. The projected ecological effects of climate disruption result from the buildup of greenhouse gas concentrations, which itself is the result of the emissions from billions of sources from around the globe. As a result, prevention of many of the most severe impacts of climate disruption is impossible in the absence of the combined efforts of the world's industrialized and rapidly industrializing nations.

The ensuing chapters of this book will discuss other aspects of climate disruption in much greater detail along with the potential solutions provided by various legal approaches to environmental protection.

 ## U.S. Global Change Research Program, U.S. National Climate Assessment
Global Climate Change Impacts in the United States (2014)

Overview

Climate change is already affecting the American people in far-reaching ways. Certain types of extreme weather events with links to climate change have become more frequent and/or intense, including prolonged periods of heat, heavy downpours, and, in some regions, floods and droughts. In addition, warming is causing sea level to rise and glaciers and Arctic sea ice to melt, and oceans are becoming more acidic as they absorb carbon dioxide. These and other aspects of climate change are disrupting people's lives and damaging some sectors of our economy.

Climate Change: Present and Future

Evidence for climate change abounds, from the top of the atmosphere to the depths of the oceans. . . . Evidence of climate change is also visible in the observed and measured changes in location and behavior of species and functioning of ecosystems. Taken together, this evidence tells an unambiguous story: the planet is warming, and over the last half century, this warming has been driven primarily by human activity.

Multiple lines of independent evidence confirm that human activities are the primary cause of the global warming of the past 50 years. The burning of coal, oil, and gas, and clearing of forests have increased the concentration of carbon dioxide in the atmosphere by more than 40 percent since the Industrial Revolution, and it has been known for almost two centuries that this carbon dioxide traps heat. Methane and nitrous oxide emissions from agriculture and other human activities add to the atmospheric burden of heat-trapping gases. Data show that natural factors like the sun and volcanoes cannot have caused the warming observed over the past 50 years. Sensors on satellites have measured the sun's output with great accuracy and found no overall increase during the past half century. Large volcanic eruptions during this period, such as Mount Pinatubo in 1991, have exerted a short-term cooling influence. In fact, if not for human activities, global climate would actually have cooled slightly over the past 50 years. The pattern of temperature change through the layers of the atmosphere, with warming near the surface and cooling higher up in the stratosphere, further confirms that it is the buildup of heat-trapping gases (also known as "greenhouse gases") that has caused most of the Earth's warming over the past half century.

Because human-induced warming is superimposed on a background of natural variations in climate, warming is not uniform over time. Short-term fluctuations in the long-term upward trend are thus natural and expected. . . .

U.S. average temperature has increased by 1.3°F to 1.9°F since 1895, and most of this increase has occurred since 1970. The most recent decade was the nation's and the world's hottest on record, and 2012 was the hottest year on record in the continental United States. All U.S. regions have experienced warming in recent decades, but the extent of warming has not been uniform. . . .

The amount of warming projected beyond the next few decades is directly linked to the cumulative global emissions of heat-trapping gases and particles. By the end of this century, a roughly 3°F to 5°F rise is projected under a lower emissions scenario, which would require substantial reductions in emissions . . . and a 5°F to 10°F rise for a higher emissions scenario assuming continued increases in emissions, predominantly from fossil fuel combustion. . . . These projections are based on results from 16 climate models. . . . The range of model projections for each emissions scenario is the result of the differences in the ways the models represent key factors such as water vapor, ice and snow reflectivity, and clouds, which can either dampen or amplify the initial effect of human influences on temperature. . . .

Prolonged periods of high temperatures and the persistence of high nighttime temperatures have increased in many locations (especially in urban areas) over the past half century. High nighttime temperatures have widespread impacts because people, livestock, and wildlife get no respite from the heat. In some regions, prolonged periods of high temperatures associated with droughts contribute to conditions that lead to larger wildfires and longer fire seasons. As expected in a warming climate, recent trends show that extreme heat is becoming more common, while extreme cold is becoming less common. . . .

Human-induced climate change means much more than just hotter weather. Increases in ocean and freshwater temperatures, frost-free days, and heavy downpours have all been documented. Global sea level has risen, and there have been large reductions in snow-cover extent, glaciers, and sea ice. These changes and other climatic changes have affected and will continue to affect human health, water supply, agriculture, transportation, energy, coastal areas, and many other sectors of society, with increasingly adverse impacts on the American economy and quality of life.

* * *

Some impacts that occur in one region ripple beyond that region. For example the dramatic decline of summer sea ice in the Arctic—a loss of ice cover roughly equal to half the area of the continental United States—exacerbates global warming by reducing the reflectivity of Earth's surface and increasing the amount of heat absorbed. Similarly, smoke from wildfires in one location can contribute to poor air quality in faraway regions, and evidence suggests that particulate matter can affect atmospheric properties and therefore weather patterns. Major storms and the higher storm surges exacerbated by sea level rise that hit the Gulf Coast affect the entire country through their cascading effects on oil and gas production and distribution.

Water expands as it warms, causing global sea levels to rise; melting of land-based ice also raises sea level by adding water to the oceans. Over the past century, global average sea level has risen by about 8 inches. . . . Sea level is projected to rise by another 1 to 4 feet in this century, although the rise in sea level in specific regions is expected to vary from this global average for a number of reasons. . . . The stakes are high, as nearly five million Americans and hundreds of billions of dollars of property are located in areas that are less than four feet above the local high tide level.

In addition to causing changes in climate, increasing levels of carbon dioxide from the burning of fossil fuels and other human activities have a direct effect on the world's oceans. Carbon dioxide interacts with ocean water to form carbonic acid, increasing the ocean's acidity. Ocean surface waters have become 30 percent more acidic over the last 250 years as they have absorbed large amounts of carbon dioxide from the atmosphere. This ocean acidification makes water more corrosive, reducing the capacity of marine organisms with shells or skeletons made of calcium carbonate (such as corals, krill, oysters, clams, and crabs) to survive, grow, and reproduce, which in turn will affect the marine food chain.

Widespread Impacts

* * *

Sectors affected by climate changes include agriculture, water, human health, energy, transportation, forests, and ecosystems. Climate change poses a major challenge to U.S. agriculture because of the critical dependence of agricultural systems on climate. Climate change has the potential to both positively and negatively affect the location, timing, and productivity of crop, livestock, and fishery systems at local, national, and global scales. The United States produces nearly $330 billion per year in agricultural commodities. This productivity is vulnerable to direct impacts on crops and livestock from changing climate conditions and extreme weather events and indirect impacts through increasing pressures from pests and pathogens. Climate change will also alter the stability of food supplies and create new food security challenges for the United States as the world seeks to feed nine billion people by 2050 . . . .

Water quality and quantity are being affected by climate change. Changes in precipitation and runoff, combined with changes in consumption and withdrawal, have reduced surface and groundwater supplies in many areas. These trends are expected to continue, increasing the likelihood of water shortages for many uses. Water quality is also diminishing in many areas, particularly due to sediment and contaminant concentrations after heavy downpours.

Sea level rise, storms and storm surges, and changes in surface and groundwater use patterns are expected to compromise the sustainability of coastal freshwater aquifers and wetlands. . . .

Climate change affects human health in many ways. For example, increasingly frequent and intense heat events lead to more heat related illnesses and deaths and, over time, worsen drought and wildfire risks, and intensify air pollution. Increasingly frequent extreme precipitation and associated flooding can lead to injuries and increases in waterborne disease. Rising sea surface temperatures have been linked with increasing levels and ranges of diseases. Rising sea levels intensify coastal flooding and storm surge, and thus exacerbate threats to public safety during storms. Certain groups of people are more vulnerable to the range of climate change related health impacts, including the elderly, children, the poor, and the sick. Others are vulnerable because of where they live, including those in floodplains, coastal zones, and some urban areas. . . .

Climate change also affects the living world, including people, through changes in ecosystems and biodiversity. . . . Climate change driven disruptions to ecosystems have direct and indirect human impacts, including reduced water supply and quality, the loss of iconic species and landscapes, effects on food chains and the timing and success of species migrations, and the potential for extreme weather and climate events to destroy or degrade the ability of ecosystems to provide societal benefits.

Questions on Climate Disruption's Characteristics

1. *Does climate disruption exemplify the unique aspects of environmental injuries?* Consider each unique aspect of environmental injuries highlighted by Richard Lazarus and assess whether climate disruption exemplifies this characteristic and, if so, why.

2. *Scientific uncertainty.* What are the major uncertainties associated with climate disruption and how should we address those uncertainties? Which projected impacts of climate disruption are considered the most uncertain and which the most certain?

2

Common Law Solutions

Students of environmental law soon learn that complex federal and state statutes currently dominate the field. Even longer sets of implementing regulations and policies dwarf these statutes. These regulatory regimes usually employ a somewhat comprehensive approach, *i.e.*, they might address all sources of a particular type of pollution or regulate entire industries as opposed to individual polluters. For the most part, however, this statutory and regulatory regime only began to develop over the past several decades.[1] Before then, someone who felt sufficiently aggrieved by pollution to seek legal redress would have to resort to common law remedies on a case-by-case basis.

This chapter first explores the major common law doctrines used to redress pollution and other environmental problems. In doing so, we have multiple goals. First, despite the overlay of modern statutes and regulations, the common law is not dead as a tool for addressing environmental problems. Plaintiffs continue to bring common law actions to redress environmental harm for a variety of reasons: There are gaps in the statutory system; the common law may provide superior remedies for particular plaintiffs; and some plaintiffs may believe that a local judge or jury might provide a more receptive audience than a distant bureaucrat. Some have argued that the common law can and should function as a strong and vibrant force of legal change in law, informing the development of contemporary environmental statutes. Alexandra B. Klass, *Common Law and Federalism in the Age of the Regulatory State*, 92 Iowa L. Rev. 545, 580 (2007). Thus, environmental lawyers should be familiar with the kinds of common law cases that remain available to address environmental issues.

---

1. There are, of course, some exceptions. For example, the Supreme Court construed the Rivers and Harbors Act of 1899, a law originally designed to protect waterways from refuse that would impede navigation for commerce and national defense, in part as an anti-pollution law. *See* United States v. Republic Steel Corp., 362 U.S. 482 (1960); United States v. Standard Oil Co., 384 U.S. 224 (1966). The direct precursor to the modern Clean Water Act was the Water Pollution Control Act of 1948, and the first incarnation of the Clean Air Act was passed in 1955. For the most part, however, common law approaches to most environmental problems were dominant until the 1960s and 1970s.

Second, our environmental statutes were not written on a blank slate. In many cases, Congress (and state legislatures) borrowed concepts from the existing common law, either intact or in modified form, as the basis for statutory regulation. The clearest example is the federal "Superfund" statute,[2] in which Congress adopted certain common law liability rules as the governing substantive law, but less explicit use of common law principles is evident in other statutes as well. Thus, a grounding in common law approaches to environmental problems will enhance your understanding of the evolving statutory system.

Third, Congress adopted our modern environmental laws in significant part due to the perceived inadequacy of common law approaches to address the full range and magnitude of environmental problems in an increasingly industrialized world. To understand why those laws were passed, and what they sought to accomplish, it is useful to evaluate both the strengths and the weaknesses of common law approaches.

A. COMMON LAW APPROACHES—FROM STRICT RIGHTS TO BALANCE

Solutions to early environmental problems derived mainly from the law of property and the law of torts. We begin by outlining the most prevalent premises of common law doctrine that are potentially useful for environmental law. Then, we present some of the most noted common law cases in the United States as examples of how those doctrines apply to environmental problems. As you read each of these cases, take note of the ways in which common law doctrines provide useful solutions to environmental problems, and the limitations that might have prompted the development of statutory regimes to augment or replace the common law.

As with many aspects of the common law, some doctrines establish strict rights-based approaches in which any impairment of established rights is unlawful *per se*, leaving the nature of the remedy as the only remaining issue. Other doctrines seek to balance the rights and interests of one party against those of others, including the public at large. In some cases, strict rights-based doctrines evolved to reflect more of a balancing approach, as the aesthetic values of once-pastoral societies gave way to the practical needs of the industrial revolution. Pay attention to which aspects of common law doctrine reflect a strict rights-based approach, and which reflect more of a balancing method. Both concepts have parallels in various statutory systems you will study later in the book.

---

2. This law is known more formally as the Comprehensive Environmental Response, Compensation, and Liability Act (CERCLA), and is codified at 42 U.S.C. §§9601 *et seq.*

TRESPASS AND NUISANCE PROBLEM: CARBON STORAGE AND SEQUESTRATION

Juanita Rozwell's house is rising. In fact, the one-acre parcel of land on which Juanita's house sits in a sparsely populated part of the Texas panhandle has risen by six inches since the beginning of last year. As a result, Juanita, a small-scale farmer, has experienced ruptures in the piping that conveys water, electricity, and gas to her home, causing her and her three children to move in with relatives for the foreseeable future. In trying to determine the cause, Juanita has learned that, for the past year, CarbonX, Inc., which owns a nearby parcel of land, has been engaged in a climate disruption mitigation technique known as carbon capture and sequestration, or "CCS," only a half mile from her house. CarbonX has been capturing carbon dioxide emissions from the stacks of a nearby coal-fired electricity plant, compressing the gas into a liquid form, and then piping the liquid to an injection point near Juanita's house where it is pumped 2,600 feet below the surface into an existing geological formation that subsurface geological maps show runs under Juanita's land. According to a government website, CarbonX's CCS project is a pilot project to determine the suitability of large-scale CCS in this region of the country, potentially piping CO_2 from power plants up to a hundred miles away. With further investigation, Juanita has also determined that several nearby family farms, as well as a new windfarm, have also sustained damages attributable to land disturbances that have all occurred shortly after the CarbonX injection activities commenced.

Suppose Juanita wants to stop CarbonX's CCS activities and obtain compensation for the damages she has sustained. As you read the following information about common law causes of action, please think about which common law actions might lie for this problem. Then, draft a complaint on her behalf and prepare a bench memo for the judge deciding a motion by CarbonX to dismiss the case.

---

1. Trespass

The common law of trespass, an important element of property law, prevents someone from intentionally interfering with your physical possession of land, whether by treading across your prize flower beds or building their new garage on your side of the property line. Likewise, contaminated water or other pollutants flowing onto your fields or into your groundwater can constitute a physical invasion of property. *See, e.g.*, Castles Auto & Truck Service v. Exxon Corp., 16 Fed. Appx. 163, 167 (4th Cir. 2001) (affirming jury verdict of trespass based on migration of petroleum onto plaintiff's property). Should wafts of thick smoke from a nearby factory constitute a physical invasion of property? *See* Stacy v. VEPCO, 7 ENVTL. REP. CASES (BNA) 1443 (E.D. Va. 1975) (finding "negligence and/or trespass" from power plant emissions that, based on expert testimony, damaged trees 22 miles away). What about invisible but unpleasant odors emanating from a neighboring hog farm?

Trespass is a strict liability doctrine for any intentional (and non-consensual) physical invasion of land. Strict liability means that once the elements of the cause of action are established (intentional physical invasion without consent), liability attaches. The intent element of trespass does not require that a defendant act with the purpose of entering another's property, but that the defendant know that his conduct will, inevitably or with substantial certainty, result in such an entry. Restatement (Second) of Torts, §163 cmts. b & c (1963). Thus, trespass reflects a rights-based approach. Property owners are entitled to physical control and enjoyment of their property free from unwanted physical invasions, and the courts strictly protect those rights. Under trespass law, we do not balance the needs and interests of the property owner against those of the intruder.

Questions concerning the scope of a property owner's possessory interest in land that he or she owns free of an actionable trespass or nuisance frequently arise in common law cases. Are there any limits to its vertical extent? At common law, ownership of the land extended to the periphery of the universe — *cujus est solum ejus est usque ad coelum*, which, according to Black's Law Dictionary, is Latin for "the rights of the surface owner extend upward to the heavens." 1 COKE, INSTITUTES ch. 1, §1(4a) (19th ed. 1832). But that view is rejected by modern courts as inconsistent with the public right to a navigable airspace, limiting a landowner's possessory claim to the immediate reaches of the superjacent airspace that he or she can use and occupy. United States v. Causby, 328 U.S. 256, 263-65 (1946). What about the subsurface? The Latin maxim above is often provided with the ending "*ad inferos*," extending the scope of a surface owner's rights not only up to the heavens, but also downward to the center of the earth. Courts continue to repeat this view, though they have been loath to apply it beyond the immediate (tree root deep) subsurface. Summarizing the law, one commentator states, "Broadly speaking, the deeper the dispute, the less likely courts are to recognize the surface owner's title." John G. Spankling, *Owning the Center of the Earth*, 55 UCLA L. REV. 979, 1004 (2008). *See, e.g.*, Chance v. BP Chemicals, 77 Ohio St. 3d 17, 24-28 (1996) (rejecting trespass and nuisance claims against company injecting hazardous waste into a formation 2,430 feet below the surface).

A common law protection against water pollution somewhat related to trespass, also grounded in the law of property, is the doctrine of riparian rights. Law students most commonly study riparian rights in courses in Water Law, with an emphasis on the amount of water flowing past or through one's land. Under the traditional form of this doctrine, developed in England, and then adopted in the eastern United States,[3] riparian landowners are entitled to the "natural flow" of a stream through their property, undiminished in quantity and unimpaired in quality, regardless of hardship to the interests of other users of the waterway. As such, riparian rights resemble trespass in that both doctrines protect property absolutely against pollution and other forms of impairment. Unlike trespass, however, the law

---

3. The western states adopted the very different prior appropriation doctrine, which in its traditional form protects those who divert water from streams for beneficial uses, regardless of impacts to the environment or to junior (more recent) appropriators.

of riparian rights evolved such that courts typically balance the rights, needs, and interests of riparian landowners against those of other water users and the general public. As uses of water grew more common and more intensive, the strict riparian rights doctrine gave way to a "reasonable use" approach in which competing uses of water and waterways — included waste disposal — were weighed, based on factors such as economic utility and the feasibility of abating the harm. *See, e.g.,* Snow v. Parsons, 28 Vt. 459, 464 (1856) (rejecting absolute riparian doctrine in favor of assessment of reasonableness in challenge to discharge of tannery wastes). The Restatement (Second) of Torts (1979), §§850 and 850A, also embodies those principles. A similar development occurred in the law of nuisance.

2. Nuisance

As noted by Professor William Rodgers, who penned one of the seminal treatises on modern environmental law, the common law of nuisance has had a formative influence on the entire field of environmental law:

> To a surprising degree, the legal history of the environment has been written by nuisance law. There is no common law doctrine that approaches nuisance in comprehensiveness or detail as a regulator of land use and of technological abuse. Nuisance actions reach pollution of all physical media — air, water, land, groundwater — by a variety of means. Nuisance actions have challenged virtually every major industrial and municipal activity that today is the subject of comprehensive environmental regulation — the operation of landfills, incinerators, sewage treatment plants, activities at chemical plants, aluminum, lead and copper smelters, oil refineries, pulp mills, rendering plants, quarries and mines, textile mills and a host of other manufacturing activities. Nuisance litigation has influenced energy policy at all stages — fuel exploration, transportation, siting of facilities, fuel combustion, waste disposal and reclamation. Nuisance theory is the common law backbone of modern environmental and energy law.

WILLIAM H. RODGERS, JR., ENVIRONMENTAL LAW §2.1, at 112-13 (2d ed. 1994).

One main reason for this pervasive influence of nuisance law is that, whereas trespass law protects against physical invasion of property, nuisance goes further and protects against any substantial interference with the use and enjoyment of land. *See* Restatement (Second) of Torts §822. To the extent that no physical invasion is required, nuisance law potentially reaches a broader range of actions that may cause environmental harm. *See, e.g.,* O'Neill v. Carolina Freight Carriers Corp., 244 A.2d 372, 374 (Conn. 1968) (affirming jury verdict awarding damages to homeowner and granting injunctive relief against truck terminal due to excessive noise during nighttime hours); Washington Suburban Sanitary Commission v. CAE-Link Corp., 622 A.2d 745, 761 (Md. 1993) (holding that odors from sewage sludge composting facility constituted a nuisance). This breadth is tempered, however, by an accompanying limitation that actual interference be shown (as opposed to mere physical presence under trespass law) and that the interference be "substantial."

Nuisance law is divided into two related doctrines, private nuisance and public nuisance, each of which has its own relevance to environmental law. Private nuisance allows private parties to seek redress for injuries to their property rights due to the activities of others. As a result, private nuisance claims are available only to those whose property rights are harmed by a particular activity. Public nuisance protects against injuries to the broader public.

Although private nuisance is grounded in property law because of its focus on protecting property rights, it also encompasses various elements of the law of torts. A private nuisance consists of an invasion of property that adversely and substantially affects the use and enjoyment of land and is either intentional and unreasonable or unintentional but otherwise actionable. As in trespass law, under the Restatement (Second) of Torts, a person's interference is "intentional" where she acts for the purpose of causing the interference or knows, or is substantially certain, that an interference will result from her conduct. §822. An interference is "unreasonable" whether either the gravity of the harm outweighs the utility of the conduct, or the harm is serious and the defendant is financially incapable of compensating the plaintiff for the harm. "Otherwise actionable" can encompass any otherwise valid cause of action but most commonly means either negligence or strict liability for abnormally dangerous activities, both of which are common law torts. Finally, a defendant is liable in nuisance only to a person who sustains "significant harm" as a result of the interference. Restatement (Second) of Torts §821F.

Nuisance has functioned as a primitive type of land use regulation, encouraging the siting of compatible uses and discouraging incompatible uses. For instance, in determining the reasonableness of a given interference, the Restatement (Second) of Torts asks whether the use or enjoyment interfered with and the interfering conduct is "suitable" to the locality. Is residential use suitable to a locality when it adjoins a corridor of petrochemical plants? Similarly, a potent defense to a nuisance claim is that the plaintiff "came to the nuisance." While not a complete defense, in all states it will be harder for the plaintiff to prevail where she arrived after the use about which she complains. JOSEPH SINGER, PROPERTY LAW: RULES, POLICIES, AND PRACTICES (6th ed. 2014). Does nuisance law retard the evolution to "greener" land uses, i.e., a neighborhood's reliance upon windmills for energy as opposed to a coal-fired power plant? To the extent the "coming to the nuisance" defense highlights the priority placed by the common law in protecting an owner's investment in a given land use, can the law facilitate a change in land use and yet still protect that owner's investment? See Spur Industries v. Del E. Webb Development, Inc., 108 Ariz. 178 (1972) (granting retirement community an injunction against a feedlot operation but requiring the community to indemnify the feedlot for its losses).

In its original form, nuisance doctrine imposed strict liability in the same manner as trespass law on the theory that the right to use and enjoy property should be protected against any unlawful or unreasonable invasion, with the appropriate remedy varying with degree of harm. As industrial activity intensified, however, this strict rights-based approach shifted to a balancing test in which courts weighted the gravity of harm against the utility of the challenged activity. In striking this balance, courts now consider factors such as the extent of harm, the nature of harm, the social value of the competing uses, the suitability of the activity to the place, and the feasibility (or burden) of avoiding the alleged harm. Many modern environmental laws reflect this balancing approach.

Private nuisance cases have only limited utility in redressing widespread environmental harm because those cases require one or more plaintiffs with the requisite degree and kind of harm, as well as sufficient economic means and incentive, to invoke the doctrine. Private nuisance law is less useful where a large number of property owners suffer lesser individual (but cumulatively significant) harm, or where harm occurs to public as opposed to private resources (such as public forests or water bodies). Public nuisance law fills the gap by protecting against an unreasonable interference common to the public. In deciding whether to abate a public nuisance, courts consider the extent to which an activity interferes with public health, safety, peace, and convenience; whether the activity is proscribed by statute or regulation or is otherwise unlawful; and the length and degree of permanence of the harm. *See* Restatement (Second) of Torts, §821C. Traditionally, only public officials could bring public nuisance cases. However, individuals also may bring public nuisance claims if they suffer injuries that are different in kind, not just degree, than those inflicted on the public at large. While monetary damages may be sufficient to redress a private nuisance to a small number of individual property owners, public nuisances are more likely to justify injunctive relief.

3. Trespass or Nuisance?

A frequently litigated issue in common law environmental cases is whether the conduct complained of—often a polluting factory or minerals processing facility—is a trespass or a nuisance. Why might a plaintiff seek to convince the court that the activity is a trespass, rather than relying solely on nuisance? How difficult do you think it could be to demonstrate that the interferences caused by polluting emissions from a lead smelter or an oil production facility or the pesticide spray from a crop-duster are "unreasonable"? For cases struggling to categorize the dispersal of microscopic particulates as either a "trespass" or a "nuisance," see Johnson v. Paynesville Farmers Union Cooperative Oil Co., 817 N.W.2d 693 (Minn. 2012); Borland v. Sanders Lead Co., 369 So. 2d 523 (1979); Martin v. Reynolds Metals Co., 342 P.2d 790 (1959).

4. Strict Liability for Abnormally Dangerous Activities

The concept of "abnormally dangerous activities" has obvious application to environmental cases involving such activities as petrochemical plants or the transportation of toxic or otherwise hazardous materials. Under the principle first established in Fletcher v. Rylands, L.R. 3 H.L. 330, 340 (1868) (finding liability without fault due to dam failure), strict liability may attach to an unduly dangerous thing or activity that a court finds inappropriate to a particular place. *See, e.g.,* Crawford v. National Lead Co., 784 F. Supp. 439, 443-44 (S.D. Ohio 1989) (finding liability for emotional distress and reduced property values due to emissions of uranium and other harmful substances). Under the modern version of the doctrine set forth in the Restatement (Second) of Torts, §520, in deciding whether an activity is abnormally dangerous, courts consider the risk of harm, the gravity of harm, whether the risk can be avoided with reasonable care, whether the activity is a "common usage," whether it is inappropriate to a particular place, and the value of the activity to the community. This modern version reflects a balancing of interests rather than a strict protection of property rights.

B.   THE PROMISE AND LIMITS OF COMMON LAW SOLUTIONS

Common law environmental cases are legion. We set forth below some of the most noted cases that have defined common law environmental jurisprudence in the United States. As you read these cases, ask yourself the following questions: (1) In what respects are common law doctrines useful in addressing the range of environmental problems identified in Chapter 1? (2) In what respects are common law approaches potentially inadequate to address those issues and problems? (3) Do these cases suggest anything about whether rights-based or balancing approaches are most appropriate to address environmental issues? (4) What do these cases teach about whether common law doctrines adequately address environmental problems?

1.   Remedies: Injunctive Relief or Damages?

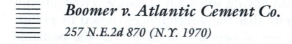

Boomer v. Atlantic Cement Co.
257 N.E.2d 870 (N.Y. 1970)

BERGAN, JUDGE.

Defendant operates a large cement plant near Albany. These are actions for injunction and damages by neighboring land owners alleging injury to property from dirt, smoke and vibration emanating from the plant. A nuisance has been found after trial, temporary damages have been allowed; but an injunction has been denied.

The public concern with air pollution arising from many sources in industry and in transportation is currently accorded ever wider recognition accompanied by a growing sense of responsibility in State and Federal Governments to control it. Cement plants are obvious sources of air pollution in the neighborhoods where they operate.

But there is now before the court private litigation in which individual property owners have sought specific relief from a single plant operation. The threshold question raised by the division of view on this appeal is whether the court should resolve the litigation between the parties now before it as equitably as seems possible; or whether, seeking promotion of the general public welfare, it should channel private litigation into broad public objectives.

A court performs its essential function when it decides the rights of parties before it. Its decision of private controversies may sometimes greatly affect public issues. Large questions of law are often resolved by the manner in which private litigation is decided. But this is normally an incident to the court's main function to settle controversy. It is a rare exercise of judicial power to use a decision in private litigation as a purposeful mechanism to achieve direct public objectives greatly beyond the rights and interests before the court.

Effective control of air pollution is a problem presently far from solution even with the full public and financial powers of government. In large measure adequate technical procedures are yet to be developed and some that appear possible may be economically impracticable. It seems apparent that the amelioration of air pollution will depend on technical research in great depth; on a carefully balanced consideration of the economic impact of close regulation; and of the actual effect on public health. It is likely to require massive public expenditure and to demand more than any local community can accomplish and to depend on regional and interstate controls.

A court should not try to do this on its own as a by-product of private litigation and it seems manifest that the judicial establishment is neither equipped in the limited nature of any judgment it can pronounce nor prepared to lay down and implement an effective policy for the elimination of air pollution. This is an area beyond the circumference of one private lawsuit. It is a direct responsibility for government and should not thus be undertaken as an incident to solving a dispute between property owners and a single cement plant—one of many—in the Hudson River valley.

The cement making operations of defendant have been found by the court of Special Term to have damaged the nearby properties of plaintiffs in these two actions. That court, as it has been noted, accordingly found defendant maintained a nuisance and this has been affirmed at the Appellate Division. The total damage to plaintiffs' properties is, however, relatively small in comparison with the value of defendant's operation and with the consequences of the injunction which plaintiffs seek.

The ground for the denial of injunction, notwithstanding the finding both that there is a nuisance and that plaintiffs have been damaged substantially, is the large disparity in economic consequences of the nuisance and of the injunction. This theory cannot, however, be sustained without overruling a doctrine which has been consistently reaffirmed in several leading cases in this court and which has never been disavowed here, namely that where a nuisance has been found and where there has been any substantial damage shown by the party complaining an injunction will be granted.

The rule in New York has been that such a nuisance will be enjoined although marked disparity be shown in economic consequence between the effect of the injunction and the effect of the nuisance . . . but to follow the rule literally in these cases would be to close down the plant at once. This court is fully agreed to avoid that immediately drastic remedy; the difference in view is how best to avoid it.*

* Respondent's investment in the plant is in excess of $45,000,000.00. There are over 300 people employed there.

One alternative is to grant the injunction but postpone its effect to a specified future date to give opportunity for technical advances to permit defendant to eliminate the nuisance; another is to grant the injunction conditioned on the payment of permanent damages to plaintiffs which would compensate them for the total economic loss to their property present and future caused by defendant's operations. For reasons which will be developed the court chooses the latter alternative.

If the injunction were to be granted unless within a short period — e.g., 18 months — the nuisance be abated by improved methods, there would be no assurance that any significant technical improvement would occur.

The parties could settle this private litigation at any time if defendant paid enough money and the imminent threat of closing the plant would build up the pressure on defendant. If there were no improved techniques found, there would inevitably be applications to the court at Special Term for extensions of time to perform on showing of good faith efforts to find such techniques. Moreover, techniques to eliminate dust and other annoying by-products of cement making are unlikely to be developed by any research the defendant can undertake within any short period, but will depend on the total resources of the cement industry nationwide and throughout the world. The problem is universal wherever cement is made.

For obvious reasons the rate of the research is beyond control of defendant. If at the end of 18 months the whole industry has not found a technical solution a court would be hard put to close down this one cement plant if due regard be given to equitable principles.

On the other hand, to grant the injunction unless defendant pays plaintiffs such permanent damages as may be fixed by the court seems to do justice between the contending parties. All of the attributions of economic loss to the properties on which plaintiffs' complaints are based will have been redressed.

The nuisance complained of by these plaintiffs may have other public or private consequences, but these particular parties are the only ones who have sought remedies and the judgment proposed will fully redress them. The limitation of relief granted is a limitation only within the four corners of these actions and does not foreclose public health or other public agencies from seeking proper relief in a proper court.

It seems reasonable to think that the risk of being required to pay permanent damages to injured property owners by cement plant owners would itself be a reasonable effective spur to research for improved techniques to minimize nuisance.

The power of the court to condition on equitable grounds the continuance of an injunction on the payment of permanent damages seems undoubted. . . .

JASEN, JUDGE (dissenting).

I agree with the majority that a reversal is required here, but I do not subscribe to the newly enunciated doctrine of assessment of permanent damages, in lieu of an injunction, where substantial property rights have been impaired by the creation of a nuisance.

It has long been the rule in this State, as the majority acknowledges, that a nuisance which results in substantial continuing damage to neighbors must be enjoined. To now change the rule to permit the cement company to continue polluting the air indefinitely upon the payment of permanent damages is, in my opinion, compounding the magnitude of a very serious problem in our State and Nation today. . . .

The harmful nature and widespread occurrence of air pollution have been extensively documented. Congressional hearings have revealed that air pollution causes substantial property damage, as well as being a contributing factor to a rising incidence of lung cancer, emphysema, bronchitis and asthma. . . .

I see grave dangers in overruling our long-established rule of granting an injunction where a nuisance results in substantial continuing damage. In permitting the injunction to become inoperative upon the payment of permanent damages, the majority is, in effect, licensing a continuing wrong. It is the same as saying to the cement company, you may continue to do harm to your neighbors so long as you pay a fee for it. Furthermore, once such permanent damages are assessed and paid, the incentive to alleviate the wrong would be eliminated, thereby continuing air pollution of an area without abatement.

It is true that some courts have sanctioned the remedy here proposed by the majority in a number of cases, but none of the authorities relied upon by the majority are analogous to the situation before us. In those cases, the courts, in denying an injunction and awarding money damages, grounded their decision on a showing that the use to which the property was intended to be put was primarily for the public benefit. Here, on the other hand, it is clearly established that the cement company is creating a continuing air pollution nuisance primarily for its own private interest with no public benefit. . . .

I would enjoin the defendant cement company from continuing the discharge of dust particles upon its neighbors' properties unless, within 18 months, the cement company abated this nuisance.

It is not my intention to cause the removal of the cement plant from the Albany area, but to recognize the urgency of the problem stemming from this stationary source of air pollution, and to allow the company a specified period of time to develop a means to alleviate this nuisance.

I am aware that the trial court found that the most modern dust control devices available have been installed in defendant's plant, but, I submit, this does not mean that better and more effective dust control devices could not be developed within the time allowed to abate the pollution.

Moreover, I believe it is incumbent upon the defendant to develop such devices, since the cement company, at the time the plant commenced production (1962), was well aware of the plaintiffs' presence in the area, as well as the probable consequences of its contemplated operation. Yet, it still chose to build and operate the plant at this site.

In a day when there is a growing concern for clean air, highly developed industry should not expect acquiescence by the courts, but should, instead, plan its operations to eliminate contamination of our air and damage to its neighbors.

NOTES AND QUESTIONS ON *BOOMER*
 v. ATLANTIC CEMENT

1. *Proof and basis for injunctive relief.* Did the plaintiffs in this case prove the elements of a private nuisance claim against the cement manufacturer? If so, why did the court deny them an injunction against the plant? Under prevailing New York State law when this decision was issued, any showing of "substantial damage" required the court to issue an injunction. What is the justification for this *per se* rule, and why did the *Boomer* majority reject this longstanding approach here?

2. *Conditional injunctions.* A somewhat softer form of injunction is a conditional injunction, in which the plant is allowed to operate for a fixed period of time, during which it is expected to develop and implement means to abate the nuisance. The dissent suggests the court adopt this remedy. Why does the court reject this approach? Some statutory approaches to environmental law use various means of identifying or forcing development of the "best technology" to control pollution.

3. *Measure of damages.* The court indicated that a damage award was appropriate in lieu of injunctive relief. How should the amount of damages be determined? What amount will compensate plaintiffs for their losses? What if the nature or degree of harm changes, or if new information shows that the pollution causes more harm than initially believed?

4. *Judicial solutions to public problems through private litigation.* What do you think concerns the court about using "private litigation" to achieve "broad public objectives"? Is the majority most concerned about the nature of the judicial process (resolving site-specific litigation as opposed to broader societal problems), or about its expertise and ability to deal with the complex technical issues of environmental law and management? Does the dissent simply strike a different balance with respect to the appropriate remedy in this case, or does it disagree more fundamentally about the role and capacity of courts to address environmental problems?

5. *Assessment of nuisance doctrine.* Based on the case and your answers to the previous questions, what are the major benefits and limitations of private nuisance doctrine in addressing environmental problems?

2. Common Law Goals and Coase

We have seen that, if actionable, some common law doctrines, such as trespass and strict liability, afford plaintiffs a legal right to be free from significant harm from pollution. Others, however, such as nuisance, employ some balancing, at least in deciding upon remedies. Which is the proper approach? Between the right to pollute and the right to be free of pollution, is there a "right" answer? Consider the seminal law and economics article set forth below. For which approach—a rights-based approach or a balancing approach—does Coase's concept of reciprocal harms best fit? Why does Coase's view of reciprocal harms call for private bargaining as the solution? What was Coase trying to achieve with private bargaining? To the extent private bargaining is impossible in a given context (why?), should society step in and mandate the outcome that *would* have been achieved if private bargaining was not impeded by transactions costs?

R.H. Coase, *The Problem of Social Cost*
3 J.L. & Econ. 1 (1960)

The Problem to Be Examined

This paper is concerned with those actions of business firms which have harmful effects on others. The standard example is that of a factory the smoke from which has harmful effects on those occupying neighboring properties. The economic analysis of such a situation has usually proceeded in terms of a divergence between the private and social product of the factory, in which economists have largely followed the treatment of Pigou in *The Economics of Welfare*. The conclusions to which this kind of analysis seems to have led most economists is that it would be desirable to make the owner of the factory liable for the damage caused to those injured by the smoke, or alternatively, to place a tax on the factory owner varying with the amount of smoke produced and equivalent in money terms to the damage it would cause, or finally, to exclude the factory from residential districts (and presumably from other areas in which the emission of smoke would have harmful effects on others). It is my contention that the suggested courses of action are inappropriate, in that they lead to results which are not necessarily, or even usually, desirable.

The Reciprocal Nature of the Problem

The traditional approach has tended to obscure the nature of the choice that has to be made. The question is commonly thought of as one in which A inflicts harm on B and what has to be decided is: how should we restrain A? But this is wrong. We are dealing with a problem of a reciprocal nature. To avoid the harm to B would inflict harm on A. The real question that has to be decided is: should A be allowed to harm B or should B be allowed to harm A? The problem is to avoid the more serious harm. I instanced in my previous article the case of a confectioner the noise and vibrations from whose machinery disturbed a doctor in his work. To avoid harming the doctor would inflict harm on the confectioner. The problem posed by this case was essentially whether it was worth while, as a result of restricting the methods of production which could be used for the confectioner, to secure more doctoring at the cost of a reduced supply of confectionery products. Another example is afforded by the problem of straying cattle which destroy crops on neighboring land. If it is inevitable that some cattle will stray, an increase in the supply of meat can only be obtained at the expense of a decrease in the supply of crops. The nature of the choice is clear: meat or crops. What answer should be given is, of course, not clear unless we know the value of what is obtained was well as the value of what is sacrificed to obtain it. To give another example, Professor George J. Stigler instances the contamination of a stream. If we assume that the harmful effect of the pollution is that it kills the fish, the question to be decided is: is the value of the fish lost greater or less than the value of the product which the contamination of the stream makes possible. . . .

[Coase proceeds to demonstrate, through a hypothetical arithmetic example, which we have spared you, that even absent legal intervention, the parties affected by such choices will bargain to reach the economically optimal result in terms of the values of the resources at issue. Thus, in the case of the cattle straying onto a neighbor's land, if the value of the increased cattle exceeds that of the lost crops, the rancher will pay the farmer the value of the lost crops. If the value of the lost crops exceeds that of the cattle, the farmer will pay the rancher to keep the cattle away. In either instance, he argues, both parties will be better off through this arm's length bargaining process. Moreover, Coase shows that in order to reach such optimal results, it does not matter whether the initial assumption is that the rancher has a right to allow his cattle to roam, or that the farmer has the right to exclude the cattle from her land. Thus, according to Coase, a background rule that automatically places liability on the party causing harm — a presumptive initial delineation of rights — is not necessarily appropriate. In the following section of the article, however, Coase explains a key limitation in this thesis.]

The Cost of Market Transactions Taken into Account

The argument has proceeded up to this point on the assumption . . . that there were no costs involved in carrying out market transactions. This is, of course, a very unrealistic assumption. In order to carry out a market transaction it is necessary to discover who it is that one wishes to deal with, to inform people that one wishes to deal and on what terms, to conduct negotiations leading up to a bargain, to draw up the contract, to undertake the inspection needed to make sure that the terms of the contract are being observed, and so on. These operations are often extremely costly, sufficiently costly at any rate to prevent many transactions that would be carried out in a world in which the pricing system worked without cost.

In earlier sections, when dealing with the problem of the rearrangement of legal rights through the market, it was argued that such a rearrangement would be made through the market whenever this would lead to an increase in the value of production. But this assumed costless market transactions. Once the costs of carrying out market transactions are taken into account it is clear that such a rearrangement of rights will only be undertaken when the increase in the value of production consequent upon the rearrangement is greater than the costs which would be involved in bringing it about. When it is less, the granting of an injunction (or the knowledge that it would be granted) or the liability to pay damages may result in an activity being discontinued (or may prevent its being started) which would be undertaken if market transactions were costless. In these conditions the initial delimitation of legal rights does have an effect on the efficiency with which the economic system operates. One arrangement of rights may bring about a greater value of production than any other. But unless this is the arrangement of rights established by the legal system, the costs of reaching the same result by altering and combining rights through the market may be so great that this optimal arrangement of rights, and the greater value of production which it would bring, may never be achieved. . . .

NOTES AND QUESTIONS ON COASE

1. *Pollution as a reciprocal problem.* Do you agree with Coase that pollution is a reciprocal problem? Does a breather of fumes harm the owner of the factory polluting the air? Can one abate pollution without harming the factory or its customers?

   2. *Economic efficiency.* Does it make sense to force a cattle rancher to fence in her property, if her neighbor's crops are not as valuable as the extra meat produced when cattle can eat the neighbor's crops? Does it make sense to force a factory owner to abate pollution when doing so will impose a cost on her customers exceeding the value of the fish that the pollution kills? Economists would consider it "inefficient" to impose costs on polluters that exceed the value associated with the resulting environmental benefits. We will return to the efficiency concept when we address cost-benefit analysis.

   3. *Coasian solutions to nuisance cases.* How would you resolve the *Boomer* case under Coase's approach? Would the approach be different if the plaintiffs consisted of an entire town of several hundred people? Can a homeowner bargain with a factory to obtain payments to offset an increased risk of cancer to the homeowner and her family?

   4. *Private bargaining and public pollution.* Do you read Coase to argue that private bargaining alone provides an adequate solution to pollution problems?

3. Public and Private Nuisance

   Indivisible resources such as the air space, large water bodies, and undeveloped land pose special problems for environmental protection. First, such resources are often not owned by private persons. Should the plaintiff's status as a government entity make a difference when it sues to enjoin the polluting activity of a private landowner? When there has been an unreasonable interference with an indivisible resource (water, air, and public rights of way) shared by the public, courts have typically found a public nuisance, as opposed to a private nuisance. The potential difference between private and public nuisance cases is illustrated by two famous cases regarding the exact same Tennessee smelter. The same year that the Tennessee Supreme Court denied injunctive relief to landowners neighboring the smelter in the case of Madison v. Ducktown Sulphur, 83 S.W.2d 658 (Tenn. 1904), the State of Georgia filed an original jurisdiction action in the U.S. Supreme Court to enjoin operation of the smelters because of extensive alleged property damage from emissions that crossed the state border. That case follows.

Georgia v. Tennessee Copper Co.
206 U.S. 230 (1907)

MR. JUSTICE HOLMES delivered the opinion of the court:
   This is a bill in equity filed in this court by the state of Georgia, in pursuance of a resolution of the legislature and by direction of the governor of the state, to enjoin the defendant copper companies from discharging noxious gas from their works in Tennessee over the plaintiff's territory. It alleges that, in consequence of such discharge, a wholesale destruction of forests, orchards, and crops is going on, and other injuries are done and threatened in five counties of the state. It alleges also a vain application to the state of Tennessee for relief.

. . . The case has been argued largely as if it were one between two private parties; but it is not. The very elements that would be relied upon in a suit between fellow-citizens as a ground for equitable relief are wanting here. The state owns very little of the territory alleged to be affected, and the damage to it capable of estimate in money, possibly, at least, is small. This is a suit by a state for an injury to it in its capacity of quasi-sovereign. In that capacity the state has an interest independent of and behind the titles of its citizens, in all the earth and air within its domain. It has the last word as to whether its mountains shall be stripped of their forests and its inhabitants shall breathe pure air. It might have to pay individuals before it could utter that word, but with it remains the final power. The alleged damage to the state as a private owner is merely a makeweight, and we may lay on one side the dispute as to whether the destruction of forests has led to the gullying of its roads.

Some peculiarities necessarily mark a suit of this kind. If the state has a case at all, it is somewhat more certainly entitled to specific relief than a private party might be. It is not lightly to be required to give up quasi-sovereign rights for pay; and, apart from the difficulty of valuing such rights in money, if that be its choice it may insist that an infraction of them shall be stopped. The states, by entering the Union, did not sink to the position of private owners, subject to one system of private law. This court has not quite the same freedom to balance the harm that will be done by an injunction against that of which the plaintiff complains, that it would have in deciding between two subjects of a single political power. Without excluding the considerations that equity always takes into account, we cannot give the weight that was given them in argument to a comparison between the damage threatened to the plaintiff and the calamity of a possible stop to the defendants' business, the question of health, the character of the forests as a first or second growth, the commercial possibility or impossibility of reducing the fumes to sulphuric acid, the special adaptation of the business to the place.

It is a fair and reasonable demand on the part of a sovereign that the air over its territory should not be polluted on a great scale by sulphurous acid gas, that the forests on its mountains, be they better or worse, and whatever domestic destruction they have suffered, should not be further destroyed or threatened by the act of persons beyond its control, that the crops and orchards on its hills should not be endangered from the same source. If any such demand is to be enforced this must be notwithstanding the hesitation that we might feel if the suit were between private parties, and the doubt whether, for the injuries which they might be suffering to their property, they should not be left to an action at law.

. . . The proof requires but a few words. It is not denied that the defendants generate in their works near the Georgia line large quantities of sulphur dioxide which becomes sulphurous acid by its mixture with the air. It hardly is denied, and cannot be denied with success, that this gas often is carried by the wind great distances and over great tracts of Georgia land. On the evidence the pollution of the air and the magnitude of that pollution are not open to dispute. Without any attempt to go into details immaterial to the suit, it is proper to add that we are satisfied, by a preponderance of evidence, that the sulphurous fumes cause and threaten damage on so considerable a scale to the forests and vegetable life, if not to health, within the plaintiff state, as to make out a case within the requirements of Missouri v. Illinois. Whether Georgia, by insisting upon this claim, is doing more harm than good to her own citizens, is for her to determine. The possible disaster to those outside the state must be accepted as a consequence of her standing upon her extreme rights.

. . . If the state of Georgia adheres to its determination, there is no alternative to issuing an injunction, after allowing a reasonable time to the defendants to complete the structures that they now are building, and the efforts that they are making to stop the fumes. The plaintiff may submit a form of decree on the coming in of this court in October next.

Injunction to issue.

NOTES AND QUESTIONS ON *GEORGIA v. TENNESSEE COPPER CO.*

1. Per se *injunctive relief.* What is the justification for providing injunctive relief as of right in a public nuisance case brought by a state (or other political subdivision), but making it a matter of equitable discretion in a private nuisance suit?

2. *Limiting the scope of public nuisance claims.* Some courts, however, limit the scope of public rights that public nuisance can address. *See* Rhode Island v. Lead Industries Ass'n, 951 A.2d 428, 454 (R.I. 2008) (finding injuries resulting from lead paint exposure within homes does not constitute a public nuisance). Why do you suppose the court found that the widespread exposure of large numbers of children to lead-based paint does not constitute a public nuisance?

4. The Usefulness of the Common Law in Addressing Environmental-Mediated Harms

Missouri v. Illinois
200 U.S. 496 (1906)

JUSTICE HOLMES delivered the opinion of the court.

This is a suit brought by the state of Missouri to restrain the discharge of the sewage of Chicago through an artificial channel into the Desplaines river, in the state of Illinois. That river empties into the Illinois river, and the latter empties into the Mississippi at a point about 43 miles above the city of St. Louis. It was alleged in the bill that the result of the threatened discharge would be to send 1,500 tons of poisonous filth daily into the Mississippi, to deposit great quantities of the same upon the part of the bed of the last-named river belonging to the plaintiff, and so to poison the water of that river, upon which various of the plaintiff's cities, towns, and inhabitants depended, as to make it unfit for drinking, agricultural, or manufacturing purposes. It was alleged that the defendant sanitary district was acting in pursuance of a statute of the state of Illinois, and as an agency of that state. . . . A supplemental bill alleges that since the filing of the original bill the drainage canal has been opened and put into operation, and has produced and is producing all the evils which were apprehended when the injunction first was asked. The answers deny the plaintiff's case, allege that the new plan sends the water of the Illinois river into the Mississippi much purer than it was before, that many towns and cities of the plaintiff along the Missouri and Mississippi discharge their sewage into those rivers, and that if there is any trouble the plaintiff must look nearer home for the cause.

. . . The nuisance set forth in the bill was one which would be of international importance,—a visible change of a great river from a pure stream into a polluted and poisoned ditch. The only question presented was whether, as between the states of the Union, this court was competent to deal with a situation which, if it arose between independent sovereignties, might lead to war. Whatever differences of opinion there might be upon matters of detail, the jurisdiction and authority of this court to deal with such a case as that is not open to doubt. But the evidence now is in, the actual facts have required for their establishment the most ingenious experiments, and for their interpretation the most subtle speculations, of modern science, and therefore it becomes necessary at the present stage to consider somewhat more nicely than heretofore how the evidence in it is to be approached.

. . . Before this court ought to intervene, the case should be of serious magnitude, clearly and fully proved, and the principle to be applied should be one which the court is prepared deliberately to maintain against all considerations on the other side.

As to the principle to be laid down, the caution necessary is manifest. It is a question of the first magnitude whether the destiny of the great rivers is to be the sewers of the cities along their banks or to be protected against everything which threatens their purity. To decide the whole matter at one blow by an irrevocable fiat would be at least premature. If we are to judge by what the plaintiff itself permits, the discharge of sewage into the Mississippi by cities and towns is to be expected. We believe that the practice of discharging into the river is general along its banks, except where the levees of Louisiana have led to a different course. The argument for the plaintiff asserts it to be proper within certain limits. These are facts to be considered. Even in cases between individuals, some consideration is given to the practical course of events. In the black country of England parties would not be expected to stand upon extreme rights. Where, as here, the plaintiff has sovereign powers, and deliberately permits discharges similar to those of which it complains, it not only offers a standard to which the defendant has the right to appeal, but, as some of those discharges are above the intake of St. Louis, it warrants the defendant in demanding the strictest proof that the plaintiff's own conduct does not produce the result, or at least so conduce to it, that courts should not be curious to apportion the blame.

We have studied the plaintiff's statement of the facts in detail, and have perused the evidence, but it is unnecessary for the purposes of decision to do more than give the general result in a very simple way. At the outset we cannot but be struck by the consideration that if this suit had been brought fifty years ago it almost necessarily would have failed. There is no pretense that there is a nuisance of the simple kind that was known to the older common law. There is nothing which can be detected by the unassisted senses,—no visible increase of filth, no new smell. On the contrary, it is proved that the great volume of pure water from Lake Michigan, which is mixed with the sewage at the start, has improved the Illinois river in these respects to a noticeable extent. Formerly it was sluggish and ill smelling. Now it is a comparatively clear stream to which edible fish have returned. Its water is drunk by the fishermen, it is said without evil results. The plaintiff's case depends upon an inference of the unseen. It draws the inference from two propositions. First, that typhoid fever has increased considerably since the change, and that other explanations have been disproved; and second, that the bacillus of typhoid can and does survive the journey and reach the intake of St. Louis in the Mississippi.

We assume the now-prevailing scientific explanation of typhoid fever to be correct. But when we go beyond that assumption, everything is involved in doubt. The data upon which an increase in the deaths from typhoid fever in St. Louis is alleged are disputed. The elimination of other causes is denied. The experts differ as to the time and distance within which a stream would purify itself. No case of an epidemic caused by infection at so remote a source is brought forward and the cases which are produced are controverted. The plaintiff obviously must be cautious upon this point, for, if this suit should succeed, many others would follow, and it not improbably would find itself a defendant to a bill by one or more of the states lower down upon the Mississippi. The distance which the sewage has to travel (357 miles) is not open to debate, but the time of transit, to be inferred from experiments with floats, is estimated as varying from eight to eighteen and a half days, with forty-eight hours more from intake to distribution, and when corrected by observations of bacteria is greatly prolonged by the defendants. The experiments of the defendant's experts lead them to the opinion that a typhoid bacillus could not survive the journey, while those on the other side maintain that it might live and keep its power for twenty-five days or more, and arrive at St. Louis. Upon the question at issue, whether the new discharge from Chicago hurts St. Louis, there is a categorical contradiction between the experts on the two sides.

The Chicago drainage canal was opened on January 17, 1900. The deaths from typhoid fever in St. Louis, before and after that date, are stated somewhat differently in different places. We give them mainly from the plaintiff's brief: 1890, 140; 1891, 165; 1892, 441; 1893, 215; 1894, 171; 1895, 106; 1896, 106; 1897, 125; 1898, 95; 1899, 131; 1900, 154; 1901, 181; 1902, 216; 1903, 281. It is argued for the defendant that the numbers for the later years have been enlarged by carrying over cases which in earlier years would have been put into a miscellaneous column (intermittent, remittent, typho-malaria, etc., etc.), but we assume that the increase is real. Nevertheless, comparing the last four years with the earlier ones, it is obvious that the ground for a specific inference is very narrow, if we stopped at this point. The plaintiff argues that the increase must be due to Chicago, since there is nothing corresponding to it in the watersheds of the Missouri or Mississippi. On the other hand, the defendant points out that there has been no such enhanced rate of typhoid on the banks of the Illinois as would have been found if the opening of the drainage canal were the true cause.

Both sides agree that the detection of the typhoid bacillus in the water is not to be expected. But the plaintiff relies upon proof that such bacilli are discharged into the Chicago sewage in considerable quantities; that the number of bacilli in the water of the Illinois is much increased, including the bacillus coli communis, which is admitted to be an index of contamination, and that the chemical analyses lead to the same inference. To prove that the typhoid bacillus could make the journey an experiment was tried with the bacillus prodigiosus, which seems to have been unknown, or nearly unknown, in these waters. After preliminary trials, in which these bacilli emptied into the Mississippi near the mouth of the Illinois were found near the St. Louis intake and in St. Louis in times varying from three days to a month, one hundred and seven barrels of the same, said to contain one thousand million bacilli to the cubic centimeter, were put into the drainage canal near the starting point on November 6, and on December 4 an example was found at the St. Louis intake tower. Four others were found on the three following days, two at the tower and two at the mouth of the Illinois. As this bacillus is asserted to have about the same length of life in sunlight in living waters as the bacillus typhosus, although it is a little more hardy, the experiment is thought to prove one element of the plaintiff's case, although the very small number found in many samples of water is thought by the other side to indicate that practically no typhoid germs would get through. It seems to be conceded that the purification of the Illinois by the large dilution from Lake Michigan (nine parts or more in ten) would increase the danger, as it now generally is believed that the bacteria of decay, the saprophytes, which flourish in stagnant pools, destroy the pathogenic germs. Of course, the addition of so much water to the Illinois also increases its speed.

On the other hand, the defendant's evidence shows a reduction in the chemical and bacterial accompaniments of pollution in a given quantity of water, which would be natural in view of the mixture of nine parts to one from Lake Michigan. It affirms that the Illinois is better or no worse at its mouth than it was before, and makes it at least uncertain how much of the present pollution is due to Chicago and how much to sources further down, not complained of in the bill. It contends that if any bacilli should get through, they would be scattered and enfeebled and would do no harm. The defendant also sets against the experiment with the bacillus prodigiosus a no less striking experiment with typhoid germs suspended in the Illinois river in permeable sacs. According to this the duration of the life of these germs has been much exaggerated, and in that water would not be more than three or four days. It is suggested, by way of criticism that the germs may not have been of normal strength, that the conditions were less favorable than if they had floated down in a comparatively unchanging body of water, and that the germs may have escaped; but the experiment raises at least a serious doubt. Further, it hardly is denied that there is no parallelism in detail between the increase and decrease of typhoid fever in Chicago and St. Louis. The defendant's experts maintain that the water of the Missouri is worse than that of the Illinois, while it contributes a much larger portion to the intake. The evidence is very strong that it is necessary for St. Louis to take preventive measures, by filtration or otherwise, against the dangers of the plaintiff's own creation or from other sources than Illinois. What will protect against one will protect against another. The presence of causes of infection from the plaintiff's action makes the case weaker in principle as well as harder to prove than one in which all came from a single source.

Some stress was laid on the proposition that Chicago is not on the natural watershed of the Mississippi, because of a rise of a few feet between the Des Plaines and the Chicago rivers. We perceive no reason for distinction on this ground. The natural features relied upon are of the smallest. And if, under any circumstances, they could affect the case, it is enough to say that Illinois brought Chicago into the Mississippi watershed in pursuance, not only of its own statutes, but also of the acts of Congress . . . the validity of which is not disputed. . . . Of course these acts do not grant the right to discharge sewage, but the case stands no differently in point of law from a suit because of the discharge from Peoria into the Illinois, or from any other or all the other cities on the banks of that stream.

We might go more into detail, but we believe that we have said enough to explain our point of view and our opinion of the evidence as it stands. What the future may develop, of course we cannot tell. But our conclusion upon the present evidence is that the case proved falls so far below the allegations of the bill that it is not brought within the principles heretofore established in the cause.

Bill dismissed without prejudice.

NOTES AND QUESTIONS ON *MISSOURI v. ILLINOIS*

1. *Nuisance doctrine and new kinds of harm.* Courts developed nuisance doctrine to address obvious sources of annoyance, such as noxious odors, visible wastes, etc. Here, the alleged harm was bacterial, but the water that carried those pathogens looked and smelled better than it did previously. How well suited was nuisance law to handle this new kind of harm?

2. *Causation and injunctive relief.* Proving harm can be difficult at the frontiers of science. Should the opponent of a polluting activity have to prove an activity is harmful before it can be stopped (the general rule in civil litigation), or should the proponent of the activity bear the burden of proving that the activity is *safe* in the face of uncertainty? As an example, does the following graphic depiction of some of the key evidence indicate that plaintiffs proved that harm was caused by the defendant's conduct?

Missouri v Illinois—Typhoid incidence before and after river re-routed

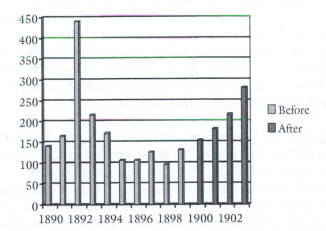

3. *"Unclean hands."* How was the strength of Missouri's case affected by the fact that many cities and towns in the state also disposed of their sewage and waste into the Mississippi River? While Georgia's status as a sovereign worked to its advantage in *Georgia v. Tennessee Copper*, Missouri's sovereign status presented the plaintiff with an argument that Missouri was holding Illinois to an impossibly high standard. Both cases highlight the fact that a state government is a special type of party in common law environmental litigation. For states, taking an aggressive environmental stand can come back to haunt them in future cases (as suggested by Justice Holmes' question, in the *Georgia* case, as to whether the state was doing more harm than good by standing on her "extreme rights") or may be impossible to sustain given the state's own contradictory behavior (as seen in *Missouri*). What

does this say about relying upon states to protect the environment through the common law? Is the federal government hobbled by the same dynamic?

4. *Prevention versus remediation.* What does this issue say about the ability of the common law to adopt a preventive as opposed to a remedial approach to environmental harm?

Garrett Hardin, The Tragedy of the Commons
162 Science 1243 (1968)

The tragedy of the commons develops in this way. Picture a pasture open to all. It is to be expected that each herdsman will try to keep as many cattle as possible on the commons. Such an arrangement may work reasonably satisfactorily for centuries because tribal wars, poaching, and disease keep the numbers of both man and beast well below the carrying capacity of the land. Finally, however, comes the day of reckoning, that is, the day when the long-desired goal of social stability becomes reality. At this point, the inherent logic of the commons remorselessly generates tragedy.

As a rational being, each herdsman seeks to maximize his gain. Explicitly or implicitly, more or less consciously, he asks, "What is the utility *to me* of adding one more animal to my herd?" This utility has one negative and one positive component.

1. The positive component is a function of the increment of one animal. Since the herdsman receives all the proceeds from the sale of the additional animal, the positive utility is nearly +1.
2. The negative component is a function of the additional overgrazing created by one more animal. Since, however, the effects of overgrazing are shared by all the herdsmen, the negative utility for any particular decision-making herdsman is only a fraction of −1.

Adding together the component partial utilities, the rational herdsman concludes that the only sensible course for him to pursue is to add another animal to his herd. And another; and another. . . . But this is the conclusion reached by each and every rational herdsman sharing a commons. Therein is the tragedy. Each man is locked into a system that compels him to increase his heard without limit—in a world that is limited. Ruin is the destination toward which all men rush, each pursuing his own best interest in a society that believes in the freedom of the commons. Freedom in a commons brings ruin to all. . . .

The National Parks present another instance of the working out of the tragedy of the commons. At present, they are open to all, without limit. The parks themselves are limited in extent—there is only one Yosemite Valley—whereas population seems to grow without limit. The values that visitors seek in the parks are steadily eroded. Plainly we must soon cease to treat the parks as commons or they will be of no value to anyone.

What shall we do? We have several options. We might sell them off as private property. We might keep them as public property, but allocate the right to enter them. . . .

Pollution

In a reverse way, the tragedy of the commons reappears in problems of pollution. Here it is not a question of taking something out of the commons, but of putting something in — sewage, or chemical, radioactive, and heat wastes into water; noxious and dangerous fumes into the air; and distracting and unpleasant advertising signs into the line of sight. The calculations of utility are much the same as before. The rational man finds that his share of the cost of the wastes he discharges into the commons is less than the cost of purifying his wastes before releasing them. Since this is true for everyone, we are locked into a system of "fouling our own nest," so long as we behave only as independent, rational, free-enterprisers.

The tragedy of the commons as a food basket is averted by private property, or something formally like it. But the air and waters surrounding us cannot readily be fenced, and so the tragedy of the commons as a cesspool must be prevented by different means, by coercive laws or taxing devices that make it cheaper for the polluter to treat his pollutants than to discharge them untreated. We have not progressed as far with the solution of this problem as we have with the first. Indeed, our particular concept of private property, which deters us from exhausting the positive resources of the earth, favors pollution. The owner of a factory on the bank of a stream whose property extends to the middle of the stream, often has difficulty seeing why it is not his natural right to muddy the waters flowing past his door. The law, always behind the times, requires elaborate stitching and fitting to adapt it to this newly perceived aspect of the commons.

The pollution problem is a consequence of population. It did not much matter how a lonely American frontiersman disposed of his waste. "Flowing water purifies itself every 10 miles," my grandfather used to say, and the myth was near enough to the truth when he was a boy, for there were not too many people. But as population became denser, the natural chemical and biological recycling processes became overloaded, calling for a redefinition of property rights. . . .

The laws of our society . . . are poorly suited to governing a complex, crowded, changeable world. Our . . . solution is to augment statutory law with administrative law. Since it is practically impossible to spell out all the conditions under which it is safe to burn trash in the back yard or to run an automobile without smog-control, by law we delegate the details to bureaus.

NOTES AND QUESTIONS ON HARDIN

1. *Privatization versus government allocation.* How would Hardin remedy the problem of too many cattle grazing on the commons? Is privatizing the commons a better solution than government allocation of grazing rights? What would Coase have to say about that question?

2. *Role of costs.* Would Hardin favor reducing pollution to levels where all fish survive, regardless of the costs of doing so? Would Coase?

3. *Administrative versus statutory solutions.* Notice that Hardin favors an administrative law solution to the tragedy of the commons over a statutory solution. A statutory solution might involve Congress setting standards for how to burn trash safely or what sort of smog control we should use on automobiles. An administrative approach might have Congress delegating the detailed decisions on these matters to an administrative agency. Why does Hardin favor administrative to statutory law? As you read the next chapter, think about whether a system of statutes granting agencies substantial authority for detailed decisions enjoys important advantages over common law solutions.

CLIMATE DISRUPTION COMMON LAW REVIEW PROBLEM

As mentioned in the beginning of this chapter, the common law is not dead as a tool for addressing environmental problems. Plaintiffs continue to bring common law actions to redress environmental harm for a variety of reasons: gaps in the statutory system or the availability of superior remedies for particular plaintiffs.

Nothing better illustrates this point than the use of the common law to address harms from climate disruption. The first of several such lawsuits, *Connecticut v. American Electric Power Company, Inc.*, was filed in 2003 by several states and the City of New York against the five largest power companies in the United States, alleging liability attributable to the companies' emissions of greenhouse gases under various common law causes of action. At the time the *AEP* case was filed, many bills to regulate carbon dioxide emissions from the electricity sector had been introduced in Congress, but none had passed. Similarly, EPA had yet to promulgate or propose regulations for emissions of greenhouse gases. All of the plaintiff states and the City of New York were engaged in the process of regulating greenhouse gas emissions in some fashion.

Below are paragraphs from the plaintiff's complaint in the *American Electric Power* case. By reading the complaint and answering the questions that follow, you will get a better understanding of the attraction of the common law for persons alleging harm from climate disruption as well as the difficulties posed by unique aspects of climate disruption. We end by asking you to draft a complaint and a judge's bench memo in a hypothetical case that, unlike that of *American Electric Power*, requires you to apply private nuisance concepts to the problem of climate disruption.

IN THE UNITED STATES DISTRICT COURT
FOR THE SOUTHERN DISTRICT OF NEW YORK
COMPLAINT

1. The States of Connecticut, New York, California, Iowa, New Jersey, Rhode Island, Vermont, Wisconsin and the City of New York bring this action against defendant electric power corporations under federal

common law and, in the alternative, state law, to seek abatement of defendants' ongoing contributions to a public nuisance.

2. Defendants, by their annual emissions of approximately 650 million tons of carbon dioxide, are substantial contributors to elevated levels of carbon dioxide and global warming. Defendants are the five largest emitters of carbon dioxide in the United States and are among the largest in the world. Defendants' emissions constitute approximately one quarter of the U.S. electric power sector's carbon dioxide emissions and approximately ten percent of all carbon dioxide emissions from human activities in the United States.

Injuries to the Plaintiffs and Their Citizens and Residents from Global Warming

110. Global warming is expected to cause intensified and prolonged summertime heat waves in the plaintiffs' jurisdictions, resulting in increases in heat deaths, heat illnesses, and heat-related hospitalizations. . . . The elderly and poor will be at highest risk.

111. [Defendant's emissions] . . . will increase smog levels [which will in turn] cause increased incidence of, and susceptibility to, respiratory illnesses including asthma, pneumonia and bronchitis.

113-118. Global warming will cause accelerated sea-level rise . . . [that will] inundate low-lying property, especially during coastal storms, in the coastal plaintiffs' jurisdictions [and] cause saltwater intrusion into groundwater aquifers or other water supplies. . . .

119. In California, the mountain snowpack is the single largest freshwater source. . . . Global warming will severely reduce the size of the snowpack. . . .

120. Global warming will result in more intense precipitation events.

126. A drop in Great Lakes levels from global warming will reduce access to marinas and docks for recreational boaters, require thousands of municipal water intakes and wells to be moved or extended, and damage wetlands that are important for fish and other wildlife.

130. Global warming will . . . increase stress to crops, thereby reducing crop yields.

133. The hardwood forests that give Vermont, Connecticut, New York, New Jersey, Rhode Island and Wisconsin their fall colors and that give Vermont and several other plaintiff States their maple sugar industry are threatened by global warming. . . .

141. . . . Global warming will . . . increase[e] the number of escaped wildfires, increasing the area burned by wildfires and shortening the return period of wildfires.

CLAIMS FOR RELIEF

First Claim for Relief—Federal Common Law of Public Nuisance

153. . . . Defendants, by their emissions of carbon dioxide from the combustion of fossil fuels at electric generating facilities, are knowingly,

        intentionally or negligently creating, maintaining or contributing to a public nuisance—global warming—injurious to the plaintiffs and their citizens and residents.

154. Defendants' emissions . . . constitute a substantial and unreasonable interference with public rights in the plaintiffs' jurisdictions, including, *inter alia*, the right to public comfort and safety, the right to protection of vital natural resources and public property, and the right to use, enjoy, and preserve the aesthetic and ecological values of the natural world.

155. Carbon dioxide emissions and global warming are inherently interstate in nature.

156. Defendants could generate the same amount of electricity while emitting significantly less carbon dioxide by employing readily available processes and technologies.

157. Defendants know or should know that their emissions of carbon dioxide contribute to global warming and to the resulting injuries and threatened injuries to the plaintiffs, their citizens and residents, and their environment.

158. Defendants' carbon dioxide emissions are a direct and proximate contributing cause of global warming and of the injuries and threatened injuries to the plaintiffs, their citizens and residents, and their environment, from global warming.

159. Defendants, individually and collectively, are substantial contributors to global warming and to the injuries and threatened injuries claimed herein.

160. The injuries and threatened injuries from global warming are indivisible injuries.

161. The injuries from global warming claimed herein are imminent.

162. The injuries from global warming claimed herein are irreparable and monetary damages are inadequate to remedy the injuries.

164. Defendants are jointly and severally liable under the federal common law of public nuisance. . . .

PRAYER FOR RELIEF

WHEREFORE, plaintiffs pray that judgment be entered against defendants as follows:

    Holding each defendant jointly and severally liable for creating, contributing to, and/or maintaining a public nuisance;

    Permanently enjoining each defendant to abate its contribution to the nuisance by requiring it to cap its carbon dioxide emissions and then reduce them by a specified percentage each year for at least a decade; and

    Granting such other relief as this Court deems just and proper.

Questions

1. *The attraction of the common law.* Which of the reasons for the continued viability of the common law mentioned at the beginning of the chapter might explain why plaintiffs are turning to the common law for redress with respect to climate disruption? What does the common law have to offer that legislation does not? Is the common law an appropriate alternative to legislation or administrative law? How might they work in tandem to meet the plaintiffs' goals?

2. *The propriety of the common law.* Can common law nuisance lawsuits, filed on a case-by-case basis against sources of greenhouse gases such as electric generating plants, realistically do much to reduce climate disruption? Is there an analogy to the *Boomer* majority's admonition that "amelioration of air pollution will depend on technical research in great depth" and is "likely to require massive public expenditure and to demand more than any local community can accomplish and to depend on regional and interstate controls"? If so, should climate disruption be fodder for common law public nuisance actions or, as some courts have suggested, is it better left to the political branches?

3. *Why these defendants?* What is special about these particular defendants' contributions to climate disruption? Is that a sufficient reason to require them to bear a disproportionate burden of mitigating climate disruption when there exist scores of other large contributors throughout the United States and the world?

4. *Elements of a public nuisance.* What are the elements of a public nuisance cause of action? Have the plaintiffs adequately pled facts to support these elements so as to survive a potential motion by the defendants to have the complaint dismissed under Federal Rule of Civil Procedure 12(b)(6)? Indeed, can they? Should the plaintiffs survive a 12(b)(6) motion, what types of evidence would you suggest they introduce to prove causation at trial?

5. *Remedy.* What remedy do the plaintiffs seek and what do you think of their chances of success? Why do you think the plaintiffs are not seeking damages? Which of the nuisance cases that you have read is the best predictor of the outcome of this case and why? How would the analysis be different if the plaintiffs were private landowners as opposed to state and city governments?

3

From Common Law to Administrative Law

In the last chapter, you examined common law solutions to environmental problems. Hopefully, you identified the ways in which common law approaches may be useful in addressing environmental issues, as well as the ways in which those approaches alone may be inadequate in the face of the complexity, uncertainty, and ubiquity of modern environmental problems.

Congress and state legislatures responded to these perceived deficiencies in common law approaches by adopting regulatory statutes designed to address environmental problems in a more comprehensive fashion. Some of these laws are relatively brief. Others, however, are mind-boggling in their length and complexity.[1]

Why are statutory and regulatory approaches useful to solve problems for which the common law was perceived as insufficient? In this chapter, we address this issue in three parts. First, we discuss the basic reasons for statutory approaches to environmental problems, and describe the kinds of mechanisms used to implement those approaches, using the Clean Air Act as an example. Second, we explain the roles of administrative agencies in implementing and enforcing those schemes, and of judicial oversight in ensuring that implementing agencies administer the statutes fairly and reasonably. Third, we revisit the residual role of the common law, which in most respects remains in place, notwithstanding the comprehensive statutory overlay, and explore how the two systems—common law and statutory—relate to each other.

---

1. The National Environmental Policy Act, 42 U.S.C. §§4321-4370, for example, takes just 46 pages in the United States Code. The Clean Air Act, by contrast, now consumes some 1,386 pages in the United States Code, and, as noted by Justice Rehnquist, the provisions "virtually swim before one's eyes." United States Steel Corp. v. United States EPA, 444 U.S. 1035, 1038 (1980) (Rehnquist, J., dissenting from denial of certiorari). Some commentators believe that the modern regulatory regime has become far too complex and inefficient as a result. *See, e.g.*, Richard Lazarus, *The Tragedy of Distrust in the Implementation of Federal Environmental Law*, 54 Law & Contemp. Probs. 311 (1991).

A.   THE IDEA OF STATUTORY SCHEMES

1.   *Boomer v. Atlantic Cement*: A Reprise

Recall the reluctance shown by the majority opinion in *Boomer* regarding the appropriate role of common law judges in addressing widespread environmental problems:

> Effective control of air pollution is a problem presently far from solution even with the full public and financial powers of government. In large measure adequate technical procedures are yet to be developed and some that appear possible may be economically impracticable. It seems apparent that the amelioration of air pollution will depend on technical research in great depth; on a carefully balanced consideration of the economic impact of close regulation; and of the actual effect on public health. It is likely to require massive public expenditure and to demand more than any local community can accomplish and to depend on regional and inter-state controls.
>
> A court should not try to do this on its own as a by-product of private litigation and it seems manifest that the judicial establishment is neither equipped in the limited nature of any judgment it can pronounce nor prepared to lay down and implement an effective policy for the elimination of air pollution. This is an area beyond the circumference of one private lawsuit. It is a direct responsibility for government and should not thus be undertaken as an incident to solving a dispute between property owners and a single cement plant—one of many—in the Hudson River valley.

The majority in *Boomer* also believed that it was unfair and inappropriate to place on a single company—the defendant in that case—the obligation to research and develop technological solutions to air pollution on behalf of an entire industry:

> Moreover, techniques to eliminate dust and other annoying by-products of cement making are unlikely to be developed by any research the defendant can undertake within any short period, but will depend on the total resources of the cement industry nationwide and throughout the world. The problem is universal wherever cement is made.
>
> For obvious reasons the rate of the research is beyond control of defendant. If at the end of 18 months the whole industry has not found a technical solution a court would be hard put to close down this one cement plant if due regard be given to equitable principles.

The *Boomer* court identified several areas in which it believed that the elected branches of government both bore the responsibility and were better equipped to make the kinds of broad technical and public policy decisions necessary to regulate air pollution at large. In addition to expertise and resources, what other factors might suggest that such decisions are best placed in the hands of the executive and legislative branches of government, rather than the courts?

Consider the problems inherent in determining what pollution controls, or levels of pollution controls, should be imposed not just on one cement plant, but on all cement plants in a region, state, or the country as a whole. Also consider that cement plants might differ in size, materials used, manufacturing methods, energy sources, proximity to homes or other places where the resulting pollution might cause harm, and other factors. In part because of its lack of technological expertise, the *Boomer* court declined to order the defendants to adopt any particular form of pollution controls. Instead, it directed the lower court to assess damages proven by the plaintiffs in this case, leaving it to the defendants to decide whether it would be cheaper to adopt pollution controls in the future to avoid additional monetary damages, and to determine what those controls might be.

Would a statutory system address these issues differently, and if so, how? Among the various pollution control strategies that could be adopted for the entire cement industry, government simply could impose a system of pollution charges similar to the damages assessed in *Boomer*, leaving it to individual plant owners or managers to decide what, if any, controls to adopt. Alternatively, government might choose a single technology for all cement plants, regardless of size, location, and other factors. Or, pollution controls could be set at particular levels, leaving it to each plant to decide how those standards should be met. Are those kinds of choices best made by courts, by legislatures as part of a comprehensive statute, or by government agency officials as part of a broad delegation of authority to regulate air pollution?

Next, consider that cement plants are just one of many sources of air pollution in any community, and in the nation as a whole. Pollution controls that work for cement plants may be inadequate for, or even entirely inapplicable to, coal-fired power plants. Moreover, citizens in any community are likely to breathe a complex mix of pollution from different kinds of factories, power plants, smaller sources, and the ubiquitous motor vehicle. Air pollution might be addressed by focusing on individual pollution sources alone, or by deciding how much *aggregate* pollution is acceptable given the economic and other benefits that might be lost if some sources are shut down or forced to install expensive control systems. Should standards be established to control this aggregate pollution, and if so, for which of the thousands of chemicals that are released into the air routinely from the many different sources of pollution? Which of those sources should be controlled, and to what degree, to assure that the aggregate standards are met?

Congress was also motivated to adopt comprehensive statutory regimes because of public pressure to solve significant environmental problems that simply were not being addressed by common law cases alone. In 1969, the Cuyahoga River in Cleveland, Ohio literally caught fire due to the oil and other industrial wastes floating downstream.[2] Acute air pollution episodes in industrial towns like Donora, Pennsylvania caused large numbers of deaths and serious illnesses. Toxic chemicals buried for decades in the "Love Canal" near Buffalo, New York forced the evacuation of an entire suburban community. A massive oil spill off the coast of Santa Barbara, California (similar in nature and public impact to the more recent *Deepwater Horizon* spill in the Gulf of Mexico, with which current readers may be more familiar) highlighted the danger of producing and transporting large quantities of dangerous materials. While these are just some of the more dramatic examples, the problem of pollution was thrust into the public arena at a time when many citizens were demanding more government intervention in a number of areas, from civil rights to social services to environmental protection. And a number of scholars believe that government regulation is more effective than tort law in addressing the

---

2. *See* Robert W. Adler, Jessica C. Landman & Diane M. Cameron, The Clean Water Act, Twenty Years Later (1993). For more horror stories about water pollution by the late 1960s, see David Zwick & Marcy Benstock, Water Wasteland (1971).

problems of modern environmental pollution. Professor Christopher Schroeder, for example, writes:

> With respect to remedies, environmental regulations seek prevention rather than cure. With respect to substance, the levels of environmental quality that our current environmental regulatory system embodies cannot be achieved under current tort standards, because the collectively chosen levels differ from the cost-beneficial levels of environmental quality tort is geared to achieve.

Christopher H. Schroeder, *Lost in the Translation: What Environmental Regulation Does That Tort Cannot Duplicate*, 41 WASHBURN L.J. 583, 583 (2002).

Congress responded to these problems with a series of federal statutes designed to address a range of environmental issues. Below, we summarize the Clean Air Act as one example of how a comprehensive statutory scheme differs from the common law approach. (We include a more detailed "Trail Guide to the Clean Air Act" and similar guides to other key environmental statutes later in the book.)

2. Statutory Responses: The Clean Air Act as an Example

The appellate decision in *Boomer* was issued in 1970, when the American public and its elected officials increasingly were recognizing the perils of air pollution. On New Year's Eve of the same year, Congress adopted comprehensive amendments to the Clean Air Act (CAA).[3] The House Report on the 1970 Act stated:

> "A review of achievements to date . . . make abundantly clear that the strategies which we have pursued in the war against air pollution have been inadequate in several important respects, and the methods employed in implementing those strategies often have been slower and less effective than they might have been."

H.R. Rep. 1146, 91st Cong., 2d Sess. 1, *reprinted at* 1970 U.S. Cong. Code & Admin. News 5356.

As you review the main elements of the Clean Air Act statutory program, ask yourself how Congress sought to address the various problems as compared with the common law approach you identified in the last chapter, and in our reprise of *Boomer* above. In what respects do you think that the statutory approach is superior, and in what ways might it portend problems?

---

3. As with some of the other federal environmental laws, in the case of air pollution Congress did not act on a clean slate in 1970. Congress adopted the original "Clean Air Act" in 1955, with amendments in 1963, 1965, 1966, and 1967. The Air Pollution Control Act of 1955, Pub. L. No. 84-159 (July 14, 1955), extended by Pub. L. No. 86-365 (1959); the Clean Air Act of 1963, Pub. L. No. 88-206 (Dec. 17, 1963), as amended by Pub. L. No. 89-272 (Oct. 20, 1965); the Air Quality Act of 1967, Pub. L. No. 90-148, codified at 42 U.S.C. §§1857 *et seq.* (1967). Earlier legislation, however, was limited largely to authorizing grants and research and development on potential auto emission controls and air quality standards. The 1970 amendments established a comprehensive federal *regulatory* program for air pollution control. The Clean Air Act of 1970, Pub. L. No. 91-604, codified at 42 U.S.C. §§1857 *et seq.* (1970). For a complete history of the 1970 law and later amendments, see A.W. REITZE, JR., AIR POLLUTION CONTROL LAW: COMPLIANCE AND ENFORCEMENT (2001), A.W. Reitze, Jr., *Overview and Critique: A Century of Air Pollution Control Law: What's Worked; What's Failed; What Might Work*, 21 ENVTL. L. 1549 (1991).

a. Setting Standards for Clean Air

Under the common law approach, the most a judge can do in a single case is require that the pollution at a single plant be abated. The quality of the air actually breathed will depend on the aggregate emissions from all sources that contribute to pollution at a given location, some of which might be lowered due to common law liability, and others of which will remain uncontrolled. In the Clean Air Act, Congress directed the federal government (through the U.S. Environmental Protection Agency (EPA)) to identify those pollutants that may endanger public health or welfare and that derive from numerous or diverse sources (and thus are not likely to be controlled adequately by individual source controls alone). CAA §108, 42 U.S.C. §7408. For those pollutants (at present, EPA has identified six, the sources and effects of which we identified in Chapter 1), EPA establishes national ambient air quality standards, which become the mandatory target for clean air programs everywhere in the country. We discuss these kinds of standards further in Chapter 5.

b. Setting Standards for Particular Source Controls

The *Boomer* court was also reluctant to decide what level of air pollution control to impose on the defendant cement plant, much less to decide what kinds of controls were available, appropriate, and feasible. Citing technological complexity and other factors, the court used the device of liability to induce pollution control decisions by the plant owners or managers. In the CAA, Congress established a complex system in which EPA and state officials make decisions about the levels of pollution control that can be achieved using various definitions of the "best technology" for particular kinds of pollution sources, from cars to factories to power plants.

c. Planning for Overall Air Quality

Because the common law approach operates primarily at a site-specific level, discrete decisions by even a large number of individual sources cannot assure that the combination of pollution controls in a region will suffice to "solve" the air pollution problems there. The CAA includes a planning and accounting system in which government officials identify all of the pollution sources, and determine how much pollution is emitted from each and how much total pollution control is necessary in order for the national ambient air quality standards to be met. Then, they allocate control requirements among sources so that the air quality standards will be met in each region.

B. THE ROLE OF ADMINISTRATIVE AGENCIES AND JUDICIAL REVIEW

The comprehensive statutory scheme discussed above (and other statutory schemes as well) require an enormous number of decisions regarding very technical issues. Congress cannot possibly make all of these decisions itself, especially when circumstances frequently change (*e.g.*, new facilities, changing technology, more research on health and environmental impacts). As a result, Congress delegated significant responsibilities to administrative agencies, which operate under various doctrines of administrative law to ensure that agencies act only within the scope of their delegated powers, and otherwise in accordance with law. Thus, to understand and to practice environmental law, you need to understand both the substantive environmental law, and how it is implemented and reviewed under the rules and procedures of applicable administrative law. For example, you need to understand the rules governing how agencies issue regulations, permits, and other documents; the rights and obligations of other parties with respect to those actions; and how courts review those actions.

The following is a brief survey of the most important rules and principles of *federal* administrative law that are useful in understanding the cases and other materials in this book. These principles are dictated largely by the federal Administrative Procedure Act (APA) and cases applying and interpreting that law, but many environmental statutes and regulations also dictate more specific rules for particular circumstances. Thus, to practice environmental law effectively, lawyers often need to understand (1) the relevant substantive law under applicable federal and state statutes, regulations, and cases; (2) the general principles of administrative law and procedure under the federal APA and potentially its state counterparts; (3) specific procedural requirements in the governing substantive statute and regulations; and (4) how all of those components fit together.

Four main sets of questions dominate federal administrative law as applied to environmental law. First, what kinds of decisions do administrative agencies make, and how much lawmaking authority may be delegated to them? Second, how do federal agencies make those decisions, and how can outside parties influence them (including decisions about what actions to take)? Third, who can challenge agency decisions, and under what circumstances? Fourth, what standards do courts apply in reviewing agency decisions?

1. The Scope of Administrative Agency Authority (Delegation and Nondelegation)

In theory, delegation of legislative authority to agency officials is prohibited by Article I, section 1 of the Constitution, which provides: "All legislative Powers herein granted shall be vested in a Congress of the United States. . . ." As students learn in Constitutional Law classes, on rare occasions dating back to the early New Deal period, the Supreme Court invalidated legislative delegations of authority where there was inadequate definition of the bounds of that power. *See* Panama Refining Co. v. Ryan, 293 U.S. 388 (1935); A.L.A. Schecter Poultry Corp. v. United States, 295 U.S. 495 (1935). *See also* Carter v. Carter Coal Co., 298 U.S. 238, 310-12 (1936) (holding that delegation of law-making authority to a private board offends due process). Since that time, however, the Supreme Court has regularly upheld delegations of quasi-legislative authority to administrative agencies even when accompanied by very vague statutory instructions. The Court recently reaffirmed that Congress need only set forth some "intelligible principle" to guide agency action in upholding the delegation of authority to EPA to adopt national ambient air quality standards protecting public health. Whitman v. American Trucking Ass'ns, Inc., 531 U.S. 457 (2001).

From a more practical perspective, however, it is important for lawyers to learn how to identify the breadth of delegation conferred in any particular statute or statutory provision. Agency actions can be challenged on the grounds that they exceed (or are outside the bounds of) the delegated authority. In passing environmental laws, Congress has fluctuated between generality and specificity; *i.e.*, between grants of broad and narrow discretion, depending on the program or circumstances, or the politics of the time. In general, Congress has delegated to EPA and other agencies significant amounts of discretion within which to act. In other instances, frustrated with either the pace or manner in which agencies have acted, Congress has adopted far more detailed and specific instructions, choosing to "micro-manage" some agency programs.

Where Congress delegates power broadly, agency lawyers will advise their clients that the agency has more latitude to make different policy choices, and outside parties will have less chance of arguing that an agency has exceeded or otherwise violated its power. Where Congress delegates narrowly, or with very specific rules and conditions, agencies have a smaller ambit within which to act and outside parties have more ammunition to mount legal challenges to agency actions that deviate from those limitations or requirements. From a policy perspective, are broad delegations of quasi-legislative authority appropriate? Does it depend on the issues involved? The magnitude and breadth of regulatory impacts? Other factors?

2. Agency Decision Procedures and the Role of Outside Parties

One possible "check" on the ability of administrative agencies to "make law" under legislative delegations of authority involves the procedures that agencies must use to adopt regulations, to issue permits, and to make other decisions. The APA sets forth the general rules governing federal agencies' actions. However, each substantive statute may set forth different or additional procedures that apply for particular actions. Moreover, where neither the APA nor other statutes specify procedures for particular actions, agencies are free to adopt their own practices and procedures, so long as they comport with basic requirements of due process. *See* Vermont Yankee Nuclear Power Corp. v. Natural Resources Defense Council, 435 U.S. 519, 524 (1978) (rejecting challenge to agency rule-making procedures for nuclear power plant licensing where agency followed minimum statutory procedural requirements); Chemical Waste Management, Inc. v. U.S. Environmental Protection Agency, 873 F.2d 1477, 1482 (D.C. Cir. 1989) (upholding informal agency hearing procedures in proceedings regarding corrective actions at contaminated waste sites). Below, we outline the basic procedures by which environmental (and other) agencies operate under the APA.

The APA sets forth two main kinds of actions that agencies may take, rules and orders, with two associated sets of procedures. A "rule" is typically an action that applies prospectively to a class or category of activities, and establishes principles of general applicability. An "order" generally applies to a particular party (or parties) to address particular sites or circumstances. Thus, in the APA, a "rule" is defined as "an agency statement of general or particular applicability and future effect designed to implement, interpret, or prescribe law or policy or describing the organization, procedure, or practice requirements of an agency. . . ." 5 U.S.C. §551(4). An "order," by contrast, constitutes "a final disposition, whether affirmative, negative, injunctive, or declaratory in form, of an agency in a matter other than rule making but including licensing." *Id.* §551(6). For example, EPA might issue a rule requiring all factories of a given type to reduce their emissions by 50 percent. It might issue a site-specific permit dictating exactly how many pounds of pollution a particular factory must reduce to comply with that rule, or an adjudication to decide whether the rule has been violated at that site. This distinction can be deceptive, however, because agency applications of law to particular cases can "make law" analogous to the actions of common law judges.

The procedures by which agencies promulgate rules and issue orders and other actions also vary. In general, agencies adopt "rules" most often through informal "notice and comment" procedures, and issue "orders" through more formal adjudicative procedures. In between those two extremes, however, lies a spectrum of procedures (sometimes called "informal adjudications") that may apply to particular actions. The procedures outlined below, along with judicial review discussed in the following section, are important "checks" to ensure that agencies and officials consider a spectrum of views and factors before exercising their authority.[4]

Agency adjudications are trial-type hearings, typically with live witnesses, cross-examination, rules of evidence, and other trial-type procedures. *See* 5 U.S.C. §§556, 557. The basic format resembles civil adjudication and is, therefore, familiar to lawyers and law students and requires no particular elaboration. Informal rule making is a much different process, and is less familiar and perhaps even somewhat strange to many practicing lawyers. Informal rule making consists of three basic steps: (1) notice, (2) opportunity for comment, and (3) evaluation and explanation. 5 U.S.C. §553. Each step is designed to ensure that when agencies exercise their authority, they bear some accountability to diverse interests and values.

First, agencies generally must publish in the Federal Register a "notice of proposed rule making," including:

(1) a statement of the time, place, and nature of public rule-making proceedings;
(2) reference to the legal authority under which the rule is proposed; and
(3) either the terms or substance of the proposed rule or a description of the subjects and issues involved.

5 U.S.C. §553(b). This "notice" step ensures that all interested parties—either those who are subject to a regulation or those the regulation should benefit—know about the pending rule and have an opportunity to participate to try to influence the final result.

---

4. Additional transparency is provided by "open government" statutes such as the Freedom of Information Act, 5 U.S.C. §552, and requirements for open meetings, *see id.* §552b.

The second phase of informal rule making provides:

> After notice required by this section, the agency shall give interested persons an opportunity to participate in the rule making through submission of written data, views, or arguments with or without opportunity for oral presentation. After consideration of the relevant matter presented, the agency shall incorporate in the rules adopted a concise general statement of their basis and purpose.

Id. §553(c). The "opportunity to participate" allows parties to submit not only their opinions about whether and how the agency should regulate, but also "data" and "arguments" in support of their positions. This does not typically involve live "witnesses" with cross-examination and formal rules of evidence, although agencies might provide a "public hearing" at which anyone may "testify," *i.e.*, make an oral statement or presentation, as well as the chance to submit written comments, data, studies, etc. This means that there is no formal "gate keeping" process by which the agency may admit or exclude particular "evidence." *Cf.* Daubert v. Merrell Dow Pharmaceuticals, 509 U.S. 579, 597 (1993) (allowing courts to exclude certain kinds of expert testimony from civil trials on grounds of reliability and other factors) (now embodied in Fed. R. Evid. 702; *see* United States v. Parra, 402 F.3d 752 (7th Cir. 2005) (explaining that the new rule incorporates the same principles as articulated in *Daubert*)). Moreover, there is no limit to *who* may submit comments in an informal rule making, *i.e.*, there are no "standing" or other threshold requirements for interested parties.

The open-ended aspect of informal rule-making procedure can be significant given the final step mandated by the statute: "After consideration of the relevant matter presented, the agency shall incorporate in the rules adopted a concise general statement of their basis and purpose." In some cases, agencies must reasonably respond to all significant comments, which requires them to sort through massive volumes of comments and carefully address many or all of them.

NOTES AND QUESTIONS ON AGENCY PROCEDURES

1. *Detail in regulatory proposals.* The APA obligates the agency to provide notice of a proposed rule, but in remarkably brief terms: "either the terms or substance of the proposed rule or a description of the subjects and issues involved." In a complex environmental rule making, does this suffice to give interested parties a fair opportunity to comment? The usual agency practice is to publish the full text of the proposed rule, along with a detailed explanation of its purposes, alternatives, and key issues the agency is considering.

2. *Detail in agency explanations of final rules.* The APA calls for a "concise" explanation of the final agency rule or decision. Given that agencies must offer the opportunity for comment to any outside party, and the nature and volume of information that outside parties might present in a complex environmental rule making just how "concise" would you expect EPA's explanation to be? In practice, EPA and other agencies typically publish very detailed explanations of the final rule, responses to comments, and reasons why they rejected various alternatives proposed by outside parties. The rule-making record may include tens of thousands of

pages of supporting data and studies. How do you think this affects the agency's ability to promulgate final rules in a timely fashion?

3. *Changes in final regulations.* When an outside party submits comments that are critical of an agency proposal, the agency has several choices. It can stay the course, in which case it must explain why it rejected the comments (for example, why the information submitted is flawed, or why the agency information is superior, or why legal or policy reasons suggest or require the agency approach). It can withdraw the proposal, in which case it must explain why it has done so, especially where other parties supported the proposal. Or, it can modify the proposal to address the information and concerns raised in the comments. In the last option, can the agency simply explain why it changed the proposal, or must it circulate the modified proposal for additional comments? The general rule is that an agency need not seek additional public comment so long as the final rule is a "logical outgrowth" of the original proposal. *See* NRDC v. U.S. EPA, 824 F.2d 1258, 1285 (1987) (invalidating groundwater protection regulations because the final rule was not a logical outgrowth of the proposed rule). Can an agency simply withdraw a final regulation without an opportunity for notice and comment? *See* Natural Resources Defense Council v. U.S. EPA, 683 F.2d 752 (3d Cir. 1982) (invalidating EPA's decision to indefinitely postpone the effective date of amendments to regulations promulgated under the Clean Water Act, because postponement of duly adopted regulation constituted a "rule" for purposes of the APA and therefore could only be promulgated after public notice and comment).

4. *Failure to comment.* The APA affords parties an opportunity to comment, but what are the ramifications if they fail to do so? The general rule is that parties who fail to raise an issue during the comment period are barred from doing so in subsequent litigation. Sims v. Apfel, 530 U.S. 103 (2000). (One might say that the most fundamental rule of practice in this area is to "comment early and comment often.") There are, however, exceptions for purely legal issues and other circumstances. *See* Chemical Manufacturers Ass'n v. U.S. Environmental Protection Agency, 870 F.2d 177, 263 (5th Cir. 1989) (finding the NRDC was not precluded from raising a purely legal issue that was not raised during the notice and comment period).

3.   The Role of the Courts

Judicial review constitutes the second major "check" on the delegation of significant authority to agencies to formulate national environmental law and policy as they implement statutory schemes. As a practical matter, the availability of judicial review, the ability of parties to compel agencies to act, and the standards under which agency actions are reviewed, all affect the actual breadth of the agency's discretion. The more opportunities parties have to compel and to challenge an agency action, and the stricter the standards for review, the narrower the bounds within which agencies can dictate environmental law and policy. Conversely, where opportunities for judicial review are constrained, and where the standards of review are deferential, agencies enjoy much wider latitude. Where judicial review is constrained, parties usually have better opportunities to influence outcomes by persuading agency officials than they may have of prevailing in court. The combination of various limits on judicial review, relatively narrow, deferential standards for judicial review, and broad delegations of quasi-legislative authority confers substantial authority to "make" environmental law and policy on federal agencies and their state counterparts.

a. The Availability of Judicial Review

The Administrative Procedure Act provides specifically for judicial review of administrative agency actions, under prescribed circumstances. Section 701 first states:

> (a) This chapter applies, according to the provisions hereof, except to the extent that—
> (1) statutes preclude judicial review; or
> (2) agency action is committed to agency discretion by law.

5 U.S.C. §701(a). In some statutes, although relatively rarely, Congress expressly prohibits judicial review of certain agency actions and decisions. For example, the Unfunded Mandates Reform Act of 1995, Pub. L. No. 104-4, 109 Stat. 48 (1995), imposes a series of procedural and analytical requirements on various kinds of federal action, most of which are designed to ensure that actions (including laws passed by Congress) are taken with full awareness of the fiscal impacts on state and local governments (and in some cases, the private sector). However, the statute expressly precludes judicial challenges based on alleged violations of those requirements. On the other hand, many environmental statutes expressly provide for direct judicial review of agency decisions. See, e.g., 33 U.S.C. §1369(b) (authorizing direct review in the U.S. Courts of Appeals of specified actions under the Clean Water Act); 42 U.S.C. §7607(b) (same with respect to specified EPA actions under the Clean Air Act).

The bigger *potential* limitation on judicial review is for "agency action that is committed to agency discretion by law." If interpreted broadly, this language would preclude judicial review of a wide range of agency environmental decisions. The courts, however, have interpreted this provision very narrowly to encompass only those agency decisions that are so completely subject to agency discretion that there is "no law to apply," an extremely rare situation. See Heckler v. Chaney, 470 U.S. 821, 838 (1985) (finding an agency decision not to pursue an enforcement action to be entirely committed to agency discretion and thus not subject to judicial review).[5] This is consistent with the Supreme Court's holding in Abbott Laboratories v. Gardner, 387 U.S. 136, 140 (1967), that administrative agency action is subject to a "presumption of reviewability." Section 704 of the APA reinforces this presumption by providing that "[a]gency action made reviewable by

---

5. Synthesizing the law of nondelegation with the law of judicial review, however, produces another odd situation. As discussed above, the Supreme Court has found no unlawful delegation of legislative authority so long as the agency's action is subject to "some intelligible principle" to guide the agency action. One might ask whether there can be "some intelligible principle" if there is "no law to apply" to a particular agency action.

statute and final agency action *for which there is no other adequate remedy in a court* are subject to judicial review." 5 U.S.C. §704 (emphasis added).

Finally, the issue of *who* may challenge a particular agency action is defined in §702 of the APA: "A person suffering legal wrong because of agency action, or adversely affected or aggrieved by agency action within the meaning of a relevant statute, is entitled to judicial review thereof." 5 U.S.C. §702. The issue of who suffers "legal wrong" or is "adversely affected or aggrieved" by agency action is related to principles of standing, which we discuss in Chapter 16. Does it appear that allowing any aggrieved person to challenge agency action offers broader or narrower opportunities to address pollution through litigation than the common law provides? Who could bring suit at common law?

Other principles of justiciability may limit access to court. These principles are based upon statutory, constitutional (Article III "case or controversy") or prudential (gate keeping) factors. For example, under APA §704, as well as the related doctrine of ripeness, only "final agency" action is reviewable, as opposed to "preliminary, procedural, or intermediate agency action." *See, e.g.*, Louisiana Environmental Action Network v. Browner, 87 F.3d 1379, 1385 (D.C. Cir. 1996) (EPA rules identifying standards to be used in later final approvals not ripe for review); Clean Air Implementation Project v. EPA, 150 F.3d 1200, 1208 (D.C. Cir. 1998) (industry challenge to EPA "any credible evidence" rule not ripe where factual application needed to determine impact of the rule). At the other end of the time spectrum, challenges may be precluded on grounds of mootness where harm no longer exists. *See, e.g.*, City of Newport Beach v. Civil Aeronautics Board, 665 F.2d 1280, 1284 (D.C. Cir. 1981) (observing that a lawsuit seeking to compel preparation of an environmental impact statement (EIS) is mooted once the EIS is fully completed). Other potential barriers include exhaustion of administrative remedies,[6] statutes of limitations,[7] abstention and primary jurisdiction,[8] and defenses based on sovereign immunity and the Eleventh Amendment.[9] Those issues are best addressed in courses on federal courts and administrative law.

---

6. *See* the *Chemical Manufacturers Ass'n* case *infra*.

7. *See, e.g.*, Sierra Club v. Slater, 120 F.3d 623, 631 (6th Cir. 1997) (six-year statute of limitations applied to NEPA challenge to highway project); Florida Keys Citizens Coalition v. Army Dep't, 996 F. Supp. 1254, 1256 (S.D. Fla. 1998) (challenge to regulation barred by statute of limitations).

8. *See* National Solid Waste Management Council v. Ohio, 763 F. Supp. 244, 256 (S.D. Ohio 1991), *rev'd on other grounds*, 959 F.2d 590 (6th Cir. 1992) (abstention not appropriately invoked where challenge was to facial constitutionality of state statute under the Commerce Clause and federal court was not asked to pass on matters of state policy); Culbertson v. Coast American, Inc., 913 F. Supp. 1572, 1578 (N.D. Ga. 1995) (abstention raised as defense to citizen suit); Davies v. National Cooperative Refinery Ass'n, 1996 WL 529208, at *6-7 (D. Kan. 1996) (primary jurisdiction and abstention defenses rejected in RCRA case).

9. *See* Maine v. Department of the Navy, 973 F.2d 1007, 1012 (1st Cir. 1992) (federal government enjoys sovereign immunity with regard to state-imposed penalties under CERCLA and RCRA); NRDC v. California Department of Transportation, 96 F.3d 420, 423 (9th Cir. 1996) (barring claims against the Department for alleged CWA violations due to the Eleventh Amendment); Mancuso v. N.Y. State Thruway Authority, 86 F.3d 289, 296 (2d Cir. 1996) (highway authority not entitled to immunity in Clean Water Act case); New Jersey v. Gloucester Environmental Management Services, 923 F. Supp. 651, 664 (D.N.J. 1995) (state hospital but not state colleges entitled to immunity, but New Jersey waived this immunity by participating in litigation); California v. Campbell, 138 F.3d 784, 787 (9th Cir. 1998) (court-appointed receiver is not arm of the state for purposes of Eleventh Amendment immunity).

b. *Forcing Agency Action*

Parties may use the courts to influence the agency agenda by asking judges to order agencies to issue particular rules or to take other actions. When Congress adopts statutory schemes in which it delegates significant implementing authority and responsibility to EPA and other agencies, the force of an agency's power may lie first and foremost in which portions of the statute it elects to implement. Often, Congress establishes an agency agenda by identifying a series of rule-making tasks. Sometimes, Congress prioritizes those tasks by setting statutory deadlines within which agencies must issue rules. If the agency fails to promulgate an essential set of implementing regulations, or to do so within the prescribed deadlines, that part of the statutory scheme might lie dormant. Likewise, if a statute prohibits someone from acting (discharging pollutants into air or water, for instance) without a permit, agency failure to act on a permit application may hinder that party's operations. An agency might decide not to act because it has too much to do and too few resources; because of lengthy, cumbersome procedural requirements; because it is reluctant to make difficult policy choices; or because it disagrees with a particular program as a matter of policy. (That decision, of course, constitutes a virtual statutory amendment if left unchallenged.) A remarkable amount of environmental law and policy, therefore, has been the product of litigation designed to force an agency to act in particular areas.

Several agency-forcing mechanisms are available to various parties to move matters along. First, most of the major environmental statutes include "citizen suit" provisions that allow "any person" to sue the Administrator of EPA or other agency officials (depending on the statute) for failure to perform any action that is "not discretionary." *See, e.g.*, Clean Water Act §505(a)(2), 33 U.S.C. §1365(a)(2). Obviously, a key determination is whether the official's action is mandatory or discretionary, but agencies clearly have a mandatory duty to comply with a statutory deadline. This kind of citizen suit litigation has driven significant statutory programs. *See, e.g.*, NRDC v. Train, 8 ENVTL. REP. CASES (BNA) 2120 (D.D.C. 1976) (approving a settlement that dictated EPA's long-term agenda for the regulation of toxic water pollutants and other industrial discharges for decades). What are the policy implications of this kind of citizen suit? On the plus side, clearly it can be used to force a reluctant agency to do the job set out for it by Congress. But where Congress assigns the agency too much to do, with too few resources, who should decide what programs and activities are most important or most pressing: outside groups, the courts, or the agencies themselves? *See, e.g.*, D. Noah Greenwald, Kieran F. Suckling & Martin Taylor, *The Listing Record, in* I THE ENDANGERED SPECIES ACT AT THIRTY, RENEWING THE CONSERVATION PROMISE 51, 63 (Goble, Scott & Davis eds., 2006) (discussing and presenting data on the tension between political opposition to new listings of threatened and endangered species and citizen suit pressure to do so).

Second, in some instances Congress takes the initiative in dealing with chronic agency inaction by legislating a default result if the agency fails to act, sometimes known as legislative "hammer provisions." One example is the so-called land ban provisions Congress adopted as part of the 1984 amendments to the Resource Conservation and Recovery Act (RCRA). Under this provision, adopted as part of section 3004 of RCRA, 42 U.S.C. §6924, Congress enforced a requirement that

EPA write regulations establishing treatment requirements by prohibiting industry from disposing of certain categories of hazardous waste in landfills after certain prescribed dates unless they complied with these new treatment requirements, or met other extremely onerous requirements.

Finally, the APA includes a mandamus-type provision, which may be used where no specific citizen suit authority exists, or where the statute includes no specific deadline for action. The APA requires federal agencies to "give an interested person the right to petition for the issuance, amendment, or repeal of a rule." 5 U.S.C. §553(e). Asking, however, does not mean getting. The statute, therefore, authorizes a reviewing court to "compel agency action unlawfully withheld or unreasonably delayed." 5 U.S.C. §706(1). Suits to remedy unreasonable delay are typically less effective than suits to enforce a firm statutory deadline for several reasons. The issue of what constitutes unreasonable delay is inherently subjective. Further, filing a rule-making petition under section 553(e) is a prerequisite to a mandamus action under section 706(1), meaning that one must first petition the agency for rule making, and then wait a respectable time for the agency to act (or not), before even seeking judicial review of the agency's action or inaction. *See* Oljato Chapter of the Navajo Tribe v. Train, 515 F.2d 654, 667 (D.C. Cir. 1975) (affirming dismissal of challenge to EPA's failure to revise air pollution regulation absent petition for rule making and supporting materials, followed by agency decision on petition). The Supreme Court's decision in Norton v. Southern Utah Wilderness Alliance, 542 U.S. 55, 65 (2004), further limits efforts to force agency action under section 706 of the APA, because the Court held that the term "agency action" does not include discretionary implementation of broad agency programs, such as land use plans, as opposed to discrete actions that laws specifically mandate.

c. Challenges on the Merits—Standards of Judicial Review

The APA also provides for judicial review of completed agency action. The standards governing judicial review of agency actions significantly affect the breadth of agency authority to establish environmental law and policy. Along with the authority in section 706(1) to compel agency action unlawfully withheld or unreasonably delayed, section 706 of the APA directs courts to:

(2) hold unlawful and set aside agency action, findings, and conclusions found to be—

(A) arbitrary, capricious, an abuse of discretion, or otherwise not in accordance with law;

(B) contrary to constitutional right, power, privilege, or immunity;

(C) in excess of statutory jurisdiction, authority, or limitations, or short of statutory right;

(D) without observance of procedure required by law;

(E) unsupported by substantial evidence in a case subject to sections 556 and 557 of this title or otherwise reviewed on the record of an agency hearing provided by statute; or

(F) unwarranted by the facts to the extent that the facts are subject to trial de novo by the reviewing court.

5 U.S.C. §706(2).

First, it is important to understand which of these standards applies to a particular case. Obviously, all agency decisions must be constitutional (subsection B), and comply with the applicable statutes (subsection C) and procedural requirements (subsection D). The standards in subsections E and F, requiring specific degrees of factual support for decisions, apply only to adjudications. The majority of informal agency actions, therefore, such as promulgation of rules and issuance of permits, will be subject to the "arbitrary and capricious" standard set forth in subsection A. The Supreme Court explained the meaning of this key standard in an environmental context in the following seminal case.

Citizens to Preserve Overton Park v. Volpe
401 U.S. 402 (1971)

Opinion of the Court by JUSTICE MARSHALL, announced by JUSTICE STEWART.

The growing public concern about the quality of our natural environment has prompted Congress in recent years to enact legislation designed to curb the accelerating destruction of our country's natural beauty. We are concerned in this case with §4(f) of the Department of Transportation Act of 1966, as amended, and §18(a) of the Federal-Aid Highway Act of 1968. These statutes prohibit the Secretary of Transportation from authorizing the use of federal funds to finance the construction of highways through public parks if a "feasible and prudent" alternative route exists. If no such route is available, the statutes allow him to approve construction through parks only if there has been "all possible planning to minimize harm" to the park.

Petitioners, private citizens as well as local and national conservation organizations, contend that the Secretary has violated these statutes by authorizing the expenditure of federal funds for the construction of a six-lane interstate highway through a public park in Memphis, Tennessee.

Overton Park is 342-acre city park located near the center of Memphis. The park contains a zoo, a nine-hole municipal golf course, an outdoor theater, nature trails, a bridle path, an art academy, picnic areas, and 170 acres of forest. The proposed highway, which is to be a six-lane, high-speed, expressway, will sever the zoo from the rest of the park. Although the roadway will be depressed below ground level except where it crosses a small creek, 26 acres of the park will be destroyed. The highway is to be a segment of Interstate Highway I-40, part of the National System of Interstate and Defense Highways. I-40 will provide Memphis with a major east-west expressway which will allow easier access to downtown Memphis from the residential areas on the eastern edge of the city.

. . . Neither announcement approving the route and design of I-40 was accompanied by a statement of the Secretary's factual findings. He did not indicate why he believed there were no feasible and prudent alternative routes or why design changes could not be made to reduce the harm to the park. . . .

Respondents argue that it was unnecessary for the Secretary to make formal findings, and that he did, in fact, exercise his own independent judgment which was supported by the facts. In the District Court, respondents introduced affidavits, prepared specifically for this litigation, which indicated that the Secretary had made the decision and that the decision was supportable.

We agree that formal findings were not required. But we do not believe that in this case judicial review based solely on litigation affidavits was adequate.

[T]he existence of judicial review is only the start: the standard for review must also be determined. For that we must look to §706 of the Administrative Procedure Act, which provides that a "reviewing court shall . . . hold unlawful and set aside agency action, findings, and conclusions found" not to meet six separate standards. In all cases agency action must be set aside if the action was "arbitrary, capricious, an abuse of discretion, or otherwise not in accordance with law" or if the action failed to meet statutory, procedural, or constitutional requirements. . . . [T]he generally applicable standards of §706 require the reviewing court to engage in a substantial inquiry. Certainly, the Secretary's decision is entitled to a presumption of regularity. But that presumption is not to shield his action from a thorough, probing, in-depth review.

The court is first required to decide whether the Secretary acted within the scope of his authority. This determination naturally begins with a delineation of the scope of the Secretary's authority and discretion. As has been shown, Congress has specified only a small range of choices that the Secretary can make. Also involved in this initial inquiry is a determination of whether on the facts the Secretary's decision can reasonably be said to be within that range. The reviewing court must consider whether the Secretary properly construed his authority to approve the use of parkland as limited to situations where there are no feasible alternative routes or where feasible alternative routes involve uniquely difficult problems. And the reviewing court must be able to find that the Secretary could have reasonably believed that in this case there are no feasible alternatives or that alternatives do involve unique problems.

Scrutiny of the facts does not end, however, with the determination that the Secretary has acted within the scope of his statutory authority. Section 706(2)(A) requires a finding that the actual choice made was not "arbitrary, capricious, an abuse of discretion, or otherwise not in accordance with law." To make this finding the court must consider whether the decision was based on a consideration of the relevant factors and whether there has been a clear error of judgment. Although this inquiry into the facts is to be searching and careful, the ultimate standard of review is a narrow one. The court is not empowered to substitute its judgment for that of the agency. The final inquiry is whether the Secretary's action followed the necessary procedural requirements. Here the only procedural error alleged is the failure of the Secretary to make formal findings and state his reason for allowing the highway to be built through the park.

Undoubtedly, review of the Secretary's action is hampered by his failure to make such findings, but the absence of formal findings does not necessarily require that the case be remanded to the Secretary. Neither the Department of Transportation Act nor the Federal-Aid Highway Act requires such formal findings. Moreover, the Administrative Procedure Act requirements that there be formal findings in certain rulemaking and adjudicatory proceedings do not apply to the Secretary's action here. And, although formal findings may be required in some cases in the absence of statutory directives when the nature of the agency action is ambiguous, those situations are rare. Plainly, there is no ambiguity here; the Secretary has approved the construction of I-40 through Overton Park and has approved a specific design for the project. . . .

Moreover, there is an administrative record that allows the full, prompt review of the Secretary's action that is sought without additional delay which would result from having a remand to the Secretary.

That administrative record is not, however, before us. The lower courts based their review on the litigation affidavits that were presented. These affidavits were merely "post hoc" rationalizations, which have traditionally been found to be an inadequate basis for review. And they clearly do not constitute the "whole record" compiled by the agency: the basis for review required by §706 of the Administrative Procedure Act.

Thus it is necessary to remand this case to the District Court for plenary review of the Secretary's decision. That review is to be based on the full administrative record that was before the Secretary at the time he made his decision. But since the bare record may not disclose the factors that were considered or the Secretary's construction of the evidence it may be necessary for the District Court to require some explanation in order to determine if the Secretary acted within the scope of his authority and if the Secretary's action was justifiable under the applicable standard. The court may require the administrative officials who participated in the decision to give testimony explaining their action. Of course, such inquiry into the mental processes of administrative decisionmakers is usually to be avoided. And where there are administrative findings that were made at the same time as the decision . . . there must be a strong showing of bad faith or improper behavior before such inquiry may be made. But here there are no such formal findings and it may be that the only way there can be effective judicial review is by examining the decisionmakers themselves.

The District Court is not, however, required to make such an inquiry. It may be that the Secretary can prepare formal findings . . . that will provide an adequate explanation for his action. Such an explanation will, to some extent, be a "post hoc rationalization" and thus must be viewed critically. If the District Court decides that additional explanation is necessary, that court should consider which method will prove the most expeditious so that full review may be had as soon as possible.

Reversed and remanded.

NOTES AND QUESTIONS ON *OVERTON PARK*

1. *The APA as the basis for judicial review.* The Court found that the agency decision was subject to review under the APA. (Note that the Supreme Court later clarified that the APA provides the necessary cause of action to challenge administrative actions under the appropriate circumstances, but not an independent source of federal subject matter jurisdiction. Califano v. Sanders, 430 U.S. 100, 104-07 (1977).) Because challenges to federal agency action tend to arise under federal statutes, subject matter jurisdiction exists under 28 U.S.C. §1311, rendering this distinction trivial as a matter of principle but important as a matter of pleading. This ruling exposed to judicial scrutiny under various

environmental laws a huge range of decisions by federal agencies whose basic missions have little to do with environmental protection (agencies that build or permit the building of highways, dams, and other projects, or who allow development activities on public lands). It also rendered those decisions subject to review under underlying agency substantive statutes (such as the highway laws at issue in this case), whether or not those laws have independent provisions for judicial review. This holding was particularly significant given the passage of the National Environmental Policy Act (NEPA) just two years earlier, under which all federal agencies, whether or not they have "environmental" responsibilities as part of their primary missions, must evaluate and disclose the environmental impacts of proposed actions and alternatives. Because NEPA itself contains no independent provision for judicial review, the APA provides the only cause of action to challenge an agency NEPA violation. *See* Marsh v. Oregon Natural Resources Council, 490 U.S. 360 (1989) (holding the "arbitrary and capricious" standard of review as the appropriate standard to evaluate the Army Corps decision not to supplement an EIS).

2. *Deferential standard of review.* At the same time, however, the *Overton Park* decision signaled that the standard of review under the APA arbitrary and capricious language is narrow and, ultimately, deferential to agency policy choices:

> . . . [T]he court must consider whether the decision was based on a consideration of the relevant factors and whether there has been a clear error of judgment. Although this inquiry into the facts is to be searching and careful, the ultimate standard of review is a narrow one. The court is not empowered to substitute its judgment for that of the agency.

3. *Motor vehicles.* In Motor Vehicle Manufacturers Ass'n v. State Farm Mutual Auto Insurance Co., 463 U.S. 29 (1983), the Supreme Court elaborated on the arbitrary and capricious standard of review. While this case involved passive restraint standards for automobile safety, rather than environmental issues, it stands as one of the most revealing articulations of the applicable standard of review under APA §706(2)(A):

> The scope of review under the "arbitrary and capricious" standard is narrow and a court is not to substitute its judgment for that of the agency. Nevertheless, the agency must examine the relevant data and articulate a satisfactory explanation for its action including a "rational connection between the facts found and the choice made." In reviewing that explanation, we must "consider whether the decision was based on a consideration of the relevant factors and whether there has been a clear error of judgment." Normally, an agency rule would be arbitrary and capricious if the agency has relied on factors which Congress has not intended it to consider, entirely failed to consider an important aspect of the problem, offered an explanation for its decision that runs counter to the evidence before the agency, or is so implausible that it could not be ascribed to a difference in view or the product of agency expertise. The reviewing court should not attempt itself to make up for such deficiencies: "We may not supply a reasoned basis for the agency's action that the agency itself has not given." We will, however, "uphold a decision of less than ideal clarity if the agency's path may reasonably be discerned." For purposes of this case, it is also relevant that Congress required a record of the rulemaking proceedings to be compiled and submitted to a reviewing court, and intended that agency findings would be supported by "substantial evidence on the record considered as a whole."

463 U.S. at 43-44.

This brief excerpt can serve as a template for agency lawyers who want to ensure that agency decisions are likely to withstand judicial review, and for outside parties to guide potential challenges to unfavorable decisions. It can also serve as a list of the various ways in which agency decisions might be found unlawful, as you read the substantive cases later in the book.

4. *Administrative record.* Last, but not least, the Supreme Court in *Overton Park* clarified the materials a reviewing court may use when evaluating the validity of an agency decision, a process known as "administrative record review." The "administrative record" is comprised of all of the documents and other information that the agency relied upon in reaching its decision, and the agency must compile it contemporaneously throughout the agency's decision-making process. It should include background materials, data, reports and analysis, the agency proposal (or proposals), comments submitted by outside parties, and the agency's responses to those comments, as well as the final decision and any accompanying analysis and rationale for that decision. The concept that review of agency decisions is limited to materials included in the administrative record may have come as a surprise to lawyers used to presenting and cross-examining live witnesses and hand-choosing the documents and other exhibits they want to court to review. It is, however, fundamental to understanding how many environmental decisions are made, and the grounds on which they can be challenged. In addition, it further underscores a point we made earlier in the chapter—the critical importance of submitting comments and relevant data, studies, and other materials on the record during the public comment period. Matters not raised on the record may be precluded from later consideration, although this general rule is subject to several exceptions. *See* Animal Defense Council v. Hodel, 840 F.2d 1432 (9th Cir. 1988) (stating that in deciding a challenge to an agency rule, a district court may look beyond the administrative record and/or pursue any necessary discovery only where (1) the agency relied on materials not included in the administrative record, (2) the court finds review or discovery beyond the administrative record to be "necessary to explain the agency action," or (3) the court finds that the agency has acted in bad faith).

5. *Deference to agencies.* Is the level of deference to agency policy decisions afforded in cases like *Overton Park* and *Motor Vehicle Manufacturers* appropriate? Why or why not?

Arguably, the "arbitrary and capricious" portion of the APA standard applies to agency policy decisions that are within the bounds of discretion delegated by Congress, while more of a purely legal determination is involved when a party challenges agency actions as "not in accordance with law" (subsection A) or "in excess of statutory jurisdiction, authority, or limitations, or short of statutory right" (subsection C). The opening sentence of section 706 provides: "To the extent necessary to decision and when presented, the reviewing court shall decide all relevant questions of law, interpret constitutional and statutory provisions, and determine the meaning or applicability of the terms of an agency action." Does this language suggest more of a de novo judicial review of purely legal issues? Is this not the primary role of the judiciary? Before making a final call on this issue, read the following case.

Chevron, U.S.A. v. Natural Resources Defense Council
467 U.S. 837 (1984)

JUSTICE STEVENS delivered the opinion of the Court.

In the Clean Air Act Amendments of 1977, Congress enacted certain requirements applicable to States that had not achieved the national air quality standards established by the Environmental Protection Agency (EPA) pursuant to earlier legislation. The amended Clean Air Act required these "nonattainment" States to establish a permit program regulating "new or modified major stationary sources" of air pollution. Generally, a permit may not be issued for a new or modified major stationary source unless several stringent conditions are met.[1] The EPA regulation promulgated to implement this permit requirement allows a State to adopt a plantwide definition of the term "stationary source."[2] Under this definition, an existing plant that contains several pollution-emitting devices may install or modify one piece of equipment without meeting the permit conditions if the alteration will not increase the total emissions from the plant. The question presented by these cases is whether EPA's decision to allow States to treat all of the pollution-emitting devices within the same industrial grouping as though they were encased within a single "bubble" is based on a reasonable construction of the statutory term "stationary source." . . .

The Court of Appeals set aside the regulations. . . .

The court observed that the relevant part of the amended Clean Air Act "does not explicitly define what Congress envisioned as a 'stationary source,' to which the permit program . . . should apply," and further stated that the precise issue was not "squarely addressed in the legislative history." In light of its conclusion that the legislative history bearing on the question was "at best contradictory," it reasoned that "the purposes of the nonattainment program should guide our decision here." Based on two of its precedents concerning the applicability of the bubble concept to certain Clean Air Act programs, the court stated that the bubble concept was "mandatory" in programs designed merely to maintain existing air quality, but held that it was "inappropriate" in programs enacted to improve air quality. Since the purpose of the permit program—its "raison d'être," in the court's view—was to improve air quality, the court held that the bubble concept was inapplicable in these cases under its prior precedents. It therefore set aside the regulations embodying the bubble concept as contrary to law. We granted certiorari to review that judgment, and we now reverse. The basic legal error of the Court of Appeals was to adopt a static judicial definition of the term "stationary source" when it had decided that Congress itself had not commanded that definition. . . .

---

1. Section 172(b)(6), 42 U.S.C. §7502(b)(6), provides: "The plan provisions required by subsection (a) shall—

   '(6) require permits for the construction and operation of new or modified major stationary sources in accordance with section 173 (relating to permit requirements).'" 91 Stat. 747.

   2. "(i) 'Stationary source' means any building, structure, facility, or installation which emits or may emit any air pollutant subject to regulation under the Act. (ii) 'Building, structure, facility, or installation' means all of the pollutant-emitting activities which belong to the same industrial grouping, are located on one or more contiguous or adjacent properties, and are under the control of the same person (or persons under common control) except the activities of any vessel." 40 CFR §§51.18(j)(1)(i) and (ii) (1983).

II

When a court reviews an agency's construction of the statute which it administers, it is confronted with two questions. First, always, is the question whether Congress has directly spoken to the precise question at issue. If the intent of Congress is clear, that is the end of the matter; for the court, as well as the agency, must give effect to the unambiguously expressed intent of Congress.[9] If, however, the court determines Congress has not directly addressed the precise question at issue, the court does not simply impose its own construction on the statute, as would be necessary in the absence of an administrative interpretation. Rather, if the statute is silent or ambiguous with respect to the specific issue, the question for the court is whether the agency's answer is based on a permissible construction of the statute.[11]

"The power of an administrative agency to administer a congressionally created . . . program necessarily requires the formulation of policy and the making of rules to fill any gap left, implicitly or explicitly, by Congress." If Congress has explicitly left a gap for the agency to fill, there is an express delegation of authority to the agency to elucidate a specific provision of the statute by regulation. Such legislative regulations are given controlling weight unless they are arbitrary, capricious, or manifestly contrary to the statute. Sometimes the legislative delegation to an agency on a particular question is implicit rather than explicit. In such a case, a court may not substitute its own construction of a statutory provision for a reasonable interpretation made by the administrator of an agency.

We have long recognized that considerable weight should be accorded to an executive department's construction of a statutory scheme it is entrusted to administer, and the principle of deference to administrative interpretations.

In light of these well-settled principles it is clear that the Court of Appeals misconceived the nature of its role in reviewing the regulations at issue. Once it determined, after its own examination of the legislation, that Congress did not actually have an intent regarding the applicability of the bubble concept to the permit program, the question before it was not whether in its view the concept is "inappropriate" in the general context of a program designed to improve air quality, but whether the Administrator's view that it is appropriate in the context of this particular program is a reasonable one. Based on the examination of the legislation and its history . . . we agree with the Court of Appeals that Congress did not have a specific intention on the applicability of the bubble concept in these cases, and conclude that the EPA's use of that concept here is a reasonable policy choice for the agency to make. . . .

9. The judiciary is the final authority on issues of statutory construction and must reject administrative constructions which are contrary to clear congressional intent. If a court, employing traditional tools of statutory construction, ascertains that Congress had an intention on the precise question at issue, that intention is the law and must be given effect.

11. The court need not conclude that the agency construction was the only one it permissibly could have adopted to uphold the construction, or even the reading the court would have reached if the question initially had arisen in a judicial proceeding.

Policy

The arguments over policy that are advanced in the parties' briefs create the impression that respondents are now waging in a judicial forum a specific policy battle which they ultimately lost in the agency and in the 32 jurisdictions opting for the "bubble concept," but one which was never waged in the Congress. Such policy arguments are more properly addressed to legislators or administrators, not to judges. In these cases, the Administrator's interpretation represents a reasonable accommodation of manifestly competing interests and is entitled to deference: the regulatory scheme is technical and complex, the agency considered the matter in a detailed and reasoned fashion, and the decision involves reconciling conflicting policies. Congress intended to accommodate both interests, but did not do so itself on the level of specificity presented by these cases. Perhaps that body consciously desired the Administrator to strike the balance at this level, thinking that those with great expertise and charged with responsibility for administering the provision would be in a better position to do so; perhaps it simply did not consider the question at this level; and perhaps Congress was unable to forge a coalition on either side of the question, and those on each side decided to take their chances with the scheme devised by the agency. For judicial purposes, it matters not which of these things occurred. Judges are not experts in the field, and are not part of either political branch of the Government. Courts must, in some cases, reconcile competing political interests, but not on the basis of the judges' personal policy preferences. In contrast, an agency to which Congress has delegated policy-making responsibilities may, within the limits of that delegation, properly rely upon the incumbent administration's views of wise policy to inform its judgments. While agencies are not directly accountable to the people, the Chief Executive is, and it is entirely appropriate for this political branch of the Government to make such policy choices—resolving the competing interests which Congress itself either inadvertently did not resolve, or intentionally left to be resolved by the agency charged with the administration of the statute in light of everyday realities. When a challenge to an agency construction of a statutory provision, fairly conceptualized, really centers on the wisdom of the agency's policy, rather than whether it is a reasonable choice within a gap left open by Congress, the challenge must fail. In such a case, federal judges—who have no constituency—have a duty to respect legitimate policy choices made by those who do. The responsibilities for assessing the wisdom of such policy choices and resolving the struggle between competing views of the public interest are not judicial ones: "Our Constitution vests such responsibilities in the political branches."

We hold that the EPA's definition of the term "source" is a permissible construction of the statute which seeks to accommodate progress in reducing air pollution with economic growth. "The Regulations which the Administrator has adopted provide what the agency could allowably view as . . . [an] effective reconciliation of these twofold ends. . . ."

The judgment of the Court of Appeals is reversed.

NOTES AND QUESTIONS ON *CHEVRON*

1. *Holding.* Articulate the two-part test identified in this decision for when a court reviews an agency decision involving statutory interpretation. Does this standard of review comport with the role of courts articulated in the first sentence of APA §706, set forth above? What are the implications of this standard for the breadth of agency authority to "make" environmental law and policy?

2. *Strategy.* What prong of the two-part test do parties who challenge agency decisions prefer? What prong do agency lawyers who defend those decisions prefer?

3. *Plain language versus legislative history.* Among other factors, the *Chevron* doctrine reaffirms the traditional role of legislative history in construing statutes. Courts use various canons of construction, as well as relevant statements in congressional reports and debates, to ascertain what Congress intended in the face of otherwise ambiguous statutory text. However, the Court has also tended in recent years to decline *Chevron* deference by construing statutes based on the plain statutory text where possible. *See, e.g.*, City of Chicago v. Environmental Defense Fund, 511 U.S. 328, 337 (1994) ("it is the statute, not the Committee Report, which is the authoritative expression of the law") (Scalia, J.); Solid Waste Agency of Northern Cook County v. U.S. Army Corps of Engineers, 531 U.S. 159, 172 (2001) (declining *Chevron* deference where statutory text is clear). *See generally* ANTONIN SCALIA, A MATTER OF INTERPRETATION: FEDERAL COURTS AND THE LAW 23 (1997) (arguing that the plain meaning of statutes should be construed "reasonably, to contain all that it fairly means"); Thomas Merrill, *Textualism and the Future of the* Chevron *Doctrine*, 72 WASH. U. L.J. 351 (1994).

4. *Evolution of* Chevron *doctrine.* Lest you begin to think that it is virtually impossible to challenge administrative agency decisions, in addition to the trend toward textualism discussed above, the *Chevron* doctrine has experienced some significant erosion since it was adopted. Perhaps most notably, in United States v. Mead, 533 U.S. 218 (2001), the Supreme Court clarified that *Chevron* deference is appropriate only where Congress delegates rule-making authority to an agency, and the agency promulgates rules pursuant to that authority. *See, e.g.*, Catskill Mountains Chapter of Trout Unlimited, Inc. v. The City of New York, 273 F.3d 481 (2d Cir. 2001) (declining to defer to EPA interpretation of Clean Water Act that was not embodied in a rule-making action). Other agency actions are entitled to a weaker form of deference, the weight of which depends on the thoroughness and validity of the agency's reasoning, consistency with other agency pronouncements, and other factors relevant to the persuasiveness of the agency decision. Skidmore v. Swift & Co., 323 U.S. 134 (1944). At the other end of the spectrum, an agency's interpretation of its own regulations is entitled to deference unless it is plainly erroneous or inconsistent with the regulation. Auer v. Robbins, 519 U.S. 452 (1997). In *Solid Waste Agency of Northern Cook County*, the Court also declined to afford *Chevron* deference where the administrative interpretation would raise "serious constitutional problems," unless the result would plainly contradict Congress' intent. 531 U.S. at 160.

Review—Key APA Provisions Governing Administrative Process

Section of APA	Provision
5 U.S.C. §551(4)	Defines "rule" as "an agency statement of general or particular applicability and future effect designed to implement, interpret or prescribe law or policy. . . ."
5 U.S.C. §551(6)	Defines "order" as "a whole or a part of a final disposition, whether affirmative, negative, injunctive, or declaratory in form, of an agency in a matter other than rule making but including licensing."
5 U.S.C. §553(a)-(c)	Establishes "notice and comment" rule-making process in which agencies must (1) publish notices of proposed rule making (including a description of the substance of the proposal or its subjects and issues); (2) allow interested persons an opportunity to comment on the proposal or otherwise to participate in the rule making; and (3) consider and respond to comments before issuing a final rule.
5 U.S.C. §553(e)	Requires agencies to provide any interested person the right to petition for the issuance, amendment, or repeal of rules.
5 U.S.C. §§554, 556	Establishes procedures for administrative adjudications.
5 U.S.C. §702	Allows judicial review by any person who suffers legal wrong or is adversely affected or aggrieved by agency action.
5 U.S.C. §704	Provides for judicial review of agency actions made reviewable by statute, or other final agency actions for which there is no other adequate remedy in court.
5 U.S.C. §706(1)	Allows parties to ask a reviewing court to "compel agency action unlawfully withheld or unreasonably delayed."
5 U.S.C. §706(2)	Establishes standards of judicial review of agency actions, providing relief for actions which are (A) "arbitrary, capricious, an abuse of discretion, or otherwise not in accordance with law," (B) unconstitutional, (C) beyond the scope of agency authority, (D) adopted contrary to applicable procedures, or (E) and (F) insufficiently supported by evidence or facts.

CLIMATE DISRUPTION ADMINISTRATIVE LAW PROBLEM

Section 202(a) of the Clean Air Act provides:

The Administrator shall by regulation prescribe . . . standards applicable to the emission of any air pollutant from any class or classes of new motor vehicles or new motor vehicle engines, which in his judgment cause, or contribute to, air pollution which may reasonably be anticipated to endanger public health or welfare.

42 U.S.C. §7521. The Act further defines an "air pollutant" as

any air pollution agent or combination of such agents, including any physical, chemical, biological, radioactive . . . substance or matter which is emitted into or otherwise enters the ambient air.

42 U.S.C. §7602(g).

1. Suppose you represent a coalition of environmental organizations and several state governments eager to see the federal EPA issue uniform greenhouse gas emission standards for motor vehicles. You believe this provision requires EPA to issue tailpipe standards for greenhouse gas emissions from motor vehicles, but EPA has publicly disavowed any intent to issue such regulations. What procedural options do you have to compel EPA to issue such regulations? What do you deem your best option and why?

Suppose that, on behalf of the environmental organizations, you file a petition requesting EPA to issue rules regulating greenhouse gas emissions from motor vehicles but that EPA denies the petition in a final rule making. EPA's rationale is that greenhouse gases do not constitute Clean Air Act "air pollutants" because the Act does not apply to pollutants that affect the global climate, but only pollutants that affect air pollution levels in the locality where the pollutants are emitted. Is EPA's denial of your rule-making petition subject to judicial review? Upon what grounds might you challenge it? How might *Chevron* apply and what legal result would it dictate?

2. Suppose you succeed in obtaining a court decision that rejects EPA's holding that only substances with local effects are air pollutants under section 202 and remands the matter back to the agency. However, several months have now gone by without any follow-up regulatory action by EPA. Now what can you do? Can you file suit against EPA? For what, exactly? How likely is it to be successful?

Suppose EPA proposes, in a Notice of Proposed Rulemaking published in the Federal Register, to find that emissions of greenhouse gases "cause, or contribute to, air pollution which may reasonably be anticipated to endanger public health or welfare" under section 202 of the Clean Air Act (proposed "endangerment finding"). This time you represent North American Motors, Inc., a maker of passenger vehicles. Would you want to comment on this rule? If so, what will be the gist of your comments? Suppose your client asks you to convey one of two messages in your comments: Message 1 is that EPA's tailpipe standards for greenhouse gas emissions will be too stringent and will thus cause your company financial hardship and message 2 is that the current observed warming of the climate is just part of a natural cycle and has nothing to do with emissions of greenhouse gases. Which message is the most appropriate, and why?

3. Suppose instead that you represent the national environmental organization mentioned above. Your client is fairly happy with EPA's proposed endangerment finding and has informed you not to bother filing comments. Would you advise the organization any differently? What risks does the organization run by not commenting on the proposal? What might be the gist of the organization's comments?

Suppose that EPA heeds the comments from industry and issues a final rule withdrawing its proposed endangerment finding.[14] The agency states that the dangers to human health and welfare from climate disruption are not so severe as to meet the standard of "endangerment." Consider that EPA justified its proposed rule in part upon the U.S. Global Change Research Program's 2009 report on global climate change impacts in the United States (excerpted in Chapter 1). Put yourself again in the shoes of an attorney representing a national environmental organization. Is EPA's final endangerment finding subject to judicial review? What arguments would you make in an effort to invalidate the final rule?

14. Note that, in reality, EPA finalized its proposed endangerment finding and the D.C. Circuit upheld it. *See* Coalition for Responsible Regulation v. EPA, 684 F.3d 102 (D.C. Cir. 2012), *reversed in part on other grounds sub nom.* Utility Air Regulatory Group v. EPA, 134 S. Ct. 2427 (2014).

ESTABLISHING ENVIRONMENTAL STANDARDS

The remaining chapters in this book explain and illustrate the concepts underlying the statutory schemes that dominate modern environmental law. Many of these statutory schemes address pollution in a particular medium. Thus, the Clean Air Act (CAA) addresses air pollution and the Clean Water Act (CWA) addresses water pollution. The Resource Conservation and Recovery Act (RCRA) addresses solid waste disposal, thereby protecting land. The Comprehensive Environmental Response, Compensation, and Liability Act (CERCLA) complements RCRA's effort to prevent harmful disposal on land by requiring cleanup of already contaminated sites. By contrast, the Federal Insecticide, Fungicide, and Rodenticide Act (FIFRA) and the Toxic Substances Control Act (TSCA) focus on toxic pollutants regardless of the environmental medium that they might pollute.

Each of these statutes contains a vast array of specific provisions. Practitioners often become experts in a particular statute or, more commonly, a particular part of one of these statutes. It is not possible to master every provision in all of these statutes or even all of the provisions in one of the more detailed statutes in a single environmental law course. You should aim as you study these materials to acquire the skills needed to understand the specifics of any statutory provision you may encounter by carefully learning and giving meaning to each statutory provision you read.

At the same time, skilled practitioners regularly understand specific provisions in light of their place in the entire statutory scheme. So, you must also understand the statutory scheme as a whole, even when a specific issue primarily implicates a single provision or a limited number of provisions. Even the most skilled practitioners rarely know each provision in the more complex statutes intimately. But they do know how the statutory scheme functions and where the provisions they know well fit in that scheme, so they can then more easily research specific provisions as needed.

Skilled practitioners understand statutory schemes as an arrangement of conceptual choices made by Congress. A fairly typical choice in many of these schemes involves setting an effects-based standard as an overall goal for a statutory program — meaning a standard limiting pollution sufficiently to prevent undesirable effects (such as human illness or harm to an ecosystem). The statute then requires administrative agencies to use technology-based standards—standards based on the capabilities of pollution control technologies for specific pollution sources to take steps toward these broader goals. Understanding environmental law's key concepts prepares one to understand statutory schemes well and to better understand any provision's role and meaning in the statutory scheme. Each of the following chapters will explore a key environmental law concept in depth.

A. A CONCEPTUAL ROADMAP

This roadmap will address environmental standard setting. In particular, this part presents the key concepts underlying statutory criteria for regulatory standards—the criteria that guide agency decisions about how strictly to limit pollution. It then discusses the means of environmental protection, which one might think of as the methods through which agencies effectuate environmental standards. Finally, it discusses statutory allocation of authority to establish standards to state and federal government agencies. Along the way, we will provide summary overviews of entire statutory schemes (which we call "Trail Guides" to the statutes), so you can see how the law employs the concepts you are learning.

1. Criteria for Standard Setting

Congress enacted the environmental statutes in order to achieve specific purposes, which sometimes appear in the first sections of the statutes. Practitioners regularly refer to these goals as aids to interpreting the statutes, and those aids can influence judicial interpretations of specific provisions and administrative agency implementation decisions.

Congress usually delegates authority to EPA and its state counterparts to enact standards that help achieve these goals pursuant to statutory criteria guiding agency decisions about how much pollution reduction to demand. These criteria all serve a very general goal of advancing environmental protection. But they also embody more particularized policy decisions that in effect decide in a more precise way what goals the agency should pursue in particular rule-making proceedings to establish new standards. Some criteria suggest that particular standards should protect the public from all significant environmental harms. The goal of other standard-setting exercises might be more modest—to effectuate some sort of balance between environmental goals and other goals. We saw examples of this choice in common law decisions about when to issue injunctions.

We divide statutory criteria into three basic types of goals: effects-based, technology-based, and cost-benefit–based criteria. We briefly introduce each of these in turn.

An effects-based goal seeks to wholly avoid a set of environmental or health effects deemed undesirable. This sort of goal requires an agency to determine what level of pollution is safe when data about the precise effects of pollution is usually incomplete and uncertain—a very difficult task. This sort of goal commonly functions as a major goal for an entire statute. Thus, for example, the Clean Air Act aims to protect public health and the Clean Water Act aims to provide swimmable and fishable waters. 42 U.S.C. §§7401(b)(1), 7409(b); 33 U.S.C. §1251(2). But it can also guide specific standards for a particular type of industry. *See, e.g.,* Natural Resources Defense Council v. EPA, 529 F.3d 1077 (D.C. Cir. 2008) (discussing health-based standards for hazardous air pollutants).

Most standard-setting provisions in the major environmental statutes for particular industries or other pollution sources, however, reflect a technology-based criterion. They require agencies to set pollution standards reflecting what known (or in some cases, future) technology can achieve. This sort of goal turns standard setting into something of an engineering exercise, evaluating the pollution control potential of various technologies. These sorts of standards require agencies to evaluate the economic and technological feasibility of various pollution control techniques. Notice that this implies a very different technical focus than that emanating from effects-based standards.

Finally, courts have interpreted FIFRA, TSCA, and the Safe Drinking Water Act to require agencies to set some standards under those statutes through cost-benefit analysis (CBA). Even under statutes that do not contemplate CBA, CBA can play a role, because executive orders require that agencies only promulgate major rules where the costs justify the benefits "to the extent permitted by law." E.O. 12291, 46 Fed. Reg. 13193 (Feb. 17, 1981). CBA requires agencies to quantify the costs of pollution reductions, much as they would in evaluating the economic feasibility of a technology-based standard, and also to consider environmental and health effects, as they do when setting effects-based standards. It also demands that agencies convert health and environmental effects into dollar terms to the extent possible to facilitate a comparison of costs to benefits. This conversion is controversial, because it involves putting a dollar value on human life, illness, and ecological destruction. It also places a premium on quantification of effects.

CBA might be thought of as making economic efficiency a goal. The term economic efficiency in this context refers to what economists call allocative efficiency—the balancing of costs and benefits to society of taking a particular regulatory action.

Although we present these concepts in separate chapters for the sake of clarity, they can sometimes overlap and cause conflict in practice. The most obvious example involves cases where statutes require a technology-based approach, but the executive orders call for CBA. *See* American Textile Manufacturers Institute, Inc. v. Donovan, 452 U.S. 490, 509-20 (1981) (holding that a technology-based provision of the Occupational Health and Safety Act does not require CBA); Entergy Corp. v. Riverkeeper, Inc., 556 U.S. 208, 226 (2009) (holding that EPA may rely on CBA in establishing technology-based standards for water intake under the Clean Water Act). The question of what criteria law should embrace obviously implicates value choices.

2. The Means of Environmental Protection

Setting standards involves choices about means as well as ends: How should polluters achieve the reductions demanded in a particular standard? The literature usually talks about the choice between economic incentives and command and control regulation as a means of achieving regulatory standards. This book uses the term "traditional regulation" as a substitute for the term "command and control," which is pejorative and potentially misleading, and contrasts traditional regulation with economic incentives. This book also discusses other means of achieving environmental goals that do not neatly fit this typology.

Traditional regulation consists of performance standards, work practice standards, and, less commonly, bans. Performance standards establish a level of performance that polluters must meet, but leaves them with some flexibility in choosing how to meet the level. So, for example, a rule limiting greenhouse gas emissions from power plants might call for power plants to meet targets expressed in pounds of pollution per megawatt hour (a megawatt hour measures the amount of electricity produced). *See, e.g.*, Electric Utility Generating Units, Proposed Rule, 79 Fed. Reg. 1430, 1432 (Jan. 8, 2014). Coal-fired power plants could meet the proposed level of emissions either by switching to natural gas or by using carbon capture and storage technology, but the rule would allow utilities to use different techniques they invent, if they achieved the limits. Performance standards have traditionally been the most commonly employed means of implementing pollution control standards.

By contrast, agencies sometimes establish a work practice standard, which dictates use of a particular pollution control technique. If the proposed rule had, for example, commanded all new plants to use natural gas, it would have been a work practice standard. When, if ever, do you think agencies should use work practice standards, rather than performance standards?

Occasionally, the government bans a particular practice or chemical as a means of protecting the environment. A leading example involves the Montreal Protocol for Ozone Depleting Substances, which phased out many ozone-depleting chemicals, but other examples exist. All three of these techniques exemplify traditional regulation.

Since the 1980s, policy makers have increasingly relied on "economic incentive" measures as a means of reaching environmental goals. The classic economic incentive measure involves imposing a pollution tax, but in the United States, use of this measure is a rarity. We have, however, increasingly relied upon emissions trading as a means of meeting environmental goals. An emissions trading program involves establishing performance standards, but then making them tradable. In such a scheme, a polluter facing high control costs can avoid making reductions at its own facility, if the management purchases reductions reflecting additional non-required reductions at some other facility. These trades tend to maximize the use of the cheapest pollution reduction measures, thereby reducing the cost of achieving environmental goals. A successful trading program reduced sulfur dioxide emissions contributing to acid rain in the 1990s, and many countries have used the trading approach to address climate disruption, with mixed results.

3.   Allocation of Responsibility

Statutory schemes always include some sort of allocation of responsibility to set (and enforce) standards. The Clean Air Act, Clean Water Act, RCRA, and CERCLA all feature fairly complex allocations of governmental authority. These statutes all employ forms of "cooperative federalism," which distributes authority between state and local governments. You have already seen one example of this allocation in Chapter 3. You may have noted that the Clean Air Act mentioned in that chapter assigns the federal government (more precisely, the federal EPA) the task of establishing effects-based national ambient air quality standards to protect public health and the environment. These standards are "ambient" standards because they address the levels of overall air quality in the air around them. In order to achieve these ambient standards, however, some government authority must limit pollution outputs from particular sources. The Clean Air Act delegates much of the responsibility to set output standards, many of them technology-based, to the states. Conversely, you will learn, the Clean Water Act relies on states to set water quality standards, but requires the federal EPA to establish technology-based output standards for the major point sources. You will learn that the allocation of authority under these statutory schemes has some overlap and that each of the general allocation rules described above have important exceptions. (For example, the federal government sets output standards for new vehicles under the Clean Air Act, and the state governments have lead responsibility for output standards for nonpoint sources under the Clean Water Act.) The main point here is simple: Understanding the allocation of authority under a particular statute provides a key to understanding statutory schemes as a whole.

B.   CRITERIA FOR STANDARD SETTING

This subpart discusses the main criteria governing standard setting—the effects-based, technology-based, and cost-benefit–based criteria introduced above. As you learn about these criteria think about which make the most sense as a value choice. Also, think about what information and analysis the various criteria make relevant to agency decision making. The materials should help understand not just the legal provisions you will find in statutes, but also the challenges and dilemmas that agencies face under different criteria.

4

Effects-Based Standards

One potential answer to the question of what the goal of environmental law should be is that the basic goal of environmental statutes should be to control or prevent the adverse *effects* of pollution and other sources of environmental harm. This, you might think, seems incredibly obvious. What other purpose is there to environmental law if not to control or prevent adverse environmental effects? Establishing environmental standards on the basis of adverse effects, however, implies far more than is immediately apparent.

All environmental standards seek to reduce adverse effects in some way. Effects-based environmental standards, often referred to as "health-based" or "environment-based" standards, do so by expressly determining the level of environmental quality deemed acceptable as a goal. (This could be viewed from the opposite perspective as the residual level of environmental harm permitted.) In establishing effects-based standards, we ask what level of environmental quality is adequate, or necessary, to protect health or environmental resources. The difficult part is deciding what is "adequate." That question is answered in part by the language of particular statutes, and in part by the manner in which the statutes are interpreted and administered by agencies and courts.

In Section A, we introduce the basic idea of effects-based standards, the threshold for deciding when such standards are needed, and the degree to which a precautionary as opposed to a reactive approach is used in writing those standards. One kind of effects-based standard, known as an "ambient standard," dictates acceptable levels of environmental quality in the ambient environment, such as the air we breathe or the water we use in rivers for swimming or drinking. Key examples are the National Ambient Air Quality Standards promulgated by EPA under the Clean Air Act, and water quality standards generally developed by states under the Clean Water Act. Rather than focusing upon individual pollution sources, or even categories of sources, ambient standards govern aggregate impacts from all of the sources that contribute to a particular kind of pollution in a defined geographic region (an airshed or a stretch of river, for example). We explore those kinds of standards in Section B of this chapter. Alternatively, effects-based standards can control the health or environmental impacts of particular pollution sources or categories of sources (automobiles, for example). "Output standards" or "release standards" define how much pollution a particular type of source may release into the environment, rather than how dirty the environmental medium may become. While output or release standards from individual sources can also be based on other concepts, such as the best available control technology approach discussed in Chapter 5, in Section C of this chapter we describe output or release standards, the stringency of which is determined by reference to health and environmental effects.

A. DEFINING "EFFECTS"—CONCEPTS OF RISK AND PRECAUTION

The following case addresses EPA's authority under section 211(c) of the Clean Air Act either to control, or to prohibit altogether, motor vehicle fuels or fuel additives. Section 211 is a very long, complex provision, which Congress amended several times after this case was decided. To understand this case, you only need to read the portions of the statute included in the case excerpt. To put the case in context, you should understand that: (1) automobiles and other motor vehicles are one of the major sources of air pollution nationally; (2) the manner in which gasoline and other fuels are manufactured can contribute significantly to that pollution; and (3) the use of lead as a fuel additive was the principal gasoline component of concern when Congress first adopted this section of the law. Therefore, in addition to regulating tailpipe emissions from cars and trucks directly, Congress authorized EPA to regulate motor vehicle fuels that contribute to those emissions. In section 211, Congress authorized EPA to regulate fuel additives in two separate circumstances. In the provision not at issue in this case, EPA could prohibit or regulate fuels or fuel additives that would interfere with the new technologies designed to control tailpipe emissions (especially catalytic converters). Under the subsection at issue here, EPA could regulate fuels or fuel components that, at the time this case was decided, the Administrator of EPA found "will endanger the public health or welfare. . . ." In reading this case, focus on the threshold of harm, *i.e.*, what "effects" were necessary to justify EPA regulation under this provision, and with what degree of certainty.

≡ *Ethyl Corporation v. Environmental Protection Agency*
  541 F.2d 1 (D.C. Cir. 1976) (en banc)

J. SKELLY WRIGHT, CIRCUIT JUDGE.

[Environmental agencies] must deal with predictions and uncertainty, with developing evidence, with conflicting evidence, and, sometimes, with little or no evidence at all. Today we address the scope of the power delegated one such watchdog, the Environmental Protection Agency (EPA). We must determine the certainty required by the Clean Air Act before EPA may act to protect the health of our populace from the lead particulate emissions of automobiles.

Section 211(c)(1)(A) of the Clean Air Act authorizes the Administrator of EPA to regulate gasoline additives whose emission products "will endanger the public health or welfare. . . ." Acting pursuant to that power, the Administrator, after notice and comment, determined that the automotive emissions caused by leaded gasoline present "a significant risk of harm" to the public health. Accordingly, he promulgated regulations that reduce, in step-wise fashion, the lead content of leaded gasoline. We must decide whether the Administrator properly interpreted the meaning of Section 211(c)(1)(A) and the scope of his power thereunder, and, if so, whether the evidence adduced at the rule-making proceeding supports his final determination. Finding in favor of the Administrator on both grounds, and on all other grounds raised by petitioners, we affirm his determination.

I. The Facts, the Statute, the Proceedings, and the Regulations

Hard on the introduction of the first gasoline-powered automobiles came the discovery that lead "antiknock" compounds, when added to gasoline, dramatically increase the fuel's octane rating. Increased octane allows for higher compression engines, which operate with greater efficiency. Since 1923 antiknocks have been regularly added to gasoline, and a large industry has developed to supply those compounds. Today, approximately 90 percent of motor gasoline manufactured in the United States contains lead additives, even though most 1975 and 1976 model automobiles are equipped with catalytic converters, which require lead-free gasoline. From the beginning, however, scientists have questioned whether the addition of lead to gasoline, and its consequent diffusion into the atmosphere from the automobile emission, poses a danger to the public health. As use of automobiles, and emission of lead particulates, has accelerated in the last quarter century, this concern has mounted. The reasons for concern are obvious (and essentially undisputed by petitioners): (1) lead in high concentrations in the body is toxic; (2) lead can be absorbed into the body from the ambient air; and (3) lead particulate emissions from gasoline engines account for approximately 90 percent of the lead in our air. Despite these apparent reasons for concern, hard proof of any danger caused by lead automotive emissions has been hard to come by. Part of the reason for this lies in the multiple sources of human exposure to lead.

Lead is an ubiquitous element. It is found in the land, in the sea, in plants, in animals, and, ultimately, in humans. Traces of lead ranging from 10 to 40 micrograms per 100 grams of blood (10-40 µg/100 g) are found in everyone, including those living in environments with almost no atmospheric lead. Despite its universal presence, however, lead serves no known purpose in the human body, and at higher concentrations is toxic, causing anemia, severe intestinal cramps, paralysis of nerves, fatigue, and even death. Clinical symptoms of lead poisoning appear at blood lead levels of 80-100 µg or higher, and symptomatic lead poisoning may appear at levels of 50-60 µg, particularly in the presence of anemia.

Human body lead comes from three major sources. In most people, the largest source is the diet. EPA estimates daily dietary lead intake for adults to average 200-300 µg per day, with a range of 100-500 µg a day. Absorption of dietary lead into the bloodstream is estimated at about 10 percent, although in children absorption may be as high as 50 percent. Thus the average adult adds 20-30 µg of lead to his bloodstream daily from his diet alone. This daily intake, which may be highly variable depending on individual diets, is generally regarded as, for all practical purposes, uncontrollable.

A second major source of the body's lead burden, at least among urban children, is regarded as controllable, although effective control may be both difficult and expensive to achieve. Ingestion of lead paint by children with pica (the abnormal ingestion of non-food substances, a relatively common trait in pre-school children, particularly ages 1-3) is generally regarded as "the principal environmental source in cases of severe acute lead poisoning in young children." . . .

The last remaining major source of lead exposure for humans is the ambient air. This source is easily the most controllable, since approximately 90 percent of lead in the air comes from automobile emissions, and can be simply eliminated by removing lead from gasoline. While the extent to which such lead actually enters the body is vigorously contested by petitioners and lies at the heart of this appeal, all parties agree that, to some extent at least, airborne lead can be absorbed through the lungs as a person breathes lead-contaminated air and that it can be eaten by children with pica after larger lead particles fall to the ground and mix with dust. Once the lead is in the body, however, its source becomes irrelevant; all lead in the bloodstream, from whatever source, is essentially fungible. Thus so long as there are multiple sources of lead exposure it is virtually impossible to isolate one source and determine its particular effect on the body. The effect of any one source is meaningful only in cumulative terms.

The multiple sources of human exposure to lead explain in part why it has been difficult to pinpoint automobile lead emissions as a danger to public health. Obviously, any danger is caused only by the additive effect of lead emissions on the other, largely uncontrollable, sources of lead. For years the lead antiknock industry has refused to accept the developing evidence that lead emissions contribute significantly to the total human lead body burden. In the Clean Air Act Amendments of 1970, however, Congress finally set up a legal mechanism by which that evidence could be weighed in a more objective tribunal. It gave the newly-created EPA authority to control or prohibit the sale or manufacture of any fuel additive whose emission products "will endanger the public health or welfare. . . ." 42 U.S.C. §1857f–6c(c)(1)(A) (1970). It is beyond question that the fuel additive Congress had in mind was lead. . . .

On October 28, 1973 . . . this court ordered EPA to reach within 30 days a final decision on whether lead additives should be regulated for health reasons. . . . Under the final regulations, lead in all gasoline would be reduced over a five-year period to an average of 0.5 grams per gallon.

Petitioners, various manufacturers of lead additives and refiners of gasoline, appealed the promulgation of low-lead regulations to this court under Section 307 of the Clean Air Act. . . .

The regulations are challenged by petitioners on a variety of grounds, all of which will be addressed below. Their primary claims, and the ones on which the division majority based its reversal, are that the Administrator misinterpreted the statutory standard of "will endanger" and that his application of that standard is without support in the evidence and arbitrary and capricious.

II. The Statutory Requirements

Under Section 211(c)(1)(A) the Administrator may, on the basis of all the information available to him, promulgate regulations that control or prohibit the manufacture, introduction into commerce, offering for sale, or sale of any fuel or fuel additive for use in a motor vehicle or motor vehicle engine (A) if any emission products of such fuel or fuel additive will endanger the public health or welfare. . . . The Administrator cannot act under Section 211(c)(1)(A), however, until after "consideration of all relevant medical and scientific evidence available to him, including consideration of other technologically or economically feasible means of achieving emission standards under (Section 202)." Section 211(c)(2)(A). Section 202 of the Act allows the Administrator to set standards for emission of pollutants from automobiles (as opposed to standards for the composition of the gasoline that produces the emissions), and is thus the preferred although not the mandatory alternative under the statutory scheme, presumably because it minimizes Agency interference with manufacturer prerogatives.[14]

The Administrator is also required, before prohibiting a fuel or fuel additive under Section 211(c)(1)(A), to find, and publish the finding, that in his judgment any fuel or fuel additive likely to replace the prohibited one will not "endanger the public health or welfare to the same or greater degree. . . ." Section 211(c)(2)(C). It is significant that this is the only conclusion the Administrator is expressly required to "find" before regulating a fuel or fuel additive for health reasons.

A. The Threshold Determination

In making his threshold determination that lead particulate emissions from motor vehicles "will endanger the public health or welfare," the Administrator provided his interpretation of the statutory language by couching his conclusion in these words: such emissions "present a significant risk of harm to the health of urban populations, particularly to the health of city children." By way of further interpretation, he added that it was his view that the statutory language . . . does not require a determination that automobile emissions alone create the endangerment on which controls may be based. Rather, the Administrator believes that in providing this authority, the Congress was aware that the public's exposure to harmful substances results from a number of sources which may have varying degrees of susceptibility to control. It is petitioners' first claim of error that the Administrator has erroneously interpreted Section 211(c)(1)(A) by not sufficiently appreciating the rigor demanded by Congress in establishing the "will endanger" standard. Therefore, petitioners argue, the Administrator's action is "short of statutory right," in violation of Section 10(e)(2)(C) of the Administrative Procedure Act (APA).

Petitioners argue that the "will endanger" standard requires a high quantum of factual proof, proof of actual harm rather than of a "significant risk of harm."

---

14. When EPA acts under §211(c)(1)(A) it is essentially telling manufacturers how to make their fuels, a task Congress felt the Agency should enter upon only with trepidation. *See, e.g.,* 116 Cong. Rec. 32920 (1970) (remarks of Sen. Baker); *id.* at 19229 (remarks of Reps. Rogers & Waggoner). On the other hand, when the Agency acts under §202, it is only mandating an end product[—]regulated emissions. The method for achieving the required result is entirely in the hands of the manufacturers.

Since, according to petitioners, regulation under Section 211(c)(1)(A) must be premised upon factual proof of actual harm, the Administrator has, in their view, no power to assess risks or make policy judgments in deciding to regulate lead additives. Moreover, petitioners argue, regulation must be based on the danger presented by lead additives "in and of themselves," so it is improper to consider, as the Administrator did, the cumulative impact of lead additives on all other sources of human exposure to lead. We have considered these arguments with care and find them to be without merit. It is our view that the Administrator's interpretation of the standard is the correct one.

1. The Precautionary Nature of "Will Endanger"

Simply as a matter of plain meaning, we have difficulty crediting petitioners' reading of the "will endanger" standard. The meaning of "endanger" is not disputed. Case law and dictionary definition agree that endanger means something less than actual harm.[17] When one is endangered, harm is threatened; no actual injury need ever occur. Thus, for example, a town may be "endangered" by a threatening plague or hurricane and yet emerge from the danger completely unscathed. A statute allowing for regulation in the face of danger is, necessarily, a precautionary statute. Regulatory action may be taken before the threatened harm occurs; indeed, the very existence of such precautionary legislation would seem to demand that regulatory action precede, and, optimally, prevent, the perceived threat. As should be apparent, the "will endanger" language of Section 211(c)(1)(A) makes it such a precautionary statute.

The Administrator read it as such, interpreting "will endanger" to mean "presents a significant risk of harm." We agree with the Administrator's interpretation. . . .

In the context of this environmental legislation, we believe that Congress used the term "endangering" in a precautionary or preventive sense, and, therefore, evidence of potential harm as well as actual harm comes within the purview of that term. . . .

Perhaps because it realized that the above interpretation was the only possible reading of the statutory language, petitioner Ethyl addresses this interpretation and argues that even if actual harm is not required for action under Section 211(c)(1)(A), the occurrence of the threatened harm must be "probable" before regulation is justified. While the dictionary admittedly settles on "probable" as its measure of danger, we believe a more sophisticated case-by-case analysis is appropriate. Danger, the Administrator recognized, is not set by a fixed probability of harm, but rather is composed of reciprocal elements of risk and harm, or probability and severity. *Cf.* Carolina Environmental Study Group v. United States, 510 F.2d 796,

---

17. It is linguistically clear, of course, that one can be "endangered" without actually being harmed. Nonetheless, some risk of harm is necessary. State v. Fine, 324 Mo. 194, 23 S.W.2d 7, 9 (1929). Webster defines "endanger" as "to bring into danger or peril of *probable* harm or loss." Webster's Third New International Dictionary 748 (1961) (emphasis added).

799 (1975); Reserve Mining Co. v. EPA, *supra*, 514 F.2d at 519-520. That is to say, the public health may properly be found endangered both by a lesser risk of a greater harm and by a greater risk of a lesser harm.[32] Danger depends upon the relation between the risk and harm presented by each case, and cannot legitimately be pegged to "probable" harm, regardless of whether that harm be great or small. As the Eighth Circuit found in *Reserve Mining*, these concepts "necessarily must apply in a determination of whether any relief should be given in cases of this kind in which proof with certainty is impossible." 514 F.2d at 520. . . .

NOTES AND QUESTIONS ON *ETHYL CORPORATION*

1. *Uncertainty.* Identify all of the components of uncertainty that complicated EPA's decision and ultimately caused the industry to challenge EPA's finding of "endangerment." Then, explain how EPA and the court's interpretation of the statutory language justified the regulation of lead in motor vehicle fuels notwithstanding this uncertainty.

2. *Precautionary principle.* The Court refers to the "precautionary nature" of the statutory language. A similarly phrased "precautionary principle" has been adopted as one of the bedrock principles of international environmental law. *See* Rio Declaration on Environment and Development, U.N. Conference on Environment and Development, U.N. Doc. A/CONF.151/5/Rev.1, 31 I.L.M. 874 (1992). How does the CAA statutory approach compare with the common law standards studied in Chapter 2 under which lead hazards might otherwise be addressed?

3. Reserve Mining *and the Clean Water Act.* EPA's and the Court's precautionary interpretation of the "will endanger" standard was also supported in part by the Eighth Circuit's holding in Reserve Mining Co. v. EPA, 514 F.2d 492 (8th Cir. 1975) (en banc). *Reserve Mining* involved EPA's request, under the statutory predecessor to the current Clean Water Act, for an injunction against the continued discharge of mine tailings that contained asbestos fibers into waters of Lake Superior used as public water supply for the City of Duluth, Minnesota. As in *Ethyl Corp.*, considerable scientific uncertainty surrounded the issue of whether the fibers caused demonstrable harm to public health. While the Eighth Circuit held that the degree of scientific uncertainty should be considered in determining the nature and terms of the injunction, it ruled that uncertainty does not preclude such relief under the language of the statute in effect at the time: "In the context of this environmental legislation, we believe that Congress used the term 'endangering' in a precautionary or preventive sense, and, therefore, evidence of potential harm

---

32. This proposition must be confined to reasonable limits, however. In Carolina Environmental Study Group v. United States, 510 F.2d 796 (1975), a division of this court found the possibility of a Class 9 nuclear reactor disaster, a disaster of ultimate severity and horrible consequences, to be so low that the Atomic Energy Commission's minimal consideration of the effects of such a disaster in an environmental impact statement prepared for a new reactor was sufficient. Likewise, even the absolute certainty of de minimis harm might not justify government action. Under §211 the threatened harm must be sufficiently significant to justify health-based regulation of national impact. Ultimately, of course, whether a particular combination of slight risk and great harm, or great risk and slight harm, constitutes a danger must depend on the facts of each case.

as well as actual harm comes within the purview of that term." *Id.* at 528. The D.C. Circuit noted in *Ethyl Corp.* that similar provisions of the Clean Air Act and the Clean Water Act, adopted contemporaneously, often are interpreted similarly. 541 F.2d at 17. This is one of many examples. *See also* Natural Resources Defense Council v. Train, 510 F.2d 692, 701-02 (D.C. Cir. 1975).

4. *Statutory amendment.* The panel decision preceding the en banc opinion presented above struck down the lead rule as contrary to the "will endanger" standard. 5 ENVTL. L. REP. (ENVTL. L. INST.) 20,096 (D.C. Cir. 1975). Congress later amended the relevant statutory language to: "(A) if in the judgment of the Administrator any emission product of such fuel or fuel additive causes, or contributes to, air pollution which may reasonably be anticipated to endanger the public health or welfare." 42 U.S.C. §7545(c)(1)(A). In what ways does this amendment affect EPA's ability to regulate fuels or fuel additives under this provision?

5. *Health-based trigger.* The Court referred to the standards reviewed in *Ethyl Corp.* as "health-based regulations," apparently to distinguish them from standards adopted under the "sister provision" in section 211(b)(1)(B), which regulates fuel additives to protect the operation of emissions control devices in motor vehicles. This terminology, however, is potentially misleading. EPA evaluated and made findings regarding the potential health effects of leaded gasoline in making the threshold determination that it had authority to adopt the lead phase-out regulation. It did not, however, explicitly tie the "pooled average" levels of lead allowed under the agency's final regulation to particular health effects, and did not seek to justify the regulatory level on health-protection grounds. As you read the provisions addressed in the following section, and in the cases interpreting them, make sure you understand the conceptual differences between an effects-based trigger for regulation and an effects-based regulatory level. Also consider the practical implications of that difference in terms of what issues the agency can and cannot consider in writing the rules, and in what information interested parties should include in comments on proposed rules.

6. *Implied cost-consideration trigger.* In Michigan v. EPA, 135 S. Ct. 2699 (2015), the Supreme Court held that EPA acted unreasonably (and therefore was not entitled to *Chevron* deference to its statutory interpretation) when it refused to consider costs in deciding whether it was "appropriate and necessary" for the agency to regulate mercury emissions from power plants under the Clean Air Act. Does it make sense to require an agency to consider costs at the initial step of deciding whether to regulate even in the absence of explicit statutory language mandating the consideration of costs at that stage? Does the fact that costs vary with the stringency of the regulation ultimately adopted change your answer?

B. AMBIENT EFFECTS-BASED STANDARDS

Some effects-based standards define environmental quality goals in the ambient environment. "Ambient" means "surrounding on all sides." In this context, it means setting effects-based standards in the environment at large—such as the air we breathe and the water in rivers and lakes. The most notable examples of ambient environmental standards are the National Ambient Air Quality Standards (NAAQS) promulgated by EPA under the Clean Air Act, and water quality standards (WQS) generally issued by individual states under the Clean Water Act. These two main examples are similar in many respects, but different in others. Read the following two cases, one regarding NAAQS and the other WQS, for two main purposes. First, try to ascertain the major characteristics of ambient effects-based standards. What factors and information can the issuing agencies consider, and what is out of bounds? What is the scope of the standards, and what kinds of environmental harm can they address? Second, in what ways are ambient standards similar or different under the two statutes, and what are the practical implications of those differences?

1.   National Ambient Air Quality Standards

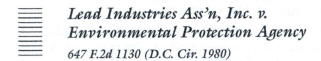

Lead Industries Ass'n, Inc. v. Environmental Protection Agency
647 F.2d 1130 (D.C. Cir. 1980)

J. SKELLY WRIGHT, CHIEF JUDGE.

   . . . In the present consolidated cases we are asked to review EPA regulations establishing national ambient air quality standards for lead. These air quality standards prescribe the maximum concentrations of lead that will be permitted in the air of our country. We must decide whether EPA's Administrator acted within the scope of his statutory authority in promulgating these regulations and, if so, whether the evidence adduced at the rulemaking proceeding supports his final determinations. . . .

II.   The Statutory Scheme

   The first step toward establishing national ambient air quality standards for a particular pollutant is its addition to a list, compiled by EPA's Administrator, of pollutants that cause or contribute to air pollution "which may reasonably be anticipated to endanger public health or welfare(.)" Section 108(a)(1), 42 U.S.C. §7408(a)(1). Within twelve months of the listing of a pollutant under Section 108(a) the Administrator must issue "air quality criteria" for the pollutant. Section 108 makes it clear that the term "air quality criteria" means something different from the conventional meaning of "criterion"; such "criteria" do not constitute "standards" or "guidelines," but rather refer to a document to be prepared by EPA which is to provide the scientific basis for promulgation of air quality standards for the pollutant. This criteria document must "accurately reflect the latest scientific knowledge useful in indicating the kind and extent of all identifiable effects on public health or welfare which may be expected from the presence of such pollutant in the ambient air, in varying quantities." Section 108(a)(2), 42 U.S.C. §7408(a)(2).

At the same time as he issues air quality criteria for a pollutant, the Administrator must also publish proposed national primary and secondary air quality standards for the pollutant. Section 109(a)(2), 42 U.S.C. §7409(a)(2). National primary ambient air quality standards are standards "the attainment and maintenance of which in the judgment of the Administrator, based on such criteria and allowing an adequate margin of safety, are requisite to protect the public health." Section 109(b)(1), 42 U.S.C. §7409(b)(1). Secondary air quality standards "specify a level of air quality the attainment and maintenance of which in the judgment of the Administrator, based on such criteria, is requisite to protect the public welfare from any known or anticipated adverse effects associated with the presence of such air pollutant in the ambient air." Section 109(b)(2), 42 U.S.C. §7409(b)(2). Effects on "the public welfare" include "effects on soils, water, crops, vegetation, man-made materials, animals, wildlife, weather, visibility, and climate, damage to and deterioration of property, and hazards to transportation, as well as effects on economic values and on personal comfort and well-being." Section 302(h), 42 U.S.C. §7602(h). The Administrator is required to submit the proposed air quality standards for public comment in a rulemaking proceeding, the procedure for which is prescribed by Section 307(d) of the Act, 42 U.S.C. §7607(d).

Within six months of publication of the proposed standards the Administrator must promulgate final primary and secondary ambient air quality standards for the pollutant. Section 307(d)(10), 42 U.S.C. §7607(d)(10). Once EPA has promulgated national ambient air quality standards, responsibility under the Act shifts from the federal government to the states. Within nine months of promulgation of the standards each state must prepare and submit to EPA for approval a state implementation plan. Section 110(a)(1), 42 U.S.C. §7410(a)(1). These state implementation plans must contain emission limitations and all other measures necessary to attain the primary standards "as expeditiously as practicable," but no later than three years after EPA approval of the plan, and to attain the secondary standards within a reasonable period of time. Section 110(a)(2)(A) & (B), 42 U.S.C. §7410(a)(2)(A) & (B). . . .

III.   The Lead Standards Rulemaking Proceedings

As required by statute, EPA's first step toward promulgating air quality standards for lead was to prepare a criteria document. The Lead Criteria Document was the culmination of a process of rigorous scientific and public review, and thus is a comprehensive and thoughtful analysis of the most current scientific information on the subject. . . .

[The opinion summarized the adverse health effects of lead identified in EPA's Criteria Document. Lead levels in blood are measured in micrograms of lead per deciliter of blood (μg Pb/dl). The ambient air quality standards are expressed as micrograms of lead per cubic meter of air (μg Pb/m³). EPA found that people with elevated blood lead (about 40 μg Pb/dl in children and about 50 μg Pb/dl in adults) experienced anemia due to destruction of red blood cells, and due to impaired synthesis of hemoglobin, the protein that carries oxygen in the blood. EPA also identified "subclinical effects" at lower blood levels. Subclinical effects include impairment of various physiological functions, but at levels that do not produce the kinds of symptoms discovered in routine medical examinations. EPA found one such effect, lead-related elevation of erythrocyte protoporphyrin (EP elevation), in children and women is at blood lead levels of 15-20 µg Pb/dl, and 25-30 µg Pb/dl in adult males.]

In addition to examining the health effects of lead exposure, the Criteria Document also discussed other issues critical to the task of setting air quality standards for lead. One of these issues is the relationship between air lead exposure and blood lead levels, a relationship commonly referred to as the air lead/blood lead ratio. . . . [A]ir lead/blood lead ratios fall within a range of 1:1 to 1:2 (µg Pb/m³ air):(µg Pb/dl blood) at the levels of lead exposure generally encountered by the population, i.e., blood lead levels increase by between 1 and 2 µg Pb/dl of blood for every 1 µg Pb/m³ of air. . . . The Criteria Document reported that the studies indicate that the ratio for children is at the upper end of this range or even slightly above it.

Finally, the Criteria Document also examined the distribution of blood lead levels throughout the population, concluding that there is a significant variability in individual blood lead responses to any particular level of air lead exposure. . . . [P]reschool-age children and pregnant women are particularly sensitive to lead exposure, the latter mainly because of the risk to the unborn child. . . .

D. *The Final Air Quality Standards for Lead*

The Administrator promulgated the final air quality standards on October 5, 1978, prescribing national primary and secondary ambient air quality standards for lead of 1.5 µg Pb/m³, averaged over a calendar quarter. . . . The Administrator . . . focused on two key questions: (1) What is the maximum safe individual blood lead level for children? and (2) what proportion of the target population should be kept below this blood lead level? Addressing the first issue required a review of the health effects of lead exposure discussed in the Criteria Document. The Administrator concluded that, although EP elevation beginning at blood lead levels of 15-20 µg Pb/dl is potentially adverse to the health of children, only when blood lead concentration reaches a level of 30 µg Pb/dl is this effect significant enough to be considered adverse to health. Accordingly, he selected 30 µg Pb/dl as the maximum safe individual blood lead level for children. The Administrator based this choice on three mutually supporting grounds. First, it is at this blood lead level that the first adverse health effect of lead exposure impairment of heme synthesis begins to occur in children. Second, a maximum safe individual blood lead level of 30 µg Pb/dl would allow an adequate margin of safety in protecting children against more serious effects of lead exposure anemia, symptoms of which begin to appear in children at blood lead levels of 40 µg Pb/dl, and central nervous system deficits which start to occur in children at blood lead levels of 50 µg Pb/ dl. Third, the Administrator reasoned that the maximum safe individual blood lead level should be no higher than the blood lead level used by the Centers for Disease Control in screening children for lead poisoning[:] 30 µg Pb/dl.

Having determined the maximum safe individual blood lead level for the target population, the Administrator next focused on the question of what percentage of children between the ages of 1 and 5 years the standard should attempt to keep below this blood lead level. According to the 1970 census, there are approximately 20 million children under the age of 5 years in the United States, 12 million of them in urban areas and 5 million in inner cities where lead exposure may be especially high. The Administrator concluded that in order to provide an adequate margin of safety, and to protect special high risk sub-groups, the standards should aim at keeping 99.5% of the target population below the maximum safe individual blood lead level of 30 µg Pb/dl. . . . The result was an ambient air quality standard of 1.5 µg Pb/m^3. . . .

V. Statutory Authority

The petitioners' first claim is that the Administrator exceeded his authority under the statute by promulgating a primary air quality standard for lead which is more stringent than is necessary to protect the public health because it is designed to protect the public against "sub-clinical" effects which are not harmful to health. According to petitioners, Congress only authorized the Administrator to set primary air quality standards that are aimed at protecting the public against health effects which are known to be clearly harmful. They argue that Congress so limited the Administrator's authority because it was concerned that excessively stringent air quality standards could cause massive economic dislocation.

In developing this argument St. Joe contends that EPA erred by refusing to consider the issues of economic and technological feasibility in setting the air quality standards for lead. St. Joe's claim that the Administrator should have considered these issues is based on the statutory provision directing him to allow an "adequate margin of safety" in setting primary air quality standards. In St. Joe's view, the Administrator must consider the economic impact of the proposed standard on industry and the technological feasibility of compliance by emission sources in determining the appropriate allowance for a margin of safety. St. Joe argues that the Administrator abused his discretion by refusing to consider these factors in determining the appropriate margin of safety for the lead standards, and maintains that the lead air quality standards will have a disastrous economic impact on industrial sources of lead emissions.

This argument is totally without merit. St. Joe is unable to point to anything in either the language of the Act or its legislative history that offers any support for its claim that Congress, by specifying that the Administrator is to allow an "adequate margin of safety" in setting primary air quality standards, thereby required the Administrator to consider economic or technological feasibility. To the contrary, the statute and its legislative history make clear that economic considerations play no part in the promulgation of ambient air quality standards under Section 109.

Where Congress intended the Administrator to be concerned about economic and technological feasibility, it expressly so provided. For example, Section 111 of the Act directs the Administrator to consider economic and technological feasibility in establishing standards of performance for new stationary sources of air pollution based on the best available control technology. In contrast, Section 109(b) speaks only of protecting the public health and welfare. Nothing in its language suggests that the Administrator is to consider economic or technological feasibility in setting ambient air quality standards.

The legislative history of the Act also shows the Administrator may not consider economic and technological feasibility in setting air quality standards; the absence of any provision requiring consideration of these factors was no accident; it was the result of a deliberate decision by Congress to subordinate such concerns to the achievement of health goals. . . .

For its part, LIA [Lead Industries Ass'n] maintains that its claim that the Administrator exceeded the bounds of his statutory authority does not depend on the supposition that he is required, or even permitted, to consider economic and technological feasibility in setting air quality standards. LIA contends that, instead, its argument is based on the fact that Congress itself was concerned about the question of the economic feasibility of compliance with air quality standards, a concern which was reflected in the statute it enacted. According to LIA, Congress was mindful of the possibility that air quality standards which are too stringent could cause severe economic dislocation. For this reason it only granted the Administrator authority to adopt air quality standards which are "designed to protect the public from adverse health effects that are clearly harmful(.)" LIA finds support for its interpretation of congressional intent in various portions of the legislative history of the Act. . . . LIA then argues that the Administrator based the lead air quality standards on protecting children from "subclinical" effects of lead exposure which have not been shown to be harmful to health, that in so doing the Administrator ignored the clear limitation that Congress imposed on his standard-setting powers, and that the Administrator's action will in fact cause the very result that Congress was so concerned about avoiding. . . .

Section 109(b) does not specify precisely what Congress had in mind when it directed the Administrator to prescribe air quality standards that are "requisite to protect the public health." The legislative history of the Act does, however, provide some guidance. The Senate Report explains that the goal of the air quality standards must be to ensure that the public is protected from "adverse health effects." And the report is particularly careful to note that especially sensitive persons such as asthmatics and emphysematics are included within the group that must be protected. It is on the interpretation of the phrase "adverse health effects" that the disagreement between LIA and EPA about the limits of the Administrator's statutory authority appears to be based. LIA argues that the legislative history of the Act indicates that Congress only intended to protect the public against effects which are known to be clearly harmful to health, maintaining that this limitation on the Administrator's statutory authority is necessary to ensure that the standards are not set at a level which is more stringent than Congress contemplated. The Administrator, on the other hand, agrees that primary air quality standards must be based on protecting the public from "adverse health effects," but argues that the meaning LIA assigns to that phrase is too limited. In particular, the Administrator contends that LIA's interpretation is inconsistent with the precautionary nature of the statute, and will frustrate Congress' intent in requiring promulgation of air quality standards.

The Administrator begins by pointing out that the Act's stated goal is "to protect and enhance the quality of the Nation's air resources so as to promote the public health and welfare and the productive capacity of its population(.)" Section 101(b)(1). This goal was reaffirmed in the 1977 Amendments. For example, the House Report accompanying the Amendments states that one of its purposes is "(t)o emphasize the preventive or precautionary nature of the act, i.e., to assure that regulatory action can effectively prevent harm before it occurs; to emphasize the predominant value of protection of public health(.)" The Administrator notes that protecting the public from harmful effects requires decisions about exactly what these harms are, a task Congress left to his judgment. He notes that the task of making these decisions is complicated by the absence of any clear thresholds above which there are adverse effects and below which there are none. Rather, as scientific knowledge expands and analytical techniques are improved, new information is uncovered which indicates that pollution levels that were once considered harmless are not in fact harmless. Congress, the Administrator argues, was conscious of this problem, and left these decisions to his judgment partly for this reason. In such situations the perspective that is brought to bear on the problem plays a crucial role in determining what decisions are made. Because it realized this, Congress, the Administrator maintains, directed him to err on the side of caution in making these judgments. First, Congress made it abundantly clear that considerations of economic or technological feasibility are to be subordinated to the goal of protecting the public health by prohibiting any consideration of such factors. Second, it specified that the air quality standards must also protect individuals who are particularly sensitive to the effects of pollution. Third, it required that the standards be set at a level at which there is "an absence of adverse effect" on these sensitive individuals. Finally, it specifically directed the Administrator to allow an adequate margin of safety in setting primary air quality standards in order to provide some protection against effects that research has not yet uncovered. The Administrator contends that these indicia of congressional intent, the precautionary nature of the statutory mandate to protect the public health, the broad discretion Congress gave him to decide what effects to protect against, and the uncertainty that must be part of any attempt to determine the health effects of air pollution, are all extremely difficult to reconcile with LIA's suggestion that he can only set standards which are designed to protect against effects which are known to be clearly harmful to health.

We agree that LIA's interpretation of the statute is at odds with Congress' directives to the Administrator. . . .

NOTES AND QUESTIONS ON *LEAD INDUSTRIES*

1. *Holding.* What is the textual basis for the court's holding that EPA may not consider economic factors in setting ambient air quality standards? What is the relationship between section 108 and section 109 of the statute, *i.e.*, how does section 108 govern the appropriate interpretation of section 109? Is this the only plausible way to interpret this statutory language?

2. *Rule-making practice and administrative record.* What kinds of issues and information may EPA consider in establishing (or revising) an ambient air quality standard? What other issues and information, in addition to purely economic factors, is EPA prohibited from considering? Is it realistic to assume that EPA can ignore economic factors entirely?

3. *Policy.* What are the policy implications of developing ambient air quality standards solely on the basis of health and environmental factors, and with no

consideration of economic impacts or attainability? The NAAQS drive much of the rest of the statute, but taken alone impose no requirements on sources of air pollution. In the opening section of the opinion describing the overall legal scheme, the court identifies the State Implementation Plans (SIPs), which must include emissions limitations and other requirements on particular pollution sources, as necessary to implement the NAAQS. In later chapters, you will learn the extent to which costs and other factors may be taken into account in adopting those source control requirements.

4. *Later cases.* The D.C. Circuit repeatedly reaffirmed in later decisions that EPA may not consider cost in setting the NAAQS. American Petroleum Institute v. Costle, 665 F.2d 1176 (D.C. Cir. 1981), 455 U.S. 1034 (1982); Natural Resources Defense Council v. Administrator, U.S. EPA, 902 F.2d 962 (D.C. Cir. 1990) (per curiam), *opinion dismissed in part and vacated in part*, 921 F.2d 326 (D.C. Cir. 1991); American Lung Ass'n v. EPA, 134 F.3d 388 (D.C. Cir. 1998). The cost issue later reached the U.S. Supreme Court in the context of allegations that EPA surreptitiously (that is, not on the record) considered economic factors in amending some of the NAAQS. Justice Scalia rejected the argument that EPA may consider cost in establishing the NAAQS:

> The text of §109(b), interpreted in its statutory and historical context and with appreciation for its importance to the CAA as a whole, unambiguously bars cost considerations from the NAAQS-setting process, and thus ends the matter for us as well as the EPA.

Whitman v. American Trucking Ass'ns, Inc., 531 U.S. 457, 471 (2001). With respect to the argument that EPA secretly did consider economic factors, the Court said:

> Respondents' speculation that the EPA is secretly considering the costs of attainment without telling anyone is irrelevant to our interpretive inquiry. If such an allegation could be proved, it would be grounds for vacating the NAAQS, because the Administrator had not followed the law.

Id. n.4.

5. *Complexity.* This case provides a sense of some of the scientific, policy, ethical, and other issues involved in identifying a numeric criterion that defines, for the ambient air in the entire nation, what level of air quality is "requisite to protect the public health" with an "adequate margin of safety." Here is a summary of the lead health effects considered in this rule making:

Threshold Lead Impacts (µg Pb/dl)

*	15-20	EP elevation children (subclinical)
*	5-20	EP elevation in adults
*	30	CDC screening level
*	40	Anemia in children
*	50	Anemia in adults
*	80-100	Neurological effects in children
*	100-200	Neurological effects in adults

While a full understanding of those complex issues requires a much more detailed inquiry, consider the following issues raised by the lead rule making:

a. Why can EPA consider "subclinical" health effects in establishing NAAQS? What kinds of "effects" count as "public health impairment"? Irritation to eyes and lungs, at levels that are annoying but present no long-term risk of illness or diminution of life span? What if you are a runner and shortness of breath from air pollution adds a minute to your time in your next recreational 5K race?

b. What portion of the population should be the focal point of health-effects–based regulations? Certain sub-populations may be more susceptible to adverse health effects than the general population, including children, the elderly, and individuals who already suffer respiratory, cardiovascular, or other illnesses. Are those sub-populations the appropriate focus for rules designed to protect the "public health" nationally?

c. Should the most susceptible individuals be protected in the standards, or a population average? For an interesting analysis of the degree to which genetic predisposition to illness should be considered in effects-based rules, see Jamie A. Grodsky, *Genetics and Environmental Law: Redefining Public Health*, 93 CAL. L. REV. 171 (2005).

d. What if certain racial or ethnic groups face disproportionate impacts from a particular air pollutant, either because of where they live or other risk factors? Should EPA modify a national air quality standard to protect such sub-populations?

6. *Primary and secondary standards.* What is the difference between "primary" and "secondary" ambient air quality standards? From a practical perspective, EPA has almost invariably determined that human health impacts occur at lower levels than other adverse air pollution effects to "human welfare." As a result, the primary and secondary standards are identical in most cases. *See* 40 C.F.R. §§50.6-50.12 (NAAQS for particulate matter, carbon monoxide, ozone, nitrogen dioxide, and lead). For sulfur oxides, EPA has established somewhat different primary and secondary standards. *Id.* §§50.4, 50.5.

2. Critiques of National Ambient Air Quality Standards

From the outset, the concept of uniform national ambient air quality standards has been controversial. Consider the following critique, published just a few years after the 1970 Clean Air Act was passed:

James E. Krier, The Irrational National Air Quality Standards: Macro- and Micro-Mistakes
22 UCLA L. Rev. 323 (1974-1975)

. . . I begin with the assertion that uniform national ambient standards represent a fundamental error in our approach to air pollution control. . . .

A.   Test for Resource Allocation

It is well worth keeping in mind that the air is a resource used by all of us (although in many different ways) and valued by all of us (although to varying degrees, depending upon our own individual frame of preferences and upon the uses to which we put the air environment). Government long ago concluded, quite justifiably, that a laissez-faire market could not adequately allocate this resource among all the differently valued divergent uses, and that government intervention was necessary. The task of government is then to allocate the resource *wisely.*

At a minimum, wise resource allocation entails recognition of two propositions: *First,* that while use of a resource in certain ways may result in costs, avoidance of those uses (or the costs of those uses) also results in costs; *second,* that society is using a resource most efficiently (though not necessarily most fairly, an important point to which we shall return) when the total of these costs is as low as possible. Applying these propositions to the air resource, we should first recognize that using the air as a pollutant receptacle entails costs such as discomfort, ill health, crop damage, materials damage, and scenic blight. But we should also realize that avoiding these pollution costs requires expenditures of time, effort, and money. At least from the standpoint of efficiency, therefore, our goal for air quality—for allocating the air to polluting and nonpolluting uses—appears to be quite clear: The air should be cleaned (or polluted, depending upon one's perspective) to the level that minimizes the sum of (a) the costs of pollution, plus (b) the costs of avoiding the costs of pollution.

B.   Applying the Test to Uniform Air Quality Standards

Let us turn to applying the resource allocation test to the federal requirement of uniform national air quality standards. Do such standards represent an efficient allocation of the air resource?

I think it clear that at one level of analysis the answer to this question must be no. To justify uniform standards as efficient in cost-minimization terms one would have to assume that the costs of a given level of pollution and a given level of control are the same across the nation. This assumption, however, is manifestly not valid. For example, aesthetic costs and materials losses will be functions of the varying resource endowments, degrees of development, and human attitudes that exist in different regions. Even health costs—which were of the greatest concern to Congress in passing the 1970 legislation—vary from place to place. Since such costs represent the aggregate of individual health effects, and since population varies significantly by region, so too will health costs. If one believes that per capita and not aggregate health costs should be the relevant factor, efficiency considerations would still suggest some variation in air quality levels. This is because the costs of pollution control will also vary, depending upon population, density and nature of development, and meteorological and topographical conditions in any particular region. In short, since the costs of pollution and the costs of control vary across the country, it is difficult to see how a uniform standard can begin to take the varying costs into account. The standard that minimizes total costs for a region in Iowa is hardly likely to do so for all the regions of California or New York or Colorado as well. To require adherence to the same stringent standard everywhere will in many areas result in the imposition of control costs which are much larger than the pollution costs avoided. . . .

NOTES AND QUESTIONS ON KRIER CRITIQUE

1. *Allocating clean air.* Do you agree with Professor Krier that air pollution control is a matter of "resource allocation," *i.e.*, that air is a resource to be allocated among "polluting and nonpolluting uses"? If not, what other perspective on the issue would you suggest, and how does that affect the issue of what approach we take to air quality control?

2. *Uniformity.* Professor Krier criticizes the national uniformity inherent in the NAAQS. Professor Krier prefers an approach in which decisions about ambient air quality standards are based on more localized assessments of the impacts of air pollution in different areas, and the costs of controlling it. Later in this chapter, you will see that Congress adopted such an approach in the Clean Water Act, in which states adopt their own water quality criteria, subject to EPA review and approval. Do not, however, confuse the issue of uniformity with the level of government at which more localized decisions might be made. In theory, EPA, rather than the states could adopt air quality standards that vary in stringency around the country. Indeed, Professor Krier states that he prefers federally promulgated non-uniform standards. *See* James E. Krier, *On the Topology of Uniform Environmental Standards in a Federal System—and Why It Matters*, 54 Md. L. Rev. 1226 (1995). What are the advantages and disadvantages of adopting non-uniform ambient standards at the national as opposed to the state (or local) levels?

3. *Costs versus benefits.* Krier's critique of the effects-based standards approach, however, also runs much deeper. He suggests that ambient air quality standards should reflect the health and other costs of air pollution relative to the costs of controlling that pollution, in order to reach an "optimal" level of pollution (or air quality) from an overall societal perspective. In essence, Krier argues that ambient air quality standards should be set based on a cost-benefit analysis, rather than the assumption that all adverse air pollution effects should be eliminated or at least minimized.

Clean Air Act Trail Guide, 42 U.S.C. §§7401-7671(q)

Introduction and Overview

Title I of the Clean Air Act establishes a program based on effects-based National Ambient Air Quality Standards (NAAQS), which establish air quality goals for the program as a whole with respect to ubiquitous criteria pollutants. States must then design state implementation plans (SIPs), which frequently employ technology-based standards, to meet these air quality goals. States, however, get some federal regulatory assistance. The federal government establishes technology-based new source performance standards for new and modified major sources of air pollution. 42 U.S.C. §7411. States, however, must supplement these standards with Lowest Achievable Emission Rate standards for pollutants in nonattainment areas (areas that have not achieved the NAAQS) and Best Available Technology standards in attainment areas (where the NAAQS have been achieved) for many new and existing sources. 42 U.S.C. §§7501(3), 7503(a)(2), 7475(a)(4), 7479. Under

Title II, EPA also regulates vehicle pollution. These programs should deliver some of the pollution reductions states would otherwise need to deliver in order to meet the NAAQs, but states must make up shortfalls with their own regulatory programs.

In addition, the statute requires the federal government to regulate major sources of hazardous air pollutants, 42 U.S.C. §7412, which are associated with serious health effects like cancer and birth defects, but are not as ubiquitous as criteria pollutants. Under the Act as amended in 1990, this program uses technology-based standards in phase one and effects-based standards to eliminate any residual risk in phase II. 42 U.S.C. §7411(d) authorizes state regulation of existing source pollutants not regulated as criteria pollutants or hazardous air pollutants subject to federal guidance based on the technology-based principles for new source performance standards.

The Act also regulates acid rain, principally through a federal emissions trading program (Title IV) for power plant sulfur dioxide emissions. Title VI regulates ozone-depleting chemicals, primarily through a federal phase-out.

In order to facilitate compliance, the Act requires owners of stationary sources (like factories) to obtain an operating permit showing how the source plans to comply with its obligations under the Act. Like most environmental statutes, the Clean Air Act provides for enforcement of pollution standards through citizen suits, federal enforcement, and state enforcement. It also provides for enforcement against the EPA through citizen suits (for failures to complete regulations) and through judicial review of completed agency actions.

Key Provisions of the Clean Air Act

Declaration of Purpose, 42 U.S.C. §7401, including protecting and enhancing air quality so as to promote public health and welfare.

Title I: Stationary Sources

Listing and Air Quality "Criteria," 42 U.S.C. §7408: Requires listing of pollutants that may endanger public health or welfare stemming from multiple sources and promulgation of "air quality criteria"—descriptions of the science relevant to understanding the pollutants' effects—for these listed pollutants.

National Ambient Air Quality Standards, 42 U.S.C. §7409: Requires National Ambient Air Quality Standards (NAAQS) for criteria pollutants (listed under 42 U.S.C. §7408) adequate to protect public health and welfare.

State Implementation Plans, 42 U.S.C. §§7410, 7501, 7502-7515: Detailed requirements for state implementation plans imposing emission limits and other measures to reduce emissions so that the national ambient air quality standards (42 U.S.C. §7409) are met. Many of these standards are technology-based standards based on available pollution control technology.

New Source Performance Standards, 42 U.S.C. §7411: Requires federal standards reflecting emission levels achievable through the best system of emission reductions (considering cost) for new stationary sources of air pollution and some existing sources of air pollution. Requires similar state standards under EPA guidance for existing sources of air pollutants not subject to regulation as either criteria pollutants or hazardous air pollutants.

Hazardous Air Pollution, 42 U.S.C. §7412: Requires regulation of sources of hazardous air pollutants in two phases. First, EPA must promulgate standards reflecting the maximum achievable emission reductions (MACT), 42 U.S.C. §7412(d). Second, EPA must promulgate additional stricter standards if necessary to provide an ample margin of safety to protect public health.

Prevention of Significant Deterioration, 42 U.S.C. §§7470-7492: Requires regulation of new sources as needed to prevent significant deterioration of air quality in areas that have attained the NAAQS and as needed to protect visibility in areas where visibility is important, such as national parks. These requirements include use of Best Available Control Technology for many new and existing sources.

Title II: Emissions from Mobile Sources (*e.g.*, cars)

Emissions Standards for New Motor Vehicles, 42 U.S.C. §7521: Requires regulation of pollutants from new motor vehicles that may endanger public health or welfare. Establishes numerical standards for certain pollutants from motor vehicles. Regulations under this section must take effect after a period of time sufficient to permit development of the appropriate technology. These standards are sometimes considered technology-forcing.

Regulation of Fuels, 42 U.S.C. §7545: Authorizes regulation or banning of fuels or fuel additives that may endanger public health or welfare or will significantly impair pollution control equipment. This section has a host of more specific requirements, including a schedule for increasing the amount of renewable fuel sold in the United States. *See* 42 U.S.C. §7545(o).

Clean Fuel Vehicle Programs, 42 U.S.C. §7581-7590: Requires states to demand that fleets of vehicles (*e.g.*, garbage trucks, school buses) use clean fuels in seriously polluted areas. These state clean fuel fleet programs form part of the SIPs required in Title One.

Title III: Administrative Provisions

Citizen Suit Provision, 42 U.S.C. §7604: Authorizes citizens to sue in order to enforce the Act's standards against polluters or to correct certain administrative failures to take actions.

Judicial Review, 42 U.S.C. §7606: Describes rule-making procedures and authorizes judicial review of completed agency actions.

Title IV: Acid Rain, 42 U.S.C. §§7651-7651o: Creates an emissions trading program for sulfur dioxide emissions and requires reductions in nitrogen oxide emissions in order to address acid rain.

Title V: Permits, 42 U.S.C. §§7661-7661f: Requires major industrial sources to obtain permits and enhance emissions monitoring.

Title VI: Stratospheric Ozone Protection, 42 U.S.C. §§7671-7671q: Requires a phase-out of chemicals depleting the stratospheric ozone layer.

Practice Under the Clean Air Act

An understanding of this structure makes it possible to figure out how the Act applies in practice. The analysis below leaves out numerous details that experts in this area must master, but shows some of the basics of how one might proceed.

The Act draws a fundamental distinction between mobile sources (vehicles) and stationary sources (*e.g.*, factories). If the activity regulated involves emissions from a vehicle, one looks at specific statutory provisions and regulations under Title II to identify relevant requirements, most of which will be technology-based regulations.

For major stationary sources, one begins by identifying the type of pollutant emitted and the nature of the facility. Title III applies to hazardous air pollutants, Title IV to sulfur dioxide and nitrogen oxides from power plants, Title VI to ozone-depleting substances, and Title I to criteria pollutants (listed under 42 U.S.C. §7408) and their precursors (the pollutants that react with each other to form a criteria pollutant).

With respect to criteria pollutants and their precursors, most of the regulatory requirements vary regionally. For each pollutant one must ask whether the region in which the facility operates has attained the health-based NAAQS or not. Generally, state and local regulations (mostly technology-based) apply to existing sources in nonattainment areas, but in attainment areas existing sources may not be subject to local and state requirements. (Notice that a polluter may be in an attainment area with respect to some pollutants and in a nonattainment area with respect to others.)

Modifications of existing facilities and construction of new facilities emitting criteria air pollutants (and some other pollutants, including carbon dioxide) implicate Title I's new source review provisions. In nonattainment areas the relevant requirements include federal new source performance standards. In attainment areas, the requirements stem from the Act's program for prevention of significant deterioration. Generally, the technology-based standards for new sources will be stricter than the technology-based standards for existing sources.

Operators of stationary sources must collect any requirements that they are subject to and explain how they plan to comply in an operating permit application to the local or state authorities. The state or local government reviews these operating permits and usually have the primary responsibility for enforcing compliance with their terms.

3. Water Quality Standards

In some major respects, ambient air and water quality standards share common characteristics. In some ways they are quite different. While EPA establishes uniform ambient air quality standards for the entire nation, Congress directed each state to adopt its own water quality standards specific to individual bodies of water or categories of waters, subject to EPA review and approval. Therefore, developing water quality standards involves a two-step process. States first designate the particular uses for which each kind of water body is to be protected (such as drinking water, cold water fish, or swimming). Second, they adopt standards deemed adequate to protect those uses. While air quality standards have focused primarily on human health impacts, water quality standards address a wide range of factors that impair the "physical, chemical, and biological integrity of the nation's waters," the overriding objective of the CWA. Therefore, while water quality standards may focus on human health issues related to fishing, swimming, or drinking water, they also address toxicity and other adverse impacts to fish and aquatic life. Protecting so many different kinds of uses requires states to adopt different kinds of water quality standards. These variations can pose different kinds of issues and challenges for the water quality standards process than for the NAAQS process, as illustrated in the following case:

Mississippi Commission on Natural Resources v. Costle
625 F.2d 1269 (5th Cir. 1980)

FAY, CIRCUIT JUDGE.

The Mississippi Commission on Natural Resources (Commission) challenges the authority of the United States Environmental Protection Agency (EPA) to promulgate a water quality standard on dissolved oxygen for Mississippi. . . .

I.   Statutory Framework

Prior to 1972, the Federal Water Pollution Control Act (FWPCA) relied primarily upon state-promulgated water quality standards as the means for reaching its goal of enhancing the quality of the nation's waters. A water quality standard has two components. The first is the use for the water in an area. Possible uses are for industry, agriculture, propagation and protection of fish and wildlife, recreation, and public water supply. The second component is the water quality criteria necessary to meet the designated use. For most pollutants, criteria are expressed as specific numerical concentration limits. For example, a state might set the water quality standard for a certain creek by designating it as a fishing area and requiring that the chloride concentration be no greater than 250 milligrams per liter of water.

In 1965, Congress considered whether the states or a federal administrator should establish water quality standards. Concerned that federal promulgation would discourage state plans for water quality and "would place in the hands of a single Federal official the power to establish zoning measures to control the use of land within watershed areas" throughout the nation, Congress gave the states primary authority to set water quality standards. The state standards and plans were submitted to the federal administrator, who determined whether they were consistent with the Act's requirements. If the state did not adopt complying standards, the administrator promulgated water quality uses and criteria.

As the Act was passed, states promulgate water quality standards, which are submitted to EPA for approval. EPA can promulgate standards if the state does not set standards consistent with the Act or whenever EPA determines that another "standard is necessary to meet the requirements of (the Act)." State standards are reviewed every three years. 33 U.S.C. §1313 (1976). NPDES permits must contain not only any [technology-based] effluent limitations set by EPA and the states, but also any more stringent limits necessary to reach the water quality standards. *Id*. §1311(b). In addition, EPA must develop and publish "criteria for water quality accurately reflecting the latest scientific knowledge." *Id*. §1314.

II.　Facts

The dispute in this case arises from EPA's refusal to approve the Mississippi water quality standard for dissolved oxygen (DO) and EPA's subsequent promulgation of a DO standard. Dissolved oxygen is necessary for the protection and propagation of fish and aquatic life, and is generally measured in milligrams per liter (mg/l).

VI.　Disapproval of Mississippi's Standard

A.　*Scope of Authority*

The Commission contends that EPA exceeded its statutory authority by tipping the balance of federal and state power created by Congress in the FWPCA. The Commission argues that EPA may substitute its judgment only if a state fails to act or acts irresponsibly. Furthermore, the Commission asserts that EPA misconstrues its authority as allowing disapprovals of standards that do not meet the requirements of EPA policy instead of those not meeting the requirements of the Act.

Congress did place primary authority for establishing water quality standards with the states. Furthermore,

> it is the policy of the Congress to recognize, preserve, and protect the primary responsibilities and rights of States to prevent, reduce, and eliminate pollution, to plan the development and use (including restoration, preservation, and enhancement) of land and water resources, and to consult with the Administrator in the exercise of his authority under this chapter.

33 U.S.C. §1251(b) (1976). As noted above, the legislative history reflects congressional concern that the Act not place in the hands of a federal administrator absolute power over zoning watershed areas. The varied topographies and climates in the country call for varied water quality solutions.

Despite this primary allocation of power, the states are not given unreviewable discretion to set water quality standards. All water quality standards must be submitted to the federal Administrator. 33 U.S.C. §1313(c)(2) (1976). The state must review its standards at least once every three years and make the results of the review available to the Administrator. *Id*. §1313(c)(1). EPA is given the final voice on the standard's adequacy:

> If the Administrator determines that any such revised or new standard is not consistent with the applicable requirements of this chapter, he shall not later than the ninetieth day after the date of submission of such standard notify the State and specify the changes to meet such requirements. If such changes are not adopted by the State within ninety days after the date of notification, the Administrator shall promulgate such standard pursuant to paragraph (4) of this subsection.

Id. §1313(c)(3). EPA's role also is more dominant when water quality criteria are in question. Although the designation of uses and the setting of criteria are interrelating chores, the specification of a waterway as one for fishing, swimming, or public water supply is closely tied to the zoning power Congress wanted left with the states. The criteria set for a specific use are more amenable to uniformity. Congress recognized this distinction by placing with EPA the duty to develop and publish water quality criteria reflecting the latest scientific knowledge shortly after the amendment's passage and periodically thereafter. *Id.* §1314(a)(1). EPA correctly points out that by leaving intact the Mississippi use designations it has acted in the manner least intrusive of state prerogatives. Nothing indicates a congressional intent to restrict EPA's review of state standards to the issue of whether the state acted arbitrarily or capriciously. The FWPCA requires EPA to determine whether the standard is "consistent with" the Act's requirements. The Commission argues that the Administrator has improperly construed his power as authorizing disapproval of state standards that do not meet EPA policy as embodied in the Red Book.

The statute enumerates the following requirements for water quality standards:

> Such standards shall be such as to protect the public health or welfare, enhance the quality of water and serve the purposes of this chapter. Such standards shall be established taking into consideration their use and value for public water supplies, propagation of fish and wildlife, recreational purposes, and agricultural, industrial, and other purposes, and also taking into consideration their use and value for navigation.

33 U.S.C. §1313(c)(2) (1976). One purpose of the Act is

> the national goal that wherever attainable, an interim goal of water quality which provides for the protection and propagation of fish, shellfish, and wildlife and provides for recreation in and on the water be achieved by July 1, 1983.

Id. §1251(a)(2). The EPA administrator did not improperly construe his authority by interpreting the FWPCA as allowing him to translate these broad statutory guidelines and goals into specifics that could be used to evaluate a state's standard. One "requirement of the Act" is that EPA formulate these policies for water quality criteria. *Id.* §1314(a)(1). It was not unreasonable for the EPA Administrator to interpret the Act as allowing him to require states to justify standards not in conformance with the criteria policy.

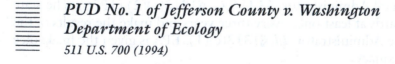

PUD No. 1 of Jefferson County v. Washington Department of Ecology
511 U.S. 700 (1994)

JUSTICE O'CONNOR delivered the opinion of the Court.

Petitioners, a city and a local utility district, want to build a hydroelectric project on the Dosewallips River in Washington State. We must decide whether respondent state environmental agency (hereinafter respondent) properly conditioned a permit for the project on the maintenance of specific minimum stream flows to protect salmon and steelhead runs.

I

This case involves the complex statutory and regulatory scheme that governs our Nation's waters, a scheme that implicates both federal and state administrative responsibilities. The Federal Water Pollution Control Act, commonly known as the Clean Water Act, 86 Stat. 816, as amended, 33 U.S.C. §1251 et seq., is a comprehensive water quality statute designed to "restore and maintain the chemical, physical, and biological integrity of the Nation's waters." §1251(a). The Act also seeks to attain "water quality which provides for the protection and propagation of fish, shellfish, and wildlife." §1251(a)(2).

To achieve these ambitious goals, the Clean Water Act establishes distinct roles for the Federal and State Governments. Under the Act, the Administrator of the Environmental Protection Agency (EPA) is required, among other things, to establish and enforce technology-based limitations on individual discharges into the country's navigable waters from point sources. *See* §§1311, 1314. Section 303 of the Act also requires each State, subject to federal approval, to institute comprehensive water quality standards establishing water quality goals for all intrastate waters. §§1311(b)(1)(C), 1313. These state water quality standards provide "a supplementary basis . . . so that numerous point sources, despite individual compliance with effluent limitations, may be further regulated to prevent water quality from falling below acceptable levels."

A state water quality standard "shall consist of the designated uses of the navigable waters involved and the water quality criteria for such waters based upon such uses." 33 U.S.C. §1313(c)(2)(A). In setting standards, the State must comply with the following broad requirements:

> Such standards shall be such as to protect the public health or welfare, enhance the quality of water and serve the purposes of this chapter. Such standards shall be established taking into consideration their use and value for public water supplies, propagation of fish and wildlife, recreational [and other purposes.]

Ibid. See also §1251(a)(2).

A 1987 amendment to the Clean Water Act makes clear that §303 also contains an "antidegradation policy"—that is, a policy requiring that state standards be sufficient to maintain existing beneficial uses of navigable waters, preventing their further degradation. Specifically, the Act permits the revision of certain effluent limitations or water quality standards "only if such revision is subject to and consistent with the antidegradation policy established under this section." §1313(d)(4)(B). Accordingly, EPA's regulations implementing the Act require that state water quality standards include "a statewide antidegradation policy" to ensure that "[e]xisting instream water uses and the level of water quality necessary to protect the existing uses shall be maintained and protected." 40 CFR §131.12 (1993). At a minimum, state water quality standards must satisfy these conditions. The Act also allows States to impose more stringent water quality controls. *See* 33 U.S.C. §§1311(b)(1)(C), 1370. *See also* 40 CFR §131.4(a) (1993) ("As recognized by section 510 of the Clean Water Act [33 U.S.C. §1370], States may develop water quality standards more stringent than required by this regulation").

The State of Washington has adopted comprehensive water quality standards intended to regulate all of the State's navigable waters. The State created an inventory of all the State's waters, and divided the waters into five classes. Each individual fresh surface water of the State is placed into one of these classes. The Dosewallips River is classified AA, extraordinary. The water quality standard for Class AA waters . . . identifies the designated uses of Class AA waters as well as the criteria applicable to such waters.

In addition to these specific standards applicable to Class AA waters, the State has adopted a statewide antidegradation policy. That policy provides:

> "(a) Existing beneficial uses shall be maintained and protected and no further degradation which would interfere with or become injurious to existing beneficial uses will be allowed.
>
> "(b) No degradation will be allowed of waters lying in national parks, national recreation areas, national wildlife refuges, national scenic rivers, and other areas of national ecological importance . . . .
>
> "(f) In no case, will any degradation of water quality be allowed if this degradation interferes with or becomes injurious to existing water uses and causes long-term and irreparable harm to the environment."

As required by the Act, EPA reviewed and approved the State's water quality standards. Upon approval by EPA, the state standard became "the water quality standard for the applicable waters of that State." 33 U.S.C. §1313(c)(3). . . .

III

The principal dispute in this case concerns whether the minimum stream flow requirement that the State imposed on the Elkhorn Project is a permissible condition . . . under the Clean Water Act. [The Court first determined the breadth of the State's authority to condition federal licenses and permits under section 401 of the CWA, one of the provisions that authorizes states to implement and enforce WQS. In the following section of the opinion, the Court decided whether states can establish minimum stream flows as part of their WQS:]

B

Having concluded that, pursuant to §401, States may condition certification upon any limitations necessary to ensure compliance with state water quality standards or any other "appropriate requirement of State law," we consider whether the minimum flow condition is such a limitation. Under §303, state water quality standards must "consist of the designated uses of the navigable waters involved and the water quality criteria for such waters based upon such uses." In imposing the minimum stream flow requirement, the State determined that construction and operation of the project as planned would be inconsistent with one of the designated uses of Class AA water, namely "[s]almonid [and other fish] migration, rearing, spawning, and harvesting." The designated use of the river as a fish habitat directly reflects the Clean Water Act's goal of maintaining the "chemical, physical, and biological integrity of the Nation's waters." 33 U.S.C. §1251(a). Indeed, the Act defines pollution as "the man-made or man induced alteration of the chemical, physical, biological, and radiological integrity of water." §1362(19). Moreover, the Act expressly requires that, in adopting water quality standards, the State must take into consideration the use of waters for "propagation of fish and wildlife." §1313(c)(2)(A).

Petitioners assert, however, that §303 requires the State to protect designated uses solely through implementation of specific "criteria." According to petitioners, the State may not require them to operate their dam in a manner consistent with a designated "use"; instead, say petitioners, under §303 the State may only require that the project comply with specific numerical "criteria."

We disagree with petitioners' interpretation of the language of §303(c)(2)(A). Under the statute, a water quality standard must "consist of the designated uses of the navigable waters involved *and* the water quality criteria for such waters based upon such uses." 33 U.S.C. §1313(c)(2)(A) (emphasis added). The text makes it plain that water quality standards contain two components. We think the language of §303 is most naturally read to require that a project be consistent with both components, namely, the designated use and the water quality criteria. Accordingly, under the literal terms of the statute, a project that does not comply with a designated use of the water does not comply with the applicable water quality standards. . . .

EPA has not interpreted §303 to require the States to protect designated uses exclusively through enforcement of numerical criteria. In its regulations governing state water quality standards, EPA defines criteria as "*elements* of State water quality standards, expressed as constituent concentrations, levels, or narrative statements, representing a quality of water that supports a particular use." 40 CFR §131.3(b) (1993) (emphasis added). The regulations further provide that "[w]hen criteria are met, water quality will *generally* protect the designated use." *Ibid.* (emphasis added). Thus, the EPA regulations implicitly recognize that in some circumstances, criteria alone are insufficient to protect a designated use.

Petitioners also appear to argue that use requirements are too open ended, and that the Act only contemplates enforcement of the more specific and objective "criteria." But this argument is belied by the open-ended nature of the criteria themselves. As the Solicitor General points out, even "criteria" are often expressed in broad, narrative terms, such as "'there shall be no discharge of toxic pollutants in toxic amounts.'" *See* American Paper Institute, Inc. v. EPA, 996 F.2d 346, 349 (CADC 1993). In fact, under the Clean Water Act, only one class of criteria, those governing "toxic pollutants listed pursuant to section 1317(a)(1)," need be rendered in numerical form. *See* 33 U.S.C. §1313(c)(2)(B); 40 CFR §131.11(b)(2) (1993).

Washington's Class AA water quality standards are typical in that they contain several open-ended criteria which, like the use designation of the river as a fishery, must be translated into specific limitations for individual projects. For example, the standards state that "[t]oxic, radioactive, or deleterious material concentrations shall be less than those which may affect public health, the natural aquatic environment, or the desirability of the water for any use." Similarly, the state standards specify that "[a]esthetic values shall not be impaired by the presence of materials or their effects, excluding those of natural origin, which offend the senses of sight, smell, touch, or taste." We think petitioners' attempt to distinguish between uses and criteria loses much of its force in light of the fact that the Act permits enforcement of broad, narrative criteria based on, for example, "aesthetics."

Petitioners further argue that enforcement of water quality standards through use designations renders the water quality criteria component of the standards irrelevant. We see no anomaly, however, in the State's reliance on both use designations and criteria to protect water quality. The specific numerical limitations embodied in the criteria are a convenient enforcement mechanism for identifying minimum water conditions which will generally achieve the requisite water quality. And, in most circumstances, satisfying the criteria will, as EPA recognizes, be sufficient to maintain the designated use. Water quality standards, however, apply to an entire class of water, a class which contains numerous individual water bodies. For example, in the State of Washington, the Class AA water quality standard applies to 81 specified fresh surface waters, as well as to all "surface waters lying within the mountainous regions of the state assigned to national parks, national forests, and/or wilderness areas," all "lakes and their feeder streams within the state," and all "unclassified surface waters that are tributaries to Class AA waters." While enforcement of criteria will in general protect the uses of these diverse waters, a complementary requirement that activities also comport with designated uses enables the States to ensure that each activity—even if not foreseen by the criteria—will be consistent with the specific uses and attributes of a particular body of water.

Under petitioners' interpretation of the statute, however, if a particular criterion, such as turbidity, were missing from the list contained in an individual state water quality standard, or even if an existing turbidity criterion were insufficient to protect a particular species of fish in a particular river, the State would nonetheless be forced to allow activities inconsistent with the existing or designated uses. We think petitioners' reading leads to an unreasonable interpretation of the Act. The criteria components of state water quality standards attempt to identify, for all the water bodies in a given class, water quality requirements generally sufficient to protect designated uses. These criteria, however, cannot reasonably be expected to anticipate all the water quality issues arising from every activity that can affect the State's hundreds of individual water bodies. Requiring the States to enforce only the criteria component of their water quality standards would in essence require the States to study to a level of great specificity each individual surface water to ensure that the criteria applicable to that water are sufficiently detailed and individualized to fully protect the water's designated uses. Given that there is no textual support for imposing this requirement, we are loath to attribute to Congress an intent to impose this heavy regulatory burden on the States.

The State also justified its minimum stream flow as necessary to implement the "antidegradation policy" of §303. When the Clean Water Act was enacted in 1972, the water quality standards of all 50 States had antidegradation provisions. These provisions were required by federal law. By providing in 1972 that existing state water quality standards would remain in force until revised, the Clean Water Act ensured that the States would continue their antidegradation programs. EPA has consistently required that revised state standards incorporate an antidegradation policy. And, in 1987, Congress explicitly recognized the existence of an "antidegradation policy established under [§303]."

EPA has promulgated regulations implementing §303's antidegradation policy, a phrase that is not defined elsewhere in the Act. These regulations require States to "develop and adopt a statewide antidegradation policy and identify the methods for implementing such policy." 40 CFR §131.12 (1993). These "implementation methods shall, at a minimum, be consistent with the . . . [e]xisting instream water uses and the level of water quality necessary to protect the existing uses shall be maintained and protected." *Ibid*. EPA has explained that under its antidegradation regulation, "no activity is allowable . . . which could partially or completely eliminate any existing use." Thus, States must implement their antidegradation policy in a manner "consistent" with existing uses of the stream. The State of Washington's antidegradation policy in turn provides that "[e]xisting beneficial uses shall be maintained and protected and no further degradation which would interfere with or become injurious to existing beneficial uses will be allowed." The State concluded that the reduced stream flows would have just the effect prohibited by this policy. The Solicitor General, representing EPA, asserts, and we agree, that the State's minimum stream flow condition is a proper application of the state and federal antidegradation regulations, as it ensures that an "existing instream water us[e]" will be "maintained and protected."

Petitioners also assert more generally that the Clean Water Act is only concerned with water "quality," and does not allow the regulation of water "quantity." This is an artificial distinction. In many cases, water quantity is closely related to water quality; a sufficient lowering of the water quantity in a body of water could destroy all of its designated uses, be it for drinking water, recreation, navigation or, as here, as a fishery. In any event, there is recognition in the Clean Water Act itself that reduced stream flow, i.e., diminishment of water quantity, can constitute water pollution. First, the Act's definition of pollution as "the man-made or man induced alteration of the chemical, physical, biological, and radiological integrity of water" encompasses the effects of reduced water quantity. 33 U.S.C. §1362(19). This broad conception of pollution—one which expressly evinces Congress' concern with the physical and biological integrity of water—refutes petitioners' assertion that the Act draws a sharp distinction between the regulation of water "quantity" and water "quality." . . .

NOTES AND QUESTIONS ON *JEFFERSON COUNTY* AND *MISSISSIPPI COMMISSION*

1. *Designated uses and water quality criteria.* Ambient air quality standards consist of one component, the standards themselves. Water quality standards consist of two major components: designated uses and water quality criteria to protect those uses. What explains this difference? Is the dissolved oxygen standard at issue in *Mississippi Commission* an example of a water quality criteria or a designated use? Suppose that Mississippi decides to remove fishing as a designated use of the Mississippi River and EPA disallows it. Should a reviewing court uphold this decision?

2. *Enforceability.* What did the Supreme Court say in *Jefferson County* about the enforceable nature of both components of the standards (designated uses and

criteria), and why is that important? How does it further distinguish ambient water quality standards from ambient air quality standards?

3. *Scope.* EPA has adopted ambient air quality standards for only six pollutants. By contrast, it has issued water quality criteria guidance under section 304 of the CWA for over a hundred toxic and other water pollutants. Under pressure from Congress, most states have adopted water quality standards for most of those pollutants, as well as others. What explains this difference? *Compare* CAA section 108(a), 42 U.S.C. §7408(a), *with* CWA section 303(c)(2)-(4), 33 U.S.C. §1313(c)(2)-(4).

4. *Format.* Ambient air quality criteria are universally expressed in numeric terms, in concentrations of a particular pollutant over a specified unit of time. For example, the primary NAAQS for sulfur dioxide is 80 micrograms per cubic meter as an annual arithmetic mean, and 365 micrograms per cubic meter over a 24-hour period. Setting different standards for different time periods can protect against different kinds of adverse health and other impacts. For example, some kinds of illness (shortness of breath or other acute respiratory impacts) can occur during brief periods of very high exposure. Other effects can occur due to long-term exposure at somewhat lower concentrations.

Water quality standards, by contrast, come in more flavors that have evolved over time and that continue to evolve in order to address a suite of factors that determine whether various uses of water bodies will be protected:

a. *Narrative criteria.* As discussed in *Jefferson County*, the most general forms of water quality standards are narrative standards, which articulate in plain English the acceptable condition of a water body. Examples of narrative criteria include statements that water bodies must be "free from floatable wastes" or contain "no toxics in toxic amounts." *See* Environmental Defense Fund v. Costle, 657 F.2d 275, 288 (D.C. Cir. 1981) (approving the use of narrative rather than numeric criteria for salinity). From the perspective of an environmental agency, what is useful about such broad narrative criteria? What might make them difficult to implement in practice?

b. *Numeric criteria.* States also adopt specific numeric water quality criteria similar in nature to the numeric air quality standards. The Supreme Court highlighted the utility of numeric standards in EPA v. California ex rel. State Water Resources Control Board, 426 U.S. 200 (1976), noting that one of the key purposes of the 1972 amendments was to translate general water quality requirements into specific obligations of individual dischargers. *See also* Natural Resources Defense Council v. EPA, 915 F.2d 1314 (9th Cir. 1990) (describing water quality criteria as the "maximum concentration of pollutants that could occur without jeopardizing the use").

c. *Whole effluent toxicity criteria.* Why might numeric criteria for a long list of pollutants not suffice to protect water body uses? To address the additive and synergistic effects of multiple pollutants on aquatic life, states also may issue "whole effluent toxicity" (WET) criteria, which measure the combined effects of toxic pollutants on test organisms that may be in the polluted water body. The legality of these criteria was upheld in American Paper Institute, Inc. v. EPA, 996 F.2d 346 (D.C. Cir. 1993), and in Natural Resources Defense Council v. EPA, 859 F.2d 156 (D.C. Cir. 1988).

d. *Biocriteria.* All of the above forms of water quality criteria address the "chemical" aspect of the Clean Water Act's overriding objective to restore the chemical, physical, and biological integrity of the nation's waters. Physical and biological impairments to water bodies are notably absent from the criteria described above, but are far more difficult to articulate as criteria. A more recent innovation to fill this gap is the establishment of biological water quality criteria (biocriteria), which define the health of aquatic ecosystems by comparing the biota in a given water body with those in the least-altered natural system of the same or similar type, using a rigorous set of statistical measurements. *See* Robert W. Adler, *The Two Lost Books in the Water Quality Trilogy: The Elusive Objectives of Physical and Biological Integrity*, 33 ENVTL. L. 29, 70-75 (2003).

e. *Antidegradation criteria.* Yet another form of "ambient water quality standard" is reflected in the "antidegradation" provisions of EPA's regulations, 40 C.F.R. §131.12, as discussed in the *Jefferson County* decision. Antidegradation standards require the protection of all designated uses and water quality at levels necessary to protect those uses, and further require that water quality above that level be maintained and protected except under prescribed conditions. Similar requirements are included in the Prevention of Significant Deterioration (PSD) provisions of the Clean Air Act. Briefly, the PSD provisions in the CAA require states to limit air quality degradation even where air quality is better than required by the NAAQS. These provisions are designed to prevent future violations due to additional growth or other factors, and to protect visibility afforded by particularly clean air, especially in National Parks and other scenic places.

5. *The Endangered Species Act.* The ESA can be viewed as an example of an effects-based statute. The purpose of the statute is to provide "means whereby the ecosystems upon which endangered species depend may be conserved. . . ." 16 U.S.C. §1531(b). Preventing impairment of healthy ecosystems on which species depend, therefore, is the primary statutory goal, and areas of "critical habitat" are identified to serve that goal. *Id.* §1533(b)(6)(C). Congress defined "conserve" to mean "all methods and procedures which are necessary to bring any endangered species or threatened species to the point at which" additional corrective actions are not necessary. *Id.* §1532(3). Species recovery, therefore, is the effect by which statutory implementation is gauged, and species-specific recovery plans are adopted to define the actions necessary to achieve recovery, and the criteria by which recovery will be ascertained. *Id.* §1533(f).

C. EFFECTS-BASED OUTPUT STANDARDS (RELEASE LIMITS)

A key characteristic of both the ambient air quality standards and the ambient water quality standards is that they define how clean the air and water, respectively, must be in the environment as a whole. As such, to provide for attainment of the ambient standards, we must consider the combined effects of all sources of that pollutant within a given area. Effects-based standards, however, also can be written at the level of individual pollution sources. Effects-based output standards (or release limits) dictate the amount of pollution that can be released from a particular smokestack or pipe or similar facility, and are known as "emission limits" in the CAA and "effluent standards" in the CWA. Like effects-based ambient standards, regulators dictate effects-based output standards based on adverse health and environmental effects. The scientific and regulatory problems inherent in establishing effects-based output standards, therefore, closely resemble those confronted in setting ambient effects-based standards. These issues are described in the following two cases, which pondered the establishment of effects-based source standards for toxic air pollutants under the pre-1990 and post-1990 versions of the Clean Air Act, respectively.

Natural Resources Defense Council v. EPA
824 F.2d 1146 (D.C. Cir. 1987)

BORK, CIRCUIT JUDGE [*en banc*].

Current scientific knowledge does not permit a finding that there is a completely safe level of human exposure to carcinogenic agents. The Administrator of the Environmental Protection Agency, however, is charged with regulating hazardous pollutants, including carcinogens, under section 112 of the Clean Air Act by setting emission standards "at the level which in his judgment provides an ample margin of safety to protect the public health." 42 U.S.C. §7412(b)(1)(B) (1982). We address here the question of the extent of the Administrator's authority under this delegation in setting emission standards for carcinogenic pollutants.

Petitioner Natural Resources Defense Council ("NRDC") contends that the Administrator must base a decision under section 112 exclusively on health-related factors and, therefore, that the uncertainty about the effects of carcinogenic agents requires the Administrator to prohibit all emissions. The Administrator argues that in the face of this uncertainty he is authorized to set standards that require emission reduction to the lowest level attainable by best available control technology whenever that level is below that at which harm to humans has been demonstrated. We find no support for either position in the language or legislative history of the Clean Air Act. We therefore grant the petition for review and remand to the Administrator for reconsideration in light of this opinion.

I

Section 112 of the Clean Air Act provides for regulation of hazardous air pollutants, which the statute defines as "air pollutant[s] to which no ambient air quality standard is applicable and which in the judgment of the Administrator cause[ ], or contribute[ ] to, air pollution which may reasonably be anticipated to result in an increase in mortality or an increase in serious irreversible, or incapacitating reversible, illness." 42 U.S.C. §7412(a)(1) (1982). . . . The statute directs the Administrator to set an emission standard promulgated under section 112 "at the level which in his judgment provides an ample margin of safety to protect the public health." *Id.*

This case concerns vinyl chloride regulations. Vinyl chloride is a gaseous synthetic chemical used in the manufacture of plastics and is a strong carcinogen. . . . EPA asserted that available data linked vinyl chloride to carcinogenic, as well as some noncarcinogenic, disorders and that "[r]easonable extrapolations" from this data suggested "that present ambient levels of vinyl chloride may cause or contribute to . . . [such] disorders." The EPA also noted that vinyl chloride is "an apparent non-threshold pollutant," which means that it appears to create a risk to health at all non-zero levels of emission. Scientific uncertainty, due to the unavailability of dose-response data and the twenty-year latency period between initial exposure to vinyl chloride and the occurrence of disease, makes it impossible to establish any definite threshold level below which there are no adverse effects to human health. [EPA's] notice also stated the "EPA's position that for a carcinogen it should be assumed, in the absence of strong evidence to the contrary, that there is no atmospheric concentration that poses absolutely no public health risk."

Because of this assumption, the EPA concluded that it was faced with two alternative interpretations of its duty under section 112. First, the EPA determined that section 112 might require a complete prohibition of emissions of non-threshold pollutants because a "zero emission limitation would be the only emission standard which would offer absolute safety from ambient exposure." The EPA found this alternative "neither desirable nor necessary" because "[c]omplete prohibition of all emissions could require closure of an entire industry," a cost the EPA found "extremely high for elimination of a risk to health that is of unknown dimensions."

The EPA stated the second alternative as follows:

> An alternative interpretation of section 112 is that it authorizes setting emission standards that require emission reduction to the lowest level achievable by use of the best available control technology in cases involving apparent non-threshold pollutants, where complete emission prohibition would result in widespread industry closure and EPA has determined that the cost of such closure would be grossly disproportionate to the benefits of removing the risk that would remain after imposition of the best available control technology.

The EPA adopted this alternative on the belief that it would "produce the most stringent regulation of hazardous air pollutants short of requiring a complete prohibition in all cases."

III

The NRDC's challenge . . . is simple: because the statute adopts an exclusive focus on considerations of health, the Administrator must set a zero level of emissions when he cannot determine that there is a level below which no harm will occur.

. . . We find no support in the text or legislative history for the proposition that Congress intended to require a complete prohibition of emissions whenever the EPA cannot determine a threshold level for a hazardous pollutant. Instead, there is strong evidence that Congress considered such a requirement and rejected it.

Section 112 commands the Administrator to set an "emission standard" for a particular "hazardous air pollutant" which in his "judgment" will provide an "ample margin of safety." Congress' use of the term "ample margin of safety" is inconsistent with the NRDC's position that the Administrator has no discretion in the face of uncertainty. The statute nowhere defines "ample margin of safety." The Senate Report, however, in discussing a similar requirement in the context of setting ambient air standards under section 109 of the Act, explained the purpose of the "margin of safety" standard as one of affording "a reasonable degree of protection . . . against hazards which research has not yet identified." This view comports with the historical use of the term in engineering as "a safety factor . . . meant to compensate for uncertainties and variabilities." Furthermore, in a discussion of the use of identical language in the Federal Water Pollution Control Act, this court has recognized that, in discharging the responsibility to assure "an ample margin of safety," the Administrator faces "a difficult task, indeed, a veritable paradox—calling as it does for knowledge of that which is unknown—[but] . . . the term 'margin of safety' is Congress's directive that means be found to carry out the task and to reconcile the paradox." Environmental Defense Fund v. EPA, 598 F.2d 62, 81 (D.C. Cir. 1978). And while Congress used the modifier "ample" to exhort the Administrator not to allow "the public [or] the environment . . . to be exposed to anything resembling the maximum risk" and, therefore, to set a margin "greater than 'normal' or 'adequate,'" Congress still left the EPA "great latitude in meeting its responsibility."

Congress' use of the word "safety," moreover, is significant evidence that it did not intend to require the Administrator to prohibit all emissions of non-threshold pollutants. As the Supreme Court has recently held, "safe" does not mean "risk-free." Industrial Union Dep't, AFL-CIO v. American Petroleum Inst., 448 U.S. 607, 642 (1980). Instead, something is "unsafe" only when it threatens humans with "a significant risk of harm." *Id.*

Thus, the terms of section 112 provide little support for the NRDC's position. The uncertainty about the effects of a particular carcinogenic pollutant invokes the Administrator's discretion under section 112. In contrast, the NRDC's position would eliminate any discretion and would render the standard "ample margin of safety" meaningless as applied to carcinogenic pollutants.[1] Whenever any scientific uncertainty existed about the ill effects of a nonzero level of hazardous air pol-

---

1. With the exception of mercury, every pollutant the Administrator has listed or intends to list under §112 is a non-threshold carcinogen. . . .

lutants—and we think it unlikely that science will ever yield absolute certainty of safety in an area so complicated and rife with problems of measurement, modeling, long latency, and the like—the Administrator would have no discretion but would be required to prohibit all emissions. Had Congress intended that result, it could very easily have said so by writing a statute that states that no level of emissions shall be allowed as to which there is any uncertainty. But Congress chose instead to deal with the pervasive nature of scientific uncertainty and the inherent limitations of scientific knowledge by vesting in the Administrator the discretion to deal with uncertainty in each case. . . .

IV

We turn now to the question whether the Administrator's chosen method for setting emission levels above zero is consistent with congressional intent. The Administrator's position is that he may set an emission level for non-threshold pollutants at the lowest level achievable by best available control technology when that level is anywhere below the level of demonstrated harm and the cost of setting a lower level is grossly disproportionate to the benefits of removing the remaining risk. The NRDC argues that this standard is arbitrary and capricious because the EPA is never permitted to consider cost and technological feasibility under section 112 but instead is limited to consideration of health-based factors. Thus, before addressing the Administrator's method of using cost and technological feasibility in this case, we must determine whether he may consider cost and technological feasibility at all.

A.

On its face, section 112 does not indicate that Congress intended to preclude consideration of any factor. Though the phrase "to protect the public health" evinces an intent to make health the primary consideration, there is no indication of the factors the Administrator may or may not consider in determining, in his "judgment," what level of emissions will provide "an ample margin of safety." Instead, the language used, and the absence of any specific limitation, gives the clear impression that the Administrator has some discretion in determining what, if any, additional factors he will consider in setting an emission standard. . . .

The legislative history is simply ambiguous with respect to the question of whether the Administrator may permissibly consider cost and technological feasibility under section 112. In the course of the compromise, the House lost a provision which would have permitted consideration of non-health based factors and the Senate lost a provision which would have limited the Administrator to consideration of health-based factors. The resulting standard neither permits nor prohibits consideration of any factor. Thus, we cannot find a clear congressional intent in the language, structure, or legislative history of the Act to preclude consideration of cost and technological feasibility under section 112. . . .

C.

The petitioner argues next that a finding that section 112 does not preclude consideration of cost and technological feasibility would render the Clean Air Act structurally incoherent and would be inconsistent with the Supreme Court's interpretation of section 110 of the Act . . . , and this court's interpretation of section 109 of the Act, *see* Lead Indus. Ass'n v. EPA, as precluding consideration of these factors. We do not believe that our decision here is inconsistent with either the holding or the statutory interpretation. . . .

First, as discussed below, the court in [*Lead Industries* and *Union Electric, infra*] rejected an argument that the EPA must consider cost and technological feasibility as factors equal in importance to health. We reject the same argument here. In this case, however, we must also address the question of whether the Administrator may consider these factors if necessary to further protect the public health. This issue was not addressed in . . . *Lead Industries*. . . .

In *Lead Industries*, we held that the Administrator is not required to consider cost and technology under the mandate in section 109 of the Clean Air Act to promulgate primary air quality standards which "allow[ ] an adequate margin of safety . . . to protect the public health." 42 U.S.C. §7409(b)(1) (1982). The NRDC argues that the decision in *Lead Industries*, which involved the more permissive language "adequate," rather than "ample," "margin of safety," compels the conclusion that section 112 precludes consideration of economic and technological feasibility. We think not.

The *Lead Industries* court did note that the statute on its face does not allow consideration of technological or economic feasibility, but the court based its decision that section 109 does not allow consideration of these factors in part on structural aspects of the ambient air pollution provisions that are not present here. First, besides "allowing an adequate margin of safety," ambient air standards set under section 109(b) must be based on "air quality criteria," which section 108 defines as comprising several elements, all related to health. The court reasoned that the exclusion of economic and technological feasibility considerations from air quality criteria also foreclosed reliance on such factors in setting the ambient air quality standards based on those criteria. The court also relied on the fact that state implementation plans, the means of enforcement of ambient air standards, could not take into account economic and technological feasibility if such consideration interfered with the timely attainment of ambient air standards, and that the Administrator could not consider such feasibility factors in deciding whether to approve the state plans. This provided further grounds for the court to believe that Congress simply did not intend the economics of pollution control to be considered in the scheme of ambient air regulations.

In *Lead Industries*, moreover, the relevant Senate Report stated flatly that "existing sources of pollutants either should meet the standard of the law or be closed down." This is a far clearer statement than anything in the present case that Congress considered the alternatives and chose to close down sources or even industries rather than to allow risks to health.

The substantive standard imposed under the hazardous air pollutants provisions of section 112, by contrast with sections 109 and 110, is not based on criteria that enumerate specific factors to consider and pointedly exclude feasibility. Section 112(b)(1)'s command "to provide an ample margin of safety to protect the public health" is self-contained, and the absence of enumerated criteria may well evince a congressional intent for the Administrator to supply reasonable ones. . . .

Thus, in *Lead Industries*, the court found clear evidence that Congress intended to limit the factors the Administrator is permitted to consider in setting a "margin of safety" under section 109. The "margin of safety" standard in section 112 is not so adorned. For that reason, *Lead Industries* does not control this case. . . .

V

. . . Given the foregoing analysis of the language and legislative history of section 112, it seems to us beyond dispute that Congress was primarily concerned with health in promulgating section 112. Every action by the Administrator in setting an emission standard is to be taken "to protect the public health." In setting an emission standard for vinyl chloride, however, the Administrator has made no finding with respect to the effect of the chosen level of emissions on health. Nor has the Administrator stated that a certain level of emissions is "safe" or that the chosen level will provide an "ample margin of safety." Instead, the Administrator has substituted "best available technology" for a finding of the risk to health. . . .

Thus, in setting emission standards for carcinogenic pollutants, the Administrator has decided to determine first the level of emissions attainable by best available control technology. He will then determine the costs of setting the standard below that level and balance those costs against the risk to health below the level of feasibility. If the costs are greater than the reduction in risk, then he will set the standard at the level of feasibility. This exercise, in the Administrator's view, will always produce an "ample margin of safety." . . .

We find that the congressional mandate to provide "an ample margin of safety" "to protect the public health" requires the Administrator to make an initial determination of what is "safe." This determination must be based exclusively upon the Administrator's determination of the risk to health at a particular emission level. Because the Administrator in this case did not make any finding of the risk to health, the question of how that determination is to be made is not before us. We do wish to note, however, that the Administrator's decision does not require a finding that "safe" means "risk-free," or a finding that the determination is free from uncertainty. Instead, we find only that the Administrator's decision must be based upon an expert judgment with regard to the level of emission that will result in an "acceptable" risk to health. In this regard, the Administrator must determine what inferences should be drawn from available scientific data and decide what risks are acceptable in the world in which we live. This determination must be based solely upon the risk to health. The Administrator cannot under any circumstances consider cost and technological feasibility at this stage of the analysis. The latter factors have no relevance to the preliminary determination of what is safe. Of course, if the Administrator cannot find that there is an acceptable risk at any level, then the Administrator must set the level at zero.

Congress, however, recognized in section 112 that the determination of what is "safe" will always be marked by scientific uncertainty and thus exhorted the Administrator to set emission standards that will provide an "ample margin" of safety. This language permits the Administrator to take into account scientific uncertainty and to use expert discretion to determine what action should be taken in light of that uncertainty. In determining what is an "ample margin" the

Administrator may, and perhaps must, take into account the inherent limitations of risk assessment and the limited scientific knowledge of the effects of exposure to carcinogens at various levels, and may therefore decide to set the level below that previously determined to be "safe." This is especially true when a straight line extrapolation from known risks is used to estimate risks to health at levels of exposure for which no data is available. This method, which is based upon the results of exposure at fairly high levels of the hazardous pollutants, will show some risk at every level because of the rules of arithmetic rather than because of any knowledge. In fact the risk at a certain point on the extrapolated line may have no relationship to reality; there is no particular reason to think that the actual line of the incidence of harm is represented by a straight line. Thus, by its nature the finding of risk is uncertain and the Administrator must use his discretion to meet the statutory mandate. It is only at this point of the regulatory process that the Administrator may set the emission standard at the lowest level that is technologically feasible. In fact, this is, we believe, precisely the type of policy choice that Congress envisioned when it directed the Administrator to provide an "ample margin of safety." Once "safety" is assured, the Administrator should be free to diminish as much of the statistically determined risk as possible by setting the standard at the lowest feasible level. Because consideration of these factors at this stage is clearly intended "to protect the public health," it is fully consistent with the Administrator's mandate under section 112. . . .

≣ *Natural Resources Defense Council v. EPA*
≣ *529 F.3d 1077, 1078-83 (D.C. Cir. 2008)*

SILBERMAN, SENIOR CIRCUIT JUDGE.

Synthetic organic chemicals have few direct consumer uses, but they often serve as raw materials in the production of plastics, rubbers, fibers, protective coatings, and detergents. Petitioners . . . challenge EPA's residual risk rulemaking under subsection 112(f) of the Clean Air Act for facilities that use or produce synthetic organic chemicals ("the industry"). . . . We deny the petition.

I.

Section 112 of the Clean Air Act regulates hazardous air pollutants. When the Act was passed in 1970, hazardous air pollutant was defined as a substance "which may reasonably be anticipated to result in an increase in mortality or an increase in serious irreversible, or incapacitating irreversible, illness." The Administrator of the EPA was required to prepare a list of air pollutants that fell within this definition, then promulgate standards to protect the public health from these substances with an "ample margin of safety."

. . . In 1990, Congress sought to hasten the process by adopting a new regulatory approach for hazardous air pollutants. Rather than have EPA list one-by-one those substances likely to be harmful, the amended version of section 112 provides a list of 191 substances that Congress deemed to be hazardous.

Instead of basing its regulations on health risks (the "ample margin of safety"), EPA was required by the 1990 amendments to adopt technology-based standards in the first instance. That is to say, in the first round of regulation, the agency was obliged to look to the best available control technology to control emissions for each category of major sources that emits one or more of the listed hazardous air pollutants. (The control technology used to meet this standard is referred to as the "maximum achievable control technology" or "MACT.") . . .

In the second stage of regulation, EPA was obliged to review any residual health risks that had not been eliminated by the initial technology-based standards. This second stage is described as "risk-based" or "health-based" because it requires EPA to set a standard based on a medical assessment of a given pollutant's health risks (as was true of the pre-1990 statute), rather than the current state of control technology. Within six years of promulgating the technology-based standards, EPA was required to prepare a report to Congress analyzing any residual health risks. If Congress did not act on the report, then EPA was to conduct residual risk analysis under subsection 112(f)(2).

EPA initially promulgated technology-based emission standards for the industry in 1994. . . . After submitting the required report to Congress in 1999, the agency commenced residual risk rulemaking, apparently because—as we discuss below—it read the statute as requiring a rulemaking proceeding to consider whether to revise the technology-based standards, since the industry's emissions pose lifetime excess cancer risks of greater than one-in-one million.

In the notice of proposed rulemaking, EPA listed two options for the residual risk rulemaking, one of which would have imposed somewhat stricter standards. But the other, which EPA adopted in the final rule, was a reaffirmation of the existing rule. EPA determined that under the existing technology-based standard, no individual would face an excess lifetime cancer risk of greater than 100-in-one million, which EPA regards as the "presumptively acceptable" level under its precedents. . . .

[Petitioners'] primary argument is one of statutory construction. They contend that the statute obliged EPA, in the residual risk rulemaking, to tighten the standards for the industry so that the lifetime excess cancer risk to exposed persons would be no greater than one-in-one million.

II.

A.

Petitioners contend that subsection 112(f)(2)(A) obliged EPA to revise industry standards to reduce lifetime excess cancer risk to one-in-one million. Petitioners rely primarily on the last sentence of that subsection, whereas EPA looks to the whole subsection. That provision states in full:

> If Congress does not act on any recommendation submitted under paragraph (1), the Administrator shall, within 8 years after promulgation of standards for each category or subcategory of sources pursuant to subsection (d) of this section, promulgate standards for such category or subcategory if promulgation of such standards is required in order to provide an

ample margin of safety to protect public health in accordance with this section (as in effect before November 15, 1990) or to prevent, taking into consideration costs, energy, safety, and other relevant factors, an adverse environmental effect. Emissions standards promulgated under this subsection shall provide an ample margin of safety to protect public health in accordance with this section (as in effect before November 15, 1990), unless the Administrator determines that a more stringent standard is necessary to prevent, taking into consideration costs, energy, safety, and other relevant factors, an adverse environmental effect. If standards promulgated pursuant to subsection (d) of this section and applicable to a category or subcategory of sources emitting a pollutant (or pollutants) classified as a known, probable or possible human carcinogen do not reduce lifetime excess cancer risks to the individual most exposed to emissions from a source in the category or subcategory to less than one in one million, the Administrator shall promulgate standards under this subsection for such source category.

42 U.S.C. §7412(f)(2)(A).

It is undisputed that facilities that produce or use synthetic organic chemicals emit carcinogens and are, therefore, within the reach of the last sentence. It is also undisputed that, in light of the fact that existing technology-based standards do not reduce the risk to less than one-in-one million, EPA was obliged to "promulgate standards" under subsection 112(f). Petitioners contend that the third sentence obviously means that residual risk standards must meet the threshold test—*i.e.*, EPA must reduce such risks to one-in-one million. That may well be a possible interpretation, but the sentence contains a glaring omission; it does not say what petitioners would like us to infer. Rather, that sentence instructs the Administrator to "promulgate standards," but it says nothing about the substantive content of those standards. If Congress had wished to set a "bright line" standard, it would have been rather easy for the draftsmen to say just that. The failure to do so could not have been accidental. In light of the rest of the subsection's language (and other provisions), it seems to us that the subsection was drafted as a deliberately ambiguous compromise.[4]

We reach that conclusion because the second sentence, which sets forth the substantive standard to be applied, simply calls for standards that "provide an ample margin of safety to protect public health" (unless the Administrator wishes to go further to avoid adverse environmental effects). No distinction is drawn between carcinogens and non-carcinogens. The third sentence, on which petitioners rely, not only lacks the language that petitioners ask us to infer; it also specifically states that if the one-in-one million trigger is met, the Administrator must promulgate standards "under this subsection," which, perforce, takes us back to the second sentence. . . .

NOTES AND QUESTIONS ON THE SECTION 112 CASES

1. *Zero risk.* If EPA was required before 1990 to adopt effects-based standards at levels necessary to "protect public health," and if some cancer may occur at any level of vinyl chloride emissions, why was EPA *not* required to establish a zero

---

4. Congress rejected the Senate version of the bill—which mandated a bright line standard for carcinogens—in favor of the House version, which gave the Secretary more discretion under the "ample margin of safety" standard.

emissions level? Did the *Vinyl Chloride* decision prohibit EPA from adopting a zero emission standard?

2. Lead Industries. Does the *Vinyl Chloride* court convincingly distinguish section 109 of the CAA, as interpreted in *Lead Industries*? In choosing an effects level at which some risk to public health remains, are we not at least implicitly allowing EPA to balance economic impacts (closing factories, losing jobs) against the remaining risk of cancer?

3. *Technology-based approach*. Why did the *Vinyl Chloride* court reject EPA's approach of reducing releases to the maximum extent possible given available technology? Why was it not within EPA's discretion to find that reducing emissions by the maximum amount possible provides the largest margin of safety possible? Why, then, do you imagine Congress adopted that same basic approach in the 1990 amendments? Did EPA lose the battle in *Vinyl Chloride* but win the war in Congress?

4. *Residual risk under the 1990 amendments*. Did the *Synthetic Organic Chemicals* court rule correctly that EPA is allowed to choose a residual risk level higher than one in a million? If so, what factors should EPA consider in deciding an appropriate residual risk level? What guidance did the *Vinyl Chloride* court give as to how EPA should develop toxic air pollutant emissions standards, *i.e.*, when and how may EPA consider economic and similar factors, and when is it prohibited from doing so? What continued relevance does this guidance have in interpreting the 1990 version of the statute?

5. *Clean Water Act*. A similar regulatory/legislative saga unfolded under the CWA, but with somewhat different results. Under the version of section 307(a) of the CWA enacted in 1972, Congress directed EPA to identify and issue effects-based source standards (known in the water context as "effluent standards" rather than "emissions standards") for toxic water pollutants. The CWA standards, however, required a lengthy quasi-adjudicative hearing process, which made the issuance of those standards even more difficult administratively. The long saga of one of EPA's rule-making proceedings under this provision is described in Environmental Defense Fund v. EPA, 598 F.2d 62 (D.C. Cir. 1978). Due to EPA's glacial pace of issuing effects-based effluent standards for toxic water pollutants, Congress amended the CWA in both 1977 and 1987, in ways designed to promote more efficient attention to the problem of toxic water pollution. Section 307(a) now requires EPA to develop technology-based requirements, by categories and subcategories of sources, for all toxic pollutants identified on a list compiled in the legislative history. 33 U.S.C. §1317(a). EPA retains the discretion to adopt effects-based standards on a pollutant-specific basis, but has not done so since the 1977 amendments were adopted. (Unlike the amended section 112 of the CAA, EPA's residual authority to adopt effects-based effluent standards under the CWA is entirely discretionary.) In 1987, Congress also required individual states, or EPA if they fail to do so, to promulgate ambient water quality criteria for toxic pollutants. 33 U.S.C. §1313(c)(2)(B). The history of EPA's implementation of the original provision, and Congress' response, is detailed in Oliver A. Houck, *The Regulation of Toxic Pollutants Under the Clean Water Act*, 21 ENVTL. L. REP. (ENVTL. L. INST.) 10,528 (1991).

D. ISSUES IN RISK ASSESSMENT AND DECISION MAKING

General Background on Risk Assessment and Management

> "The risks are all acceptable; acceptable to who?"
> Folksinger/songwriter Charlie King

While environmental lawyers do not need to become experts in risk assessment and related disciplines, in part because they will work with experts in those fields, they do need to understand the basics of how risk assessment methodology is used in the regulatory process. As you saw in the above cases, changes in methods, assumptions, and data can have a dramatic influence on the final regulatory standards. We will begin with some basic terminology:

- **Risk assessment** is a process by which we try to characterize the risk of harm from exposure to a particular environmental cause. Risk assessment can consist solely of a qualitative assessment, as in the *Ethyl* case. Quantitative risk assessment involves an effort to evaluate the magnitude of particular harm from a particular cause. Quantitative risk assessment might involve estimating the lifetime incremental risk of getting cancer due to exposure to a particular chemical, with "incremental risk," meaning the added probability of cancer from that exposure above the background cancer rate in the population. Or, it might predict that a certain number of people will experience difficulty breathing due to a certain level of an air pollutant, or that there is an X percent chance that the population of an endangered species might decline by another Y percent if a particular highway is built. Risk assessment relies upon scientific data, but usually requires extrapolation from limited scientific evidence and interpretation of relevant science.
- **Risk management** is a policy inquiry in which we make regulatory and other decisions based on the risk assessment process and results. Using risk management, we might decide to choose regulatory standard A over standard B based on the degree of risk we are willing to tolerate. Or, we might choose to site a new hazardous waste landfill at site C rather than D based on the relative risks between the sites, or issue the landfill permit or not, based on how severe we predict the risks will be.

Risk assessment requires an understanding of several factors. First, how much of a pollutant is emitted into the environment? Second, what is the pathway by which the pollutant reaches an individual who might be harmed? This inquiry, in turn, involves questions about the fate and persistence of the pollutant. (Does it break down into another substance? Does it dissipate over time or through dilution? Does it evaporate into the air? Does it concentrate in various places in the environment, for example, through bioconcentration or biomagnification?) Third, what is the effect or potential effect on the recipient? This last inquiry might involve what parts of the individual are exposed, what kinds of effects might occur, and the probability that those effects will occur, all of which involve complex and difficult data collection and analysis.

Based on this information, to what degree is risk assessment a purely "objective" scientific inquiry? Where might more subjective policy factors enter the risk assessment process? What additional factors are considered in risk management? To what degree are those decisions guided by science, law, policy, economics, ethics, or other factors? Revisit these issues after you evaluate the example below.

Figure 5-1—The Risk Assessment Process

Risk Assessment

SOURCE   ⟶   RECIPIENT   ⟶   IMPACTS
(Exposure pathway)   (Impacts Analysis)

CLIMATE DISRUPTION, TOXICS, AND RISK

Although rising temperatures, sea level rise and coastal inundation, increased storm intensity, and melting glaciers are among the more frequently cited effects of climate disruption, experts predict a surprisingly wide range of other possible impacts as well. This renders climate disruption risk assessment an extremely complex endeavor. How might climate disruption increase risk from toxic chemicals? As an example, consider the following:

Weeds benefit more than cash crops from higher temperatures and carbon dioxide levels. One concern with continued warming is the northward expansion of invasive weeds. Southern farmers currently lose more of their crops to weeds than do northern farmers. . . . As temperatures continue to rise, these weeds will expand their ranges northward into important agricultural areas. . . .

Controlling weeds currently costs the United States more than $11 billion a year, with the majority spent on herbicides; so both herbicide use and costs are likely to increase as temperatures and carbon dioxide levels rise. At the same time, the most widely used herbicide in the United States, glyphosate (RoundUp®), loses its efficacy on weeds grown at carbon dioxide levels that are projected to occur in the coming decades. Higher concentrations of the chemical and more frequent spraying thus will be needed, increasing economic and environmental costs associated with chemical use.

Many insect pests and crop diseases thrive due to warming, increasing losses and necessitating greater pesticide use. Warming aids insects and diseases in several ways. Rising temperatures allow both insects and pathogens to expand their ranges northward. In addition, rapidly rising winter temperatures allow more insects to survive over the winter, whereas cold winters once controlled their populations. . . . The longer growing season will allow some insects to produce more generations in a single season, greatly increasing their populations. Finally, plants grown in higher carbon dioxide conditions tend to be less nutritious, so insects must eat more to meet their protein requirements, causing greater destruction to crops.

Due to the increased presence of pests, spraying is already much more common in warmer areas than in cooler areas. . . . In addition, higher temperatures are known to reduce the effectiveness of certain classes of pesticides. . . .

Farmers are likely to respond to more aggressive and invasive weeds, insects, and pathogens with increased use of herbicides, insecticides, and fungicides. Where increases in . . . chemical inputs become necessary, this will increase costs for the farmer, as well as having society-wide impacts by . . . increasing . . . pesticide loads to the environment, and increasing risks to food safety and human exposure to pesticides.

U.S. Global Change Research Program, Global Climate Change Impacts in the United States (2009).

E.   POSTSCRIPT: A SEGUE FROM EFFECTS-BASED TO TECHNOLOGY-BASED REGULATION

This chapter explored effects-based regulations. The following chapter will discuss technology-based regulation. In some statutory provisions, however, Congress did not choose so clearly among those options. Some statutes reflect what may be called a "hybrid" of the two approaches, and provide a useful way for us to transition between these two concepts. The following excerpt is from the case in which the U.S. Supreme Court most squarely addressed issues of human health risk assessment, in the context of the Occupational Safety and Health Act. As you read the case, often known as the "Benzene" case, ask yourself the following questions. First, what role is risk assessment playing in this case? Second, under the relevant statutory provisions, when and in what ways should the Occupational Safety and Health Administration (OSHA) consider health effects, and when should it consider technological feasibility?

Industrial Union Department, AFL-CIO v. American Petroleum Institute
448 U.S. 607 (1980)

JUSTICE STEVENS announced the judgment of the Court and delivered an opinion, in which THE CHIEF JUSTICE and MR. JUSTICE STEWART joined and in Parts I, II, III-A, III-B, III-C and III-E of which MR. JUSTICE POWELL joined.

The Occupational Safety and Health Act of 1970 (Act) was enacted for the purpose of ensuring safe and healthful working conditions for every working man and woman in the Nation. This litigation concerns a standard promulgated by the Secretary of Labor to regulate occupational exposure to benzene, a substance which has been shown to cause cancer at high exposure levels. The principal question is whether such a showing is a sufficient basis for a standard that places the most stringent limitation on exposure to benzene that is technologically and economically possible.

The Act delegates broad authority to the Secretary to promulgate different kinds of standards. The basic definition of an "occupational safety and health standard" is found in §3(8), which provides:

The term "occupational safety and health standard" means a standard which requires conditions, or the adoption or use of one or more practices, means, methods, operations, or processes, reasonably necessary or appropriate to provide safe or healthful employment and places of employment.

Where toxic materials or harmful physical agents are concerned, a standard must also comply with §6(b)(5), which provides:

> The Secretary, in promulgating standards dealing with toxic materials or harmful physical agents under this subsection, shall set the standard which most adequately assures, to the extent feasible, on the basis of the best available evidence, that no employee will suffer material impairment of health or functional capacity even if such employee has regular exposure to the hazard dealt with by such standard for the period of his working life. . . .

Wherever the toxic material to be regulated is a carcinogen, the Secretary has taken the position that no safe exposure level can be determined and that §6(b)(5) requires him to set an exposure limit at the lowest technologically feasible level that will not impair the viability of the industries regulated. In this case, after having determined that there is a causal connection between benzene and leukemia (a cancer of the white blood cells), the Secretary set an exposure limit on airborne concentrations of benzene of one part benzene per million parts of air (1 ppm), regulated dermal and eye contact with solutions containing benzene, and imposed complex monitoring and medical testing requirements on employers whose workplaces contain 0.5 ppm or more of benzene.

On pre-enforcement review, the United States Court of Appeals for the Fifth Circuit held the regulation invalid. The court concluded that the Occupational Safety and Health Administration (OSHA) had exceeded its standard-setting authority because it had not shown that the new benzene exposure limit was "reasonably necessary or appropriate to provide safe or healthful employment" as required by §3(8), and because §6(b)(5) does "not give OSHA the unbridled discretion to adopt standards designed to create absolutely risk-free workplaces regardless of costs." Reaching the two provisions together, the Fifth Circuit held that the Secretary was under a duty to determine whether the benefits expected from the new standard bore a reasonable relationship to the costs that it imposed. The court noted that OSHA had made an estimate of the costs of compliance, but that the record lacked substantial evidence of any discernible benefits.

We agree with the Fifth Circuit's holding that §3(8) requires the Secretary to find, as a threshold matter, that the toxic substance in question poses a significant health risk in the workplace and that a new, lower standard is therefore "reasonably necessary or appropriate to provide safe or healthful employment and places of employment." Unless and until such a finding is made, it is not necessary to address the further question whether the Court of Appeals correctly held that there must be a reasonable correlation between costs and benefits, or whether, as the federal parties argue, the Secretary is then required by §6(b)(5) to promulgate a standard that goes as far as technologically and economically possible to eliminate the risk. . . .

I

The entire population of the United States is exposed to small quantities of benzene, ranging from a few parts per billion to 0.5 ppm, in the ambient air. Over one million workers are subject to additional low-level exposures as a consequence of their employment. . . .

As early as 1928, some health experts theorized that there might also be a connection between benzene in the workplace and leukemia. . . .

Between 1974 and 1976 additional studies were published which tended to confirm the view that benzene can cause leukemia, at least when exposure levels are high. In . . . August 1976 . . . NIOSH [OSHA's research arm] stated that these studies provided "conclusive" proof of a causal connection between benzene and leukemia. Although it acknowledged that none of the intervening studies had provided the dose-response data it had found lacking two years earlier, NIOSH nevertheless recommended that the exposure limit be set low as possible. As a result of this recommendation, OSHA contracted with a consulting firm to do a study on the costs to industry of complying with the 10 ppm standard then in effect or, alternatively, with whatever standard would be the lowest feasible.

In October 1976, NIOSH sent another memorandum to OSHA, seeking acceleration of the rulemaking process and "strongly" recommending the issuance of an emergency temporary standard pursuant to §6(c) of the Act for benzene and two other chemicals believed to be carcinogens. NIOSH recommended that a 1 ppm exposure limit be imposed for benzene.

In [response to new evidence], OSHA issue[d] an emergency standard effective May 21, 1977, reducing the benzene exposure limit from 10 ppm to 1 ppm, the ceiling for exposures of up to 10 minutes from 25 ppm to 5 ppm, and eliminating the authority for peak concentrations of 50 ppm. 42 Fed. Reg. 22516 (1977). In its explanation accompanying the emergency standard, OSHA stated that benzene had been shown to cause leukemia at exposures below 25 ppm and that, in light of its consultant's report, it was feasible to reduce the exposure limit to 1 ppm. . . . [OSHA then proposed to make this standard permanent.]

In its published statement giving notice of the proposed permanent standard, OSHA did not ask for comments as to whether or not benzene presented a significant health risk at exposures of 10 ppm or less. Rather, it asked for comments as to whether 1 ppm was the minimum feasible exposure limit. [T]his formulation of the issue to be considered by the Agency was consistent with OSHA's general policy with respect to carcinogens. Whenever a carcinogen is involved, OSHA will presume that no safe level of exposure exists in the absence of clear proof establishing such a level and will accordingly set the exposure limit at the lowest level feasible. The proposed 1 ppm exposure limit in this case thus was established not on the basis of a proven hazard at 10 ppm, but rather on the basis of "OSHA's best judgement at the time of the proposal of the feasibility of compliance with the proposed standard by the [a]ffected industries." Given OSHA's cancer policy, it was in fact irrelevant whether there was any evidence at all of a leukemia risk at 10 ppm. The important point was that there was no evidence that there was *not* some risk, however small, at that level. The fact that OSHA did not ask for comments on whether there was a safe level of exposure for benzene was indicative of its further view that a demonstration of such absolute safety simply could not be made. The final standard was issued on February 10, 1978. In its final form, the benzene standard is designed to protect workers from whatever hazards are associated with low-level benzene exposures by requiring employers to . . . institute whatever engineering or other controls are necessary to keep exposures at or below 1 ppm.

As presently formulated, the benzene standard is an expensive way of providing some additional protection for a relatively small number of employees. According to OSHA's figures, the standard will require capital investments in engineering controls of approximately $266 million, first-year operating costs (for monitoring, medical testing, employee training, and respirators) of $187 million to $205 million and recurring annual costs of approximately $34 million. The figures outlined in OSHA's explanation of the costs of compliance to various industries indicate that only 35,000 employees would gain any benefit from the regulation in terms of a reduction in their exposure to benzene. . . .

Although OSHA did not quantify the benefits to each category of worker in terms of decreased exposure to benzene, it appears from the economic impact study done at OSHA's direction that those benefits may be relatively small. Thus, although the current exposure limit is 10 ppm, the actual exposures outlined in that study are often considerably lower. For example, for the period 1970-1975 the petrochemical industry reported that, out of a total of 496 employees exposed to benzene, only 53 were exposed to levels between 1 and 5 ppm and only 7 (all at the same plant) were exposed to between 5 and 10 ppm.

II

The critical issue at this point in the litigation is whether the Court of Appeals was correct in refusing to enforce the 1 ppm exposure limit on the ground that it was not supported by appropriate findings.

Any discussion of the 1 ppm exposure limit must, of course, begin with the Agency's rationale for imposing that limit. The written explanation of the standard fills 184 pages of the printed appendix. Much of it is devoted to a discussion of the voluminous evidence of the adverse effects of exposure to benzene at levels of concentration well above 10 ppm. This discussion demonstrates that there is ample justification for regulating occupational exposure to benzene and that the prior limit of 10 ppm, with a ceiling of 25 ppm (or a peak of 50 ppm) was reasonable. It does not, however, provide direct support for the Agency's conclusion that the limit should be reduced from 10 ppm to 1 ppm. . . .

The Agency made no finding that . . . any . . . empirical evidence, or any opinion testimony demonstrated that exposure to benzene at or below the 10 ppm level had ever in fact caused leukemia.

In the end OSHA's rationale for lowering the permissible exposure limit to 1 ppm was based, not on any finding that leukemia has ever been caused by exposure to 10 ppm of benzene and that it will *not* be caused by exposure to 1 ppm, but rather on a series of assumptions indicating that some leukemias might result from exposure to 10 ppm and that the number of cases might be reduced by reducing the exposure level to 1 ppm. In reaching that result, the Agency first unequivocally concluded that benzene is a human carcinogen. Second, it concluded that industry had failed to prove that there is a safe threshold level of exposure to benzene below which no excess leukemia cases would occur. . . .

Third, the Agency applied its standard policy with respect to carcinogens, concluding that, in the absence of definitive proof of a safe level, it must be assumed that *any* level above zero presents *some* increased risk of cancer. . . .

Fourth, the Agency reiterated its view of the Act, stating that it was required by §6(b)(5) to set the standard either at the level that has been demonstrated to be safe or at the lowest level feasible, whichever is higher. If no safe level is established, as in this case, the Secretary's interpretation of the statute automatically leads to the selection of an exposure limit that is the lowest feasible. Because of benzene's importance to the economy, no one has ever suggested that it would be feasible to eliminate its use entirely, or to try to limit exposures to the small amounts that are omnipresent. Rather, the Agency selected 1 ppm as a workable exposure level, and then determined that compliance with that level was technologically feasible and that "the economic impact of . . . [compliance] will not be such as to threaten the financial welfare of the affected firms or the general economy." It therefore held that 1 ppm was the minimum feasible exposure level within the meaning of §6(b)(5) of the Act.

Finally, although the Agency did not refer in its discussion of the pertinent legal authority to any duty to identify the anticipated benefits of the new standard, it did conclude that some benefits were likely to result from reducing the exposure limit from 10 ppm to 1 ppm. This conclusion was based, again, not on evidence, but rather on the assumption that the risk of leukemia will decrease as exposure levels decrease. . . .

III

Our resolution of the issues in these cases turns, to a large extent, on the meaning of and the relationship between §3(8), which defines a health and safety standard as a standard that is "reasonably necessary and appropriate to provide safe or healthful employment," and §6(b)(5), which directs the Secretary in promulgating a health and safety standard for toxic materials to "set the standard which most adequately assures, to the extent feasible, on the basis of the best available evidence, that no employee will suffer material impairment of health or functional capacity. . . ."

In the Government's view, §3(8)'s definition of the term "standard" has no legal significance or at best merely requires that a standard not be totally irrational. It takes the position that §6(b)(5) is controlling and that it requires OSHA to promulgate a standard that either gives an absolute assurance of safety for each and every worker or reduces exposures to the lowest level feasible. The Government interprets "feasible" as meaning technologically achievable at a cost that would not impair the viability of the industries subject to the regulation. The respondent industry representatives, on the other hand, argue that the Court of Appeals was correct in holding that the "reasonably necessary and appropriate" language of §3(8), along with the feasibility requirement of §6(b)(5), requires the Agency to quantify both the costs and the benefits of a proposed rule and to conclude that they are roughly commensurate.

In our view, it is not necessary to decide whether either the Government or industry is entirely correct. For we think it is clear that §3(8) does apply to all permanent standards promulgated under the Act and that it requires the Secretary, before issuing any standard, to determine that it is reasonably necessary and appropriate to remedy a significant risk of material health impairment. Only after the Secretary has made the threshold determination that such a risk exists with respect to a toxic substance, would it be necessary to decide whether §6(b)(5) requires him to select the most protective standard he can consistent with economic and technological feasibility, or whether, as respondents argue, the benefits of the regulation must be commensurate with the costs of its implementation. Because the Secretary did not make the required threshold finding in these cases, we have no occasion to determine whether costs must be weighed against benefits in an appropriate case.

A

Under the Government's view, §3(8), if it has any substantive content at all, merely requires OSHA to issue standards that are reasonably calculated to produce a safer or more healthy work environment. Apart from this minimal requirement of rationality, the Government argues that §3(8) imposes no limits on the Agency's power, and thus would not prevent it from requiring employers to do whatever would be "reasonably necessary" to eliminate all risks of any harm from their workplaces. With respect to toxic substances and harmful physical agents, the Government takes an even more extreme position. Relying on §6(b)(5)'s direction to set a standard "which most adequately assures . . . that no employee will suffer material impairment of health or functional capacity," the Government contends that the Secretary is required to impose standards that either guarantee workplaces that are free from any risk of material health impairment, however small, or that come as close as possible to doing so without ruining entire industries.

If the purpose of the statute were to eliminate completely and with absolute certainty any risk of serious harm, we would agree that it would be proper for the Secretary to interpret §§3(8) and 6(b)(5) in this fashion. But we think it is clear that the statute was not designed to require employers to provide absolutely risk-free workplaces whenever it is technologically feasible to do so, so long as the cost is not great enough to destroy an entire industry. Rather, both the language and structure of the Act, as well as its legislative history, indicate that it was intended to require the elimination, as far as feasible, of significant risks of harm.

B

By empowering the Secretary to promulgate standards that are "reasonably necessary or appropriate to provide safe or healthful employment and places of employment," the Act implies that, before promulgating any standard, the Secretary must make a finding that the workplaces in question are not safe. But "safe" is not the equivalent of "risk-free." There are many activities that we engage in every day—such as driving a car or even breathing city air—that entail some risk of accident or material health impairment; nevertheless, few people would consider these activities "unsafe." Similarly, a workplace can hardly be considered "unsafe" unless it threatens the workers with a significant risk of harm.

Therefore, before he can promulgate *any* permanent health or safety standard, the Secretary is required to make a threshold finding that a place of employment is unsafe—in the sense that significant risks are present and can be eliminated or lessened by a change in practices. This requirement applies to permanent standards promulgated pursuant to §6(b)(5), as well as to other types of permanent standards. For there is no reason why §3(8)'s definition of a standard should not be deemed incorporated by reference into §6(b)(5). The standards promulgated pursuant to §6(b)(5) are just one species of the genus of standards governed by the basic requirement. That section repeatedly uses the term "standard" without suggesting any exception from, or qualification of, the general definition; on the contrary, its directs the Secretary to select "*the* standard"—that is to say, one of various possible alternatives that satisfy the basic definition in §3(8)—that is most protective. Moreover, requiring the Secretary to make a threshold finding of significant risk is consistent with the scope of the regulatory power granted to him by §6(b)(5), which empowers the Secretary to promulgate standards, not for chemicals and physical agents generally, but for "*toxic* materials" and "*harmful* physical agents."

Thus, in this case, the Secretary was required to find that exposures at the current permissible exposure level of 10 ppm present a significant risk of harm in the workplace.

In the absence of a clear mandate in the Act, it is unreasonable to assume that Congress intended to give the Secretary the unprecedented power over American industry that would result from the Government's view of §§3(8) and 6(b)(5), coupled with OSHA's cancer policy. Expert testimony that a substance is probably a human carcinogen—either because it has caused cancer in animals or because individuals have contracted cancer following extremely high exposures—would justify the conclusion that the substance poses some risk of serious harm no matter how minute the exposure and no matter how many experts testified that they regarded the risk as insignificant. That conclusion would in turn justify pervasive regulation limited only by the constraint of feasibility. In light of the fact that there are literally thousands of substances used in the workplace that have been identified as carcinogens or suspect carcinogens, the Government's theory would give OSHA power to impose enormous costs that might produce little, if any, discernible benefit. . . .

If the Government was correct in arguing that neither §3(8) nor §6(b)(5) requires that the risk from a toxic substance be quantified sufficiently to enable the Secretary to characterize it as significant in an understandable way, the statute would make such a "sweeping delegation of legislative power" that it might be unconstitutional under the Court's reasoning in A.L.A. Schechter Poultry Corp. v. United States, 295 U.S. 495 and Panama Refining Co. v. Ryan, 293 U.S. 388. A construction of the statute that avoids this kind of open-ended grant should certainly be favored. . . .

D

Given the conclusion that the Act empowers the Secretary to promulgate health and safety standards only where a significant risk of harm exists, the critical issue becomes how to define and allocate the burden of proving the significance of the risk in a case such as this, where scientific knowledge is imperfect and the precise quantification of risks is therefore impossible. The Agency's position is that there is substantial evidence in the record to support its conclusion that there is no absolutely safe level for a carcinogen and that, therefore, the burden is properly on industry to prove, apparently beyond a shadow of a doubt, that there *is* a safe level for benzene exposure. The Agency argues that, because of the uncertainties in this area, any other approach would render it helpless, forcing it to wait for the leukemia deaths that it believes are likely to occur before taking any regulatory action.

We disagree. As we read the statute, the burden was on the Agency to show, on the basis of substantial evidence, that it is at least more likely than not that long-term exposure to 10 ppm of benzene presents a significant risk of material health impairment. Ordinarily, it is the proponent of a rule or order who has the burden of proof in administrative proceedings.

In this case OSHA did not even attempt to carry its burden of proof. The closest it came to making a finding that benzene presented a significant risk of harm in the workplace was its statement that the benefits to be derived from lowering the permissible exposure level from 10 to 1 ppm were "likely" to be "appreciable." The Court of Appeals held that this finding was not supported by substantial evidence. Of greater importance, even if it were supported by substantial evidence, such a finding would not be sufficient to satisfy the Agency's obligations under the Act. . . .

OSHA is not required to support its finding that a significant risk exists with anything approaching scientific certainty. Although the Agency's findings must be supported by substantial evidence, 29 U.S.C. §655(f), §6(b)(5) specifically allows the Secretary to regulate on the basis of the "best available evidence." As several Courts of Appeals have held, this provision requires a reviewing court to give OSHA some leeway where its findings must be made on the frontiers of scientific knowledge. Thus, so long as they are supported by a body of reputable scientific thought, the Agency is free to use conservative assumptions in interpreting the data with respect to carcinogens, risking error on the side of overprotection rather than underprotection. . . .

The judgment of the Court of Appeals remanding the petition for review to the Secretary for further proceedings is affirmed.

JUSTICE POWELL, concurring in part and concurring in the judgment.

I agree that §§6(b)(5) and 3(8) of the Occupational Safety and Health Act of 1970, 29 U.S.C. §§655(b)(5) and 652(8), must be read together. They require OSHA to make a threshold finding that proposed occupational health standards are reasonably necessary to provide safe workplaces. When OSHA acts to reduce existing national consensus standards, therefore, it must find that (i) currently permissible exposure levels create a significant risk of material health impairment; and (ii) a reduction of those levels would significantly reduce the hazard.

[Justice Powell argues that OSHA did find significant risk, but that substantial evidence does not support this finding.]

II

I conclude that the statute also requires the agency to determine that the economic effects of its standard bear a reasonable relationship to the expected benefits.

An occupational health standard is neither "reasonably necessary" nor "feasible," as required by statute, if it calls for expenditures wholly disproportionate to the expected health and safety benefits. . . .

Although one might wish that Congress had spoken with greater clarity, the legislative history and purposes of the statute do not support OSHA's interpretation of the Act. It is simply unreasonable to believe that Congress intended OSHA to pursue the desirable goal of risk-free workplaces to the extent that the economic viability of particular industries—or significant segments thereof—is threatened. . . .

I therefore would not lightly assume that Congress intended OSHA to require reduction of health risks found to be significant *whenever* it also finds that the affected industry can bear the costs. Perhaps more significantly, however, OSHA's interpretation of §6(b)(5) would force it to regulate in a manner inconsistent with the important health and safety purposes of the legislation we construe today. Thousands of toxic substances present risks that fairly could be characterized as "significant." Even if OSHA succeeded in selecting the gravest risks for earliest regulation, a standard-setting process that ignored economic considerations would result in a serious misallocation of resources and a lower effective level of safety than could be achieved under standards set with reference to the comparative benefits available at a lower cost. I would not attribute such an irrational intention to Congress.

I join the Court's judgment affirming the judgment of the Court of Appeals.

JUSTICE MARSHALL, with whom JUSTICE BRENNAN, JUSTICE WHITE, and JUSTICE BLACKMUN join, dissenting.

The plurality ignores the plain meaning of the Occupational Safety and Health Act of 1970 in order to bring the authority of the Secretary of Labor in line with the plurality's own views of proper regulatory policy. The unfortunate consequence is that the Federal Government's efforts to protect American workers from cancer and other crippling diseases may be substantially impaired. . . .

In this case the Secretary of Labor found, on the basis of substantial evidence, that (1) exposure to benzene creates a risk of cancer, chromosomal damage, and a variety of nonmalignant but potentially fatal blood disorders, even at the level of 1 ppm; (2) no safe level of exposure has been shown; (3) benefits in the form of saved lives would be derived from the permanent standard; (4) the number of lives that would be saved could turn out to be either substantial or relatively small; (5) under the present state of scientific knowledge, it is impossible to calculate even in a rough way the number of lives that would be saved, at least without making assumptions that would appear absurd to much of the medical community; and (6) the standard would not materially harm the financial condition of the covered industries. The Court does not set aside any of these findings. Thus, it could not be plainer that the Secretary's decision was fully in accord with his statutory mandate "most adequately [to] assur[e] . . . that no employee will suffer material impairment of health or functional capacity. . . ."

The plurality's conclusion to the contrary is based on its interpretation of 29 U.S.C. §652(8), which defines an occupational safety and health standard as one "which requires conditions . . . reasonably necessary or appropriate to provide safe or healthful employment. . . ." According to the plurality, a standard is not "reasonably necessary or appropriate" unless the Secretary is able to show that it is "at least more likely than not" that the risk he seeks to regulate is a "significant" one. Nothing in the statute's language or legislative history, however, indicates that the "reasonably necessary or appropriate" language should be given this meaning. Indeed, both demonstrate that the plurality's standard bears no connection with the acts or intentions of Congress and is based only on the plurality's solicitude for the welfare of regulated industries. And the plurality uses this standard to evaluate not the agency's decision in this case, but a strawman of its own creation.

Unlike the plurality, I do not purport to know whether the actions taken by Congress and its delegates to ensure occupational safety represent sound or unsound regulatory policy. The critical problem in cases like the ones at bar is scientific uncertainty. While science has determined that exposure to benzene at levels above 1 ppm creates a definite risk of health impairment, the magnitude of the risk cannot be quantified at the present time. The risk at issue has hardly been shown to be insignificant; indeed, future research may reveal that the risk is in fact considerable. But the existing evidence may frequently be inadequate to enable the Secretary to make the threshold finding of "significance" that the Court requires today. If so, the consequence of the plurality's approach would be to subject American workers to a continuing risk of cancer and other fatal diseases, and to render the Federal Government powerless to take protective action on their behalf. Such an approach would place the burden of medical uncertainty squarely on the shoulders of the American worker, the intended beneficiary of the Occupational Safety and Health Act. It is fortunate indeed that at least a majority of the Justices reject the view that the Secretary is prevented from taking regulatory action when the magnitude of a health risk cannot be quantified on the basis of current techniques. . . .

I

Congress enacted the Occupational Safety and Health Act as a response to what was characterized as "the grim history of our failure to heed the occupational health needs of our workers." . . .

The Act is enforced primarily through two provisions. First, a "general duty" is imposed upon employers to furnish employment and places of employment "free from recognized hazards that are causing or are likely to cause death or serious physical harm. . . ." Second, the Secretary of Labor is authorized to set "occupational safety and health standards," defined as standards requiring "conditions, or the adoption or use of one or more practices, means, methods, operations, or processes, reasonably necessary or appropriate to provide safe or healthful employment and places of employment."

The legislative history of the Act reveals Congress' particular concern for health hazards of "unprecedented complexity" that had resulted from chemicals whose toxic effects "are only now being discovered." Members of Congress made repeated references to the dangers posed by carcinogens and to the defects in our knowledge of their operation and effect. One of the primary purposes of the Act was to ensure regulation of these "insidious 'silent' killers."

This special concern led to the enactment of the first sentence of 29 U.S.C. §655(b)(5), which, as noted above, provides:

> The Secretary, in promulgating standards dealing with toxic materials or harmful physical agents under this subsection, shall set the standard which most adequately assures, to the extent feasible, on the basis of the best available evidence, that no employee will suffer material impairment of health or functional capacity even if such employee has regular exposure to the hazard dealt with by such standard for the period of his working life.

This directive is designed to implement three legislative purposes. First, Congress recognized that there may be substances that become dangerous only upon repeated or frequent exposure. The Secretary was therefore required to provide protection even from substances that would cause material impairment only upon exposure occurring throughout an employee's working life. Second, the requirement that the Secretary act on the basis of "the best available evidence" was intended to ensure that the standard-setting process would not be destroyed by the uncertainty of scientific views. Recognizing that existing knowledge may be inadequate, Congress did not require the Secretary to wait until definitive information could be obtained. Thus "it is not intended that the Secretary be paralyzed by debate surrounding diverse medical opinions." Third, Congress' special concern for the "silent killers" was felt to justify an especially strong directive to the Secretary in the standard-setting process.

The authority conferred by §655(b)(5), however, is not absolute. The subsection itself contains two primary limitations. The requirement of "material" impairment was designed to prohibit the Secretary from regulating substances that create a trivial hazard to affected employees. Moreover, all standards promulgated under the subsection must be "feasible." During the floor debates Congress expressed concern that a prior version of the bill, not clearly embodying the feasibility requirement, would require the Secretary to close down whole industries in order to eliminate risks of impairment. This standard was criticized as unrealistic. The feasibility requirement was imposed as an affirmative limit on the standard-setting power.

The remainder of §655(b)(5), applicable to all safety and health standards, requires the Secretary to base his standards "upon research, demonstrations, experiments, and such other information as may be appropriate." In setting standards, the Secretary is directed to consider "the attainment of the highest degree of health and safety protection for the employee" and also "the latest available scientific data in the field, the feasibility of the standards, and experience gained under this and other health and safety laws." . . .

II

The plurality's discussion of the record in this case is both extraordinarily arrogant and extraordinarily unfair. It is arrogant because the plurality presumes to make its own factual findings with respect to a variety of disputed issues relating to carcinogen regulation. It should not be necessary to remind the Members of this Court that they were not appointed to undertake independent review of adequately supported scientific findings made by a technically expert agency. And the plurality's discussion is unfair because its characterization of the Secretary's report bears practically no resemblance to what the Secretary actually did in this case. Contrary to the plurality's suggestion, the Secretary did not rely blindly on some Draconian carcinogen "policy." If he had, it would have been sufficient for him to have observed that benzene is a carcinogen, a proposition that respondents do not dispute. Instead, the Secretary gathered over 50 volumes of exhibits and testimony and offered a detailed and evenhanded discussion of the relationship between exposure to benzene at all recorded exposure levels and chromosomal damage, aplastic anemia, and leukemia. In that discussion he evaluated, and took seriously, respondents' evidence of a safe exposure level. . . .

The Secretary discussed the contention that a safe level of exposure to benzene had been demonstrated. From the testimony of numerous scientists, he concluded that it had not. He also found that although no dose-response curve could be plotted, the extent of the risk would decline with the exposure level. Exposure at a level of 1 ppm would therefore be less dangerous than exposure at one of 10 ppm. The Secretary found that the existing evidence justified the conclusion that he should not "wait for answers" while employees continued to be exposed to benzene at hazardous levels.

Finally, the Secretary responded to the argument that the permissible exposure level should be zero or lower than 1 ppm. Even though many industries had already achieved the 1 ppm level, he found that a lower level would not be feasible.

Costs and benefits. The Secretary offered a detailed discussion of the role that economic considerations should play in his determination. He observed that standards must be "feasible," both economically and technologically. In his view the permanent standard for benzene was feasible under both tests. The economic impact would fall primarily on the more stable industries, such as petroleum refining and petrochemical production. These industries would be able readily to absorb the costs or to pass them on to consumers. None of the 20 affected industries, involving 157,000 facilities and 629,000 exposed employees[,] would be unable to bear the required expenditures. He concluded that the compliance costs were "well within the financial capability of the covered industries." . . .

III

A

This is not a case in which the Secretary found, or respondents established, that no benefits would be derived from a permanent standard, or that the likelihood of benefits was insignificant. Nor was it shown that a quantitative estimate of benefits could be made on the basis of "the best available evidence." Instead, the Secretary concluded that benefits will result, that those benefits "may" be appreciable, but that the dose-response relationship of low levels of benzene exposure and leukemia, nonmalignant blood disorders, and chromosomal damage was impossible to determine. The question presented is whether, in these circumstances, the Act permits the Secretary to take regulatory action, or whether he must allow continued exposure until more definitive information becomes available.

As noted above, the Secretary's determinations must be upheld if supported by "substantial evidence in the record considered as a whole." This standard represents a legislative judgment that regulatory action should be subject to review more stringent than the traditional "arbitrary and capricious" standard for informal rulemaking. We have observed that the arbitrary and capricious standard itself contemplates a searching "inquiry into the facts" in order to determine "whether the decision was based on a consideration of the relevant factors and whether there has been a clear error of judgment." Careful performance of this task is especially important when Congress has imposed the comparatively more rigorous "substantial evidence" requirement. As we have emphasized, however, judicial review under the substantial evidence test is ultimately deferential. The agency's decision is entitled to the traditional presumption of validity, and the court is not authorized to substitute its judgment for that of the Secretary. If the Secretary has considered the decisional factors and acted in conformance with the statute, his ultimate decision must be given a large measure of respect.

The plurality is insensitive to three factors which, in my view, make judicial review of occupational safety and health standards under the substantial evidence test particularly difficult. First, the issues often reach a high level of technical complexity. In such circumstances the courts are required to immerse themselves in matters to which they are unaccustomed by training or experience. Second, the factual issues with which the Secretary must deal are frequently not subject to any definitive resolution. Often "the factual finger points, it does not conclude." Causal connections and theoretical extrapolations may be uncertain. Third, when the question involves determination of the acceptable level of risk, the ultimate decision must necessarily be based on considerations of policy as well as empirically verifiable facts. Factual determinations can at most define the risk in some statistical way; the judgment whether that risk is tolerable cannot be based solely on a resolution of the facts.

The decision to take action in conditions of uncertainty bears little resemblance to the sort of empirically verifiable factual conclusions to which the substantial evidence test is normally applied. Such decisions were not intended to be unreviewable; they too must be scrutinized to ensure that the Secretary has acted reasonably and within the boundaries set by Congress. But a reviewing court must be mindful of the limited nature of its role. It must recognize that the ultimate decision cannot be based solely on determinations of fact, and that those factual conclusions that have been reached are ones which the courts are ill-equipped to resolve on their own.

Under this standard of review, the decision to reduce the permissible exposure level to 1 ppm was well within the Secretary's authority. The Court of Appeals upheld the Secretary's conclusions that benzene causes leukemia, blood disorders, and chromosomal damage even at low levels, that an exposure level of 10 ppm is more dangerous than one of 1 ppm, and that benefits will result from the proposed standard. It did not set aside his finding that the number of lives that would be saved was not subject to quantification. Nor did it question his conclusion that the reduction was "feasible."

In these circumstances, the Secretary's decision was reasonable and in full conformance with the statutory language requiring that he "set the standard which most adequately assures, to the extent feasible, on the basis of the best available evidence, that no employee will suffer material impairment of health or functional capacity even if such employee has regular exposure to the hazard dealt with by such standard for the period of his working life." 29 U.S.C. §655(b)(5). On this record, the Secretary could conclude that regular exposure above the 1 ppm level would pose a definite risk resulting in material impairment to some indeterminate but possibly substantial number of employees. Studies revealed hundreds of deaths attributable to benzene exposure. Expert after expert testified that no safe level of exposure had been shown and that the extent of the risk declined with the exposure level. There was some direct evidence of incidence of leukemia, nonmalignant blood disorders, and chromosomal damage at exposure levels of 10 ppm and below. Moreover, numerous experts testified that existing evidence required an inference that an exposure level above 1 ppm was hazardous. We have stated that "well-reasoned expert testimony—based on what is known and uncontradicted by empirical evidence—may in and of itself be 'substantial evidence' when first-hand evidence on the question is unavailable." Nothing in the Act purports to prevent the Secretary from acting when definitive information as to the quantity of a standard's benefits is unavailable. Where, as here, the deficiency in knowledge relates to the extent of the benefits rather than their existence, I see no reason to hold that the Secretary has exceeded his statutory authority. . . .

In passing the Occupational Safety and Health Act of 1970, Congress was aware that it was authorizing the Secretary to regulate in areas of scientific uncertainty. But it intended to require stringent regulation even when definitive information was unavailable. In reducing the permissible level of exposure to benzene, the Secretary applied proper legal standards. His determinations are supported by substantial evidence. The Secretary's decision was one, then, which the governing legislation authorized him to make.

IV

In recent years there has been increasing recognition that the products of technological development may have harmful effects whose incidence and severity cannot be predicted with certainty. The responsibility to regulate such products has fallen to administrative agencies. Their task is not an enviable one. Frequently no clear causal link can be established between the regulated substance and the harm to be averted. Risks of harm are often uncertain, but inaction has considerable costs of its own. The agency must decide whether to take regulatory action against possibly substantial risks or to wait until more definitive information becomes available—a judgment which by its very nature cannot be based solely on determinations of fact.

Those delegations, in turn, have been made on the understanding that judicial review would be available to ensure that the agency's determinations are supported by substantial evidence and that its actions do not exceed the limits set by Congress. In the Occupational Safety and Health Act, Congress expressed confidence that the courts would carry out this important responsibility. But in these cases the plurality has far exceeded its authority. The plurality's "threshold finding" requirement is nowhere to be found in the Act and is antithetical to its basic purposes. "The fundamental policy questions appropriately resolved in Congress . . . are *not* subject to re-examination in the federal courts under the guise of judicial review of agency action." Surely this is no less true of the decision to ensure safety for the American worker than the decision to proceed with nuclear power.

Because the approach taken by the plurality is so plainly irreconcilable with the Court's proper institutional role, I am certain that it will not stand the test of time. In all likelihood, today's decision will come to be regarded as an extreme reaction to a regulatory scheme that, as the Members of the plurality perceived it, imposed an unduly harsh burden on regulated industries. But as the Constitution "does not enact Mr. Herbert Spencer's Social Statics," Lochner v. New York, 198 U.S. 45, 75 (1905) (Holmes, J., dissenting), so the responsibility to scrutinize federal administrative action does not authorize this Court to strike its own balance between the costs and benefits of occupational safety standards. I am confident that the approach taken by the plurality today, like that in *Lochner* itself, will eventually be abandoned, and that the representative branches of government will once again be allowed to determine the level of safety and health protection to be accorded to the American worker.

NOTES AND QUESTIONS ON *BENZENE*

1. *Holding.* Does the case resolve the question decided in the Court of Appeals, whether OSHA must find a reasonable relationship between costs and benefits? Is there a majority opinion? Does Justice Stevens' opinion require effects-based standards?

2. *Basis for ruling.* What section of the statute does the plurality opinion rely upon? What parts of the statute do the dissenters rely upon? Does the section relied upon by the plurality justify the requirement to find a significant risk before regulating?

3. *Safety and risk.* Does safe mean "risk free"? If not, what does it mean?

4. *Quantification.* Must the agency quantify the risk in order to meet the burden of proof imposed by the plurality opinion?

OSHA justified setting the benzene standard at the lowest feasible level by stating that "there is no safe level of exposure . . . and that it is impossible to precisely quantify the anticipated benefits." This approach reflected a generic cancer policy being advocated in the federal government as a method of avoiding revisiting similar cancer scientific policy issues in each chemical-specific rule making.

The Court claimed that a requirement to demonstrate significant risk will not stymie regulation of carcinogens for the following reasons:

First, the requirement that a "significant" risk be identified is not a mathematical straitjacket. It is the Agency's responsibility to determine, in the first instance, what it considers to be a "significant" risk. Some risks are plainly acceptable and others are plainly unacceptable. If, for example, the odds are one in a billion that a person will die from cancer by taking a drink of chlorinated water, the risk clearly could not be considered significant. On the other hand, if the odds are one in a thousand that regular inhalation of gasoline vapors that are 2% benzene will be fatal, a reasonable person might well consider the risk significant and take appropriate steps to decrease or eliminate it. Although the Agency has no duty to calculate the exact probability of harm, it does have an obligation to find that a significant risk is present before it can characterize a place of employment as "unsafe."

If the agency is not able to quantify the risks, are these suggestions helpful? Can OSHA justify a finding of significant risk without quantification? If not, can it adequately protect workers' health?

5. *Agency response.* Suppose that you are counsel for OSHA. The head of OSHA and her staff remain convinced that the existing 10 ppm standard does not adequately protect workers and would like to promulgate a stricter standard. How would you recommend that the agency justify this standard?

6. *Aftermath.* Although the *Benzene* case produced no majority opinion, it had a profound impact upon agency practice. It led federal regulatory agencies to abandon formal generic cancer policy, articulating general presumptions to apply in cases of uncertainty in favor of case-by-case quantitative risk assessment. Thomas O. McGarity, *The Story of the Benzene Case: Judicially Imposed Regulatory Reform Through Risk Assessment, in* ENVIRONMENTAL LAW STORIES 165-68 (Richard J. Lazarus & Oliver A. Houck eds., 2005).

Nevertheless, as a science policy matter, the federal agencies, with support from the Scientific Advisory Board, have continued to assume, as OSHA had in the "Benzene" case, that absent contrary evidence for a particular carcinogen, no safe threshold exists for carcinogens. Industry and the conservative think tanks it funds have attacked this presumption for many years.

5

Technology-Based Standard Setting

Many statutory provisions require agencies to set standards that available (or potentially available) technologies are capable of achieving. Typically, agencies establish these standards by asking some variation of the following question: What level of emission reductions can the best technology for this kind of pollution from this kind of facility allow a polluter to achieve? Answering this sort of question can prove deceptively difficult.

The Clean Water Act relies heavily upon this approach in its national pollutant discharge elimination standards (NPDES) program for point sources (pollutants discharged through some sort of discrete conveyance). *See, e.g.*, 33 U.S.C. §§1311, 1362(11), (14). The Clean Air Act relies heavily upon technology-based standards as well. *See, e.g.*, 42 U.S.C. §§7411, 7412(d). Many technology-based provisions require the maximum feasible reductions of pollution. *See, e.g.*, 42 U.S.C. §7412(d); 33 U.S.C. §1316(a)(1). But others are less demanding, for example, by requiring only "reasonably available" means of pollution reduction. *See, e.g.*, 42 U.S.C. §7502(c)(1).

This chapter will explore the major concepts and problems associated with technology-based standards, using a few examples. These concepts will help you understand any technology-based standard setting provision and will enable you to address any problem under such a provision, even one you have not encountered before.

A. FEASIBILITY

The *Benzene* case might lead one to expect that the technology-based approach to standard setting plays no role in setting toxics standards under the OSH Act. The *Cotton Dust* case, decided one year after *Benzene*, addresses the question of how OSHA should determine the stringency of toxics standards under that statute.

American Textile Manufacturers Institute, Inc. v. Donovan [Cotton Dust Case]
452 U.S. 490 (1981)

BRENNAN, J.

Congress enacted the Occupational Safety and Health Act of 1970 (Act) "to assure so far as possible every working man and woman in the Nation safe and healthful working conditions." . . . 29 U.S.C. §651(b). The Act authorizes the Secretary of Labor to establish, after notice and opportunity to comment, mandatory nationwide standards governing health and safety in the workplace. 29 U.S.C. §§655(a), (b). In 1978, the Secretary, acting through the Occupational Safety and Health Administration (OSHA), promulgated a standard limiting occupational exposure to cotton dust, an airborne particle byproduct of the preparation and manufacture of cotton products, exposure to which induces a "constellation of respiratory effects" known as "byssinosis." This disease was one of the expressly recognized health hazards that led to passage of the Act. . . .

Byssinosis, known in its more severe manifestations as "brown lung" disease, is a serious and potentially disabling respiratory disease primarily caused by the inhalation of cotton dust. . . .

The Cotton Dust Standard promulgated by OSHA establishes mandatory [permissible exposure limits] PELs over an 8-hour period of 200 [micrograms per cubic meter of air] $\mu g/m^3$ for yarn manufacturing, 750 $\mu g/m^3$ for slashing and weaving operations, and 500 $\mu g/m^3$ for all other processes in the cotton industry. These levels represent a relaxation of the proposed PEL of 200 $\mu g/m^3$ for all segments of the cotton industry. . . .

In promulgating the Cotton Dust Standard, OSHA interpreted the Act to require adoption of the most stringent standard to protect against material health impairment, bounded only by technological and economic feasibility. . . .

The Court of Appeals upheld the Standard in all major respects. The court held that "Congress itself struck the balance between costs and benefits in the mandate to the agency" under §6(b)(5) of the Act, 29 U.S.C. §655(b)(5), and that OSHA is powerless to circumvent that judgment by adopting less than the most protective feasible standard. Finally, the court held that the agency's determination of technological and economic feasibility was supported by substantial evidence in the record as a whole.

We affirm. . . .

II

The principal question presented in these cases is whether the Occupational Safety and Health Act requires the Secretary, in promulgating a standard pursuant to §6(b)(5) of the Act, 29 U.S.C. §655(b)(5), to determine that the costs of the standard bear a reasonable relationship to its benefits. Relying on §§6(b)(5) and 3(8) of the Act, 29 U.S.C. §§655(b)(5) and 652(8), petitioners urge not only that OSHA must show that a standard addresses a significant risk of material health impairment, see Industrial Union Dept. v. American Petroleum Institute, 448 U.S., at 639 (plurality opinion), but also that OSHA must demonstrate that the reduction in risk of material health impairment is significant in light of the costs of attaining that reduction. Respondents on the other hand contend that the Act requires OSHA to promulgate standards that eliminate or reduce such risks "to the extent such protection is technologically and economically feasible." To resolve this debate, we must turn to the language, structure, and legislative history of the Act.

A

The starting point of our analysis is the language of the statute itself. Section 6(b)(5) of the Act, 29 U.S.C. §655(b)(5) (emphasis added), provides:

> The Secretary, in promulgating standards dealing with toxic materials or harmful physical agents under this subsection, shall set the standard which most adequately assures, *to the extent feasible*, on the basis of the best available evidence, that no employee will suffer material impairment of health or functional capacity even if such employee has regular exposure to the hazard dealt with by such standard for the period of his working life.

Although their interpretations differ, all parties agree that the phrase "to the extent feasible" contains the critical language in §6(b)(5) for purposes of these cases. The plain meaning of the word "feasible" supports respondents' interpretation of the statute. According to Webster's Third New International Dictionary of the English Language 831 (1976), "feasible" means "capable of being done, executed, or effected." Thus, §6(b)(5) directs the Secretary to issue the standard that "most adequately assures . . . that no employee will suffer material impairment of health," limited only by the extent to which this is "capable of being done." In effect then, as the Court of Appeals held, Congress itself defined the basic relationship between costs and benefits, by placing the "benefit" of worker health above all other considerations save those making attainment of this "benefit" unachievable. Any standard based on a balancing of costs and benefits by the Secretary that strikes a different balance than that struck by Congress would be inconsistent with the command set forth in §6(b)(5). Thus, cost-benefit analysis by OSHA is not required by the statute because feasibility analysis is. *See* Industrial Union Dept. v. American Petroleum Institute, 448 U.S., at 718-719 (Marshall, J., dissenting). When Congress has intended that an agency engage in cost-benefit analysis, it has clearly indicated such intent on the face of the statute. One early example is the Flood Control Act of 1936: "[T]he Federal Government should improve or participate in the improvement of navigable waters or their tributaries, including watersheds thereof, for flood-control purposes *if the benefits to whomsoever they may accrue are in excess of the estimated costs. . . .*"

B

Even though the plain language of §6(b)(5) supports this construction, we must still decide whether §3(8), the general definition of an occupational safety and health standard, either alone or in tandem with §6(b)(5), incorporates a cost-benefit requirement for standards dealing with toxic materials or harmful physical agents. Section 3(8) of the Act, 29 U.S.C. §652(8) (emphasis added), provides:

The term "occupational safety and health standard" means a standard which requires conditions, or the adoption or use of one or more practices, means, methods, operations, or processes, *reasonably necessary or appropriate* to provide safe or healthful employment and places of employment.

Taken alone, the phrase "reasonably necessary or appropriate" might be construed to contemplate some balancing of the costs and benefits of a standard. Petitioners urge that, so construed, §3(8) engrafts a cost-benefit analysis requirement on the issuance of §6(b)(5) standards, even if §6(b)(5) itself does not authorize such analysis. We need not decide whether §3(8), standing alone, would contemplate some form of cost-benefit analysis. For even if it does, Congress specifically chose in §6(b)(5) to impose separate and additional requirements for issuance of a subcategory of occupational safety and health standards dealing with toxic materials and harmful physical agents: it required that those standards be issued to prevent material impairment of health *to the extent feasible*. Congress could reasonably have concluded that health standards should be subject to different criteria than *safety* standards because of the special problems presented in regulating them. *See* Industrial Union Dept. v. American Petroleum Institute, 448 U.S., at 649, n.54 (plurality opinion).

Agreement with petitioners' argument that §3(8) imposes an additional and overriding requirement of cost-benefit analysis on the issuance of §6(b)(5) standards would eviscerate the "to the extent feasible" requirement. Standards would inevitably be set at the level indicated by cost-benefit analysis, and not at the level specified by §6(b)(5). For example, if cost-benefit analysis indicated a protective standard of 1,000 µg/m³ PEL, while feasibility analysis indicated a 500 µg/m³ PEL, the agency would be forced by the cost-benefit requirement to choose the less stringent point. We cannot believe that Congress intended the general terms of §3(8) to countermand the specific feasibility requirement of §6(b)(5).

Adoption of petitioners' interpretation would effectively write §6(b)(5) out of the Act. We decline to render Congress' decision to include a feasibility requirement nugatory, thereby offending the well-settled rule that all parts of a statute, if possible, are to be given effect. Congress did not contemplate any further balancing by the agency for toxic material and harmful physical agents standards, and we should not "'impute to Congress a purpose to paralyze with one hand what it sought to promote with the other.'"

C

The legislative history of the Act, while concededly not crystal clear, provides general support for respondents' interpretation of the Act. The congressional Reports and debates certainly confirm that Congress meant "feasible" and nothing else in using that term. Congress was concerned that the Act might be thought to require achievement of absolute safety, an impossible standard, and therefore insisted that health and safety goals be capable of economic and technological accomplishment. Perhaps most telling is the absence of any indication whatsoever that Congress intended OSHA to conduct its own cost-benefit analysis before promulgating a toxic material or harmful physical agent standard. The legislative history demonstrates conclusively that Congress was fully aware that the Act would impose real and substantial costs of compliance on industry, and believed that such costs were part of the cost of doing business. . . .

Not only does the legislative history confirm that Congress meant "feasible" rather than "cost-benefit" when it used the former term, but it also shows that Congress understood that the Act would create substantial costs for employers, yet intended to impose such costs when necessary to create a safe and healthful working environment. Congress viewed the costs of health and safety as a cost of doing business. . . .

Accordingly, the judgment of the Court of Appeals is affirmed. It is so ordered.

NOTES AND QUESTIONS ON THE *COTTON DUST CASE*

1. *Consistency with* Benzene. Is the *Cotton Dust* case (as the *Donovan* case above is often called) consistent with *Benzene*? How does the *Cotton Dust* Court seek to reconcile these cases?

2. *Criterion.* What criterion determines the stringency of standards under *Cotton Dust*? Does the *Cotton Dust* Court embrace or reject cost-benefit analysis as the method for determining the stringency of standards under the OSH Act? Does it reject consideration of cost altogether?

3. *Congressional balance.* The Court explains that Congress itself determined the balance to be struck between costs and benefits. What does it mean by that? Should Congress perform that role, or should administrative agencies?

Notice that Congress has apparently agreed not to fully protect the health of workers, if doing so is not feasible. This suggests a general point about technology-based standards. If one uses technological capability to determine the amount of cleanup to demand, that level might inadequately protect health or the environment. Conversely, it is possible that the level of cleanup demanded may be more than is needed to fully protect health and the environment. While technology-based standards by themselves have no clear relationship to health or environmentally protective goals, they often serve as mechanisms to advance those goals. For example, the Clean Air Act requires states with unhealthy air quality to impose "reasonably available control" technology on major sources of pollution as a means toward the end of meeting the health-based NAAQS. *See* 42 U.S.C. §7502(c)(1).

The *Cotton Dust* case leads to some questions not only about the OSH Act, but also about technology-based standard setting in general. How should an administrative agency determine what is feasible, *i.e.*, what a regulated industry is "capable of doing"? The courts, in interpreting relevant statutory provisions, have generally answered this question (both before and after the *Cotton Dust* decision) by requiring that agency standards meet tests of both technical and economic feasibility.

1. Technical Feasibility

a. Demonstrated Technology

The case below is fairly typical of cases raising concerns about technical feasibility. EPA set a new source performance standard (NSPS) for air pollution emissions from lime kilns. NSPS is a type of technology-based standard that EPA writes for major new stationary sources under the Clean Air Act, based on its assessment of technological capability. The owners of these facilities challenged the standards in court, arguing that the technology on which EPA based its standards is not capable of meeting the performance standard EPA promulgated. Therefore, they argue, compliance with the standard is not feasible. Owners of regulated facilities have made similar arguments with varying degrees of success in dozens of reported cases. *See, e.g.*, National Petrochemical & Refiners Ass'n v. EPA, 287 F.3d 1130, 1151 (D.C. Cir. 2002) (upholding limits on diesel engine exhaust emissions); Husqvarna AB v. EPA, 254 F.3d 195, 203 (D.C. Cir. 2001) (upholding air pollution standards for new handheld non-road engines); AFL-CIO v. OSHA, 965 F.2d 962, 981 (11th Cir. 1992) (rejecting agency conclusion that "existing engineering controls are available" to meet its standards for air contaminants, because of lack of information about how specific industries will meet the standards); FMC Corp. v. Train, 539 F.2d 973, 982 (4th Cir. 1976) (rejecting reliance upon single plant's achievement and prediction that the regulated parties could apply their expertise to meet limits, when record does not identify plant or provide details); Tanners' Council of America v. Train, 540 F.2d 1188, 1193 (4th Cir. 1976) (rejecting regulation of tannery effluent).

National Lime Ass'n v. Environmental Protection Agency

627 F.2d 416 (D.C. Cir. 1980)

WALD, CIRCUIT JUDGE.

The National Lime Ass'n (NLA), representing ninety percent of this country's commercial producers of lime and lime hydrate (the industry), challenges the new source performance standards (NSPS) for lime manufacturing plants issued by the Environmental Protection Agency (EPA, Administrator or Agency) under §111 of the Clean Air Act (the Act). The standards limit the mass of particulate that may be emitted in the exhaust gas from all lime-hydrating and from certain lime-manufacturing facilities and limit the permitted visibility of exhaust gas emissions from some facilities manufacturing lime. We find inadequate support in the administrative record for the standards promulgated and therefore remand to the Administrator.

* * *

II. PROCEDURAL HISTORY

Section 111 of the Clean Air Act . . . authorizes the Administrator to limit the air pollutants that can lawfully be emitted from newly constructed[22] or modified[23] plants. This the Administrator can do by promulgating new source performance standards requiring new or modified plants to meet standards which can be met through application of the best system of emission reduction (considering costs) which has been "adequately demonstrated." The purpose is to assure that new or modified plants will not create significant new air pollution problems. . . .

III. PREVIOUS REVIEW UNDER SECTION 111

As amended in 1977, section 111 of the Clean Air Act requires the Administrator to prescribe standards of performance for new statutory sources that reflect the degree of emission limitation and the percentage reduction achievable through the application of the best technological system of continuous emission reduction which (taking into consideration the cost of achieving such emission reduction, any nonair quality health and environmental impact and energy requirements), the Administrator determines has been adequately demonstrated. . . . 42 U.S.C. §7411(a).

[Our] decisions have established a rigorous standard of review under section 111. . . . [W]hile we remain diffident in approaching problems of this technical complexity, . . . the necessity to review agency decisions, if it is to be more than a meaningless exercise, requires enough steeping in technical matters to determine whether the agency "has exercised a reasoned discretion." . . . We cannot substitute our judgment for that of the agency, but it is our duty to consider whether "the decision was based on a consideration of the relevant factors and whether there has been a clear error of judgment." Ultimately, we believe, that the cause of a clean environment is best served by reasoned decision-making.

Section 111 requires that the emissions control system considered able to meet the standard be "adequately demonstrated" and the standard itself "achievable." 42 U.S.C. §7411(a).

The issue presented here is primarily one of the adequacy of EPA's test data on which the industry standards are based. NLA disagrees with EPA's conclusion that the standards are achievable under the "best technological system of continuous emission reduction which . . . the Administrator determines has been adequately demonstrated." Specifically, NLA claims that the test data underlying the development of the standards do not support the Administrator's conclusion that the promulgated emission levels are in fact "achievable" on a continuous basis. Promulgation of standards based upon inadequate proof of achievability would

---

22. A "new source" is defined by the Act to mean: any stationary source, the construction or modification of which is commenced after the publication of regulations (or, if earlier, proposed regulations) prescribing a standard of performance under this section which will be applicable to such source.

23. "Modification" of a source is defined to mean: any physical change in, or change in the method of operation of, a stationary source which increases the amount of any air pollutant emitted by such source or which results in the emission of any air pollutant not previously emitted. Conversion of a kiln from natural gas or fuel oil to coal firing may constitute a "modification," triggering application of the NSPS here promulgated.

defy the Administrative Procedure Act's mandate against action that is "arbitrary, capricious, an abuse of discretion, or otherwise not in accordance with law."

IV.   ASSESSMENT OF THE OBJECTIONS RAISED BY THE INDUSTRY

Our review has led us to conclude that the record does not support the "achievability" of the promulgated standards for the industry as a whole. This conclusion is a cumulative one, resulting from our assessment of the many points raised by the industry at the administrative level and in this court; no one point made is so cogent that remand would necessarily have followed on that basis alone. In the analysis that follows, common threads will be discerned in our discussions of individual points. Chief among these common threads is a concern that the Agency consider the representativeness for the industry as a whole of the tested plants on which it relies, at least where its central argument is that the standard is achievable because it has been achieved (at the tested plants). The Agency's failure to consider the representativeness along various relevant parameters of the data relied upon is the primary reason for our remand. The locus of administrative burdens of going forward or of persuasion may shift in the course of a rulemaking proceeding, but we think an initial burden of promulgating and explaining a non-arbitrary, non-capricious rule rests with the Agency and we think that by failing to explain how the standard proposed is achievable under the range of relevant conditions which may affect the emissions to be regulated, the Agency has not satisfied this initial burden.

Bearing this initial burden will involve first, identifying and verifying as relevant or irrelevant specific variable conditions that may contribute substantially to the amount of emissions, or otherwise affect the efficiency of the emissions control systems considered. And second, where test results are relied upon, it should involve the selection or use of test results in a manner which provides some assurance of the achievability of the standard for the industry as a whole, given the range of variable factors found relevant to the standards' achievability.

EPA itself acknowledged in this case that "standards of performance . . . must . . . meet these conditions for all variations of operating conditions being considered anywhere in the country." As set forth in the standards support statement, EPA's guidelines require data to be assessed with consideration of the "representativeness" of the source tested, including the "feedstock, operation, size and age" of the source. Furthermore, the record strongly suggests other factors that may affect the particulate emissions from lime plants. Yet at no point does EPA evaluate the relevance or irrelevance of such factors to regulable emissions; nor does the Agency explain how such factors might have been taken into account in choosing test plant sites or in analyzing the data from the sites it chose.

The critical question presented here is whether the regulated industry, through its trade association, should have borne the entire burden of demonstrating the unreliability for the industry as a whole of the conclusions drawn by the EPA. In this connection we are candidly troubled by the industry's failure to respond, at a crucial juncture in the standards development process, to the Agency's invitation to submit data supporting a fundamental industry objection to the achievability of the standard. We would have expected the industry to have been eager to supply supporting data for its position, assuming the "cost" of obtaining such data were less than the "cost" of compliance with a standard that was argued to be unachievable on any reliably repetitive basis for the industry as a whole. We cannot help but wonder if the industry's failure to supply such data means that the data available or obtained would not be favorable to the industry's position. Nevertheless we remand because we think, on balance, EPA must affirmatively show that its standard reflects consideration of the range of relevant variables that may affect emissions in different plants.

The showing we require does not mean that EPA must perform repeated tests on every plant operating within its regulatory jurisdiction. It does, however, mean that due consideration must be given to the possible impact on emissions of recognized variations in operations and some rationale offered for the achievability of the promulgated standard given the tests conducted and the relevant variables identified. To facilitate public comment, we think this rationale should have appeared in the Agency's initial standards support statement.

We must remand to the Agency for a more adequate explanation or, if necessary, for supplementary data to justify the standard in terms of the "representativeness" of the sources tested. The specific doubts generated by our review of the record in light of the lime industry's attack on the standard are more fully explained below.

A. *The Particulate Emission Standards*

1. **Rotary Kilns**

EPA tested emissions at six plants before it proposed its mass emission standard for rotary lime kilns. These six plants were selected for testing on the basis of visits to thirty-nine plants, during which the visibility of emissions was observed and information obtained on the emissions control systems employed. The thirty-nine plants were themselves selected because they had been identified as effectively controlled after a review of the literature and contact with industry representatives. The results of the tests of one plant (Plant A) which could not meet the proposed standard were excluded from consideration because the plant was thought not to represent best technology. From what we can gather from the record, three plants were able to meet the standard consistently.

Our doubts about the representativeness of the data relied upon are grouped under [these] subheadings. Variations in Quantity of Particulate Generated in the Kiln [and] Variations in Controllability of Particulate Generated. . . . Under the subheading Variations in Quantity of Particulate Generated in the Kiln, we discuss the possible impact on the standard's achievability of composite dust levels generated by the tested plants and two factors (feedstock variations and gas velocity) that may contribute to composite dust levels. Under the subheading Variations in Controllability of Particulate Generated, we discuss two factors apart from sheer quantity of dust that may affect emissions control: coal usage and particulate size. . . .

a.   Variations in Quantity of Particulate Generated in the Kiln

That the quantity of dust produced in the kilns would affect the controllability of emissions and the achievability of the standards does not seem an unreasonable expectation. The Agency, however, appears to have taken conflicting positions on the reasonableness of this expectation and perhaps as a consequence has devoted inadequate attention to several variables which EPA's own documents and the industry suggest may affect the volume of dust produced in different kilns.

(1)   Feedstock Variations

For example, the record suggests that the size and chemical composition of the limestone feedstock used will affect the amount of dust produced.

This suggests to us that some analysis should have been performed or tests conducted which took into account significant variations in limestone feed, or other variables relevant to dust generation.

For all we know, the six plants tested could be using kinds and sizes of feed which are representative of only a small segment of the industry spectrum. If that were true the plants may not be "representative" and the regulation might not be "achievable" by the industry as a whole. . . .

(2)   Gas Velocity and Operation Levels

According to the [consultant's] [r]eport [found in the record], dust generation is in part a function of gas velocity in the kiln. Gas velocity appears in turn to depend on several factors, including the percentage of capacity at which the kiln is operating. Thus the level of capacity at which the plant was operating at the time of sampling and the gas velocity would appear relevant to the representativeness of the test data.

Data on the production level and air flow rate (velocity) at the tested plants were included in the support document filed in this case. . . .

Having stated that much, however, the Agency did not explain how the range of test results fully takes account of any significant differences in operating conditions in the industry. The support document is totally devoid of analysis of the relevance or irrelevance of operating level or gas velocity to the achievability of the standard, notwithstanding assertions in the EPA's own contracted-for report that gas velocity bears upon dust generation rates.

(3)   Dust Levels at the Tested Plants . . .

As laypersons it seems entirely logical to us to suppose that dust generation levels would directly affect emissions controllability, viz., the higher the dust generation, the more difficult the achievability of the standard by the technological control device. But the exact relationship between volume of dust generated and the efficiency of the emissions control systems is never clearly stated or explained by the Agency. Instead, the Agency sends us several mixed signals. . . .

Our examination of the record thus yields a conflict: while in one breath EPA appears to acknowledge the relevance of dust generation levels to the proposed standard, in another breath the relevance is denied. In our view, the conflict is not adequately explained, nor is the industry-wide achievability of the standard adequately justified, in light of the acknowledged possibility that heavy dusting creates a more difficult control problem. From what appears in the record, both variations in dust volume produced and its contributing factors received inadequate attention from the Agency in the development and explanation of this standard.

b.   Variations in Controllability of Particulate Generated

The record points to other variables which were also given short shrift in the stated rationale: the use of coal to fuel the kiln (as it relates to controllability of emissions); and variations in size of emitted particles. The record strongly supports the relevance of coal usage to the efficiency of at least the [electrostatic precipitator] (ESP) . . . control method and it also suggests a relationship between particle size and the efficiency of both the ESP and the baghouse control method. Nothing indicates how if at all variations in these factors were considered in proposing an "achievable" standard. . . .

(2)   Particle Size

Although there is (a) considerable evidence in the record that the efficiency of available control technology varies with emitted particle size and (b) that lime dust particle size varies regionally (probably due to feedstock variation), the EPA (c) undertook no analysis of the impact of particle size distribution on the achievability of its standard. Each of these points is discussed under separate subheadings below.

(a)   The relationship of particle size to efficiency of control methods

That particle size affects the efficiency of at least two of the three "best" technological control systems seems clear. . . .

(b)   Regional variations in particle size

Two early studies on which EPA relies in support of its standard strongly suggest regional or temporal variations in lime particle size. . . . When particle size was identified as a potentially important variable, both the Agency and the industry failed to pick up the ball.

(c)   EPA's lack of analysis

As far as we can tell the Agency gathered no data on particle size distribution at the tested plants or in the industry generally, either before or after the industry meeting which focused on this factor. Whether the EPA took particle size into account in developing and promulgating its proposed standard cannot be determined from this record.

Understandably, the Agency's main defense in court centers on the industry's total failure to respond positively to EPA's suggestion that the industry either suggest additional test sites or submit data on the basis of which EPA might reconsider or subcategorize the standard to conform to local variations. EPA's point is a sympathetic one, but not, we think, dispositive. EPA has a statutory duty to promulgate achievable standards. This requires that they approach that task in a systematic manner that identifies relevant variables and ensures that they are taken account of in analyzing test data. EPA's own support document recognizes particle size as a variable but enigmatically does not discuss it at any length or explain its importance in emissions control. That the industry did not assist the Agency in any meaningful way by data or even by suggestions for additional testing is certainly discouraging. But we do not think that inaction lamentable though it may be lifted the burden from the Agency of pursuing what appears to be a relevant variable or at the least discussing in its document why it was not considered important.

In this respect, we believe that the industry's comments, concerning particle size distribution, when viewed in light of the material contained in EPA's own support statement and in light of the background documents on which it relied, met a "threshold requirement of materiality," mandating an Agency response which was not forthcoming here.

B. The Opacity Standard . . .

Both in this court and at the administrative level EPA emphasizes the overwhelming extent to which the plants tested were able to meet the ten percent opacity standard. But without knowing the representativeness of the plants tested or of test conditions, we cannot say that the standard is neither arbitrary nor capricious. Certainly the fact that virtually all plants tested were able to meet the standard is an important consideration, but our doubts are sufficient, when coupled with our doubts concerning the mass emissions standard (discussed above), to remand to the Agency for amplification of the record.

V.   THE STANDARD OF REVIEW AS APPLIED

Our requirement that the EPA consider the representativeness of the test data relied upon in the development and justification of its standard does not presage any new or more stringent standard of judicial review. The rigorousness of the review in which this court has engaged in previous NSPS decisions known to some as the "hard look" standard has already been described. . . .

Both decisions reviewing the NSPS and those reviewing other administrative determinations under the Clean Air Act evince a concern that variables be accounted for, that the representativeness of test conditions be ascertained, that the validity of tests be assured and the statistical significance of results determined. Collectively, these concerns have sometimes been expressed as a need for "reasoned decision-making" and sometimes as a need for adequate "methodology." However expressed, these more substantive concerns have been coupled with a requirement that assumptions be stated, that process be revealed, that the rejection of alternate theories or abandonment of alternate courses of action be explained and that the rationale for the ultimate decision be set forth in a manner which permits the public to exercise its statutory prerogative of comment and the courts to exercise their statutory responsibility upon review. . . .

Our opinion should not suggest the necessity of "ninety-five percent certainty" in all the "facts" which enter into the Agency's decision. We would require only that the Agency provide sufficient data to demonstrate a systematic approach to problems, not that it adduce vast quantities of factual data. However, where the facts pertinent to the standard's feasibility are available and easily discoverable by conventional technical means, there is somewhat less reason for so limited a data base. Nothing in the record suggests the relevant facts are not readily accessible to the Agency; the number of plants is large, use of the control methods found by the

Agency to represent the "best systems" is widespread, and stack emission measurement techniques have been known and applied for many years.

With respect to the standard's achievability we are thus not presented with the question how much deference is owed a judgment predicated on limited evidence when additional evidence cannot be adduced or adduced in the near future. We do not depart from some of the most carefully considered and closely reasoned decisions of this court which permit an agency latitude to exercise its discretion in accordance with the remedial purposes of the controlling statute where relevant facts cannot be ascertained or are on the frontiers of scientific inquiry.

A systematic approach may not necessarily require a conclusion grounded in actual test results. We do not intend to bridle the Agency's discretion to make well-founded assumptions even where the assumption could be replaced by valid test results, but we think first, the assumption should be stated and second, where test data could have verified the assumption, a reason for not testing or relying on such data should be given.

We recognize, for example, that the finding of facts, especially through elaborate testing, is costly and the costs of additional testing may be added by the Agency to the costs of delay in issuing the proposed rule and the sum of these costs weighed against the benefit of proposing a rule without additional data.

We leave to the Agency on remand the decision whether additional Agency-conducted testing is appropriate in this case. Data may already be available to the Administrator which would support the achievability of these standards for the industry as a whole. If so, satisfaction of the concerns we have expressed in this opinion may be a fairly simple matter.

To ensure that the Agency has engaged in reasoned decision-making, we remand. We have outlined our substantive misgivings; the Agency may choose the appropriate method of response.

Remanded.

NOTES AND QUESTIONS ON *NATIONAL LIME*

1. *Burden of production.* One could imagine a court holding that EPA had met its initial burden by showing that some facilities could meet EPA's standards. Once this initial burden is met, the regulated industry must bring forth test data to show that variability in operating conditions makes achievement of the standards impossible. But the court did not do this. Should the court have put the burden upon EPA of showing in the administrative record that EPA's standards are achievable by the whole industry?

2. *Information asymmetry.* Judge Wald expresses dismay at the industry's failure to come forward with test results. A significant problem afflicting technology-based standards involves what economists call an information asymmetry. Often the regulated industry has better information about its own operations, and thus the potential for (or problems with) pollution control, than the agency. Does the *National Lime* case provide the proper incentives to overcome problems of information asymmetry?

3. *Remand.* What should EPA do on remand, assuming it does not have a sufficient budget to test all of the plants in the industry? EPA has authority under the Clean Air Act (as it has under other statutes) to order industry to monitor and report its emissions and to inspect facilities in order to facilitate standard setting. *See* 42 U.S.C. §7414(a). Would this authority suffice to develop the information needed to address the court's concern on remand?

One might think that this authority to require emissions reports would overcome some information asymmetries. The Paperwork Reduction Act, which authorizes the Office of Management and Budget (OMB) to review the burdens involved in government paperwork requirements, may provide a disincentive to liberal exercise of this authority. *See* UNITED STATES GENERAL ACCOUNTING OFFICE, ENVIRONMENTAL REGULATION: DIFFERENCES REMAIN BETWEEN EPA AND OMB OVER PAPERWORK REQUIREMENTS (RCED-94-254) (1994) (describing the difficulties EPA has experienced in seeking and obtaining approval of reporting requests). Also, polluters may require significant amounts of time to provide useful information, which can delay standard setting unless begun well in advance of a rule-making effort. Information procured early in the rule-making process, on the other hand, can become outdated before a rule is promulgated. Also, in using this information, EPA may not disclose trade secrets. *See* 42 U.S.C. §7414(c). This can limit opportunities for the public to use facility-provided information to influence the outcome of rules and of the agencies to rely upon the information to justify a rule publicly.

In *National Lime*, EPA itself took the position that it must show that the industry could meet its standard under the operating conditions prevailing in the industry. Suppose that EPA instead took the position that the owners of the plants could control all of the operational variables that might make meeting promulgated emission standards problematic. This position might be tenable with respect to some of the variables at issue in *National Lime*. For example, owners might have a choice of feedstock materials, a variable that industry and EPA agreed might affect emissions. And the agency could take the position that pollution control considerations should influence industry feedstock selection. Does CAA section 111 authorize EPA to assume that companies can adjust their feedstock materials or other operating conditions, even if the test data do not adequately account for the variables that might influence emissions?

A Note on the Follow-the-Leader Principle, the Problem of Categorization, and Variances

In the 1990 Amendments to the Clean Air Act, Congress responded to the dampening effect the *National Lime* case had on stringent standard setting when it created, for the first time, technology-based requirements for sources of hazardous air pollutants (recall that Congress used a health-based approach to these pollutants prior to 1990). *See* 42 U.S.C. §7412(d). Practitioners refer to these standards as "MACT" standards because they generally require standards reflecting the "maximum achievable control technology."

In order to relieve the agency of the burden of proving that all sources could meet a standard, Congress required EPA to set standards for existing sources that were at least as strict as the "average emission limit achieved by the best performing 12 percent of the existing sources . . ." in an industrial category or subcategory. 42 U.S.C. §7412(d)(3). With respect to new sources of hazardous air pollutants, Congress required EPA to set standards at least as stringent as that achieved by the "best controlled similar source." Practitioners refer to these requirements as the "MACT floor" provisions, because the statute authorizes EPA to set standards even stricter than those achieved by the best performing sources, but does not allow standards less strict than the best source (for new sources) or the average of the best 12 percent (for existing sources). Yet, Congress did not enact similar amendments to section 111, the section at issue in *National Lime*, which governs standard setting applying to new sources for non-hazardous pollutants. In spite of this congressional fix to the *National Lime* problem in section 112, EPA has been reluctant to impose standards for hazardous air pollutants without a high degree of confidence that all regulated plants are capable of achieving the standards with a technology the agency knows about. *See, e.g.,* Sierra Club v. EPA, 167 F.3d 658 (D.C. Cir. 1999) (remanding rule because EPA did not adequately explain its determination of the "MACT floor"); National Lime Ass'n v. EPA, 233 F.3d 625, 632 (D.C. Cir. 2000) (same, with EPA trying to defend its method as justified by the need to show that all sources can achieve the standards set under the most adverse conditions). Why do you suppose that EPA feels compelled to show that all facilities can meet its emission limits, even when there is some indication that Congress is trying to give it more latitude?

The MACT floor provides an example of congressional adoption of a "follow-the-leader" principle for determining feasibility. This principle requires that EPA set standards at least as stringent as those achieved in practice by the best-controlled similar plants. The Supreme Court recognized that Congress has intended this principle to govern best practicable control technology (BPT) standards under the Clean Water Act. *See* E.I. du Pont de Nemours v. Train, 430 U.S. 112, 131 n.21 (1977) (BPT limitations should be based upon the average of the best performers). BPT standards form part of the Clean Water Act's suite of technology-based standards, serving as a prelude to more stringent best available technology (BAT) standards. Is the follow-the-leader principle consistent with the EPA's position that it must show that all plants can meet the standard it imposed? If this principle is not followed, will the agency be forced to adopt extremely lax standards in order to make sure that the most antiquated poorly equipped plants can meet them? If so, how will pollution control methods improve over time?

Notice that the follow-the-leader principle may have some harsh consequences. It could require an implementing agency to set a standard that some facilities cannot comply with, because of the kinds of variations in operating conditions that *National Lime* discusses, which may cause some plants to close. The legislative history of several technology-based provisions, however, shows that Congress did intend to require standards sufficiently stringent to allow marginal or laggard facilities to go out of business. *See, e.g.,* Industrial Union Dep't, AFL-CIO v. Hodgson, 499 F.2d 467, 477 (D.C. Cir. 1974) (Occupational Safety and Health Act allows a laggard in protecting the health and safety of workers to go out of business). Does the desire for a level playing field justify this approach? *See* Wendy A. Wagner, *Innovations in Environmental Policies: The Triumph of Technology-Based Standards,*

2000 U. ILL. L. REV. 83, 103-04 (technology-based standards create a level playing field by treating all companies in the same class the same). Should all companies that compete with each other have to meet the same standards regardless of variations in circumstances?

The statutes contain several mechanisms to ameliorate the potential harshness of strict uniform standards for a broad category of facilities. First, they sometimes authorize agencies to set different standards for different subcategories of facilities. *See, e.g.,* American Iron & Steel Inst. v. EPA, 568 F.2d 284, 297-300 (3d Cir. 1977) (adjudicating dispute about subcategorization). For example, the agency could subcategorize an industry based on available feedstock materials (such as different kinds of coal), different manufacturing processes, or different environmental conditions (such as climate), all of which might affect pollution control feasibility. Does subcategorization undercut the follow-the-leader principle?

What policy goals should guide EPA in its use of authority to subcategorize? Should it only consider physical differences among plants, or also take differences in economic capabilities into account? There is some evidence that Congress intended that this authority be used to avoid widespread shutdowns, but not to avoid the shutdown of a few laggard facilities:

> [T]he [Clean Water] Act's supporters in both Houses acknowledged and accepted the possibility that its 1977 requirements might cause individual plants to go out of business. They self-consciously made the legislative determination that the health and safety gains that achievement of the Act's aspirations would bring to future generations will in some cases outweigh the economic dislocation it causes to the present generation.

Weyerhaeuser Co. v. Costle, 590 F.2d 1011, 1036-37 (D.C. Cir. 1978). Is that the right policy?

Another technique for ameliorating the potential harshness of imposing strict standards on a broad category of plants involves offering variances for individual plants that have difficulty in complying. If an adjustment mechanism is desired, which mechanism is better, subcategorization or variances? In EPA v. National Crushed Stone Ass'n, 449 U.S. 64, 76-77 (1980), the Supreme Court disallowed a general variance from BPT standards under the Clean Water Act based on the individual polluter's economic capabilities as inconsistent with the follow-the-leader approach. On the other hand, the Court stated that a variance might be appropriate if the polluter can show that "its situation, including its costs of compliance, is outside the range or circumstances" EPA considered when establishing the standards. *Id.* at 77.

By contrast, consider the variance criterion that section 301(c) of the Clean Water Act applies to polluters subject to BAT standards, stricter standards imposed to limit water pollution after laxer BPT standards have been met. That section allows a variance if the applicant shows that the modified requirements represent "the maximum use of technology within" the owner's "economic capability" and produces "reasonable further progress" toward the "elimination" of pollution discharges. Notice that this does allow a limited variance based on the polluter's economic capability. *See Crushed Stone,* 449 U.S. at 73. Why would Congress allow EPA to take economic capability into account in granting BAT variances, but not in granting BPT variances? Does allowing a variance for lack of economic capability undermine the level playing field ideal?

A Note on the Value of Uniformity

Congress in many instances required EPA to set uniform standards for polluters in a source category. Why not adopt individually tailored standards instead, since different facilities have different physical characteristics and different owners have different economic capabilities?

Congress clearly hoped to achieve economies of scale through uniform standard setting. Setting individual standards for each facility can prove enormously resource intensive. Setting a uniform standard for an entire industrial subcategory allows simultaneous regulation of a large number of facilities. The level playing field idea also helps explain why Congress (and sometimes industry) supports uniform standards. Of course, the provisions for subcategorization and variances raise questions about whether the standards are as uniform in practice as they appear to be in theory. We will consider some criticisms of uniformity at the end of this chapter.

b. *Technology-Forcing*

In *National Lime*, EPA claimed that existing technology that it had identified and already tested could enable lime kilns to meet the adopted standard. Section 111 requires standards reflecting the capabilities of the best emission reduction system that EPA "determines has been adequately demonstrated." 42 U.S.C. §7411(a). While an early decision interpreted this language to allow EPA to base standards on technology that has not been used but might be created in response to its standard setting, *see* Portland Cement Ass'n v. Ruckelshaus, 486 F.2d 375, 391 (D.C. Cir. 1973) (analogizing NSPS provisions to technology-forcing standards for mobile sources), EPA has generally based its NSPS standards on existing technology, *cf.* Lignite Energy Council v. EPA, 198 F.3d 930, 933 (D.C. Cir. 1999) (new source performance standards are not technology-forcing).

By contrast, the subsection of the Clean Air Act requiring EPA to regulate non-road engines (such as those found in power mowers and weed trimmers) requires EPA to set standards to "achieve the greatest degree of emission reduction achievable through the application of technology which the Administrator determines *will be* available. . . ." 42 U.S.C. §7547(a)(3). The United States Court of Appeals for the District of Columbia Circuit has held that this provision authorizes or requires technology-forcing regulation, *i.e.*, regulation that might force companies to come up with technology not yet developed or successfully employed. *See* Husqvarna AB v. EPA, 254 F.3d 195, 201 (D.C. Cir. 2001).

In general, the Supreme Court has explained that the Clean Air Act is a "technology forcing" statute. *See* Union Electric v. EPA, 427 U.S. 246, 257 (1976). The idea of technology-forcing comes from the legislative history of the Clean Air Act Amendments of 1970, which established the modern statute's basic contours. Congress feared that industry would resist standards by claiming that cleanup was impossible. Such claims might defeat efforts to establish the standards needed to produce clean air.

Senator Muskie responded to concerns that achievement of clean air might be impossible in a very interesting way. He did not simply deny the validity of the concern, by claiming that achievement of the 1970 Amendment's standards was possible. Rather, he argued that Congress' proper role is to protect public health, leaving industry to figure out how to clean up. 116 Cong. Rec. 32901-32902 (1970) (statement of Senator Muskie). If after a good faith effort to comply with the 1970 Amendments, industry could not do so, it should then come back to Congress for relief. Industry has done this many times over the years, and received exemptions and extensions of deadlines. The legislative history specifically reflects an intention to force the development of technology that would make it possible to achieve levels of cleanup that might "appear" impossible. *Id. See Union Electric*, 427 U.S. at 259.

Two features of the 1970 Amendments are most closely associated with the technology-forcing philosophy. The rejection of administrative consideration of cost in setting the health-based National Ambient Air Quality Standards (recall *Lead Industries*) implies that states must ultimately come up with sufficiently stringent emission standards to protect public health. *Union Electric*, 427 U.S. at 258-59. Congress deemed this cost-blindness appropriate in part because it believed that industry would develop the technologies needed to protect health if required to do so. Thus, health-based standards (or other effects-based standards) can force technology, because EPA sets them without considering cost or technological feasibility in establishing a standard's stringency.

Second, statutory provisions governing emissions from automobiles also reflected the technology-forcing philosophy. These provisions required industry to meet strict numerical limits that Congress wrote into the 1970 Amendments, notwithstanding auto industry claims that the standards were impossible to meet. But Congress provided an escape valve, authorizing EPA to delay compliance with these standards, which it did.

In 1970, Congress also authorized EPA to set "feasible" technology-forcing limits on its own to supplement the specific limits Congress created. These provisions are technology-based standards that require the consideration of cost and technology. But they permit the agency to rely upon technologies not yet adequately developed in justifying a standard. Similar provisions in the subsequent 1977 Amendments gave rise to the following case:

Natural Resources Defense Council v. U.S. Environmental Protection Agency
655 F.2d 318 (D.C. Cir. 1981)

Mikva, Circuit Judge.

These consolidated cases present a variety of challenges to actions of the EPA in setting standards to govern emissions of particulate matter and oxides of nitrogen from diesel vehicles. . . . General Motors Corporation (GM) and Intervenors Mercedes-Benz of North America, Inc., and Volkswagen of America, Inc., assert that . . . the standards are too strict. Finding that the agency has stated adequate reasons for its decisions . . . we uphold the challenged regulations in their entirety. . . .

B. Technological Feasibility

The EPA's choice of the 0.20 gpm [grams per mile] standard for light-duty diesels in 1985 was the result of adjusting current diesel particulate emission data by the percentage of reduction expected from certain technological improvements, most notably the trap-oxidizer. The manufacturers' attack on the standard focuses on the EPA's prediction concerning the probable pace of development of trap-oxidizer technology. Before examining the details of the agency's reasoning and the industry challenges, however, we find it useful to discuss the legal standard that governs our inquiry.

1. *The Standard of Review*

The standard of review in this case is the traditional one for judicial scrutiny of agency rulemaking: we are to set aside any action found to be "arbitrary, capricious, an abuse of discretion, or otherwise not in accordance with law." Act §307(d)(9)(A). As nonscientists, we must recall that "(o)ur 'expertise' is not in setting standards for emission control but in determining if the standards as set are the result of reasoned decisionmaking." Despite this limited role, our examination of the record must be searching, for the necessity to review agency decisions, if it is to be more than a meaningless exercise, requires enough steeping in technical matters to determine whether the agency "has exercised a reasoned discretion." . . . We cannot substitute our own judgment for that of the agency, but it is our duty to consider whether "the decision was based on a consideration of the relevant factors and whether there has been a clear error of judgment."

In the present case, GM attacks the EPA's estimation of the period of time "necessary to permit the development and application of the requisite technology" to achieve compliance with the 1985 particulate standards. The agency has determined that the technology will be available in time, and now seeks to defend its conclusion as a product of reasoned decisionmaking. Such predictions inherently involve a greater degree of uncertainty than estimations of the effectiveness of current technology. If we judge the EPA's action by the standard of certainty appropriate to current technology, the agency will be unable to set pollutant levels until the necessary technology is already available.

The legislative history of both the 1970 and the 1977 amendments demonstrates that Congress intended the agency to project future advances in pollution control capability. . . .

This court has upheld the agency's power to make such projections, while recognizing that it is "subject to the restraints of reasonableness, and does not open the door to ' "crystal ball" inquiry.' " [sic] The Clean Air Act requires the EPA to look to the future in setting standards, but the agency must also provide a reasoned explanation of its basis for believing that its projection is reliable. This includes a defense of its methodology for arriving at numerical estimates.

The EPA has generally been granted "considerable latitude in extrapolating from today's technology" when it predicts future technological developments for the purposes of the Clean Water Act. The courts have had numerous occasions to review EPA determinations that a given control technique constitutes the "best available technology economically achievable" in the 1980s. Most of the opinions . . . steer close by the shores of their factual contexts and yield little in the way of explicit doctrine. But their essential requirement is that the agency provide "a reasonable basis for belief that a new technology will be available and economically achievable." When a technology is already in use in other industries, the court often expects more solid evidence that the technology can be transferred to the industry in question, or at least that relevant dissimilarities have been considered.

The EPA's decision must be judged in terms of record evidence available in early 1980, allowing a "time frame of 2–2½ years for completion of the design development phase (and) 2–2½ years of production lead time."

Given this time frame, we feel that there is substantial room for deference to the EPA's expertise in projecting the likely course of development. The essential question in this case is the pace of that development, and absent a revolution in the study of industry, defense of such a projection can never possess the inescapable logic of a mathematical deduction. We think that the EPA will have demonstrated the reasonableness of its basis for prediction if it answers any theoretical objections to the trap-oxidizer method, identifies the major steps necessary in refinement of the device, and offers plausible reasons for believing that each of those steps can be completed in the time available. If the agency can make this showing, then we cannot say that its determination was the result of crystal ball inquiry, or that it neglected its duty of reasoned decisionmaking. . . .

2. Time "Necessary to Permit the Development and Application of the Requisite Technology" . . .

The EPA has predicted that trap-oxidizers will be available for use in model year 1985 vehicles. As the agency has repeatedly observed, the trap-oxidizer is familiar and unobjectionable as a concept. It is not only theoretically sound—experimental data demonstrate that periodic incineration can maintain efficiency for over 10,000 miles. But to date, no filter material has been found that can withstand periodic incineration of the accumulated particulates throughout the 50,000-mile useful life of the vehicle while maintaining a high level of trapping efficiency. . . .

The EPA is not obliged to provide detailed solutions to every engineering problem posed in the perfection of the trap-oxidizer. In the absence of theoretical objections to the technology, the agency need only identify the major steps necessary for development of the device, and give plausible reasons for its belief that the industry will be able to solve those problems in the time remaining. The EPA is not required to rebut all speculation that unspecified factors may hinder "real world" emission control.

The EPA has identified as the necessary remaining steps in development of trap-oxidizer technology—the choice of a durable, efficient filter material, the selection of an incineration method, and the refinement of a control mechanism to bring about automatic initiation of the regeneration process. GM agrees with the agency's specification of these aspects of the trap-oxidizer as the ones requiring further research.

a. Development of a Durable Filter

The most vigorously controverted issue in this case concerns durability, which the EPA has recognized as the key remaining problem. "Collection efficiencies and regeneration techniques have progressed to the point where the most critical issue is whether the efficiency and regeneration mechanism can be maintained over the useful life of the vehicle." Both parties focus on the GM Opel test, in which a metal mesh trap survived over 12,000 miles; the EPA views this test as a stirring demonstration of how far research had progressed in the brief springtime of trap-oxidizer research, while GM sees the 12,000-mile mark as insubstantial compared to the 50,000- to 100,000-mile goal.

The EPA has predicted that the necessary work can be accomplished in time for 1985 model year production. The agency points to the wide variety of materials that have demonstrated appropriate initial efficiencies; several of these are hybrids, suggesting that new combinations of present candidates, rather than hitherto untested substances, may provide the answer. The EPA noted the rapid pace of achievement since attention turned to trap-oxidizers. . . .

Considerable progress has occurred in the last 1½ years. . . .

We conclude that these are plausible reasons for a determination that the industry is capable of solving the durability problem in the allotted time. The EPA could reasonably refuse to be discouraged by the limited initial success, as the project is relatively young. The rapidity of recent progress is a factor that the agency may consider in making a prediction of future capabilities. And the industry's own predictions, while not determinative, support the view that success in this kind of research can realistically be expected within the proposed time frame. We conclude that the EPA's durability prediction, though uncertain, is no more uncertain than such estimates inherently must be, and that the EPA has met the requirement of "reasoned decisionmaking." . . .

d. Conclusion

In summary, we find sufficient support for the EPA's necessarily predictive judgment and therefore uphold the EPA's particulate standard. The agency has given the manufacturers substantial lead time, and there is room for interim adjustments to the standard without significant hardship. Under those circumstances, the applicable standard of review allows the EPA considerable latitude to exercise its expertise through reasoned projections. We find that the agency has given an adequate explanation of its reasons for believing that the necessary steps in improving trap-oxidizer technology can be completed in the time remaining. . . .

V. Conclusion

In the Clean Air Act, Congress encouraged the EPA to set standards for the future without specifying the methodology the agency must follow to determine the probable course of future technological growth. In these circumstances, a reviewing court's role is to make sure that the agency has acted responsibly in formulating a reasoned prediction. It is not our task to decide whether the agency is correct, or to require proof to a mathematical certainty. We must be satisfied if the agency has undertaken its analysis with the degree of precision and clarity that the subject inherently permits. The EPA has done so in this case. . . .

The regulations reviewed in this proceeding, in their entirety, are Affirmed.

NOTES AND QUESTIONS ON *NRDC v. EPA* AND TECHNOLOGY-FORCING

1. *1970 Amendments.* Both EPA and Congress delayed implementation of the numerical standards for automobile emissions many times. But ultimately, the game of chicken worked, and the automobile industry did comply with the standards enacted. Some scholars, however, have claimed that these standards did not truly force development of new technology, but instead simply forced adoption of already existing technology that industry was resisting as impracticable. D. Bruce La Pierre, *Technology-Forcing and Federal Environmental Protection Statutes*, 62 IOWA L. REV. 771, 796 (1977) (concluding that the automobile standards have not sparked efforts "to develop a variety of innovative controls"); Richard B. Stewart, *Regulation, Innovation, and Administrative Law: A Conceptual Framework*, 69 CAL. L. REV. 1256, 1304 (1981) (automobile standards forced "the rapid commercialization and diffusion of add-on catalysts," but failed to produce "basic changes in engine technologies").

2. *California LEV standards.* The State of California has always played a leading role in developing automobile standards and forcing technology. In the 1990s, California introduced low emission vehicle (LEV) standards to force further technological development and cleanup from the automobile industry. As originally enacted, these standards demanded improvements in emission levels that would require increasingly radical technological change over a long period of time, culminating in a zero emission standard that probably would require some sort of electric vehicle not using gasoline at all. Industry has successfully pressured California to relax and delay these standards in various ways, largely out of concern about the zero emission mandate. Still, these standards, which a number of states have copied, have led to the introduction of cars with substantially lower emissions, some of which use new "hybrid technology." Hybrid technology uses a combination of gasoline and electric power to reduce fuel consumption and emissions, and sales of hybrid vehicles have been rising. In 2010, the federal government made California's work in establishing LEV standards for carbon dioxide the basis for a federal rule requiring greenhouse gas reductions equivalent to a fleet average fuel economy of 35.5 miles per gallon. Now, electric vehicles that achieve the zero emissions mandate are beginning to penetrate the market, but very slowly. But are electric cars truly "zero emission vehicles"? Does it depend on the source of the electricity used to charge the vehicle battery?

3. *What must government know about technology?* Should Congress or administrative agencies impose standards (such as LEV) without knowing how companies can meet them? Do the standards the D.C. Circuit has developed provide a sufficient framework for judicial review of such standards?

2. Economic Feasibility

The technology-based standard setting provisions generally require agencies to consider the costs of compliance, not just the technical feasibility of installing and operating particular pollution control technologies. But how should they analyze costs and take them into account?

The law could require agencies to consider costs to determine whether facility owners can afford the cost of compliance, *i.e.*, to analyze whether a standard is economically feasible. Agencies might instead compare the costs to the societal benefits of regulation (in reduced health and environmental impacts), *i.e.*, engage in cost-benefit analysis. Or agencies might analyze the dollars that must be expended for each marginal increment in pollution reduction, a marginal cost effectiveness analysis.

One of us has described the restraints the feasibility principle imposes in the following manner:

> The feasibility principle . . . generally requires stringent regulation, but presumptively subjects this demand for stringency to two constraints. First, the principle authorizes government agencies to forego physically impossible environmental improvements. Second, the principle authorizes government agencies to forego constraints so costly that they cause widespread plant shutdowns. . . . The cost constraint requires assessment of cost and the technological constraint requires assessment of engineering possibilities, i.e. a technological assessment. But cost assessment presupposes technological assessment. The cost of making any environmental improvement equals the cost incurred in making the physical changes necessary to accomplish it. Nobody can begin to estimate the cost of an environmental improvement until an engineer describes the technologies regulated parties will use to make that improvement. . . .
>
> The cost constraint, however, implies that the regulator must analyze whether the cost of implementing the technologically possible reductions would lead to plant shutdowns. This implies that regulators must compare cost, not to benefits, but to net earnings prior to regulation and the value of corporate assets. Costs significant enough to render plants *unprofitable* could lead their owners to shut them down. For that reason, feasibility analysis also includes an assessment of the cost's impact on shutdowns. . . .
>
> The feasibility principle does not, however, consist wholly of constraints. This principle requires maximum reductions at least up to the point where plant closures begin to occur.

David M. Driesen, *Distributing the Costs of Environmental, Health and Safety Protection: The Feasibility Principle, Cost-Benefit Analysis, and Regulatory Reform*, 32 B.C. Envtl. Aff. L. Rev. 1, 9-16 (2005).

Does the idea that regulators should "avoid widespread plant shutdowns" offer a good interpretation of what it means for a regulation to be feasible? What else might the idea of economic feasibility mean?

Agencies and courts have not been clear and consistent in how they interpret the economic constraint on feasibility. Furthermore, Professor Driesen only argues that the requirement to maximize reductions that do not shut down plants offers a good presumptive interpretation of statutory provisions employing maximizing language, such as requirements for the "maximum" achievable emissions reduction, *see* 42 U.S.C. §7412(d), and the "best" available technology, *see* 33 U.S.C. §1311(b)(2). He does not argue, for example, that the provision of the Clean Air Act requiring states to impose limits reflecting "reasonably available control technology" on major existing sources, for example, requires regulators to maximize reductions up to the point of widespread plant closures. For that provision does not have any language indicating intent to "maximize" reductions or employ the "best" technology.

In the case below, EPA established effluent limitations (a form of technology-based regulation governing water pollution) under two separate statutory provisions of the Clean Water Act. One requires it to set standards based on the "best practicable control technology" (BPT); another required standards based on the "best available technology" (BAT). Consider whether the statutory language of either of these standards embodies something like the feasibility principle. Does it demand consideration of economic feasibility, cost-benefit analysis, or marginal cost effectiveness analysis?

Ass'n of Pacific Fisheries v. EPA
615 F.2d 794 (9th Cir. 1980)

KENNEDY, CIRCUIT JUDGE.

In 1972 Congress, intending "to restore and maintain the chemical, physical, and biological integrity of the Nation's waters," amended the Federal Water Pollution Control Act (Act). Congress established national pollution goals to be achieved by specific dates. By July 1, 1977, industries discharging pollutants into the nation's waters were to have achieved "the best practicable control technology currently available (BPT)." Section 301(b)(1)(A), 33 U.S.C. §1311(b)(1)(A). By 1983, industry is to achieve "the best available technology economically achievable [BAT]." Section 301(b)(2)(A), 33 U.S.C. §1311(b)(2)(A). The Environmental Protection Agency (EPA or Agency) was entrusted with the responsibility of defining and policing the efficient and prompt achievement of these goals.

This case involves a challenge to regulations promulgated by the Agency establishing effluent guidelines for the Canned and Preserved Seafood Processing Point Source Category. . . . The effluent which is the subject of the regulations consists of unused fish residuals. This discharge includes heads, tails, and internal residuals of the processed fish. Substantial quantities of water are used at various stages of the plant operations. This water comes into contact with the fish residuals and contains pollutants when discharged. The regulations prescribe limitations on discharge, and utilize three measures of pollution: five-day biochemical oxygen demand (BOD 5); total suspended solids (TSS); and oil and grease (O & G). The regulations establish daily maximum levels and monthly average levels for each subcategory, and are measured in terms of the amount of pollutant per thousand pounds of fish processed.

The prescribed 1977 BPT for processors not located in Alaska, and Alaska processors located in "population or processing centers," is the installation of screens to trap the larger fish particles before the effluent is discharged from the plant. . . .

By 1983 the fisheries must comply with more rigorous technology requirements and effluent limitations. For nonremote facilities, the Agency directed that a dissolved air flotation unit be installed at each location and that the end-of-pipe effluent be channeled through this system before it is discharged into the receiving water. These regulations apply to all nonremote subcategories except Subpart V,

Conventional Bottomfish. There, the Administrator has prescribed aerated lagoons as the BAT. Remote Alaska fish processors will be required by the 1983 regulations to screen the effluent before discharging it into the receiving waters.

Scope of Review

The scope of our review in cases like this is well-settled and need not be restated at length. Our task is to insure that the Agency has accumulated sufficient material upon which to make a reasoned decision, reviewed that material, and promulgated regulations that are the result of reasoned decisionmaking. . . .

1977 Regulations

The petitioners contend that the cost of operating the required technology is wholly disproportionate to the resulting pollution control benefits, and that both costs and benefits were erroneously calculated by the Agency. . . .

B. Cost-Benefit Comparisons and the Question of Screening

The parties dispute whether or not the requirement of screening plus barging or land-based disposal was reached after a proper evaluation of costs and benefits. The disagreement extends both to questions of interpreting the statute and to whether the Agency followed the Act even assuming its own interpretation is correct.

Section 304(b)(1)(B) of the Act provides in part:

> Factors relating to the assessment of best practicable control technology currently available to comply with subsection (b)(1) of section 301 of this Act shall include consideration of the total cost of application of technology in relation to the effluent reduction benefits to be achieved from such application. . . .

We think it plain that, as a general rule, the EPA is required to consider the costs and benefits of a proposed technology in its inquiry to determine the BPT. The Agency has broad discretion in weighing these competing factors, however. When considering different levels of technology, it must be shown that increased costs are wholly disproportionate to potential effluent reduction before the Agency is permitted to rely on a cost-benefit comparison to select a lower level of technology as the BPT. This conclusion is consistent with the interpretation of section 304(b)(1)(B) given in the Conference Report on the bill which ultimately became the Act. The Report states:

> The balancing test between total cost and effluent reduction benefits is intended to limit the application of technology only where the additional degree of effluent reduction is wholly out of proportion to the costs of achieving such marginal level of reduction for any class or category of sources.

It is relevant in this case, moreover, to consider the definition of the benefits the Agency is directed to weigh. We agree with the Agency's contention that Congress intended BPT standards to be based primarily on employment of available technology for reducing effluent discharge, and not primarily on demonstrated changes in water quality. Congress was aware that prior enforcement efforts based on water quality standards had not been successful. It determined, accordingly, that the Agency should have the authority to require effluent reduction benefits as defined by the amount or degree of reduction achieved by a level of technology applied to discharge, without the necessity of demonstrating the incremental effect of that technology on the quality of the receiving water. . . . [T]he "effluent reduction benefits" referred to in the Act are not primarily water quality benefits; rather, "(e)ffluent reduction occurs whenever less effluent is discharged, i.e., whenever a plant treats its wastes before discharge. . . ."

The costs of screening were also considered by the Agency. . . . After estimating the costs for affected subcategories, the Agency concluded the total internal costs of the 1977 effluent limitations would be $6.2 million for investment and $1.3 million of annual expenditures. External costs included a minor effect on prices and the expected closure of some processing plants because of inability to comply economically with the regulations. The effect of these closures on the domestic industry capacity was anticipated to be small.

Petitioners argue that the number of plants estimated to close as a result of the regulations demonstrates that the costs of implementing the technology are wholly out of proportion to the effluent reduction benefits, and thus that the regulations do not prescribe a practicable technology. We do not find the Agency's action can be set aside on this issue.

Precisely how many plants in nonremote locations the EPA estimated would close as a result of the 1977 BPT is not completely clear from the record. In the Preamble to the Regulations, 40 Fed. Reg. 55777, the Agency states only that "a number of small plants are projected to be adversely affected by the effluent limitations." The record shows that in affected subcategories 28 out of 172 plants were projected to close as a result of the 1977 BPT. In its brief, the Agency argues that for several reasons, stated in the record, its original estimate of the number of plant closings was too high. It does not, however, point to any revised estimate. Thus, the most concrete estimate available is that contained in EPA's Economic Analysis. These data also disclose that in Alaska nonremote subcategories the Alaska subcategories where screening is the BPT seven out of sixteen plants were predicted to close as a result of inability to meet BPT.

Petitioners agree Congress contemplated that implementing BPT might result in plant closures in some industries. The proportion of plants estimated to close in the nonremote Alaska subcategories (57% for nonremote Alaskan fresh and frozen salmon and 33% for nonremote Alaskan salmon canning) is substantially higher than that approved in some other cases. See, e.g., *Weyerhaeuser*, 590 F.2d at 1047 (summarizing facts in American Paper Inst. v. Train, 543 F.2d 328, 338-39 (D.C. Cir.) (out of 270 mills and 120,000 people, 8 mills estimated to close and 1800 people laid off; in three subcategories, of 30 mills, 3 estimated to close). The Agency determined, however, that the effect on prices of implementing the BPT would be small: "price increases generally in the range of 0.3 to 0.5 percent are projected," 40 Fed. Reg. at 55777. It also found that "domestic industry capacity is not expected to be affected by the potential closure of these particular small plants." *Id.* The percentage of estimated plant closures in the seafood processing category generally is low. Given these findings, the estimated number of plant closings in the nonremote Alaska subcategories, standing by itself, does not invalidate its cost/benefit analysis or require us to set aside the Agency's determination that the required technology was practicable.

The Agency need not balance the costs of compliance against effluent reduction benefits with pinpoint precision, in part because many of the benefits resulting from the effluent reduction are incapable of precise quantification. *Cf.* American Petroleum Inst. v. EPA, 540 F.2d 1023, 1038 (10th Cir. 1976) ("The value of the resulting benefits is not capable of present-day determination."). *See also* Appalachian Power Co. v. Train, 545 F.2d 1351, 1361 (4th Cir. 1976) ("(W)e (reject) Industry's contention that benefits derived from a particular level of effluent reduction must be quantified in monetary terms. This reflects the simple fact that such benefits often cannot be reduced to dollars and cents.").

The Agency, upon consideration of the effluent reduction benefits thought to be achieved by screening, both the water quality benefits and the amount of pollutants discharged into the receiving waters, determined that the costs of screening were justified. We conclude the Agency complied with the Act's mandate to consider the costs of technology in relation to effluent reduction benefits.

1983 Regulations

The regulations promulgated by the Administrator for 1983 are to reflect the "best available technology economically achievable." Section 301(b)(2)(A), 33 U.S.C. §1311(b)(2)(A). For the regulations to be affirmed, the Agency must demonstrate that the technology required is "available" and the effluent limitations are "economically achievable."

. . . [The court upheld the EPA's conclusion that its BAT limits were technically achievable.]

The next question is whether the Agency properly evaluated the costs of meeting the 1983 guidelines. In describing the role of costs in promulgating [BAT], the Conference Report stated:

> While cost should be a factor in the Administrator's judgment, no balancing test will be required. The Administrator will be bound by a test of reasonableness. In this case, the reasonableness of what is "economically achievable" should reflect an evaluation of what needs to be done to move toward the elimination of the discharge of pollutants and what is achievable through the application of available technology without regard to cost.

Although the wording of the statute clearly states that the 1983 limitations must be "economically achievable," there is some disagreement among the circuits as to whether the costs of compliance should be considered in a review of the 1983 limitations. We hold . . . that the EPA must consider the economic consequences of the 1983 regulations, along with the other factors mentioned in section 304(b)(2)(B), 33 U.S.C. §1314(b)(2)(B).

Petitioners maintain that the Agency must balance the ecological benefits against the associated costs in determining whether the technology is economically achievable. They cite in support of this proposition Appalachian Power Co. v. Train, *supra*. In remanding the 1983 regulations affecting electrical power companies, the court there stated:

(I)n choosing among alternative strategies, EPA must not only set forth the cost of achieving a particular level of heat reduction but must also state the expected environmental benefits, that is to say the effect on the environment, which will take place as a result of reduction, for it is only after EPA has fully explicated its course of conduct in this manner that a reviewing court can determine whether the agency has, in light of the goal to be achieved, acted arbitrarily or capriciously in adopting a particular effluent reduction level.

According to petitioners, the Agency did not consider the incremental benefit to the environment to be achieved by the dissolved air flotation units, and the regulations must be set aside. We cannot agree. As noted by the court in *Weyerhaeuser*, the language of the statute indicates that the EPA's consideration of costs in determining BPT and [BAT] was to be different. In prescribing the appropriate 1977 technology, the Agency was to "include consideration of the total cost of application of technology *in relation to the effluent reduction benefits to be achieved from such application*." Section 304(b)(1)(B) (emphasis added). In determining the 1983 control technology, however, the EPA must "take into account . . . the cost of achieving such effluent reduction," along with various other factors. Section 304(b)(2)(B). The conspicuous absence of the comparative language contained in section 304(b)(1)(B) leads us to the conclusion that Congress did not intend the Agency or this court to engage in marginal cost-benefit comparisons.

The intent of Congress is stated in 33 U.S.C. §1251(a)(1): "(I)t is the national goal that the discharge of pollutants into the navigable waters be eliminated by 1985." The regulations that will be applied in 1983 are intended to result "in reasonable further progress toward the national goal of eliminating the discharge of all pollutants. . . ." 33 U.S.C. §1311(b)(2)(A). These express declarations of congressional intent cannot be ignored in determining the reasonableness of the 1983 regulations. So long as the required technology reduces the discharge of pollutants, our inquiry will be limited to whether the Agency considered the cost of technology, along with the other statutory factors, and whether its conclusion is reasonable. Of course, at some point extremely costly more refined treatment will have a de minimis effect on the receiving waters. But that point has not been reached in these [BAT] regulations.

The record discloses that the Agency studied the cost of complying with the 1983 regulations. It set forth the cost of compliance for plants that produced various amounts of effluent per minute, both in terms of capital costs and operation and maintenance costs. The projections include estimates of the costs of construction, labor, power, chemicals and fuel. Although land acquisition costs were not considered, the amount of land necessary for the air flotation unit is minimal. In contrast to our conclusion regarding aerated lagoons, the Agency was not arbitrary in concluding that the DAF unit could be installed on existing plant locations without necessitating additional land acquisitions. . . .

Finally, it does not appear that the cost of complying with the 1983 regulations is unreasonable. The cost of compliance for the Northwest Canned Salmon subcategory, for example, is estimated to be $157,000 for initial investment and $32,000 of annual expenditures for the average size plants. According to the EPA's economic analysis, the total annual costs of pollution abatement averaged between one and two percent of the total sales figures of each subcategory. Depreciation is available for the capital outlays and tax deductions are available for business expenses. The Agency concluded that the benefits justified the costs, and petitioners have not shown that conclusion to be arbitrary or capricious.

Although the number of plants estimated to close as a result of the 1983 regulations was not stated clearly to us, it appears to be a lesser proportion of affected plants than that which we approved for the 1977 regulations. Since Congress contemplated the closure of some marginal plants, we do not consider the regulations to be arbitrary and capricious.

For these reasons, we conclude that the 1983 regulations requiring dissolved air flotation units for West Coast fish processors should be upheld.

[The court remanded part of the regulation, because EPA had not adequately demonstrated the technical feasibility of plants achieving the limits EPA said that aerated lagoons can enable them to achieve or the costs of land acquisition associated with this technology.]

AFFIRMED in part and REMANDED in part.

NOTES AND QUESTIONS ON *PACIFIC FISHERIES* AND ECONOMIC FEASIBILITY

1. *Considering cost.* The Clean Water Act requires EPA to consider the cost of its technology-based effluent regulations. According to this case, how precisely must the agency do so, and in what respects?

2. *CBA?* In the next chapter, we will consider cost-benefit analysis (CBA) and its role in regulation. Some commentators regard any regulatory process that involves consideration and analysis of cost as an instance of CBA. Does the Clean Water Act require CBA in this sense? This book and most commentators who write about this subject frequently employ a narrower definition of CBA. Under this definition, CBA requires a comparison between the costs of regulation and its benefits, and the benefits must be monetized, *i.e.*, expressed in dollar terms. Do the statutory provisions governing BPT and BAT require CBA in this sense? Do these provisions differ in how they treat cost, and if so, how?

3. *Facility closure.* EPA predicted that its regulations would close some facilities. Did that make the standards unachievable in the court's view? What degree of plant closures would make a regulation "unachievable"? The court noted that this regulation would close a larger number of facilities than is typical. For many regulations, EPA projects no plant closures at all. *See* Driesen, *Feasibility Principle, supra*, at 43. When it does project plant closures, it usually expects that 3 percent or less of regulated plants will close. *See id.*

4. *Feasibility and cost.* Note that if the economic feasibility test is understood as a prohibition against widespread plant closures, decisions about feasibility do not depend upon the relationship between costs and benefits. Rather, they depend upon the relationship between costs and the economic capabilities of regulated industry. *See, e.g.*, National Wildlife Federation v. EPA, 286 F.3d 554, 564 (D.C. Cir. 2002) (plant closures predicted when net earnings fall below the salvage value of a regulated mill).

5. *Definition of benefits for BPT.* With respect to BPT, the court defined the benefit of the regulation in terms of the amount of effluent reduction, rather than in terms of "water quality benefits." In Weyerhauser v. Costle, 590 F.2d 1011 (D.C. Cir. 1978), the court explained the reasons to avoid considering water quality benefits in rejecting paper mill owners' argument that EPA must consider the capacity of ocean waters to dilute effluent in setting BPT limits:

> [For 24 years], Congress attempted to use receiving water quality as a basis for setting effluent standards. At the end of that period, Congress realized not only that its water pollution efforts . . . had failed, but also that reliance on receiving water capacity as a crucial test for permissible pollution levels had contributed greatly to that failure.
>
> Based on this experience, Congress adopted a new approach in 1972. Under the Act, "a discharger's performance is . . . measured against strict technology-based effluent limitations—specified levels of treatment—to which it must conform, rather than against limitations derived from water quality standards to which it and other polluters must collectively conform."
>
> The new approach reflected developing views on practicality and rights. Congress concluded that water pollution seriously harmed the environment, and that although the cost of control would be heavy, the nation would benefit from controlling that pollution. Yet scientific uncertainties made it difficult to assess the benefits to particular bodies of receiving water. Even if the federal government eventually could succeed at the task at which [sic] had failed for 24 years and thus could determine benefits and devise water quality standards, Congress concluded that the requisite further delay was too long for the nation to wait.
>
> Moreover, by eliminating the issue of the capacity of particular bodies of receiving water, Congress made nationwide uniformity in effluent limitations possible. . . .
>
> More fundamentally, the new approach implemented changing views as to the relative rights of the public and of industrial polluters. Hitherto, the right of the polluter was pre-eminent, unless the damage caused by pollution could be proven. Henceforth, the right of the public to a clean environment would be pre-eminent, unless pollution treatment was impractical or unachievable. . . . This view of relative rights was based in part on hard-nosed assessment of our scientific ignorance. . . .

Weyerhauser, 590 F.2d at 1042-43.

One cannot monetize the benefits of regulation without taking into account the impact of specific dischargers on specific water bodies. To monetize benefits, EPA would have to assess not just the tons of pollution reduced and the cost of pollution control, but also the degree of benefit these reductions would bring to fish, wildlife, aesthetics, water-based recreation, and other discrete values associated with improved water quality. Such an analysis would prove difficult or impossible in the context of national standard setting, because the water quality benefit of a particular quantity of reduction would vary with the quality of particular receiving waters, and the state of controls on sources other than the ones being regulated. The benefit would not be uniform nationally. Because the legislative history on the BPT cost-benefit provision recognizes this problem, courts have rejected the claim that the requirement to consider the costs and benefits of effluent reductions for purposes of establishing BPT requires consideration of water quality.

6. *Costs disproportionate to benefits.* The *Pacific Fisheries* court interpreted the statutory language governing BPT standards to allow EPA to set less stringent regulations than a feasibility test might indicate if costs are wholly disproportionate to benefits. If a regulation required removal of 100 million pounds of total suspended solids, how would EPA determine the point at which costs would be "wholly

disproportionate" to those benefits? ($100 million? $200 million? $500 million?) Is it possible to make that determination without translating the amount of effluent reduction into water quality benefits? Would translation of the benefit into estimates of water quality benefits make it possible to determine proportionality?

Cost Per Ton of Pollution Removed

7. *Marginal cost effectiveness analysis.* EPA has relied primarily upon marginal cost effectiveness analysis in comparing costs to effluent reduction benefits for purposes of setting BPT standards. Thus, in a subsequent case, EPA successfully defended BPT standards for the chemical industry by asserting that $76.6 million of annualized compliance cost after an initial capital investment of $215.8 million was reasonable, since its regulations would remove 108 million pounds of conventional pollutants annually. *See* Chemical Mfrs. Ass'n v. EPA, 870 F.2d 177, 204 (5th Cir. 1989). In *Chemical Mfrs. Ass'n*, the chemical industry invoked marginal cost effectiveness analysis to challenge EPA's BPT requirements. It argued that in going from 96 to 99 percent removal, costs increased from 38 cents per pound to 71 cents per pound. *Id.* at 205.

The court upheld the regulations anyway, refusing to require a "knee of the curve test" that would prohibit regulations that made a curve drawn showing the marginal cost per marginal pound of abatement sloping sharply upward. *Id.* at 204.

Did the court properly interpret the BPT requirements, and if so, are they appropriate? Suppose that the average costs were reasonable, but the curve did rise sharply in going from 96 to 99 percent. Should the agency avoid the sharp rise in marginal abatement cost?

8. *Rationale for the feasibility principle.* Consider the following defense of the feasibility principle:

> If one believes, as many CBA proponents do, that environmental regulators should consider the distribution of costs and benefits of environmental regulation, the feasibility principle has much to recommend it. This approach focuses regulators' attention on significant costs and avoids wasting resources considering finely calibrated responses to costs having minor impacts on society.
>
> This approach relies primarily upon information about the distribution of costs to separate significant from insignificant costs. When economic losses become concentrated in ways that devastate individuals, they can have drastic effects, even if the total amount of cost is low. Conversely, widely distributed costs can have minor effects, even if total aggregate costs are

high. This "concentration" principle suggests that the distribution of costs can tell us a lot about their significance. . . .

As a general rule, environmental regulations may lead owners of regulated facilities to increase employment. Regulations often force companies to hire more workers or pay contractors to install and operate pollution controls or to redesign processes to prevent pollution. Indeed, more stringent and costly regulation may force more pollution-control related hiring than less stringent and costly regulation, as long as the regulation does not make plants unprofitable and lead to shutdowns.

Often costs imposed on companies become distributed so widely that they have little real impact on human lives. . . . Furthermore, firms can creatively compensate for or avoid costs. Indeed, when environmental regulation has been demanding, firms have often engaged in innovative changes to avoid the costs of regulation. . . .

By contrast, regulations that force a plant owner to shutdown decrease employment, at least in the short run. This can concentrate severe economic losses on small numbers of workers who can ill afford them. This sort of loss can have a devastating impact on workers' lives, leading to depression, a terrible feeling of loss, and an inability to cope economically, especially if unemployment or very severe underemployment proves permanent. . . .

While firms often can systematically distribute regulatory costs widely or avoid them altogether, harms from pollution often devastate randomly selected individuals. Cancer, for example, can lead to a long slow painful death for some unfortunates. Birth defects can ruin the lives of children born with them and afflict their parents with enormous burdens. Asthma can make its victims gasp for air, send asthmatics to hospital emergency rooms in summer, and force children from the playground on hot days. As these examples demonstrate, we should think of most pollution control programs as efforts to ameliorate concentrated harms.

Furthermore, while imposition of regulatory costs tends to spawn cost avoidance behavior, some of which can be very socially productive, pollution can impose burdens that one cannot easily escape. Since people must breathe, they cannot escape air pollution. Of course, relatively wealthy individuals can choose among the cleanest areas and escape some of the worst effects of pollution. But others have fewer options. . . .

The feasibility constraint focuses analytical attention on costs likely to be significant, in the sense of having a distribution likely to have a serious impact on people's lives. It avoids lavishing administrative resources on calibrating responses to what one might call de minimis costs.

The feasibility principle offers an appropriate response to problems characterized by de minimis cost and concentrated harms. It calls for stringent regulation. On the other hand, it constrains regulation when the costs concentrate in ways likely to produce greater than de minimis impacts.

Driesen, *Feasibility Principle, supra*, at 34-41. *Cf.* Jonathan S. Masur & Eric A. Posner, *Against Feasibility Analysis*, 77 U. CHI. L. REV. 657 (2010); David M. Driesen, *Two Cheers for Feasible Regulation: A Modest Response to Masur and Posner*, 35 HARV. ENVTL. L. REV. 313 (2012).

If you were a member of Congress, would you vote to eliminate or to expand EPA's authority to reject feasible requirements where costs are wholly disproportionate to benefits? Or would you substitute a cost-benefit test for the feasibility tests found in many existing statutory provisions?

9. *Overestimating cost.* In practice, EPA usually overestimates the cost of its regulations. It often relies upon regulated industry for estimates of the cost of the technologies involved, and regulated industry has an incentive to exaggerate costs in order to persuade EPA to set lax standards. *See* Thomas O. McGarity & Ruth Ruttenberg, *Counting the Cost of Health Safety and Environmental Regulation*, 80 TEX. L. REV. 1997, 1998 (2002) (*ex ante* cost estimates have been higher than actual costs incurred, sometimes by orders of magnitude); Winston Harrington,

Richard D. Morgenstern & Peter Nelson, *On the Accuracy of Regulatory Cost Estimates*, 19 J. Pol'y Analysis & Mgmt. 297 (2000). Also, once a regulation is promulgated, industry acquires an incentive to lower the cost of compliance as much as possible, either through competitive bidding processes or through innovation in applying new approaches or technologies. David M. Driesen, *The Societal Cost of Environmental Protection: Beyond Administrative Cost-Benefit Analysis*, 24 Ecology L.Q. 545, 600-01 (1997). Should this influence how the agencies or courts evaluate technological achievability? If so, how?

A TRAIL GUIDE TO THE CLEAN WATER ACT (CWA)
(also known as the Federal Water Pollution Control Act)

Introduction and Overview

In Chapter 4, you learned about effects-based standards, known as water quality standards (WQS) in the CWA. In this chapter, you learned about technology-based standards, of which there are several varieties in the CWA, including effluent limitations for existing point source dischargers (a term we define and explain below), new source performance standards for new point sources, and pretreatment standards for point sources that discharge effluent into public sewer systems. In the section of Chapter 3 describing the Clean Air Act statutory scheme, and in the Trail Guide to the Clean Air Act in Chapter 4, you also learned about the planning program (the SIP process) designed to ensure that the combination of pollution controls adopted through technology-based controls, controls on automobiles and other mobile source emissions, and other programs result in attainment of the Clean Air Act version of effects-based standards — the National Ambient Air Quality Standards (NAAQS).

In the CWA statutory scheme, Congress adopted a similar triad of effects-based standards, technology-based standards, and planning. The effects-based WQS establish goals for protecting and maintaining the health of individual water bodies. Technology-based controls on point source discharges, and a range of other programs designed to control water pollution from other sources, such as contaminated runoff from farms, ranches, urban areas, and other dispersed or so-called nonpoint sources, as well as a range of financial incentives and education and training programs, promote improved water pollution control from particular sources or categories of sources. While the CAA incorporates all planning into a single SIP process, the CWA employs a somewhat confusing combination of different planning programs, the most important of which are summarized below, to ensure that water pollution control from a wide range of aggregate sources within a watershed is sufficient to attain and maintain the WQS in all water bodies.

In other respects, however, the CWA is markedly different from the CAA. First, the CAA allows for some air emissions from any given source so long as the NAAQS are met and air quality is otherwise sufficient to protect the public health and welfare. By contrast, the CWA establishes an ambitious and controversial "zero discharge" goal, at least for point sources of pollution, resulting in "the elimination . . . ." Thus, rather than serving simply as a tool to attain WQS, technology-based controls under the CWA in theory are supposed to force technology until point source water pollution discharges are eliminated entirely. The theory behind this ambitious goal is that we will never know enough about the effects of water pollution to eliminate harm entirely — and to adopt and implement WQS with sufficient confidence to protect human health and the aquatic environment completely — and therefore that elimination of water pollution discharges is the safest course.

A second key difference between the CAA and the CWA is the scope of objectives. The CAA has a singular, although phenomenally important, goal of protecting public health and welfare from the adverse effects of air pollution emissions, and the atmosphere we breathe is a single, nationwide resource. The overarching objective of the CWA, by contrast, is to "restore and maintain the chemical, physical and biological integrity of the Nation's waters." The "Nation's waters" encompass a diverse array of rivers, lakes, estuaries, wetlands, and other aquatic ecosystems, which support a wide range of ecosystem services beyond human health protection, and are impaired by an even wider scope of human activities such as filling, damming, channelization, diversion, water depletion, urbanization, and other activities that go well beyond the direct discharge of chemical pollutants. The CWA, therefore, includes programs designed to address those additional forms of water pollution, activities that impair the chemical, physical, and biological integrity of the nation's waters. Those programs have led to some of the most intense controversies regarding the scope and purpose of the Act, and the respective roles of the federal and state governments in issues involving land and water use and management.

Key Provisions of the Clean Water Act

Title I is labeled "Research and Related Programs," and does include those kinds of provisions along with programs aimed at protecting major individual water bodies or watersheds, including the Hudson River, the Chesapeake Bay, the Great Lakes, Long Island Sound, Lake Champlain, and the Lake Pontchartrain Basin.

The most significant provision in Title I, however, and one of the most notable in the entire Act, is the *Declaration of Purpose*, 33 U.S.C. §1251. That provision includes the overriding statutory objective "to restore and maintain the chemical, physical, and biological integrity of the Nation's waters." Among the more important subsidiary statutory goals and objectives are:

- 33 U.S.C. §1251(a)(1), defining "the national goal that the discharge of pollutants into the navigable waters be eliminated by 1985" (the so-called zero discharge goal);
- 33 U.S.C. §1251(a)(2), articulating a "national goal that, wherever attainable, an interim goal of water quality which provides for the protection and propagation of fish, shellfish, and wildlife and provides

for recreation in and on the water be achieved by July 1, 1983" (the so-called fishable and swimmable goal); and

- 33 U.S.C. §1251(a)(3), establishing a "national policy that the discharge of toxic pollutants in toxic amounts be prohibited."
- 33 U.S.C. §1251(b) and (g) articulate a policy of state responsibility to take the lead role in controlling water pollution, while retaining their traditional control over land and water use.

Titles II and VI established programs of federal financial assistance to state and local governments to construct and operate modern sewage treatment plants (also known as publicly owned treatment works, or POTWs). In 1987, Congress replaced the original program of massive federal grants to states and cities under Title II (adopted in 1972), with a revolving loan program in Title VI.

In 33 U.S.C. §1288, Congress also adopted a program for comprehensive areawide plans to address multiple, aggregate sources of pollution, including both point and nonpoint sources of pollution, in areas with "substantial water quality control problems," encouraging a regional approach to water pollution control.

Title III includes the core regulatory provisions of the Act, including key standard-setting and enforcement provisions, including the following:

- 33 U.S.C. §1311(a) incorporates the most fundamental substantive requirement of the statute that, "except as in compliance with [various permitting and pollution control requirements] the discharge of any pollutant by any person shall be unlawful."
- 33 U.S.C. §1311(b)-(n), along with *id.* §§1314(b), 1316, and 1317, define and establish the procedures for promulgation of the key technology-based pollution control standards applicable to various categories of discharger.
- 33 U.S.C. §1313(a)-(e) along with §1314(a) establish the requirements and procedures to establish the effects-based water quality standards (WQS) applicable to individual water bodies or categories of water bodies within individual states, the "total maximum daily load" (TMDL) process for ensuring that the WQS are not violated due to excessive aggregate pollution, and a "continuing planning process" to incorporate those requirements into permits and other control mechanisms.
- 33 U.S.C. §1319 provides federal administrative, civil, and criminal enforcement authority for violations of the Act.
- 33 U.S.C. §1321 establishes a cleanup and liability regime for the unlawful release of oil and hazardous substances, and was the historical predecessor and model for the more comprehensive "Superfund" law.
- 33 U.S.C. §1319 requires states to develop comprehensive plans for nonpoint sources of pollution, which are not subject to the permitting requirements for discharges from discrete point sources.

Title IV incorporates the most important certification and permitting provisions of the Act, including the following:

- 33 U.S.C. §1341 requires all applicants for any federal license or permit that may result in a discharge into the navigable waters to obtain a certification from the state in which the discharge originates that the discharge will not result in a violation of any WQS or other key water pollution control standards or requirements.

- 33 U.S.C. §1342 authorizes EPA, or states with delegated programs, to issue National Discharge Elimination Permits to all point source dischargers, incorporating technology-based and water quality–based pollution controls and other requirements.
- 33 U.S.C. §1344 authorizes the U.S. Army Corps of Engineers, or delegated states, to issue permits for the discharge of "dredged or fill material" into waters of the United States, incorporating pollution controls and mitigation requirements adopted by EPA and Corps of Engineers regulations, including discharges of material used to fill wetlands and other water bodies for development.

Title V, called "General Provisions," includes EPA rule-making authority in 33 U.S.C. §1361, the very important statutory definitions in 33 U.S.C. §1362, authority for citizen enforcement suits in 33 U.S.C. §1365, and procedures and jurisdiction for judicial review of EPA actions in 33 U.S.C. §1369.

An Analytical Approach to the Clean Water Act

An alternative, potentially useful approach to understanding the CWA statutory scheme is to ask how you would analyze and apply the statute to a particular activity or proposed activity in the real world that might cause water pollution, and therefore that might be subject to one or more of the statute's regulatory or other controls. That analysis might proceed as follows:

First, is there (or will there be) a discharge of a pollutant, meaning an "addition" of a "pollutant" from a "point source" into a "water of the United States"? If so, the CWA prohibits that discharge without a valid permit. If not, but if there is pollution from a "nonpoint source," does the state in which the pollution occurs impose any requirements or otherwise address the pollution through its nonpoint source pollution control programs under 33 U.S.C. §1288 or §1329?

Second, if there is a point source discharge requiring a permit, is the discharge of "dredged or fill" material or of any other kind of pollutant?

- If the discharge involves dredged or fill material, including the most common example of material used to fill wetlands for development, the permit must be issued under 33 U.S.C. §1344 by the U.S. Army Corps of Engineers (ACE), or by one of the small number of states with a delegated program to issue such permits. Permits issued by ACE (commonly known as "404 permits") also require a state certification under 33 U.S.C. §1341 documenting that the discharge will comply with state WQS.
- If the discharge involves other pollutants, the permit must be issued under 33 U.S.C. §1342 by the state water pollution control agency (almost all states have delegated authority to issue these permits), or by EPA for those few states that lack such authority. These are known as National Pollutant Discharge Elimination System (or NPDES) permits.

Third, what substantive pollution control conditions and requirements apply to each form of permit?

- For 404 permits, EPA and the Army Corps of Engineers have promulgated a lengthy set of rules to determine whether the discharge may occur. In brief, discharges of dredged and fill material to waters of the United States are permissible only if there is "no practicable alternative" to doing so. If a discharge is allowed, the discharger must assure compliance with state WQS, including through state water quality certification under 33 U.S.C. §1341, and mitigate the discharge by restoring or replacing the lost aquatic resources elsewhere.
- NPDES permits require a two-part analysis:
  - What technology-based standards apply to this discharge? Some kind (or sometimes multiple kinds) of technology-based standard applies to every point source discharge, so this is a matter of determining the category of discharger and identifying the applicable regulation. This inquiry depends on a number of factors, such as whether the discharger is municipal or industrial, a new or existing source, processes waste or storm water, and what source category or subcategory the discharger belongs to, etc. Even where no regulation applies, the permit-writer must determine the applicable "best technology" based on her "best professional judgment." The main point for now is that some kind of technology-based controls must be used to control every discharge whether or not WQS are violated in the receiving water body.
  - Once the applicable technology-based standard is applied to an individual discharge, the follow-up question is whether that level of control is sufficient to ensure attainment of water quality standards in the receiving water. If not, as determined through a permit-specific analysis or as part of a "total maximum daily load" (TMDL) calculation for the water body, stricter WQ-based permit limits must be imposed.

B. THE VARIETY OF TECHNOLOGY-BASED STANDARDS

While it is impossible to learn all of the statutory details for each of the technology-based provisions Congress has drafted in an introductory environmental law course, you should be aware of some of the patterns found in technology-based provisions.

First, the statutes often apply stricter standards to new sources than to existing sources. This reflects Congress' view that costs of retrofitting old sources might be very high, but that the installation of new equipment provides an opportunity for cost effective emissions control. Thus, for example, the Clean Air Act requires that new and modified sources conform to federal new source performance standards (NSPS), which we as have seen envision limits reflecting the best adequately demonstrated emission control technology, considering cost and some other factors. *See* 42 U.S.C. §7411(a). *See also* 33 U.S.C. §1316 (requiring strict new source performance standards under the Clean Water Act). Yet, states need only require emission levels reflecting "reasonably available control technology" (RACT) of major existing sources. 42 U.S.C. §7502(c)(1).

Second, the Clean Air Act tends to apply more comprehensive and strict standards to areas that have not attained the NAAQS than to areas that have met them. Thus, states must require new and modified major sources to attain the "lowest achievable emission" rate (LAER) in nonattainment areas (where the NAAQS have not been attained) and the emission level reflecting the best available control technology (BACT) in attainment areas (where the NAAQS has been attained). *See* 42 U.S.C. §§7501(3), 7503(a)(2), 7479. LAER is generally considered stricter. Can you see why?

Overall, this scheme looks like this:

Selected Clean Air Act Technology-Based Standards

	Attainment Area	*Nonattainment Area*
Existing Sources		RACT
New Sources	NSPS, BACT	NSPS, LAER

Notice the blank in the upper left-hand corner (standards for existing sources in attainment areas). Why do you suppose Congress did not generally require technology-based regulation of existing sources in attainment areas? By contrast, Congress does require technology-based controls for all point source dischargers under the Clean Water Act, regardless of compliance with the effects-based water quality standards. Why the difference, and is it justified?

The NSPS standards are federal standards promulgated for selected categories of sources. The BACT and LAER standards are source-specific standards applicable to any major source. Why do we have both? Given the limitations that *National Lime* places on national standard setting, can you see why BACT and LAER requirements might usefully supplement NSPS standards?

Third, a common pattern involves progressing from relatively undemanding standards for "reasonably available" control technology to stricter standards governed by the feasibility principle. This is most obvious in the Federal Water Pollution Control Act, which, as we have seen, required best practicable control technology (BPT) by July 1, 1977 and best available technology (BAT) by July 1, 1983. *See* 33 U.S.C. §1311(b)(1), (2). *Cf.* 33 U.S.C. §1317(a) (requiring BAT for toxic pollutants). Since the Clean Air Act applies strict new source standards to modified sources, and most facility owners eventually modify their facilities, one can likewise view the Clean Air Act as contemplating a progression toward stricter standards.

Fourth, Congress has tended to treat toxic pollutants, those associated with acute hazards like cancer, differently. Thus, while Congress only requires states to apply RACT under the Clean Air Act to existing sources of conventional pollutants in nonattainment areas, it has required the emission limits based on the maximum achievable control technology (MACT) nationwide for the first phase of regulation of toxic (or hazardous) air pollutants. *See* 42 U.S.C. §7412(d).

Do these patterns reflect sound policy? Why or why not?

TECHNOLOGY-BASED STANDARD SETTING PROBLEM

During the George W. Bush Administration, states and environmental groups petitioned EPA to regulate greenhouse gas emissions from new motor vehicles under the endangerment standard put in place after *Ethyl*. EPA refused, arguing for various policy reasons that Congress did not intend the term "pollutant" to apply to gases causing global problems. In Massachusetts v. EPA, 549 U.S. 497 (2007), the Supreme Court reversed and remanded this ruling and EPA issued a formal finding that greenhouse gases constitute pollutants endangering public health and the environment. Endangerment and Cause or Contribute Findings for Greenhouse Gases Under Section 202(a) of the Clean Air Act, 74 Fed. Reg. 66496 (Dec. 15, 2009). Since a number of Clean Air Act provisions require regulation of pollutants, this finding led to regulation beyond the motor vehicle sector. See Utility Air Regulatory Group v. EPA, 134 S. Ct. 2427 (2014) (addressing some of the regulation following the finding). An important component of EPA's plan for reducing greenhouse gas emissions is to limit emissions of carbon dioxide from fossil fuel–fired electric generating units, or power plants, under section 111 of the Clean Air Act, 42 U.S.C. §7411. Fossil fuel–fired electric generating units include natural gas–fired units employing a natural gas combined cycle (NGCC) design and coal-fired units.

Section 111 of the Clean Air Act is set out in relevant part below:

42 U.S.C. §7411: Standards of Performance for New Sources

(a) Definitions
For purposes of this section:

(1) The term "standard of performance" means a standard for emissions of air pollutants which reflects the degree of emission limitation achievable through the application of the best system of emission reduction which (taking into account the cost of achieving such reduction and any nonair quality health and environmental impact and energy requirements) the Administrator determines has been adequately demonstrated.

(2) The term "new source" means any stationary source, the construction or modification of which is commenced after the publication of regulations (or, if earlier, proposed regulations) prescribing a standard of performance under this section which will be applicable to such source. . . .

(4) The term "modification" means any physical change in, or change in the method of operation of, a stationary source which increases the amount of any air pollutant emitted by such source or which results in the emission of any air pollutant not previously emitted. . . .

(6) The term "existing source" means any stationary source other than a new source.

(7) The term "technological system of continuous emission reduction" means—

(A) a technological process for production or operation by any source which is inherently low-polluting or nonpolluting, or

(B) a technological system for continuous reduction of the pollution generated by a source before such pollution is emitted into the ambient air, including precombustion cleaning or treatment of fuels. . . .

(b) List of categories of stationary sources; standards of performance; information on pollution control techniques; sources owned or operated by United States; particular systems; revised standards

(1)

(A) The Administrator shall, within 90 days after December 31, 1970, publish (and from time to time thereafter shall revise) a list of categories of stationary sources. He shall include a category of sources in such list if in his judgment it causes, or contributes significantly to, air pollution which may reasonably be anticipated to endanger public health or welfare.

(B) Within one year after the inclusion of a category of stationary sources in a list under subparagraph (A), the Administrator shall publish proposed regulations, establishing Federal standards of performance for new sources within such category. . . . After considering . . . comments, he shall promulgate, within one year after such publication, such standards with such modifications as he deems appropriate. The Administrator shall, at least every 8 years, review and, if appropriate, revise such standards. . . .

(2) The Administrator may distinguish among classes, types, and sizes within categories of new sources for the purpose of establishing such standards.

(4) The provisions of this section shall apply to any new source owned or operated by the United States.

(5) Except as otherwise authorized under subsection (h), nothing in this section shall be construed to require, or to authorize the Administrator to require, any new or modified source to install and operate any particular technological system of continuous emission reduction to comply with any new source standard or performance.
. . .

(e) Prohibited acts

After the effective date of standards of performance promulgated under this section, it shall be unlawful for any owner or operator of any new source to operate such source in violation of any standard of performance applicable to such source.

EPA promulgated section 111 "New Source Performance Standards" (NSPS) for new (meaning "greenfield" sources made from scratch) large fossil fuel–fired power plants based upon the statutory standard and a review of technologies available to reduce emissions from power plants. EPA adopted separate standards for coal-fired units on the one hand and NGCC units on the other.

EPA required that coal-fired units meet a limit of 1,400 pounds of carbon dioxide per megawatt hour (lb. CO_2/MWh). EPA, Standards of Performance for Greenhouse Gas Emissions from New Stationary Sources: Electric Utility Generating Units, 80 Fed. Reg. 64510 (Oct. 23, 2015). With respect to coal-fired units, EPA stated that it found that partial implementation of carbon capture and storage (CCS), where carbon is captured and stored underground, is the "best system of emission reduction" for such units and that partial CCS can meet the 1,400 lb. CO_2/MWh limit.

EPA required that NGCC units meet a standard of 1,000 lb. CO_2/MWh. The agency found that NGCC technology constitutes the best system of emission reduction for NGCC units and that plants constructed using an NGCC design can meet this limit without add-on control devices.

EPA estimates that its proposed rule will impose little or no cost on electric utilities. EPA does not anticipate construction of new coal-fired electric steam generating units, because low natural gas prices have made natural gas–fired units cheaper than coal-fired units. Accordingly, it expects utilities to generally construct NGCC units, which can meet the rule's standards without add-on equipment.

If natural gas prices rise enough to make coal economical or coal-mining states refuse to switch to natural gas, however, utilities might wish to construct coal-fired units. Accordingly, EPA has considered the costs of carbon capture and storage. EPA suggests that the cost of "full capture" CCS would be between $97 and $143 per MWh. It finds this cost unreasonable because such costs are outside the range of costs that utilities are considering for comparable generation in their future plans. In particular, these costs would be higher than nuclear power, biomass generation, or geothermal energy production. By contrast, EPA estimates the costs of "partial" CCS for coal-fired units at $92 to $117 per MWh. It finds these costs reasonable because they are within the range of costs generated by these other non–natural gas technologies. Furthermore, it finds that most projects under development already incorporate partial CCS, so that requiring partial use of CCS would not have a significant economic impact.

In general, EPA finds that full CCS has produced 90 percent reductions in emissions from coal-fired units. EPA's proposed 1,400 lb. CO_2/MWh standard for coal-fired units would produce a 16 percent reduction in emissions.

EPA finds that partial carbon capture and storage represents the best system of emission reduction for coal-fired units because it ensures that utilities will achieve meaningful CO_2 reductions, has reasonable cost, and will encourage greater use and development of CCS technologies. It concludes that partial CCS is adequately demonstrated because it has been implemented in a number of facilities over the years.

With respect to natural gas—NGCC—units, EPA compared an efficiently designed modern NGCC unit without add-on controls to an efficient modern NGCG unit with CCS added on. EPA concludes that CCS was not an adequately demonstrated technology for NGCC units for several reasons. First, it knows of only one project that had applied CCS to a NGCC unit. EPA does not consider the experience with applying CCS to coal-fired power plants probative with respect to the feasibility of applying it to NGCC units, because the CO_2 is much more concentrated in the flue gas from a coal-fired plant than from a gas-fired unit. Accordingly, EPA chose an emission limit based on NGCC technology without CCS.

EPA adopted standards for modified and reconstructed coal-fired electric generating units requiring them to meet an emission limit based on their best historical emission rate since 2002, but no more stringent than 1,800 lb. CO_2/MWh. This represents emissions achievable through equipment upgrades and best operating practices. EPA did not base its limits for modified and reconstructed facilities on CCS because it did not have sufficient information about the costs of applying partial CCS to modified or reconstructed facilities, which would vary depending on the size and configuration of the unit. EPA also noted that it lacked information that would be needed to evaluate the costs of a retrofit, which would depend on site-specific details.

1) *Likely arguments against the rule.* Suppose that you are in the EPA general counsel's office. You receive an assignment to evaluate the arguments that an environmental group might advance that the agency's rule governing absolutely new (rather than modified or reconstructed) sources is illegally lax and those arguments that industry advocates might advance to argue that it is illegally stringent. Identify the best arguments and assess their likelihood of success.

2) *Modified sources.* EPA initially proposed emission limits for entirely new sources and specifically refrained from proposing any limits for modified sources. EPA, Standards of Performance for Greenhouse Gas Emissions for New Stationary Sources: Electric Generating Units, Proposed Rule, 77 Fed. Reg. 22392, 22394 (Apr. 13, 2012). Why do you think it subsequently proposed a rule establishing limits (however modest) for modified sources? Is it good policy to write laxer limits for modified sources than for new "greenfield" sources as EPA did in the final rule?

3) *Fuel-specific limits.* In its initial 2012 proposal, EPA had also proposed to treat all new greenfield electric power plants as part of a single source category, imposing a 1,000 lb. CO_2/MWh limit on all of them. But in its January 2014 proposals, the agency developed separate standards for coal-fired units, and for gas-fired units, and it finalized a rule with a wide disparity between the two standards. Is this breaking apart of the power plant source category legal or illegal given the rationale suggested by the 2014 proposal? Is distinguishing plants based primarily on the fuel used good policy? How would a uniform limit influence utility choices about what sort of plants to build? Would that effect be good or bad?

4) *Renewable energy.* At the same time that EPA promulgated the new source performance standards mentioned above, it promulgated standards for existing sources of emissions under 42 U.S.C. §7411(d). These standards relied in part on the reductions achievable through increased use of renewable energy. Construction of renewable energy facilities, such as solar power plants and wind turbines, should reduce the total amount of electricity produced by coal-fired power plants, thereby lowering annual carbon dioxide emissions. Is renewable

energy an appropriate technological basis for emission reduction measures under 42 U.S.C. §7411(d), which requires EPA to establish a procedure under which states will submit plans establishing "standards of performance" defined the same way as NSPS standards under section 111(a) above? Would including renewable energy as a technology justify stricter or laxer emission limits?

5) *Carbon capture and storage.* CCS involves storing the captured carbon underground. EPA's proposal acknowledges that some of the carbon stored in this way might leak out eventually. Suppose that based on comments EPA concludes that some existing storage sites probably will leak carbon into the atmosphere in significant quantities one hundred years from now. Should it modify the rule? If so, how?

C. TECHNOLOGY-BASED STANDARD SETTING'S RECORD

Congress introduced technology-based output standards into the Clean Water Act in 1972 in response to failed efforts to base reduction requirements on ambient water quality standards in earlier versions of the law. As the *Weyerhauser* Court suggested, the process of back calculating emission or effluent limitations from ambient air quality or water quality standards has always been extraordinarily complex and difficult. The Supreme Court explained:

> Before it was amended in 1972, the Federal Water Pollution Control Act employed ambient water quality standards specifying acceptable levels of pollution in a State's interstate navigable waters as the primary mechanism for the control of water pollution. This program based on water quality standards, which were to serve both to guide performance by polluters and to trigger legal action to abate pollution, proved ineffective. The problems stemmed from the character of the standards themselves, which focused on the tolerable effects rather than the preventable causes of water pollution, from the awkwardly shared federal and state responsibility for promulgating such standards, and from the cumbersome enforcement procedures. These combined to make it very difficult to develop and enforce standards to govern the conduct of individual polluters.

EPA v. California ex rel. State Water Resources Control Bd., 426 U.S. 200, 202-03 (1976).

Oliver Houck, a leading water pollution expert, has written that "[a]mbient-based management has not worked well in any media—air, water, or waste." *See, e.g.*, OLIVER A. HOUCK, THE CLEAN WATER ACT TMDL PROGRAM: LAW, POLICY, AND IMPLEMENTATION 165 (2d ed. 2002). By contrast, a consensus exists that technology-based regulations have produced significant reductions in pollution. *See, e.g., id.* at 3; Wendy A. Wagner, *Innovations in Environmental Policies: The Triumph of Technology-Based Standards*, 2000 U. ILL. L. REV. 83, 94; Sidney A. Shapiro & Thomas O. McGarity, *Not So Paradoxical: The Rationale for Technology-Based Regulation*, 1991 DUKE L.J. 729, 739-42. While the standard-setting process has been somewhat treacherous, understanding technological possibilities is not as difficult as risk-based standard setting. And technology-based standards, once promulgated, can produce large amounts of reduction in a variety of pollutants across a wide geographic area. We shall see, however, that scholars have harshly criticized "command and control" regulation as inefficient and otherwise defective.

The history of pollution control efforts in the United States contains many instances of Congress converting risk-based programs into technology-based programs, because the risk-based programs did not work. For example, the 1970 Clean Air Act Amendments required EPA to regulate hazardous air pollutants to achieve an ample margin of safety. (Recall the *Vinyl Chloride* case, *supra*.) EPA only regulated 7 pollutants in 20 years under this risk-based approach. *See* David M. Driesen, *Getting Our Priorities Straight: One Strand of the Regulatory Reform Debate*, 31 Envtl. L. Rep. (Envtl. L. Inst.) 10003, 10007 (2001). Some observers attribute this to EPA's fear of having to put industry out of business in order to implement a mandate to protect public health. Others attribute it to the difficulty of analyzing the health effects data. But Congress clearly concluded in 1990 that this program had failed and substituted a technology-based standard setting program for 189 pollutants that Congress listed in the statute. This program generated 97 standards governing 174 source category and reduced air toxic emissions by 1.5 million tons. EPA, National Air Toxics Program: The Second Integrated Urban Air Toxics Report to Congress xiii, 3-3 (2014).[1] The statute still contemplates a second phase of regulation to eliminate residual risk. *See* 42 U.S.C. §7412(f); *cf.* Natural Resources Defense Council v. EPA, 529 F.3d 1077 (D.C. Cir. 2008) (upholding EPA's decision not to promulgate a residual risk standard for the largest emitter of air toxics, the chemical industry).

A similar history comes from the Clean Water Act. The Natural Resources Defense Council (NRDC), an environmental group, sued EPA for failing to implement that statute's mandate for protective regulation of toxic water pollutants. NRDC, industry, and EPA agreed to regulate a list of "priority" pollutants negotiated between the parties. They agreed that rather than strictly following the risk-based approach in the statute, EPA would base these limits on technological capability. Congress subsequently ratified this approach when it amended the Clean Water Act. This approach has produced significant reductions in toxic effluent.

On the other hand, industry lobbyists frequently criticize technology-based standard setting as "control for control's" sake. They have a point, don't they? After all, we regulate to achieve environmental benefits. Technology-based standard setting becomes simple at the cost of not considering the precise environmental benefit involved. It focuses primarily on what can be done, rather than the value of reductions to the environment.

Scholars have frequently criticized technology-based standards as inefficient. They rely on the sort of variability in plant conditions that *National Lime* discusses. These variations imply that the cost of achieving a given level of pollution reduction is relatively high at some plants and low at others, something nobody

---

1. This number includes reductions from a parallel program for waste combustors under section 129 of the Clean Air Act. *See* id. at 3-3.

doubts. Uniform standards can prove inefficient because they do not take this variability into account. Does this criticism apply only to technology-based uniform standards? Would it apply to health-based uniform standards? Cost-benefit–based uniform standards?

Scholars have also attacked technology-based standard setting as providing insufficient incentives for innovation. For example, Bruce Ackerman and Richard Stewart write:

> BAT controls can ensure the diffusion of established control technologies. But they do not provide strong incentives for the development of new environmentally superior strategies and may actually discourage their development. Such innovations are essential if we are to maintain economic growth in the long run without simultaneously increasing pollution and other forms of environmental degradation.

Reforming Environmental Law: The Democratic Case for Market Incentives, 13 COLUM. J. ENVTL. L. 171, 174 (1988).

Because of a dearth of post-compliance studies, we do not know how often technology-based regulations encourage innovation. Nevertheless, a number of scholars share Ackerman's and Stewart's views. On the other hand, we know that in some instances technology-based regulation has encouraged innovation. *See* DAVID M. DRIESEN, THE ECONOMIC DYNAMICS OF ENVIRONMENTAL LAW 53 (2003); David Popp, *Pollution Control Innovations and the 1990 Clean Air Act Amendments*, 22 J. POL'Y ANALYSIS & MGMT. 641 (2003); UNITED STATES CONGRESS, OFFICE OF TECHNOLOGY ASSESSMENT, GAUGING CONTROL TECHNOLOGY AND REGULATORY IMPACTS IN OCCUPATIONAL SAFETY AND HEALTH—AN APPRAISAL OF OSHA'S ANALYTICAL APPROACH 64 (1995); Nicholas A. Ashford, Christine Ayers & Robert F. Stone, *Using Regulation to Change the Market for Innovation*, 9 HARV. ENVTL. L. REV. 419, 440-41 (1985); Nicholas A. Ashford & George R. Heaton Jr., *Regulation and Technological Innovation in the Chemical Industry*, 46 LAW & CONTEMP. PROBS. 109, 139-40 (1983).

What variables do you suppose might influence innovation rates? Do you think that more stringent and costly regulation would increase or decrease incentives for innovation? Would health-based standards encourage innovation better than technology-based regulation? What about standards based on cost-benefit analysis?

Many scholars have argued that the law's tendency to impose stricter standards on new sources than on existing sources also tends to discourage innovation. Is this really a criticism of technology-based standard setting? Suppose that the federal government amended the environmental statutes to impose equally strict requirements on new and existing sources, but based both on technological capability. Would this solve the problem of discouraging cleaner new sources? Recall (from *National Lime, supra*) that new source controls under the Clean Air Act apply to modified sources as well as existing sources. The Clean Air Act defines modification as a physical or operational change at an existing pollution source that increases emissions. Can one argue, given the applicability of new source controls to modified existing sources, that existing law discourages emission decreasing modernization by imposing stricter requirements on new sources than on existing ones? Would strict application of new source controls to modified sources remove the disincentives for new sources? Are pollution control costs significant enough to influence firms' technological choices in a significant way? What data would you like to have to answer this question?

Scholars who criticize technology-based regulation for imposing too much cost while discouraging innovation usually recommend emissions trading programs as a remedy. In the next chapter, we consider the alternative to technology-based standard setting advocated by industry in the *Benzene* and *Pacific Fisheries* cases.

6

Cost-Benefit Approaches

In recent decades, government has placed a great deal of emphasis on using cost-benefit analysis (CBA) to guide environmental decision making, which had a relatively confined role in the 1970s. CBA involves comparing the costs of a proposed action to its benefits. This chapter focuses primarily upon the use of CBA to guide pollution control decisions.

When the action subject to CBA consists of a government regulation requiring reduction or elimination of pollution, the direct costs typically consist of the monies regulated firms or individuals must spend to comply with regulatory requirements. CBA may also include estimates of indirect impacts upon employment and the economy. Calculating the direct costs of environmental regulation for purposes of CBA is basically the same as calculating direct costs to set a technology-based standard. (Recall that the technology-based standard provisions typically required consideration of cost, but did not require CBA.)

The benefits consist of the environmental improvements the pollution reduction will bring about. Estimating the value of these benefits proves more difficult than the estimation of compliance cost. Estimation of benefits involves two steps. First, the analyst must engage in quantitative risk assessment. Then, she must monetize the benefits, *i.e.*, assign a dollar value to the health and environmental consequences of the regulation. Conversion of environmental benefits into dollars allows the regulator to compare the value of environmental benefits to the costs.

The quantitative risk assessment step requires government officials to estimate the number of deaths, illnesses, and other consequences a proposed regulation would prevent. Usually, the agency is unable to quantify many significant environmental and health effects, because of lack of sufficient data.

Monetizing the amount of ecological damage a regulation might avoid usually proves especially difficult. How much is it worth to have bald eagles, to see a beautiful view unmarred by haze, or to be able to exercise outdoors without harm to one's health? While economists have tried to estimate the dollar value of some environmental amenities, *see, e.g.*, Ohio v. Dep't of Interior, 880 F.2d 432, 475 (D.C. Cir. 1989) (discussing various ways of assessing natural resource damages), critics question whether these techniques adequately capture the true value.

Almost always, quantification involves substantial uncertainties. For example, carcinogens usually command regulatory attention because data from experiments on animals indicate that the animals contract cancer when consuming a lot of a substance. *See* Wendy E. Wagner, *The Science Charade in Toxic Risk Regulation*, 95 COLUM. L. REV. 1613, 1625 (1995) (discussing the problem of extrapolating human health effects from high dose animal experiments). If we have human exposure data, those data usually come from rare accidental occupational exposures to unusually high doses of the chemical, much higher and of shorter duration than typical environmental exposures. Estimation of the effects of continuous low dose exposure upon humans requires extrapolation from the animal data and (if it exists) data about human response to temporary high doses. Unfortunately, we do not understand cancer well enough to know how to make this extrapolation. For that reason, the National Academy of Sciences has recommended providing a range of estimates, rather than a point estimate. Frequently, the range of plausible estimates is so large as to provide relatively little guidance. Cass R. Sunstein, *The Arithmetic of Arsenic*, 90 GEO. L.J. 2255, 2257 (2002). *See also* Donald T. Hornstein, *Reclaiming Environmental Law: A Normative Critique of Comparative Risk Analysis*, 92 COLUM. L. REV. 562, 572 (1992) (the National Academy of Sciences has identified 50 "inference options," where a policy decision must be made to extrapolate a risk assessment from limited data).

The agency must then attempt to monetize the benefits, such as the saving of human life and the prevention of serious illness. This monetization is extremely controversial. Critics claim that we ought not treat life like a commodity and that assigning it a dollar value is arbitrary. Furthermore, they claim that data limitations make a lot of this monetization ludicrous and question the value choices imbedded in the assumptions underlying the choice of dollar values. *See* FRANK ACKERMAN & LISA HEINZERLING, PRICELESS: ON KNOWING THE PRICE OF EVERYTHING AND THE VALUE OF NOTHING (2004). Others, however, believe this process appropriate, even if imprecise, because of the need to improve priority setting, advance overall well-being (including economic well-being), and improve the rationality of regulation. *See, e.g.*, CASS R. SUNSTEIN, THE COST-BENEFIT STATE: THE FUTURE OF REGULATORY PROTECTION (2002); CASS R. SUNSTEIN, RISK AND REASON: SAFETY, LAW, AND THE ENVIRONMENT (2002); Matthew D. Adler & Eric A. Posner, *Rethinking Cost-Benefit Analysis*, 109 YALE L.J. 165 (1999). After monetizing benefits, the agency must then compare costs and benefits in some fashion.

A. CBA IN THE TOXIC SUBSTANCES CONTROL ACT, THE FEDERAL INSECTICIDE, FUNGICIDE, AND RODENTICIDE ACT, AND THE SAFE DRINKING WATER ACT

The following case history involves an EPA proposal to ban most uses of asbestos under the Toxic Substances Control Act (TSCA). This proposal followed a series of actions seeking to limit asbestos exposure in various settings. For example, the *Reserve Mining* case sought to limit asbestos as a water pollutant. Asbestos is a fire-proofing material often used in construction and brake linings. Asbestos causes two diseases not significantly associated with other causes, asbestosis and mesothelioma. It also causes a number of cancers, such as lung and gastrointestinal cancers, that other toxic substances can also trigger. By the time EPA promulgated its asbestos ban, successful toxic tort suits were well on their way to driving the asbestos industry into bankruptcy. Apparently, juries were satisfied that asbestos was causing serious injuries to those who had worked with the substance.

Consider first the following questions. Does section 6 of the Toxic Substances Control Act require CBA? How should EPA go about deciding whether a ban is appropriate? Section 6 (15 U.S.C. §2605) provides:

Regulation of hazardous chemical substances and mixtures

(a) Scope of regulation. If the Administrator finds that there is a reasonable basis to conclude that the manufacture, processing, distribution in commerce, use, or disposal of a chemical substance or mixture, or that any combination of such activities, presents or will present an unreasonable risk of injury to health or the environment, the Administrator shall by rule apply one or more of the following requirements to such substance or mixture to the extent necessary to protect adequately against such risk using the least burdensome requirements:

(1) A requirement (A) prohibiting the manufacturing, processing, or distribution in commerce of such substance or mixture, or (B) limiting the amount of such substance or mixture which may be manufactured, processed, or distributed in commerce.

(2) A requirement—

(A) prohibiting the manufacture, processing, or distribution in commerce of such substance or mixture for (i) a particular use or (ii) a particular use in a concentration in excess of a level specified by the Administrator in the rule imposing the requirement, or

(B) limiting the amount of such substance or mixture which may be manufactured, processed, or distributed in commerce for (i) a particular use or (ii) a particular use in a concentration in excess of a level specified by the Administrator in the rule imposing the requirement.

(3) A requirement that such substance or mixture or any article containing such substance or mixture be marked with or accompanied by clear and adequate warnings and instructions with respect to its use, distribution in commerce, or disposal or with respect to any combination of such activities. The form and content of such warnings and instructions shall be prescribed by the Administrator.

(4) A requirement that manufacturers and processors of such substance or mixture make and retain records of the processes used to manufacture or process such substance or mixture and monitor or conduct tests which are reasonable and necessary to assure compliance with the requirements of any rule applicable under this subsection.

(5) A requirement prohibiting or otherwise regulating any manner or method of commercial use of such substance or mixture.

(6) (A) A requirement prohibiting or otherwise regulating any manner or method of disposal of such substance or mixture, or of any article containing such substance or mixture, by its manufacturer or processor or by any other person who uses, or disposes of, it for commercial purposes.

(B) A requirement under subparagraph (A) may not require any person to take any action which would be in violation of any law or requirement of, or in effect for, a State or political subdivision, and shall require each person subject to it to notify each State and political subdivision in which a required disposal may occur of such disposal.

(7) A requirement directing manufacturers or processors of such substance or mixture (A) to give notice of such unreasonable risk of injury to distributors in commerce of such substance or mixture and, to the extent reasonably ascertainable, to other persons in possession of such substance or mixture or exposed to such substance or mixture, (B) to give public notice of such risk of injury, and (C) to replace or repurchase such substance or mixture as elected by the person to which the requirement is directed.

Does this language require that the benefits of an asbestos ban outweigh the costs? Suppose that EPA concludes that all of the options except a ban would not adequately prevent a risk of contracting cancer. May it still choose one of the less drastic options? Would your answer change if the cost of a ban outweighed the benefits? *See* Thomas O. McGarity, *The Courts and the Ossification of Rulemaking: A Response to Professor Seidenfeld*, 75 Tex. L. Rev. 525, 541-49 (1997).

EPA decided to phase out most uses of asbestos. But it exempted particular asbestos uses from the ban if an applicant could demonstrate that she "has made demonstrable good faith efforts to develop substitutes for its product and that granting the exemption will not result in an unreasonable risk of injury to human health." EPA's decision and interpretation of section 6 are explained in the Federal Register notice announcing the asbestos ban:

Asbestos; Manufacture, Importation, Processing, and Distribution in Commerce Prohibitions

54 Fed. Reg. 29460 (July 12, 1989)

* * *

V. Regulatory Assessment

Section 6 of TSCA authorizes EPA to promulgate a rule prohibiting or limiting the amount of a chemical substance that may be manufactured, processed, or distributed in commerce in the U.S. if EPA finds that there is a reasonable basis to conclude that the manufacturer, processing, distribution in commerce, use, or disposal of the chemical substance, or any combination of these activities, presents or will present an unreasonable risk of injury to human health or the environment.

Section 6(c)(1) of TSCA requires EPA to consider the following factors when determining whether a chemical substance presents an unreasonable risk:

1. The effects of such substance on human health and the magnitude of the exposure of human beings to such substance.
2. The effects of such substance on the environment and the magnitude of the exposure of the environment to such substance or mixture.
3. The benefits of such substance for various uses and the availability of substitutes for such uses.
4. The reasonably ascertainable economic consequences of the rule, after consideration of the effect on the national economy, small businesses, technological innovation, the environment, and public health.

To determine whether a risk from activities involving asbestos-containing products presents an unreasonable risk, EPA must balance the probability that harm will occur from the activities against the effects of the proposed regulatory action on the availability to society of the benefits of asbestos. EPA has considered these factors in conjunction with the extensive record gathered in the development of this rule. EPA has concluded that the continued manufacture, importation, processing, and distribution in commerce of most asbestos-containing products poses an unreasonable risk to human health. This conclusion is based on information summarized in the following paragraphs and discussed in the units that follow.

EPA has concluded that exposure to asbestos during the life cycles of many asbestos-containing products poses an unreasonable risk of injury to human health. EPA has also concluded that section 6 of TSCA is the ideal statutory authority to regulate the risks posed by asbestos exposure. This rule's pollution prevention actions under TSCA are both the preferable and the least burdensome means of controlling the exposure risks posed throughout the life cycle of asbestos-containing products. Findings supporting this conclusion include the following:

1. Exposure to asbestos causes many painful, premature deaths due to mesothelioma and lung, gastrointestinal, and other cancers, as well as asbestosis and other diseases. Risks attributable to asbestos exposure and addressed by this rule are serious and are calculated for this rule using direct evidence from numerous human epidemiological studies. Studies show that asbestos is a highly potent carcinogen and that severe health effects occur after even short-term, high-level or longer-term, low-level exposures to asbestos. Asbestos exposure is compatible with a linear, nonthreshold dose-response model for lung cancer. In addition, there is no undisputed evidence of quantitative differences in potency based on fiber size or type.

   For the quantitative risk assessment performed as part of this rulemaking, EPA used dose-response constants for lung cancer and mesothelioma that were the geometric means of the "best estimates" from a number of epidemiological studies. If EPA had instead used an upper bound estimate, as is normally done by the scientific community and in EPA regulatory risk assessment when only data from animal studies is available to extrapolate human health risk, predicted lung cancer deaths could increase by a factor of 10 and mesothelioma deaths could increase by a factor of 20.

2. People are frequently unknowingly exposed to asbestos and are rarely in a position to protect themselves. Asbestos is generally invisible, odorless, very durable, and highly aerodynamic. It can travel long distances and exist in the environment for extended periods. Therefore, exposure can take place long after the release of asbestos and at a distant location from the source of release.

3. Additions to the current stock of asbestos-containing products would contribute to the environmental loading of asbestos. This poses the potential for an increased risk to the general population of asbestos-related disease and an increased risk to future generations because of asbestos' longevity.

4. Asbestos fibers are released to the air at many stages of the commercial life of the products that are subject to this rule. Activities that might lead to the release of asbestos include mining of the substance, processing asbestos fibers into products, and transport, installation, use, maintenance, repair, removal, and disposal of asbestos-containing products. EPA has found that the occupational and non-occupational exposure existing over the entire life cycles of each of the banned asbestos-containing products poses a high level of individual risk. EPA has determined that thousands of persons involved in the manufacture, processing, transport, installation, use, repair, removal, and disposal of the asbestos-containing products affected by this rule are exposed to a serious lifetime asbestos exposure risk, despite OSHA's relatively low workplace PEL. In addition, according to the EPA Asbestos Modeling Study, millions of members of the general U.S. population are exposed to elevated levels of lifetime risk due to asbestos released throughout the life cycle of asbestos-containing products. EPA believes that the exposure quantified for the analyses supporting this rule represent an understatement of actual exposure.

5. Release of asbestos fibers from many products during life cycle activities can be substantial. OSHA stated in setting its PEL of 0.2 f/cc [fibers per cubic centimeter of air] that remaining exposures pose a serious risk because of limitations on available exposure control technologies. Even with OSHA's controls, thousands of workers involved in the manufacture and processing of asbestos-containing products are exposed to a lifetime risk of 1 in 1,000 of developing cancer. Many other exposures addressed by this rule are not affected by engineering controls required by OSHA's PEL or by other government regulation. Because asbestos is a highly potent carcinogen, the uncontrolled high peak episodic exposures that are faced by large populations pose a significant risk.

6. Because of the life cycle or "cradle-to-grave" nature of the risk posed by asbestos, attempts by OSHA, the Consumer Product Safety Commission (CPSC), and other EPA offices to regulate the continued commercial use of asbestos still leave many persons unprotected from the hazards of asbestos exposure. Technological limitations inhibit the effectiveness of existing or possible exposure control actions under non-TSCA authorities. Many routes of asbestos exposure posed by the products subject to this rule are outside the jurisdictions of regulatory authorities other than TSCA. EPA has determined that the residual exposure to asbestos that exists despite the

actions taken under other authorities poses a serious health risk throughout the life cycle of many asbestos-containing products. This residual exposure can only be adequately controlled by the exposure prevention actions taken in this rule.

7. Despite the proven risks of asbestos exposure and the current or imminent existence of suitable substitutes for most uses of asbestos, asbestos continues to be used in large quantities in the U.S. in the manufacture or processing of a wide variety of commercial products. Total annual U.S. consumption of asbestos dropped from a 1984 total of about 240,000 metric tons to less than 85,000 metric tons in 1987, according to the U.S. Department of Interior, Bureau of Mines data. This change suggests that the use of substitutes has increased markedly since the proposal. However, the 1987 consumption total indicates that significant exposure due to the commercial use of asbestos and the resultant risks would continue for the foreseeable future absent the actions taken in this rule.

Evidence supports the conclusion that substitutes already exist or will soon exist for each of the products that are subject to the rule's bans. In scheduling products for the different stages of the bans, EPA has analyzed the probable availability of non-asbestos substitutes. In the rule, the various asbestos products are scheduled to be banned at times when it is likely that suitable non-asbestos substitutes will be available. However, the rule also includes an exemption provision to account for instances in which technology might not have advanced sufficiently by the time of a ban to produce substitutes for certain specialized or limited uses of asbestos.

8. EPA has calculated that the product bans in this rule will result in the avoidance of 202 quantifiable cancer cases, if benefits are not discounted, and 148 cases, if benefits are discounted at 3 percent. The figures decrease to 164 cases, if benefits are not discounted, and 120 cases, if benefits are discounted at 3 percent, if analogous exposures are not included in the analysis. In all likelihood, the rule will result in the avoidance of a large number of other cancer cases that cannot be quantified, as well as many cases of asbestos related diseases. Estimates of benefits resulting from the action taken in this rule are limited to mesothelioma and lung and gastro-intestinal cancer-cases-avoided, and do not include cases of asbestosis and other diseases avoided and avoided costs from treating asbestos diseases, lost productivity, or other factors. EPA has estimated that the cost of this rule, for the 13-year period of the analyses performed, will be approximately $458.89 million, or $806.51 million if a 1 percent annual decline in the price of substitutes is not assumed. This cost will be spread over time and a large population so that the cost to any person is likely to be negligible. In addition, the rule's exemption provision is a qualitative factor that supports the actions taken in this rule. EPA has concluded that the quantifiable and unquantifiable benefits of the rule's staged-ban of the identified asbestos-containing products will outweigh the resultant economic consequences to consumers, producers, and users of the products.

9. EPA has determined that, within the findings required by section 6 of TSCA, only the staged-ban approach employed in this final rule will adequately control the asbestos exposure risk posed by the product categories affected by this rule. Other options either fail to address significant portions of the life cycle risk posed by products subject to the rule or are unreasonably burdensome. EPA has, therefore, concluded that the actions taken in this rule represent the least burdensome means of reducing the risk posed by exposure to asbestos during the life cycles of the products that are subject to the bans.

10. Based on the reasons summarized in this preamble, this rule bans most asbestos-containing products in the U.S. because they pose an unreasonable risk to human health. These banned products account for approximately 94 percent of U.S. asbestos consumption, based on 1985 consumption figures. The actions taken will result in a substantial reduction in the unreasonable risk caused by asbestos exposure in the U.S.

A few minor uses of asbestos and asbestos products are not included in the ban. These uses, which account for less than 6 percent of U.S. asbestos consumption based on 1985 data, do not pose an unreasonable risk, based on current knowledge. . . .

The United States Court of Appeals for the Fifth Circuit reversed EPA's ban. Focus on whether the court's statutory interpretation differed from that of EPA, and if so, how.

Corrosion Proof Fittings v. EPA

947 F.2d 1201 (5th Cir. 1991)

SMITH, CIRCUIT JUDGE.

The Environmental Protection Agency (EPA) issued a final rule under section 6 of the Toxic Substances Control Act (TSCA) to prohibit the future manufacture, importation, processing, and distribution of asbestos in almost all products. Petitioners claim that the EPA's . . . rule was not promulgated on the basis of substantial evidence. . . . Because the EPA failed to muster substantial evidence to support its rule, we remand this matter to the EPA for further consideration in light of this opinion.

I. Facts and Procedural History . . .

The EPA began these proceedings in 1979, when it issued an Advanced Notice of Proposed Rulemaking announcing its intent to explore the use of TSCA "to reduce the risk to human health posed by exposure to asbestos." *See* 54 Fed. Reg. 29,460 (1989). While these proceedings were pending, other agencies continued their regulation of asbestos uses, in particular the Occupational Safety and Health Administration (OSHA), which in 1983 and 1984 involved itself with lowering standards for workplace asbestos exposure.

An EPA-appointed panel reviewed over one hundred studies of asbestos and conducted several public meetings. Based upon its studies and the public comments, the EPA concluded that asbestos is a potential carcinogen at all levels of exposure, regardless of the type of asbestos or the size of the fiber. The EPA concluded in 1986 that exposure to asbestos "poses an unreasonable risk to human health" and thus proposed at least four regulatory options for prohibiting or restricting the use of asbestos, including a mixed ban and phase-out of asbestos over ten years; a two-stage ban of asbestos, depending upon product usage; a three-stage ban on all asbestos products leading to a total ban in ten years; and labeling of all products containing asbestos.

Over the next two years, the EPA updated its data, received further comments, and allowed cross-examination on the updated documents. In 1989, the EPA issued a final rule prohibiting the manufacture, importation, processing, and distribution in commerce of most asbestos-containing products. Finding that asbestos constituted an unreasonable risk to health and the environment, the EPA promulgated a staged ban of most commercial uses of asbestos. The EPA estimates that this rule will save either 202 or 148 lives, depending upon whether the benefits are discounted, at a cost of approximately $450-800 million, depending upon the price of substitutes.

[P]etitioners challenge the EPA's final rule, claiming that the EPA's rulemaking procedure was flawed and that the rule was not promulgated based upon substantial evidence. . . .

IV. The Language of TSCA

A. Standard of Review

Our inquiry into the legitimacy of the EPA rulemaking begins with a discussion of the standard of review governing this case. EPA's phase-out ban of most commercial uses of asbestos is a TSCA §6(a) rulemaking. TSCA provides that a reviewing court "shall hold unlawful and set aside" a final rule promulgated under §6(a) "if the court finds that the rule is not supported by substantial evidence in the rulemaking record . . . taken as a whole."

Substantial evidence requires "something less than the weight of the evidence, and the possibility of drawing two inconsistent conclusions from the evidence does not prevent an administrative agency's finding from being supported by substantial evidence." This standard requires (1) that the agency's decision be based upon the entire record, taking into account whatever in the record detracts from the weight of the agency's decision; and (2) that the agency's decision be what "a reasonable mind might accept as adequate to support [its] conclusion." Thus, even if there is enough evidence in the record to support the petitioners' assertions, we will not reverse if there is substantial evidence to support the agency's decision. . . .

In evaluating whether the EPA has presented substantial evidence, we examine (1) whether the quantities of the regulated chemical entering into the environment are "substantial" and (2) whether human exposure to the chemical is "substantial" or "significant." An agency may exercise its judgment without strictly relying upon quantifiable risks, costs, and benefits, but it must "cogently explain why it has exercised its discretion in a given manner" and "must offer a 'rational connection between the facts found and the choice made.'"

We note that in undertaking our review, we give all agency rules a presumption of validity, and it is up to the challenger to any rule to show that the agency action is invalid. The burden remains on the EPA, however, to justify that the products it bans present an unreasonable risk, no matter how regulated. Finally, as we discuss in detail *infra*, because TSCA instructs the EPA to undertake the least burdensome regulation sufficient to regulate the substance at issue, the agency bears a heavier burden when it seeks a partial or total ban of a substance than when it merely seeks to regulate that product.

B. *The EPA's Burden Under TSCA*

TSCA provides, in pertinent part, as follows:

(a) Scope of regulation.—If the Administrator finds that there is a *reasonable basis* to conclude that the manufacture, processing, distribution in commerce, use, or disposal of a chemical substance or mixture, or that any combination of such activities, presents or will present an *unreasonable risk of injury* to health or the environment, the Administrator shall by rule apply one or more of the following requirements to such substance or mixture to the extent necessary *to protect adequately* against such risk using the *least burdensome* requirements.

As the highlighted language shows, Congress did not enact TSCA as a zero-risk statute. The EPA, rather, was required to consider both alternatives to a ban and the costs of any proposed actions and to "carry out this chapter in a reasonable and prudent manner [after considering] the environmental, economic, and social impact of any action." 15 U.S.C. §2601(c).

We conclude that the EPA has presented insufficient evidence to justify its asbestos ban. We base this conclusion upon two grounds: the failure of the EPA to consider all necessary evidence and its failure to give adequate weight to statutory language requiring it to promulgate the least burdensome, reasonable regulation required to protect the environment adequately. Because the EPA failed to address these concerns, and because the EPA is required to articulate a "reasoned basis" for its rules, we are compelled to return the regulation to the agency for reconsideration.

1. Least Burdensome and Reasonable

TSCA requires that the EPA use the least burdensome regulation to achieve its goal of minimum reasonable risk. This statutory requirement can create problems in evaluating just what is a "reasonable risk." Congress's rejection of a no-risk policy, however, also means that in certain cases, the least burdensome yet still adequate solution may entail somewhat more risk than would other, known regulations that are far more burdensome on the industry and the economy. The very language of TSCA requires that the EPA, once it has determined what an acceptable level of non-zero risk is, choose the least burdensome method of reaching that level.

In this case, the EPA banned, for all practical purposes, all present and future uses of asbestos—a position the petitioners characterize as the "death penalty alternative," as this is the *most* burdensome of all possible alternatives listed as open to the EPA under TSCA. TSCA not only provides the EPA with a list of alternative actions, but also provides those alternatives in order of how burdensome they are. The regulations thus provide for EPA regulation ranging from labeling the least toxic chemicals to limiting the total amount of chemicals an industry may use. Total bans head the list as the most burdensome regulatory option.

By choosing the harshest remedy given to it under TSCA, the EPA assigned to itself the toughest burden in satisfying TSCA's requirement that its alternative be the least burdensome of all those offered to it. Since, both by definition and by the terms of TSCA, the complete ban of manufacturing is the most burdensome alternative—for even stringent regulation at least allows a manufacturer the chance to invest and meet the new, higher standard—the EPA's regulation cannot stand if there is any other regulation that would achieve an acceptable level of risk as mandated by TSCA.

We reserve until a later part of the opinion a product-by-product review of the regulation. Before reaching this analysis, however, we lay down the inquiry that the EPA should undertake whenever it seeks total ban of a product.

The EPA considered, and rejected, such options as labeling asbestos products, thereby warning users and workers involved in the manufacture of asbestos-containing products of the chemical's dangers, and stricter workplace rules. EPA also rejected controlled use of asbestos in the workplace and deferral to other government agencies charged with worker and consumer exposure to industrial and product hazards, such as OSHA, the CPSC, and the MSHA. The EPA determined that deferral to these other agencies was inappropriate because no one other authority could address all the risks posed "throughout the life cycle" by asbestos, and any action by one or more of the other agencies still would leave an unacceptable residual risk.

Much of the EPA's analysis is correct, and the EPA's basic decision to use TSCA as a comprehensive statute designed to fight a multi-industry problem was a proper one that we uphold today on review. What concerns us, however, is the manner in which the EPA conducted some of its analysis. TSCA requires the EPA to consider, along with the effects of toxic substances on human health and the environment, "the benefits of such substance[s] or mixture[s] for various uses and the availability of substitutes for such uses," as well as "the reasonably ascertainable economic consequences of the rule, after consideration for the effect on the national economy, small business, technological innovation, the environment, and public health." *Id.* §2605(c)(1)(C-D).

The EPA presented two comparisons in the record: a world with no further regulation under TSCA, and a world in which no manufacture of asbestos takes place. The EPA rejected calculating how many lives a less burdensome regulation would save, and at what cost. Furthermore the EPA, when calculating the benefits of its ban, explicitly refused to compare it to an improved workplace in which currently available control technology is utilized. This decision artificially inflated the purported benefits of the rule by using a baseline comparison substantially lower than what currently available technology could yield.

Under TSCA, the EPA was required to evaluate, rather than ignore, less burdensome regulatory alternatives. TSCA imposes a least-to-most-burdensome hierarchy. In order to impose a regulation at the top of the hierarchy—a total ban of asbestos—the EPA must show not only that its proposed action reduces the risk of the product to an adequate level, but also that the actions Congress identified as less burdensome also would not do the job. The failure of the EPA to do this constitutes a failure to meet its burden of showing that its actions not only reduce the risk but do so in the Congressionally-mandated *least burdensome* fashion.

Thus it was not enough for the EPA to show, as it did in this case, that banning some asbestos products might reduce the harm that could occur from the use of these products. If that were the standard, it would be no standard at all, for few indeed are the products that are so safe that a complete ban of them would not make the world still safer.

This comparison of two static worlds is insufficient to satisfy the dictates of TSCA. While the EPA may have shown that a world with a complete ban of asbestos might be preferable to one in which there is only the current amount of regulation, the EPA has failed to show that there is not some intermediate state of regulation that would be superior to both the currently-regulated and the completely-banned world. Without showing that asbestos regulation would be ineffective, the EPA cannot discharge its TSCA burden of showing that its regulation is the least burdensome available to it.

Upon an initial showing of product danger, the proper course for the EPA to follow is to consider each regulatory option, beginning with the least burdensome, and the costs and benefits of regulation under each option. The EPA cannot simply skip several rungs, as it did in this case, for in doing so, it may skip a less-burdensome alternative mandated by TSCA. Here, although the EPA mentions the problems posed by intermediate levels of regulation, it takes no steps to calculate the costs and benefits of these intermediate levels. Without doing this it is impossible, both for the EPA and for this court on review, to know that none of these alternatives was less burdensome than the ban in fact chosen by the agency.

The EPA's offhand rejection of these intermediate regulatory steps is "not the stuff of which substantial evidence is made." While it is true that the EPA considered five different ban options, these differed solely with respect to their effective dates. The EPA did not calculate the risk levels for intermediate levels of regulation, as it believed that there was no asbestos exposure level for which the risk of injury or death was zero. Reducing risk to zero, however, was not the task that Congress set for the EPA in enacting TSCA. The EPA thus has failed "cogently [to] explain why it has exercised its discretion in a given manner," by failing to explore in more than a cursory way the less burdensome alternatives to a total ban.

2. The EPA's Calculations

Furthermore, we are concerned about some of the methodology employed by the EPA in making various of the calculations that it did perform. In order to aid the EPA's reconsideration of this and other cases, we present our concerns here.

First, we note that there was some dispute in the record regarding the appropriateness of discounting the perceived benefits of the EPA's rule. In choosing between the calculated costs and benefits, the EPA presented variations in which it discounted only the costs, and counter-variations in which it discounted both the costs and the benefits, measured in both monetary and human injury terms. As between these two variations, we choose to evaluate the EPA's work using its discounted benefits calculations.

Although various commentators dispute whether it ever is appropriate to discount benefits when they are measured in human lives, we note that it would skew the results to discount only costs without according similar treatment to the benefits side of the equation. Adopting the position of the commentators who advocate not discounting benefits would force the EPA similarly not to calculate costs in present discounted real terms, making comparisons difficult. Furthermore, in evaluating situations in which different options incur costs at varying time intervals, the EPA would not be able to take into account that soon-to-be-incurred costs are more harmful than postponable costs. Because the EPA must discount costs to perform its evaluations properly, the EPA also should discount benefits to preserve an apples-to-apples comparison, even if this entails discounting benefits of a non-monetary nature. *See What Price Posterity?*, The Economist, March 23, 1991, at 73 (explaining use of discount rates for non-monetary goods). . . .

Of more concern to us is the failure of the EPA to compute the costs and benefits of its proposed rule past the year 2000, and its double-counting of the costs of asbestos use. In performing its calculus, the EPA only included the number of lives saved over the next thirteen years, and counted any additional lives saved as simply "unquantified benefits." 54 Fed. Reg. at 29,486. The EPA and intervenors now seek to use these unquantified lives saved to justify calculations as to which the benefits seem far outweighed by the astronomical costs. For example, the EPA plans to save about three lives with its ban of asbestos pipe, at a cost of $128-227 million (*i.e.*, approximately $43-76 million per life saved). Although the EPA admits that the price tag is high, it claims that the lives saved past the year 2000 justify the price.

Such calculations not only lessen the value of the EPA's cost analysis, but also make any meaningful judicial review impossible. While TSCA contemplates a useful place for unquantified benefits beyond the EPA's calculation, unquantified benefits never were intended as a trump card allowing the EPA to justify any cost calculus, no matter how high.

The concept of unquantified benefits, rather, is intended to allow the EPA to provide a rightful place for any remaining benefits that are impossible to quantify after the EPA's best attempt, but which still are of some concern. But the allowance for unquantified costs is not intended to allow the EPA to perform its calculations over an arbitrarily short period so as to preserve a large unquantified portion.

Unquantified benefits can, at times, permissibly tip the balance in close cases. They cannot, however, be used to effect a wholesale shift on the balance beam. Such a use makes a mockery of the requirements of TSCA that the EPA weigh the costs of its actions before it chooses the least burdensome alternative.

We do not today determine what an appropriate period for the EPA's calculations would be, as this is a matter better left for agency discretion. We do note, however, that the choice of a thirteen-year period is so short as to make the unquantified period so unreasonably large that any EPA reliance upon it must be displaced. . . .

4. Unreasonable Risk of Injury

The final requirement the EPA must satisfy before engaging in any TSCA rulemaking is that it only take steps designed to prevent "unreasonable" risks. In evaluating what is "unreasonable," the EPA is required to consider the costs of any proposed actions and to "carry out this chapter in a reasonable and prudent manner [after considering] the environmental, economic, and social impact of any action." 15 U.S.C. §2601(c).

As the District of Columbia Circuit stated when evaluating similar language governing the Federal Hazardous Substances Act, "the requirement that the risk be 'unreasonable' necessarily involves a balancing test like that familiar in tort law: The regulation may issue if the severity of the injury that may result from the product, factored by the likelihood of the injury, offsets the harm the regulation itself imposes upon manufacturers and consumers. . . ."

That the EPA must balance the costs of its regulations against their benefits further is reinforced by the requirement that it seek the least burdensome regulation. While Congress did not dictate that the EPA engage in an exhaustive, full-scale cost-benefit analysis, it did require the EPA to consider both sides of the regulatory equation, and it rejected the notion that the EPA should pursue the reduction of workplace risk at any cost. Thus, "Congress also plainly intended the EPA to consider the economic impact of *any* actions taken by it under . . . TSCA."

Even taking all of the EPA's figures as true, and evaluating them in the light most favorable to the agency's decision (non-discounted benefits, discounted costs, analogous exposure estimates included), the agency's analysis results in figures as high as $74 million per life saved. For example, the EPA states that its ban of asbestos pipe will save three lives over the next thirteen years, at a cost of $128-227 million ($43-76 million per life saved), depending upon the price of substitutes; that its ban of asbestos shingles will cost $23-34 million to save 0.32 statistical lives ($72-106 million per life saved); that its ban of asbestos coatings will cost $46-181 million to save 3.33 lives ($14-54 million per life saved); and that its ban of asbestos paper products will save 0.60 lives at a cost of $4-5 million ($7-8 million per life saved). Were the analogous exposure estimates not included, the cancer risks from substitutes such as ductile iron pipe factored in, and the benefits of the ban appropriately discounted from the time of the manifestation of an injury rather than the time of exposure, the costs would shift even more sharply against the EPA's position.

While we do not sit as a regulatory agency that must make the difficult decision as to what an appropriate expenditure is to prevent someone from incurring the risk of an asbestos-related death, we do note that the EPA, in its zeal to ban any and all asbestos products, basically ignored the cost side of the TSCA equation. The EPA would have this court believe that Congress, when it enacted its requirement that the EPA consider the economic impacts of its regulations, thought that spending $200-300 million to save approximately seven lives (approximately $30-40 million per life) over thirteen years is reasonable.

As we stated in the OSHA context, until an agency "can provide substantial evidence that the benefits to be achieved by [a regulation] bear a reasonable relationship to the costs imposed by the reduction, it cannot show that the standard is reasonably necessary to provide safe or healthful workplaces." Although the OSHA statute differs in major respects from TSCA, the statute does require substantial evidence to support the EPA's contentions that its regulations both have a reasonable basis and are the least burdensome means to a reasonably safe workplace.

The EPA's willingness to argue that spending $23.7 million to save less than one-third of a life reveals that its economic review of its regulations, as required by

TSCA, was meaningless. As the petitioners' brief and our review of EPA case law reveals, such high costs are rarely, if ever, used to support a safety regulation. If we were to allow such cavalier treatment of the EPA's duty to consider the economic effects of its decisions, we would have to excise entire sections and phrases from the language of TSCA. Because we are judges, not surgeons, we decline to do so. . . .

VI. Conclusion

In summary, of most concern to us is that the EPA has failed to implement the dictates of TSCA and the prior decisions of this and other courts that, before it impose a ban on a product, it first evaluate and then reject the less burdensome alternatives laid out for it by Congress. While the EPA spent much time and care crafting its asbestos regulation, its explicit failure to consider the alternatives required of it by Congress deprived its final rule of the reasonable basis it needed to survive judicial scrutiny.

We regret that this matter must continue to take up the valuable time of the agency, parties and, undoubtedly, future courts. The requirements of TSCA, however, are plain, and the EPA cannot deviate from them to reach its desired result. We therefore GRANT the petition for review, VACATE the EPA's proposed regulation, and REMAND to the EPA for further proceedings in light of this opinion.

NOTES AND QUESTIONS ON *CORROSION PROOF FITTINGS*, TSCA, FIFRA, AND THE SDWA

1. *Remand.* Can the agency expect to meet the Fifth Circuit's demands on remand? What should it do if it wants to try?

2. *Aftermath.* The court was wrong to think that this matter would continue to take up valuable judicial time. After this decision, EPA never again regulated any new substance under section 6 of the Toxic Substances Control Act and it never again sought to apply section 6 authority to asbestos. Why do you think paralysis followed this decision? EPA spent ten years preparing the rule reversed in *Corrosion Proof Fittings* and it spent between $5 and $10 million on consultants as part of its cost-benefit analysis. *See* ECONOMIC ANALYSIS AT EPA: ASSESSING REGULATORY IMPACT 173 (Richard Morgenstern ed., 1997) [*Economic Analysis*].

3. *Statutory interpretation.* How did the court's statutory interpretation differ from that of EPA in the Federal Register notice, and why? The court demanded more than an EPA finding that the benefits of banning asbestos outweigh the costs, and a finding that the alternatives to a ban failed to protect public health. It required EPA to weigh the costs and benefits of each alternative to the ban.

4. *The most burdensome option.* The court says that the ban chosen by EPA is the "most burdensome" option. If a substitute for asbestos proves no more costly than asbestos itself, will the substitution impose any net burden on consumers? On the manufacturer? *Cf.* Honeywell Int'l, Inc. v. EPA, 374 F.3d 1363 (D.C. Cir. 2004) (discussing the potential economic benefits of bans for manufacturers of substitutes and issues posed by the variations in costs among the substitutes). Which burden should matter the most in deciding whether to ban the substance?

For more information on how EPA quantified the costs of switching products, see *Economic Analysis, supra,* at 182-89.

5. *Non-quantified benefits.* The court said that EPA could consider non-quantified benefits, but could not assign them great weight. Does the fact that a benefit cannot be quantified mean that it is trivial? Should it matter that EPA considered its monetization of benefits an understatement? Consider the following:

> There were . . . many instances where there was good reason to believe that exposure occurred, but there were no data as to the level of exposure. . . . Although benefits were estimated assuming zero exposure where no data was available, unless the exposures to asbestos from those products was in fact zero, this procedure would clearly bias the benefit-cost information in the direction of not supporting a regulation when regulation is warranted.

Economic Analysis, supra, at 191-92. What should EPA do in this circumstance?

6. *Discounting.* The court requires discounting future benefits, *i.e.,* assigning a future benefit a lower value than the same benefit would receive if realized immediately. The notion that agencies should discount future compliance *costs* in assessing regulations is not controversial. The reason is fairly simple. Suppose that the prevailing interest rate today is 5 percent. If a manufacturer needs to spend $1 million to comply with a regulation, it needs $1 million. Suppose, however, that the manufacturer must spend $1 million five years from now to comply. The manufacturer need not put aside $1 million today to fund that obligation. Because the money put aside will earn 5 percent interest, the manufacturer can put aside significantly less than $1 million, because the money saved will earn interest at a 5 percent rate. To take this into account, regulators must discount future compliance expenditures, applying a discount rate corresponding to estimates of prevailing interest rates.

Most economists believe that regulatory agencies monetizing benefits should discount future benefits in a similar fashion. But is a life saved tomorrow worth less than a life saved today? Why does the court insist on discounting benefits? Do you agree with its reasoning? Should it defer to the agency's judgment on this?

The decision to use a discount rate and the choice of which discount rate to apply can have an enormous impact on the calculations of costs and benefits.[1] For example, a regulation saving 100 lives 30 years from now at a discount rate of 3 percent has a present value of 41.2 lives. If one increases the discount rate to 6 percent, the regulation saves the equivalent of 17.41 lives today, less than half the number of present lives saved with a 3 percent assumption. *See* http://www.progres-siveregulation.org/perspectives/costbenefit.cfm (online calculator). If the regulator values each life saved at $6.3 million, then selecting the higher discount rate (6 percent) can reduce the estimate of the regulatory benefit by $150 million.

---

1. *See* Douglas A. Kysar, *Climate Change, Cultural Transformation, and Comprehensive Rationality,* 31 B.C. Envtl. Aff. L. Rev. 555, 578-85 (2004) (discussing discounting's moral issues in the climate change context); Lisa Heinzerling, *The Rights of Statistical People,* 24 Harv. Envtl. L. Rev. 189 (2000); Armatya Sen, *The Discipline of Cost-Benefit Analysis,* 29 J. Legal Stud. 931 (2000); Henry Richardson, *The Stupidity of Cost-Benefit Analysis,* 29 J. Legal Stud. 971 (2000); Richard L. Revesz, *Environmental Regulation, Cost-Benefit Analysis, and the Discounting of Human Lives,* 99 Colum. L. Rev. 941 (1999); Lisa Heinzerling, *Discounting Life,* 108 Yale L.J. 1911 (1999); John J. Donohue, III, *Why We Should Discount the Views of Those Who Discount Discounting,* 108 Yale L.J. 1901 (1999); Daniel A. Farber & Paul A. Hemmersbaugh, *The Shadow of the Future: Discount Rates, Later Generations, and the Environment,* 46 Vand. L. Rev. 267 (1993). *See also* Edith Brown Weiss, *The Planetary Trust: Conservation and Intergenerational Equity,* 11 Ecology L.Q. 495 (1984).

7. *FIFRA.* The courts have also interpreted the Federal Insecticide, Fungicide, and Rodenticide Act to apply a cost-benefit test to decisions about whether to register a pesticide. EPA has authority to ban or drastically limit the use of pesticides, but it rarely uses that authority. Experts on this statute agree that the requirement to quantify the risks of pesticides has paralyzed EPA:

> The informational demands of risk analysis doom the regulatory process to a perpetual state of slow motion. . . . "[A]fter 20 years collecting data to reevaluate the health and environmental effects of 19,000 older pesticides, EPA . . . had reregistered only 2 products."

Donald Hornstein, *Lessons from Federal Pesticide Regulation on the Paradigm and Politics of Environmental Law Reform,* 10 YALE J. ON REG. 369, 437-38 (1993).

8. *The Safe Drinking Water Act.* The SDWA generally requires health protective goals and standards approximating those goals as closely as feasible. 42 U.S.C. §300g-1(b)(4), (A), (B). The 1996 Amendments to this statute, however, require CBA of most new standards and authorize relaxation of new standards where the Administrator of EPA determines that "the benefits of a [standard] would not justify the costs of complying with the [standard]." *Id.* §300g-1(b)(6); *see* City of Portland v. EPA, 507 F.3d 706, 710 (D.C. Cir. 2007). This marks the first time Congress expressly required CBA in a modern environmental statute and shows how acceptance of the technique has grown since the 1970s.

B.   REVIEW UNDER THE EXECUTIVE ORDERS

President Reagan heavily promoted cost-benefit analysis in order to "reduce the burdens" on regulated industry. *See* E.O. 12291, 46 Fed. Reg. 13193 (Feb. 17, 1981). He issued an executive order requiring the Office of Management and Budget (OMB) to apply a cost-benefit test to major regulations to the extent consistent with applicable law. Specifically, the Executive Order required "to the extent permitted by law" that "regulation shall not be undertaken unless the potential benefits to society . . . outweigh the potential costs. . . ." *Id.* §2(b).

Does the law permit this cost-benefit test to apply to decisions to set national ambient air quality standards under section 109? *See* Whitman v. American Trucking Ass'ns, 531 U.S. 457, 464-71 (2001). Recall that this section requires health protective standards and does not authorize the consideration of cost. Does the law permit a cost-benefit test to apply to a cost-sensitive technology-based decision, like those undertaken in setting best available technology and best practicable control technology decisions under the Clean Water Act? Recall *Pacific Fisheries'* discussion of the consideration of cost.

Reagan's order led to charges that OMB was forcing EPA to violate the law. *See* Erik Olson, *The Quiet Shift of Power: Office of Management and Budget Supervision of Environmental Protection Agency Rulemaking Under Executive Order 12,291,* 4 VA. J. NAT. RES. L. 1, 51 (1984). Would a requirement that benefits must outweigh costs ever require the agency to make a regulation more stringent? Or is it a one-way ratchet making regulations less stringent? *See* David M. Driesen, *Is Cost-Benefit Analysis Neutral?,* 77 U. COLO. L. REV. 335, 387-89 (2006). *Cf.* E.O. 12291 §2 (requiring that regulatory objectives be chosen to maximize net benefits to society). Critics also accused OMB of functioning as a secretive back channel helping industry undermine environmental, health, and safety protection. *See* Olson, *supra*, at 55-57.

Support for CBA, however, clearly became wider during the 1980s. When President Clinton came into office, he continued the practice of OMB review ostensibly based on CBA. *See* E.O. 12866, 58 Fed. Reg. 51735 (Sept. 30, 1993). This order stated that regulation should only be adopted if "the benefits of the . . . regulation justify the costs." *Id.* §1(b)(6). Does this criterion differ materially from that imposed by President Reagan? Is it a one-way ratchet or not? *Cf. id.* §1(a) (agencies should select "approaches" that "maximize net benefits"); Driesen, *supra*, at 341, 386-87 (discussing the "indeterminate position" that regulators should consider CBA). The Clinton order aimed to increase the transparency of the process and focus it on economically significant rules. *Cf.* UNITED STATES GENERAL ACCOUNTING OFFICE, RULEMAKING: OMB'S ROLE IN REVIEWS OF AGENCIES' DRAFT RULES AND THE TRANSPARENCY OF THOSE REVIEWS (2003) (discussing the extent to which transparency had taken hold during the Bush Administration). Congress, which had initially been very skeptical of CBA, lent its support in 1995 when it passed the Unfunded Mandates Reform Act (UMRA), Pub. L. No. 104-4, §202, codified at 2 U.S.C. §1532. UMRA required CBA of rules generating over $100 million in annual compliance expenditures "unless otherwise prohibited by law."

The executive orders mention another criterion, maximizing net benefits. *See, e.g.,* E.O. 13563, 76 Fed. Reg. 3821, 3821 (Jan. 21, 2011). As a technical economic matter, this should mean that marginal costs are set equal to marginal benefits. HORST SIEBERT, ECONOMICS OF THE ENVIRONMENT: THEORY AND POLICY 65 (5th rev. ed. 1998). Economists define "optimal pollution levels" as those reflecting equalization of costs and benefits at the margin. This means that the cost of the last increment of pollution control should provide a benefit equal to the cost. Since marginal pollution control cost (*i.e.*, the cost associated with each increment of stringency) typically rises as standards become more stringent, one can graph this concept as follows:

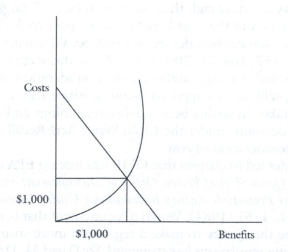

Does this criterion act as a one-way ratchet?

Assume that controlling air emissions at a plant producing atrazine using mediocre pollution control equipment costs $50 per pound for the last unit of control. And assume that this last unit of control produces $75 worth of benefit at the margin (*i.e.*, for last unit of control only). A more stringent approach would cost $80 per pound at the margin, and would produce $80 worth of benefits.

Which option does the maximize net benefits criterion suggest the regulator should choose? Does this criterion make sense as a policy matter?

The question of whether an agency may allow cost-benefit analysis under the Executive Order to influence its decisions depends on operable statutory provisions and their interpretations. In reading this case, think not only about whether you agree with the Supreme Court's statutory interpretation, but also about what goal-setting method you would prefer for the problem described.

 ### *Entergy Corp. v. Riverkeeper, Inc.*
556 U.S. 208 (2009)

JUSTICE SCALIA delivered the opinion of the Court.

These cases concern a set of regulations adopted by the Environmental Protection Agency (EPA or agency) under §316(b) of the Clean Water Act, 33 U.S.C. §1326(b). Respondents—environmental groups and various States—challenged those regulations, and the Second Circuit set them aside. The issue for our decision is whether, as the Second Circuit held, the EPA is not permitted to use cost-benefit analysis in determining the content of regulations promulgated under §1326(b).

I

Petitioners operate . . . large powerplants. In the course of generating power, those plants also generate large amounts of heat. To cool their facilities, petitioners employ "cooling water intake structures" that extract water from nearby water sources. These structures pose various threats to the environment, chief among them the squashing against intake screens (elegantly called "impingement") or suction into the cooling system ("entrainment") of aquatic organisms that live in the affected water sources. Accordingly, the facilities are subject to regulation under the Clean Water Act, which mandates:

> Any standard established pursuant to section 1311 of this title or section 1316 of this title and applicable to a point source shall require that the location, design, construction, and capacity of cooling water intake structures reflect the best technology available for minimizing adverse environmental impact. §1326(b).

. . .

To address those environmental impacts, the EPA set "national performance standards," requiring Phase II facilities (with some exceptions) to reduce "impingement mortality for all life stages of fish and shellfish by 80 to 95 percent from the calculation baseline"; a subset of facilities must also reduce entrainment of such aquatic organisms by "60 to 90 percent from the calculation baseline." Those targets are based on the environmental improvements achievable through deployment of a mix of remedial technologies, which the EPA determined were "commercially available and economically practicable[.]"

In its Phase II rules, however, the EPA expressly declined to mandate adoption of closed-cycle cooling systems or equivalent reductions in impingement and entrainment, as it had done for new facilities subject to the Phase I rules. It refused to take that step in part because of the "generally high costs" of converting existing facilities to closed-cycle operation, and because "other technologies approach the performance of this option." . . . The EPA concluded that "[a]lthough not identical, the ranges of impingement and entrainment reduction are similar under both options. . . . [Benefits of compliance with the Phase II rules] can approach those of closed-cycle recirculating at less cost with fewer implementation problems."

. . .

Respondents challenged the EPA's Phase II regulations, and the Second Circuit granted their petition for review and remanded the regulations to the EPA. The Second Circuit identified two ways in which the EPA could permissibly consider costs under 33 U.S.C. §1326(b): (1) in determining whether the costs of remediation "can be 'reasonably borne' by the industry," and (2) in determining which remedial technologies are the most cost-effective, that is, the technologies that reach a specified level of benefit at the lowest cost. It concluded, however, that cost-benefit analysis, which "compares the costs and benefits of various ends, and chooses the end with the best net benefits" is impermissible under §1326(b).

. . . We then granted certiorari limited to the following question: "Whether [§1326(b)] . . . authorizes the [EPA] to compare costs with benefits in determining 'the best technology available for minimizing adverse environmental impact' at cooling water intake structures."

II

In setting the Phase II national performance standards . . . , the EPA relied on its view that §1326(b)'s "best technology available" standard permits consideration of the technology's costs and of the relationship between those costs and the environmental benefits produced. That view governs if it is a reasonable interpretation of the statute — not necessarily the only possible interpretation, nor even the interpretation deemed *most* reasonable by the courts. Chevron U.S.A. Inc. v. Natural Resources Defense Council, 467 U.S. 837, 843-844 (1984).

As we have described, §1326(b) instructs the EPA to set standards for cooling water intake structures that reflect "the best technology available for minimizing adverse environmental impact." The Second Circuit took that language to mean the technology that achieves the greatest reduction in adverse environmental impacts at a cost that can reasonably be borne by the industry. That is certainly a plausible interpretation of the statute. The "best" technology—that which is "most advantageous," Webster's New International Dictionary 258 (2d ed. 1953)—may well be the one that produces the most of some good, here a reduction in adverse environmental impact. But "best technology" may also describe the technology that *most efficiently* produces some good. In common parlance one could certainly use the phrase "best technology" to refer to that which produces a good at the lowest per-unit cost, even if it produces a lesser quantity of that good than other available technologies.

Respondents contend that this latter reading is precluded by the statute's use of the phrase "for minimizing adverse environmental impact." Minimizing, they argue, means reducing to the smallest amount possible, and the "best technology available for minimizing adverse environmental impacts," must be the economically feasible technology that achieves the greatest possible reduction in environmental harm. But "minimize" is a term that admits of degree and is not necessarily used to refer exclusively to the "greatest possible reduction." For example, elsewhere in the Clean Water Act, Congress declared that the procedures implementing the Act "shall encourage the drastic minimization of paperwork and interagency decision procedures." If respondents' definition of the term "minimize" is correct, the statute's use of the modifier "drastic" is superfluous.

Other provisions in the Clean Water Act also suggest the agency's interpretation. When Congress wished to mandate the greatest feasible reduction in water pollution, it did so in plain language: The provision governing the discharge of toxic pollutants into the Nation's waters requires the EPA to set "effluent limitations [which] shall require the *elimination* of discharges of all pollutants if the Administrator finds . . . that such elimination is technologically and economically achievable." *See also* §1316(a)(1) (mandating "where practicable, a standard [for new point sources] permitting *no discharge* of pollutants" (emphasis added)). Section 1326(b)'s use of the less ambitious goal of "minimizing adverse environmental impact" suggests, we think, that the agency retains some discretion to determine the extent of reduction that is warranted under the circumstances. That determination could plausibly involve a consideration of the benefits derived from reductions and the costs of achieving them. It seems to us, therefore, that the phrase "best technology available," even with the added specification "for minimizing adverse environmental impact," does not unambiguously preclude cost-benefit analysis.

Respondents' alternative (and, alas, also more complex) argument rests upon the structure of the Clean Water Act. The Act provided that during its initial implementation period existing "point sources"—discrete conveyances from which pollutants are or may be discharged, 33 U.S.C. §1362(14)—were subject to "effluent limitations . . . which shall require the application of the *best practicable control technology* currently available." §1311(b)(1)(A) (emphasis added). (We shall call this the "BPT" test.) Following that transition period, the Act initially mandated adoption, by July 1, 1983 (later extended to March 31, 1989), of stricter effluent limitations requiring "application of the *best available technology economically achievable* for such category or class, which will result in reasonable further progress toward the national goal of eliminating the discharge of all pollutants." §1311(b)(2)(A) (emphasis added). (We shall call this the "BATEA" test.) Subsequent amendment limited application of this standard to toxic and nonconventional pollutants and for the remainder established a (presumably laxer) test of "best conventional-pollutant control technology." §1311(b)(2)(E). (We shall call this "BCT.") Finally, §1316 subjected certain categories of new point sources to "the greatest degree of effluent reduction which the Administrator determines to be achievable through application of the *best available demonstrated control technology.*" §1316(a)(1) (emphasis added); §1316(b)(1)(B). (We shall call this the "BADT" test.) The provision at issue here, applicable not to effluents but to cooling water intake structures, requires, as we have described, "the *best technology available for minimizing adverse environmental impact,*" §1326(b) (emphasis added). (We shall call this the "BTA" test.)

The first four of these tests are elucidated by statutory factor lists that guide their implementation. To take the standards in (presumed) order of increasing stringency: In applying the BPT test the EPA is instructed to consider, among other factors, "the total cost of application of technology in relation to the effluent reduction benefits to be achieved." §1314(b)(1)(B). In applying the BCT test it is instructed to consider "the *reasonableness of the relationship* between the costs of attaining a reduction in effluents and the effluent reduction benefits derived." §1314(b)(4)(B) (emphasis added). And in applying the BATEA and BADT tests the EPA is instructed to consider the "cost of achieving such effluent reduction." §§1314(b)(2)(B), 1316(b)(1)(B). There is no such elucidating language applicable to the BTA test at issue here. . . .

The Second Circuit, in rejecting the EPA's use of cost-benefit analysis, relied in part on the propositions that (1) cost-benefit analysis is precluded under the BATEA and BADT tests; and (2) that, insofar as the permissibility of cost-benefit analysis is concerned, the BTA test (the one at issue here) is to be treated the same as those two. It is not obvious to us that the first of these propositions is correct, but we need not pursue that point, since we assuredly do not agree with the second. It is certainly reasonable for the agency to conclude that the BTA test need not be interpreted to permit only what those other two tests permit. Its text is not identical to theirs. It has the relatively modest goal of "minimizing adverse environmental impact" as compared with the BATEA's goal of "eliminating the discharge of all pollutants." And it is unencumbered by specified statutory factors of the sort provided for those other two tests, which omission can reasonably be interpreted to suggest that the EPA is accorded greater discretion in determining its precise content.

Respondents and the dissent argue that the mere fact that §1326(b) does not expressly authorize cost-benefit analysis for the BTA test, though it does so for two of the other tests, displays an intent to forbid its use. This surely proves too much. For while it is true that two of the other tests authorize cost-benefit analysis, it is also true that *all four* of the other tests expressly authorize *some* consideration of costs. Thus, if respondents' and the dissent's conclusion regarding the import of §1326(b)'s silence is correct, it is *a fortiori* true that the BTA test permits *no consideration of cost whatsoever*, not even the "cost-effectiveness" and "feasibility" analysis that the Second Circuit approved, that the dissent would approve, and that respondents acknowledge. The inference that respondents and the dissent would draw from the silence is, in any event, implausible, as §1326(b) is silent not only with respect to cost-benefit analysis but with respect to all potentially relevant factors. If silence here implies prohibition, then the EPA could not consider *any* factors in implementing §1326(b)—an obvious logical impossibility. It is eminently reasonable to conclude that §1326(b)'s silence is meant to convey nothing more than a refusal to tie the agency's hands as to whether cost-benefit analysis should be used, and if so to what degree.

Contrary to the dissent's suggestion, our decisions in Whitman v. American Trucking Assns., Inc. . . . and American Textile Mfrs. Institute, Inc. v. Donovan . . . do not undermine this conclusion. In *American Trucking,* we held that the text of §109 of the Clean Air Act, "interpreted in its statutory and historical context . . . unambiguously bars cost considerations" in setting air quality standards under that provision. The relevant "statutory context" included other provisions in the Clean Air Act that expressly authorized consideration of costs, whereas §109 did not. *American Trucking* thus stands for the rather unremarkable proposition that sometimes statutory silence, when viewed in context, is best interpreted as limiting agency discretion. For the reasons discussed earlier, §1326(b)'s silence cannot bear that interpretation.

In *American Textile,* the Court relied in part on a statute's failure to mention cost-benefit analysis in holding that the relevant agency was not required to engage in cost-benefit analysis in setting certain health and safety standards. But under *Chevron,* that an agency is not *required* to do so does not mean that an agency is not *permitted* to do so.

This extended consideration of the text of §1326(b), and comparison of that with the text and statutory factors applicable to four parallel provisions of the Clean Water Act, lead us to the conclusion that it was well within the bounds of reasonable interpretation for the EPA to conclude that cost-benefit analysis is not categorically forbidden. Other arguments may be available to preclude such a rigorous form of cost-benefit analysis as that which was prescribed under the statute's former BPT standard, which required weighing "the total cost of application of technology" against "the . . . benefits to be achieved." But that question is not before us.

In the Phase II requirements challenged here the EPA sought only to avoid extreme disparities between costs and benefits. . . . In defining the "national performance standards" . . . the EPA assumed the application of technologies whose benefits "approach those estimated" for closed-cycle cooling systems at a fraction of the cost: $389 million per year, as compared with (1) at least $3.5 billion per year to operate compliant closed-cycle cooling systems, (or $1 billion per year to impose similar requirements on a subset of Phase II facilities), and (2) significant reduction in the energy output of the altered facilities. And finally, EPA's assessment of the relatively meager financial benefits of the Phase II regulations that it adopted—reduced impingement and entrainment of 1.4 billion aquatic organisms, with annualized use-benefits of $83 million and non-use benefits of indeterminate value, when compared to annual costs of $389 million, demonstrates quite clearly that the agency did not select the Phase II regulatory requirements because their benefits equaled their costs.

. . .

In the last analysis, even respondents ultimately recognize that some form of cost-benefit analysis is permissible. They acknowledge that the statute's language is "plainly not so constricted as to require EPA to require industry petitioners to spend billions to save one more fish or plankton." This concedes the principle—the permissibility of at least some cost-benefit analysis—and we see no statutory basis for limiting its use to situations where the benefits are *de minimis* rather than significantly disproportionate.

. . .

We conclude that the EPA permissibly relied on cost-benefit analysis in setting the national performance standards. . . . The Court of Appeals' reliance in part on the agency's use of cost-benefit analysis in invalidating the site-specific cost-benefit variance provision was therefore in error, as was its remand of the national performance standards for clarification of whether cost-benefit analysis was impermissibly used. . . . The judgment of the Court of Appeals is reversed, and the cases are remanded for further proceedings consistent with this opinion. . . .

* * *

JUSTICE STEVENS, with whom JUSTICE SOUTER and JUSTICE GINSBURG join, dissenting.

Section 316(b) of the Clean Water Act (CWA), 33 U.S.C. §1326(b), which governs industrial powerplant water intake structures, provides that the Environmental Protection Agency (EPA or Agency) "shall require" that such structures "reflect the best technology available for minimizing adverse environmental impact." The EPA has interpreted that mandate to authorize the use of cost-benefit analysis in promulgating regulations under §316(b). For instance, under the Agency's interpretation, technology that would otherwise qualify as the best available need not be used if its costs are "significantly greater than the benefits" of compliance.

Like the Court of Appeals, I am convinced that the EPA has misinterpreted the plain text of §316(b). Unless costs are so high that the best technology is not "available," Congress has decided that they are outweighed by the benefits of minimizing adverse environmental impact. Section 316(b) neither expressly nor implicitly authorizes the EPA to use cost-benefit analysis when setting regulatory standards; fairly read, it prohibits such use.

I

As typically performed by the EPA, cost-benefit analysis requires the Agency to first monetize the costs and benefits of a regulation, balance the results, and then choose the regulation with the greatest net benefits. The process is particularly controversial in the environmental context in which a regulation's financial costs are often more obvious and easier to quantify than its environmental benefits. And cost-benefit analysis often, if not always, yields a result that does not maximize environmental protection.

For instance, although the EPA estimated that water intake structures kill 3.4 billion fish and shellfish each year, the Agency struggled to calculate the value of the aquatic life that would be protected under its §316(b) regulations. To compensate, the EPA took a shortcut: Instead of monetizing all aquatic life, the Agency counted only those species that are commercially or recreationally harvested, a tiny slice (1.8 percent to be precise) of all impacted fish and shellfish. This narrow focus in turn skewed the Agency's calculation of benefits. When the EPA attempted to value all aquatic life, the benefits measured $735 million. But when the EPA decided to give zero value to the 98.2 percent of fish not commercially or recreationally harvested, the benefits calculation dropped dramatically—to $83 million. The Agency acknowledged that its failure to monetize the other 98.2 percent of affected species "could result in serious misallocation of resources," because its "comparison of complete costs and incomplete benefits does not provide an accurate picture of net benefits to society."

Because benefits can be more accurately monetized in some industries than in others, Congress typically decides whether it is appropriate for an agency to use cost-benefit analysis in crafting regulations. Indeed, this Court has recognized that "[w]hen Congress has intended that an agency engage in cost-benefit analysis, it has clearly indicated such intent on the face of the statute." American Textile Mfrs. Institute, Inc. v. Donovan. . . . Accordingly, we should not treat a provision's silence as an implicit source of cost-benefit authority, particularly when such authority is elsewhere expressly granted and it has the potential to fundamentally alter an agency's approach to regulation. Congress, we have noted, "does not alter the fundamental details of a regulatory scheme in vague terms or ancillary provisions—it does not, one might say, hide elephants in mouseholes." Whitman v. American Trucking Assns., Inc.

When interpreting statutory silence in the past, we have sought guidance from a statute's other provisions. Evidence that Congress confronted an issue in some parts of a statute, while leaving it unaddressed in others, can demonstrate that Congress meant its silence to be decisive. We concluded as much in *American Trucking*. In that case, the Court reviewed the EPA's claim that §109 of the Clean Air Act (CAA), 42 U.S.C. §7409(a) (2000 ed.), authorized the Agency to consider implementation costs in setting ambient air quality standards. We read §109, which was silent on the matter, to prohibit Agency reliance on cost considerations. After examining other provisions in which Congress had given the Agency authority to consider costs, the Court "refused to find implicit in ambiguous sections of the CAA an authorization to consider costs that has elsewhere, and so often, been expressly granted." Studied silence, we thus concluded, can be as much a prohibition as an explicit "no."

. . .

American Trucking's approach should have guided the Court's reading of §316(b). Nowhere in the text of §316(b) does Congress explicitly authorize the use of cost-benefit analysis as it does elsewhere in the CWA. And the use of cost-benefit analysis, like the consideration of implementation costs in *American Trucking*, "pad[s]" §316(b)'s environmental mandate with tangential economic efficiency concerns. Yet the majority fails to follow *American Trucking* despite that case's obvious relevance to our inquiry.

II

In 1972, Congress amended the CWA to strike a careful balance between the country's energy demands and its desire to protect the environment. The Act required industry to adopt increasingly advanced technology capable of mitigating its detrimental environmental impact. Not all point sources were subject to strict rules at once. Existing plants were granted time to retrofit with the best technology while new plants were required to incorporate such technology as a matter of design. Although Congress realized that technology standards would necessarily put some firms out of business, the statute's steady march was toward stricter rules and potentially higher costs.

Section 316(b) was an integral part of the statutory scheme. The provision instructs that "[a]ny standard established pursuant to section 1311 of this title or section 1316 of this title and applicable to a point source shall require that the location, design, construction, and capacity of cooling water intake structures reflect the *best technology available for minimizing adverse environmental impact.*" 33 U.S.C. §1326(b) (emphasis added). The "best technology available," or "BTA," standard delivers a clear command: To minimize the adverse environmental impact of water intake structures, the EPA must require industry to adopt the best technology available.

Based largely on the observation that §316(b)'s text offers little guidance and therefore delegates some amount of gap-filling authority to the EPA, the Court concludes that the Agency has discretion to rely on cost-benefit analysis. . . . Silence, in the majority's view, represents ambiguity and an invitation for the Agency to decide for itself which factors should govern its regulatory approach.

Powerful evidence of Congress' decision not to authorize cost-benefit analysis in the BTA standard lies in the series of standards adopted to regulate the outflow, or effluent, from industrial powerplants. Passed at the same time as the BTA standard at issue here, the effluent limitation standards imposed increasingly strict technology requirements on industry. In each effluent limitation provision, Congress distinguished its willingness to allow the EPA to consider costs from its willingness to allow the Agency to conduct a cost-benefit analysis. And to the extent Congress permitted cost-benefit analysis, its use was intended to be temporary and exceptional.

The first tier of technology standards applied to existing plants—facilities for which retrofitting would be particularly costly. Congress required these plants to adopt "effluent limitations . . . which shall require the application of the best practicable control technology currently available." 33 U.S.C. §1311(b)(1)(A). Because this "best practicable," or "BPT," standard was meant to ease industry's transition to the new technology-based regime, Congress gave BPT two unique features: First, it would be temporary, remaining in effect only until July 1, 1983. Second, it specified that the EPA was to conduct a cost-benefit analysis in setting BPT requirements by considering "the total cost of application of technology in relation to the effluent reduction benefits to be achieved from such application." §1314(b)(1)(B). Permitting cost-benefit analysis in BPT gave the EPA the ability to cushion the new technology requirement. For a limited time, a technology with costs that exceeded its benefits would not be considered "best."

The second tier of technology standards required existing powerplants to adopt the "best available technology economically achievable" to advance "the national goal of eliminating the discharge of all pollutants." §1311(b)(2)(A). In setting this "best available technology," or "BAT," standard, Congress gave the EPA a notably different command for deciding what technology would qualify as "best": The EPA was to consider, among other factors, "the cost of achieving such effluent reduction," but Congress did not grant it authority to balance costs with the benefits of stricter regulation. §1314(b)(2)(B). . . .

. . .

The third and strictest regulatory tier was reserved for new point sources—facilities that could incorporate technology improvements into their initial design. These new facilities were required to adopt "the best available demonstrated control technology," or "BADT," which Congress described as "a standard . . . which reflect[s] the greatest degree of effluent reduction." §1316(a)(1). In administering BADT, Congress directed the EPA to consider "the cost of achieving such effluent reduction." §1316(b)(1)(B). But because BADT was meant to be the most stringent standard of all, Congress made no mention of cost-benefit analysis. Again, the silence was intentional. The House's version of BADT originally contained an exemption for point sources for which "the economic, social, and environmental costs bear no reasonable relationship to the economic, social, and environmental benefit to be obtained." That this exemption did not appear in the final legislation demonstrates that Congress considered, and rejected, reliance on cost-benefit analysis for BADT.

It is in this light that the BTA standard regulating water intake structures must be viewed. The use of cost-benefit analysis was a critical component of the CWA's structure and a key concern in the legislative process. We should therefore conclude that Congress intended to forbid cost-benefit analysis in one provision of the Act in which it was silent on the matter when it expressly authorized its use in another. This is particularly true given Congress' decision that cost-benefit analysis would play a temporary and exceptional role in the CWA to help existing plants transition to the Act's ambitious environmental standards. Allowing cost-benefit analysis in the BTA standard, a permanent mandate applicable to all powerplants, serves no such purpose and instead fundamentally weakens the provision's mandate.

Accordingly, I would hold that the EPA is without authority to perform cost-benefit analysis in setting BTA standards. . . . Because the Court unsettles the scheme Congress established, I respectfully dissent.

NOTES AND QUESTIONS ON *ENTERGY CORP. v. RIVERKEEPER*

1. *Who is correct?* Do you agree with the majority or the dissent? Is *Entergy* consistent with *Donovan*?

2. *Change in the law?* You may recall that the *Pacific Fisheries* court held, in a decision echoed by many other courts of appeals, that EPA may not rely on CBA to set BAT standards (referred to as BATEA by the *Entergy* Court) and need not quantify benefits in dollar terms in establishing BPT standards. To what extent, if at all, does *Entergy* undermine this line of cases?

3. *The executive order.* EPA often conducts CBA of technology-based standards, because OMB demands it under the executive order. Should the executive order influence the statutory question of whether a given provision authorizes CBA?

4. *Effects-based standards.* This case features a contest between proponents of CBA and of technology-based approaches to setting goals. How would one employ an effects-based approach to addressing the problem of water intake killing aquatic organisms and disrupting ecosystems? What effects-based criterion might one use?

C. THE POLICY DEBATE

1. Tradeoffs

Proponents of CBA argue that environmental law must take tradeoffs into account and that CBA helps it do that. *See, e.g.,* Sunstein, *supra,* at 5. Resources used for environmental protection will not be available for other uses. *See* WILLIAM BAXTER, PEOPLE OR PENGUINS: THE CASE FOR OPTIMAL POLLUTION (1974). Regulatory reformers argue that regulations costing more than they are worth waste money that could be used to save even more lives. Does relaxing a regulation limiting emissions of hazardous air pollutants help fund childhood vaccinations, which might deserve higher priority from a public health standpoint?

The degree of stringency, CBA proponents argue, should reflect the magnitude of the harm and the amount of costs. Otherwise, in the words politicians use to advocate CBA, we might impose regulations that do more harm than good. Should environmental regulation countenance tradeoffs or should it involve an uncompromising search for full protection of the environment and public health? *See* JOSEPH SAX, MOUNTAINS WITHOUT HANDRAILS: REFLECTIONS ON THE NATIONAL PARKS (1980). If tradeoffs must be taken into account, does it follow that we must use CBA to do so? *See BP Exploration, supra.* Do health-based standards take tradeoffs into account? What about technology-based standards? Does the feasibility principle take tradeoffs into account? What about a system that forbids agencies from taking tradeoffs into account? Would such a system forbid Congress from countermanding overly aggressive agency action from time to time? Is such an approach, combining absolutist administrative law with occasional political intervention to correct abuses, an adequate way to take tradeoffs into account?

A number of statutes seek to protect natural resources from a broad array of threats, rather than only prevent pollution. Natural resources suffer threats from economic development of land; extraction of timber, oil, minerals, and other resources; and many other human activities. A number of federal and state statutes address these issues, with most of the federal statutes addressing the use of federal lands, such as National Parks and National Forests.

Most statutes addressing natural resources destruction stop short of banning all activities harming a resource. For example, under the Multiple Use Sustained Yield Act, which governs National Forests, the Forest Service must balance competing uses of the national forests in some fashion. Thus, the statute clearly contemplates some use of forests as sources of timber, notwithstanding logging operations' potential to harm the environment. Many other public land statutes likewise envision some sort of balancing.

But Congress employed a much firmer approach to address the extinction of species, as the case below illustrates. As you read the case, think about whether tradeoffs should be considered in protecting endangered species as a policy matter.

Tennessee Valley Authority v. Hill
437 U.S. 153 (1978)

CHIEF JUSTICE BURGER delivered the opinion of the Court.

The question[ ] presented in this case [is] . . . whether the Endangered Species Act of 1973 requires a court to enjoin the operation of a virtually completed federal dam—which had been authorized prior to 1973—when, pursuant to authority vested in him by Congress, the Secretary of the Interior has determined that operation of the dam would eradicate an endangered species. . . .

[T]he Tennessee Valley Authority, a wholly owned public corporation of the United States, began constructing the Tellico Dam and Reservoir Project in 1967, shortly after Congress appropriated initial funds for its development. Tellico is a multipurpose regional development project designed principally to stimulate shoreline development, generate sufficient electric current to heat 20,000 homes, and provide flatwater recreation and flood control, as well as improve economic conditions in "an area characterized by underutilization of human resources and out migration of young people." . . .

Exploring the area around [the damn site] a University of Tennessee ichthyologist, Dr. David A. Etnier, found a previously unknown species of perch, the snail darter. . . . This three-inch, tannish-colored fish, whose numbers are estimated to be in the range of 10,000 to 15,000, would soon engage the attention of environmentalists, the TVA, the Department of the Interior, the Congress of the United States, and ultimately the federal courts, as a basis to halt construction of the dam.

Until recently the finding of a new species of animal life would hardly generate a cause célèbre. This is particularly so in the case of darters, of which there are approximately 130 known species, 8 to 10 of these having been identified only in the last five years. The moving force behind the snail darter's sudden fame came some four months after its discovery, when the Congress passed the Endangered Species Act of 1973 (Act). This legislation, among other things, authorizes the Secretary of the Interior to declare species of animal life "endangered" and to identify the "critical habitat" of these creatures. When a species or its habitat is so listed, the following portion of the Act—relevant here—becomes effective:

> The Secretary [of the Interior] shall review other programs administered by him and utilize such programs in furtherance of the purposes of this chapter. All other Federal departments and agencies shall, in consultation with and with the assistance of the Secretary, utilize their authorities in furtherance of the purposes of this chapter by carrying out programs for the conservation of endangered species and threatened species listed pursuant to section 1533 of this title and *by taking such action necessary to insure that actions authorized, funded, or carried out by them do not jeopardize the continued existence of such endangered species and threatened species or result in the destruction or modification of habitat of such species* which is determined by the Secretary, after consultation as appropriate with the affected States, to be critical.

16 U.S.C. §1536 (1976 ed.) (emphasis added).

In January 1975, the respondents in this case . . . petitioned the Secretary of the Interior to list the snail darter as an endangered species. [T]he Secretary formally listed the snail darter as an endangered species on October 8, 1975. In so acting, . . . the Secretary determined that the snail darter apparently lives only in that portion of the Little Tennessee River which would be completely inundated by the reservoir created as a consequence of the Tellico Dam's completion. The Secretary went on to explain the significance of the dam to the habitat of the snail darter:

> "[The] snail darter occurs only in the swifter portions of shoals over clean gravel substrate in cool, low-turbidity water. Food of the snail darter is almost exclusively snails which require a clean gravel substrate for their survival. *The proposed impoundment of water behind the proposed Tellico Dam would result in total destruction of the snail darter's habitat.*" *Ibid.* (emphasis added).

Subsequent to this determination, the Secretary declared the area of the Little Tennessee which would be affected by the Tellico Dam to be the "critical habitat" of the snail darter. Using these determinations as a predicate, and notwithstanding the near completion of the dam, the Secretary declared that pursuant to §7 of the Act, "all Federal agencies must take such action as is necessary to insure that actions authorized, funded, or carried out by them do not result in the destruction or modification of this critical habitat area." This notice, of course, was pointedly directed at TVA and clearly aimed at halting completion or operation of the dam. . . .

The District Court found that closure of the dam and the consequent impoundment of the reservoir would "result in the adverse modification, if not complete destruction, of the snail darter's critical habitat," making it "highly probable" that "the continued existence of the snail darter" would be "jeopardize[d]." Despite these findings, the District Court declined to embrace the plaintiffs' position on the merits: that once a federal project was shown to jeopardize an endangered species, a court of equity is compelled to issue an injunction restraining violation of the Endangered Species Act.

In reaching this result, the District Court stressed that the entire project was then about 80% complete and, based on available evidence, "there [were] no alternatives to impoundment of the reservoir, short of scrapping the entire project." The District Court also found that if the Tellico Project was permanently enjoined, "[s]ome $53 million would be lost in nonrecoverable obligations," meaning that a large portion of the $78 million already expended would be wasted. . . .

To accept the plaintiffs' position, the District Court argued, would inexorably lead to what it characterized as the absurd result of requiring "a court to halt impoundment of water behind a fully completed dam if an endangered species were discovered in the river on the day before such impoundment was scheduled to take place. We cannot conceive that Congress intended such a result."

Thereafter, in the Court of Appeals, respondents argued that the District Court had abused its discretion by not issuing an injunction in the face of "a blatant statutory violation." The Court of Appeals agreed, and on January 31, 1977, it reversed, remanding "with instructions that a permanent injunction issue halting all activities incident to the Tellico Project which may destroy or modify the critical habitat of the snail darter." . . .

We granted certiorari to review the judgment of the Court of Appeals.

II

We begin with the premise that operation of the Tellico Dam will either eradicate the known population of snail darters or destroy their critical habitat. Petitioner does not now seriously dispute this fact. In any event, under §4(a)(1) of the Act the Secretary of the Interior is vested with exclusive authority to determine whether a species such as the snail darter is "endangered" or "threatened" and to ascertain the factors which have led to such a precarious existence. By §4(d) Congress has authorized—indeed commanded—the Secretary to "issue such regulations as he deems necessary and advisable to provide for the conservation of such species." 16 U.S.C. §1533(d) (1976 ed.). As we have seen, the Secretary promulgated regulations which declared the snail darter an endangered species whose critical habitat would be destroyed by creation of the Tellico Dam. . . .

Starting from the above premise, two questions are presented: (a) would TVA be in violation of the Act if it completed and operated the Tellico Dam as planned? (b) if TVA's actions would offend the Act, is an injunction the appropriate remedy for the violation? For the reasons stated hereinafter, we hold that both questions must be answered in the affirmative.

(A)

It may seem curious to some that the survival of a relatively small number of three-inch fish among all the countless millions of species extant would require the permanent halting of a virtually completed dam for which Congress has expended more than $100 million. . . .

One would be hard pressed to find a statutory provision whose terms were any plainer than those in §7 of the Endangered Species Act. Its very words affirmatively command all federal agencies "to *insure* that actions *authorized, funded*, or *carried out* by them do not *jeopardize* the continued existence" of an endangered species or "*result* in the destruction or modification of habitat of such species." 16 U.S.C. §1536 (1976 ed.) (emphasis added.) This language admits of no exception. Nonetheless, petitioner urges, as do the dissenters, that the Act cannot reasonably be interpreted as applying to a federal project which was well under way when Congress passed the Endangered Species Act of 1973. To sustain that position, however, we would be forced to ignore the ordinary meaning of plain language. It has not been shown, for example, how TVA can close the gates of the Tellico Dam without "carrying out" an action that has been "authorized" and "funded" by a federal agency. Nor can we understand how such action will "*insure*" that the snail darter's habitat is not disrupted. Accepting the Secretary's determinations, as we must, it is clear that TVA's proposed operation of the dam will have precisely the opposite effect, namely the *eradication* of an endangered species.

Concededly, this view of the Act will produce results requiring the sacrifice of the anticipated benefits of the project and of many millions of dollars in public funds. But examination of the language, history, and structure of the legislation under review here indicates beyond doubt that Congress intended endangered species to be afforded the highest of priorities.

By 1973, when Congress held hearings on what would later become the Endangered Species Act of 1973, it was informed that species were . . . being lost at the rate of about one per year, 1973 House Hearings 306 (statement of Stephen R. Seater, for Defenders of Wildlife), and "the pace of disappearance of species" appeared to be "accelerating." H.R. Rep. No. 93-412, p. 4 (1973). Moreover, Congress was also told that the primary cause of this trend was something other than the normal process of natural selection:

> [Man] and his technology has [*sic*] continued at an ever-increasing rate to disrupt the natural ecosystem. This has resulted in a dramatic rise in the number and severity of the threats faced by the world's wildlife. The truth in this is apparent when one realizes that half of the recorded extinctions of mammals over the past 2,000 years have occurred in the most recent 50-year period.

1973 House Hearings 202 (statement of Assistant Secretary of the Interior).

That Congress did not view these developments lightly was stressed by one commentator:

> The dominant theme pervading all Congressional discussion of the proposed [Endangered Species Act of 1973] was the overriding need *to devote whatever effort and resources were necessary* to avoid further diminution of national and worldwide wildlife resources. Much of the testimony at the hearings and much debate was devoted to the biological problem of extinction. Senators and Congressmen uniformly deplored the irreplaceable loss to aesthetics, science, ecology, and the national heritage should more species disappear.

The legislative proceedings in 1973 are, in fact, replete with expressions of concern over the risk that might lie in the loss of *any* endangered species. Typifying these sentiments is the Report of the House Committee on Merchant Marine and Fisheries on H.R. 37, a bill which contained the essential features of the subsequently enacted Act of 1973; in explaining the need for the legislation, the Report stated:

> As we homogenize the habitats in which these plants and animals evolved, and as we increase the pressure for products that they are in a position to supply (usually unwillingly) we threaten their — and our own — genetic heritage.
> *The value of this genetic heritage is, quite literally, incalculable.*
> From the most narrow possible point of view, *it is in the best interests of mankind to minimize the losses of genetic variations.* The reason is simple: they are potential resources. They are keys to puzzles which we cannot solve, and may provide answers to questions which we have not yet learned to ask.
> To take a homely, but apt, example: one of the critical chemicals in the regulation of ovulations in humans was found in a common plant. Once discovered, and analyzed, humans could duplicate it synthetically, but had it never existed — or had it been driven out of existence before we knew its potentialities — we would never have tried to synthesize it in the first place.
> Who knows, or can say, what potential cures for cancer or other scourges, present or future, may lie locked up in the structures of plants which may yet be undiscovered, much less analyzed? Sheer self-interest impels us to be cautious.
> *The institutionalization of that caution* lies at the heart of H.R. 37 . . . H.R. Rep. No. 93-412, pp. 4-5 (1973). (Emphasis added.)

As the examples cited here demonstrate, Congress was concerned about the *unknown* uses that endangered species might have and about the *unforeseeable* place such creatures may have in the chain of life on this planet.

In shaping legislation to deal with the problem thus presented, Congress started from the finding that "[t]he two major causes of extinction are hunting and destruction of natural habitat." Of these twin threats, Congress was informed that the greatest was destruction of natural habitats. Witnesses recommended, among other things, that Congress require all land-managing agencies "to avoid damaging critical habitat for endangered species and to take positive steps to improve such habitat." . . .

As it was finally passed, the Endangered Species Act of 1973 represented the most comprehensive legislation for the preservation of endangered species ever enacted by any nation. Its stated purposes were "to provide a means whereby the ecosystems upon which endangered species and threatened species depend may be conserved," and "to provide a program for the conservation of such species."

16 U.S.C. §1531(b) (1976 ed.). In furtherance of these goals, Congress expressly stated in §2(c) that "all Federal departments and agencies *shall* seek *to conserve endangered species* and threatened species." 16 U.S.C. §1531(c) (1976 ed.) (emphasis added.) Lest there be any ambiguity as to the meaning of this statutory directive, the Act specifically defined "conserve" as meaning "to use and the use of *all methods and procedures which are necessary* to bring *any endangered species* or threatened species to the point at which the measures provided pursuant to this chapter are no longer necessary." §1532(2). (Emphasis added.) Aside from §7, other provisions indicated the seriousness with which Congress viewed this issue: Virtually all dealings with endangered species, including taking, possession, transportation, and sale, were prohibited, 16 U.S.C. §1538 (1976 ed.), except in extremely narrow circumstances, *see* §1539(b). The Secretary was also given extensive power to develop regulations and programs for the preservation of endangered and threatened species. . . .

The plain intent of Congress in enacting this statute was to halt and reverse the trend toward species extinction, whatever the cost. This is reflected not only in the stated policies of the Act, but in literally every section of the statute. All persons, including federal agencies, are specifically instructed not to "take" endangered species, meaning that no one is "to harass, harm, pursue, hunt, shoot, wound, kill, trap, capture, or collect" such life forms. 16 U.S.C. §§1532(14), 1538(a)(1)(B) (1976 ed.). Agencies in particular are directed by §§2(c) and 3(2) of the Act to "use . . . *all methods* and procedures which are necessary" to preserve endangered species. 16 U.S.C. §§1531(c), 1532(2) (1976 ed.) (emphasis added). In addition, the legislative history undergirding §7 reveals an explicit congressional decision to require agencies to afford first priority to the declared national policy of saving endangered species. The pointed omission of the type of qualifying language previously included in endangered species legislation reveals a conscious decision by Congress to give endangered species priority over the "primary missions" of federal agencies. . . .

One might dispute the [ESA's] applicability of . . . to the Tellico Dam by saying that in this case the burden on the public through the loss of millions of unrecoverable dollars would greatly outweigh the loss of the snail darter. But neither the Endangered Species Act nor Art. III of the Constitution provides federal courts with authority to make such fine utilitarian calculations. On the contrary, the plain language of the Act, buttressed by its legislative history, shows clearly that Congress viewed the value of endangered species as "incalculable." Quite obviously, it would be difficult for a court to balance the loss of a sum certain—even $100 million—against a congressionally declared "incalculable" value, even assuming we had the power to engage in such a weighing process, which we emphatically do not.

In passing the Endangered Species Act of 1973, Congress was also aware of certain instances in which exceptions to the statute's broad sweep would be necessary. Thus, §10, 16 U.S.C. §1539 (1976 ed.), creates a number of limited "hardship exemptions," none of which would even remotely apply to the Tellico Project. In fact, there are no exemptions in the Endangered Species Act for federal agencies, meaning that under the maxim *expressio unius est exclusio alterius,* we must presume that these were the only "hardship cases" Congress intended to exempt.

(B)

* * *

Here we are urged to view the Endangered Species Act "reasonably," and hence shape a remedy "that accords with some modicum of common sense and the public weal." But is that our function? We have no expert knowledge on the subject of endangered species, much less do we have a mandate from the people to strike a balance of equities on the side of the Tellico Dam. Congress has spoken in the plainest of words, making it abundantly clear that the balance has been struck in favor of affording endangered species the highest of priorities, thereby adopting a policy which it described as "institutionalized caution."

Our individual appraisal of the wisdom or unwisdom of a particular course consciously selected by the Congress is to be put aside in the process of interpreting a statute. Once the meaning of an enactment is discerned and its constitutionality determined, the judicial process comes to an end. . . .

JUSTICE POWELL, with whom JUSTICE BLACKMUN joins, dissenting.

The Court today holds that §7 of the Endangered Species Act requires a federal court, for the purpose of protecting an endangered species or its habitat, to enjoin permanently the operation of any federal project, whether completed or substantially completed. This decision casts a long shadow over the operation of even the most important projects, serving vital needs of society and national defense, whenever it is determined that continued operation would threaten extinction of an endangered species or its habitat. This result is said to be required by the "plain intent of Congress" as well as by the language of the statute.

In my view §7 cannot reasonably be interpreted as applying to a project that is completed or substantially completed when its threat to an endangered species is discovered. Nor can I believe that Congress could have intended this Act to produce the "absurd result"—in the words of the District Court—of this case. If it were clear from the language of the Act and its legislative history that Congress intended to authorize this result, this Court would be compelled to enforce it. It is not our province to rectify policy or political judgments by the Legislative Branch, however egregiously they may disserve the public interest. But where the statutory language and legislative history, as in this case, need not be construed to reach such a result, I view it as the duty of this Court to adopt a permissible construction that accords with some modicum of common sense and the public weal. . . .

JUSTICE REHNQUIST, dissenting.

In the light of my Brother Powell's dissenting opinion, I am far less convinced than is the Court that the Endangered Species Act of 1973 was intended to prohibit the completion of the Tellico Dam. But the very difficulty and doubtfulness of the correct answer to this legal question convinces me that the Act did *not* prohibit the District Court from refusing, in the exercise of its traditional equitable powers, to enjoin petitioner from completing the Dam. . . .

. . . [T]he District Court's refusal to issue an injunction was not an abuse of its discretion. I therefore dissent from the Court's opinion holding otherwise.

NOTES AND QUESTIONS ON THE ENDANGERED SPECIES ACT

1. *The case.* Do you agree with the majority opinion or the dissent, and why?

2. *Tradeoffs?* Is it appropriate to protect species regardless of cost? *See* John Copeland Nagle, *Playing Noah*, 82 MINN. L. REV. 1171 (1998) (discussing biblical lessons about endangered species). Should the obligation to protect endangered species trump Indian treaty rights to hunt and fish? *See* Mary Gray Holt, *Choosing Harmony: Indian Rights and the Endangered Species Act, in* ENDANGERED SPECIES ACT: LAW, POLICY, AND PERSPECTIVES 155-78 (Donald C. Baur & Wm. Robert Irvin eds., 2002). What if the obligation to avoid harming a species effectively eliminated the economy of a ranching community that has persisted for generations? Should all pollutants that can kill a human being be banned? What about all pollutants that can kill thousands of human beings?

3. *Escape valves.* The ESA is not as absolute as it might seem at first glance. Do the escape valves described below imply that Congress authorized the use of CBA to determine whether to protect a species? Do they suggest that the Act authorizes some consideration of tradeoffs?

Congress enacted the Act's most well-known escape hatch, the so-called God Squad provision, in response to the *Snail Darter* case. That provision allows a committee made up of cabinet members to exempt a particular federal action from the section 7(a)(2) prohibition on harming species or their habitat. *See* 16 U.S.C. §1536(a)(2), (e)-(h).

While readers of *TVA v. Hill* might assume that the snail darter saga involved an extreme example of economic folly, the halting of a nearly completed dam to save a minor species, the subsequent history, which includes the first use of the God Squad, demonstrates that the converse was true. The decision to halt the dam made good economic sense, but did not prove essential to the snail darter's survival. The God Squad unanimously decided not to exempt the Tellico dam from operation of the ESA on economic, not environmental grounds. The chair of Council of Economic Advisors prompted this decision by arguing that the costs of finishing off the mostly completed dam exceeded the benefits. Patrick A. Parenteau, *The Exemption Process and the God Squad, in Endangered Species, supra*, at 144. Congress, however, passed an appropriations rider ordering the dam to begin operation, in spite of information indicating that it made no economic or environmental sense. But the snail darter had the last laugh. Other populations of the snail darter appeared in tributaries of the Little Tennessee River. *Id.* at 145.

In 20 years, the God Squad has only met twice. *Id.* at 143. The second meeting (after the meeting on the Tellico and Grey Rocks dam projects) approved 13 timber sales, but denied exemptions for 31 additional sales, in land designated as habitat for the listed spotted owl. *Id.* at 150. Nor is the God Squad the leading check on absolutism. A leading natural resources scholar explains:

While the God Squad provision only rarely applies, still the ESA rarely stops projects: "In the Act's implementation, 'mitigation' is the watchword." Mitigation essentially means a new form of accommodative flexibility.

George Cameron Coggins, *A Premature Evaluation of American Endangered Species Law, in Endangered Species Act, supra*, at 7. *TVA v. Hill* explains that agencies have a duty not to jeopardize an endangered species. To carry out this obligation, they must consult with the Fish and Wildlife Service or the National Marine Fisheries Service, which advises agencies about the effects of their actions on listed species. *Cf.* National Ass'n of Home Builders v. Defenders of Wildlife, 551 U.S. 644 (2007) (upholding regulation limiting consultation to cases involving discretionary federal action). The following statutory provisions govern these "jeopardy findings."

16 U.S.C. §1536(b) . . .

(3) (A) . . . If jeopardy or adverse modification is found, the Secretary shall suggest those reasonable and prudent alternatives which he believes would not violate subsection (a)(2) of this section and can be taken by the Federal agency or applicant in implementing the agency action. . . .

(4) If after consultation under subsection (a)(2) of this section, the Secretary concludes that—

(A) the agency action will not violate such subsection, or offers reasonable and prudent alternatives which the Secretary believes would not violate such subsection;

(B) the taking of an endangered species or a threatened species incidental to the agency action will not violate such subsection; and

(C) if an endangered species or threatened species of a marine mammal is involved, the taking is authorized pursuant to section 1371(a)(5) of this title;

the Secretary shall provide the Federal agency and the applicant concerned, if any, with a written statement that—

(i) specifies the impact of such incidental taking on the species,

(ii) specifies those reasonable and prudent measures that the Secretary considers necessary or appropriate to minimize such impact,

(iii) in the case of marine mammals, specifies those measures that are necessary to comply with section 1371(a)(5) of this title with regard to such taking, and

(iv) sets forth the terms and conditions (including, but not limited to, reporting requirements) that must be complied with by the Federal agency or applicant (if any), or both, to implement the measures specified under clauses (ii) and (iii).

You can see that these provisions emphasize mitigation of impacts and alternatives to the precise projects proposed, rather than necessarily stopping projects altogether. In the 1980s, less than 1 percent of the jeopardy consultations called for in these provisions produced an opinion that a project would jeopardize a listed species. Of this 1 percent, the government cancelled only one in eight projects. *Id.*

Mitigation of potential impacts upon endangered species through adjustments as to how and when projects are carried out occur far more commonly than project cancellations.

The Act generally prohibits private actions harming an endangered species, including actions that degrade critical habitat. *See* Babbitt v. Sweet Home Chapter for Communities for a Greater Oregon, 515 U.S. 687 (1995). But the Act also authorizes incidental take permits in that context under similar conditions and other exceptions.

2. The Supermandate Idea

About the time that Congress passed the Unfunded Mandates Reform Act, it considered superseding almost all environmental statutory provisions with a "supermandate" applying a cost-benefit test to all environmental statutes. Do you think such a supermandate is a good idea? *See* William W. Buzbee, *Regulatory Reform or Statutory Muddle: The "Legislative Mirage" of Single Statute Regulatory Reform*, 5 N.Y.U. ENVTL. L.J. 298 (1996). Many legislators, even some who favored a supermandate, would have limited the use of judicial review in enforcing it. Does the *Corrosion Proof Fittings* case counsel against judicially reviewable CBA?

3. Priority Setting and Dollars Per Life Saved Tables

Supporters of CBA claim that environmental law has been very bad at priority setting. They cite tables developed by an OMB economist showing that the dollars per lives saved for various regulatory interventions have varied wildly and argue that CBA is needed as a rationalizing reform. *See, e.g.*, CASS SUNSTEIN, RISK AND REASON: SAFETY, LAW, AND THE ENVIRONMENT 19-27 (2002). Opponents of CBA claim that these tables include regulations that were never promulgated and that the table's authors used their own questionable assumptions to doctor government estimates of costs and benefits. *See* Richard W. Parker, *Grading Government*, 70 U. CHI. L. REV. 1345 (2003); Lisa Heinzerling, *Regulatory Costs of Mythic Proportions*, 107 YALE L.J. 1981 (1998). *Cf.* John F. Morrall, *Saving Lives: A Review of the Record*, 27 J. RISK & UNCERTAINTY (2003) (defending his tables). If regulation does have discrepancies in dollars per life saved, does that make regulation irrational *per se*? Suppose that regulation is technology-based. Will that approach produce even cost-benefit ratios? Is it irrational to base regulation on what the regulated are capable of doing? What if a regulation with very high dollars per life saved brings an enormous ecological benefit? Does that matter? Is it correct to think of decisions about regulatory stringency as priority-setting decisions? *See* David M. Driesen, *Getting Our Priorities Straight: One Strand of the Regulatory Reform Debate*, 31 ENVTL. L. REP. (ENVTL. L. INST.) 10003 (2001); STEPHEN BREYER, BREAKING THE VICIOUS CIRCLE: TOWARD EFFECTIVE RISK REGULATION (1993).

4. Quantifying Risk and Ecological Harm

The argument that environmental law should consider the magnitude of the harm leads directly to efforts to quantify the risks. But even proponents of CBA recognize that many harms cannot be quantified, because of data gaps. Quantifying ecological harms can be especially difficult. *See generally* Amy Sinden, *The Economics of Endangered Species: Why Less Is More in the Economic Analysis of Critical Habitat Designations*, 28 HARV. ENVTL. L. REV. 129, 146-51 (2004) (explaining the difficulties of quantifying benefits in the Endangered Species Act context). CBA proponents usually argue that regulators should consider the non-quantified harms as well as the quantified ones. Suppose that the monetized costs exceed the monetized benefits, but the EPA Administrator believed that the non-monetized benefits justify the regulation. How could she rationally explain why these unquantified benefits outweigh a particular cost? Could she make an explanation that would survive judicial review?

How helpful is CBA when not all of the benefits can be monetized? Consider this statement by an EPA senior scientist:

> Typically, only a few potential health or other benefits can be quantified, and even fewer can be valued monetarily. Consequently, when the sum of the limited subset of benefits that can be quantified and monetized is shown to be less than the estimated costs, it is often impossible to conclude anything about the relative magnitude of the full benefits.

Ronnie Levin, *Lead in Drinking Water*, in *Economic Analysis, supra*, at 230. Is the opposite true? If the monetizable benefits are shown to be more than the estimated costs, is it possible to tell whether the benefits outweigh the costs?

When risks can be quantified, the benefits range can be quite large, depending upon the underlying assumptions chosen in the risk assessment and monetization process. Professors Shapiro and McGarity state that the range of risk estimates for a carcinogen approximates the difference between the size of the national debt (circa 1990) and the price of a cup of coffee (regular coffee, not lattes). *See* Sidney A. Shapiro & Thomas O. McGarity, *Not So Paradoxical: The Rationale for Technology-Based Regulation*, 1991 DUKE L.J. 729, 731. If that's true, how useful can CBA be in decision making? *See* Amy Sinden, *Cass Sunstein's Cost-Benefit Lite: Economics for Liberals*, 29 COLUM. J. ENVTL. L. 191, 210-11 (2004) (arguing that CBA expands agency discretion and exacerbates problems of special interest influence).

5. Preferences and Statistical Life

The dollar value figures for the value of human life comes from surveys that economists have interpreted as showing that labor markets charge "risk premiums." In other words, jobs with greater danger from occupational hazards command higher wages. The hypothesis underlying the number assumes that these differentials reflect how much the worker is willing to accept to put up with greater risk. Some, however, have questioned whether that is so. *See* Ackerman & Heinzerling, *supra*, at 77 (pointing out that workers may have limited choices in jobs and may not understand the risks that they supposedly have accepted).

Climate Disruption Problem:
A Cost-Benefit Analysis of EPA's Emission Guidelines for Greenhouse Gas Emissions from Existing Power Plants

EPA has prepared a regulatory impact analysis (RIA) of its rule addressing existing power plant emissions of CO_2 (carbon dioxide). EPA, Regulatory Impact Analysis for the Clean Power Plan Final Rule (August 2015) [hereinafter RIA]. This RIA includes a cost-benefit analysis (CBA) of the rule and provides a basis for OIRA review under E.O. 12866 and 13563. Information and questions based primarily on this CBA follow.

1. Nonquantified Benefits

The following table lists the benefits of EPA's power plant rule and shows which benefits EPA could not quantify and monetize. As you read this, ask yourself the following questions. How significant are the unquantified benefits? What does the existence of these unquantified benefits say about the overall value of the analysis?

Quantified and Unquantified Benefits		
Benefits Category	*Specific Effect*	*Effect Has Been Monetized*
Improved Environment		
Reduced climate effects	Global climate impacts from CO_2	Yes
	Climate impacts from ozone and black carbon (directly emitted PM)	No
	Other climate impacts (e.g., other GHGs such as methane, aerosols, other impacts)	No
Improved Human Health (Co-Benefits)		
Reduced incidence of premature mortality from exposure to $PM_{2.5}$	Adult premature mortality based on cohort study estimates and expert elicitation estimates (age>25 or age>30)	Yes
	Infant mortality (age<1)	Yes
Reduced incidence of morbidity from exposure to $PM_{2.5}$	Non-fatal heart attacks (age>18)	Yes
	Hospital admissions—respiratory (all ages)	Yes
	Hospital admissions—cardiovascular (age>20)	Yes
	Emergency room visits for asthma (all ages)	Yes
	Acute bronchitis (age 8-12)	Yes
	Lower respiratory symptoms (age 7-14)	Yes
	Upper respiratory symptoms (asthmatics age 9-11)	Yes
	Asthma exacerbation (asthmatics age 6-18)	Yes

Quantified and Unquantified Benefits		
Benefits Category	Specific Effect	Effect Has Been Monetized
	Lost work days (age 18-65)	Yes
	Minor restricted-activity days (age 18-65)	Yes
	Chronic bronchitis (age>26)	No
	Emergency room visits for cardiovascular effects (all ages)	No
	Strokes and cerebrovascular disease (age 50-79)	No
	Other cardiovascular effects (e.g., other ages)	No
	Other respiratory effects (e.g., pulmonary function, non-asthma ER visits, non-bronchitis chronic diseases, other ages and populations)	No
	Reproductive and developmental effects (e.g., low birth weight, pre-term births, etc.)	No
	Cancer, mutagenicity, and genotoxicity effects	No
Reduced incidence of mortality from exposure to ozone	Premature mortality based on short-term study estimates (all ages)	Yes
	Premature mortality based on long-term study estimates (age 30-99)	No
Reduced incidence of morbidity from exposure to ozone	Hospital admissions—respiratory causes (age>65)	Yes
	Hospital admissions—respiratory causes (age<2)	Yes
	Emergency department visits for asthma (all ages)	Yes
	Minor restricted-activity days (age 18-65)	Yes
	School absence days (age 5-17)	Yes
	Decreased outdoor worker productivity (age 18-65)	No
	Other respiratory effects (e.g., premature aging of lungs)	No
	Cardiovascular and nervous system effects	No
	Reproductive and developmental effects	No
Reduced incidence of morbidity from exposure to NO_2	Asthma hospital admissions (all ages)	No
	Chronic lung disease hospital admissions (age>65)	No
	Respiratory emergency department visits (all ages)	No
	Asthma exacerbation (asthmatics age 4-18)	No
	Acute respiratory symptoms (age 7-14)	No
	Premature mortality	No
	Other respiratory effects (e.g., airway hyperresponsiveness and inflammation, lung function, other ages and populations)	No

Quantified and Unquantified Benefits		
Benefits Category	*Specific Effect*	*Effect Has Been Monetized*
Reduced incidence of morbidity from exposure to SO_2	Respiratory hospital admissions (age>65)	No
	Asthma emergency department visits (all ages)	No
	Asthma exacerbation (asthmatics age 4-12)	No
	Acute respiratory symptoms (age 7-14)	No
	Premature mortality	No
	Other respiratory effects (e.g., airway hyperresponsiveness and inflammation, lung function, other ages and populations)	No
Reduced incidence of morbidity from exposure to methylmercury	Neurologic effects—IQ loss	No
	Other neurologic effects (e.g., developmental delays, memory, behavior)	No
	Cardiovascular effects	No
	Genotoxic, immunologic, and other toxic effects	No
Reduced incidence of morbidity from exposure to HAP	Effects associated with exposure to hydrogen chloride	No
Improved Environment (Co-Benefits)		
Reduced visibility impairment	Visibility in Class 1 areas	No
	Visibility in residential areas	No
Reduced effects on materials	Household soiling	No
	Materials damage (e.g., corrosion, increased wear)	No
Reduced PM deposition (metals and organics)	Effects on individual organisms and ecosystems	No
Reduced vegetation and ecosystem effects from exposure to ozone	Visible foliar injury on vegetation	No
	Reduced vegetation growth and reproduction	No
	Yield and quality of commercial forest products and crops	No
	Damage to urban ornamental plants	No
	Carbon sequestration in terrestrial ecosystems	No
	Recreational demand associated with forest aesthetics	No
	Other non-use effects	No
	Ecosystem functions (e.g., water cycling, biogeochemical cycles, net primary productivity, leaf-gas exchange, community composition)	No

Quantified and Unquantified Benefits		
Benefits Category	*Specific Effect*	*Effect Has Been Monetized*
Reduced effects from acid deposition	Recreational fishing	No
	Tree mortality and decline	No
	Commercial fishing and forestry effects	No
	Recreational demand in terrestrial and aquatic ecosystems	No
	Other no-use effects	No
	Ecosystem functions (e.g., biogeochemical cycles)	No
Reduced effects from nutrient enrichment	Species composition and biodiversity in terrestrial and estuarine ecosystems	No
	Coastal eutrophication	No
	Recreational demand in terrestrial and estuarine ecosystems	No
	Other non-use effects	
	Ecosystem functions (e.g., biogeochemical cycles, fire regulation)	No
Reduced vegetation effects from exposure to SO_2 and NO_x	Injury to vegetation from SO_2 exposure	No
	Injury to vegetation from NO_x exposure	No
Reduced ecosystem effects from exposure to methylmercury	Effects on fish, birds, and mammals (e.g., reproductive effects)	No
	Commercial, subsistence and recreational fishing	No

Id. ES-12-14.

2. The Social Cost of Carbon: Missing Effects

EPA's claim that it could monetize the reduced climate effects from CO_2 emissions was based on an interagency effort to monetize the social cost of carbon. *See* Interagency Working Group on Social Cost of Carbon, Technical Support Document: Social Cost of Carbon for Regulatory Impact Analysis Under Executive Order 12866, http://www.whitehouse.gov/sites/default/files/omb/inforeg/For-agencies/Social-Cost-of-Carbon-for-RIA.pdf [hereinafter 2010 TSD]; Interagency Working Group on Social Cost of Carbon, Technical Update of the Social Cost of Carbon for Regulatory Impact Analysis (November 2013), http://www.whitehouse.gov/sites/default/files/omb/assets/inforeg/technical-update-social-cost-of-carbon-for-regulatory-impact-analysis.pdf; FRANK ACKERMAN & ELIZABETH STANTON, THE SOCIAL COST OF CARBON: A REPORT FOR THE ECONOMICS FOR EQUITY AND THE ENVIRONMENT NETWORK (2010) (critiquing the 2010 carbon cost estimate); Jonathan Masur & Eric Posner, *Climate Regulation and the Limits of Cost-Benefit Analysis*, 99 CAL. L. REV. 1557 (2011) (same).

The social cost of carbon is the dollar value of negative impacts associated with a metric ton of CO_2. Conversely, for a measure reducing CO_2 emissions, such as the power plant rule, the social cost of carbon provides an estimate of the monetized benefit associated with a metric ton of reduction in CO_2 emissions. Suppose that EPA estimates the social cost of carbon at $100 per metric ton and that it requires a 100 metric ton reduction in CO_2 emissions in its rule. What is the estimated dollar value of the reduction in climate disruption produced by the 100 ton CO_2 emission reduction?

EPA, however, noted that the models it used to generate these estimates "do not assign value to all of the important physical, ecological, and economic impacts of climate change recognized in the climate change literature." RIA at ES-16. Furthermore, the models used are extremely limited in their treatment of catastrophic climate disruption, which the scientific literature treats seriously. *Id.* The social cost of carbon is based on averaging results from three models. One of these models assumes away catastrophic climate disruption altogether and the others treat it as a low probability event, even though there is little scientific basis for finding catastrophic climate disruption improbable or probable. 2010 TSD at 31-32. Was EPA correct to claim that it could monetize the climate disruption impacts associated with carbon dioxide in light of these limitations?

3. Discount Rates

Economists usually apply discount rates to both costs and benefits of future emission reductions. The following table, derived from EPA's RIA, shows the influence of discount rates on benefits estimates. There is no professional consensus on what discount rates are appropriate. The first three rows show benefits estimates based on the average values found in the models used for monetized benefits. The last row uses estimates based on the upper ranges of values from the model (*i.e.*, the 95th percentile), used as a very imperfect proxy for catastrophic climate disruption. What does this table suggest about the utility of CBA for this rule?

Estimated Global Climate Benefits for the Final Emission Guidelines in 2025 (Billions of 2011$)[2]

Discount Rate	Monetized Benefits
5% (average)	$3.6
3% (average)	$12
2.5% (average)	$17
3% (95th percentile)	$35

2. This table is derived from RIA, at 4-5, Table 4-3.

4. Monetization

EPA usually bases its monetization of human life on statistical studies of the "risk premiums" paid to workers in high-risk jobs and did so here with respect to the co-benefits of the rule (*e.g.*, avoided deaths because of less emissions of particulate matter), estimating the value of a statistical life saved in 2020 at $9.6 million. For climate disruption, however, developing countries (where scientists predict the worst effects will occur) often do not generate adequate risk premium data and economists turn to a method for valuing human lives based on the ratio between risk premiums and per capita lifetime income. Economists sometimes estimate that the value of a life saved as determined by risk premium studies is about 140 times per capita income. An economist accepting this estimate would multiply the average per capital income of a country times 140 to estimate the value of a statistical life in that country. Suppose that per capita income in Bangladesh rises to $1,000 a year. What would the value of a statistical life be in Bangladesh based on this methodology and ratio? Is this procedure fair and appropriate? What effect does using this procedure have on climate benefit estimates?

For many health effects, EPA cannot reliably estimate the value of the pain and suffering illness causes. It therefore uses treatment costs as an estimate of the value of an illness. How would that influence the benefits analysis?

5. The Bottom Line

EPA estimated that the most stringent option it proposed would generate $7.5 billion in compliance costs but realize between $35 and $58 billion in monetized benefits by 2020. Its least stringent option for individual state implementation would generate $5.5 billion in compliance costs and between $28 and $36 billion in monetized benefits. Which option looks best based on the CBA? Should EPA have made the rule more or less stringent than either of these options based on the CBA alone?

These rules are promulgated under section 111(d) of the Clean Air Act, which requires that these rules reflect the best demonstrated technology. Can EPA consider its CBA in deciding whether to alter its proposed rule? If so, what sorts of adjustments, if any, are appropriate based on the CBA? Are there any constraints on adjustments EPA might legally make based on the CBA?

≡ THE MEANS OF ENVIRONMENTAL PROTECTION

The previous subpart focused on how agencies make decisions about the stringency of environmental standards (both ambient and output standards). We saw that environmental law uses effects-based, technological, or cost-benefit criteria to guide agency stringency determinations.

These stringency determinations set enforceable objectives for improving the environment. This part discusses the means of realizing these environmental improvements. Once the agency has chosen a level of protection, it must decide whether to command use of a particular technology or technique, require a particular level of performance from regulated parties, employ an "economic incentive" to encourage reduced environmental damage, use information to motivate change, or try to encourage or require pollution prevention or recycling. The legislature faces the same choices if it decides to make detailed decisions itself, rather than delegate them to an administrative agency.

We explore the choice of means through chapters on traditional regulation, economic incentive approaches, informational approaches, pollution prevention, and environmental restoration. The choice about the means of meeting environmental goals can influence cost, enforceability, and fairness, so it raises extremely important practical issues that influence policy making.

7

Traditional Regulation

This book uses the term "traditional regulation" to refer to performance standards, work practice standards, and bans. For convenience, this chapter uses the term "work practice standards" in a generic sense to refer to any standard dictating a particular method of obtaining emission reductions, a definition that includes design, equipment, or operational standards. *Cf.* 42 U.S.C. §7412(h)(1). We contrast traditional regulation with approaches, such as emissions trading, that most experts think of as economic incentive programs.

Most writing about the means of environmental regulation contrasts "command and control regulation" with economic incentives. Some writers use the term "command and control regulation" to refer to work practice standards. Others use the term to refer to both work practice standards and standards requiring a particular level of performance. This book's use of the term "traditional regulation" generally tracks this broader definition of command and control regulation.

A. PERFORMANCE STANDARDS

A performance standard quantitatively limits the amount of pollution or natural resource destruction. For example, EPA has traditionally limited air emissions from electric utilities with standards limiting the pounds per million British Thermal Units (BTUs are a measure of heat energy) that the utility can emit. It has often regulated vehicle emissions by limiting the grams of a pollutant emitted per mile. Here's one court's description of a traditional utility performance standard promulgated under section 111 of the Clean Air Act:

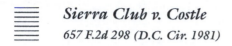

Sierra Club v. Costle
657 F.2d 298 (D.C. Cir. 1981)

WALD, CIRCUIT JUDGE.

I. Introduction

A. The Challenged Standards

The Clean Air Act provides for direct federal regulation of emissions from new stationary sources of air pollution by authorizing EPA to set performance standards for significant sources of air pollution which may be reasonably anticipated to endanger public health or welfare. In June 1979 EPA promulgated the NSPS [New Source Performance Standards] involved in this case. The new standards increase pollution controls for new coal-fired electric power plants by tightening restrictions on emissions of sulfur dioxide and particulate matter. Sulfur dioxide emissions are limited to a maximum of 1.2 lbs./MBtu[6] . . . and a 90 percent reduction of potential uncontrolled sulfur dioxide emissions is required except when emissions to the atmosphere are less than 0.60 lbs./MBtu. When sulfur dioxide emissions are less than 0.60 lbs./MBtu potential emissions must be reduced by no less than 70 percent. In addition, emissions of particulate matter are limited to 0.03 lbs./MBtu.

II. The Variable Percentage Reduction Option

[T]he final NSPS adopted by EPA include an optional variable percentage reduction standard. Under this optional standard a utility plant can permissibly reduce its sulfur dioxide emissions by less than 90 percent of potential uncontrolled emissions if the amount of sulfur dioxide emitted following the use of pollution control technology is less than 0.60 lbs./MBtu. In no instance, however, can a plant reduce emissions by less than 70 percent of potential uncontrolled emissions. As a result of this option, the NSPS requirements for percentage reduction of sulfur dioxide removal vary on a sliding scale ranging from a minimum of 70 percent to a maximum of 90 percent. There is no dispute that the 70 percent floor in the standard necessarily means that, given the present state of pollution control technology, utilities will have to employ some form of flue gas desulfurization (. . . "scrubbing") technology.

NOTES AND QUESTIONS ON THE PERFORMANCE STANDARD IN *SIERRA CLUB v. COSTLE*

1. *Flexibility of performance standards.* The court states, "*[G]iven the present state of pollution control technology,* utilities will have to employ some form of

---

6. MBtu refers to Million British thermal units which is a measure of heat energy. A single Btu is the amount of energy required to raise the temperature of one pound of water one degree Fahrenheit. This measure is appropriate here because utility plants combust coal to heat water which produces steam used for generating electricity.

flue gas desulfurization ("FGD" or "scrubbing") technology" (emphasis added). *Sierra Club*, 657 F.2d at 316. Suppose that a utility invents a new form of technology capable of meeting the numerical standards in the regulation. May the utility use this alternative technology under this standard as written?

2. *Coal washing.* On the other hand, coal-washing technology, which would usually cost much less than scrubbing, reduces emissions by 20-40 percent. *See* BRUCE A. ACKERMAN & WILLIAM T. HASSLER, CLEAN COAL/DIRTY AIR: OR HOW THE CLEAN AIR ACT BECAME A MULTIBILLION-DOLLAR BAIL-OUT FOR HIGH SULFUR COAL PRODUCERS AND WHAT SHOULD BE DONE ABOUT IT 15, 66-68 (1981). Does the standard described in this case preclude complete reliance upon coal washing for compliance? Why did EPA rule out a nice cheap control option?

3. *CWA statutory language.* Many statutes contain language calling for performance standards. For example, section 304(b)(2)(A) of the Clean Water Act requires technology-based standards identifying "the degree of effluent reduction attainable through the application of the best control measures and practices achievable including treatment techniques, process and procedure innovations, operating methods, and other alternatives. . . ." 33 U.S.C. §1314(b)(2)(A). Do you see why this language requires a performance standard, rather than a specification of technique? If that is so, why does the provision mention techniques?

4. *Ends and means.* In *Costle*, the Clean Air Act required EPA to use a technology-based approach to choosing its performance standard. *See* 42 U.S.C. §7411(a)(1). Can an agency use a health-based approach or a cost-benefit approach to setting a performance standard? Would these sorts of standards look any different in the Code of Federal Regulations, which codifies the standards themselves but omits the explanation for standards found in the Federal Register?

While performance standards seem to allow technological innovations that make equal or better environmental performance possible at lower cost, some writers have claimed that in practice performance standards discourage innovation. Consider the views of Professor Stewart:

Richard Stewart, Regulation, Innovation, and Administrative Law: A Conceptual Framework
69 Cal. L. Rev. 1256, 1268-69 (1981)

3. Performance, Specification, and Engineering Standards

The conduct required by standards may be expressed in terms of a performance characteristic (*e.g.*, m.p.g. fuel economy, quantity of emissions, toxicity of ingredients). Alternately, a standard may specify a particular input, such as low-sulphur fuel oil, or a particular engineering design or piece of equipment, such as a flue gas desulphurization "scrubber." Performance standards allow regulated firms flexibility to select the least costly or least burdensome means of achieving compliance. For instance, cost considerations might cause a firm to change its internal processes rather than to incorporate an "end-of-pipe" control to meet standards. Specification standards, on the other hand, offer administrative simplicity and ease of enforcement. Technology to monitor emissions, particularly from industrial sources, in many cases has been expensive, cumbersome, and not very accurate. These drawbacks have allowed regulated firms to resist enforcement through legal challenges related to evidentiary and technical issues. Also, agency monitoring and enforcement resources are often quite limited. With specification standards, enforcement personnel need only check fuel supply invoices or determine whether control equipment is operating.

Engineering standards are a hybrid of performance standards and specifications. In form, they are expressed as pure performance standards. In practice, they are based upon the level of performance that can be achieved by a specific input or technology. Administrators rely on these specific control measures to determine the required level of performance in order to simplify standard setting, to meet legal challenges to standards' feasibility, and to facilitate enforcement. While regulated firms are in theory free to meet the required level of performance any way they choose, they have strong incentives to adopt the particular technology underlying the standard because its use will readily persuade regulators of compliance.

NOTES AND QUESTIONS ON TECHNOLOGICAL INNOVATION

1. *Does technology-based goal setting discourage innovation?* Professor Stewart's statement suggesting that in practice technology-based performance standards discourage even compliant innovations seems to assume that the work of evaluating a technology's feasibility in setting a limit influences firms' decisions about what technology to adopt. Does this argument that performance standards discourage innovation apply to a performance standard adopted using a health-based approach to standard setting? In that situation, the regulator might not have relied upon the performance of any particular technology to arrive at the decision about what level of reductions to require. Would his argument apply to a standard set using CBA? Professor Stewart's argument, while very influential, has been contested:

> Professor Richard Stewart of New York University, however, has stated that polluters have "strong incentives to adopt the particular technology underlying" a technology-based performance standard because "its use will readily persuade regulators of compliance." He does not explain why this countervailing persuasion incentive would overcome the economic incentive to realize savings through an effective and cheaper innovation, even if the persuasiveness incentive were powerful. Polluters, after all, have a number of means of persuading regulators that their innovations perform adequately if they in fact do so. First, polluters may monitor their pollution directly to demonstrate compliance. Second, in some cases polluters may eliminate regulated chemicals, which certainly demonstrates compliance.

DAVID M. DRIESEN, THE ECONOMIC DYNAMICS OF ENVIRONMENTAL LAW 52 (2003).

2. *Client counseling.* Imagine that you represent a company required to comply with a performance standard. Suppose that your client's engineers have figured out how to eliminate the pollution the performance standard regulates. What factors would you consider in deciding whether to counsel your client to adopt this

pollution prevention method? What if your client has a control technology that it thinks superior, but the regulator has never seen it?

If your client thinks there is some risk of not meeting the standard both with the technology the agency evaluated in setting the standard and an alternative being offered by a vendor, which would you select? In the event of a failure to meet the performance standard, would (or should) the choice of technology influence the court's decision about the size of the penalty?

3. *Empirical information.* The question of whether performance standards discourage innovation should be empirically testable. The literature does show some cases where polluters have innovated in response to performance standards. *See* Kurt Strasser, *Clean Technology, Pollution Prevention, and Environmental Regulation*, 9 FORDHAM ENVTL. L.J. 1, 32 (1997); U.S. CONGRESS, OFFICE OF TECHNOLOGY ASSESSMENT, GAUGING CONTROL TECHNOLOGY AND REGULATORY IMPACTS IN OCCUPATIONAL SAFETY AND HEALTH—AN APPRAISAL OF OSHA'S ANALYTICAL APPROACH 64 (1995); Nicholas A. Ashford, Christine Ayers & Robert F. Stone, *Using Regulations to Change the Market for Innovation*, 9 HARV. ENVTL. L. REV. 419, 440-41 (1985); Nicholas Ashford & George R. Heaton Jr., *Regulation and Technological Innovation in the Chemical Industry*, 46 LAW & CONTEMP. PROBS. 109, 139-40 (1983). Yet, we simply have no good information about precisely how polluters have responded to most standards. And many experts believe that traditional regulation has not proven very successful at promoting innovation.

B. WORK PRACTICE STANDARDS

In contrast to performance standards, work practice standards specifically require use of a particular technique. Why would a regulatory agency ever mandate a technique, rather than at least provide some potential for flexibility through a performance standard? Consider a typical provision governing the use of work practice standards from section 112 of the Clean Air Act:

42 U.S.C. §7412. Hazardous air pollutants

(h) Work practice standards and other requirements

(1) In general

For purposes of this section, if it is not feasible in the judgment of the Administrator to prescribe or enforce an emission standard for control of a hazardous air pollutant or pollutants, the Administrator may, in lieu thereof, promulgate a design, equipment, work practice, or operational standard, or combination thereof. . . .

(2) Definition

For the purpose of this subsection, the phrase "not feasible to prescribe or enforce an emission standard" means any situation in which the Administrator determines that—

(A) a hazardous air pollutant or pollutants cannot be emitted through a conveyance designed and constructed to emit or capture such pollutant . . . or

(B) the application of measurement methodology to a particular class of sources is not practicable due to technological and economic limitations. . . .

(4) Numerical standard required

Any standard promulgated under paragraph (1) shall be promulgated in terms of an emission standard whenever it is feasible to promulgate and enforce a standard in such terms.

Section 112(h) distinguishes work practice standards from design, equipment, or operational standards. Recall, however, that this textbook uses the term "work practice" standard to include these similar prescriptive requirements. If it is impossible to measure pollution, can a performance standard be enforced? Does the statute favor or disfavor work practice standards? The following case offers an example of a work practice standard.

 Adamo Wrecking Co. v. United States
434 U.S. 275 (1978)

JUSTICE REHNQUIST delivered the opinion of the Court.

The Clean Air Act authorizes the Administrator of the Environmental Protection Agency to promulgate "emission standards" for hazardous air pollutants "at the level which in his judgment provides an ample margin of safety to protect the public health." The emission of an air pollutant in violation of an applicable emission standard is prohibited by section 112(c)(1)(B) of the Act. The knowing violation of the latter section, in turn, subjects the violator to fine and imprisonment under the provisions of §113(c)(1)(C) of the Act. The final piece in this statutory puzzle is §307(b) of the Act, which provides in pertinent part:

(1) A petition for review of action of the Administrator in promulgating . . . any emission standard under section 112 . . . may be filed only in the United States Court of Appeals for the District of Columbia. . . . Any such petition shall be filed within 30 days from the date of such promulgation or approval, or after such date if such petition is based solely on grounds arising after such 30th day.

(2) Action of the Administrator with respect to which review could have been obtained under paragraph (1) shall not be subject to judicial review in civil or criminal proceedings for enforcement.

It is within this legislative matrix that the present criminal prosecution arose. Petitioner was indicted in the United States District Court for the Eastern District of Michigan for violation of §112(c)(1)(B). The indictment alleged that petitioner, while engaged in the demolition of a building in Detroit, failed to comply with 40 CFR §61.22(d)(2)(I) (1975). That regulation, described in its caption as a "National Emission Standard for Asbestos," specifies procedures to be followed in connection with building demolitions, but does not by its terms limit emissions of asbestos which occur during the course of a demolition. The District Court granted petitioner's motion to dismiss the indictment on the ground that no violation of §112(c)(1)(B), necessary to establish criminal liability under §113(c)(1)(C), had been alleged, because the cited regulation was not an "emission standard" within the meaning of §112(c). The United States Court of Appeals for the Sixth Circuit reversed holding that Congress had in §307(b) precluded petitioner from questioning in a criminal proceeding whether a regulation ostensibly promulgated under §112(b)(1)(B) was in fact an emission standard. We granted certiorari, and we now reverse.

I

We do not intend to make light of a difficult question of statutory interpretation when we say that the basic question in this case may be phrased: "When is an emission standard not an emission standard?" Petitioner contends, and the District Court agreed, that while the preclusion and exclusivity provisions of §307(b) of the Act prevented his obtaining "judicial review" of an emission standard in this criminal proceeding, he was nonetheless entitled to claim that the administrative regulation cited in the indictment was actually not an emission standard at all. The Court of Appeals took the contrary view. It held that a regulation designated by the Administrator as an "emission standard," however different in content it might be from what Congress had contemplated when it authorized the promulgation of emission standards, was sufficient to support a criminal charge based upon §112(c), unless it had been set aside in an appropriate proceeding commenced in the United States Court of Appeals for the District of Columbia Circuit pursuant to §307(b). . . .

III

. . . A federal court in which a criminal prosecution under §113(c)(1)(C) of the Clean Air Act is brought may determine whether or not the regulation which the defendant is alleged to have violated is an "emission standard" within the meaning of the Act. We are aware of the possible dangers that flow from this interpretation; district courts will be importuned, under the guise of making a determination as to whether a regulation is an "emission standard," to engage in judicial review in a manner that is precluded by §307(b)(2) of the Act. This they may not do. The narrow inquiry to be addressed by the court in a criminal prosecution is not whether the Administrator has complied with appropriate procedures in promulgating the regulation in question, or whether the particular regulation is arbitrary, capricious, or supported by the administrative record. Nor is the court to pursue any of the other familiar inquiries which arise in the course of an administrative review proceeding. The question is only whether the regulation which the defendant is alleged to have violated is on its face an "emission standard" within the broad limits of the congressional meaning of that term.

IV

It remains to be seen whether the District Court reached the correct conclusion with regard to the regulation here in question. In the Act, Congress has given a substantial indication of the intended meaning of the term "emission standard." Section 112 on its face distinguishes between emission standards and the techniques to be utilized in achieving those standards. Under §112(c)(1)(B)(ii), the Administrator is empowered temporarily to exempt certain facilities from the burden of compliance with an emission standard, "if he finds that such period is necessary for the installation of controls." In specified circumstances, the President, under §112(c)(2), has the same power, "if he finds that the technology to implement such standards is not available." Section 112(b)(2) authorizes the Administrator to issue information on "pollution control techniques."

Most clearly supportive of petitioner's position that a standard was intended to be a quantitative limit on emissions is this provision of §112(b)(1)(B): "The Administrator shall establish any such standard *at the level* which in his judgment provides an ample margin of safety to protect the public health from such hazardous air pollutant." (Emphasis added.) All these provisions lend force to the conclusion that a standard is a quantitative "level" to be attained by use of "techniques," "controls," and "technology." This conclusion is fortified by recent amendments to the Act, by which Congress authorized the Administrator to promulgate a "design, equipment, work practice, or operational standard" when "it is not feasible to prescribe or enforce an emission standard." Clean Air Act Amendments of 1977, Pub. L. 95-95, §110, 91 Stat. 703.

This distinction, now endorsed by Congress, between "work practice standards" and "emission standards" first appears in the Administrator's own account of the development of this regulation. Although the Administrator has contended that a "work practice standard" is just another type of emission standard, the history of this regulation demonstrates that he chose to regulate work practices only when it became clear he could not regulate emissions. The regulation as originally proposed would have prohibited all visible emissions of asbestos during the course of demolitions. In adopting the final form of the regulation, the Administrator concluded "that the no visible emission requirement would prohibit repair or demolition in many situations, since it would be impracticable, if not impossible, to do such work without creating visible emissions." Therefore the Administrator chose to "specif[y] certain work practices" instead.

The Government concedes that, prior to the 1977 Amendments, the statute was ambiguous with regard to whether a work-practice standard was properly classified as an emission standard, but argues that this Court should defer to the Administrator's construction of the Act. While such deference is entirely appropriate under ordinary circumstances, in this case the 1977 Amendments to the Clean Air Act tend to undercut the administrative construction. The Senate Report reiterated its "strong preference for numerical emission limitations," but endorsed the addition of §112(e) to the Act to allow the use of work-practice standards "in a very few limited cases." Although the Committee agreed that the Amendments would authorize the regulation involved here, it refrained from endorsing the Administrator's view that the regulation had previously been authorized as an emission standard under §112(c). The clear distinction drawn in §112(e) between work-practice standards and emission standards practically forecloses any such inference.

For all of the foregoing reasons, we conclude that the work-practice standard involved here was not an emission standard. The District Court's order dismissing the indictment was therefore proper, and the judgment of the Court of Appeals is Reversed.

JUSTICE STEVENS, dissenting.

The regulation which petitioner is accused of violating requires that asbestos insulation and fireproofing in large buildings be watered down before the building is demolished.

The reason Congress attached "the most stringent criminal liability" to the violation of an emission standard for a "hazardous air pollutant" is that substances within that narrow category pose an especially grave threat to human health. That is also a reason why the Court should avoid a construction of the statute that would deny the Administrator the authority to regulate these poisonous substances effectively.

The reason the Administrator did not frame the emission standard for asbestos in numerical terms is that asbestos emissions cannot be measured numerically. For that reason, if Congress simultaneously commanded him (a) to regulate asbestos emissions by establishing and enforcing emission standards and (b) never to use any kind of standard except one framed in numerical terms, it commanded an impossible task.

Nothing in the language of the 1970 statute, or in its history, compels so crippling an interpretation of the Administrator's authority. On the contrary, I am persuaded (1) that the Administrator's regulation of asbestos emissions was entirely legitimate; (2) that if this conclusion were doubtful, we would nevertheless be required to respect his reasonable interpretation of the governing statute; (3) that the 1977 Amendments, fairly read, merely clarified his pre-existing authority; and (4) that the Court's reading of the statute in its current form leads to the anomalous conclusion that work-practice rules, even though properly promulgated, are entirely unenforceable. Accordingly, . . . I cannot accept Part IV's disposition of the most important issue in this case.

The regulation which petitioner is accused of violating requires that asbestos insulation and fireproofing in large buildings be watered down before the building is demolished. The effect of the regulation is to curtail the quantity of asbestos which is emitted into the open air during demolition. Because neither the rule nor its limiting effect is expressed in numerical terms, the Court holds that the asbestos regulation cannot be a "standard" within the meaning of §112(b)(1) of the Clean Air Act. This conclusion is not compelled by the use of the word "standard" or by Congress' expectation that standards would normally be expressed in numerical terms; for the statute contains no express requirements that standards always be framed in such language. There is no semantic reason why the word "standard" may not be used to describe the watered down asbestos standard involved in this case.

The promulgated standard is entirely consistent with congressional intent. Congress had indicated a preference for numerical emission standards.[13] Congress

---

13. Congress apparently believed that too frequent resort to work-practice rules or equipment specifications would discourage the private market's pursuit of "the most economic, acceptable technique to apply." S. Rep. No. 91-1196, at 17.

had also expressed a willingness to accept the serious economic hardships that a total prohibition of asbestos emissions would have caused. But there is no evidence that Congress intended to require the Administrator to make a choice between the extremes of closing down an entire industry and imposing no regulation on the emission of a hazardous pollutant; Congress expressed no overriding interest in using a numerical standard when industry is able to demonstrate that a less drastic control technique is available,[14] and that it provides an ample margin of safety to the public health. . . .

IV

A reading of the entire statute, as amended in 1977, confirms my opinion that the asbestos regulation is, and since its promulgation has been, an emission standard. If this is not true, as the Court holds today, it is unenforceable, and will continue to be unenforceable even if promulgated anew pursuant to the authority expressly set forth in the 1977 Amendments.

The Clean Air Act treats the Administrator's power to promulgate emission standards separately from his power to enforce them. While it is §112(b) that gives the Administrator authority to promulgate an "emission standard," it is §112(c) that prohibits the violation of an "emission standard." Presumably the Court's holding that a work-practice rule is not an "emission standard" applies to both of these sections. Under that holding a work-practice rule may neither be enforced nor promulgated as an emission standard. This holding will not affect the Administrator's power to promulgate work-practice rules, because the 1977 Amendments explicitly recognize that power. But Congress has not amended §112(c), which continues to permit enforcement only of "emission standards." Accordingly, the Court's holding today has effectively made the asbestos regulation, and any other work-practice rule as well, unenforceable.

Ironically, therefore, the 1977 Amendments, which were intended to lift the cloud over the Administrator's authority, have actually made his exercise of that authority ineffectual. This is the kind of consequence a court risks when it substitutes its reading of a complex statute for that of the Administrator charged with the responsibility of enforcing it. Moreover, it is a consequence which would be entirely avoided by recognizing that the Administrator acted well within his statutory authority when he promulgated the asbestos regulation as an "emission standard" for hazardous air pollutants. I would affirm the judgment of the Court of Appeals for the Sixth Circuit.

---

14. A summary of the conference agreement states that §112 "could mean, effectively, that a plant would be required to close because of the absence of control techniques." This statement implies that the Administrator should avoid setting emission standards that will require plant closings if alternative control techniques—including work-practice rules—can provide an ample margin of safety. It is unlikely that Congress intended, by expressing a modest preference for numerical standards, to mandate plant closings under a numerical standard when a work-practice rule would achieve the same level of protection with less economic disruption.

NOTES AND QUESTIONS ON *ADAMO WRECKING* AND WORK PRACTICE STANDARDS

1. *Subsequent history.* Congress promptly superseded this decision with a statutory amendment making sure that EPA could criminally enforce work practice standards promulgated under section 112. *See* United States v. Ethyl Corp., 576 F. Supp. 80, 82 (M.D. La. 1983), *rev'd on other grounds*, 761 F.2d 1153 (5th Cir. 1985), *cert. denied*, 474 U.S. 1070 (1986). No authority, however, has called the Court's description of the difference between work practice and emission standards into question. Even though that distinction has ceased to matter for purposes of the applicability of criminal sanctions, the choice between those forms of standards remains an issue that arises regularly in agency rule making. Agencies must implement the congressional policies respecting which type of standard to promulgate.

2. *Why?* Why did EPA write a work practice standard instead of an emissions standard?

3. *Reasons to prefer performance standards.* Note that in explaining the congressional preference for emission standards rather than work practice standards, Justice Stevens explains:

> Congress apparently believed that too frequent resort to work-practice rules or equipment specifications would discourage the private market's pursuit of "the most economic, acceptable technique to apply."

Adamo Wrecking, 434 U.S. at 299 n.13 (Stevens, J., dissenting).

4. *Other statutory provisions.* The strong congressional preference for emissions standards is not unique to section 112 of the Clean Air Act. *See* 42 U.S.C. §7411(h); PPG Industries v. Harrison, 660 F.2d 628, 636 (5th Cir. 1981) (authority to set performance standards does not include authority to specify fuels); American Petroleum Institute v. EPA, 52 F.3d 1113 (1995) (EPA may not limit use of ethanol in reformulated gasoline, because Clean Air Act mandates performance standards).

5. *Counseling EPA.* You are an EPA attorney advising EPA's Office of Solid Waste. That office has drafted regulations addressing the treatment of hazardous waste exempted from RCRA's ban on land disposal of certain waste. This ban proceeds in phases, but allows EPA to exempt waste from the ban if the ban "is not required in order to protect human health and the environment." 42 U.S.C. §6924(d)-(g). While that office believes that it is possible to measure the levels of waste being released into the environment, it would prefer to simply mandate its preferred treatment technology in order to reduce enforcement and monitoring costs. Would you recommend that it do so? The relevant statutory language follows:

> [T]he Administrator shall promulgate regulations specifying those levels or methods of treatment, if any, which substantially diminish the toxicity of waste or substantially reduce the likelihood of migration of hazardous constituents from the waste so that short-term and long-term threats to human health and the environment are minimized.

42 U.S.C. §6924(m)(1).

Suppose that you transfer to the Office of Air and Radiation and confront the same question, *i.e.*, that office would prefer to mandate its preferred technology even though measurement of pollution levels is possible. Would you give the same advice in a rule making governed by CAA section 112(h), the provision involved in *Adamo Wrecking*?

C. BANS

As an alternative to performance standards or work practice standards, governments may choose to simply ban environmentally destructive substances and practices. Although a ban may seem to be the most prescriptive and absolute form of traditional regulation, a number of factors can mitigate that apparent harshness. First, although a ban can be absolute, that is, government can ban the manufacture and use of a chemical or other product entirely, it can also impose a more tailored ban. For example, it can ban only particular uses of a chemical, or only the disposal of a chemical to a particular environmental medium. Or, it can ban an activity pursuant to a phase-out to allow industry economic transition or identification of viable alternatives. Second, government can also issue a conditional ban. The ban might apply unless the regulated party takes certain actions, such as mitigation of harm from the activity or restoration of any resources damaged by the use or activity; or, the ban may apply unless the regulated party can meet certain requirements, such as information and analysis sufficient to demonstrate that there are no feasible alternatives to the otherwise banned use or activity. As you can see, there are a wide variety of potential variations on the kinds of bans that might be imposed. As you read the following, consider what kinds of justifications dictate whether a ban is appropriate, and what forms of bans are best suited to what circumstances.

1. Absolute Bans

Congress and EPA have occasionally elected to simply ban hazardous substances of various kinds. Congress, for example, generally banned manufacture of polychlorinated biphenyls (PCBs) when it passed TSCA. *See* 15 U.S.C. §2605(e)(3)(A). EPA banned use in the United States of the pesticide DDT under the Federal Insecticide, Fungicide, and Rodenticide Act (FIFRA). Note that the former prohibited all new manufacture and commercial distribution of PCBs, but not necessarily the use of existing stocks. *See id.* §2606(e)(3)(C). By contrast, the latter banned the use of DDT in the United States but not its manufacture, *see* Environmental Defense Fund v. EPA, 489 F.2d 1247 (D.C. Cir. 1973) (affirming ban of DDT), and DDT use continues in other countries. *See* Henk van den Berg, *Global Status of DDT and Its Alternatives for Use in Vector Control to Prevent Disease*, 117 ENVTL. HEALTH PERSP. 1656 (2009).

Congress also required EPA to phase out ozone-depleting substances under the 1990 Amendments to the Clean Air Act. Scientists had found that a host of substances used as refrigerants, solvents, and pesticides were depleting the stratospheric ozone layer, which shields us from ultraviolet rays. This depletion posed serious risks of producing skin cancer, cataracts, and immune deficiencies. Accordingly, the United States spearheaded an international agreement to phase out the most serious ozone-depleting substances, called the Montreal Protocol to the Vienna Convention on Ozone Depleting Substances. Title VI of the Clean Air Act Amendments of 1990 implements this agreement, and indeed, requires more rapid phase-out than the agreement requires in some respects. *See* 42 U.S.C. §§7671-7671q.

Prior to the signing of the Montreal Protocol, ozone-depleting substances were widely used and well entrenched. It was not clear whether adequate substitutes could be found and it was considered likely that any substitutes would prove costly. *See* Edward A. Parson, Protecting the Ozone Layer: Science and Strategy 9 (2003). Nevertheless, all principal manufacturing countries agreed to phase out production of ozone-depleting chemicals. The phase-out proved relatively inexpensive and produced a raft of innovative substitutes in a variety of applications.

At first glance, it might appear that a ban is simply an extremely stringent performance standard, a zero emissions standard. Alternatively, one might think of it as a very specific work practice standard.

While both of these views are plausible, a complete ban on the manufacture or use of a chemical has special characteristics that require some discussion. First of all, as both EPA and the *Corrosion Proof Fittings* court recognized when EPA attempted to phase out asbestos, a ban does more than reduce releases to zero in a given medium. It eliminates a particular substance as a future threat to all media—air, water, and land. *See, e.g.*, Richard B. Alexander & Richard A. Smith, *Trends in Lead Concentrations in Major U.S. Rivers and Their Relation to Historical Changes in Gasoline-Lead Consumption*, 24 Water Res. Bull. 557, 568 (1988) (ban on lead in gasoline, while motivated by concerns about air emissions, reduced water pollution).

On the other hand, a production ban does not address continuing use of substances already manufactured. Thus, for example, even as EPA banned future production of Freon, an ozone-depleting substance that auto manufacturers used as a coolant for vehicle air conditioners, EPA found it necessary to write work practice standards to govern the disposal of Freon already in use. Still, over the long term, bans can be extremely effective. On the other hand, they can, as the *Corrosion Proof Fittings* court recognized, raise risk/risk tradeoffs. For example, some of the substitutes for ozone-depleting chemicals in solvents were as benign as soap and water, but others were toxic chemicals that posed cancer risks.

A work practice standard like that in *Adamo* may appear to share a lot in common with a ban. Both involve very specific government orders. But there's a significant difference. The work practice standard told asbestos contractors what to do, *i.e.*, to wet down buildings undergoing demolition. A ban tells manufacturers what not to do, *i.e.*, do not continue to use or manufacture the dangerous substance.

While orders telling people precisely what to do by their nature greatly limit flexibility, orders prohibiting a dangerous substance allow manufacturers to do anything but that which is prohibited. Thus, phase-outs can serve as catalysts for innovation. *Accord* Strasser, *supra*, at 38-40. They prohibit manufacture of substances with an established market niche and thus open up space for competitors to do something new. Indeed, if the old way of doing something is forbidden, manufacturers have to attempt something new if they want to profit from meeting the need that created the demand for a product in the first place.

Bans can obviously disrupt existing industry. The degree of the disruption, however, may vary. For example, manufacturers of ozone-depleting chemicals ultimately supported the phase-out of ozone-depleting chemicals, because they believed that they could manufacture profitable substitutes. Would you expect the same reaction if EPA announced that it was banning all chemical pesticides, because organic agriculture or genetically modified organisms make them unnecessary? What if EPA decided to phase out the use of coal in power plants, either to control the health effects of air pollution or to reduce greenhouse gas emissions? When government wishes to ban a material, it frequently phases it out over time to give industry time to adjust and to minimize disruption.

2. Partial Bans

Absolute bans are premised on a legislative or administrative agency determination that a particular chemical or other activity is so inherently dangerous that the chemical should not be used or disposed of anywhere, for any purpose. What if a chemical can be used safely in some applications, however, but not others? Or what if it can be disposed of safely to one environmental medium where it is isolated from human or environmental exposure, but other disposal means pose unacceptable hazards? Or what if an agency simply has authority under a particular statute to impose a partial but not absolute ban? In those or other circumstances, an agency might choose a partial rather than an absolute ban.

One example noted above was Congress' decision to ban the use of lead in gasoline under the Clean Air Act. 42 U.S.C. §7545(n). Lead may be dangerous in a range of other applications (for example, in paint, which was banned under separate statutory authority), but in the Clean Air Act, Congress banned only a single economic use to address a specific environmental problem—the dangerous concentrations of lead in the air in U.S. cities due to the combustion of leaded gasoline, along with the negative effect of leaded gasoline on catalytic converter pollution control technology in automobiles. As noted above, however, this partial ban also had the beneficial side effect of reducing lead contamination of surface waters, because runoff of lead-contaminated stormwater from roads and parking lots was a major source of water pollution. *See* Alexander & Smith, *supra*.

The pollution control statutes (particularly the Clean Air Act and Clean Water Act) tend to employ more modest approaches that limit rather than ban pollution. Feasibility-based standards limit pollution releases only to the extent technologically and economically practicable. In the case of the CWA, however, Congress expressly mandated that those standards eliminate discharges into surface waters whenever possible. *See, e.g.,* 33 U.S.C. §1311(b)(2)(A) ("best available technology" must require elimination of discharges when achievable). Indeed, one of the principal goals of the 1972 CWA was to "eliminate the discharge of pollutants into the Nation's waters. . . ." 33 U.S.C. §1251(a)(1). In this context, a technology-based effluent limitation under the CWA merges with a discharge ban to one specified environmental medium defined by the statute as "waters of the United States." Although the "zero discharge" goal has turned out—at least to date—to be largely aspirational, EPA has adopted zero discharge effluent limitations, effectively discharge bans, for some categories of discharges. *See, e.g.*, Texas Oil & Gas Ass'n v. EPA, 161 F.3d 923 (5th Cir. 1998) (upholding zero discharge effluent limitations for certain offshore oil and gas wastes).

Likewise, effects-based standards under both the Clean Air Act and the Clean Water Act limit pollution discharges to air and water, respectively, only to the extent necessary to prevent identified harm to human health or the environment. Typically, those standards allow some discharges so long as ambient concentrations of pollutants do not exceed levels the agency deems safe. What about non-threshold pollutants such as PVC? If a discharge causes some harm at any level, does that justify a ban on that kind of release? In the *Vinyl Chloride* case, the D.C. Circuit rejected NRDC's argument that the statute required a ban on vinyl chloride emissions under the then-applicable version of CAA section 112. By contrast, in earlier cases the D.C. Circuit upheld EPA's decision to ban water pollutant discharges for certain particularly dangerous chemicals under an analogous provision of the CWA, as discussed in the following case.

Environmental Defense Fund v. Environmental Protection Agency
598 F.2d 62 (D.C. Cir. 1978)

TAMM, CIRCUIT JUDGE.

We are called upon in these consolidated cases to review challenges to the Environmental Protection Agency's (EPA) first regulations prohibiting discharge into the nation's waterways of a toxic substance, polychlorinated biphenyls (PCBs), under the [CWA]. For the reasons that follow, we uphold the EPA's regulations.

I.   Facts and Prior Proceedings

A.   Factual Background on PCBs

PCBs are a group of related chlorinated hydrocarbon chemicals useful in several industrial processes and toxic to a wide variety of organisms, including man. . . . PCBs fall into two chemical categories: PCBs with a low chlorine content (less chlorinated PCBs) and PCBs with a high chlorine content (more chlorinated PCBs). More chlorinated PCBs have been manufactured and used since 1929. For decades, they served in a variety of industrial uses such as ink solvents, plasticizers, adhesives, and textile coatings, but their principal use was and is in electrical equipment. PCBs are nonflammable liquids that are highly resistant to electrical current. Therefore, they have been widely used to fill electrical devices such as capacitors and transformers, aiding in the storage of electrical charge without creating the fire hazard that would occur if a flammable filler were used.

Awareness of the danger from PCBs to the environment and to man was slow to develop. Although large quantities of PCBs were manufactured and leaked into the environment, the PCBs detected in the environment were long mistaken for pesticide residues, which they resemble chemically. It was not until the mid-1960's that the presence of PCBs in the environment and the harm they inflict were recognized and distinguished from the pesticide problem. As we shall discuss below, it became apparent from scientific studies that more chlorinated PCBs built up to dangerous levels in the sediments of waterways, in the water, in fish, and ultimately in humans, creating a serious risk of death for aquatic organisms and disease (particularly cancer) for man.

In 1971-72, in response to public and government pressure, PCBs manufacturers and users took initial steps to reduce the PCBs danger. Manufacture was shifted from the more chlorinated PCBs to the less chlorinated PCBs, because it was hoped that less chlorinated PCBs were less dangerous. PCBs use was limited to closed electrical equipment, where the need was greatest and the leakage was least. Some effort was made to control discharge of PCBs into waterways.

. . . EPA's initial effort to control discharge of PCBs into waterways, the precursor of the proceeding now on review, ended in failure in 1973-74. Discharges of PCBs into the nation's waterways continued.

Developments in the early and mid-1970's heightened the public concern about PCBs and resulted in new regulatory efforts in late 1975 and early 1976. Monitoring of residues in fish revealed that industrial discharges of PCBs were rendering fish in many waterways unhealthy for human consumption. . . .

Following the 1975 renewal of EPA's regulatory effort, further information accumulated with respect to the health hazards posed by PCBs. Moreover, substitutes for PCBs were developed in this country and in Japan that would serve adequately in electrical equipment without creating a fire hazard. Congress became impatient and wrote a special provision devoted solely to PCBs into the Toxic Substances Control Act of 1976. See section 6(e), 15 U.S.C. §2605(e) (1976). Considering that there are few statutes aimed so particularly at control of an individual chemical, we construe this provision as a significant comment on the failure of existing regulatory mechanisms. Failure of existing regulatory mechanisms to control PCBs contributed materially both to passage of the preventive sections of the Toxic Substances Control Act and to strengthening, in 1977, of the toxics provision of Federal Water Pollution Control Act Amendments of 1972. See 33 U.S.C.A. §1317(a) (1977). . . .

B. PCBs Proceedings

. . . The 1972 [Clean Water] Act prescribed a rigid schedule for promulgation of effluent standards for toxic substances. Section 307(a), 33 U.S.C. §1317(a) (1976), directed EPA to publish a list of toxic substances within ninety days, propose effluent standards for the listed substances within 180 days after listing, and promulgate final effluent standards within six months after the proposed standards. Thus, EPA was to promulgate toxic effluent regulations by early 1974.

[The Court described regulatory delay and the rule-making process.] The final standards . . . prohibited any PCBs in discharges of manufacturers of electrical equipment. . . .

II.   Statutory Framework

The [1972 CWA] authorized a series of steps to be taken to achieve the goal of eliminating all discharges of pollutants into the Nation's waters by 1985, §101(a)(1). The steps to be taken included promulgation by EPA of effluent standards, or regulations limiting discharges of various kinds of pollutants, under a number of statutory provisions covering industrial sources, municipal sources, sources that discharge into public treatment facilities (pretreatment standards), and sources that discharge toxic pollutants.

. . . Prior to 1972, there was no special provision in the federal water pollution laws to cope with toxic pollutants. As the number and amount of chemicals discharged into the nation's waterways increased in recent decades, it became apparent that some groups of chemicals posed a special danger to public health and the environment. There were two leading examples of such groups: chlorinated hydrocarbons, a group that included both pesticides (such as DDT, endrin, and toxaphene) and industrial chemicals (such as PCBs); and heavy metals, a group that included cadmium, mercury, and others.

Toxic substances, such as these, create a special danger in several ways. As demonstrated by a number of disasters involving widespread human poisoning or massive kills or contamination of fish, shellfish, birds, and other wildlife, many chemicals discharged into waters are lethal or injurious even in minute doses. Toxic chemicals have been identified repeatedly as a cause of cancer, through studies both of persons exposed to such chemicals on the job and elsewhere, and of animals in the laboratory and the field. Moreover, toxic substances often have characteristics besides toxicity that magnify their danger. These characteristics include (1) physical and chemical factors such as resistance to detoxification by sunlight and water, and mobility in the air and water; and (2) biological factors, such as tendencies not to be safely degraded by organisms, but rather to accumulate in organisms or to degrade into other toxic substances. Finally a most troubling characteristic of toxic substances is how little they are understood by scientists. New discoveries about their nature and effects are made constantly, but existing knowledge seems inadequate to measure their full danger.

Congress's response to the toxics problem was section 307 of the 1972 Act. Other interlocking sections gave prominence to section 307. Section 101(a)(3) of the Act, 33 U.S.C. §1251(a)(3) (1976), stated that "it is the national policy that the discharge of toxic pollutants in toxic amounts be prohibited." . . .

Section 307(a) sets forth the substantive considerations and procedures for EPA to use in formulating toxics standards. . . . Section 307(a)(4) directs EPA to set the standards at a level that provides "an ample margin of safety," a phrase that is the section's polestar, its guiding principle in protecting against incompletely understood dangers. . . .

IV.   Interaction with Toxic Substances Control Act

Congress enacted the Toxic Substances Control Act (TSCA), 15 U.S.C. §§2601-2629 (1976), during the pendency of EPA's proceedings on the proposed PCBs effluent standards. TSCA requires notice of intent to manufacture, and pre-manufacture testing of chemical substances, and confers authority on EPA to regulate the manufacture, processing, distribution in commerce, use, or disposal of such substances. In addition to the provisions applicable to chemical substances in general, TSCA includes a specific provision concerned solely with polychlorinated biphenyls, section 6(e), 15 U.S.C. §2605(e) (1976). Section 6(e) provides for a gradual phasing out of PCBs use over a two and one-half year period with limited provision for exemptions.

Industry petitioners contend that this section of TSCA was intended to "pre-empt" EPA's authority under the [Clean Water] Act. They assert that EPA's ban on discharges of PCBs into waterways makes manufacture and processing of PCBs impossible and that TSCA's phase-out timetable and exemption authority show that Congress did not intend PCBs to be completely and immediately phased out. Therefore, the argument goes, EPA should not achieve this result by the use of its authority under another regulatory provision, the toxics section of the [Clean Water] Act. EPA responds that Congress did not intend section 6(e) to deprive it of its authority under the 1972 [Clean Water] Act.

We agree with EPA. Strictly speaking, the claim made by industry petitioners is one of "repeal by implication," the overriding of one statute by a later enactment sub silentio, rather than a claim of "preemption." [The Court cited cases ruling that repeals by implication are disfavored, and can be found only where there is an "irreconcilable conflict" between the two statutes.]

Not only is there no "clearly expressed congressional intention" that TSCA repeal EPA's prior regulatory authority, and no "irreconcilable conflict" between TSCA and the 1972 Act, but, in fact, Congress carefully and explicitly harmonized TSCA with prior enactments.

Section 9(b) of TSCA, 15 U.S.C. §2608(b) (1976) (emphasis added), provides, in part:

> If the Administrator determines that a risk to health or the environment associated with a chemical substance or mixture could be eliminated or reduced to a sufficient extent by actions taken under the authorities contained in . . . other Federal laws, the Administrator shall use such authorities to protect against such risk unless the Administrator determines, in the Administrator's discretion, that it is in the public interest to protect against such risk by actions taken under this chapter. This subsection shall not be construed to relieve the Administrator of any requirement imposed on the Administrator by such other Federal laws.

Section 9(b) leaves EPA the choice of regulating toxic substances under TSCA, other statutes (such as the 1972 Act), or both. . . . Congress determined that a choice among regulatory authorities was necessary so that EPA could use the most effective means available to combat unknown and potentially extreme risks from toxic substances, and that judicial review of EPA's choice was inappropriate. Our interpretation of section 9(b) is reinforced by section 6(e)(5), 15

U.S.C. §2605(e)(5) (1976), which states: "(t)his subsection (6(e) (governing PCBs)) does not limit the authority of the Administrator, under any other provision of this chapter or any other Federal law, to take action respecting any polychlorinated biphenyl." . . .

V.   Evidentiary Basis for Regulation of Less Chlorinated PCBs

A.   *Arguments of the Parties*

The principal claim of industry petitioners is that EPA's regulations lack an adequate basis in the record to the extent that they cover less chlorinated PCBs because the record consists, in large part, of studies of related, but different substances (more chlorinated PCBs). . . .

. . . Most of the available scientific studies on PCBs concern more chlorinated PCBs, either because the studies were conducted over the decades when more chlorinated PCBs were the main PCBs in use, or because, even after the early 1970's, scientists continued to study the more chlorinated PCBs.

Accordingly, EPA faced a familiar choice in this proceeding. On one hand, it could regulate a substance whose properties were incompletely understood (less chlorinated PCBs) by relying, in major part, upon its knowledge about more familiar substances (more chlorinated PCBs), despite the uncertainties of extrapolation from one substance to another. On the other hand, it could delay regulation until science could more fully explore the risks of the new substance.

Industry petitioners contend that EPA lacked an adequate basis for regulation because of this incompleteness in the scientific knowledge about less chlorinated PCBs mixtures. . . . Petitioners assert, in effect, that EPA cannot rely upon merely suggestive evidence or upon extrapolation from data concerning related substances to justify regulation of the less chlorinated PCBs. They insist that EPA must trace a line of direct causation from each substance it regulates to the danger requiring regulation.

In response, EPA disputes that it must produce such direct proof concerning the danger posed by every regulated substance. EPA notes that the statutory standard calls for setting discharge levels at the level that will provide "an ample margin of safety.". . . In EPA's view, action need not be delayed while a risky situation persists, that is, until the extent of the danger is fully ascertained. EPA contends that ample evidence showing the danger of more chlorinated PCBs together with scientific reasoning and evidence that less chlorinated PCBs share some dangerous qualities of more chlorinated PCBs, constitutes an adequate basis for regulation.

B.   *Applicable Legal Standards*

Section 307(a)(2) sets forth the relevant factors for setting toxic effluent standards. It requires EPA to "take into account" six factors in proposing such standards: "the toxicity of the pollutant, its persistence, degradability, the usual or potential presence of the affected organisms in any waters, the importance of the affected organisms and the nature and extent of the effect of the toxic pollutant on such organisms."

. . . Based on these factors, section 307(a)(4) directs EPA to set discharge standards at a level providing an "ample margin of safety." The parties dispute the significance of this important subsection. EPA argues that this subsection gives it latitude to protect against risks that are incompletely understood, in essence to "err" on the side of "overprotection" with respect to known risks in order to provide safety from unknown dangers. Industry petitioners disagree.

On examination of the wording of the statute and the legislative background, we find ourselves in agreement with EPA, whose interpretation of the complex statutes it administers is, of course, entitled to some deference. Despite the problems associated with estimating the scale of incompletely understood dangers, Congress required EPA to set standards that would protect against them.

The "ample margin of safety" standard was taken originally from technical jargon for use in section 112 of the Clean Air Act Amendments of 1970, the hazardous pollutants provision. . . .

The . . . term "margin of safety" was intended to provide protection "against hazards which research has not yet identified." Moreover, the public and the environment were not to be exposed to anything resembling the maximum risk. Not only was EPA to provide a "margin of safety," but the margin was to be greater than "normal" or "adequate": the margin was to be "ample." If administrative responsibility to protect against unknown dangers presents a difficult task, indeed, a veritable paradox calling as it does for knowledge of that which is unknown then, the term "margin of safety" is Congress's directive that means be found to carry out the task and to reconcile the paradox. Addition of a generous measure "ample" is Congress's recognition that the EPA would need great latitude in meeting its responsibility. . . .

D. Adequacy of the Basis for EPA Regulations

1. EPA's Policy Judgments Concerning Extrapolation

Industry petitioners contend that EPA lacked an adequate basis for the regulations under review because of the incomplete scientific knowledge about less chlorinated PCBs. In effect, they assert that EPA must demonstrate the toxicity of each chemical it seeks to regulate through studies demonstrating a clear line of causation between a particular chemical and harm to public health or the environment. We do not agree.

The principal basis for rejecting petitioners' views is the wording of the statute. As we stated, the "ample margin of safety" provision directs EPA to guard against incompletely known dangers. EPA, in its expert policy judgment, relied on its knowledge about a known substance to assess the danger of one about which less is known. Petitioners suggest no alternative approach for the agency short of waiting for conclusive proof about the danger posed by a less understood substance. However, by requiring EPA to set standards providing an "ample margin of safety," Congress authorized and, indeed, required EPA to protect against dangers before their extent is conclusively ascertained. The statute thus does not deny EPA the authority that petitioners would have us withhold. Indeed, the legislative history indicates that Congress intended EPA to take into account "the availability of data on similar substances or compounds." Moreover, the Clean Water Act of

1977 supports the notion that extrapolation from data about related substances is a valid approach. In 1977, Congress did not list individual substances, but rather listed families of substances, recognizing that similarities among substances render them susceptible to regulation by group.

. . . The risks posed by toxic substances, and the extent to which one substance has effects similar to those of related substances, are matters on the frontiers of scientific knowledge. EPA, not the court, has the technical expertise to decide what inferences may be drawn from the characteristics of related substances and to formulate policy with respect to what risks are acceptable.

Moreover, we are currently in a period of rapid change in assessing and regulating toxic substances. TSCA has established new regulatory mechanisms that may well lead to wholesale estimation of the risks of toxic substances. A holding from this court that only one technique of risk assessment (such as "extensive studies on comparative mammalian toxicity," Brief of Industry Petitioners at 53) is acceptable to the detriment of others would unnecessarily inhibit EPA from evaluating new approaches and formulating appropriate policy.

Finally, in reviewing EPA's policy of regulating less chlorinated PCBs in part on the basis of what is known about more chlorinated PCBs, we must recognize considerations of administrative feasibility. The number of toxic substances subject to regulation seems very large. Regulation of so many substances could well be extremely difficult if EPA were precluded from drawing inferences from available data on well-known, related substances. Moreover, requiring proof of causation for each chemical would force EPA to expend resources in areas that are well-enough known so that inference is acceptable, when those resources could be otherwise employed in areas where knowledge is inadequate. In ruling on the type of proof and procedure required for making individual determinations, the Supreme Court has construed statutes protecting the environment and public health in light of considerations of administrative feasibility.

2. EPA's Factual Determination of the Particular Risks Here

. . . EPA did not rely on a single approach or study, but acted on the basis of a variety of studies and types of evidence. Under the substantial evidence test, it is not necessary that all the evidence, or even most of the evidence, point in one direction. The evidence supporting the agency's conclusion must be such, in light of all of the evidence on the record as a whole, that "a reasonable mind might accept (it) as adequate to support (the) conclusion." Consolidated Edison Co. v. NLRB, 305 U.S. at 229, 59 at 217. . . .

a. Toxicity

The evidence presented concerning toxicity may be divided into (i) evidence bearing on aquatic organisms, (ii) evidence bearing on man, and (iii) evidence concerning the special quality of carcinogenicity. [The Court evaluated the scientific evidence considered by EPA regarding toxicity to aquatic organisms, toxicity to humans and other mammals, and carcinogenicity, and found substantial evidence to support EPA's findings of harm.]

b. Persistence

EPA summarized studies showing that PCBs tend to accumulate in the environment over many years, are mobile, and adhere to sediments. This court has noted before that such characteristics intensify the dangers posed by toxic substances, because they increase the exposure of persons and vulnerable organisms of all kinds to those substances. . . .

c. Degradability

EPA summarized a number of studies concerning the degradation of both less and more chlorinated PCBs by living organisms. PCBs were shown to resist degradation, to bioaccumulate (build up) to high levels in simple organisms, and then to bioaccumulate further as those simple organisms are consumed by higher organisms. When degradation does occur, it may result in creation of other harmful substances, either as intermediates, or as end products of degradation. . . .

. . . On this record, it is clear that EPA's prohibition on discharges of PCBs must be upheld. . . .

NOTES AND QUESTIONS ON *ENVIRONMENTAL DEFENSE FUND*

1. *Legal justification for the ban.* Did CWA section 307(a) mandate a ban of PCB discharges? In answering that question, consider the various bases for environmental standard setting you studied in Part II.A of this book. Given that the opinion begins with a recitation of the significant economic utility of PCBs, under what circumstances do you think a ban would be justified using a rule making based on cost-benefit analysis? Given that the opinion also notes the fire-prevention benefits of PCBs in its various applications, and the possibility that substitutes for PCBs might not do such a good job in preventing fires, under what circumstances do you think a ban would be justified using a rule making based on risk-risk analysis? Now, what was the actual legal basis for this rule making, and why were issues related to cost-benefit analysis and risk-risk analysis not relevant to the agency's decision?

2. *Scientific justification for the ban.* Based on the information summarized in the opinion, did EPA demonstrate enough harm from PCBs in the aquatic environment to justify a complete discharge prohibition as opposed to a very low effluent limit? (If you want to delve more deeply into EPA's scientific rationale before answering this question, the unedited opinion contains a much more detailed summary of the scientific information EPA relied on in justifying its decision.) What scientific factors do you think best justified a zero discharge standard, and why? Were the industry petitioners correct that a ban should not be justified based on an incomplete scientific record, or does the precautionary principle suggest that agencies should err on the side of caution, particularly when a statute calls for an "ample margin of safety"?

3. *Justification for a ban as the means of implementing the standard.* Once EPA decided that there was not an acceptable level of PCBs in the aquatic environment,

did it have any alternative to a regulatory ban to effectuate the zero discharge standard?

4. *Effect of the partial ban.* The prohibition reviewed in this case is a partial ban because it applies only to discharges of PCBs to the waters of the United States. It does not prohibit the manufacture or use of PCBs. It also does not prohibit the release of PCBs to other environmental media, such as land or air or groundwater, not covered by the CWA. In this rule making, did EPA have any legal choice about that limitation? Given the limitation, what did EPA achieve (and not achieve) through this rule making? At a minimum, of course, it protected the aquatic environment from the dangers of PCBs. Beyond that defined but still very important goal, might the water discharge prohibition have achieved broader collateral goals as well? Conversely, once the statutory phase-out of PCB manufacture under section 6(e) of TSCA was implemented, did the CWA discharge prohibition have any continued effect? Note, for one thing, that the TSCA phase-out included some exceptions, even if modest, which could result in PCB discharges to water. And what if PCBs are created incidentally in some other industrial process and might be in a resulting wastewater discharge subject to the CWA? Does the Court's legal rationale for rejecting industry's repeal by implication argument make more sense given those factors?

5. *Clean Air Act comparison.* Why did the D.C. Circuit uphold EPA's ban on surface water discharges of PCBs in this case, but later remand EPA's ban on air emissions of vinyl chloride under an analogous provision of the CAA? Is there a significant difference in the statutory language relied on by EPA at the time of each case? *Compare* 33 U.S.C. §1317(a) (1972) *with* 42 U.S.C. §7412(a) (1970). (As the Court notes, the "ample margin of safety" language in CWA section 307(a) was taken directly from CAA section 112, but note that Congress subsequently amended both statutory provisions.) Was there a significant difference in the scientific records justifying the respective bans? In the legal rationale EPA used to justify its decision?

3. Conditional Bans

Another use of a ban is to induce or incentivize another action, or to prohibit a use or activity unless the party subject to the ban takes some other action. One example is the "land ban" provision of RCRA, 42 U.S.C. §6924. The land ban prohibited the land disposal of various categories of hazardous wastes after specified dates unless EPA promulgated regulations prescribing the standards and conditions under which land disposal could occur safely. Absent EPA regulation, this would have been an example of an absolute statutory ban. In practice, the ban was an inducement for EPA to promulgate the necessary regulations on time, after which land disposal was regulated but not banned.

The Endangered Species Act (ESA), 16 U.S.C. §§1531-1544, relies on a ban upon harming an endangered species as its presumptive approach. Recall that section 7 of the ESA requires consultation with the U.S. Fish and Wildlife Service (FWS) or the National Marine Fisheries Service (NMFS) whenever a federal agency action would jeopardize the existence of a threatened or endangered species or result in the destruction or modification of critical habitat for those species. As was the case in *TVA v. Hill*, a federal court can enjoin an activity—effectively a judicial ban implementing and enforcing the statute—absent such consultation. Alternatively, FWS or NMFS could ban the proposed activity by determining that it would jeopardize the continued existence of the species, in which case the statute operates as an absolute ban.

But you may also recall that numerous statutory exemptions emphasize mitigation of impacts and alternatives to the precise projects proposed, rather than necessarily stopping projects altogether. Accordingly, mitigation of potential impacts upon endangered species through adjustments as to how and when projects are carried out occur far more commonly than project cancellations.

Implemented in this way, the statute becomes a conditional ban designed to encourage the analysis and implementation of mitigation measures sufficient to avoid jeopardy rather than prohibiting activities that might affect threatened and endangered species outright. In *TVA v. Hill*, because the agency never engaged in consultation, and because the statute required the government to "insure" that federal agency actions or decisions do not jeopardize species, the Supreme Court ruled that a judicial injunction (ban) was required. In many other cases involving dams and other activities, however, agencies have identified reasonable and prudent alternatives designed to avoid jeopardy. In those cases, the court's role is to review the agency decision under the familiar arbitrary and capricious standard, with predictably variable results. *Compare* Rio Grande Silvery Minnow v. Keys, 469 F. Supp. 2d 973 (D.N.M. 2002) (upholding agency determination that minimum flow requirements and fish passage facilities on dam would avoid jeopardy to endangered silvery minnows), *with* Consol. Salmonid Cases, 713 F. Supp. 2d 1116 (E.D. Cal. 2010) (invalidating water delivery reductions where agency could not show that alternatives were either necessary or sufficient to protect endangered salmonid species).

NOTES AND QUESTIONS ON THE ENDANGERED SPECIES ACT AS A BAN

1. *Section 9.* Section 7 of the Act imposes obligations upon the federal government to protect threatened and endangered species. Section 9 of the Act limits private actions that can harm an endangered species. It generally (*i.e.*, with significant exceptions) forbids any action harming an endangered species. *See* Babbitt v. Sweet Home Chapter of Communities for a Greater Oregon, 515 U.S. 687 (1995). This prohibition may preclude private development activities that destroy habitat that a species needs for its survival. For that reason, the Act has been the focal point of significant controversy. Even though section 9's prohibition on private parties taking endangered species has been defined broadly to prohibit actions harming a species, however, section 10 of the Act sets out a variety of exceptions that mitigate the absolutism of section 9. *See* 16 U.S.C. §1539. For example, the implementing agencies can grant "incidental take" permits. Such permits can authorize federal, state, or private actions that "take" a species under some circumstances. *See* 16

U.S.C. §1539(a)(2). Would the breadth of the otherwise applicable prohibitions provide an incentive to construe these exemptions broadly? The important point here is that in practice, section 9 of the ESA, like section 7, usually acts more as a conditional than as an absolute ban, and works to promote mitigation rather than banning activities altogether.

2. *What sort of ban?* While the Endangered Species Act (ESA) does ban some activities as a regulatory technique, note that the ban operates very differently from bans enacted in pollution control statutes. For one thing, the ESA's prohibitions generally have a geographically restricted reach. Section 7's prohibition became operative in the *TVA* case only after two steps took place. First, the Secretary of the Interior listed the snail darter as endangered. Second, it designated the relevant portion of the Tennessee River as "critical habitat." The prohibition on building the dam arose from the obligation section 7 imposes on federal agencies to avoid damaging critical habitat. Thus, the ESA did not prohibit dam building as a general approach to generating electricity, but only the construction of this particular dam in this particular place.

Section 7 does not, however, only prohibit "destruction or adverse modification of habitat." *See* 16 U.S.C. §1536. It also requires all federal agencies to "insure that any action authorized, funded, or carried out by such agency is not likely to jeopardize the continued existence of any endangered or threatened species." *Id.* Because most endangered species have limited geographic ranges, this clause also tends to have a geographically limited impact.

Section 9 enacts a nationwide ban on some activities, such as importing or exporting an endangered species. *See* 16 U.S.C. §1538(a)(1)(A). Section 9's limitations on private land uses harming endangered species have been even more controversial. Since most species have a limited range, section 9 generally has a geographically limited reach. Do the geographic limits implicit in sections 7 and 9 significantly limit the potential harshness of the ESA?

3. *The debate about absolutism.* Sections 7 and 9 potentially impose broad prohibitions on activities harming endangered species. Commentators have sometimes claimed that such an absolutist approach creates perverse incentives. Think about how the possibility of stringent prohibitions might influence the Department of Interior, which administers the Act. None of these prohibitions attach until the agency lists a species as endangered. The determination of whether a species is endangered or not involves an element of judgment in the face of substantial scientific uncertainty. *See generally* Holly Doremus, *Listing Decisions Under the Endangered Species Act: Why Better Science Isn't Always Better Policy*, 75 WASH. U. L.Q. 1029 (1997). Substantial scientific evidence exists that some salmon species and sub-species are becoming extinct. But listing all endangered species and sub-species of salmon might conceivably put pressure on federal agencies not just to keep the floodgates closed on a completed dam, but to take down dams that have been providing electricity for decades. Such listing decisions would almost certainly influence water allocation decisions that greatly impact farmers, fishermen, and ranchers. Is it possible that the Department of the Interior might prove reluctant to list some salmon species or sub-species because of the potentially difficult consequences?

This same concern about counterproductive stringency arose under section 112 of the Clean Air Act prior to 1990, when it required protection of public health with an ample margin of safety from hazardous air pollutants. Since many listed pollutants had no threshold where they were known to be safe, section 112 could be read to require zero emission levels (although the court of appeals rejected this interpretation more than a decade after section 112 became law). Some commentators attributed EPA's failure to list substantial numbers of pollutants under section 112 for regulation to this potential consequence. But others attributed this failure to the general scientific difficulties of determining health-based levels.

Some commentators have also claimed that the ESA creates perverse incentives for private landholders. Since a listing may limit property development, does it create incentives to kill off species that might subsequently be listed, or will it instead encourage landlords to care for the species, so that it will breed and escape actual endangerment? *See* J.B. Ruhl, *The Endangered Species Act and Private Property: A Matter of Timing and Location*, 8 Cornell J.L. & Pub. Pol'y 37, 42-43 (1998).

Even if absolutist approaches do create some perverse incentives, does that make them bad? If one believes (as apparently the enacting Congress did) that protecting endangered species should be of paramount importance, is there an alternative likely to do a better job of protecting species than a ban of activities harming them? If the statute were less draconian, would there be less slippage (failures to list endangered species, etc.) or would the slippage just retreat from a weaker baseline to a still weaker form of protection? *See* Amy Sinden, *In Defense of Absolutes: Combating the Politics of Power in Environmental Law*, 90 Iowa L. Rev. 1405 (2005) (arguing that absolutism provides a useful counterweight to powerful interests seeking to undermine environmental protection). *See generally* Daniel A. Farber, *Taking Slippage Seriously: Noncompliance and Creative Compliance in Environmental Law*, 23 Harv. Envtl. L. Rev. 297 (1999) (discussing the problem of "slippage" where implementation seriously deviates from statutory design).

Economic Incentives

8

This chapter will address the use of economic incentives as techniques for realizing environmental goals. While traditional regulatory approaches use monetary penalties to induce compliance, thus relying on economic incentives, this chapter focuses on alternatives to traditional regulatory approaches.

Some academics have criticized environmental law because it relies, at least ostensibly, upon uniform output standards for industrial categories. Because plants have uneven compliance costs, uniform standards can produce very high costs for some plants and relatively low costs for others.

In theory, it is possible to achieve the same reduction of total pollution for less cost by requiring more reductions from facilities with low compliance costs and fewer reductions from facilities with high compliance costs. In practice, the difficulty of obtaining marginal plant-specific control cost information makes it difficult for agencies to fine-tune standards in this way. *See generally* Howard Latin, *Ideal versus Real Regulatory Efficiency: Implementation of Uniform Standards and "Fine-Tuning" Regulatory Reforms*, 37 STAN. L. REV. 1267 (1985). Consider the Supreme Court's response to the argument that Clean Water Act variances should be available for facilities facing greater than average control costs:

> The approach of giving variances to pollution controls based on economic grounds has long ago shown itself to be a risky course: All too often the variances become a tool used by powerful interests to obtain so many exemptions for pollution control standards and timetables on the flimsiest of pretenses that they become meaningless. In short, with variances, exceptions to pollution cleanup can become the rule, meaning further tragic delay in stopping the destruction of our environment.

EPA v. National Crushed Stone Ass'n, 449 U.S. 64, 81 (1980). *Cf.* Chemical Mfrs. Ass'n v. Natural Resources Defense Council, 470 U.S. 116, 129-31 (1985) (stating that "fundamentally different factor" variances do not undermine statutory goals).

Economists have suggested two reforms that might seize the opportunity to realize environmental goals at lower cost: pollution taxes and pollution trading.

They tend to favor pollution taxes. We will begin with pollution taxes, even though pollution trading has proven a much more popular reform in the United States.

A. ECO-TAXES

A tax on pollution requires the polluter to pay the government a set sum for every pound of pollution released into the environment. Pollution taxes should prove more cost effective than a uniform standard because, at least in theory, polluters will respond to the tax differently depending on their pollution control cost. Imagine a pollution tax of $1.00 per pound of carbon dioxide emitted into the air. How would a polluter who faces control costs of $1.50 per pound of carbon dioxide respond to the tax? Economists predict that such a polluter would pay the tax, rather than reduce pollution, since this would cost less. Now suppose that a different polluter can reduce carbon dioxide at a cost of 50 cents per pound. How would that polluter respond? Economists predict that this polluter would prefer to reduce her pollution in order to avoid paying the tax. Notice that a tax should produce cost effective abatement. Polluters facing relatively high control costs will pay the tax, but polluters with low control costs will prefer pollution abatement.

In fact, facilities' pollution control costs can vary with the degree of reduction. While the first pounds of reduction might prove cheap, the marginal costs of additional reduction can prove relatively expensive. Consider the following hypothetical example:

Marginal Control Costs

Pounds Reduction	Cost Per Pound of Reduction
1,000-2,000	$.50
2,001-4,000	$.75
4,001-6,000	$1.25
6,001-10,000	$2.00

Notice that the marginal cost rises steeply as more reductions are produced. This is a fairly typical pattern. How many pounds of reduction would a rational polluter facing a $1.00 per pound tax make?

While the United States used a pollution tax in conjunction with the phase-out of ozone-depleting substances, it has not relied heavily upon pollution taxes as a principal method for reducing pollution. President Clinton proposed an energy tax to address climate change, but this proposal did not pass. Some taxes, such as gasoline taxes, do not tax pollution directly, but in theory, might encourage reductions of consumption that would reduce pollution impacts. Subsidies and tax breaks, however, may offset the potentially positive environmental impacts of some taxes. The environmental statutes contain some provisions requiring permit fees. But these fee provisions seek only to recover government administrative costs. They are probably not high enough to motivate much pollution reduction. Pollution taxes only motivate pollution reduction if they exceed the cost of pollution control.

Members of the European Union have made greater use of pollution taxes than the United States. Several European countries have established effluent taxes, which some use to fund waste treatment, and carbon taxes. The Canadian province of British Columbia has also recently added a carbon tax. Most developed countries also impose higher gasoline taxes than the United States does.

Suppose that you had authority to establish a pollution tax. How would you go about establishing the tax rate? Notice that this decision, like the decision about how stringent a performance standard should be, will strongly influence the amount of pollution reduction that will be realized. A higher tax rate will induce more pollution reduction than a lower rate.

In principle, it might be possible for an administrator with taxation authority to use any of the standard setting criteria mentioned previously to establish the tax rate. Economists tend to favor establishing a tax rate equal to the dollar value of the harms the taxed pollutant causes. Notice that implementing this approach requires monetization of environmental harms, a direct analogue to the monetization of environmental benefits of regulation sought through the executive orders on cost-benefit analysis. Thus, this approach involves the same quantification and monetization difficulties that beset cost-benefit analysis. This approach would therefore prove difficult to implement.

Governments, however, can establish tax rates without cost-benefit analysis. Indeed, one of the first pollution tax proposals considered in Congress would have employed a technology-based approach to taxation.

Eco-taxes can, in theory, raise production costs and therefore deter consumption. Lessening consumption can help conserve natural resources and reduce pollution. Should the United States charge fees for water used by farmers, industry, and city dwellers that flows from federal irrigation projects? Overuse of water can leave streams and rivers depleted, thereby destroying fisheries and disrupting ecosystems. Should we at least eliminate subsidies for resource use, such as those that encourage grazing and use of scarce water in the west?

State regulators have historically regulated electricity rates. Consumption of electricity leads to the use of power plants to generate electricity. Power plants produce enormous amounts of serious air pollution. Should regulators raise electricity rates to reduce consumption? In general, pricing and taxation policy can have an impact on pollution and the use of natural resources.

B. POLLUTION TRADING

Pollution trading provides another method for improving the cost effectiveness of environmental regulation. In a pollution trading system, the government determines the amount of reductions, just as it would in establishing a performance standard. But it authorizes those subject to its limits to pay other parties to make reductions in their stead.

Consider the following simplified example. An agency wishes to secure 10 tons of cumulative reduction from two pollution sources, each of which currently emits 10 tons. It could require 5 tons of reduction from each polluter, a uniform standard:

Uniform Standards Example

Plant Name	Reductions Required	Cost Per Ton of Reduction
Expensive	5 tons	$5,000
Cheap	5 tons	$1,000

If the costs are as set out in the chart above, this requirement would produce 10 tons of reductions (5 + 5) at a total cost of $30,000 ((5 × $5,000) + (5 × $1,000)). Now suppose that the regulator set the same limits, but allowed trades. Plant Expensive could pay Plant Cheap to make reductions in its stead. If this occurred, we'd have this situation:

Trading Example

Plant Name	Reductions Made	Cost Per Ton of Reduction
Expensive	0 tons	$5,000
Cheap	10 tons	$1,000

Now the total cost of making the 10 tons of reductions has dropped from $30,000 in the uniform standards example to $10,000 (10 × $1,000) in the trading example. Notice that Plant Expensive makes less than the required reductions, but that Plant Cheap makes more than the minimum requirement, in order to make up the shortfall.

Many supporters of trading claim that trading not only encourages cost effective reductions, but also provides superior incentives for innovation. Innovation in pollution control techniques can increase our future capacity to reduce pollution without economic disruption.

1. Offset Programs

Early trading programs followed what climate policy experts now call an offset model. Under this approach a pollution source required to reduce its emissions would make reductions at a source not subject to a cap and often not regulated at all in lieu of the otherwise required reductions. This offset approach made its way into environmental law gradually, first as a means of ameliorating the Clean Air Act's impact on new pollution sources. The statute generally requires major new pollution sources to conform to pollution control requirements reflecting the capabilities of state-of-the-art technology. *See, e.g.,* 42 U.S.C. §7411. It provided, however, that existing sources would only have to conform to requirements states developed in order to meet air quality goals. *See, e.g.,* 42 U.S.C. §7502(c)(1) (requiring "reasonably available control methods" in state implementation plans). The differential reflected congressional concern that retrofitting existing facilities would prove costly. Nevertheless, Congress limited the grandfathering of existing sources. It required existing sources to conform to new source requirements when their owners "modified" their facilities. *See* 42 U.S.C. §7411(a)(2). And the statute defined modification broadly as any operational or physical change increasing emissions. 42 U.S.C. §7411(a)(4). Clean Air Act experts sometimes refer to the set of requirements applicable to new and modified sources as the new source review program.

The Act, however, imposed a ban on new construction in areas that failed to meet ambient air quality standards by the Act's deadlines. When states missed the attainment deadlines, this construction ban became very controversial. In response, EPA developed the concept of an "offset." It would allow construction of new sources in areas that had missed the deadline, but only if the owners of new sources offset their emissions by procuring greater emission reductions from some other source. Notice that this approach uses the trading concept to produce reductions of emissions, whereas a ban on new construction would only keep emissions from increasing.

Subsequent amendments incorporated this offset requirement into new source review even before states had missed revised attainment deadlines incorporated in later versions of the Act. *See, e.g.*, 42 U.S.C. §7511a(a)(4), (b)(5), (c)(10), (d)(2), (e)(1). Thus, both new and modified sources in areas that violated air quality standards would not only install state-of-the-art controls, but also deliver offsetting reductions more than compensating for the remaining emissions. This particular offset requirement leads, in principle, to improvements in air quality.

Gradually, the use of offsets expanded and EPA and many states even allowed existing sources to use offsets in lieu of otherwise required reductions. Clean Air Act experts often use the term "offset" very narrowly to refer only to programs allowing credits to offset emissions remaining after new source review. This book, however, uses the term the way climate experts use it, as a broad term for any program allowing a credit from a pollution reduction project at an uncapped source (a source not subject to a mass-based cap) to be used to satisfy a compliance obligation elsewhere. Clean Air Act experts sometimes use the term "bubble" in this manner, since the early programs allowing offset credits treated facilities with multiple pollution sources as if they were encased in a bubble.

The offset programs produced enormous cost savings. But they often did so by providing cover for various forms of evasion of requirements to provide fresh emission reductions. *See* RICHARD A. LIROFF, REFORMING AIR POLLUTION REGULATION: THE TOIL AND TROUBLE OF EPA'S BUBBLE 22, 28-29 (1986); CALIFORNIA AIR RESOURCES BOARD AND UNITED STATES ENVIRONMENTAL PROTECTION AGENCY, PHASE III RULE EFFECTIVENESS STUDY OF THE AEROSPACE COATING INDUSTRY (1990). Consider the following case:

Citizens Against the Refinery's Effects v. EPA
643 F.2d 183 (4th Cir. 1981)

HALL, CIRCUIT JUDGE.

Citizens Against the Refinery's Effects (CARE) appeals from a final ruling by the Administrator of the Environmental Protection Agency (EPA) approving the Virginia State Implementation Plan (SIP) for reducing hydrocarbon pollutants. The plan requires the Virginia Highway Department to decrease usage of a certain type of asphalt, thereby reducing hydrocarbon pollution by more than enough to offset expected pollution from the Hampton Roads Energy Company's (HREC) proposed refinery. We affirm the action of the administrator in approving the state plan.

The Act

The Clean Air Act establishes National Ambient Air Quality Standards (NAAQS) for five major air pollutants. . . . Where the standard has not been attained for a certain pollutant, the state must develop a State Implementation Plan designed to bring the area into attainment within a certain period. In addition, no new source of that pollutant may be constructed until the standard is attained.

The Clean Air Act created a no-growth environment in areas where the clean air requirements had not been attained. EPA recognized the need to develop a program that encouraged attainment of clean air standards without discouraging economic growth. Thus the agency proposed an Interpretive Ruling in 1976 which allowed the states to develop an "offset program" within the State Implementation Plans. 41 Fed. Reg. 55524 (1976). The offset program, later codified by Congress in the 1977 Amendments to the Clean Air Act, permits the states to develop plans which allow construction of new pollution sources where accompanied by a corresponding reduction in an existing pollution source. In effect, a new emitting facility can be built if an existing pollution source decreases its emissions or ceases operations as long as a positive net air quality benefit occurs. . . .

The Refinery

HREC proposes to build a petroleum refinery and offloading facility in Portsmouth, Virginia. Portsmouth has been unable to reduce air pollution enough to attain the national standard for one pollutant, photochemical oxidants, which is created when hydrocarbons are released into the atmosphere and react with other substances. Since a refinery is a major source of hydrocarbons, the Clean Air Act prevents construction of the HREC plant until the area attains the national standard. . . .

The Virginia Board proposed to offset the new HREC hydrocarbon pollution by reducing the amount of cutback asphalt used for road paving operations in three highway districts by the Virginia Department of Highways. By switching from "cutback" to "emulsified" asphalt, the state can reduce hydrocarbon pollutants by the amount necessary to offset the pollutants from the proposed refinery.

CARE insists that the offset plan should have been disapproved since the state is voluntarily reducing usage of cutback asphalt anyway. . . .

[T]he standard of review here is whether the agency action was arbitrary, capricious, an abuse of discretion, or otherwise not in accordance with law. . . .

The Geographic Area

CARE contends that the state plan should not have been approved by EPA since the three highway-district area where cutback usage will be reduced to offset refinery emissions was artificially developed by the state. The ruling permits a broad area (usually within one AQCR [Air Quality Control Region]) to be used as the offset basis.

The ruling does not specify how to determine the area, nor provide a standard procedure for defining the geographic area. Here the Virginia Board originally proposed to use four highway districts comprising one-half the state as the offset area. When this was found to be much more than necessary to offset pollution expected from the refinery, the state changed it to one highway district plus nine additional counties. Later the proposed plan was again revised to include a geographic area of three highway districts.

The agency action in approving the use of three highway districts was neither arbitrary, capricious, nor outside the statute. First, Congress intended that the states and the EPA be given flexibility in designing and implementing SIPs. Such flexibility allows the states to make reasoned choices as to which areas may be used to offset new pollution and how the plan is to be implemented. Second, the offset program was initiated to encourage economic growth in the state. Thus a state plan designed to reduce highway department pollution in order to attract another industry is a reasonable contribution to economic growth without a corresponding increase in pollution. Third, to be sensibly administered the offset plan had to be divided into districts which could be monitored by the highway department. Use of any areas other than highway districts would be unwieldy and difficult to administer. Fourth, the scientific understanding of ozone pollution is not advanced to the point where exact air transport may be predicted. Designation of the broad area in which hydrocarbons may be transported is well within the discretion and expertise of the agency.

The Base Year

Asphalt consumption varies greatly from year to year, depending upon weather and road conditions. Yet EPA must accurately determine the volume of hydrocarbon emissions from cutback asphalt. Only then can the agency determine whether the reduction in cutback usage will result in an offset great enough to account for the new refinery pollution. To calculate consumption of a material where it constantly varies, a base year must be selected. In this case, EPA's Interpretive Ruling establishes the base year as the year in which the permit application is made. EPA decided that 1977 was an acceptable base year. CARE argues that EPA illegally chose 1977 instead of 1975.

Considering all of the circumstances, including the unusually high asphalt consumption in 1977, the selection by EPA of that as the base year was within the discretion of the agency. Since the EPA Interpretive Ruling allowing the offset was not issued until 1976, 1977 was the first year after the offset ruling and the logical base year in which to calculate the offset. . . .

The Legally Binding Plan

For several years, Virginia has pursued a policy of shifting from cutback asphalt to the less expensive emulsified asphalt in road-paving operations. The policy was initiated in an effort to save money, and was totally unrelated to a State Implementation Plan. Because of this policy, CARE argues that hydrocarbon emissions were decreasing independent of this SIP and therefore are not a proper offset against the refinery. They argue that there is not, in effect, an actual reduction in pollution.

The Virginia voluntary plan is not enforceable and therefore is not in compliance with the 1976 Interpretive Ruling which requires that the offset program be enforceable. 41 Fed. Reg. 55526 (1976). The EPA, in approving the state plan, obtained a letter from the Deputy Attorney General of Virginia in which he stated that the requisites had been satisfied for establishing and enforcing the plan with the Department of Highways. Without such authority, no decrease in asphalt-produced pollution is guaranteed. In contrast to the voluntary plan, the offset plan guarantees a reduction in pollution resulting from road-paving operations.

Conclusion

In approving the state plan, EPA thoroughly examined the data, requested changes in the plan, and approved the plan only after the changes were made. There is no indication that the agency acted in an arbitrary or capricious manner or that it stepped beyond the bounds of the Clean Air Act. We affirm the decision of the administrator in approving the state plan.

NOTES AND QUESTIONS ON *CITIZENS AGAINST THE REFINERY'S EFFECTS*

1. *Surplus.* Citizens argued that the changes in highway asphalt producing the offset would have been undertaken anyway. The court apparently agrees that this is true. But what is the legal and policy significance of that fact?

2. *Actual reduction.* Citizens argued that the asphalt offset does not produce an actual emission reduction. Is that correct?

3. *Enforceability.* Does the court address Citizens' argument? Is Citizens' argument really directed at the enforceability of the offset?

4. *Baselines and net pollution.* Suppose that the switch in asphalt usage would produce a 100-ton reduction in hydrocarbon emissions. Assume that the new petroleum refinery produces 90 tons of pollution. Is net pollution increasing or decreasing? By how much?

Now assume that construction of the refinery is prohibited because of the construction ban. Are there reductions from asphalt usage? Is net pollution (from the refinery and asphalt usage) rising or decreasing? By how much?

Suppose that the refinery is built, but the regulator denies permission to use the asphalt reductions as an offset. Because of this the refinery must find other fresh offsets. Is net pollution increased or reduced? By how much?

5. *The base year.* The EPA ruling provided that the base year should be the year the permit application is filed, which in this case was 1975, a low asphalt use year. However, because EPA's ruling was in 1976, it allowed Virginia to use 1977 (a very high asphalt use year) as the base year. How did this affect the application of the offset, and was it legitimate? Should some other basis be used to determine the base year, and if so, what and why?

6. *Geography.* Why is the geographic area within which trading can occur important? In 1990, Congress amended the Act to allow offsets only from the same

nonattainment area, or from another area with an equal or higher nonattainment classification *and* where the offset emissions contribute to air quality violations in the area for which the offset is sought. 42 U.S.C. §7503(c)(1). Should the offset in *Citizens Against the Refinery's Effects* have been approved if this new provision was in place?

7. *Fraud.* Is this transaction fraudulent? Most scholarly supporters of trading recognize that trading can only work when reliable monitoring is feasible. Volatile organic compounds, the predominant target of the early offset programs, are notoriously difficult to monitor. EPA has historically been reluctant to make stringent monitoring a prerequisite for trading, but, in 1990, Congress enacted a program that required strict monitoring.

2. Cap and Trade

In the 1990 Clean Air Act Amendments, Congress created a very different type of trading program, a cap and trade program. A cap and trade program imposes a mass-based cap on regulated emitters' emissions and only allows those subject to a cap to generate credits. Congress applied the cap and trade model to address acid rain by capping emissions of sulfur dioxide from power plants, the chief precursors of acid rain. Electric utilities emit sulfur dioxide and nitrogen oxides into the air. Some of this pollution deposes in water, *i.e.*, acts as "acid rain" when wet deposition occurs (some of the deposition, however, is dry). Because these compounds are highly acidic, they tend to acidify lakes, streams, and ecosystems. This acidification has damaged ecosystems, producing a loss of fish, acidification of soils, and extensive damage to trees. Congress designed the acid rain trading program to address this problem.

Unlike the offset programs, the acid rain program featured a cap on the mass of emissions, continuous emissions monitoring, and largely game-proof rules. It has produced cost savings while delivering the planned emission reductions:

 Byron Swift, Command Without Control: Why Cap-and-Trade Should Replace Rate Standards for Regional Pollutants
31 Envtl. L. Rep. (Envtl. L. Inst.) 10330 (2001)

* * *

II. An Overview of SO$_2$ [sulfur dioxide] and NOx [nitrogen oxide] Regulation in the Power Generation Sector

A. Regulation of Existing Sources: Title IV and Ozone Transport Commission (OTC) Standards

Emissions of NOx and SO$_2$ from most existing power generation sources are regulated under Title IV of the CAA established in the CAA Amendments of 1990.

Title IV creates two very different systems to achieve major reductions in SO_2 and NOx emission from utility sources: a national emissions cap and allowance trading approach for SO2, and rate-based standards for NOx. . . .

1. Emissions Cap and Allowance Trading Program for SO_2

Electric utilities are responsible for 60% of national SO_2 emissions, and Title IV imposes a permanent cap on utility SO_2 emissions at 8.95 million tons, roughly one-half the 1980 baseline. Title IV, unlike traditional regulation that imposes source-specific rate limits, implements an industry wide mass standard known as an emissions cap. The emissions cap and allowance trading program for the SO_2 program is divided in two phases. Phase I began in 1995 and required the 263 dirtiest coal-fired electric-generating units (referred to as Table A units) to reduce their emissions to a base level of 5.7 million tons of SO_2. Phase II implements a stricter standard in the year 2000, and requires all generating units larger than 25 megawatts to reduce their emissions to the final cap amount.

To implement the cap, allowances equivalent to a ton of SO_2 are assigned to each affected generating unit based on their generation rates from the historic base period of 1985-1987, scaled down so that the aggregate emissions equaled the target emissions cap. Although the annual and the bonus allowances are allocated without charge to existing sources, a limited number of allowances also are available for purchase through an annual U.S. Environmental Protection Agency (EPA) auction. Title IV, therefore, implements a zero new source standard, as any new generating source must purchase all its needed allowances. In another departure from traditional regulation, Title IV allows individual sources to trade their unused allowances to other sources or bank them for future use.

Finally, Title IV incorporates an extremely strict monitoring and compliance system. Monitoring is required by continuous emissions monitoring devices (CEMS) that collect data every 15 minutes, with consolidated data reported hourly. The monitors must also regularly transmit data that indicates that the monitor is functioning properly. CEMS are expensive, costing almost $1 million per stack. Compliance procedures are also strict and include an automatic $2,000 fine per ton and forfeiture of an additional ton of reductions.

Utilities responded to the Title IV program by reducing SO_2 emissions by eight million tons, almost 50% below their 1990 emissions level and 30% below the cap in Phase I. The most significant use of the flexibility mechanisms of Title IV was banking, or emitting below the standards and saving the allowances for later use. About 75% of total allowances created were banked, as a more stringent cap on all units would be imposed in 2000. Another major use of a flexibility provision was trading, which was used by 30 of the 51 firms for intra-firm averaging. Although trading volume increased throughout the program as firms became more comfortable with trading and some began to trade for arbitrage purposes, only 3 of the 51 firms used inter-firm trading to emit over their allowance allocation.

Figure 9-1: 1990-1999 SO₂ Allocated Allowances and Emissions

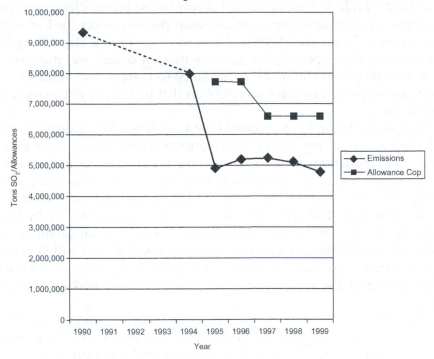

A major story of Phase I compliance under the SO_2 program was the low cost of compliance. This was due to the flexibility of Title IV, derived primarily from the cap approach, which allows greater flexibility than the rate-based standards, and also the ability to trade allowances. Initial expectations by industry in 1991 were for allowance prices of $300 to $1,000 during Phase I. In 1992 and 1993, the earliest signals began to show that prices would be substantially lower, and EPA's first auction of allowances in March 1993, revealed prices at $131. Allowance prices then continued in the $100 range until they began to climb toward $200 as Phase II approached.

The lower cost of compliance was driven by cost reductions and innovation in both of the principal means of compliance—the use of low-sulfur coal and scrubbing. The widespread use of low-sulfur coal has been a major component of compliance strategy for Phase I, resulting in over seven million tons of net reductions (over one-half of net reductions). This use was catalyzed by the flexibility afforded by Title IV, which allowed low-sulfur coal to compete with scrubbing as a compliance method. This led to experimentation and innovation in fuel blending techniques that allowed greater than expected use of low-sulfur western coals, and greater incentives to use eastern low- and medium-sulfur coals. These innovations, together with reduction in rail costs due to competition among railroads, lowered the cost premium for low-sulfur coal and dramatically increased their use, which has been a major driving force in lowering the cost of compliance in Phase I of Title IV.

Scrubbing was the second principal strategy to reduce SO_2 in Phase I, and accounts for 3.5 million tons of emissions reductions (rising to 5.5 million tons if bonus allowances allocated to scrubbed units are counted). Scrubbers were installed for 27 Table A units, promoted in part by the bonus allowances, although several firms canceled scrubber contracts when the low prices for low-sulfur coal became apparent in the early 1990s. The cost of scrubbing also fell significantly during the compliance period, due to innovation in design and materials as well as the significantly lower need for redundancy to comply with Title IV's annual standard, in comparison to previous scrubbers that had been built to meet the new source standard.

Although the Phase I cap required only a moderate SO_2 reduction of around 30%, the cap-and-trade approach exerted continuous pressure to innovate and create lower cost reductions. The cap has prompted continuing innovation in fuel blending techniques and rail infrastructure relating to low-sulfur coal, and also in scrubbing, the cost of which has declined steadily since competition was created with low-sulfur coal. The ability to trade allowances has led to a fully integrated cost of sulfur in the coal market, integrating an environmental parameter into the price of coal. Finally, the monetization of environmental costs and benefits under the cap-and-trade approach has allowed the fuller integration of environmental considerations into the regular financially based decision making throughout a company.

Overall, the shift in Title IV away from scrubber use and toward low-sulfur coal had economic, environmental, and political consequences. The investment in rail infrastructure, innovation in fuel blending and rail transport, and competition among railroads led to low compliance costs that benefitted both the industry and ratepayers. The principal environmental benefit is the reduction and permanent cap on SO_2 emissions, together with the greater political possibility of further reductions given the low cost of compliance. Other environmental benefits of the move to cleaner fuels include the benefits of pollution prevention, in avoiding the direct 1.5% energy loss and significant resource use and waste disposal consequences of scrubbing. Political consequences were also significant, and include the move from unionized coal-mining jobs in midwestern states with high-sulfur coal to western and Appalachian states with low-sulfur coal. Notwithstanding these shifts, the success of the Title IV SO_2 cap-and-trade program in overachieving a strict standard at low cost has led some to include it among the most successful programs under the CAA.

NOTES AND QUESTIONS ON THE ACID RAIN PROGRAM

1. *Cost savings.* Should one attribute the cost savings observed to trading? After all, only 3 of 51 firms engaged in inter-firm trading. In addition, post-compliance studies (where they exist) tend to show that compliance costs for traditional regulation falls below the amounts predicted. *See* Thomas O. McGarity & Ruth Ruttenberg, *Counting the Cost of Health Safety and Environmental Regulation*, 80 TEX. L. REV. 1997 (2002). Subsequently, by the way, trading increased. While one may question attribution of all of the observed cost savings to trading, surely the theoretical reasons to expect trades (even intra-facility trades) to save money justify

confidence that significant cost savings are associated with trading. Why would a facility operator engage in any trades if she did not save money by doing so?

2. *Innovation in the acid rain program.* This article, like many others, claims that the acid rain program stimulated innovation. Some commentators have cited the use of low sulfur coal and scrubbing as innovations. Consider the following Federal Register notice from 1981:

> Environmental laws have caused massive shifts in coal consumption patterns. The Clean Air Act Amendments of 1970 caused many Midwestern utilities to purchase low-sulfur "compliance coal" from Western coal producers. The subsequent geographic expansion of the market to comprise both the Midwestern and Western regions effectively lowered seller concentration levels, which were higher in the Midwest than in any other region. . . .
>
> With the implementation of the 1970 amendments, utilities could choose medium- or high-sulfur coal (usually located in the East or Midwest) with a scrubber, or use more distant low-sulfur coal (usually located in the West). . . .

Coal Competition Prospects for the 1980s: Request for Written Comments on Draft Report, 46 Fed. Reg. 10686, 10692, 10698 (1981). Is it appropriate to describe techniques available since the 1970s as innovations when employed in the 1990s?

3. *Emissions trading and innovation in general.* The standard economic theory states that emissions trading provides superior incentives to innovate, because it makes going beyond compliance profitable. While it is true that low cost sources acquire an incentive to go beyond compliance, high cost sources make fewer local reductions under a trading program than under a comparable traditional regulation. They purchase credits in lieu of making local reductions. Thus, they have less of an incentive to innovate under a trading program than they would under a traditional regulation. Do you think that trading would provide a greater net incentive to innovate than a traditional performance standard? *See* David M. Driesen, *Does Emissions Trading Encourage Innovation?*, 33 ENVTL. L. REP. (ENVTL. L. INST.) 10094 (2003).

A thorough empirical review of sulfur dioxide control technology's evolution over time concluded that the "majority of the performance and capital cost improvements in the dominant technology to achieve SO_2 control occurred before the 1990 Amendments," which contain the acid rain trading program. Margaret A. Taylor, Edward S. Rubin & David A. Hounshell, *Regulation as the Mother of Innovation: The Case for SO_2 Control*, 27 LAW & POL'Y 348, 369 (2005). Similarly, Professor Popp, an environmental economist, compared the level of patent activity associated with the new source performance standards (including the standard upheld in *Sierra Club*) and the electric utility industry with that associated with the subsequent acid rain trading program. *See* David Popp, *Pollution Control Innovations and the Clean Air Act of 1990*, 22 J. POL'Y ANALYSIS & MGMT. 641 (2003). He concludes that more patenting of new technology occurred under the old performance standard than under the trading program. But he claims that the trading program induced more patents of environmentally better technology. The traditional regulation tended to encourage patenting of cheaper methods for achieving the same amount of reductions. In both cases, companies filed patents focusing on better scrubber designs, rather than radical innovations.

4. *Radical innovation.* There seems to be no evidence that the acid rain program encouraged radical innovation, such as wider deployment of solar energy. Why not?

5. *Design.* Design of trading programs is critical. Few, if any, programs have been as well designed as the acid rain program. Yet, trading is being used extensively in a wide variety of areas. *See, e.g.*, Ann Powers, *Reducing Nitrogen Loading on Long Island Sound: Is There a Place for Pollutant Trading?*, 23 COLUM. J. ENVTL. L. 137 (1998); David M. Driesen, *Free Lunch or a Cheap Fix?: The Emissions Trading Idea and the Climate Change Convention*, 26 B.C. ENVTL. AFF. L. REV. 1 (1998); Suitum v. Tahoe Reg'l Planning Agency, 520 U.S. 725, 728-31 (1997) (discussing use of "Transferable Development Rights" under interstate compact); Robert W. Adler, *Economic Incentives for Wetlands and Water Quality Protection: A Public Perspective*, 110 ENV'T COUNSELOR 2 (1997); Royal C. Gardner, *Banking on Entrepreneurs: Wetlands, Mitigation Banking, and Takings*, 81 IOWA L. REV. 527 (1996).

3. The Hybrid Model and Climate Disruption

Trading programs addressing climate disruption, although often referred to as cap and trade programs, embody a hybrid approach that combines features of a cap and trade program with an offset model. Under the hybrid approach governments establish mass-based caps for emissions and assign allowances to regulated sources. Under a pure cap and trade approach, these capped sources would only trade allowances with each other, thereby ensuring the integrity of the cap (assuming reliable monitoring). The Kyoto Protocol (the first global climate disruption agreement to obligate developed countries to reduce emissions), however, establishes two offset programs, the clean development mechanism and the joint implementation program. These project-based mechanisms allow pollution sources without caps (unregulated sources) to generate credits. Under emissions trading programs addressing climate disruption, polluters subject to a mass-based cap can purchase offsets from these international programs or from uncapped domestic sources to meet some of their emission reduction obligations, rather than rely solely on reductions at their own facility or purchased allowances from a fellow polluter subject to a cap.

Recognizing that an offset program creates integrity problems (as we saw in the *Citizens Against the Refinery's Effects* case in Section 1), the international community and domestic governments have created review mechanisms to evaluate offset credits. Although the review procedures and the substantive standards are complex and vary somewhat, several key principles emerge:

Additionality. International and domestic law generally demands that projects generating credits produce additional reductions. This means that a project must create reductions that would not happen anyway in order to justify an emissions reduction credit. This criterion seeks to avoid scenarios analogous to that arising in *Citizens Against the Refinery's Effects*, where a non-additional credit excused an otherwise required emission reduction. Many scholars have criticized the clean development mechanism, which focuses on credit generating projects in developing countries, for generating non-additional credits. For example, in one project, a fully funded solar project in a developing country created prior to the creation of the clean development mechanism generated a credit (certified emission reductions in the language of international climate law). If a polluter subject to a cap put in place pursuant to the Kyoto Protocol purchases this credit, it could forgo reductions at its own facilities, relying on the credit to meet (*i.e.*, offset) its compliance obligation. If no credit is awarded, the solar project would go forward anyway, but the polluter who might purchase the credit would have to reduce its own emissions (unless it purchased an additional credit from elsewhere).

Leakage. Trading outside a cap creates a potential loss of emission reductions through direct leakage. Leakage can occur because of unaccounted-for demand shifts. Suppose for example, that a coal-fired power plant subject to a cap shuts down. Having reduced its emissions to zero it sells credits representing the average amount of its prior emissions to other polluters subject to a cap, who use the credits in lieu of reducing their pollution. If this is all that occurred, this might be an environmentally satisfactory trade. But suppose that demand for power has not decreased. Another coal-fired power plant not subject to a cap that had been running far below capacity now increases production, and associated emissions, in order to serve the customers previously served by the shutdown power plant (sending electricity from a jurisdiction without a cap to one that has one). Can you see that an emission reduction has leaked out of the trading system? The trading has allowed a net emission increase above the required level of reductions. (Can you see why?) Also, notice that if this were a pure cap and trade system, the power plant owner who wishes to increase production to meet the unmet demand would be constrained by a cap on her plant's emissions. The owner of the underutilized plant could not increase emissions, and so could only increase production if it took other pollution reducing steps. So, direct leakage occurs most frequently in an offset program.

These are but a few examples of the problems offset systems create. Hybrid programs combining caps on regulated facilities and offsets include the European Union's emissions trading scheme and the greenhouse gas initiative in the Northeast. Other schemes being proposed or implemented also follow this hybrid model.

CLIMATE DISRUPTION TRADING PROBLEM

You represent Coalmight, a company that owns a coal-fired power plant in Developedland, a country with a hybrid program to address greenhouse gas emissions contributing to climate disruption. Coalmight has asked you to recommend a compliance strategy for the company taking into account both economic and regulatory factors and is especially interested in your evaluation of an enticing offset offer.

Coalmight built this plant 30 years ago and has long since paid off the capital costs, so that its main cost these days is fuel. The plant currently emits 100 tons of carbon dioxide a year. Beginning next year Coalmight will receive a free allocation of 90 tons of carbon dioxide allowances. That amount declines over time, so that Developedland will only give it 80 tons of allowances in 2020 and 60 tons in 2030.

Economists estimate the slow development of an allowance-trading market such that the average price of a carbon allowance available next year may be $10 a ton and will likely go to $20 per ton in 2020 and $25 per ton in 2030. If they go to $30 a ton, a provision of the law authorizes a sale of sufficient government-held allowances to bring the price down to $25 a ton. The following chart sets out your facilities' allowance needs and expected market prices for allowances.

Year	Allowances Needed	Expected Price
Baseline	0	0
Next Year	10 tons	$10/ton
2020	20 tons	$20/ton
2030	40 tons	$25/ton

These projections assume that all countries will continue their existing cap and trade programs without modifications and is based on current prices for relevant technologies.

Your plant is capable of running on natural gas rather than coal. Your engineers estimate that a switch to natural gas would reduce your emissions by 30 tons. *Making this switch, however, would increase your production costs by $20 per ton of pollution reduction, as natural gas is a more expensive fuel than coal.* Your engineers have also identified energy efficiency measures that will reduce your carbon dioxide emissions by 5 tons at no net cost.

Mark Carbon, a broker, has offered you 10 tons of offset credits costing $5 a ton. These offsets reflect efforts to reforest areas in Developingland, where massive deforestation has occurred. Reforestation can sequester carbon, as growing young trees absorb carbon dioxide through their leaves and store it until they mature. For this reason, reforestation can be an activity generating valid offset credits.

These emission reduction credits, however, are under review by the Clean Development Mechanism Executive Board, which has the authority to disapprove or reduce the number of credits associated with offset projects in order to ensure environmental integrity. Technical experts have some concerns about the project and have been questioning it. The estimation of the amounts of credits generated depends upon the growth rates of the replanted forest and its capacity to take up carbon from the surrounding air and soil. These experts have questioned whether the project developer's estimates should be discounted to reflect the possibility of a local insect blight killing some trees or impeding their growth. Furthermore, in some adjacent deforested areas, the forest has regenerated on its own, according to the consultant Coalmight hired to evaluate this project, although at rates 50 percent lower than Mark Carbon's estimates for this offset project. Although Developingland has promised to protect the replanted forest, it has had difficulty keeping land-less peasants from chopping down forests in small random incursions into the vast forests of Developingland. Although Developingland has an excellent record in keeping loggers out of reforested lands it has pledged to protect, a minority political candidate has railed against losing logging business to rival Chaosland, which has rich forest resources and a poor forest protection effort. Mark Carbon's standard contract makes the offset credits contingent on regulatory approvals, and the law prohibits him from selling unapproved credits. Natural gas is currently in short supply, so that you will need to sign a contract to lock in a supply for next year before the review of the offset credits is completed or risk not being able to obtain any. You have also been told that it would be prudent to negotiate a long-term natural gas supply con-tract if you want a guaranteed supply into the future. The Executive Board is expected to complete its review several months before you need to comply with your cap.

The law governing clean development mechanism credits requires that credits be additional and requires project developers to account for leakage, defined as any measurable net change in greenhouse gas emissions outside the project boundary and "reasonably attributable to the CDM project activity." It also requires the Executive Board to disapprove or discount credits if the estimation does not seem realistic.

1. *Compliance choices.* Do you recommend signing a contract to meet Coalmight's regulatory requirements through a switch to natural gas now? If not, when, if ever, do you recommend that it do so? Sketch out a compliance strategy that you recommend for Coalmight for next year and in the future.

2. *Regulatory risks.* List and analyze the issues associated with the approval of the offset credits and make your best evaluation of the correct outcome.

3. *Contract.* If your client decides to purchase these offset credits, what contractual arrangements might you negotiate to fairly allocate the risk of failure of the project developer to get approval for all of the promised credits?

4. *Approval.* What decision should the CDM Executive Board make about this application for credits and why?

4. Policy Issues

a. *Environmental Justice, Hot Spots, and Currency*

A significant concern about trading involves the potential for creation of "hot spots," areas where emissions remain high or even increase, even while emissions elsewhere go down. This concern arises from the ability of pollution sources under trading to forgo reductions to the extent they purchase compensating reductions from elsewhere. If many of the polluters in a particular area fail to make reductions, then people (or environmental resources) in that area may have a disproportionate pollution burden.

For this reason, trading is generally thought appropriate only when the effects of pollution do not vary significantly with location. Where pollutants have strong local effects, trading can raise serious equitable and pragmatic issues.

The equitable concerns that trading raises become especially acute in the case of toxic pollution. Does a reduction of cancer risk in one community justify allowing a cancer risk in another community to remain high or even increase? EPA's traditional answer to this question has been no. It has generally disallowed trading of air toxics under programs aiming to reduce the risks of toxic exposures. EPA, however, did propose to apply a trading approach to reductions of mercury emissions, which depose in water and contaminate fish. This application of trading raised concerns about leaving groups that consume a lot of fish, such as some Indian tribes, exposed to high levels of mercury even as overall levels decline. *See* Catherine A. O'Neill, *Mercury, Risk and Justice*, 34 ENVTL. L. REP. (ENVTL. L. INST.) 11070 (2004); *cf.* New Jersey v. EPA, 517 F.3d 574 (D.C. Cir. 2008) (vacating this rule on the grounds that the EPA must regulate under section 112 of the Clean Air Act absent delisting).

Some environmentalists have also criticized California's RECLAIM program for volatile organic compounds as unjust to a community of color living near a petroleum refinery. The program allowed a petroleum refinery to avoid reducing its own emissions if it purchased credits for reductions from cars (obtained partly by junking older vehicles that might otherwise emit high volumes of pollutants). Both the car emissions and the refinery emissions contributed to high regional ozone pollution, which exacerbates asthma, especially in the elderly and in children. The petroleum refinery's volatile organic compounds were also highly toxic and posed risks of cancer for the community of color living near the refinery's gates. The trading program allowed these toxic emissions to continue without abatement, but the resulting reductions in vehicle emissions would not necessarily reduce the cancer risks of the community living near the refinery.

Will trading systematically disadvantage communities of color? *See* Stephen M. Johnson, *Economics versus Equity: Do Market-Based Reforms Exacerbate Environmental Injustice?*, 56 WASH. & LEE L. REV. 111 (1999).

On the other hand, Congress, EPA, and most of the environmental community embraced trading under the acid rain program, because the ecological problems were a product of atmospheric loadings across a wide area. In such situations, the location of particular pollution sources (credit buyers and sellers) becomes much less important. Nevertheless, Congress authorized EPA to set a "deposition" standard if need be. The idea is that if an ecologically sensitive area (such as New York's Adirondack Park) became a hot spot, then EPA would impose additional geographically targeted reductions to address the problem. Would such a problem arise if all of the polluters downwind of the park were credit sellers? What if they were all buyers? This problem did not arise and EPA did not establish a deposition standard.

A related concern about trading involves the issue of currency:

James Salzman & J.B. Ruhl, Currencies and the Commodification of Environmental Law

53 Stan. L. Rev. 607, 609-13 (2000)

[E]nvironmental trading markets (ETMs) now operate in a range of regulatory settings where parties exchange credits to emit air pollutants, extract natural resources, and develop habitat. In fact, every major environmental policy review in the last five years has called for even greater use of ETMs. Markets for environmental commodities represent the new wave of environmental protection and, despite critiques both subtle and shrill, they are still building.

[Yet] a basic aspect of trading has largely escaped attention. Perhaps because it is so obvious, there has been scant consideration of the simple question—what is actually being traded?

If one compares trading programs, they all seem to share a basic feature. The CFC, fisheries, and proposed greenhouse gas ETMs, for example, all exchange commodities that appear to be fungible. One molecule of CFC, kilo of halibut, or ton of carbon dioxide seems much the same as another, both in terms of identity and impact. It is trading apples for apples (or pork bellies for pork bellies). Thus ETMs are considered a type of commodity market, where environmental credits go to the highest bidder. And for good reason, since the Chicago Board of Trade now sells rights to emit sulfur dioxide alongside pork bellies, orange juice, and grain futures.

Indeed ETMs must assume fungibility—that the things exchanged are sufficiently similar in ways important to the goals of environmental protection— otherwise there would be no assurance that trading ensured environmental protection. While the precondition of fungibility may seem self-evident, this core assumption turns out to be more problematic than it first appears.

As an example of why fungibility matters, consider wetlands mitigation banking. This policy permits developers, once they have taken steps to avoid and minimize wetland loss, to compensate for wetlands that will be destroyed through development by ensuring the restoration of wetlands in another location. The regulations mandate trades that ensure equivalent value and function between destroyed and restored wetlands. In practice, however, most trades are valued in units of acreage. Within very loose guidelines, trades between productive (though soon to be destroyed) wetlands and restored wetlands are approved on an acre-for-acre basis. More sophisticated banks require ratios, trading development on one acre of productive wetlands for, say, restoring four or five acres of wetlands somewhere else. Counting acres may make for easy accounting, but it is poor policy.

Why? The social value of the habitat is absent from the transaction. The ecosystem services provided by the wetlands—positive externalities such as water purification, groundwater recharge, and flood control—are largely ignored. Opinions may differ over the value of a wetland's scenic vista, but they are in universal accord over the contributions of clean water and flood control to social welfare. Trading acres for acres provides an inadequate measure to capture what is really being traded of significance. To be sure, such a simple metric allows trades, but other important, unaccounted trade-offs are occurring. The program can suffer from a lack of accountability (or, more accurately, a lack of countability).

In fact, upon close inspection, it turns out that most ETMs involve commodities and trades that exhibit a range of fungibilities. Legal trades can range from relatively straightforward kilos of surf clams to trades involving the exchange of different types of habitat (that may provide very different social benefits). To achieve the optimal outcome from ETMs, we need to understand and account much better for the qualities being traded. To do so requires careful consideration of the measure of exchange — the currency — since in the final analysis the currency forms the very basis of the transaction. The trading currency superficially makes the commodities fungible, determining what is being traded and, therefore, protected.

Many of the currencies employed by ETMs present trades of an acre of wetland here for an acre of wetland there, or a ton of emissions here for a ton there, as a basic exchange of apples for apples. In reality, though, this is a misleading description. More times than one might think, we are trading Macintoshes for Granny Smiths, apples for oranges, and, in some cases, apples for Buicks. Put simply, we can end up trading the wrong things.

NOTES AND QUESTIONS ON HOT SPOTS AND CURRENCY

1. *Responses to currency problems.* Should regulators forgo trading where simple currencies, such as acreage in a wetlands trade, do not work? Or are the cost savings from trading so important that regulators should continue to use simple currencies even when they do not capture important environmental values? Should regulators instead use a more complex currency, and if so, what currency should they use?

2. *Wetlands example.* To make the possibility of a complex currency concrete, consider the following: Suppose that developers who choose to use wetland protection credits to justify filling in a wetland must obtain credits from projects of equivalent ecological value. Imagine that the wetland being developed and creating the debit offers very good flood control potential, habitat for some common migratory birds, and little scenic value. The wetland being protected for credit does not provide any flood control value, provides habitat for several endangered species, but no migratory birds, and appeared beautiful to one third of the surrounding community. How should a regulator decide whether protecting the creditable wetland in exchange for developing the other one constitutes a good deal? Is there a scientific basis for declaring flood control more important than protecting an endangered species, or is public input necessary to make such choices? Won't public hearings for each trade create transaction costs impeding trading? The federal government has, in fact, developed an approach that tries to distinguish between different wetland types, values, and functions for purposes of mitigation and potentially, mitigation banking — a form of trading. *See The National Action Plan to Implement the Hydrogeomorphic Approach to Assessing Wetland Functions*, 62 Fed. Reg. 33607 (June 20, 1997).

3. *Comparing contexts.* Perhaps the problem of currency is more acute in the case of wetlands protection than in the case of acid rain. Do tons of sulfur dioxide mean the same thing regardless of location? Sulfur dioxide can travel hundreds of

miles. In the Midwest and East, prevailing winds tend to blow the sulfur dioxide toward the east. In terms of impacts on lakes in the Adirondacks, in north central New York, is a ton of sulfur dioxide from a plant on Long Island (in eastern New York) the same as a ton of sulfur dioxide from a plant in West Virginia?

4. *Geographical restrictions.* One approach to trying to address the problem of equivalent masses of pollution having different effects depending upon geography has been to place geographical restrictions in trades. For example, Clean Water Act effluent trading has been confined to trades within a watershed. Would that help solve the problem of treating tons of pollution as a currency, even when the effects of that pollution vary with geography?

b. Emissions Trading versus Best Available Technology

Now that you have some understanding of emissions trading, you can start to evaluate its desirability. The article that appears below predates the acid rain program. It argues that emissions trading is superior to a "best available technology" system. Consider these arguments in light of the information presented in Chapter 5 about technology-based standard setting. How prescient have these arguments been in light of the subsequent experience with emissions trading discussed above?

 ### Bruce A. Ackerman & Richard B. Stewart, Comment: Reforming Environmental Law
37 Stan. L. Rev. 1333 (1985)

The existing system of pollution regulation . . . is primarily based on a Best Available Technology (BAT) strategy. If an industrial process or product generates some nontrivial risk, the responsible plant or industry must install whatever technology is available to reduce or eliminate this risk, so long as the costs of doing so will not cause a shutdown of the plant or industry. BAT requirements are largely determined through uniform federal regulations. Under the Clean Water Act's BAT strategy, the EPA adapts nationally uniform effluent limitations for some 500 different industries. A similar BAT strategy is deployed under the Clean Air Act for new industrial sources of air pollution, new automobiles, and industrial sources of toxic air pollutants. BAT strategies are also widely used in many fields of environmental regulation other than air and water pollution.

BAT was embraced by Congress and administrators in the early 1970s in order to impose immediate, readily enforceable federal controls on a relatively few widespread pollutants, while avoiding widespread industrial shutdowns. Subsequent experience and analysis has demonstrated:

1. Uniform BAT requirements waste many billions of dollars annually by ignoring variations among plants and industries in the cost of reducing pollution and by ignoring geographic variations in pollution effects. A more cost-effective strategy of risk reduction could free enormous resources for additional pollution reduction or other purposes.

2. BAT controls, and the litigation they provoke, impose disproportionate penalties on new products and processes. A BAT strategy typically imposes far more stringent controls on new sources because there is no risk of shut-down. Also, new plants and products must run the gauntlet of lengthy regulatory and legal proceedings to win approval; the resulting uncertainty and delay discourage new investment. By contrast, existing sources can use the delays and costs of the legal process to burden regulators and postpone or "water-down" compliance. BAT strategies also impose disproportionate burdens on more productive and profitable industries because these industries can "afford" more stringent controls. This "soak the rich" approach penalizes growth and international competitiveness.

3. BAT controls can ensure that established control technologies are installed. They do not, however, provide strong incentives for the development of new, environmentally superior strategies, and may actually discourage their development. Such innovations are essential for maintaining long-term economic growth without simultaneously increasing pollution and other forms of environmental degradation.

4. BAT involves the centralized determination of complex scientific, engineering, and economic issues regarding the feasibility of controls on hundreds of thousands of pollution sources. Such determinations impose massive information-gathering burdens on administrators, and provide a fertile ground for complex litigation in the form of massive adversary rule-making proceedings and protracted judicial review. Given the high costs of regulatory compliance and the potential gains from litigation brought to defeat or delay regulatory requirements, it is often more cost-effective for industry to "invest" in such litigation rather than to comply.

5. A BAT strategy is inconsistent with intelligent priority setting. Simply regulating to the hilt whatever pollutants happen to get on the regulatory agenda may preclude an agency from dealing adequately with more serious problems that come to scientific attention later. BAT also tends to reinforce regulatory inertia. Foreseeing that "all or nothing" regulation of a given substance under BAT will involve large administrative and compliance costs, and recognizing that resources are limited, agencies often seek to limit sharply the number of substances on the agenda for regulatory action.

When a polluter receives an air or water permit under existing law . . . the permit tries to be as quantitatively precise as possible, telling each discharger how much of the regulated pollutants he may discharge.

. . . [O]ur reforms build upon, rather than abandon, this basic permit system. Indeed, we have only two, albeit far-reaching, objections to the existing permit mechanism. First, existing permits are free. This is bad because it gives the polluter no incentive to reduce his wastes below the permitted amount. Second, they are non-transferable. This is bad because polluter A is obliged to cut back his own wastes even if it is cheaper for him to pay his neighbor B to undertake the extra cleanup instead.

Our basic reform would respond to these deficiencies by allowing polluters to buy and sell each other's permits—thereby creating a powerful financial incentive for those who can clean up most cheaply to sell their permits to those whose treatment costs are highest. This reform will, at one stroke, cure many of the basic flaws of the existing command-and-control regulatory systems discussed earlier.

A system of tradeable rights will tend to bring about a least cost allocation of control burdens, saving many billions of dollars annually. It will eliminate the disproportionate burdens that BAT imposes on new and more productive industries by treating all sources of the same pollutant on the same basis. It will provide positive economic rewards for polluters who develop environmentally superior products and processes. It will, as we show below, reduce the incentives for litigation, simplify the issues in controversy, and facilitate more intelligent setting of priorities.

Would allowing the sale of permits lead to a bureaucratic nightmare? Before proceeding to the new administrative burdens marketability will generate, it is wise to pause . . . to consider marketability's great administrative advantages.

First, marketability would immediately eliminate most of the information-processing tasks that are presently overwhelming the federal and state bureaucracies. No longer would the EPA be required to conduct endless adversary proceedings to determine the best available control technologies in each major industry of the United States, and to defend its determinations before the courts; nor would federal and state officials be required to spend vast amounts of time and energy in adapting these changing national guidelines to the particular conditions of every important pollution source in the United States. Instead of giving the job of economic and technological assessment to bureaucrats, the marketable rights mechanism would put the information-processing burden precisely where it belongs: upon business managers and engineers who are in the best position to figure out how to cut back on their plants' pollution costs. If the managers operating plant A think they can clean up a pollutant more cheaply than those in charge of plant B, they should be expected to sell some of their pollution rights to B at a mutually advantageous price; cleanup will occur at the least cost without the need for constant bureaucratic decisions about the best available technology. . . . [T]he existing system of command-and-control regulation . . . envisions inevitably ill-informed bureaucrats continually "fine-tuning" technological and economic decisions best made by the people operating the plants.

Second, marketable permits would open up enormous financial resources for effective and informed regulation. While polluters would have the right to trade their permits among themselves during the n years they are valid, they would be obliged to buy new ones when their permits expired at an auction held by the EPA in each watershed and air quality control region. These auctions would raise substantial sums of money for the government on a continuing basis. . . .

Third, the auction system would help correct one of the worst weaknesses of the present system: the egregious failure of the EPA and associated state agencies to enforce the laws on the books in a timely and effective way. Part of the problem stems from the ability of existing polluters to delay regulatory implementation by using legal proceedings to challenge the economic and engineering bases of BAT regulations and permit conditions. But agencies also invest so little in monitoring that they must rely on polluters for the bulk of their data on discharges. Since polluters are predictably reluctant to report their own violations, the current system perpetuates a Panglossian view of regulatory reality. For example, a General

Accounting Office investigation of 921 major air polluters officially considered to be in compliance revealed 200, or 22%, to be violating their permits; in one region, the number not complying was 52%. Even when illegal polluters are identified, they are not effectively sanctioned: The EPA's Inspector General in 1984 found that it was a common practice for water pollution officials to respond to violations by issuing administrative orders that effectively legitimized excess discharges. Thus, while the system may, after protracted litigation, eventually "work" to force the slow installation of expensive control machinery, there is no reason to think this machinery will run well when eventually installed. Although there are many reasons for this appalling weakness in enforcement, one stands out above all others: The present system does not put pressure on agency policymakers to make the large investments in monitoring and personnel that are required to make the tedious and unending work of credible enforcement a bureaucratic reality.

The auction system would change existing compliance incentives dramatically. It would reduce the opportunity and incentive of polluters to use the legal system for delay and obstruction by finessing the complex BAT issues, and it would limit dispute to the question of whether a source's discharges exceeded its permits. It would also eliminate the possibility of using the legal system to postpone implementation of regulatory requirements by requiring the polluter that lost its legal challenge to pay for the permits it would have been obliged to buy during the entire intervening period of noncompliance (plus interest).

The marketable permit system would also provide much stronger incentives for effective monitoring and enforcement. If polluters did not expect rigorous enforcement during the term of their permits, this fact would show up at the auction in dramatically lower bids: Why pay a lot for the right to pollute legally when one can pollute illegally without serious risk of detection? Under a marketable permit approach, this problem would be at the center of bureaucratic attention. For if, as we envisage, the size of the budget available to the EPA and state agencies would depend on total auction revenues, the bureaucracy's failure to invest adequately in enforcement would soon show up in a potentially dramatic drop in auction income available for the next budgetary period. This is not a prospect that top EPA administrators will take lightly. Monitoring and enforcement will become agency priorities of the first importance. Moreover, permit holders may themselves support strong enforcement in order to ensure that cheating by others does not depreciate the value of the permit holders' investments.

A system of marketable permits, then, not only promises to save Americans many billions of dollars a year, to reward innovative improvements in existing clean-up techniques, and to eliminate the BAT system's penalty on new, productive investment. It also offers formidable administrative advantages. It relieves agencies of the enormous information-processing burdens that overwhelm them under the BAT system; it greatly reduces litigation and delay; it offers a rich source of budgetary revenue in a period of general budgetary stringency; and it forces agencies to give new importance to the critical business of enforcing the law in a way that America's polluters will take seriously. . . .

The reformed system we have described involves the execution of four bureaucratic tasks. First, the agency must estimate how much pollution presently is permitted by law in each watershed and air quality region. Second, it must run a system of fair and efficient auctions in which polluters can regularly buy rights for limited terms. Third, it must run an efficient title registry in each region that will allow buyers and sellers to transfer rights in a legally effective way. Fourth, it must consistently penalize polluters who discharge more than their permitted amounts.

And that's that. . . .

NOTES AND QUESTIONS ON THE ACKERMAN AND STEWART CRITIQUE

1. *Waste.* Ackerman and Stewart claim that BAT controls are wasteful. What precisely do they mean by that?

2. *Regulating to the hilt.* Ackerman and Stewart criticize BAT for "regulating to the hilt whatever pollutants happen to get on the regulatory agenda," which they characterize as inconsistent with good priority setting. Would these problems be avoided by trading programs? *Cf.* Lesley McAllister, *The Overallocation Problem in Cap-and-Trade: Moving Toward Stringency,* 34 COLUM. J. ENVTL. L. 395 (2009) (finding trading programs in practice are often too lax).

3. *New sources.* Ackerman and Stewart criticize BAT for requiring more stringent controls of new sources.[1] But is this an inherent characteristic of technology-based performance standards? Is it possible to use traditional regulatory approaches that treat new and existing sources equally? Congress introduced differential treatment because it considered retrofitting costly and awkward. It required owners of existing sources to employ stricter new source controls when they modified their facilities. Should Congress require all facilities to meet strict new source standards? Should it instead relax new source standards to comport with less stringent regulation for existing sources?

Should Congress retain a differential favoring existing sources? Or should it reverse it, applying stricter standards to existing sources than it applies to new sources in hopes of pressuring plants into modernizing or shutting down? If Swift, *supra,* is correct that all new pollution sources in the acid rain program must purchase allowances, even though existing sources get them for free, then does trading solve the problem of discrimination against new sources?

4. *Information burdens.* Ackerman and Stewart criticize BAT because of the information burdens involved in determining feasibility. Would the information burdens prove lighter for health-based or cost-benefit-based standards? Recall that trading does not obviate the need to set limits. Wouldn't an agency establishing a trading program need to use some version of the standard setting rubrics used for traditional regulation to establish the limits? Are Ackerman and Stewart assuming that Congress, rather than an administrative agency, sets the trading program's limits? Could Congress set the limits for a non-trading program?

5. *Auctions.* Ackerman and Stewart call for an auction of pollution permits. While Congress adopted their recommendation to use trading in the acid rain

---

1. While Ackerman and Stewart are correct that the Clean Water Act contemplates stricter standards for new sources, in practice EPA often sets NSPS limits for new water pollution sources equal to BAT limits for existing sources.

program, Congress gave away most of the permits instead of auctioning them off. To what extent does this giveaway weaken the argument for trading? *See* David M. Driesen, *Capping Carbon*, 40 ENVTL. L. 1, 44-47 (2010) (discussing some of auctioning's advantages).

6. *Enforcement.* Will trading improve enforcement of the law? To what extent does Ackerman's and Stewart's argument on this point disappear when the government gives away rather than sells allowances? The acid rain program suggests that their argument that trading would provide incentives to improve monitoring and enforcement has proven prescient. Congress required continuous emission monitors in order to make the program credible and obviated the need for large investments in enforcement. On the other hand, some subsequent programs have not featured good monitoring. Consider the following:

> Spatial specificity . . . helps make standards enforceable. A regulatory agency, citizen group, or corporation seeking to evaluate compliance must generally look at each place where regulated pollution escapes into the environment in order to determine whether emission reductions have occurred. Hence, it seems logical to specify obligations for specific places where emission reductions can be verified. Where a company cannot reliably measure emissions, a regulator or citizen may determine whether a reduction has occurred at these places by determining whether the polluter has properly applied a technique known to reduce emissions at that particular place. An understanding of the reasons for spatial specificity need not lead to the conclusion that only traditional regulation makes sense. However, programs that lessen spatial specificity only produce real verifiable emission reductions when they adequately address the enforcement problems they create. Lack of spatial specificity complicates enforcement by increasing the number and variety of claims, transactions, and activities that a regulator must evaluate to detect noncompliance. . . .
>
> Furthermore, most scholars recognize that emissions trading requires good monitoring in order to succeed. Because pollution sources have an economic incentive to try to exaggerate the value of reduction credits and to understate the value of debits in an emissions trading scheme, good monitoring is essential. For some pollution sources, however, good monitoring simply is not technically feasible.
>
> For this reason, emissions trading cannot supplant true command and control regulation. Normally, command and control regulation exists precisely because an agency has determined that it cannot measure emission reductions. Emissions trading may sometimes provide a good alternative to performance standards, but it will function poorly if used to supplant true command and control regulation. Hence, the command and control/economic incentive dichotomy not only unfairly disparages traditional regulation, it suggests application of emissions trading precisely in areas where it cannot work.

David M. Driesen, *Is Emissions Trading an Economic Incentive Program?: Replacing the Command and Control/Economic Incentive Dichotomy*, 55 WASH. & LEE L. REV. 289, 303-04, 310-11 (1998). *See* Lesley McAllister, *Playing Banker: The Role of the Regulator in Emissions Trading*, 59 ADMIN. L. REV. 269 (2007) (arguing that agency enforcement in the trading context is more difficult than some imagine).

Do you think trading will improve compliance incentives for the reasons Ackerman and Stewart suggest? Would it instead make enforcement more difficult? Or does the choice between trading and traditional regulation make no difference? Will the answer vary with context? If so, what variables will influence compliance?

9

Information-Based Approaches

Generation and analysis of information about the environmental consequences of actions can provide a means of encouraging better environmental performance. The materials in this section address two basic functions that information plays.

First, information helps inform government decisions about how and whether to protect the environment. *See generally* Daniel C. Esty, *Environmental Protection in the Information Age*, 79 N.Y.U. L. REV. 115, 121-40 (2004) (delineating information's role in some detail). The National Environmental Policy Act (NEPA) and the testing requirements of the Toxic Substances Control Act (TSCA) provide prominent examples of laws seeking information to guide the government and the public before the government makes key decisions, and to help them in reaching those decisions. NEPA generates information about the environmental impact of significant proposed federal actions and alternatives to those actions. TSCA generates information on hazardous chemicals to inform regulatory decisions about toxic substances.

Second, information sometimes motivates private cleanup and/or avoidance of environmental problems. Prominent examples of laws that have motivated cleanup include federal "Right-to-Know" provisions requiring reporting of information about releases of toxic pollution into the environment and California's Proposition 65, which requires labels warning consumers about carcinogens in consumer products.

A. INFORMATION IN GOVERNMENT DECISION MAKING

1. NEPA and Its Analogues

Congress recognized the value of information to promote better decisions in one of the first modern environmental statutes it enacted, the National Environmental

Policy Act of 1969 (NEPA), 42 U.S.C. §§4321 *et seq.* NEPA requires analysis of the environmental impacts of major proposals for federal actions significantly affecting the environment. We begin with a Trail Guide to orient you to the key provisions of the statute and its main implementing regulations, and then proceed to cases that illuminate the ways in which courts have expanded—and limited—the law's requirements for agency use of information to inform and improve federal decisions.

TRAIL GUIDE TO THE NATIONAL ENVIRONMENTAL POLICY ACT (NEPA) AND COUNCIL ON ENVIRONMENTAL QUALITY (CEQ) GUIDELINES

Introduction and Overview

The National Environmental Policy Act (NEPA) is a succinct law whose most lasting requirement—the duty that federal agencies assess the environmental impacts of each of their major undertakings—is contained in a single, short, statutory subsection. Guidelines issued by the Council of Environmental Quality (CEQ), an office created by NEPA and housed within the Executive Office of the White House, add much more detail to this bare-bones requirement. For instance, CEQ's regulations explain when an agency must prepare an environmental impact statement, what that statement must contain, including the duty to assess alternatives to the agency's proposed action, and the requisite degree of public participation the agency must provide.

CEQ's current guidelines can be found in the Code of Federal Regulations at 40 C.F.R. Parts 1500-1508. Since an executive order issued by President Carter in 1978, CEQ guidelines have been considered binding on federal agencies. In addition to its guidelines, CEQ has issued an influential interpretive document: *Forty Most Asked Questions Concerning CEQ's National Environmental Quality Act Regulations,* 46 Fed. Reg. 18026 (1981). According to the Supreme Court, CEQ interpretations of NEPA are entitled to substantial deference. Andrus v. Sierra Club, 442 U.S. 347, 358 (1979).

According to the CEQ guidelines, each federal agency is responsible for adopting and implementing its own NEPA regulations. These agency-specific regulations serve to supplement the basic procedures provided for in the guidelines when the agency is also the lead agency on the proposal. In compliance with this directive, just about every federal agency has issued NEPA implementing regulations. Because each agency's NEPA regulations reflect each agency's unique mandate and mission, they differ from agency to agency. For example, the NEPA regulations of the Department of Defense, found at 32 C.F.R. Part 989, contain a special section for how to implement the EIS process where the action undergoing review has been classified for national defense for foreign policy purposes. *Id.* at 989.5. The NEPA regulations of the Federal Highway Administration, found at 23 C.F.R. Part

771, discuss the need for state public hearing procedures with respect to any federal-aid highway program. *Id.* at 771.111(h).

The following provides a guide to the NEPA statute and the primary provisions of the CEQ guidelines. NEPA contains strong language suggesting that it mandates environmental protection. But as you will learn from the materials in the text, the U.S. Supreme Court has chosen not to afford a substantive meaning to NEPA, limiting its provisions to a purely procedural mandate for federal agencies. As a result, and in the words of one of this book's co-authors, NEPA contains a host of "sleeping giants."

Key Provisions of NEPA

Declaration of rights and responsibilities, 42 U.S.C. §4331: Among other statements, this provision declares it to be "the continuing responsibility of the Federal Government to use all practicable means" to "assure for all Americans safe, healthful, productive, and esthetically and culturally pleasing surroundings" and that "Congress recognizes that each person should enjoy a healthful environment." In return, "each person has a responsibility to contribute to the preservation and enhancement of the environment."

Duty to prepare an environmental impact statement on major federal actions, 42 U.S.C. §4332: With respect to "every recommendation or report on proposals for legislation and other major Federal actions significantly affecting the quality of the human environment," each federal agency must include a "detailed statement" on the environmental impact of a proposed action, any unavoidable adverse environmental impacts following from the action, alternatives to the proposed action, and any "irreversible and irretrievable commitments of resources" that would occur should the proposed action be implemented.

Creation and duties of the Council on Environmental Quality, 42 U.S.C. §§4342-4346: The Council on Environmental Quality is created and housed within the Executive Office of the President. The Council is charged with the duty to prepare and submit to Congress an annual report on the quality of the national environment and to review and appraise federal programs and activities in light of the policy set forth in the Act.

Key Provisions of the CEQ Regulations

NEPA and agency planning, 40 C.F.R. §1501.2: Federal agencies are required to integrate the NEPA process into their own planning processes "at the earliest possible time" to ensure that the agency's ultimate decision reflects environmental values and avoids delays and conflicts.

Determine whether to prepare an EIS, 40 C.F.R. §1501.4: Agencies must decide whether to prepare an EIS based upon whether the action is major and significantly impacts the quality of the human environment, or is neither and hence does not require an EIS. Agencies are allowed to exclude entire classes of actions—"categorical exclusions"—from the EIS requirement on the basis that they generally do not pose significant impacts either individually or cumulatively. When in doubt, agencies are directed to prepare an Environmental Assessment (EA), the purpose of which is to indicate either that an EIS is required or that it is unnecessary, in which case the agency issues a "Finding of No Significant Impact" or FONSI.

Scoping, 40 C.F.R. §§1501.7, 1508.25: In preparing an EIS, agencies must determine the scope of the environmental impacts that will be studied. The scope must consider three types of actions: connected actions, cumulative actions, and similar actions; three types of alternatives: the "no action" alternative, other reasonable alternatives, and mitigation measures; and three types of impacts: direct, indirect, and cumulative.

Alternatives, 40 C.F.R. §1502.14: The EIS's discussion of alternatives is considered "the heart of the environmental impact statement." Agencies must present the environmental impacts of the agency's proposal, other reasonable alternatives both within and outside the agency's jurisdiction, and the alternative of taking no action at all. As part of this discussion the agency is to include a discussion of appropriate measures to mitigate identified environmental impacts. The discussion of alternatives is to be presented in a comparative form, "thus sharply defining the issues and providing a clear basis for choice among options by the decisionmaker and the public."

Tiering, 40 C.F.R. §§1502.20, 1508.28: Agencies are encouraged to "tier" their environmental impact statements such that they first prepare an analysis of the broader impacts of an entire program (actions at a general level or large geographic scale) and subsequently prepare analyses of more targeted actions, such as site-specific or regional actions or decisions that implement a somewhat narrow aspect of a larger program. In any given tier document, the agency may reference the analyses performed in a different tier.

Cumulative impacts, 40 C.F.R. §§1508.7, 1508.25, 1508.27: In determining the significance of an action's impact upon the environment and in thoroughly assessing those impacts, an EIS is to consider the action's cumulative impacts. These are defined by CEQ as the impacts that result "from the incremental impact of the action when added to other past, present, and reasonably foreseeable future actions regardless of what agency (federal or non-federal) or person undertakes such other actions."

Consideration of incomplete or unavailable information, 40 C.F.R. §1502.22: Agencies frequently confront the problem of what to do when information relevant to the reasonably foreseeable environmental impacts of an action are either unknown or unavailable because the costs of obtaining the information may be exorbitant. Replacing an earlier requirement that in such situations agencies analyze the impacts of a worst case analysis, CEQ now requires that agencies summarize the relevant "existing credible scientific information" relating to the impacts and evaluate such impacts based upon "theoretical approaches or research methods generally accepted in the scientific community."

Practice Under NEPA

Given the broad scope of NEPA, any attorney practicing law within or before federal agencies is well advised to be familiar with the NEPA process. As an attorney employed in a federal agency, the attorney will be responsible for seeing that the agency is in full compliance with NEPA with respect to its major proposed actions, even if the actual preparation of the NEPA documents is being handled by someone else, such as is often the case where the action concerns the issuance of an environmental permit. In such cases, it is common that the permit applicant will prepare the EA or the EIS, but ensuring NEPA compliance is still the agency's ultimate responsibility. Attorneys representing parties seeking a federal agency action, such as a Forest Service timber sale or federal funding for a highway project, must be familiar with NEPA, as the required action will hinge on the agency's successful completion of the NEPA process. For persons opposing federal agency action, for example, an environmental group opposing the construction of a dam, participating in the NEPA process by filing comments on draft documents or filing legal actions against the agency for inadequate compliance with NEPA's informational mandates may generate important information that can be used to sway agency officials or public opinion against the project, or, in extreme cases, cause the agency to significantly delay the project or abandon it altogether.

For any given proposed action, the agency's first task is to determine whether an EIS is required. An EIS is required of all major federal proposed actions significantly affecting the human environment. Unless the proposed action belongs to a class of actions for which the agency has promulgated a categorical exclusion, prior to concluding that no EIS is required, the agency should prepare an EA. The EA should inform the agency whether the action, when all direct, indirect, and cumulative impacts of the action are included, is of sufficient significance that an EIS is required or, alternatively, that the impacts will be relatively minor. In the latter case, the agency promulgates a "Finding of No Significant Impacts," also known as a "FONSI." Issuance of a FONSI constitutes final agency action with respect to NEPA and thus is subject to judicial review under the Administrative Procedure Act.

If an agency determines that an EIS is necessary, the agency's first step is to conduct a scoping process to determine the range of environmental impacts that the EIS must analyze. Here the agency may decide to "tier" its environmental analysis, first preparing a more general EIS addressing the broad, programmatic alternatives to the proposed action and then later preparing a more narrowly tailored EIS (or multiple EISs) addressing site-specific actions. Regardless, the agency will first issue a draft EIS on which, as with all procedural steps under NEPA, it will solicit public comments. Based upon those public comments and other documents in the public record, the agency will promulgate a final EIS. Like a FONSI, this final EIS also constitutes final agency action and is subject to judicial review.

Recall that the EIS process is performed with respect to "proposals" for federal action or legislation. By definition, then, the agency must either determine that no EIS is necessary or complete a final EIS, prior to moving forward with an agency action. Thus, the "final, final" step in the EIS process is the agency's issuance of a record of decision with respect to the action under review.

a. Is an EIS Required?

A federal obligation to prepare an EIS only applies to proposed "major federal actions," although state law sometimes requires the equivalent of an EIS for state actions. *See* Kenneth S. Weiner, *NEPA and State NEPA's: Learning from the Past, Foresight for the Future*, 39 ENVTL. L. REP. (ENVTL. L. INST.) 10675 (2009). Federal actions, however, encompass much more than purely federal projects. They include many decisions by the federal government to grant permits and licenses to others, *see, e.g.*, Davis v. Morton, 469 F.2d 593, 598 (10th Cir. 1972) (the Bureau of Indian Affairs must comply with NEPA before approving a lease for development purposes on tribal lands), and to fund projects that the federal government does not carry out, *see, e.g.*, Blue Ocean Preservation Society v. Watkins, 754 F. Supp. 1450, 1461 (D. Haw. 1991) (EIS required for state proposal to develop geothermal resources when federal funds support the project); Don't Ruin Our Park v. Stone, 749 F. Supp. 1386 (M.D. Pa. 1990), *aff'd mem.*, 931 F.2d 49 (3d Cir. 1991) (EIS required for relocation of a Pennsylvania National Guard unit to a location adjacent to a state park because of federal funding); *cf.* National Organization for the Reform of Marijuana Laws v. Drug Enforcement Administration, 545 F. Supp. 981, 985 (D.D.C. 1982) (federal technical assistance not a sufficient basis to make marijuana spraying a federal action); Sierra Club v. Stamm, 507 F.2d 788 (10th Cir. 1974) (federal subsidies used for pesticide and herbicide spraying does not make a federal action when the federal agency did not control the subsidies' use).

NEPA also requires an EIS only when a proposed federal action "significantly" affects the environment. *See* Minnesota Public Interest Research Group v. Butz (I), 498 F.2d 1314 (8th Cir. 1974); 40 C.F.R. §1508.18. Most courts assess significance by examining both the magnitude of harm emanating from a project and the extent to which it will cause adverse effects "in excess of those created by existing uses. . . ." *See* Hanly v. Kleindienst, 471 F.2d 823 (2d Cir. 1972), 40 C.F.R. §1508.27. Some courts require impact statements whenever the actions are "arguably" significant and demand a convincing agency case for insignificance before excusing agency preparation of an EIS. *See, e.g.*, Maryland-National Capital Park and Planning Commission v. United States Postal Service, 487 F.2d 1029 (D.C. Cir. 1973).

But the existence of a "major federal action" and "significant impacts" do not always suffice to justify the expenditure of time and effort necessary to gather and analyze the information necessary to prepare an EIS. In the following case, the Supreme Court held that there must be a sufficient causal connection between the federal action and the significant environmental effects to justify the preparation of an EIS:

Department of Transportation v. Public Citizen
541 U.S. 752 (2004)

JUSTICE THOMAS delivered the opinion of the Court.

In this case, we confront the question whether the National Environmental Policy Act of 1969 (NEPA) and the Clean Air Act (CAA) require the Federal

Motor Carrier Safety Administration (FMCSA) to evaluate the environmental effects of cross-border operations of Mexican-domiciled motor carriers, where FMCSA's promulgation of certain regulations would allow such cross-border operations to occur. Because FMCSA lacks discretion to prevent these cross-border operations, we conclude that these statutes impose no such requirement on FMCSA. . . .

1

Signed into law on January 1, 1970, NEPA establishes a "national policy [to] encourage productive and enjoyable harmony between man and his environment," and was intended to reduce or eliminate environmental damage and to promote "the understanding of the ecological systems and natural resources important to" the United States. 42 U.S.C. §4321. "NEPA itself does not mandate particular results" in order to accomplish these ends. Robertson v. Methow Valley Citizens Council, 490 U.S. 332, 350 (1989). Rather, NEPA imposes only procedural requirements on federal agencies with a particular focus on requiring agencies to undertake analyses of the environmental impact of their proposals and actions. At the heart of NEPA is a requirement that federal agencies

> "include in every recommendation or report on proposals for legislation and other major Federal actions significantly affecting the quality of the human environment, a detailed statement by the responsible official on—
> "(i) the environmental impact of the proposed action,
> "(ii) any adverse environmental effects which cannot be avoided should the proposal be implemented,
> "(iii) alternatives to the proposed action,
> "(iv) the relationship between local short-term uses of man's environment and the maintenance and enhancement of long-term productivity, and
> "(v) any irreversible and irretrievable commitments of resources which would be involved in the proposed action should it be implemented." 42 U.S.C. §4332(2)(C).

This detailed statement is called an Environmental Impact Statement (EIS). The Council of Environmental Quality (CEQ), established by NEPA with authority to issue regulations interpreting it, has promulgated regulations to guide federal agencies in determining what actions are subject to that statutory requirement. See 40 CFR §1500.3 (2003). The CEQ regulations allow an agency to prepare a more limited document, an Environmental Assessment (EA), if the agency's proposed action neither is categorically excluded from the requirement to produce an EIS nor would clearly require the production of an EIS. See §§1501.4(a)-(b). The EA is to be a "concise public document" that "[b]riefly provide[s] sufficient evidence and analysis for determining whether to prepare an [EIS]." §1508.9(a). If, pursuant to the EA, an agency determines that an EIS is not required under applicable CEQ regulations, it must issue a "finding of no significant impact" (FONSI), which briefly presents the reasons why the proposed agency action will not have a significant impact on the human environment. See §§1501.4(e), 1508.13. . . .

3

FMCSA, an agency within the Department of Transportation (DOT), is responsible for motor carrier safety and registration. FMCSA has a variety of statutory mandates, including "ensur[ing]" safety, establishing minimum levels of financial responsibility for motor carriers, and prescribing federal standards for safety inspections of commercial motor vehicles. Importantly, FMCSA has only limited discretion regarding motor vehicle carrier registration: It must grant registration to all domestic or foreign motor carriers that are "willing and able to comply with" the applicable safety, fitness, and financial-responsibility requirements. FMCSA has no statutory authority to impose or enforce emissions controls or to establish environmental requirements unrelated to motor carrier safety.

B

. . . Before 1982, motor carriers domiciled in Canada and Mexico could obtain certification to operate within the United States from the Interstate Commerce Commission (ICC). In 1982, Congress, concerned about discriminatory treatment of United States motor carriers in Mexico and Canada, enacted a 2-year moratorium on new grants of operating authority. Congress authorized the President to extend the moratorium beyond the 2-year period if Canada or Mexico continued to interfere with United States motor carriers, and also authorized the President to lift or modify the moratorium if he determined that doing so was in the national interest. . . .

In December 1992, the leaders of Mexico, Canada, and the United States signed the North American Free Trade Agreement (NAFTA). As part of NAFTA, the United States agreed to phase out the moratorium and permit Mexican motor carriers to obtain operating authority within the United States' interior by January 2000. On NAFTA's effective date (January 1, 1994), the President began to lift the trade moratorium by allowing the licensing of Mexican carriers to provide some bus services in the United States. The President, however, did not continue to ease the moratorium on the timetable specified by NAFTA, as concerns about the adequacy of Mexico's regulation of motor carrier safety remained.

The Government of Mexico challenged the United States' implementation of NAFTA's motor carrier provisions under NAFTA's dispute-resolution process, and in February 2001, an international arbitration panel determined that the United States' "blanket refusal" of Mexican motor carrier applications breached the United States' obligations under NAFTA. Shortly thereafter, the President made clear his intention to lift the moratorium on Mexican motor carrier certification following the preparation of new regulations governing grants of operating authority to Mexican motor carriers.

In May 2001, FMCSA published for comment proposed rules concerning safety regulation of Mexican motor carriers [the Application and Safety Monitoring Rules]. . . .

In December 2001, Congress enacted the Department of Transportation and Related Agencies Appropriations Act. Section 350 of this Act provided that no funds appropriated under the Act could be obligated or expended to review or to process any application by a Mexican motor carrier for authority to operate in the interior of the United States until FMCSA implemented specific application and safety-monitoring requirements for Mexican carriers. Some of these requirements went beyond those proposed by FMCSA in the Application and Safety Monitoring Rules. . . .

. . . FMCSA issued a programmatic EA for the proposed Application and Safety Monitoring Rules. FMCSA's EA evaluated the environmental impact associated with three separate scenarios: where the President did not lift the moratorium; where the President did but where (contrary to what was legally possible) FMCSA did not issue any new regulations; and the Proposed Action Alternative, where the President would modify the moratorium and where FMCSA would adopt the proposed regulations. The EA considered the environmental impact in the categories of traffic and congestion, public safety and health, air quality, noise, socioeconomic factors, and environmental justice. Vital to the EA's analysis, however, was the assumption that there would be no change in trade volume between the United States and Mexico due to the issuance of the regulations. FMCSA did note that §350's restrictions made it impossible for Mexican motor carriers to operate in the interior of the United States before FMCSA's issuance of the regulations. But, FMCSA determined that "this and any other associated effects in trade characteristics would be the result of the modification of the moratorium" by the President, not a result of FMCSA's implementation of the proposed safety regulations. Because FMCSA concluded that the entry of the Mexican trucks was not an "effect" of its regulations, it did not consider any environmental impact that might be caused by the increased presence of Mexican trucks within the United States.

The particular environmental effects on which the EA focused, then, were those likely to arise from the increase in the number of roadside inspections of Mexican trucks and buses due to the proposed regulations. The EA concluded that these effects (such as a slight increase in emissions, noise from the trucks, and possible danger to passing motorists) were minor and could be addressed and avoided in the inspections process itself. The EA also noted that the increase of inspection-related emissions would be at least partially offset by the fact that the safety requirements would reduce the number of Mexican trucks operating in the . . . United States. Due to these calculations, the EA concluded that the issuance of the proposed regulations would have no significant impact on the environment, and hence FMCSA . . . issued a FONSI.

On March 19, 2002, FMCSA issued the two interim rules. . . . In the regulatory preambles, FMCSA relied on its EA and its FONSI to demonstrate compliance with NEPA. . . .

In November 2002, the President lifted the moratorium on qualified Mexican motor carriers. Before this action, however, respondents filed petitions for judicial review of the Application and Safety Monitoring Rules, arguing that the rules were promulgated in violation of NEPA. . . .

The Court of Appeals concluded that the EA was deficient because it failed to give adequate consideration to the overall environmental impact of lifting the moratorium on the cross-border operation of Mexican motor carriers. According to the Court of Appeals, FMCSA was required to consider the environmental effects of the entry of Mexican trucks because "the President's rescission of the moratorium was 'reasonably foreseeable' at the time the EA was prepared and the decision not to prepare an EIS was made." [T]he Court of Appeals remanded the case for preparation of a full EIS. . . .

II

. . . Under NEPA, an agency is required to provide an EIS only if it will be undertaking a "major Federal actio[n]," which "significantly affect[s] the quality of the human environment." 42 U.S.C. §4332(2)(C). Under applicable CEQ regulations, "[m]ajor Federal action" is defined to "includ[e] actions with effects that may be major and which are potentially subject to Federal control and responsibility." 40 CFR §1508.18 (2003). "Effects" is defined to "include: (a) Direct effects, which are caused by the action and occur at the same time and place," and "(b) Indirect effects, which are caused by the action and are later in time or farther removed in distance, but are still reasonably foreseeable." §1508.8. Thus, the relevant question is whether the increase in cross-border operations of Mexican motor carriers, with the correlative release of emissions by Mexican trucks, is an "effect" of FMCSA's issuance of the [rules]; if not, FMCSA's failure to address these effects in its EA did not violate NEPA. . . .

B

[The Court rejected an argument that the agency failed to consider sufficient alternatives because it had not been raised in comments on the Draft EIS.] With this point aside, respondents have only one complaint with respect to the EA: It did not take into account the environmental effects of increased cross-border operations of Mexican motor carriers. Respondents' argument that FMCSA was required to consider these effects is simple. Under §350, FMCSA is barred from expending any funds to process or review any applications by Mexican motor carriers until FMCSA implemented a variety of specific application and safety-monitoring requirements for Mexican carriers. This expenditure bar makes it impossible for any Mexican motor carrier to receive authorization to operate within the United States until FMCSA issued the regulations challenged here. The promulgation of the regulations, the argument goes, would "caus[e]" the entry of Mexican trucks (and hence also cause any emissions such trucks would produce), and the entry of the trucks is "reasonably foreseeable." 40 CFR §1508.8 (2003). Thus, the argument concludes, under the relevant CEQ regulations, FMCSA must take these emissions into account in its EA when evaluating whether to produce an EIS.

Respondents' argument, however, overlooks a critical feature of this case: FMCSA has no ability to countermand the President's lifting of the moratorium or otherwise categorically to exclude Mexican motor carriers from operating within the United States. To be sure, §350 did restrict the ability of FMCSA to authorize cross-border operations of Mexican motor carriers, but Congress did not otherwise modify FMCSA's statutory mandates. In particular, FMCSA remains subject to the mandate . . . that FMCSA "*shall* register a person to provide transportation . . . as a motor carrier if [it] finds that the person is willing and able to comply with" the safety and financial responsibility requirements established by DOT. (Emphasis added.) Under FMCSA's entirely reasonable reading of this provision, it must certify *any* motor carrier that can show that it is willing and able to comply with the various substantive requirements for safety and financial responsibility contained in DOT regulations; only the moratorium prevented it from doing so for Mexican motor carriers before 2001. . . .

Respondents must rest, then, on a particularly unyielding variation of "but for" causation, where an agency's action is considered a cause of an environmental effect even when the agency has no authority to prevent the effect. However, a "but for" causal relationship is insufficient to make an agency responsible for a particular effect under NEPA and the relevant regulations. . . . As this Court held in Metropolitan Edison Co. v. People Against Nuclear Energy, 460 U.S. 766, 774 (1983), NEPA requires "a reasonably close causal relationship" between the environmental effect and the alleged cause. The Court analogized this requirement to the "familiar doctrine of proximate cause from tort law." *Ibid.* . . .

Also, inherent in NEPA and its implementing regulations is a "rule of reason," which ensures that agencies determine whether and to what extent to prepare an EIS based on the usefulness of any new potential information to the decisionmaking process. Where the preparation of an EIS would serve "no purpose" in light of NEPA's regulatory scheme as a whole, no rule of reason worthy of that title would require an agency to prepare an EIS.

In these circumstances, the underlying policies behind NEPA and Congress' intent, as informed by the "rule of reason," make clear that the causal connection between FMCSA's issuance of the proposed regulations and the entry of the Mexican trucks is insufficient to make FMCSA responsible under NEPA to consider the environmental effects of the entry. The NEPA EIS requirement serves two purposes. First, "[i]t ensures that the agency, in reaching its decision, will have available, and will carefully consider, detailed information concerning significant environmental impacts." *Robertson*, 490 U.S., at 349. Second, it "guarantees that the relevant information will be made available to the larger audience that may also play a role in both the decisionmaking process and the implementation of that decision." *Ibid.* Requiring FMCSA to consider the environmental effects of the entry of Mexican trucks would fulfill neither of these statutory purposes. Since FMCSA has no ability categorically to prevent the cross-border operations of Mexican motor carriers, the environmental impact of the cross-border operations would have no effect on FMCSA's decisionmaking—FMCSA simply lacks the power to act on whatever information might be contained in the EIS.

Similarly, the informational purpose is not served. The "informational role" of an EIS is to "giv[e] the public the assurance that the agency 'has indeed considered environmental concerns in its decisionmaking process,' Baltimore Gas & Electric Co. [v. Natural Resources Defense Council 462 U.S. 87, 97 (1983)], and, perhaps more significantly, provid[e] a springboard for public comment" in the agency decisionmaking process itself, *ibid.* The purpose here is to ensure that the "larger audience," *ibid.*, can provide input as necessary to the agency making the relevant decisions. See 40 CFR §1500.1(c) (2003) ("NEPA's purpose is not to generate paperwork—even excellent paperwork—but to foster excellent action. The NEPA process is intended to help public officials make decisions that are based on understanding of environmental consequences, and take actions that protect, restore, and enhance the environment"); §1502.1 ("The primary purpose of an environmental impact statement is to serve as an action-forcing device to insure that the policies and goals defined in the Act are infused into the ongoing programs and actions of the Federal Government"). But here, the "larger audience" can have no impact on FMCSA's decisionmaking, since, as just noted, FMCSA simply could not act on whatever input this "larger audience" could provide.

It would not, therefore, satisfy NEPA's "rule of reason" to require an agency to prepare a full EIS due to the environmental impact of an action it could not refuse to perform. Put another way, the legally relevant cause of the entry of the Mexican trucks is *not* FMCSA's action, but instead the actions of the President in lifting the moratorium and those of Congress in granting the President this authority while simultaneously limiting FMCSA's discretion. . . .

NOTES AND QUESTIONS ON *PUBLIC CITIZEN*

1. *Environmental assessments.* As the Court explains, agencies sometimes first prepare a shorter analysis called an Environmental Assessment (EA) to determine whether the environmental impacts of the proposed action are significant enough to warrant the time and expense of preparing an EIS. *See* DANIEL R. MANDELKER, NEPA LAW AND LITIGATION §7.11 (2006). If the agency decides not, it issues a Finding of No Significant Impact (FONSI), which is a final agency action subject to judicial review. EA/FONSI decisions have been the subject of considerable NEPA litigation. Note that even if an agency decides not to prepare an EIS, the EA generates more environmental information about the proposed decision than would have occurred absent NEPA.

2. *The fundamental purpose of information collection and analysis under NEPA.* Even though the Court makes clear that NEPA is a procedural rather than substantive statute, it also clarifies that information collection and analysis is not a mere technicality but is designed to fulfill a distinct purpose in federal agency decision making. Why was that purpose lacking here and how does it explain the holding? Is the Court's rationale that the environmental impact of Mexican carriers operating in the United States was not sufficiently "significant" as determined in the EA? If not, what was the rationale for the holding and how does the Court find it relates to the fundamental statutory purpose?

3. *Statutory interpretation.* An EIS is required for "major federal actions significantly affecting" the environment. First, whose "federal action" counts for this purpose? Why did not the action of the President, or the President combined with the action of the agency, trigger an EIS here? *See* Public Citizen v. U.S. Trade Representative, 5 F.3d 549, 554 (D.C. Cir. 1993) (holding that actions by the President are not "final agency action" subject to judicial review under the APA). Second, how does the Court interpret the word "affecting"?

4. *Whether versus when an EIS is required.* Closely related to the issue of *whether* there is a "major federal action significantly affecting the environment" is the issue of *when* in the sequence of agency decision making an "action" has become sufficiently concrete to require NEPA compliance, and to justify the time and effort necessary to prepare an EIS. If NEPA requires information too soon, before an agency faces a decision, it may result in significant unnecessary effort; but

if information comes too late, key decisions may have been made or resources committed before the information can be useful. In Kleppe v. Sierra Club, 427 U.S. 390 (1976), the Supreme Court rejected a claim that the government was required to prepare a "comprehensive environmental impact statement" on coal leasing in the Northern Great Plains region based on an "interim" study that assessed the potential social, economic, and environmental impacts from resource development in a multi-state region. The Department of the Interior had prepared a programmatic EIS on its national coal leasing program, and site-specific EISs evaluating individual leasing decisions, but argued that there was not yet a plan for a regional leasing program, and therefore no major federal "action" sufficient to trigger an EIS. Instead, it argued that, through the interim study, it was merely "contemplating" a regional leasing program. The Supreme Court agreed:

> Respondents can prevail only if there has been a report or recommendation on a proposal for major federal action with respect to the Northern Great Plains region. Our statement of the relevant facts shows there has been none; instead, all proposals are for actions of either local or national scope.
>
> The local actions are the decisions by the various petitioners to issue a lease, approve a mining plan, issue a right-of-way permit, or take other action to allow private activity at some point within the region identified by respondents. . . .
>
> But there is no evidence in the record of an action or a proposal for an action of regional scope. The District Court, in fact, expressly found that there was no existing or proposed plan or program on the part of the Federal Government for the regional development of the area described in respondents' complaint. . . .
>
> Quite apart from the fact that the statutory language requires an impact statement only in the event of a proposed action, respondents' desire for a regional environmental impact statement cannot be met for practical reasons. In the absence of a proposal for a regional plan of development, there is nothing that could be the subject of the analysis envisioned by the statute for an impact statement. Section 102(2)(C) requires that an impact statement contain, in essence a detailed statement of the expected adverse environmental consequences of an action, the resource commitments involved in it, and the alternatives to it. Absent an overall plan for regional development, it is impossible to predict the level of coal-related activity that will occur in the region identified by respondents, and thus impossible to analyze the environmental consequences and the resource commitments involved in, and the alternatives to, such activity. A regional plan would define fairly precisely the scope and limits of the proposed development of the region. Where no such plan exists, any attempt to produce an impact statement would be little more than a study along the lines of the [existing interim study], containing estimates of potential development and attendant environmental consequences. There would be no factual predicate for the production of an environmental impact statement of the type envisioned by NEPA.

427 U.S. at 399-402. How does this reasoning relate to the Supreme Court's later decision in *Public Citizen*? Do both cases hold that an EIS is required only when it will actually influence agency decisions? The opposite danger, of course, is that any EIS might come too late to effectively influence key environmental decisions. Should a regional EIS have been required if:

  a. The Interior Department had not prepared a national programmatic EIS?
  b. The national programmatic EIS provided little or no information about the cumulative impacts of coals leases on rivers in the Northern Great Plains or other large regions with multiple mining operations?

c. The agency had sent copies of the interim study to each federal manager responsible for coal leasing in the Northern Great Plains with instructions to minimize the environmental impacts identified as serious in the statement?

d. The agency had sent the interim study to each such federal manager, and the plan identified which portions of the Northern Great Plans leasing were "open" for coal leasing and which were off limits?

5. *Mitigation authority.* The Court says "FMCSA has no statutory authority to impose or enforce emissions controls or to establish environmental requirements unrelated to motor carrier safety." Should that matter? The CEQ regulations require agencies to include in an EIS "reasonable alternatives not within the jurisdiction of the lead agency," 40 C.F.R. §1502.14, under the theory that information in the EIS might inform the decisions of other actors with authority to prevent or reduce environmental impacts—in this case, the President in deciding whether to lift the moratorium.

b. What Information Must an EIS Consider?

Once an agency or court determines that there is a major federal action that may significantly affect the environment, thus triggering an EIS, how should the agency evaluate the impacts? An EIS typically involves substantial uncertainty and judgment, because it estimates the future impacts of a decision that has not yet been made. It also has to make some assumptions about how much of the project impact can be, and will be, mitigated through various regulatory and other requirements not tied directly to NEPA. The following case addresses how agencies should handle those problems.

i. What Environmental Effects Must Be Considered, and How?

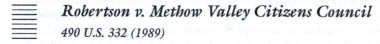

Robertson v. Methow Valley Citizens Council
490 U.S. 332 (1989)

JUSTICE STEVENS delivered the opinion of the Court.

We granted certiorari to decide two questions of law. As framed by petitioners, they are:

"1. Whether the National Environmental Policy Act requires federal agencies to include in each environmental impact statement: (a) a fully developed plan to mitigate environmental harm; and (b) a 'worst case' analysis of potential environmental harm if relevant information concerning significant environmental effects is unavailable or too costly to obtain.

"2. Whether the Forest Service may issue a special use permit for recreational use of national forest land in the absence of a fully developed plan to mitigate environmental harm."

. . .

I

The Forest Service is authorized by statute to manage the national forests for "outdoor recreation, range, timber, watershed, and wildlife and fish purposes." Pursuant to that authorization, the Forest Service has issued "special use" permits for the operation of approximately 170 Alpine and Nordic ski areas on federal lands.

The Forest Service permit process involves three separate stages. The Forest Service first examines the general environmental and financial feasibility of a proposed project and decides whether to issue a special use permit. Because that decision is a "major Federal action" within the meaning of NEPA, it must be preceded by the preparation of an Environmental Impact Statement (EIS). If the Service decides to issue a permit, it then proceeds to select a developer, formulate the basic terms of the arrangement with the selected party, and issue the permit. The special use permit does not, however, give the developer the right to begin construction. In a final stage of review, the Service evaluates the permittee's "master plan" for development, construction, and operation of the project. Construction may begin only after an additional environmental analysis (although it is not clear that a second EIS need always be prepared) and final approval of the developer's master plan. This case arises out of the Forest Service's decision to issue a special use permit authorizing the development of a major destination Alpine ski resort at Sandy Butte in the North Cascade Mountains.

. . .

In 1978, Methow Recreation, Inc. (MRI), applied for a special use permit to develop and operate its proposed "Early Winters Ski Resort" on Sandy Butte and an 1,165-acre parcel of land it had acquired adjacent to the National Forest. The proposed development would make use of approximately 3,900 acres of Sandy Butte; would entice visitors to travel long distances to stay at the resort for several days at a time; and would stimulate extensive commercial and residential growth in the vicinity to accommodate both vacationers and staff.

In response to MRI's application, the Forest Service, in cooperation with state and county officials, prepared an EIS known as the Early Winters Alpine Winter Sports Study (Early Winters Study or Study). The stated purpose of the EIS was "to provide the information required to evaluate the potential for skiing at Early Winters" and "to assist in making a decision whether to issue a Special Use Permit for downhill skiing on all or a portion of approximately 3,900 acres of National Forest System land." . . .

The Early Winters Study is a printed document containing almost 150 pages of text and 12 appendices. It evaluated five alternative levels of development of Sandy Butte that might be authorized, the lowest being a "no action" alternative and the highest being development of a 16-lift ski area able to accommodate 10,500 skiers at one time. The Study considered the effect of each level of development on water resources, soil, wildlife, air quality, vegetation, and visual quality, as well as land use and transportation in the Methow Valley, probable demographic shifts, the economic market for skiing and other summer and winter recreational activities in the Valley, and the energy requirements for the ski area and related developments. The Study's discussion of possible impacts was not limited to on-site effects, but also, as required by Council on Environmental Quality (CEQ) regulations, *see* 40 CFR §1502.16(b) (1987), addressed "off-site impacts that each alternative might have on community facilities, socio-economic and other environmental conditions in the Upper Methow Valley." As to off-site effects, the Study explained that "due to the uncertainty of where other public and private lands may become developed," it is difficult to evaluate off-site impacts, and thus the document's analysis is necessarily "not site-specific." Finally, the Study outlined certain steps that might be taken to mitigate adverse effects, both on Sandy Butte and in the neighboring Methow Valley, but indicated that these proposed steps are merely conceptual and "will be made more specific as part of the design and implementation stages of the planning process."

The effects of the proposed development on air quality and wildlife received particular attention in the Study. In the chapter on "Environmental Consequences," the first subject discussed is air quality. As is true of other subjects, the discussion included an analysis of cumulative impacts over several years resulting from actions on other lands as well as from the development of Sandy Butte itself. The Study concluded that although the construction, maintenance, and operation of the proposed ski area "will not have a measurable effect on existing or future air quality," the off-site development of private land under all five alternatives—including the "no action" alternative—"will have a significant effect on air quality during severe meteorological inversion periods." The burning of wood for space heat, the Study explained, would constitute the primary cause of diminished air quality, and the damage would increase incrementally with each of the successive levels of proposed development. The Study cautioned that without efforts to mitigate these effects, even under the "no action" alternative, the increase in automobile, fireplace, and wood stove use would reduce air quality below state standards, but added that "[t]he numerous mitigation measures discussed" in the Study "will greatly reduce the impacts presented by the model."

In its discussion of air-quality mitigation measures, the EIS identified actions that could be taken by the county government to mitigate the adverse effects of development, as well as those that the Forest Service itself could implement at the construction stage of the project. The Study suggested that Okanogan County develop an air quality management plan, requiring weatherization of new buildings, limiting the number of wood stoves and fireplaces, and adopting monitoring and enforcement measures. In addition, the Study suggested that the Forest Service require that the master plan include procedures to control dust and to comply with smoke management practices.

In its discussion of adverse effects on area wildlife, the EIS concluded that no endangered or threatened species would be affected by the proposed development and that the only impact on sensitive species was the probable loss of a pair of spotted owls and their progeny. With regard to other wildlife, the Study considered the impact on 75 different indigenous species and predicted that within a decade after development vegetational change and increased human activity would lead to a decrease in population for 31 species, while causing an increase in population for another 24 species on Sandy Butte. Two species, the pine marten and nesting goshawk, would be eliminated altogether from the area of development.

In a comment in response to the draft EIS, the Washington Department of Game voiced a special concern about potential losses to the State's largest migratory deer herd, which uses the Methow Valley as a critical winter range and as its migration route. The state agency estimated that the total population of mule deer in the area most likely to be affected was "better than 30,000 animals" and that "the ultimate impact on the Methow deer herd could exceed a 50 percent reduction in numbers." The agency asserted that "Okanogan County residents place a great deal of importance on the area's deer herd." In addition, it explained that hunters had "harvested" 3,247 deer in the Methow Valley area in 1981, and that, since in 1980 hunters on average spent $1,980 for each deer killed in Washington, they had contributed over $6 million to the State's economy in 1981. Because the deer harvest is apparently proportional to the size of the herd, the state agency predicted that "Washington business can expect to lose over $3 million annually from reduced recreational opportunity." The Forest Service's own analysis of the impact on the deer herd was more modest. It first concluded that the actual operation of the ski hill would have only a "minor" direct impact on the herd, but then recognized that the off-site effect of the development "would noticeably reduce numbers of deer in the Methow [Valley] with any alternative." Although its estimate indicated a possible 15 percent decrease in the size of the herd, it summarized the State's contrary view in the text of the EIS, and stressed that off-site effects are difficult to estimate due to uncertainty concerning private development.

As was true of its discussion of air quality, the EIS also described both on-site and off-site mitigation measures. Among possible on-site mitigation possibilities, the Study recommended locating runs, ski lifts, and roads so as to minimize interference with wildlife, restricting access to selected roads during fawning season, and further examination of the effect of the development on mule deer migration routes. Off-site options discussed in the Study included the use of zoning and tax incentives to limit development on deer winter range and migration routes, encouragement of conservation easements, and acquisition and management by local government of critical tracts of land. As with the measures suggested for mitigating the off-site effects on air quality, the proposed options were primarily directed to steps that might be taken by state and local government.

Ultimately, the Early Winters Study recommended the issuance of a permit for development at the second highest level considered—a 16-lift ski area able to accommodate 8,200 skiers at one time. On July 5, 1984, the Regional Forester decided to issue a special use permit as recommended by the Study. In his decision, the Regional Forester found that no major adverse effects would result directly from the federal action, but that secondary effects could include a degradation of existing air quality and a reduction of mule deer winter range. He therefore directed the supervisor of the Okanogan National Forest, both independently and in cooperation with local officials, to identify and implement certain mitigating measures.

Four organizations (respondents) . . . brought this action. . . . Their principal claim was that the Early Winters Study did not satisfy the requirements of NEPA. With the consent of the parties, the case was assigned to a United States Magistrate [who upheld the EIS].

Concluding that the Early Winters Study was inadequate as a matter of law, the Court of Appeals reversed. The court held that the Forest Service could not rely on "the implementation of mitigation measures" to support its conclusion that the impact on the mule deer would be minor, "since not only has the effectiveness of these mitigation measures not yet been assessed, but the mitigation measures themselves have yet to be developed." It then added that if the agency had difficulty obtaining adequate information to make a reasoned assessment of the environmental impact on the herd, it had a duty to make a so called "worst case analysis." Such an analysis is "formulated on the basis of available information, using reasonable projections of the worst possible consequences of a proposed action."

The court found a similar defect in the EIS's treatment of air quality. Since the EIS made it clear that commercial development in the Methow Valley will result in violations of state air-quality standards unless effective mitigation measures are put in place by the local governments and the private developer, the Court of Appeals concluded that the Forest Service had an affirmative duty to "develop the necessary mitigation measures *before* the permit is granted." The court . . . read the statute as imposing a substantive requirement that "action be taken to mitigate the adverse effects of major federal actions." For this reason, it concluded that "an EIS must include a thorough discussion of measures to mitigate the adverse environmental impacts of a proposed action."

. . .

II

[The Court quoted the statutory EIS requirements that appear on p. 300 *supra*.]

The statutory requirement that a federal agency contemplating a major action prepare . . . an environmental impact statement serves NEPA's "action-forcing" purpose in two important respects. It ensures that the agency, in reaching its decision, will have available, and will carefully consider, detailed information concerning significant environmental impacts; it also guarantees that the relevant information will be made available to the larger audience that may also play a role in both the decisionmaking process and the implementation of that decision.

Simply by focusing the agency's attention on the environmental consequences of a proposed project, NEPA ensures that important effects will not be overlooked or underestimated only to be discovered after resources have been committed or the die otherwise cast. Moreover, the strong precatory language of §101 of the Act and the requirement that agencies prepare detailed impact statements inevitably bring pressure to bear on agencies "to respond to the needs of environmental quality."

Publication of an EIS, both in draft and final form, also serves a larger informational role. It gives the public the assurance that the agency "has indeed considered environmental concerns in its decisionmaking process," and, perhaps more significantly, provides a springboard for public comment. Thus, in this case the final draft of the Early Winters Study reflects not only the work of the Forest Service itself, but also the critical views of the Washington State Department of Game, the Methow Valley Citizens Council, and Friends of the Earth, as well as many others, to whom copies of the draft Study were circulated. Moreover, with respect to a development such as Sandy Butte, where the adverse effects on air quality and the mule deer herd are primarily attributable to predicted off-site development that will be subject to regulation by other governmental bodies, the EIS serves the function of offering those bodies adequate notice of the expected consequences and the opportunity to plan and implement corrective measures in a timely manner.

The sweeping policy goals announced in §101 of NEPA are thus realized through a set of "action-forcing" procedures that require that agencies take a "'hard look' at environmental consequences," and that provide for broad dissemination of relevant environmental information. Although these procedures are almost certain to affect the agency's substantive decision, it is now well settled that NEPA itself does not mandate particular results, but simply prescribes the necessary process. If the adverse environmental effects of the proposed action are adequately identified and evaluated, the agency is not constrained by NEPA from deciding that other values outweigh the environmental costs. In this case, for example, it would not have violated NEPA if the Forest Service, after complying with the Act's procedural prerequisites, had decided that the benefits to be derived from downhill skiing at Sandy Butte justified the issuance of a special use permit, notwithstanding the loss of 15 percent, 50 percent, or even 100 percent of the mule deer herd. Other statutes may impose substantive environmental obligations on federal agencies, but NEPA merely prohibits uninformed—rather than unwise—agency action.

To be sure, one important ingredient of an EIS is the discussion of steps that can be taken to mitigate adverse environmental consequences. The requirement that an EIS contain a detailed discussion of possible mitigation measures flows both from the language of the Act and, more expressly, from CEQ's implementing regulations. Implicit in NEPA's demand that an agency prepare a detailed statement on "any adverse environmental effects which cannot be avoided should the proposal be implemented," is an understanding that the EIS will discuss the extent to which adverse effects can be avoided. More generally, omission of a reasonably complete discussion of possible mitigation measures would undermine the "action forcing" function of NEPA. Without such a discussion, neither the agency nor other interested groups and individuals can properly evaluate the severity of the adverse effects. An adverse effect that can be fully remedied by, for example, an inconsequential public expenditure is certainly not as serious as a similar effect that can only be modestly ameliorated through the commitment of vast public and private resources. Recognizing the importance of such a discussion in guaranteeing that the agency has taken a "hard look" at the environmental consequences of proposed federal action, CEQ regulations require that the agency discuss possible mitigation measures in defining the scope of the EIS, in discussing alternatives to the proposed action, and consequences of that action, and in explaining its ultimate decision.

There is a fundamental distinction, however, between a requirement that mitigation be discussed in sufficient detail to ensure that environmental consequences have been fairly evaluated, on the one hand, and a substantive requirement that a complete mitigation plan be actually formulated and adopted, on the other. In this case, the off-site effects on air quality and on the mule deer herd cannot be mitigated unless nonfederal government agencies take appropriate action. Since it is those state and local governmental bodies that have jurisdiction over the area in which the adverse effects need be addressed and since they have the authority to mitigate them, it would be incongruous to conclude that the Forest Service has no power to act until the local agencies have reached a final conclusion on what mitigating measures they consider necessary. Even more significantly, it would be inconsistent with NEPA's reliance on procedural mechanisms — as opposed to substantive, result-based standards — to demand the presence of a fully developed plan that will mitigate environmental harm before an agency can act.

We thus conclude that the Court of Appeals erred, first, in assuming that "NEPA requires that 'action be taken to mitigate the adverse effects of major federal actions,'" and, second, in finding that this substantive requirement entails the further duty to include in every EIS "a detailed explanation of specific measures which *will* be employed to mitigate the adverse impacts of a proposed action."

III

The Court of Appeals also concluded that the Forest Service had an obligation to make a "worst case analysis" if it could not make a reasoned assessment of the impact of the Early Winters project on the mule deer herd. Such a "worst case analysis" was required at one time by CEQ regulations, but those regulations have since been amended. Moreover, although the prior regulations may well have expressed a permissible application of NEPA, the Act itself does not mandate that uncertainty in predicting environmental harms be addressed exclusively in this manner. Accordingly, we conclude that the Court of Appeals also erred in requiring the "worst case" study.

In 1977, President Carter directed that CEQ promulgate binding regulations implementing the procedural provisions of NEPA. Exec. Order No. 11991, 3 CFR §123 (1977 Comp.). Pursuant to this Presidential order, CEQ promulgated implementing regulations. Under §1502.22 of these regulations — a provision which became known as the "worst case requirement" — CEQ provided that if certain information relevant to the agency's evaluation of the proposed action is either unavailable or too costly to obtain, the agency must include in the EIS a "worst case analysis and an indication of the probability or improbability of its occurrence." 40 CFR §1502.22 (1985). In 1986, however, CEQ replaced the "worst case" requirement with a requirement that federal agencies, in the face of unavailable information concerning a reasonably foreseeable significant environmental consequence, prepare "a summary of existing credible scientific evidence which is relevant to evaluating the adverse impacts" and prepare an "evaluation of such impacts based upon theoretical approaches or research methods generally accepted in the scientific community." 40 CFR §1502.22(b) (1987). The amended regulation thus "retains the duty to describe the consequences of a remote, but potentially severe impact, but grounds the duty in evaluation of scientific opinion rather than in the framework of a conjectural 'worst case analysis.'" 50 Fed. Reg. 32237 (1985).

The Court of Appeals recognized that the "worst case analysis" regulation has been superseded, yet held that "[t]his rescission . . . does not nullify the requirement . . . since the regulation was merely a codification of prior NEPA case law."

This conclusion, however, is erroneous in a number of respects. Most notably, review of NEPA case law reveals that the regulation, in fact, was not a codification of prior judicial decisions. The cases cited by the Court of Appeals ultimately rely on the Fifth Circuit's decision in Sierra Club v. Sigler, 695 F.2d 957 (1983). *Sigler*, however, simply recognized that the "worst case analysis" regulation codified the "judicially created principl[e]" that an EIS must "consider the probabilities of the occurrence of any environmental effects it discusses." As CEQ recognized at the time it superseded the regulation, case law prior to the adoption of the "worst case analysis" provision did require agencies to describe environmental impacts even in the face of substantial uncertainty, but did not require that this obligation necessarily be met through the mechanism of a "worst case analysis." CEQ's abandonment of the "worst case analysis" provision, therefore, is not inconsistent with any previously established judicial interpretation of the statute.

Nor are we convinced that the new CEQ regulation is not controlling simply because it was preceded by a rule that was in some respects more demanding. In Andrus v. Sierra Club, 442 U.S., at 358, we held that CEQ regulations are entitled to substantial deference. In that case we recognized that although less deference may be in order in some cases in which the "administrative guidelines" conflict "with earlier pronouncements of the agency," substantial deference is nonetheless appropriate if there appears to have been good reason for the change. Here, the amendment only came after the prior regulation had been subjected to considerable criticism. Moreover, the amendment was designed to better serve the twin functions of an EIS—requiring agencies to take a "hard look" at the consequences of the proposed action and providing important information to other groups and individuals. CEQ explained that by requiring that an EIS focus on reasonably foreseeable impacts, the new regulation "will generate information and discussion on those consequences of greatest concern to the public and of greatest relevance to the agency's decision," rather than distorting the decisionmaking process by overemphasizing highly speculative harms. In light of this well-considered basis for the change, the new regulation is entitled to substantial deference. Accordingly, the Court of Appeals erred in concluding that the Early Winters Study is inadequate because it failed to include a "worst case analysis."

* * *

V

In sum, we conclude that NEPA does not require a fully developed plan detailing what steps *will* be taken to mitigate adverse environmental impacts and does not require a "worst case analysis." . . . The judgment of the Court of Appeals is accordingly reversed, and the case is remanded for further proceedings consistent with this opinion.

It is so ordered.

NOTES AND QUESTIONS ON *ROBERTSON v. METHOW VALLEY CITIZENS COUNCIL*

1. *Information motivating action.* Even as the Court refuses to hold that NEPA requires any particular decision respecting the ski resort, it affirms that the NEPA process is "almost certain to affect the agency's substantive decision." *Robertson*, 490 U.S. at 350. If the Court is right, why is it right? The professionals in the agency might, because of their sense of professionalism, respond to significant information once they assemble it. Public disclosure of adverse environmental impacts might create sufficient political pressure to force the agency to mitigate or avoid significant environmental impacts. A third possibility is that the agency decisions will remain subject to judicial review. The agency will have to explain why it made its decision to a court. Perhaps information about negative environmental impacts makes it harder to provide non-arbitrary rationales for carrying out decisions likely to seriously harm the environment. Information in the EIS may also identify potential violations of other laws.

In spite of the Forest Service's victory in the *Methow Valley* case, the ski resort was not built. The Ninth Circuit found the EIS inadequate not only with respect to the issues raised in the Supreme Court, but on other grounds as well. As a result, the Forest Service had to revise its impact statement even after prevailing in the Supreme Court. Environmentalists continued to press their case. Eventually, the developer abandoned the plan to build the resort. Does this suggest that NEPA is working well or badly? *See* Robert W. Adler, *In Defense of NEPA: The Case of the Legacy Parkway*, 26 J. LAND, RESOURCES & ENVTL. L. 297 (2006) (addressing use of NEPA to improve as opposed to stop projects).

2. *What sort of analysis?* Does NEPA mandate formal cost-benefit analysis, in which agencies must explicitly compare, in monetary terms, the economic costs of implementing a particular action with the economic benefits to be derived, and to approve the action only where the ratio of benefits to costs is positive? Nothing in the statute says so expressly. *See* 42 U.S.C. §4332. Some courts have imposed an obligation to consider environmental costs, while others have simply overseen the content of the analysis. *See, e.g.*, Sierra Club v. Sigler, 695 F.2d 957, 974 (5th Cir. 1983) (requiring worst case analysis and analysis of the environmental costs of digging a deeper channel); Johnston v. Davis, 698 F.2d 1088 (9th Cir. 1983) (approving fairly cursory analysis of some environmental costs, but requiring the Soil Conservation Service to take the artificially low discount rate it used in evaluating its proposed project into account).

3. *Public participation.* Public participation in creating the information also plays a role in shaping decisions. NEPA creates several opportunities for the public and non-federal government entities to participate in shaping the analysis. Once an agency decides to prepare an EIS, it usually engages in a "scoping" process to determine which issues the EIS will focus upon. *See* Mandelker, *supra*, §7:12. Agencies typically solicit the views of other government agencies and the public in this process. *See* 40 C.F.R. §1501.7. *But see* Northwest Coalition for Alternatives to Pesticides v. Lyng, 844 F.2d 588 (9th Cir. 1988) (finding no prejudicial error when agency failed to notify environmental groups). Agencies also solicit public comment once they have prepared a draft environmental impact statement. 40

C.F.R. §1503.1(4). Does it appear that local and state agencies took advantage of these opportunities in the *Methow Valley* case?

The agency responds to the public comments in writing the final environmental impact statement. 40 C.F.R. §1503.4. The process culminates in a "record of decision" that explains the decision, the alternatives considered under NEPA, and whether the agency has used all practicable means to minimize environmental harm. 40 C.F.R. §1505.2. CEQ regulations also require the agency to explain why any measure capable of mitigating harm has not been adopted. 40 C.F.R. §1505.2(c). Given this last requirement, are agencies likely to seriously engage in mitigation even after *Methow Valley*?

4. *Mitigation.* Suppose that the environmental impact statement had fully discussed the environmental impacts, but failed to discuss how government officials might mitigate those impacts. Would such a statement pass muster? In this case, most of the mitigation measures discussed required local government action. Suppose an EIS identified mitigation measures that the federal government could take. Would NEPA require the federal government to take such measures if they would avoid serious environmental impacts? May the agency assume that environmental impacts are trivial, because it can envision mitigation measures that would make it trivial, without their actual adoption?

Note that under some other statutes, such as section 404 of the Clean Water Act (addressed in more detail below) and the "reasonable and prudent alternatives" requirement of the Endangered Species Act, agencies must do more than "consider" potential mitigation; they must adopt feasible mitigation measures to reduce project impacts.

a.   *Clean Water Act.* In order to preserve wetlands without completely stopping all development where wetlands exist, EPA has historically applied a structured "sequencing" approach to use of mitigation and alternatives:

> In the context of existing wetlands regulation, mitigation generally refers to avoidance, minimization, and compensation. These steps are frequently applied in a sequential manner. First, a party seeking a permit for a project that affects wetlands must demonstrate that the least environmentally damaging alternative will be used. Second, the permit applicant must develop a plan to minimize the environmental harm from any unavoidable impacts. For example, the applicant might minimize the impact of a project by scheduling construction in a manner that would reduce interference with spawning or nesting seasons. Finally, the applicant must compensate for or offset any harm done to wetland functions and values which is not avoided or minimized.

Royal C. Gardner, *Banking on Entrepreneurs: Wetlands, Mitigation Banking, and Takings*, 81 IOWA L. REV. 527, 535 (1995-96). *See* 40 C.F.R. §230.10. Why does the agency give priority to avoidance of harm, rather than mitigation? Is the requirement that permit applicants employ the least damaging alternative sufficient to meet the statutory goal of avoiding harms to aquatic ecosystems? Is avoidance more likely to achieve this goal than minimization of harm and compensation?

In the 1990s, the federal government adopted a policy of "no-net loss of wetlands." *See* WHITE HOUSE OFFICE ON ENVIRONMENTAL POLICY, PROTECTING AMERICA'S WETLANDS: A FAIR, FLEXIBLE AND EFFECTIVE APPROACH 4 (Aug. 24, 1993); *Memorandum of Agreement Between the Environmental Protection*

Agency and the Department of the Army Concerning the Determination of Mitigation Under the Clean Water Act Section 404(b)(1) Guidelines, 55 Fed. Reg. 9210, 9211 (Mar. 12, 1990). Does the sequencing approach to mitigation and alternatives adequately serve this no-net-loss goal? Does a shift from a no-loss to a no-net-loss goal have any implications for the appropriateness of sequencing? In 2008, EPA and the Army Corps of Engineers adopted comprehensive new regulations on compensatory mitigation under section 404.

b. *Endangered Species Act.* The Endangered Species Act also employs a concept of mandatory mitigation. Recall that the law as originally enacted prohibited private parties from "taking" an endangered species. But Congress amended the statute in 1982 to authorize the taking of species incidental to "otherwise lawful activity." 16 U.S.C. §1539(a)(1)(B). The United States Fish and Wildlife Service and the National Marine Fisheries Service can only grant an incidental take permit, as the permits authorizing takings are called, if "the applicant will, to the maximum extent practicable, minimize and mitigate the impact of such takings," 16 U.S.C. §1539(a)(2)(B)(ii), and "the taking will not appreciably reduce" the species' "likelihood of survival," 16 U.S.C. §1539(a)(2)(B)(iv). This provision authorizes habitat conservation plans, such as that used to preserve and enhance the habitat of endangered butterflies near the San Bruno Mountain area south of San Francisco, while authorizing limited development that might otherwise have violated section 9 of the Act. *See* Karen Donovan, *HCPs—Important Tools for Conserving Habitat and Species, in* ENDANGERED SPECIES ACT: LAW, POLICY, AND PERSPECTIVES 321 (Donald C. Baur & Wm. Robert Irvin eds., 2002). In spite of the introduction of statutory authority to sanction such habitat conservation plans (HCPs) through incidental take permits, the federal government only approved 38 such plans between 1982 and 1994. *Id.* at 326. The Clinton Administration greatly increased the use of HCPs by introducing a "no surprises" rule that forbids the agency issuing an incidental take permit based on an HCP from adding developmental restrictions later on. *Id.* at 326. Is such a "no surprises rule" good policy? *See* John Kostyack, *Tipping the Balance, in* ENDANGERED SPECIES ACT, *supra*, at 339-58 (arguing that it is not). Is such a policy consistent with section 10(a)(2)(C) of the Act, which requires revocation of a permit if the "permittee is not complying with" permit terms? 16 U.S.C. §1539(2)(C). *See* Spirit of the Sage Council v. Norton, 411 F.3d 225 (D.C. Cir. 2005) (dismissing challenge to a district court order suspending the no surprises rule while agency corrects procedural irregularities in its rule making).

5. *Worst case analysis.* Do you read the statutory language as requiring worse case analysis? *See Robertson*, 490 U.S. at 348. The Court traced the requirement for worst case analysis back to *Sierra Club v. Sigler*, which it characterizes as "simply" recognizing that the "worst case analysis" regulation codified the "judicially created principle" that an EIS "must consider the probabilities of the occurrences of any environmental effects." *Id.* at 355. The *Sigler* court, however, characterized its conclusion in the following way: "Because [the worst case requirement] is in

accord with the language and legislative history of NEPA and closely tracks NEPA case law, we conclude that it is not beyond the statutory minima of NEPA." Sierra Club v. Sigler, 695 F.2d 957, 971 (5th Cir. 1983). The *Sigler* court also states that NEPA's "literal language does not require a worst case analysis." *Id*. at 969. Should the Supreme Court have considered whether NEPA's legislative history and purposes require worst-case analysis? Which court was correct? Regardless of the results of this case, many environmental impact statements lead to measures that reduce a project's environmental impacts.

6. *Mitigation in state "NEPAs."* While the Court rejected a requirement to actually undertake mitigation measures under NEPA, such requirements do exist under some state environmental policy acts. For example:

> Mitigation plays a heightened role under the California Environmental Quality Act; once an environmental impact has been declared to be "significant" . . . the agency is required to find that sufficient mitigation measures have been taken to lessen the project's impact. If the agency finds that alternatives or mitigation measures are not feasible, the agency must adopt a statement of overriding considerations which states the specific reasons why "the project's benefit outweighs the unmitigated effects. . . ."

City of Carmel-by-the-Sea v. United States DOT, 123 F.3d 1142, 1164 (9th Cir. 1997).

7. *Worst case policy and uncertainty.* In almost all cases, the future environmental impacts of significant federal actions are uncertain. Also, scientific information that might help us make reasonable predictions usually has serious gaps. Given the pervasiveness of uncertainty, should worst-case analysis be mandatory?

Would your answer change if the possible impacts of decisions were very serious and the worst-case scenario helped inform the emergency planning of the police, fire fighters, medical personnel, and other disaster relief agencies? This is not an academic question. Chemical accidents killed or injured more than two thousand people between 1994 and 2004. As a result, the Clean Air Act requires chemical companies to create risk management plans to "detect and prevent or minimize" accidents. *See* 42 U.S.C. §7412(r)(7)(B)(ii). The planning requirements for larger plants include:

> A hazard assessment to assess the potential effects of an accidental release of any regulated substance. This assessment shall include an estimate of potential release quantities and a determination of downwind effects, including potential exposures to affected populations. Such assessments shall include a previous release history for the past 5 years, including the size concentration, and duration of release; and shall include an evaluation of *worst case accidental releases.* . . .

42 U.S.C. §7412(r)(7)(B)(ii)(I) (emphasis added). The Clean Air Act further requires that chemical plant operators make these plans public and share them with local officials. 42 U.S.C. §7412(r)(7)(H). The Emergency Planning and Community Right-to-Know-Act requires chemical plants to report accidental releases of extremely hazardous substances to local authorities and sets up a planning procedure for local governments to prepare to address chemical accidents. *See* 42 U.S.C. §§11001-11005.

After the World Trade Center attacks on September 11, 2001, the Bush Administration pulled this emergency planning information from the Internet, apparently from fear that terrorists would use it to select facilities to target. *See* 42 U.S.C. §7412(r)(7)(H)(ii)(I)(aa). Is this an appropriate response? Will public access increase the accountability of local officials for emergency planning? What information would prove most useful for terrorists? Should the problem of potential terrorism lead government to abandon worst-case analysis? Should it be available at public libraries, but not on the Internet?

ii. How and When Should Agencies Consider Cumulative Impacts and Alternatives to the Proposed Action?

The Council on Environmental Quality regulations governing NEPA practice, and NEPA case law, address a wide range of issues regarding what kinds of impacts agencies must address in the NEPA process, and how. Two of the most difficult and frequently encountered of these issues are cumulative impacts analysis and alternatives analysis, both of which go to the heart of the issue of how information is actually used in reaching environmental decisions.

First, Council on Environmental Quality regulations require agencies to consider the cumulative impacts of multiple or connected projects. 40 C.F.R. §§1502.16, 1508.7, 1508.8. Logging, coal mining, oil drilling, road construction and associated development, and other activities can create serious cumulative impacts, even if each individual instance of the activity appears insignificant. Information will look different depending on the scale of analysis. In considering why such consideration might be important, consider Professor Houck's comments about wetland permitting:

> Each of the some ten thousand permit applications processed each year is a localized event, taking one-half acre, three acres, twenty-one acres of wetlands, for this pier, that channel, a sand and gravel pit, or a building site. The indirect effects of even these individual takings—how much they will pollute, subside, or slowly asphyxiate their surroundings—are uncertain, and in any event will not be witnessed for years. The cumulative effects of these and similar activities—of one more marina on Galveston Bay, of one more logging road on the grizzly bear—may be far greater than the sum of the parts, and are even less susceptible to proof. Even those direct effects are disputable: The oysters may be able to survive a little more turbidity, the pelicans may relocate to another island. Or they may not.

Oliver A. Houck, *Hard Choices: The Analysis of Alternatives Under Section 404 of the Clean Water Act and Similar Environmental Laws*, 60 U. Colo. L. Rev. 773, 776 (1989).

Second, NEPA requires agencies to consider the environmental impacts of alternatives to its proposed action in the EIS. Council on Environmental Quality regulations require discussion of the no-action alternative—doing nothing. 40 C.F.R. §1502.14(d). But what other alternatives should the agency discuss? The Early Winters Study reviewed in *Robertson* considered five different alternative levels of development. In this context, the agency considered whether a smaller number of lifts serving fewer skiers (and therefore generating less traffic and surrounding development) might work. Suppose that the Forest Service proposes to authorize the cutting of five hundred trees in a forest. What alternatives should it study? Suppose that the Bureau of Land Management proposes to authorize oil drilling in a beautiful canyon. What alternatives should it study?

≡ ***Muckleshoot Indian Tribe v. U.S. Forest Service***
≡ *177 F.3d 800 (9th Cir. 1999)*

B. FLETCHER, REINHARDT, and THOMAS, Circuit Judges.

PER CURIAM.

Plaintiffs Muckleshoot Indian Tribe, Pilchuck Audubon Society, and Huckleberry Mountain Protection Society appeal the district court's grant of summary judgment on consolidated challenges to a land exchange between the United States Forest Service and Weyerhaeuser Company. Plaintiffs contend that the Forest Service violated the National Environmental Policy Act ("NEPA"). . . .

I. Background

Huckleberry Mountain, the land subject to the dispute in this case, is located in the Green River watershed in the Mt. Baker–Snoqualmie National Forest ("the Forest") in the state of Washington. The Forest contains sixteen percent of the wilderness in the Pacific Northwest. Thirteen percent (259,545 acres) of the 1,983,774 acres within the National Forest boundary are privately owned, primarily by Weyerhaeuser and other large corporations. Most of the privately-owned lands are in the southern portion of the Forest, and are intermingled with federal lands in a checkerboard pattern of ownership that remains from the federal land grants to railroads a century ago.

Motivated in large part by a desire to unify land ownership, the United States Forest Service ("the Forest Service") and Weyerhaeuser Company ("Weyerhaeuser") began negotiations for a series of land exchanges pursuant to 43 U.S.C. §1716, which authorizes the exchange of public lands within the National Forest system where "the public interest will be well served" by the exchange. In the 1980s, the Forest Service negotiated a land exchange with Weyerhaeuser and the Burlington Northern Railroad Company involving lands near Huckleberry Mountain. Under the terms of the Alpine Lakes Exchange, as it became known, the United States conveyed a total of 21,676 acres of federally-owned Forest land to Weyerhaeuser and Burlington Northern in exchange for other property owned by the two companies. In the present appeal, plaintiffs challenge another land exchange between Weyerhaeuser and the Forest Service, the Huckleberry Mountain Exchange ("the Exchange"), in which the Forest Service again traded old growth forest lands in the Huckleberry Mountain area. Many of the parcels conveyed by the Forest Service in the Alpine Lakes Exchange are near or contiguous to federal lands that are part of the Exchange at issue in this appeal.

Although land within the Huckleberry Mountain Exchange Area had been tentatively identified during the Alpine Lakes Exchange negotiations between 1984 and 1987, negotiations began anew in 1988 with a revised list of federal land under consideration for exchange. In July 1991, Weyerhaeuser and the Forest Service signed a Statement of Intent to enter into an exchange, which identified the parcels to be included in the exchange. Between 1992 and 1994, the Forest Service conducted surveys regarding wetlands, wildlife, rare plants, hazardous waste, cultural resources and other matters, and subsequently reduced the federal acreage proposed for transfer.

The Forest Service initiated public consultation and comment and developed a list of six exchange alternatives. In July 1996, the Forest Service released a draft Environmental Impact Statement ("EIS"). . . . It then conducted three open meetings in communities near the Forest. Among those who provided comments on the Draft EIS was the Muckleshoot Indian Tribe (the "Tribe").

On November 26, 1996, the Forest Service issued a final EIS after receiving comments on the draft EIS. The EIS considered three alternatives: a "no action" alternative, and two closely related exchange alternatives. Concurrently, the Forest Service issued a Record of Decision that called for an implementation of the Exchange through a modification of "Alternative No. 3" as evaluated in the EIS.

The Pilchuck Audubon Society and the Huckleberry Mountain Protection Society (collectively "the Societies") and the Tribe lodged separate appeals of the EIS and the ROD with the Office of the Regional Forester. These appeals were denied on March 7, 1997. On March 28, 1997, pursuant to the ROD, Weyerhaeuser and the Forest Service executed an exchange agreement under which Weyerhaeuser conveyed to the United States 30,253 acres of land in and around Mt. Baker National Forest in return for 4,362 acres of land in the Huckleberry Mountain area. In addition, Weyerhaeuser donated to the United States 962 acres to the Alpine Lakes Wilderness and 1,034 acres for Forest Service management. The National Forest lands that Weyerhaeuser received included old growth, commercial grade timber. The Forest Service also exchanged to Weyerhaeuser intact portions of the Huckleberry Divide Trail, a site important to the Tribe and that the Forest Service found eligible for inclusion in the National Register for Historic Preservation. Weyerhaeuser gave the Forest Service lands that were, for the most part, heavily logged and roaded. Weyerhaeuser intends to log the lands it received in the Exchange. . . .

* * *

III.   National Environmental Policy Act Claims

NEPA requires federal agencies such as the Forest Service to prepare a detailed environmental impact statement ("EIS") for "all major actions significantly affecting the quality of the human environment." An EIS must address the cumulative impacts of a project and consider adequate alternatives. . . .

The plaintiffs have raised several different claims under NEPA. The Tribe contends that the identification and analysis of cumulative environmental impacts in the Forest Service's EIS did not meet the requirements of NEPA. The Societies contend that the EIS inadequately defined the purpose and need for the Huckleberry Land Exchange as required by NEPA, and did not identify or evaluate sufficient alternatives for the exchange. We consider each of these issues in turn.

A. *Assessment of Cumulative Impacts Under NEPA*

We first address the Tribe's contention that the Forest Service failed to consider the cumulative impact of the exchange. A cumulative impact is defined as:

> [T]he impact on the environment which results from the incremental impact of the action when added to other past, present and reasonably foreseeable future actions regardless of what agency (Federal or non-Federal) or person undertakes such other actions. Cumulative impacts can result from individually minor but collectively significant actions taking place over a period of time.

40 C.F.R. §1508.7.

Regulations implementing NEPA require that a federal agency consider "[c]umulative actions, which when viewed with other proposed actions have cumulatively significant impacts and should therefore be discussed in the same impact statement." 40 C.F.R. §1508.25(a)(2).

In *City of Carmel-By-The-Sea v. U.S. Dept. of Transp.*, 123 F.3d 1142 (9th Cir. 1997), we noted that an EIS must "catalogue adequately the relevant past projects in the area." *Id.* at 1160. It must also include a "useful analysis of the cumulative impacts of past, present and future projects." *Id.* This requires "discussion of how [future] projects together with the proposed . . . project will affect [the environment]." *Id.* The EIS must analyze the combined effects of the actions in sufficient detail to be "useful to the decisionmaker in deciding whether, or how, to alter the program to lessen cumulative impacts." *Id.* at 1160 (internal citations omitted). Detail is therefore required in describing the cumulative effects of a proposed action with other proposed actions. . . .

The Tribe contends that the EIS gives inadequate consideration to the cumulative impacts of logging on the 1984 Alpine Lakes Exchange lands, of existing logging and other disturbances in the Green River watershed, and of a future land exchange with the Plum Creek Timber Company that involves lands in the same vicinity as the Huckleberry Mountain Exchange. The district court held that the Forest Service did not need to consider the 1984 Alpine Lake Exchange because it was part of the baseline environment and, as such, was considered in the EIS for the Mt. Baker Snoqualmie National Forest Land and Resource Management Plan, as amended by the 1994 Northwest Forest Plan ("LRMP"). The district court also held that the Plum Creek exchange was "too uncertain" to require a discussion of cumulative effects. We do not agree with those conclusions.

Appellees urge that because the final EIS for the Huckleberry Exchange is tiered to the LRMP, it sufficiently analyzes the cumulative impacts of the Exchange.

"Tiering" is defined as:

> [T]he coverage of general matters in broader environmental impact statements (such as national program or policy statements) with subsequent narrower statements or environmental analyses (such as regional or basinwide program statements or ultimately site-specific statements) incorporating by reference the general discussions and concentrating solely on the issues specific to the statement subsequently prepared.

40 C.F.R. §1508.28; *see also* 40 C.F.R. §1502.20.

We have previously interpreted the regulations to allow tiering only to another environmental impact statement. The Huckleberry Exchange EIS is tiered erroneously to the Forest Plan, not the EIS for the Forest Plan. Our review of the Forest Plan and its accompanying EIS reveals that those documents do not account for the specific impacts of the Exchange and do not remedy the Forest Service's failure to account for the impacts of the Exchange in the Huckleberry Exchange EIS. *See, e.g., Resources Ltd. v. Robertson*, 35 F.3d 1300, 1306 (9th Cir. 1993) ("specific analysis is better done when a specific development action is to be taken, not at the programmatic level").

The LRMP EIS, prepared in 1990, was prepared before the Huckleberry Exchange lands were identified with any certainty. The concept of the Huckleberry exchange was mentioned only in a pool of possible projects that would help meet the goals of the Forest Plan. There was no detail concerning those projects and their impacts. The proposed Exchange simply was not concrete enough to allow for adequate analysis. Moreover, the LRMP EIS did not analyze the impact of increased logging on the parcels that had been transferred out of federal ownership in the 1984 Alpine Lakes Exchange. Many of those parcels are in the same vicinity as the old growth forest lands the Forest Service transferred to Weyerhaeuser. If we were to adopt the Forest Service's approach, the cumulative impacts of land exchanges would escape environmental review.

The problem is compounded by the very general and one-sided analysis of the cumulative impact information that the Huckleberry Exchange EIS does contain. While the district court was correct in observing that there are "twelve sections entitled 'cumulative effects,'" these sections merely provide very broad and general statements devoid of specific, reasoned conclusions.

For example, the cumulative impact statement regarding the impact of alternatives two and three on natural vegetation simply indicates the amount of land to be exchanged, and whether or not the land will be subject to commercial harvest. It then concludes:

> Under Alternatives two and three, the Forest Service would manage for non-harvest uses an additional 16,735 (16,876 under Alternative 3) acres of young forest and non-forest vegetation. Most of this acreage . . . would over time develop greater species diversity and stand structure.

The statement notably contains no evaluation whatsoever of the impact on natural resources of timber harvesting on the lands transferred to Weyerhaeuser, nor does it assess the possible impacts that such harvesting could have upon surrounding areas. The statement focuses solely on the beneficial impact the exchange will have on lands received by the Forest Service. All of those described benefits are contingent on appropriate Forest Service action and funds to promote the recovery of the harvested lands that it will acquire. This lopsided analysis is repeated in virtually every cumulative impact statement throughout the EIS.

We hold that the cumulative impact statements that are provided in the EIS are far too general and one-sided to meet the NEPA requirements. . . .

The appellees also attempt to tier the Exchange EIS to the Green River Watershed Report to cure the deficiencies of the cumulative impact analysis of the

Exchange EIS. Such reliance is impermissible under the NEPA regulations, which only permit tiering to prior EIS's. 40 C.F.R. §§1502.20 and 1508.28.

The analysis in the Green River Watershed Report, even if appropriately allowed as a tiering document, demonstrates the need for a more thorough cumulative impact analysis. The Green River Watershed Report explicitly states that the watershed area was degraded by logging prior to the Huckleberry exchange. The Report cautions that future exchanges should be sensitive to the need to avoid additional environmental degradation. Moreover, the Report covers only a portion of the area affected by the Exchange. The Huckleberry EIS should have analyzed the cumulative effects of the logging incident to this exchange upon that damaged watershed area in conjunction with the other degradation mentioned in that document. The EIS performs no such analysis. It fails to evaluate the near term impacts of Weyerhaeuser's logging of old growth timber in any meaningful fashion. Therefore, even if the Exchange EIS could be tiered to the Watershed Report, the Watershed Report is only the starting point for the required analysis. It does not fill the gaps in the Exchange EIS.

Plaintiffs also contend that the EIS failed to analyze adequately the cumulative effects of a future land exchange involving Plum Creek Timber Company that, according to plaintiffs, was "reasonably foreseeable" at the time the Exchange EIS was prepared. An agency must analyze the incremental impact of the action "when added to other past, present, and *reasonably foreseeable* future actions. . . ." 40 C.F.R. §1508.7 (emphasis added). The district court determined that the Plum Creek Exchange was too speculative to require analysis.

Our review of the record suggests that the Plum Creek transaction was not remote or highly speculative. Rather, it was reasonably foreseeable and it should have been considered in the EIS. A summary of the proposed Plum Creek transaction already had been prepared by the Forest Service by 1995. On June 27, 1996, five months before the Huckleberry EIS was issued, Secretary of Agriculture Dan Glickman formally announced the proposed Plum Creek Exchange to the public.

Moreover, the record reflects that the Forest Service was all but certain that the National Forest lands in the upper Green River Basin would be included in the Plum Creek exchange. . . .

Given the virtual certainty of the transaction and its scope, the Forest Service was required under NEPA to evaluate the cumulative impacts of the Plum Creek transaction. In the absence of an EIS that takes into consideration the cumulative effects of the planned land sales and resultant environmental impacts, we cannot conclude that the Forest Service took the necessary "hard look" at the cumulative envionmental impacts of the Huckleberry Exchange.

Nor can the Forest Service's inappropriate use of tiering meet the requirements of the NEPA. While the LRMP EIS, which was completed in 1990, does mention the Plum Creek Exchange, it expressly indicates that at that time, its effects were too speculative to gauge. The tiering of documents that do not perform the required cumulative impact analysis falls far short of the standard articulated in *Neighbors of Cuddy Mountain*. In 1996, when the Huckleberry Exchange EIS was completed, the Plum Creek Exchange had moved well beyond mere speculation. The Forest Service abused its discretion in ignoring the impacts of that exchange.

B. Failure to Consider an Adequate Range of Alternatives

We also agree with the Societies' contention that the Forest Service violated NEPA by failing to consider a range of appropriate alternatives to the proposed exchange.

The Societies first contend that the EIS fails to properly specify the underlying purpose and need to which the proposal is responding as required by NEPA regulations. *See* 40 C.F.R. §1502.13 (requiring a statement that "shall briefly specify the underlying purpose and need to which the agency is responding in proposing the alternatives including the proposed action").

The EIS states that the purpose and need for the proposal is to "consolidate ownership and enhance future resource conservation and management by exchanging parcels of National Forest System and Weyerhaeuser land." The Societies argue that this narrowly stated purpose fails to meet the requirements of section 1502.13 as it was interpreted in *City of Carmel*, where we held that "[t]he stated goal of a project necessarily dictates the range of reasonable alternatives and an agency cannot define its objectives in unreasonably narrow terms." 123 F.3d at 1155.

While the statement of purpose contained in the EIS, taken in complete isolation, would appear too narrow to meet the standards articulated in *City of Carmel*, we note that the EIS expressly incorporates it within the LRMP's stated purpose of "creat[ing] consolidated land ownership patterns where consistent management mandates, policies and objectives apply across large blocks of land." Because the EIS's statement of purpose makes clear that an exchange of land with Weyerhaeuser would foster the desirable consolidation of ownership of the checkerboard land holdings, it is reasonable and should be upheld. *See Citizens Against Burlington v. Busey*, 938 F.2d 190, 196 (D.C. Cir. 1991) (holding that agency's stated objective should be upheld where reasonable).

However, in the course of evaluating the options that would best achieve the stated purpose of the proposed action, the Forest Service failed to consider an adequate range of alternatives. The EIS considered only a no action alternative along with two virtually identical alternatives. The selected alternative, Alternative 3, differed from Alternative 2 only in that it re-labeled a portion of the lands Weyerhaeuser transferred to the Forest Service a donation rather than an exchange, and added 141 acres of donated land.

In addressing the claims that the Forest Service erred in failing to mitigate the possible harms of the exchange, the district court concluded that there was no evidence that Weyerhaeuser would agree to plaintiffs' proposed alternative of the Forest Service purchasing the Weyerhaeuser land rather than exchanging for it and that there was no evidence that the agency failed to consider, as required by *Resources Ltd., Inc. v. Robertson*, 35 F.3d 1300, 1305 (9th Cir. 1994), "a reasonably full range of alternatives."

Our review of the record, reinforced by the statements of Weyerhaeuser's counsel at oral argument, compel us to reach the opposite conclusion. In this case, the Forest Service, after a process of "scoping" to collect the views of the public, initially considered five action alternatives and a no action alternative for the project. Three alternatives were eliminated from detailed study. Analyses were performed on the remaining two proposals and the no action plan.

One of the alternatives that was preliminarily eliminated from detailed study would have placed deed restrictions on the land traded to Weyerhaeuser, requiring that the lands be managed under National Forest Service standards, rather than allowing Weyerhaeuser to log the land pursuant to the less stringent standards of Washington state law. That alternative was rejected on the grounds that it would decrease Weyerhaeuser's incentive to trade. However, there is nothing in the record to demonstrate that the Forest Service even considered increasing Weyerhaeuser's incentive to trade either by offering additional acreage, subject to deed restrictions, or by decreasing the amount of Weyerhaeuser land transferred in the Exchange.

Although NEPA does not require the Forest Service to "consider every possible alternative to a proposed action, nor must it consider alternatives that are unlikely to be implemented or those inconsistent with its basic policy objectives," *Seattle Audubon Society v. Moseley*, 80 F.3d 1401, 1404 (9th Cir. 1996), we are troubled that in this case, the Forest Service failed to consider an alternative that was more consistent with its basic policy objectives than the alternatives that were the subject of final consideration. In this case, the applicable regulation controlling implementation of the Federal Land Policy Management Act, pursuant to which the Exchange was transacted, dictates that the agency officer authorized to conduct a land exchange "shall reserve such rights or retain such interests as are needed to protect the public interest or shall otherwise restrict the use of Federal lands to be exchanged, as appropriate." 36 C.F.R. 254.3(h). A detailed consideration of a trade involving deed restrictions or other modifications to the acreage involved is in the public interest and should have been considered.

We also recognize that an agency's discussion of alternatives must be "bounded by some notion of feasibility." *See Vermont Yankee Nuclear Power v. NRDC*, 435 U.S. 519, 551 (1978). Counsel for Weyerhaeuser conceded at oral argument that the imposition of deed restrictions was a viable alternative to the Exchange Agreement of March 28, 1997. A "viable but unexamined alternative renders [the] environmental impact statement inadequate." *Citizens for a Better Henderson v. Hodel*, 768 F.2d 1051, 1057 (9th Cir. 1985). Imposition of deed restrictions was a feasible alternative that could not be ignored.

The plaintiffs also argue that the land could have been purchased outright with funds from the Federal Land and Water Conservation Fund. While the Forest Service itself cannot appropriate these funds, it can request them. The record reflects that such a request was never made, and indeed, this option was not even considered.

The appellees respond that, because it was not clear that the funds would be available for such a purchase, the Forest Service had no obligation to consider it, as it constituted a "remote and speculative" alternative. However, NEPA regulations state that agencies shall "include reasonable alternatives not within the jurisdiction of the lead agency." 40 C.F.R. §1502.14(c). This alternative clearly falls within the range of such reasonable alternatives, and should have been considered. We also note that in presenting the beneficial cumulative impacts of the exchange, the EIS frequently relies upon references to admittedly speculative funds that will be used by the Forest Service in restoring the forest lands that it gains through the transaction. We are troubled by this selective willingness to rely upon the availability of funding sources beyond the Forest Service's direct control.

The Forest Service also contends that because the purpose of the transaction was to carry out an "exchange" and not a purchase, it was not required to consider this alternative. *Seattle Audubon Society*, 80 F.3d at 1404 (holding that an agency is not required to examine alternatives inconsistent with its basic policy objectives). To the extent that Weyerhaeuser would have been exchanging its lands for federal monies rather than federal lands, we do not recognize such an inconsistency.

* * *

NOTES AND QUESTIONS ON *MUCKLESHOOT INDIAN TRIBE*

1. *Cumulative impacts and tiering.* The Supreme Court decision in *Kleppe*, discussed in the notes following *Public Citizen*, suggest that an agency should wait until it is about to make the concrete permitting decisions that would make the contours of development clear before carrying out an EIS. While this narrows the scope of the action being evaluated and makes the assessment more concrete, it has its own problems. While one land exchange (or timber sale, or ski resort, or mining project) might have a limited effect, perhaps multiple development projects would cumulatively have a serious impact on water resources, wildlife, and the land itself. Project-specific environmental analysis might miss this bigger picture, particularly if earlier, programmatic decisions have "cast the die" for later project-specific decisions. CEQ regulations counsel the use of tiering to conduct environmental analysis prior to "irretrievable commitment of resources," to assess cumulative impacts, and to account properly for project-specific impacts. Tiering involves a sequence of program-wide and site-specific studies to assess impacts in a timely and informed manner. Here, the Forest Service claimed that it had done just that, by tiering this EIS to an earlier document. Why did the Court not accept that process? What should the Forest Service have done here to ensure that it properly considered cumulative impacts in the NEPA process?

2. *General permits.* Another technique for facilitating individually minor actions is general permits, but the process must assure that the aggregate impacts of multiple activities in a region do not have significant cumulative effects. *See* 33 U.S.C. §1344(e) (authorizing issuance of "general permits" for activities dredging and filling wetlands, but only when the activities have "minimal cumulative adverse effect on the environment"). A District Court invalidated one such form of a general permit, known as "Nationwide Permit 21" (NWP 21), in a case involving mountaintop removal coal mining because, rather than determining *ab initio* that the cumulative impacts would be minimal, the permit included the requirement that regional District Engineers determine that individual and cumulative use of NWP 21 in a region would not exceed the minimum adverse effect standard. Ohio Valley Environmental Coalition v. Bulen, 315 F. Supp. 2d 821 (S.D. W. Va.

2004) (granting a preliminary injunction), *aff'd*, 410 F. Supp. 2d 450 (S.D. W. Va. 2004), *vacated*, 429 F.3d 493 (4th Cir. 2005). In a later case, the Court of Appeals upheld the use of this practice. Ohio Valley Environmental Coalition v. Aracoma Coal, 556 F.3d 177 (4th Cir. 2009).

3. *Statement of purpose and need and agency discretion.* What was the purpose and need for the land exchange in *Muckleshoot*? Does the Forest Service statement of purpose and need unduly constrain the choice of alternatives to be considered, and if so, how? How much discretion does an agency have in choosing the breadth of the purpose and need in ways that constrain alternatives? In a case involving choices about how much wilderness to consider in roadless areas administered by the U.S. Forest Service, a majority of a Ninth Circuit panel justified allowing the Administration to consider a narrow group of alternatives, in part, on the grounds that the Forest Service need not consider alternatives "inconsistent with its basic policy objectives." Kootenai Tribe of Idaho v. Veneman, 313 F.3d 1094, 1121 (9th Cir. 2002). However, the majority conceded that the Forest Service "could not 'define its objective in unreasonably narrow terms.'" *Id.* In Citizens Against Burlington, Inc. v. Busey, 938 F.2d 190 (D.C. Cir. 1991), cited in *Muckleshoot,* then-Judge Clarence Thomas rejected a citizen group's argument that the Federal Aviation Administration needed to consider alternative locations for an airport expansion, even though the proposed expansion was near a public park, because the agency's statement of purpose and need included the need to provide new jobs in the location of the proposed airport site. In that case, did the FAA define its alternatives in "unreasonably narrow terms" in order to reach a predetermined result as to airport location? Suppose that the FAA had defined its purpose as supporting airport expansion, rather than as supporting airport expansion at the Toledo site. Would consideration of alternative sites have been consistent with this broader objective? Was it appropriate for the agency to define its objective so narrowly? Judge Buckley, writing in dissent, opined that the Federal Aviation Administration had impermissibly allowed the primary beneficiary of the airport expansion, a company that had sought to relocate to the Toledo airport from nearby Fort Wayne, to define the limits of its NEPA review. *Id.* at 207.

4. *Range of alternatives.* Since studying every alternative is not possible, how should government agencies select the range of alternatives to focus on? What legal test did the Court in *Muckleshoot* identify in reviewing the range of alternatives considered? How should a court determine when an alternative is "remote and speculative" and when it is realistic? Should a federal agency consider an alternative that only a state agency could implement? *See* 40 C.F.R. §1502.14(c) (requiring consideration of alternatives not within the jurisdiction of the lead agency). Should the agency only study alternatives that meet agency objectives? *See* Robert L. Glicksman, *Traveling in Opposite Directions: Roadless Area Management Under the Clinton and Bush Administrations,* 34 Envtl. L. 1143, 1188 (2004). Should it consider alternatives that would be illegal to implement? *Cf.* Southwest Center for Biological Diversity v. Bureau of Reclamation, 143 F.3d 515 (9th Cir. 1998) (upholding Bureau of Reclamation decision under the Endangered Species Act not to consider alternatives prohibited by applicable law governing management of the Colorado River). When an agency is considering constructing a dam as a source of

hydropower, should it limit its choices to alternative sites for the dam, or should it also consider alternative designs at the same site? Other sources of energy?

5. *Independent duty to consider alternatives.* The EIS requirement is contained in section 102(2)(C) of NEPA, 42 U.S.C. §4332(2)(C). A separate subsection, section 102(2)(E), requires all agencies to "study, develop, and describe appropriate alternatives to recommended courses of action in any proposal which involves unresolved conflicts concerning alternative uses of available resources." 42 U.S.C. §4332(2)(E). Does this require agencies to consider alternatives even if no EIS is required? *See* Trinity Episcopal School Corp. v. Romney, 523 F.2d 88, 93 (2d Cir. 1975), *judgment reversed on other grounds*, Strycker's Bay Neighborhood Council, Inc. v. Karlen, 444 U.S. 223 (1980).

6. *Information versus substance.* NEPA requires agencies to *consider* alternatives in an EIS. Section 404 of the CWA *prohibits* issuance of a permit to discharge fill into a wetland if there is a "less damaging practicable alternative." *See also* Ohio Valley Environmental Coalition v. Aracoma Coal, 556 F.3d 177, 202 (4th Cir. 2009) (citing 40 C.F.R. §230.10 (2008)). Is this distinction justified? If not, how would you propose to change the law about when one must use less damaging alternatives?

c. *Mitigating Environmental Injustice and Cumulative Impacts*

A grassroots environmental justice movement grew up in the 1980s to address the general problem of disproportionate pollution burdens in communities of color. *See* Luke Cole & Sheila Foster, From the Ground Up: Environmental Racism and the Rise of the Environmental Justice Movement (2001). This movement led a number of scholars and institutions to study the siting of industrial facilities. A number of studies found that government officials often sited hazardous waste treatment facilities and other polluting plants in communities of color. *See* Clifford Rechtschaffen & Eileen Guana, Environmental Justice: Law, Policy, and Regulation 55-76 (2002) (reviewing this claim and critiques of it). The cumulative impacts of these facilities might well subject communities of color to disproportionate health impacts.

In 1994, President Clinton signed an executive order requiring federal agencies to take environmental justice concerns into account. E.O. 12898. Since then, federal agencies have struggled with the question of how to address these concerns. The environmental justice movement has a keen interest in public participation, so that efforts by agencies to enhance effective participation of people of color in decisions about facilities in their communities can address some of the movement's concerns. But this still leaves a question about how information about disproportionate cumulative impacts should influence siting decisions and other decisions going forward.

The Council on Environmental Quality issued guidance on incorporating environmental justice concerns into NEPA. The memorandum makes the following statements regarding mitigation and the consideration of alternatives:

Council of Environmental Quality, Guidance Under the National Environmental Policy Act

(Dec. 10, 1997) available at http://www.whitehouse.gov/CEQ

* * *

. . . Mitigation measures identified as part of an environmental assessment (EA), a finding of no significant impact (FONSI), an environmental impact statement (EIS), or a record of decision (ROD) should, whenever feasible, address significant and adverse environmental effects of proposed federal actions on minority populations, and Indian tribes.

. . .

. . . When the agency has identified a disproportionately high and adverse human health or environmental effect on low-income populations, minority populations, or Indian tribes from either the proposed action or alternatives, the distribution as well as the magnitude of the disproportionate impacts in these communities should be a factor in determining the environmentally preferable alternative. In weighing this factor, the agency should consider the views it has received from the affected communities, and the magnitude of environmental impacts associated with alternatives that have a less disproportionate and adverse effect on low-income populations, minority populations, or Indian tribes.

. . .

This memorandum also urges specific measures to enhance community participation and analysis of cumulative impacts on communities. *See id.* at 10-15.

Compare this approach to that of the Department of Transportation, which manages highway projects and other projects contributing air pollution to minority communities:

Department of Transportation (DOT) Order to Address Environmental Justice in Minority Populations and Low-Income Populations

62 Fed. Reg. 18377 (Apr. 15, 1997)

* * *

8. Actions to Address Disproportionately High and Adverse Effects.

. . .

c. The Operating Administrators and other responsible DOT officials will ensure that any of their respective programs, policies or activities that will have a disproportionately high and adverse effect on minority populations or low-income populations will only be carried out if further mitigation measures or alternatives that would avoid or reduce the disproportionately high and adverse effect are not practicable. In determining whether a mitigation measure or an alternative is "practicable," the social, economic (including costs) and environmental effects of avoiding or mitigating the adverse effects will be taken into account.

d. Operating Administrators and other responsible DOT officials will also ensure that any of their respective programs, policies or activities that will have a disproportionately high and adverse effect on populations protected by Title VI ("protected populations") will only be carried out if:

(1) a substantial need for the program, policy or activity exists, based on the overall public interest; and

(2) alternatives that would have less adverse effects on protected populations (and that still satisfy the need identified in subparagraph (1) above), either (i) would have other adverse social, economic, environmental or human health impacts that are more severe, or (ii) would involve increased costs of extraordinary magnitude.

How do these two approaches differ? Which is better?

Section 3004(o)(7) of the Resource Conservation and Recovery Act requires EPA to "specify criteria for the acceptable location of new and existing treatment, storage, or disposal facilities, as necessary to protect human health and the environment." 42 U.S.C. §6924(o)(7). Should these criteria prohibit siting hazardous waste treatment facilities in communities of color suffering disproportionate cumulative impacts? *See generally* Richard J. Lazarus & Stephanie Tai, *Integrating Environmental Justice into EPA Permitting Authority*, 26 ECOLOGY L.Q. 617, 642-47 (1999) (discussing various RCRA provisions, including section 3004(o)(7) and the potential to use them to address cumulative impacts raising justice concerns).

d. NEPA's Record

Scholars vary in their assessment of NEPA. A review of NEPA's impact on the Army Corps of Engineers and the United States Forest Service reached this conclusion:

> Before the National Environmental Policy Act, most federal agencies paid scant attention to environmental values. . . . [W]hen []inside analysts are able to explore the possible environment–development trade-offs of a wide range of alternative designs, environmentally better decisions are likely to result: all projects benefitted from relatively inexpensive environmental mitigation. When, in addition, environmentally concerned outsiders pay attention to the EIS process, some of the worst projects—those projects with the great environmental costs and little political support within the agency and among its other constituencies—get eliminated.

SERGE TAYLOR, MAKING BUREAUCRACIES THINK: THE ENVIRONMENTAL IMPACT STATEMENT STRATEGY OF ADMINISTRATIVE REFORM 251 (1984). Other analysts have been more skeptical. One of NEPA's architects, Lynton Keith Caldwell, has criticized decisions like *Methow Valley* for having abandoned a serious effort to realize substantive environmental goals through NEPA. *See* LYNTON KEITH CALDWELL, THE NATIONAL ENVIRONMENTAL POLICY ACT (1998).

A 1997 assessment by the Council of Environmental Quality, which oversees NEPA implementation generally, reached the following conclusions:

> Overall, . . . NEPA is a success—it has made agencies take a hard look at the potential environmental consequences of their actions, and it has brought the public into the agency decision-making process like no other statute. . . .
>
> Despite these successes, however, NEPA's implementation at times has fallen short of its goals. For example, . . . agencies may sometimes confuse the purpose of NEPA. Some act as if the detailed statement called for in the statute is an end in itself, rather than a tool to enhance and improve decision-making. As a consequence, the exercise can be one of producing a document to no specific end. But NEPA is supposed to be about good decision-making—not endless documentation.
>
> The Study finds that agencies sometimes engage in consultation only after a decision has—for all practical purposes—been made. In such instances, other agencies and the public at large believe that their concerns have not been heard. As a result, they may find themselves opposing even worthy proposed actions. This may in turn lead to agencies seeking "litigation-proof" documents, increasing costs and time but not necessarily quality. In such cases, potential cost savings are also lost because a full range of alternatives has not been adequately examined. Other matters of concern to participants in the Study were the length of NEPA processes, the extensive detail of NEPA analyses, and the sometimes confusing overlay of other laws and regulations.

COUNCIL ON ENVIRONMENTAL QUALITY, THE NATIONAL ENVIRONMENTAL POLICY ACT: A STUDY OF ITS EFFECTIVENESS AFTER TWENTY-FIVE YEARS iii (1997).

2. TSCA and FIFRA Testing Requirements and Other Provisions Informing Pollution Control Decisions

NEPA generates information about government decisions to take actions significantly affecting the environment, such as decisions about the management of federal lands. The Toxic Substances Control Act (TSCA) and the Federal Insecticide, Fungicide, and Rodenticide Act (FIFRA) have provisions designed to obtain information to guide government decisions about regulating pollution.

Section 4 of TSCA authorizes EPA to develop test rules, requiring companies to develop basic toxicity data about individual chemicals or mixtures. In promulgating TSCA in 1976, Congress declared a policy that chemical manufacturers and processors should develop "adequate data with respect to the effect of chemical substances and mixtures on health and the environment." 15 U.S.C. §2601(b)(1). Information produced under section 4 can inform decisions about regulation of toxic chemicals under both section 6 of TSCA and under the media-specific statutes, such as the Clean Air Act, the Clean Water Act, the Resource Conservation and Recovery Act (land disposal primarily), and the Comprehensive Environmental Response, Compensation and Liability Act (cleanup of existing hazardous waste sites). Thus, section 4 can produce information to inform pollution control decisions, just as NEPA generates and organizes information useful in federal natural resources decision making.

More than 20 years after TSCA's enactment, an industry study concluded that we lack even elementary toxicity screening data for the overwhelming majority of high volume chemicals in commerce in the United States. *See* ICF KAISER

INTERNATIONAL, PUBLIC AVAILABILITY OF SIDS-RELATED TESTING DATA FOR U.S. HIGH PRODUCTION CHEMICALS (1998). The National Academy of Sciences, EPA, and environmental groups have reached similar conclusions. *See* U.S. EPA, OFFICE OF POLLUTION PREVENTION AND TOXICS, CHEMICAL HAZARD DATA AVAILABILITY STUDY: WHAT DO WE REALLY KNOW ABOUT THE SAFETY OF HIGH PRODUCTION VOLUME CHEMICALS? 2 (1998) (no basic toxicity information is available for 43 percent of high volume chemicals and a full basic set of information exists for only 7 percent); ENVIRONMENTAL DEFENSE FUND, TOXIC IGNORANCE: THE CONTINUING ABSENCE OF BASIC HEALTH TESTING FOR TOP-SELLING CHEMICALS IN THE UNITED STATES 3 (1997) (basic toxicity results cannot be found in the public record for 75 percent of the top volume chemicals in commercial use); NATIONAL RESEARCH COUNCIL, TOXICITY TESTING: STRATEGIES TO DETERMINE NEEDS AND PRIORITIES 1 (1984).

EPA has not promulgated nearly enough test rules to realize the statutory objective of providing adequate information about health and environmental effects. As of early 2005, EPA had promulgated test rules addressing 120 chemicals and published decisions not to test another 250. Lynn L. Bergeson, Lisa M. Campbell & Carla N. Hutton, *TSCA, Chemical Testing Issues*, 35 ENVTL. L. REP. (ENVTL. L. INST.) 10085, 10087 (2005). These rule-making actions did not even consider test rules for most of the 2,800 high production chemicals in commercial use in the United States. *See* ENVIRONMENTAL DEFENSE, FACING THE CHALLENGE: A STATUS REPORT ON THE U.S. HPV CHALLENGE PROGRAM 2 (2003) (noting that industry has identified nearly 3,000 high volume chemicals, 90 percent of which lacked sufficient screening data). EPA officials have reported that the "lengthy and costly rule-making process" has led the agency to eschew greater reliance on test rules.

Industry has generally resisted test rules, and, often, the disclosure of information it possesses. EPA has made some limited progress through voluntary testing rules, often negotiated in lieu of a mandatory testing rule. Why do you suppose that industry resists producing and generating information? Consider TSCA section 4(a):

(a) Testing requirements

If the Administrator finds that—

(1)(A)(i) the manufacture, distribution in commerce, processing, use, or disposal of a chemical substance or mixture, or that any combination of such activities, may present an unreasonable risk of injury to health or the environment,

(ii) there are insufficient data and experience upon which the effects of such manufacture, distribution in commerce, processing, use, or disposal of such substance or mixture or of any combination of such activities on health or the environment can reasonably be determined or predicted, and

(iii) testing of such substance or mixture with respect to such effects is necessary to develop such data; or

(B)(i) a chemical substance or mixture is or will be produced in substantial quantities, and (I) it enters or may reasonably be anticipated to enter the environment in substantial quantities or (II) there is or may be significant or substantial human exposure to such substance or mixture,

(ii) there are insufficient data and experience upon which the effects of the manufacture, distribution in commerce, processing, use, or disposal of such substance or mixture or of any combination of such activities on health or the environment can reasonably be determined or predicted, and

(iii) testing of such substance or mixture with respect to such effects is necessary to develop such data; . . .

the Administrator shall by rule require that testing be conducted on such substance or mixture to develop data with respect to the health and environmental effects for which there is an insufficiency of data and experience and which are relevant to a determination that the manufacture, distribution in commerce, processing, use, or disposal of such substance or mixture, or that any combination of such activities, does or does not present an unreasonable risk of injury to health or the environment.

15 U.S.C. §2603(a). Another provision of the statute authorizes judicial review and requires that the agency provide "substantial evidence" to support a testing rule. 15 U.S.C. §2628(c)(1)(B)(i). Given that the purpose of a testing rule is to require generation of data when data is either non-existent or inadequate, does this provision offer a sensible trigger to testing requirements? Would it be better to just require a finding that the chemical poses a significant risk, much like the NEPA finding that a proposed action will have a significant effect on the environment?

TSCA also requires "Premanufacture Notices" for new chemicals. But these notices have revealed very little toxicity data. Mary L. Lyndon, *Information Economics and Chemical Toxicity: Designing Laws to Produce and Use Data*, 87 MICH. L. REV. 1795, 1823-24 (1989).

What legal reforms might address the failure to promulgate test rules? *See* John S. Applegate, *The Perils of Unreasonable Risk: Information, Regulatory Policy and Toxic Substances Control*, 91 COLUM. L. REV. 261, 318-30 (1991) (proposing amendments to TSCA). *See generally* Wendy A. Wagner, *Commons Ignorance: The Failure of Environmental Law to Produce Needed Information on Health and the Environment*, 53 DUKE L.J. 1619 (2004). Other statutes also provide authority to gather information needed for regulatory processes. A National Toxicology Program in the Department of Health and Human Services coordinates federal toxicity research. And the Comprehensive Environmental Response, Compensation, and Liability Act maintains a Toxic Substances Disease Registry to manage data related to hazardous waste sites.

Given the enormity of the challenge, failure should hardly be surprising. EPA estimates that approximately 87,000 chemicals should be tested for their potential to disrupt the endocrine system, which regulates the body through the production of hormones. *See* Valerie J. Watnick, *Our Toxics Regulatory System and Why Risk Assessment Does Not Work: Endocrine Disrupting Chemicals as a Case in Point*, 2004 UTAH L. REV. 1305, 1308-10. And this is just one of the many health issues toxic chemicals raise. We develop new chemicals daily, thus compounding this problem. *Id.* Ideally, we should have comprehensive information about these chemicals' potential effects, including information about their potential to cause cancer, birth defects, immune system disorders, neurological problems, etc. But obtaining this information involves costly tests that can never fully resolve the uncertainties surrounding a chemical's likely effects on humans.

While EPA has authority to promulgate test rules and companies have the duty to submit pre-manufacturing notices for new chemicals, TSCA also requires companies to disclose the results of their own tests and other information. Section 8(e) provides:

> Any person who manufactures, processes, or distributes in commerce a chemical substance or mixture and who obtains information which reasonably supports the conclusion that such substance or mixture presents a substantial risk of injury to health or the environmental shall immediately inform [EPA]. . . .

15 U.S.C. §2607(e).

PROBLEM: TESTING REQUIREMENTS FOR ATRAZINE UNDER FIFRA

Like TSCA, FIFRA authorizes EPA to require manufacturers seeking registration of new pesticides to generate and report information necessary to make sound regulatory decisions. *See* 7 U.S.C. §136a(c)(1)(F). FIFRA also authorizes EPA to require registrants to collect and submit new information if "required to maintain in effect an existing registration of a pesticide. . . ." *Id.* §136a(c)(2)(B). In the notice below, EPA refers to such a requirement as a "FIFRA Section 3(c)(2)(B) Data Call-In Order (DCI)."

The atrazine re-registration process described in Chapter 4 involved two major categories of scientific uncertainty: (1) the degree to which atrazine and atrazine degradation byproducts occur in drinking water supplies and in surface water ecosystems at levels that pose risks to human health and the environment; and (2) the concentrations of atrazine that cause such adverse effects. EPA issued its interim re-registration decision (IRED) for atrazine despite these ongoing uncertainties. However, EPA conditioned the IRED on a memorandum of agreement (MOA) between EPA and the atrazine manufacturers establishing various new use restrictions (such as new labeling requirements and instructions to atrazine end product formulators), as well as requirements for the manufacturers to conduct and report additional studies. The following excerpt from the MOA includes the data collection and reporting provisions, as well as some of the pre-determined regulatory implications of that information. As you read the MOA, ask yourself the following question: Which of the major scientific uncertainties regarding atrazine registration are addressed, and which are not?

Memorandum of Agreement Between the U.S. Environmental Protection Agency and [Atrazine Manufacturers] Concerning the Registration of Pesticide Products Containing Atrazine

. . . EPA has determined that registrations pertaining to certain uses of Atrazine must be amended in order to ensure that they do not present human and ecological risks that are inconsistent with the standard for registration in FIFRA and the requirements for tolerances under the Federal Food, Drug and Cosmetic Act. . . . EPA believes that this Agreement will substantially reduce the risks posed by use of Atrazine by reducing the most significant exposures associated with Atrazine. The Atrazine Registrants believe that current Atrazine uses do not cause unreasonable adverse effects on human health or the environment. The Atrazine Registrants do not consider it appropriate to use raw water concentration measurements as triggers to require mitigation measures to protect human health. In order to reach a settlement of the issues raised by EPA, the Atrazine Registrants have agreed in this Agreement that such raw water triggers be used. Provided that the terms of this Agreement are fully implemented . . . EPA has no current intention to initiate cancellation or suspension proceedings under section 6 of FIFRA. . . .

Drinking water program: Atrazine Registrants shall conduct [a] drinking water monitoring program . . . and shall submit reports. . . . EPA has issued a FIFRA Section 3(c)(2)(B) Data Call-In Order (DCI) to require the monitoring. . . .

1) Any failure to conduct the review and analysis of SDWA compliance monitoring data . . . or to submit reports . . . may result . . . in cancellation of all Atrazine registrations without a right to a hearing.

2) Any use of Atrazine within a [listed] Watershed Area . . . contributing to a [listed] Community Water System (hereinafter "CWS") . . . and at which total chlorotriazine (hereinafter "TCT") levels have been found . . . to be at or above 37.5 ppb at the CWS raw water intake after December 31, 2003 will be prohibited. For each CWS listed . . . Atrazine Registrants must submit to EPA, no later than August 1, 2003, written Mitigation Plans including mitigation measures to be implemented within the Watershed Area containing each CWS listed and such Plans shall include consideration of Best Management Practices such as buffer strips, grass waterways, changes in tillage practices, changes in application timing, and use rate reductions, and how the Atrazine registrants intend to communicate with growers the measures included in each plan. Atrazine Registrants will submit progress reports semi-annually describing the measures taken during that quarter in each CWS, until EPA notifies Atrazine Registrants in writing that such reports may cease. . . .

4) No later than 90 days after the date of this agreement, Atrazine Registrants shall establish an Atrazine Watershed Information Center (hereinafter "AWIC").

(a) The AWIC will provide detailed information on what Watershed Areas have become subject to a prohibition on Atrazine use. . . . Only information approved by EPA may be included in the AWIC.

(b) The AWIC shall be accessible to the public daily, including weekends and holidays, through a toll-free telephone number available 24 hours a day and seven days a week, a World Wide Web site, and a regular mailing address. Contact information for the AWIC will be included on all Atrazine product labels. . . .

(d) Information provided by the AWIC regarding use prohibitions shall be prominently displayed or provided in a manner that is simple and convenient for users to access and understand and shall not be obscured by other information. . . .

6) (a) Beginning January 1, 2004, if a CWS is reported to EPA to be in violation of the Atrazine MCL, the Atrazine Registrants will initiate the watershed mitigation program . . . and develop a schedule for its implementation in consultation with the State Drinking Water Administrator of the State where such CWS is located.

(b) If the State Drinking Water Administrator, after receiving input from the State Agriculture Department and State Lead Agency for Pesticides, disapproves the mitigation schedule on the ground that it is not reasonably likely to reduce Atrazine concentrations in the CWS water supply, or the mitigation schedule is not met, the use of products containing Atrazine would be prohibited and the Watershed Area would be included in the AWIC.

[The MOA also includes monitoring requirements for rural drinking water wells and for ecological impacts to surface waters.]

1. *Sufficiency of the information required.* The DCI requires extensive monitoring and reporting of the degree to which atrazine product use results in contamination relative to EPA's existing levels of concern. It requires no new information, however, about the levels at which adverse health and environmental effects occur, and disagreement about those effects levels continues. Should EPA have addressed that issue in the MOA? Draft a new paragraph for the MOA designed to address that issue.

2. *Fox studying the henhouse?* How appropriate is it to require parties with an economic interest in the outcome to be in charge of scientific studies informing regulatory decisions? Consider the following analysis of earlier scientific studies by atrazine manufacturers:

> Tyrone Hays was the first to suspect that Atrazine was an [endocrine disrupting chemical] and brought this to media attention by publishing a paper on the topic in *Nature*, in October 2001. At the time of his initial study he was working at Syngenta, one of the world's largest producers of the herbicide, Atrazine. In response Syngenta created its own panel of scientists, called *EcoRisk*, which produced several studies that refuted Hays' findings. Ever since, there has been a huge amount of controversy over whether or not Atrazine is an [endocrine disrupting chemical] and presents a threat to the health and the environment at its present concentrations in groundwater, drinking water, etc. The EPA's Scientific Advisory Panel . . . has since reviewed all of the *EcoRisk* studies and discovered each of them to be scientifically and methodologically flawed; some on levels as basic as separating control and test subjects.

Gitanjali Deb, *Atrazine: A Case Study in the Differences Between Regulations of Endocrine Disrupting Chemicals in the EU and the U.S.*, 25 Temple J. of Sci., Tech. & Envtl. L. 173, 174 (2006).

3. *Registration now, information later?* EPA's approach was to issue an interim re-registration decision subject to specified mitigation requirements if contamination is detected, but also presumably subject to modification based on information collected and reported under the MOA. What alternative did EPA forgo in favor of this approach? (See the first paragraph of the MOA

quoted above.) Why do you think EPA adopted this approach, and which do you think is more appropriate? What revisions might you propose to the MOA to address any concerns you have about EPA's approach?

4. *Different responses to the same information.* As we saw under NEPA, information does not necessarily dictate particular results. Based on essentially the same scientific information as considered by EPA, the European Union (EU) and several individual EU countries decided to ban or phase out most uses of atrazine. Deb, *supra*, at 179-80.

5. *Other information benefits.* In addition to informing future EPA decisions about atrazine registration, who else will benefit from the information generated under the MOA, and how? What decisions by other private and public entities might this information produce?

B. INFORMATION MOTIVATING PRIVATE ACTION

Just as information generated and disclosed under NEPA or TSCA can inform and motivate government action, information can sometimes motivate private parties to protect the environment. The following materials examine this use of information as a means of "regulation."

1. Community Right to Know

The Community Right to Know Act requires factories emitting large amounts of certain hazardous pollutants to report their releases of certain hazardous chemicals to land, air, and water. EPA compiles this information in a toxic release inventory (TRI), which is available to the public. *See* http://www.epa.gov/TRI/. The media often uses this information to report on the releases of the most egregious polluters or to compare pollution levels in different regions.

This compilation, however, has some limitations. First, it only applies to very large industrial polluters, mostly chemical plants. Second, it only applies to a fraction of the chemicals that may pose risks of serious illness, like cancer. Third, it gives polluters great flexibility in choosing how they measure or estimate emissions. This flexibility has led to frequent revisions of pollution estimates and means that the data are not as reliable as data generated through carefully chosen protocols.

On the other hand, just creating this information had a much greater effect than some observers predicted. The large emissions many facilities discovered when they actually looked surprised the managers of the corporations owning the facilities and alarmed the public and regulators in some cases. These discoveries led many facilities to voluntarily reduce their emissions. *See* Bradley Karkkainen, *Information as Environmental Regulation: TRI and Performance Benchmarking, Precursor to a New Paradigm?*, 89 GEO. L.J. 257, 297 (2001). This information also helped motivate the federal and state governments to regulate hazardous air pollutants more broadly.

Are reductions in response to TRI wholly voluntary? Consider the following allegations made by Citizens for a Better Environment in a case seeking penalties and injunctive relief for a company's failure to report TRI data:

> The complaint contains claims "on behalf of both [respondent] itself and its members." It describes respondent as an organization that seeks, uses, and acquires data reported under EPCRA [the Emergency Planning and Community Right to Know Act]. It says that respondent "reports to its members and the public about storage and releases of toxic chemicals into the environment, advocates changes in environmental regulations and statutes, prepares reports for its members and the public, seeks the reduction of toxic chemicals and further seeks to promote the effective enforcement of environmental laws." The complaint asserts that respondent's "right to know about [toxic chemical] releases and its interests in protecting and improving the environment and the health of its members have been, are being, and will be adversely affected by [petitioner's] actions in failing to provide timely and required information under EPCRA." The complaint also alleges that respondent's members, who live in or frequent the area near petitioner's facility, use the EPRCA-reported information "to learn about toxic chemical releases, the use of hazardous substances in their communities, to plan emergency preparedness in the event of accidents, and to attempt to reduce the toxic chemicals in areas in which they live, work and visit." The members' "safety, health, recreational, economic, aesthetic and environmental interests" in the information, it is claimed, "have been, are being, and will be adversely affected by [petitioner's] actions in failing to file timely and required reports under EPCRA."

Steel Company v. Citizens for a Better Environment, 523 U.S. 83, 104-05 (1998). How can the citizens group use this information to "attempt to reduce" releases of "toxic chemicals"?

2.   Proposition 65 and Labeling

California's voters passed an initiative, called Proposition 65, requiring producers to affix a warning label to products containing carcinogens or reproductive toxins. *See generally* Clifford Rechtschaffen, *The Warning Game: Evaluating Warnings Under California's Proposition 65*, 23 ECOLOGY L.Q. 303 (1996). Many producers decided that they would prefer reformulating their products to announcing, in effect, that their products threatened to cause cancer or harm unborn children, or to paying fines for non-compliance with Proposition 65. *Id.* at 341-47.

3.   Radon

Indoor air pollution can expose residents to radiation when radon is present. Several states have addressed this problem by requiring measurement and disclosure of radon levels prior to a real estate sale. Many sellers and purchasers act to reduce radon levels voluntarily when confronted with the information. Is this an example of an economic incentive program? Why would a seller reduce radon levels? Why would the buyer?

4. Green Lights

Many investments in energy efficiency pay for themselves over time. For example, one can reduce use of electricity in a building by using energy-efficient light bulbs and adding insulation. While the insulation and the light bulbs have a cost, installation reduces the electricity bill, so that, after a while, the cost savings more than make up for the cost of the installation. Reductions in energy use reduce the pollutants associated with electricity generation. EPA has a Green Lights program to show businesses how to improve their energy efficiency and to convince them that it pays to do so. This program has motivated measures to increase energy efficiency. The budget for the program, however, limits the amount of people EPA can hire to spread the word. Is there any need for a government program to show companies profitable opportunities to improve the environment? Why wouldn't companies just adopt these measures on their own?

5. Certification Regimes

Various private groups have created management standards of various kinds that may prompt environmental measures. The chemical industry runs a "Responsible Care" program, which encourages "best environmental management practices" aimed at "continuous improvement" in pollution prevention. Karkkainen, *supra*, at 305-06. The International Organization for Standardization's ISO 14000 environmental management program offers another example of an obligation to establish certain management processes. Industry runs these programs. The Forest Stewardship Council's Well-Managed Forests Program, however, has some environmental representation. Environmentalists have been eager to secure voluntary commitments to more sustainable forestry, because they regard governments as ineffectual in protecting forests around the world. These voluntary programs tend to impose fairly weak inchoate obligations on their members. Fulfillment of these obligations entitles producers to put labels on their products advising consumers that they have met the voluntary standards. These obligations, even though often weak, still have some potential to lead to positive change. While some risk exists that firms will duck even mild obligations when they prove inconvenient, purchasers of products, including businesses, may demand compliance with these voluntary standards, so that some improvements may result. In part because of some of the possibilities of informal enforcement, one commentator has argued that these programs "may amount to a form of non-governmental law making." *See* Errol Meidinger, *"Private" Environmental Regulation, Human Rights, and Community,* 7 Buff. Envtl. L.J. 123, 236 (2000).

6. Some Theoretical Perspectives on Information-Based Regimes

How much potential do these approaches have to motivate voluntary action? Should we use voluntary information generation mechanisms to supplement standard setting or as a substitute? While voluntary regimes have sometimes motivated cost saving pollution prevention measures, they have not generated a whole lot of changes that have significant costs associated with them. Switches to low emission vehicles, significant efforts to limit power plant emission rates, and phase-outs of ozone-depleting chemicals all came about as a result of regulation.

Notice that Proposition 65 works by playing on industry fears about possible consumer responses to toxic substances. Douglas Kysar explicitly defends the value of consumers taking environmental values into account in making purchasing decisions, linking it with an old progressive tradition of taking social values into account in making purchasing decisions. Douglas A. Kysar, *Preferences for Processes: The Process/Product Distinction and the Regulation of Consumer Choice*, 118 HARV. L. REV. 525, 579-640 (2004). On the other hand, will consumers, acting as consumers, prove as socially conscious as citizens acting through political processes? *See* MARK SAGOFF, THE ECONOMY OF THE EARTH: PHILOSOPHY, LAW, AND THE ENVIRONMENT (1988).

Consider the problem of agricultural use of pesticides. These pesticides play a significant role in increasing water pollution and many of them are toxic. Environmentalists have long argued that organic agriculture offers an environmentally attractive alternative. Should EPA consider the possibility of organic agriculture in deciding, as a regulatory matter, whether to ban a particular pesticide? What if organic agriculture is cleaner, but more expensive? Should that matter? Regardless of what EPA should do, we know that it has historically done very little to limit pesticide use under FIFRA.

The United States Department of Agriculture (USDA) recently issued a rule setting a standard for labeling food as "organic." At one point during the rule making, the USDA proposed standards that allowed food made with genetically modified ingredients to be labeled organic. This proposal elicited a storm of protest. The USDA ultimately issued a rule that conformed fairly closely to consumers' concepts of organic practice. Organic food has been a growth industry as of late. What does this say about the potential of information regimes?

Firms producing genetically modified organisms (GMOs) have argued that GMOs offer a good alternative to agricultural practices based on large doses of pesticides. It is possible to engineer the DNA of plants to produce strains that require less use of pesticides. Some believe that GMOs may threaten biological diversity, *i.e.*, that they might crowd out native species. They have also created some concerns regarding allergies. On the other hand, some analysts regard the use of GMOs as much safer than traditional pesticide-based agriculture. The USDA has taken the position that GMOs are indistinguishable from ordinary crops from a food safety standpoint. For that reason, it has rejected labeling of food made with GMOs. Europe, on the other hand, has required labeling. Which approach is correct? *See* Kysar, *supra*, at 590 (arguing that the concept of consumer sovereignty should lead to the use of a label). Should government choose between GMOs, pesticide-based agriculture, and organic agriculture, or should it provide consumers with information as the predominant approach?

Consider the following:

While the basic idea of informing consumers about environmental impacts is straightforward, the task of educating the public is daunting. The environmental impacts of consumer product choices are manifold and complex. Most significantly, consumers have little basis for assessing these impacts when choosing among the myriad products on retail shelves or making other daily choices. Even the most diligent consumer cannot accurately assess the environmental effects caused by the extraction of raw materials, production, and transportation of the product before it reaches the store shelf and any subsequent impacts from usage and ultimate disposal. Comparing these impacts across a range of products within a particular category multiplies the problem.

Peter Menell, *Environmental Federalism: Structuring a Market-Oriented Federal Eco-Information Policy*, 54 MD. L. REV. 1435, 1436 (1995).

What about the potential to use information to investors as a strategy? An international Global Reporting Initiative is underway to create company reports about sustainability. *See* http://www.globalreporting.org/about/brief.asp. While the United Nations Environment Program has supported it, it has evolved into a private multi-stakeholder effort to develop reporting guidelines and encourage their adoption. Will private investors use information about carbon dioxide reductions, for example, to inform their decisions? What about institutional investors, like pension funds and insurance companies? The problem below explores issues associated with informing investors further as a strategy.

PROBLEM: INFORMATION APPROACHES TO CLIMATE DISRUPTION

Information to affect decisions about climate change can operate at both the public and private levels. NEPA may require federal agencies to incorporate information about climate change in an EIS. The Securities and Exchange Commission (SEC) provides an example of information requirements for public entities. The SEC issued an interpretive guidance on climate change reporting for companies ("registrants") whose securities are publicly traded. SEC, Interpretation, Commission Guidance Regarding Disclosure Related to Climate Change, 75 Fed. Reg. 6290-97 (2010) [SEC Climate Guidance]. The guidance clarifies the circumstances in which existing SEC regulations require companies to disclose, in required public financial disclosure filings, climate disruption–related information that could have "material" financial impacts upon the company. Information is deemed "material" for SEC reporting purposes "if there is a substantial likelihood that a reasonable investor would consider it important in deciding how to vote or make an investment decision, or, put another way, if the information would alter the total mix of available information." *Id.* at 6293, *citing* Basic Inc. v. Levinson, 485 U.S. 224, 231 (1988).

Specifically, the SEC's Climate Guidance highlights the following areas as examples of where climate change may trigger disclosure requirements:

Impact of Legislation and Regulation: When assessing potential disclosure obligations, a company should consider whether the impact of certain existing laws and regulations regarding climate change is material. In certain circumstances, a company should also evaluate the potential impact of pending legislation and regulation related to this topic.

Impact of International Accords: A company should consider, and disclose when material, the risks or effects on its business of international accords and treaties relating to climate change.

Indirect Consequences of Regulation or Business Trends: Legal, technological, political, and scientific developments regarding climate change may create new opportunities or risks for companies. For instance, a company may face decreased demand for goods that produce significant greenhouse gas emissions or increased demand for goods that result in lower emissions than competing products. As such, a company should consider, for disclosure purposes, the actual or potential indirect consequences it may face due to climate change related regulatory or business trends.

Physical Impacts of Climate Change: Companies should also evaluate for disclosure purposes the actual and potential material impacts of environmental matters on their business.

SEC, Press Release (Jan. 27, 2010), available at http://www.sec.gov/news/press/2010/2010-15.html. With respect to pending legislation or regulation, the SEC Interpretation gives the following compliance guidance to company management:

> First, management must evaluate whether the pending legislation or regulation is reasonably likely to be enacted. Unless management determines that it is not reasonably likely to be enacted, it must proceed on the assumption that the legislation or regulation will be enacted. Second, management must determine whether the legislation or regulation, if enacted, is reasonably likely to have a material effect on the registrant, its financial condition or results of operations. Unless management determines that a material effect is not reasonably likely, [Management's Discussion and Analysis of Financial Condition and Results of Operations] disclosure is required.

SEC Climate Guidance, 75 Fed. Reg. at 6295. Existing SEC rules require a registrant to report any material pending legal proceeding to which it or its subsidiaries are a party. *Id.* at 6293.

1. *What purpose does SEC reporting serve?* What is the purpose behind the obligation to report environmental regulation and liabilities to the SEC? How are SEC reporting obligations similar to, and different from, the Emergency Planning and Community Right-to-Know Act requirement that factories report their releases of hazardous substances into the environment? Does a publicly traded company have any obligation to report the size of its releases of greenhouse gases? Do the SEC reporting requirements protect the environment or protect companies? Do the two objectives ever merge? When?

2. *What needs to be reported?* How does the SEC interpretive guidance, as described above, affect the financial reporting by the following publicly traded companies?

    a. Serenity-by-the-Sea, a publicly traded residential development company, specializing in construction of condominium complexes on the Florida coast;

    b. Electric Power, a publicly traded electricity company with electric-generating facilities located solely in the United States which was recently named as a defendant in a lawsuit filed by environmental organizations claiming the company's greenhouse gas emissions constitute a public nuisance;

    c. Appalachian Electric Power, a publicly traded electricity company with electric-generating facilities located solely in Ohio and which has *not* been named as a defendant in a common law public nuisance climate change case;

    d. Europa Oil Co., a large oil company with refineries located throughout Europe and the United States;

    e. San Francisco Electric Power, an investor-owned utility providing electricity to the residents of San Francisco.

3. *SEC reporting and the common law: Feedback loops.* What would be the impact on SEC reporting by companies owning industrial facilities of a finding that the American Electric Power Co. is liable for a public nuisance (see Climate Disruption Problem, Chapter 2)?

4. *SEC reporting and the limits of the information approach.* Data suggest that most U.S. companies are ignoring the SEC's disclosure rule. A report by a respected public interest corporate watch dog group found that, while climate disruption imposes long- and short-term physical impacts across the entire business value chain, from raw materials through end users, 41 percent of S&P and Fortune 500 companies entirely failed to address the topic of climate change in their 2013 10-k SEC disclosure filings. Ceres, Cool Response: The SEC and Corporate Climate Change Reporting 5, 12 (February 2014). Ceres also concluded that the SEC is not prioritizing the financial risks and opportunities of climate disruption as an important corporate disclosure issue. *Id.* at 4. Is this an argument against the effectiveness of the informational approach to environmental protection?

5. *NEPA Compliance I: When do activities contributing to climate disruption trigger the duty to prepare an environmental impact statement?* NEPA compliance poses its own challenges for federal actions that contribute to climate disruption. One is determining when a major federal action "significantly affect[s] the quality of the human environment," thus triggering the duty to prepare an environmental impact statement. Should federal licensed or funded facilities that emit large quantities of greenhouse gases be considered to automatically meet this threshold, or should it depend upon a determination that the emissions will measurably enhance climate disruption? *Compare* City of Los Angeles v. National Highway Traffic Safety Administration, 912 F.2d 478 (D.C. Cir. 1990), *overruled on other grounds*, Florida Audubon Society v. Bentsen, 94 F.2d 658 (D.C. Cir. 1996) (reversing agency decision not to prepare an EIS based upon the agency's failure to explain the significance of its action within the context of the environmental harm caused by climate disruption), *with* Mid States Coalition for Progress v. Surface Transportation Board, 345 F.3d 520 (8th Cir. 2003) (requiring that agency analyze impacts of project upon climate

disruption due to the reasonable foreseeability that the project will increase demand for coal). Under the Supreme Court's decision in *Public Citizen* presented at the beginning of this chapter, does it depend on the federal decision that triggers the EIS, and if so, how? In a recent guidance document, the Council on Environmental Quality suggests that federal agencies should use 25,000 tons per year of greenhouse gases as a threshold for when agencies should consider an action-specific evaluation of the environmental impacts of the project's greenhouse gas emissions. Council on Environmental Quality, Draft NEPA Guidance on Consideration of the Effects of Climate Change and Greenhouse Gases Emissions (Feb. 18, 2010).

6. *NEPA Compliance II: How should federal agencies take climate disruption into account when analyzing the environmental impacts of their actions?* NEPA requires that federal agencies include a "detailed statement" on "the environmental impact of the proposed action." 42 U.S.C. §4332. However, the forces of climate disruption themselves could alter project impacts. For example, how should the Army Corps of Engineers take projected sea level rise into account in preparing an environmental impact statement on a new highway along the Mississippi Gulf Coast?

10

Moving Upstream: Pollution Prevention and Recycling

Traditional regulation often, but not always, encouraged polluters to install end-of-the-pipe technologies, *i.e.*, devices that reduce pollution by treating a waste stream to change its chemical composition or to concentrate contaminants into a form that can be disposed of elsewhere. A performance standard encouraging use of scrubbers offers an example of this sort of regulation. You have already seen several examples of how traditional regulation, emissions trading, and information-based approaches encourage pollution prevention, *i.e.*, changing the inputs into a process, the way something is produced, or the thing or service being produced to reduce or eliminate pollution. For example, EPA attempted to ban asbestos in order to avoid pollution in any other medium, but the judicial reversal in *Corrosion Proof Fittings* thwarted EPA's ban. While performance standards limiting pollution in particular media often lead to end-of-the-pipe controls, polluters sometimes have responded with process changes designed to lower compliance costs or seize other benefits. *See* Kurt Strasser, *Cleaner Technology, Pollution Prevention, and Environmental Regulation*, 9 FORDHAM ENVTL. L.J. 1, 28-32 (1997). The acid rain trading program encouraged electric utilities to burn low sulfur coal, which produces less sulfur dioxide emissions than burning high sulfur coal. And the Toxics Release Inventory (TRI) program encouraged a number of efforts to eliminate the use of some toxic substances in production processes.

Pollution prevention offers a number of advantages. It often proves cheaper than end-of-the-pipe controls. Indeed, sometimes pollution prevention measures save money; for example, less toxic (or non-toxic) feedstocks may also cost less money than the toxic feedstocks being replaced. Pollution prevention's cost-saving potential helps explain why polluters often adopt pollution prevention measures voluntarily, *i.e.*, without extensive regulation. Pollution prevention can also eliminate or reduce releases to all environmental media (air, land, water). By contrast, end-of-the-pipe controls sometimes reduce pollution in one medium, but create additional pollution in another. *Cf.* City of Chicago v. Environmental Defense

Fund, 511 U.S. 328, 330 (1994) (explaining that incineration of municipal waste produces an ash that may be hazardous, but was disposed of in landfills). Congress specifically recognized the value of pollution prevention in the Pollution Prevention Act of 1990:

42 U.S.C. §13101. Findings and policy

(a) **Findings—The Congress finds that:**

(1) The United States of America annually produces millions of tons of pollution and spends tens of billions of dollars per year controlling this pollution.

(2) There are significant opportunities for industry to reduce or prevent pollution at the source through cost-effective changes in production, operation, and raw materials use. Such changes offer industry substantial savings in reduced raw material, pollution control, and liability costs as well as help protect the environment and reduce risks to worker health and safety.

(3) The opportunities for source reduction are often not realized because existing regulations, and the industrial resources they require for compliance, focus upon treatment and disposal, rather than source reduction; existing regulations do not emphasize multi-media management of pollution; and businesses need information and technical assistance to overcome institutional barriers to the adoption of source reduction practices.

(4) Source reduction is fundamentally different and more desirable than waste management and pollution control. The Environmental Protection Agency needs to address the historical lack of attention to source reduction.

(5) As a first step in preventing pollution through source reduction, the Environmental Protection Agency must establish a source reduction program which collects and disseminates information, provides financial assistance to States, and implements the other activities provided for in this chapter.

(b) **Policy**—The Congress hereby declares it to be the national policy of the United States that pollution should be prevented or reduced at the source whenever feasible; pollution that cannot be prevented should be recycled in an environmentally safe manner, whenever feasible; pollution that cannot be prevented or recycled should be treated in an environmentally safe manner whenever feasible; and disposal or other release into the environment should be employed only as a last resort and should be conducted in an environmentally safe manner.

§13102. Definitions

For purposes of this chapter—
. . .

(5)(A) The term "source reduction" means any practice which—

(i) reduces the amount of any hazardous substance, pollutant, or contaminant . . . prior to recycling, treatment, or disposal; and

(ii) reduces the hazards to public health and the environment associated with . . . such substances, pollutants, or contaminants. The term includes equipment or technology modifications, reformulation or redesign of products, substitution of raw materials, and improvements in housekeeping, maintenance, training, or inventory control.

(B) The term "source reduction" does not include any practice which alters the physical, chemical, or biological characteristics or the volume of a hazardous substance, pollutant, or contaminant through a process or activity which itself is not integral to and necessary for the production of a product or the providing of a service.

———————————

1. *Recycling and prevention.* Suppose Megafarms, Inc. stopped using atrazine to grow corn, and instead relied on a new no-tilling method of planting designed to reduce weed growth on its fields. Would that involve pollution prevention or recycling? Suppose that Megafarms installed an innovative drainage and collection system at the edge of its fields, and reused that water for irrigation. Because that water contains atrazine residuals, it is able to reduce the number of atrazine applications needed to control weeds adequately. Is this an example of pollution prevention or recycling?

2. *Hierarchy of preferred approaches.* What might justify the congressional preference for pollution prevention or reduction over recycling? What might justify the preference for recycling over treatment?

3. *How to encourage pollution prevention.* While regulators often wish to promote pollution prevention, they face some difficulties in incorporating that approach into routine standard setting. While process changes can save money and create environmental benefits, mature industries worry that new approaches might compromise the performance or other characteristics of their products. Thus, California regulators ran into fierce industry resistance when they sought to require cars to meet emission limits that would require radical redesign of automobiles. It can be difficult for regulators to evaluate claims that significant changes in what is manufactured or how something is manufactured will compromise performance. Moreover, Congress has expressed a reluctance to allow federal bureaucrats to intrude too intensively into actual industrial production decisions, *i.e.*, to give them authority to dictate what will be produced, and how.

Pollution prevention advocates often suggest multimedia rule making. EPA has experimented with such rule makings. For example, EPA considered air and water pollution regulatory requirements together in regulating the pulp and paper industry. In this case, there was a fairly obvious way of eliminating a significant water pollution problem and limiting most air pollutants of concern, by eliminating the use of chlorine in paper manufacturing. Chlorine bleaching makes paper whiter, but produces dioxins and other toxic pollutants. Some companies, however, have made paper without using chlorine. Industry argued that meeting effluent and air pollution limitations based on the capabilities of chlorine-free processing would prove infeasible, cost too much, and produce an inferior product. Does a multimedia rule-making procedure provide any aid in evaluating these claims? Does it make adoption of a good pollution prevention option more likely (assuming that this option is good)?

We have already seen that information-based approaches encourage pollution prevention. These approaches do not require regulators to intrude deeply into industry decision making, because the industry can voluntarily choose how to respond to the information. In fact, the only mandatory aspect of the Pollution Prevention Act of 1990 is to require that those facilities otherwise required to file an annual report under the Toxic Release Inventory (TRI) reporting include a toxic chemical source reduction and recycling report covering each toxic chemical included as part of the TRI report. For each chemical, this source reduction and recycling report must include:

(1) [the quantity of the toxic chemical entering any waste stream (or released to the environment) prior to recycling, treatment, or disposal . . . ;

(2) the amount of the chemical from the facility which is recycled (at the facility or elsewhere) during such calendar year, the percentage change from the previous year, and the process of recycling used;

(3) the source reduction practices used . . . ;

(5) a ratio of production in the reporting year to production in the previous year . . . ;

(6) the techniques used to identify source reduction opportunities. . . .

42 U.S.C. §13106. The EPA Administrator is to make all collected information available to the general public in the same manner as the TRI data.

Regulation, however, can play a role in encouraging pollution prevention. The following materials consider how regulation of solid waste and hazardous waste, first under RCRA and second under CERCLA, has addressed both pollution prevention and recycling.

A.　THE RCRA SCHEME

Americans produce more than 251 million tons of municipal solid waste per year, approximately 4.4 pounds per person per day. This waste includes paper (more than 27 percent of the total), yard trimmings, food scraps, plastics, metals, rubber, leather, textiles, glass, and wood. In addition, in 2001, industrial facilities generated more than 34 million tons of hazardous waste.

Congress passed the Resource Conservation and Recovery Act (RCRA), Pub. L. No. 94-580, 90 Stat. 2795, in 1976, amending the Solid Waste Disposal Act, codified currently at 42 U.S.C. §§6901-6992k, to address the problem of improper disposal of this vast river of waste. RCRA responded to prevalent practices of simply dumping wastes on the ground. Congress saw RCRA's regulation of land disposal as filling the gap left when it regulated air emissions through the Clean Air Act Amendments of 1970 and effluent discharges through the Federal Water Pollution Control Act of 1972. The end-of-pipe controls used to meet air and water pollution control requirements often resulted in waste "sludges," concentrated forms of the pollutants that formerly were emitted into air or water, which then might cause problems when disposed in or on land. RCRA generally authorizes EPA regulation of "solid waste," a broad term that includes both hazardous and non-hazardous waste (in solid, liquid, and even gaseous forms). *See* 42 U.S.C. §6903(27). Paper, for example, is considered non-hazardous solid waste. But many toxic chemicals are considered hazardous solid waste, at least when disposed of.

A Trail Guide to RCRA

Overview

RCRA establishes two core programs. Subtitle D (or subchapter IV) of RCRA regulates municipal solid waste by establishing guidelines for municipal solid waste disposal programs, which primarily manage non-hazardous waste. *But see City of Chicago*, 511 U.S. at 332-34 (explaining that RCRA establishes a "household waste exclusion" that exempts hazardous waste generated by households from subtitle C, thereby allowing municipal treatment of some hazardous waste). This program, for example, did away with open dumping, requiring that municipalities line their landfills and conform to other practices designed to limit leaching of waste into groundwater and surface water. Subtitle C (or subchapter III) regulates industrial hazardous waste management. Both of these programs have an objective of encouraging source reduction and recycling. *See* 42 U.S.C. §6902(a)(6).

Subtitle C (or subchapter III) establishes a "cradle to grave" system to manage hazardous waste. Chemical Waste Management v. Hunt, 504 U.S. 334, 337 n.1 (1992). The Act employs a manifest system to track and assure proper disposal of hazardous waste. Generators and transporters of hazardous waste must employ a document called a manifest to track it and assure that it ends up at a proper treatment facility. *See* 42 U.S.C. §§6922(a)(5), 6923(a)(3). RCRA then imposes detailed obligations on facilities authorized to treat, store, or dispose of hazardous waste, called Treatment, Storage, and Disposal Facilities (TSDFs):

> TSDFs . . . are subject to much more stringent regulation than either generators or transporters, including a 4-to-5 year permitting process, burdensome financial assurance requirements, stringent design and location standards, and, perhaps most onerous of all, responsibility to take corrective action for releases of hazardous substances and to ensure safe closure of each facility, *see* 42 U.S.C. §6924; 40 CFR pt. 264 (1993).

City of Chicago, 511 U.S. at 332.

This system does not authorize EPA to require manufacturing facilities not engaged in treatment, storage, or disposal to engage in either source reduction or recycling. RCRA does, however, require generators of hazardous waste to certify in the manifest that they have a program to reduce the amount and toxicity of waste "to the degree determined by the generator to be economically practicable." *See* 42 U.S.C. §6922(b)(1). The tracking and treatment system creates some additional incentives for manufacturing facilities to practice source reduction. Because treatment at TSDF facilities can prove expensive and facilities generating waste must carefully track their hazardous waste, generators like to avoid having their waste designated as hazardous waste. As the Supreme Court noted, "RCRA's primary purpose . . . is to reduce the generation of hazardous waste and to ensure the proper treatment, storage, and disposal of that waste which is nonetheless generated, 'so as to minimize the present and future threat to human health and the environment.'" Meghrig v. KFC Western, Inc., 516 U.S. 479, 483 (1996).

Key RCRA Provisions

Subchapter I, labeled "General Provisions," includes the congressional findings, a statement of objectives and national policy, definitions, and other general provisions. As is true in most statutes, the definitions can be critical to statutory interpretation and implementation, particularly the definitions of "disposal," 42 U.S.C. §6903(3), "hazardous waste," *id.* §6903(5), "solid waste," *id.* §6903(27), and "treatment," *id.* §6903(34). As will become clear from the materials later in this chapter, the statement of "Objectives and national policy" in *id.* §6902(a), which as a rule of statutory construction have no independent legal force and effect, are also unusually important in RCRA.

Subchapter II, entitled "Office of the Solid Waste: Authorities of the Administrator," establishes EPA's organization and implementing authority under the statute.

Subchapter III, "Hazardous Waste Management," includes the pivotal provisions governing the management and treatment of hazardous waste. For hazardous waste, the statute establishes a presumption of federal (EPA) implementation unless a state adopts a regulatory program sufficient to obtain state "primacy" over the program. Key provisions of this central subchapter of the statute include:

- 42 U.S.C. §6921, articulating the rules for identification and listing of hazardous waste;
- 42 U.S.C. §6922, establishing rules governing generators of hazardous waste;
- 42 U.S.C. §6923, establishing rules governing transporters of hazardous waste;
- 42 U.S.C. §6924, establishing rules governing owners and operators of hazardous waste treatment, storage and disposal facilities (TSDFs), including EPA promulgation of hazardous waste treatment standards;
- 42 U.S.C. §6925, establishing permit requirements for TSDFs;
- 42 U.S.C. §6926, authorizing state primacy over hazardous waste management programs in their states if they meet minimum requirements adopted by EPA; and
- 42 U.S.C. §6928, providing for federal enforcement authority.

Subchapter IV governs state regulation of non-hazardous solid waste. In contrast to subchapter III regulation of hazardous waste, subchapter IV provides automatically for primary state regulation of solid waste, but subject to minimum federal guidelines promulgated by EPA. Key provisions of this subchapter of the statute include:

- 42 U.S.C. §6942, requiring EPA to adopt federal guidelines for state solid waste management plans;
- 42 U.S.C. §6943, establishing requirements for federal approval of state solid waste management plans;
- 42 U.S.C. §6944, establishing federal criteria for solid waste disposal sites (sanitary landfills); and
- 42 U.S.C. §§6946 and 6947, providing for development, federal approval, and implementation of state solid waste management plans.

Subchapter IX establishes a separate program for the regulation of underground storage tanks that contain hazardous materials and that might contaminate groundwater.

An Analytical Approach to the Resource Conservation and Recovery Act

Practitioners trying to determine whether an activity requires RCRA compliance, and if so, in what manner, would analyze the situation using the following rubric:

- First, is the material involved a "solid waste" as defined by section 6903(27) and applicable EPA regulations? If so, handling and disposal of the material is subject to some kind of RCRA regulation. If not, the statute does not apply.
- Second, if a material is "solid waste" as defined by the statute, is it also "hazardous waste"? If not, handling and disposal of the material is subject to state regulation under subchapter IV. If so, treatment, storage, transportation and disposal of the material is subject to more stringent regulation under subchapter III of RCRA, by EPA unless the state has obtained primacy for purposes of hazardous waste regulation. A solid waste is also defined as a hazardous waste if it is a listed waste, characteristic waste, mixed waste, or derived waste as defined by section 6921 and applicable EPA regulations; and
- If the waste is hazardous, does the person handling the waste qualify as a "generator," "transporter," or "treatment, storage and disposal facility," subjecting the person to differing sets of applicable regulations under sections 6922, 6923, and 6924, respectively.

B.   THE SOLID WASTE DEFINITION AND RECYCLING POLICY

Does imposing stricter cleanup standards for municipal landfills provide comparable incentives for source reduction? Will homeowners carry cloth bags to grocery stores (thereby minimizing use of plastic bags) because landfill disposal costs have gone up? Does the answer to this question depend upon who pays the disposal costs? Would it matter whether the municipality funds disposal from municipal taxes, from dedicated fees that are assessed equally to every household, or from a fee that varied with the amount of trash put out by a household? Or does it make more sense to address this problem directly through traditional regulation, as some communities have done by banning plastic bags? *See* http://www.caw-recycles.org/issues/plastic_campaign/plastic_bags/national; http://www.plasticbaglaws.org; Bridget M. Warner, *Sacking the Culture of Convenience: Regulating Plastic Shopping Bags to Prevent Further Environmental Harm*, 40 U. MEM. L. REV. 645 (2010).

A major question under RCRA involves how EPA should address recycling. EPA declined to mandate local solid waste management goals for particular materials. But EPA set a voluntary recycling and source reduction goal of 25 percent, which most states met by 1992. EPA, 25 YEARS OF RCRA: BUILDING ON OUR PAST TO PROTECT OUR FUTURE 8 (2001). Some municipalities have done better than 25 percent and some worse. If the agency is convinced that all municipalities can reduce waste by 30 percent, should it mandate such a goal through regulations? In practice, municipal policy has a big effect on recycling and source reduction. Local governments establish recycling programs. Germany, by contrast, requires manufacturers to take back packaging material or contract for its proper disposal. Does this provide a better incentive for pollution prevention? What about deposit/refund systems, where consumers get money back when they return bottles to the grocery store?

With respect to industrial and other non-municipal waste, EPA has used fine-grained regulatory definitions of solid waste to address recycling policy. These definitional choices have created a great deal of complexity and controversy. They determine the jurisdictional reach of RCRA's hazardous waste management program and profoundly influence the program's incentives for recycling and proper waste treatment. It is quite common for important policy issues to inform decisions about a program's jurisdictional reach and for interested parties to extensively lawyer these threshold questions.

United States v. ILCO, Inc.
996 F.2d 1126 (11th Cir. 1993)

FAY, CIRCUIT JUDGE:

This case is an enforcement action filed by the United States Environmental Protection Agency and the State of Alabama against a secondary lead smelter for violations of federal and state environmental law. The district court held the defendant liable and awarded civil penalties and cleanup costs to the government, and ordered compliance with the law. Although the government received a favorable decision, it has appealed the district court's conclusion that the lead components reclaimed from spent batteries are raw materials. The district court reasoned that because the smelter recycles the components into lead ingots, the components must be raw materials, and not hazardous waste subject to the provisions of the Resource Conservation and Recovery Act. The defendant has cross-appealed the district court's order awarding penalties and cleanup costs to the government. Because we find the district court's order well founded in fact and law, we affirm it in all but one respect. We reverse the court's conclusion regarding the lead components reclaimed from spent batteries because EPA, in accordance with its authority granted by Congress, has defined "discarded material" to include "recycled material."

Background

1. Industry Overview

Over the years in the United States there has been a steady increase in the number of vehicle batteries which become useless and subject to disposal. In 1986 the number stood at approximately 70,000,000. Each spent battery is a potential pollutant of the environment and can have serious deleterious effects on people and animals living in the area where the battery may be discarded. Even a small number of batteries thrown into the woods, discarded along roadways or in government designated garbage areas represent a significant threat to the water we drink, the food we eat and under limited circumstances, the air we breathe. The source of this trouble in a battery is lead. . . . Because lead is an expensive element, an industry has developed over the years to reclaim the lead from spent batteries. . . . In the mid-Seventies there were approximately 50 secondary lead smelters in the United States reclaiming the lead from about 90% of all spent batteries. The smelters were themselves a major source of pollution; surface water run-off and process water discharged by the smelters created very real health-threatening problems; on-site and off-site storage or disposition of waste became an increasing risk to the quality of life; and even the air was dangerously polluted by emissions from the smelters. In response to these problems all levels of government began to amend existing laws and to enact new laws and regulations placing much greater controls over ownership and operation of such smelters. Compliance with these new environmental laws and regulations . . . placed such a financial burden on the operation of secondary lead smelters that about 60% of the smelters operating in 1976 were out of business by 1986, and the approximately 20 smelters remaining were reclaiming only about 70% . . . of all discarded batteries. Thus in 1986 only 55,000,000 of the available 70,000,000 batteries were reclaimed, leaving the 15,000,000 unreclaimed spent batteries to endanger the health of all persons near the site of their repose. The 55,000,000 reclaimed batteries produced about 60% of all lead used in the United States. . . . This brief overview demonstrates the secondary lead smelting industry is a most vital industry not only to our economy but also to our environment. . . . Without the industry, over 70,000,000 contaminated batteries would be scattered throughout our country annually. Nevertheless, the heart of this industry centers around the handling of hazardous materials. Exempting the industry from regulation cannot be justified on the theory that its contribution to resolving our environmental problems outweighs the environmental harm caused by its operations.

2. Factual and Procedural Background

Against this industry backdrop the present case unfolds, spanning nearly a decade of interaction between the Environmental Protection Agency ("EPA"), the

Alabama Department of Environmental Management ("ADEM") and Interstate Lead Company, Inc. ("ILCO"). The voluminous facts are very briefly set forth.

ILCO owned and operated a secondary lead smelting facility in Leeds, Alabama, from the 1960's until operations ceased in 1992. As such, it was one of the 20 smelters remaining in the country which reclaimed spent batteries. In 1986 ILCO reclaimed over 2,500,000 batteries, or about 5% of those reclaimed in the United States. Diego Maffei is the president and majority shareholder of ILCO.

ILCO purchased batteries from various suppliers and placed them in a reclamation process. Incoming batteries were cracked open and drained of sulfuric acid. The rubber or black plastic battery boxes were chipped and washed to remove lead particles. The lead battery components known as "plates and groups" were then removed from the broken batteries and run through ILCO's smelting process to produce lead ingots for sale. The operation produced several waste products which were the subject of litigation in the district court: waste acid, wastewater treatment sludge, broken battery casings or "chips," and emission control dust and blast slag from the smelting process. EPA asserted, and continues to argue on appeal, that the reclaimed lead plates and groups were also waste products. The defendants viewed the plates and groups as raw materials essential to the lead recovery industry.

EPA and ADEM initiated this case as an enforcement action against ILCO and its president, Diego Maffei, seeking an injunction to curtail ongoing violations of environmental laws and regulations at ILCO's plant in Leeds and seeking penalties for past violations. The amended complaint contained six claims, but two settled during trial. Of the four remaining claims, EPA first alleged ILCO violated the Clean Water Act ("CWA"), 33 U.S.C. §§1251-1387, by improperly discharging waste water at or near the plant site in violation of its NPDES permit, and subsequent to March 1984 without any permit. The second and third claims concerned the treatment, storage and disposal of hazardous wastes since 1980 in violation of the Resource Conservation and Recovery Act ("RCRA"), as amended by the Hazardous and Solid Waste Amendments of 1984, 42 U.S.C. §§6901-92k. In the second claim EPA charged ILCO with maintaining storage areas, an incinerator and a treatment tank, all containing hazardous waste, in violation of regulations applicable to their status as an interim facility and maintaining other storage facilities and a landfill without the requisite permit. The third claim encompassed the same RCRA violation, alleging that the facility permitted releases of hazardous waste into the environment. The fourth claim focused upon alleged violations of the Comprehensive Environmental Response, Compensation, and Liability Act ("CERCLA"), 42 U.S.C. §§9601-75, at a place known as "the Church of God site," located about six miles north of the plant. ILCO was charged with dumping hazardous waste in a ravine behind the Church of God, which released or threatened to release hazardous substances into the environment. Consequently, EPA sought recovery for the excavation costs incurred in removing the waste.

This appeal arises from a finding of liability against ILCO and Maffei under the CWA and the RCRA, and a judgment awarded to EPA for cleanup costs. The district court ordered the defendants (1) to pay a $3.5 million penalty for violations of RCRA, the CWA and state laws, (2) to attain compliance with the laws, and (3) to reimburse the United States $845,033 for prejudgment interest and response costs incurred by EPA in performing a cleanup at the Church of God. The court found the lead plates and groups to be solid waste as defined in 40 C.F.R. §261.2 because they exhibit the characteristic of "Extraction Procedure toxicity" for lead and cadmium as defined in that regulation. However, the court also held the plates and groups at the ILCO facility were not "hazardous waste," accepting ILCO's argument that it did not "discard," but rather purchased the plates and groups as raw materials for the purpose of recovering lead values. EPA and ADEM appeal this ruling.

Discussion

The sole question of law raised by EPA on appeal is whether lead parts, which have been reclaimed from spent car and truck batteries for recycling purposes, are exempt from regulation under RCRA. The standard of review is *de novo*. Reviewing the interpretive decisions of an administrative agency is a two-step process: If Congress has clearly and directly spoken to the precise question at issue, effect must be given to the expressed intent of Congress. If the court finds the statute silent or ambiguous with respect to the specific issue, it must ask whether the agency's regulation is based on a "permissible" or "reasonable" construction of the statute. Chevron USA, Inc. v. National Resources Defense Council, 467 U.S. 837, 842-45 (1984). Considerable weight and deference are afforded an agency's interpretation of a statute entrusted to its administration.

Because Congress has not spoken to the precise question at issue, we must decide whether EPA has reasonably construed the RCRA to permit regulation of the recycling of hazardous materials. There is no question that the materials at issue are hazardous; the district court specifically found the plates and groups were "Extraction Procedure toxic" for lead and cadmium. If it is permissible for EPA to determine that "solid waste," as defined by Congress, includes materials that are recycled, then the lead plates and groups were "hazardous waste" and must be managed accordingly. We conclude that EPA's regulations are a reasonable exercise of its authority granted by Congress. For this reason and those to follow, we find the lead plates and groups that ILCO reclaims from spent batteries fall squarely within the law and regulations governing the storage, disposal and treatment of hazardous waste.

The RCRA, as amended, 42 U.S.C. §§6901-92k (1988), is a comprehensive environmental statute, which grants EPA authority to regulate solid and hazardous wastes from "cradle-to-grave." "Congress' 'overriding concern' in enacting RCRA was to establish the framework for a national system to insure the safe management of hazardous waste." RCRA directs EPA to promulgate regulations establishing a comprehensive management system for hazardous wastes. 42 U.S.C. §§6921-39b (1988).

Before a material can be designated and regulated as a "hazardous waste," it must first be determined to be a "solid waste." *See* 42 U.S.C. §6903(5) (1988). Solid waste includes:

> any garbage, refuse, sludge from a waste treatment plant, water supply treatment plant, or air pollution control facility *and other discarded material*, including solid, liquid, semisolid,

or contained gaseous material resulting from industrial, commercial, mining, and agricultural operations, and from community activities. . . .

42 U.S.C. §6903(27) (1988) (emphasis added). 42 U.S.C. §6921 directs the Administrator of the EPA to identify those solid wastes which are "hazardous" and whose management should therefore be governed by RCRA. In particular, §6921 requires the Administrator both to "promulgate criteria for identifying the characteristics of hazardous waste" and, using these criteria, to list "specific hazardous wastes."

Pursuant to its authority, EPA has promulgated regulations that specifically address discarded lead-acid batteries. Without clarifying the meaning of "discarded," Congress defined solid waste as "any discarded material" not otherwise exempted from regulation. EPA has filled the statutory gap by defining "discarded material" as any material which is abandoned, recycled, or inherently wastelike. 40 C.F.R. §261.2(a)(2) (1992). "Recycled material" refers to, inter alia, spent material which has been reclaimed. 40 C.F.R. §261.2(c)(3) (1992). A material is "'reclaimed' if it is processed to recover a usable product, or if it is regenerated. Examples are recovery of lead values from spent batteries. . . ." 40 C.F.R. §261.1(c)(4) (1992). "Reclaimed material" clearly includes lead values derived from the plates and groups at issue here. Furthermore, these battery components fall within the §261.1(c)(4) definition of recycled material because ILCO runs the plates and groups through a smelting process to recover a usable product, lead, which is then cast into ingots and sold. Thus, having met the definition of "recycled," the lead components are discarded material as defined in 40 C.F.R. §261.2(a)(2).

The regulations also specify those recycled materials which are solid wastes. They include "spent materials" that are recycled by "reclamation," or are "accumulated, stored, or treated before recycling" by reclamation. 40 C.F.R. §261.2(c) (1992). A "spent material" is "any material that has been used and as a result of contamination can no longer serve the purpose for which it was produced without processing." 40 C.F.R. §261.1(c)(1) (1992). Thus, the applicable regulations are unambiguous with respect to spent lead components used in a recycling process: spent materials "are solid wastes when reclaimed." 40 C.F.R. §261.2(c)(3) and Table 1 (1992).

ILCO argues that it has never "discarded" the plates and groups and, therefore, the material it recycles is not "solid waste" as defined in RCRA §6903(27). The lead plates and groups are, no doubt, valuable feedstock for a smelting process. Nevertheless, EPA, with congressional authority, promulgated regulations that classify these materials as "discarded solid waste." *Somebody* has discarded the battery in which these components are found. This fact does not change just because a reclaimer has purchased or finds value in the components.

The regulations reflect EPA's policy decision that spent batteries, including their lead components, became "part of the waste disposal problem," when the original consumer discarded the battery. It is unnecessary to read into the word "discarded" a congressional intent that the waste in question must finally and forever be discarded, as ILCO seems to argue. It is perfectly reasonable for EPA to assume Congress meant "discarded once." Were we to rule otherwise, waste such as these batteries would arguably be exempt from regulation under RCRA merely because they are potentially recyclable. Previously discarded solid waste, although it may at some point be recycled, nonetheless remains solid waste. Therefore, we find these batteries and their contents are "discarded" within the everyday sense of the word. Their secondary character as recyclable material is irrelevant to that determination.

We have found nothing in the language of the statute, and ILCO has brought forth nothing from the legislative history to show that EPA's policy choice is not one Congress would have sanctioned. On the contrary, application of these regulations to spent batteries and parts generated by consumers comports with Congress' intent in RCRA to address the problems posed by hazardous waste. The House Committee explained:

> It is not only the waste by-products of the nation's manufacturing processes with which the committee is concerned: but also the products themselves once they have served their intended purposes and are no longer wanted *by the consumer.* For these reasons the term discarded materials is used to identify collectively those substances often referred to as industrial, municipal or *post-consumer* waste; refuse, trash, garbage and sludge.

We, therefore, will not disturb an agency's policy choice that is reasonably consistent with the purpose of the statute.

Conclusion

For the foregoing reasons, we REVERSE the district court's determination that the lead plates and groups are "raw materials" and hold they are "hazardous waste" subject to regulation under RCRA, but AFFIRM its decision in every other respect. The case is REMANDED for proceedings consistent with this opinion.

NOTES AND QUESTIONS ON *UNITED STATES v. ILCO*

1. *Discouraging recycling?* If the lead from lead acid batteries can be removed and the lead can be reused, aren't secondary lead smelters providing society a benefit? Why, then, subject secondary lead recyclers to onerous regulation under RCRA? Won't that just mean fewer such recyclers will be able to stay in business? What is the justification for that?

2. *Meaning of discarded.* If secondary lead smelters are using car batteries, how is it that the car batteries are "discarded"? How far down the chain should RCRA regulation go? Should the lead ingots produced by the secondary lead recycler be regulated as hazardous wastes?

3. *Goals.* Consider the following goals that Congress established for RCRA:

Objectives and national policy

(a) **Objectives.** The objectives of this chapter are to promote the protection of health and the environment and to conserve valuable material and energy resources by—

. . .

(4) assuring that hazardous waste management practices are conducted in a manner which protects human health and the environment;

(5) requiring that hazardous waste be properly managed in the first instance thereby reducing the need for corrective action at a future date;

(6) minimizing the generation of hazardous waste and the land disposal of hazardous waste by encouraging process substitution, materials recovery, properly conducted recycling and reuse, and treatment;

. . .

42 U.S.C. §6902(a)(4)-(6). Do these objectives conflict, either inherently or as applied to the problem of recycling lead batteries?

A Note on the Closed Loop Recycling Exemption

Although EPA defines "discarded material" and hence solid waste quite broadly, the definition does have limits. *See* 40 C.F.R. §261.4 (2010). In American Mining Congress v. EPA, 824 F.2d 1177 (D.C. Cir. 1987), the D.C. Circuit held that materials "destined for . . . recycling in a continuous process by *the generating industry itself*" are not discarded material and therefore not solid waste. Can you see why the *ILCO* court did not find this holding controlling?

The D.C. Circuit interpreted *American Mining Congress (AMC I)* narrowly in several subsequent cases. In American Petroleum Institute v. EPA, 906 F.2d 729, 732, 741 (D.C. Cir. 1990), the court held that EPA unlawfully excluded slag residuals from a metals reclamation process from treatment standards. Because the slag inputs to the reclamation process were first disposed of as part of a waste treatment process prior to reclamation, the court held that they were solid wastes. *Id.* at 741. In American Mining Congress v. EPA, 907 F.2d 1179, 1186-87 (D.C. Cir. 1990) (*AMC II*), the court held that EPA may regulate sludges from wastewater that were stored in impoundments but that *may* be reclaimed in the future as solid waste. Both of these cases read *AMC I* as only exempting materials that were immediately reused in an ongoing manufacturing process.

In Ass'n of Battery Recyclers, Inc. v. EPA, 208 F.3d 1047, 1053 (D.C. Cir. 2000), however, the court held that RCRA does not apply to materials stored temporarily prior to recycling, and suggested that a reference to "immediate" reuse that appeared in *AMC I* cannot be read literally. The court distinguished *American Petroleum Institute* because the materials in that case were first classified as hazardous wastes and subject to a mandatory treatment regime, some residuals from which were subject to later reuse. It distinguished *AMC II* because the industry petitioners in that case claimed only that the materials *might* be reused, subjecting them to EPA's rule treating materials accumulated speculatively (*i.e.*, in anticipation of possible recycling) as discarded material. The court acknowledged that some of the wastes at issue in *Battery Recyclers* might also fall into the speculative accumulation category, but that other wastes might be subject to immediate reuse in a continuous industrial process and therefore were not subject to regulation.

In American Petroleum Institute v. EPA, 216 F.3d 50 (D.C. Cir. 2000), the court vacated an EPA rule regulating oil-bearing wastewater. *Id.* at 58. It applied a "primary purpose" test, under which wastewater treatment would prove subject to RCRA regulation only if the oil refiner's primary purpose was compliance with the Clean Water Act rather than recovery of used oil. *Id.* at 57-58. At the same time, the court upheld a rule prohibiting sham recycling by treating non-refinable materials in used oil as hazardous waste and limiting "speculative accumulation" of used oil. *Id.* at 58-59. In another post-*AMC I* case, the court stated that materials reused in a different industry than that which generated them can fall outside of RCRA's definition of solid waste. Safe Food and Fertilizer v. EPA, 350 F.3d 1263, 1268 (D.C. Cir. 2003), *amended,* 365 F.3d 46 (D.C. Cir. 2004). This statement stands in some tension with the early post-*AMC I* cases, which relied heavily on the narrow *AMC I* language referring to recycling at the facility generating the waste. The *Safe Food and Fertilizer* court, however, remanded to the agency, because environmentalists showed that the fertilizer made with reclaimed metal had higher concentrations of chromium than fertilizer made from virgin materials. *Id.* at 1271. The court suggested that such higher limits were only acceptable if they did not change the environmental risk.

Thus, the line between solid wastes and materials outside of EPA's jurisdiction under RCRA has proven quite blurry at times. It is clear that RCRA regulates discarded materials and does not regulate material that is not part of the waste disposal problem. It is less clear when materials will be deemed discarded, at least when a recycling process is involved. EPA and the courts have struggled to reconcile RCRA's goal of encouraging recycling with its goal of protecting public health and the environment from recycling's hazards. *See* Steven G. Davison, *EPA's Definition of "Solid Waste" Under Subtitle C of the Resource Conservation and Recovery Act: Is EPA Adequately Protecting Human Health and the Environment While Promoting Recycling?*, 30 J. Land, Resources & Envtl. L. 1, 1-7 (2010).

C. RCRA, CERCLA, AND THE ROLE OF REGULATORY LIABILITY IN POLLUTION PREVENTION

RCRA has a largely prospective orientation (although RCRA also includes "corrective action" provisions designed to require the cleanup of contamination at existing TSDFs). It seeks to regulate the disposal of solid waste to limit future environmental problems, such as creation of new sites filled with untreated hazardous waste. As a result, RCRA significantly increased the costs of waste disposal, thus creating economic incentives for waste reduction through recycling, reuse, and source reduction strategies. One of the easiest ways to avoid TSDF treatment and RCRA's tracking obligation is to avoid the generation of hazardous waste in the first place.

In economic terms, RCRA helps to internalize the costs of waste disposal, and economic theory and common sense suggest that rational businesses will take steps to avoid what might be called regulatory liability if the net costs of waste reduction are less than the costs of waste disposal in compliance with RCRA (as well as an array of similar new state waste disposal laws and regulations). One can think of the RCRA debate over recycling policy as but one example of a larger debate about the role of regulation and deregulation in encouraging pollution prevention and recycling. Does EPA encourage pollution prevention by exempting recycling processes from regulation? Would comprehensively regulating all recycling processes better encourage pollution prevention?

But prospective regulatory liability is only one part of the story. Congress adopted RCRA in its modern form in 1976. Unfortunately, quite a bit of dumping of hazardous waste had occurred before RCRA's enactment. Two years later, heavy rains washed mixtures of previously dumped hazardous chemicals into the basements of residents of a Buffalo suburb, which eventually led to the demolition of homes and the relocation of one thousand families who lived at Love Canal, as this site is called. This incident and the realization that thousands of other sites around the nation contained potent brews of previously dumped toxic waste led, a few years later, to the enactment of a law to prompt cleanup of existing disposal sites, the Comprehensive Environmental Response, Compensation, and Liability Act (CERCLA), 42 U.S.C. §§9601-9675. CERCLA made a host of parties with existing or past links to existing disposal sites liable for cleanup costs. We will discuss the CERCLA cleanup process in more detail in Chapter 11, and its allocation of liability in Chapter 12. But some discussion of the prospective effect of this imposition of retroactive liability is relevant to the question of pollution prevention.

CERCLA liability has proven extremely onerous to potentially responsible parties (PRPs, *i.e.*, those within the liable class). Cleanup can prove expensive and agreement about the division of cost among PRPs and the degree of appropriate cleanup often requires years of negotiation and litigation. Superfund liability has proven extremely irksome to PRPs, because many parties can incur a potentially expensive inchoate financial obligation that can take years to clarify. Yet, this onerous approach to liability has provided powerful incentives to avoid the creation of future disposal sites. Those who might get saddled with liability for a cleanup acquire a strong desire to avoid dumping that might create future liability. One way of making sure that a site never becomes a Superfund site is to simply avoid generating hazardous waste in the first place.

CERCLA liability applies to those associated with sites at which a "hazardous substance" is released, or where there is a threatened release. *See* 42 U.S.C. §9607(a). The definition of "hazardous substance" under CERCLA is broader than the definition of "hazardous waste" under RCRA. *See* 42 U.S.C. §9601(14). *Accord* THE RCRA PRACTICE MANUAL 26 (Theodore L. Garrett ed., 2004). This means that a company that has fully complied with RCRA might still become a PRP under CERCLA. How does this disparity in definitions influence incentives for pollution prevention?

How well have RCRA and CERCLA worked in motivating significant pollution prevention? About a decade and a half after Congress enacted RCRA and a decade after passage of CERCLA, several researchers for a group called INFORM conducted a detailed survey of source reduction activities at selected industrial facilities around the country to determine the factors that motivated those changes. The following are some of the significant findings and conclusions of that study:

More than one-third of the source reduction activities (28 out of 80) reduced between 10,000 and 99,000 pounds of waste, while another quarter (21 out of 80) reduced between 100,000 and 999,000 pounds of waste, and 18 percent (14 out of 80) reduced wastes by 1 million pounds or more. . . .

More than one-quarter of the source reduction activities with percent reductions reported (29 out of 99 activities) achieved total elimination of the target wastestream, while more than half (51 out of 99) achieved reductions of 90 percent or more. . . .

Nearly two-thirds of the 33 source reduction activities for which this information was reported (21, or 64 percent) required 6 months or less for implementation (including research and development); another 30 percent (10 out of 33) required 6 months to 3 years; and only 6 percent (2 out of 33) required more than 3 years. . . .

Sixty-eight of the 70 source reduction activities for which INFORM identified a change in product yield showed an increase in yield (one had no effect and one decreased the yield). . . .

Fifteen percent of the source reduction activities for which annual dollar savings were reported (9 out of 62) save $1 million or more annually, nearly half (28 out of 62) save between $45,000 and $1 million annually, more than one-quarter (17 out of 62) save between $6,000 and $45,000 each year, and 3 percent (8 out of 62) save less than $6,000 annually; only one out of all 181 source reduction activities documented by INFORM reported a net cost increase due to a source reduction activity. . . .

One-quarter of the source reduction activities for which capital cost information was provided (12 out of 48) required no capital investment for implementation; just under one-half (22 out of 48) required investments of less than $100,000, and these investments were recouped in savings in, on average, under 18 months. While 13 percent of the activities (6 out of 48) required investments of $1 million to $10 million to implement, these costs were paid back by savings in an average of 2.5 years. . . .

Nearly two-thirds (24 out of 38, or 63 percent) of the source reduction activities for which payback period data were reported recouped their capital investments within 6 months or less; the payback period was 6 months to 3 years for another 18 percent (7 out of 38), 3 to 10 years for 8 percent (3 out of 38), and 10 years or more for 11 percent (4 out of 38).

The problems and costs associated with waste disposal were the most frequently cited reason for implementing source reduction activities (cited for 67 out of the 162 source reduction activities for which motivation information was provided, or 41 percent), followed closely by regulations limiting waste discharge or disposal options (cited for 58 activities, or 36 percent). . . .

Environmental regulations have been the fastest growing incentive in recent years. Cited as the reason for 40 source reduction activities implemented between 1985 and 1990, as opposed to 10 activities implemented before 1985—a 300 percent increase. . . .

Process changes were the most frequently used source reduction technique (used for 78 out of 177 activities for which this information was provided, or 44 percent of the total), followed by operations changes (used for 60 activities, or 34 percent of the total). Less frequently cited techniques were equipment changes (used for 31 activities, or 18 percent), chemical substitutions (used for 18 activities, or 10 percent), and product changes (used for 8 activities, or 5 percent).

Mark H. Dorfman et al., Environmental Dividends: Cutting More Chemical Wastes 14-48 (1992).

NOTES AND QUESTIONS ON LIABILITY AND SOURCE REDUCTION

1. *Success of regulation in inducing pollution prevention.* Some commentators have suggested suggested that regulatory liability was only likely to induce

significant pollution prevention and site cleanup when property changes hands. What do the INFORM data suggest about the role of liability in inducing those activities?

2. *Motivating factors.* What factors most seem to explain business decisions to engage in pollution prevention activities? Short-term or long-term increases in profitability? Avoiding the risk and the hassle of RCRA, CERCLA, and other liability?

3. *Low hanging fruit.* Is there any reason to believe that the early success of pollution prevention activities in the late 1970s and 1980s reflected the most obvious, easy changes in industrial operations ("low hanging fruit"), but that further gains might be more difficult or more costly? Conversely, is there any reason to believe that even more pollution prevention can occur as newer facilities are designed and built, or as old facilities are modernized?

4. *Other means of inducing pollution prevention.* Information strategies sometimes motivate voluntary pollution prevention. Do you think these approaches are likely to be more or less effective than the creation of liability for disposal costs? Is emissions trading likely to encourage pollution prevention? What factors might affect your answer about which approach(es) should work best?

5. *Compliance counseling.* When a client is faced with a complex set of regulations that might cost a lot of money or reduce or delay productivity, a lawyer's role is often to guide the client through the regulatory maze, advising on various ways to comply with the law in the least onerous (or most desirable) way possible. What do these materials suggest about the range of options a good lawyer should propose that a client faced with potential hazardous waste liability should explore?

ATRAZINE SOURCE REDUCTION PROBLEM

The following is an excerpt from Institute of Agriculture and Natural Resources, University of Nebraska, *Agricultural Management Practices to Reduce Atrazine in Surface Water*, available at http://digitalcommons.unl. edu/extensionhist/1426. Assume the Nebraska Legislature, faced with the likelihood of dramatically increased atrazine use because of climate disruption, wants to take additional steps to encourage or require adoption of these measures. Which of the regulatory means presented in earlier chapters do you think would work best to encourage adoption of these measures where appropriate? Consider, but do not necessarily limit yourself to, approaches based on information, regulation, economic incentives, and liability.

Reducing Atrazine Availability

. . .

Reduced application rates—Reducing application rates will reduce potential loss in runoff. Consider applying less than the label rates if weeds can be controlled. Or use combinations with reduced rates of atrazine (see below).

. . .

Band application—Applying atrazine in a narrow band in crop rows is an effective method of reducing the total amount of atrazine applied. One or more well-timed cultivations is necessary to prevent inter-row weeds from establishing and competing with the crop. . . .

Atrazine alternatives—Atrazine, mainly a broadleaf herbicide, can be replaced either partially or totally in some cropping systems. The alternatives are usually higher in price. . . .

Rotary hoe and cultivation for weed control—Mechanical methods for weed control are effective when timed correctly. The rotary hoe should be used before weed emergence, but after the weed seed has germinated. Usually this will be within a week or 10 days after planting. The cultivator will uproot weeds and cover in-row weeds if used when weeds are small. Neither implement is as effective after weeds become established. These implements usually will complement a banded herbicide application and may reduce the need for a postemergence herbicide.

. . .

Environmental Restoration

A. THE PURPOSE AND ROLE OF RESTORATION

Thus far, we have focused largely on strategies designed to prevent or reduce future environmental harm, for example, by curtailing future pollution emissions or by banning certain substances or practices. What about soil or groundwater that is already contaminated? Or ecosystems degraded by decades if not centuries of human activity? In addition to preventing or mitigating future harm, a comprehensive system of environmental protection should seek to remediate past contamination and to restore degraded ecosystems.

The concept of restoration suggests difficult issues and tradeoffs. First, when is restoration appropriate relative to mitigation or prevention? Where a site is already degraded, the choice may be between spending scarce resources to restore, or to accept that ecological or other values have been wholly or partially lost. In some cases, future economic activities cannot occur without harm, in which case we might choose to forgo the benefits from that activity, accept the resulting harm, or condition the activity on compensatory restoration. Second, what are the goals of environmental restoration; that is, to what state is it possible, reasonable, or desirable to restore a particular damaged site or ecosystem, and how should those decisions be made? Before you study specific environmental restoration requirements presented later in the chapter, consider the two overriding issues of when restoration is appropriate ("whether restoration?") and what restoration should accomplish ("whither restoration?").

1. Whether Restoration?

The Supreme Court decision in the *Entergy* case addressed technology-based standards under the Clean Water Act (CWA) to protect fish and other aquatic life from being killed in cooling water intake structures at electric power plants. In a portion of the Second Circuit decision not reviewed by the Supreme Court, then-Judge (now Justice) Sotomayor ruled on the legality of relying on restoration to meet the Act's technology-based requirements:

> The [rule] allows a facility to meet the national performance standards . . . through the use of restoration measures such as restocking fish killed by a cooling water system and improving the habitat surrounding the intake structure in order, as the EPA explains, "to provide additional flexibility to facilities in complying with the rule. . . ." The state and environmental petitioners contend that the EPA exceeded its authority by allowing compliance with section 316(b) through restoration measures because . . . the statute's meaning is plain and that restoration measures cannot substitute for the "best technology available for minimizing adverse environmental impact" in cooling water intake structures. The EPA contends that its interpretation of the statute to permit restoration measures as a means of compliance is entitled to deference. . . .
>
> . . . Restoration measures are not part of the location, design, construction, or capacity of cooling water intake structures, and a rule permitting compliance with the statute through restoration measures allows facilities to avoid adopting *any* cooling water intake structure technology at all, in contravention of the Act's clear language as well as its technology-forcing principle. [R]estoration measures substitute after-the-fact compensation for adverse environmental impacts that have already occurred for the minimization of those impacts in the first instance. The Agency's attempt to define the word "minimize" to include "compensati[on] . . . after the fact," is simply inconsistent with that word's dictionary definition: "to reduce to the smallest possible extent," Webster's Third New Int'l Dictionary 1438 (1986).

Riverkeeper, Inc. v. EPA, 475 F.3d 83, 108-10 (2d Cir. 2007), *reversed on other grounds sub nom.* Entergy Corp v. Riverkeeper, Inc., 556 U.S. 208 (2009).

NOTES AND QUESTIONS ON WHEN RESTORATION IS PROPER

1. *Restoration and technology-based standards.* Why is it inappropriate generally to rely on *post hoc* restoration to meet the technology-based standards in the CWA? Why do you think Congress made that choice? Conversely, can you envision a statutory provision establishing a technology-based approach to restoration, and what would such a provision look like? (We will see some technology-based restoration requirements later in the chapter.)

2. *When is restoration appropriate?* If restoration isn't appropriate to meet the kinds of technology-based standards Congress adopted in the CWA, when is it an appropriate environmental strategy? Only to redress past harm that can no longer be prevented? That is the example discussed in Section B below on remediation of contaminated waste sites. Or might restoration play a role in offsetting future harm in some circumstances? Those are the key issues addressed in Section C below on compensatory mitigation as a condition of future development under the Surface Mining Conservation and Reclamation Act and under section 404 of the CWA.

2.   Whither Restoration?

[Restoration] raises perplexing issues of what we mean by a "healthier" ecosystem. Restoration requires difficult judgments about what we want to restore, to what condition, and to what purpose. In its seminal report on restoration of aquatic ecosystems, a National

Research Council committee defined "restoration" as "the reestablishment of predisturbance aquatic functions and related physical, chemical, and biological characteristics." But what do we mean by "predisturbance"? Over the course of even recent geological history, the Colorado River has hardly been a static place. About a million years ago, a lava dam rose to 2,330 feet within the Grand Canyon—over three times higher than Glen Canyon Dam—and may have backed up the river for 179 miles upstream of Lees Ferry until the river eroded away the dam in about a quarter of a million years. In the face of massive changes wrought by natural forces, as well as significant artificial modifications, to what condition should we "restore" the river now? The Society for Ecological Restoration International defined restoration as "the process of assisting the recovery of an ecosystem that has been degraded, damaged, or destroyed. This, of course, still requires judgments about what we mean by 'recovery.'"

Scientists have developed a variety of tools to characterize "natural" (or predisturbance) ecosystems. . . . But because ecosystems constantly change, due to both natural and human forces, there is no single, fixed target condition for purposes of restoration. As just one example . . . humans introduced wild horses and burros to the American West, species now protected by federal law but not native to North America at the time of European arrival. Does restoration of western range lands require removal of wild horses and burros? A more ecologically significant and plausible restoration target may be to identify natural processes (such as annual inundation of floodplains) and natural ranges of variation within which species and ecosystems fluctuate.

Restoration ecologist Eric Higgs described this quandary as "the dark waters of defining restoration," and noted that "[t]here is no *original* condition for an ecosystem in any meaningful sense; one cannot fix a specific point in time." Ultimately, Higgs argued that defining restoration goals is as much a function of values as of science. Below Glen Canyon Dam, for example, full restoration of the ecosystem competes with environmental amenities such as a superb trout fishery that have thrived under the new conditions. Defining values, then, requires attention not just to scientific but also to political processes. Although scientists continue to make progress in defining ways to identify restoration goals and means to achieve them, in the Colorado River basin and elsewhere our legal and political institutions have not always followed so quickly in helping us to make the choices necessary to adopt and implement restoration efforts with clearly defined purposes.

Even when we identify restoration goals, uncertainty can plague our efforts to achieve them. Often the reasons for ecosystem impairment are difficult to identify, especially in complex systems with multiple sources of harm. We may not know which of those causes to redress, in which order, and to which degree. A large degree of real-world experimentation may be necessary to test which restoration strategies are effective, usually under variable conditions that can cloud experimental results with additional uncertainty, due to both natural and artificial changes. Did fish return to a particular stretch of river this year because of increased flows from the upstream dam (the restoration action), or was it because of an unusually large supply of food (environmental variability)? Did fish continue to decline because the restoration action (more water) was ill-conceived, or because of polluted runoff from a new construction project?

. . . The issues become even more complex as the scale of ecosystem restoration increases from a local wetland to a small river within a single state or community to a huge watershed like that of the Colorado River, which crosses both state and international boundaries. Professionals are now beginning to grapple with the problem of restoration on a large, ecosystem scale, rather than at a smaller, project-specific level. From the Columbia River watershed to the Florida Everglades, from the Chesapeake Bay to the San Francisco Bay delta, we are trying to reverse long-term ecosystem declines. We are doing so not just by reducing or eliminating new sources of harm, but by rejuvenating some of the physical, hydrological, and biological features and processes that support those systems.

ROBERT W. ADLER, RESTORING COLORADO RIVER ECOSYSTEMS: A TROUBLED SENSE OF IMMENSITY 7-11 (2007).

NOTES AND QUESTIONS ON THE NATURE OF RESTORATION

1. *Dam removal.* Removal of existing dams is one striking example of the difficult choices that must be made in ecosystem restoration. The above excerpt refers to ongoing efforts to restore the Colorado River to promote recovery of endangered fish and for other purposes. The most dramatic proposed restoration strategy is to decommission the Glen Canyon Dam, which provides electric power for millions of residents in the Southwest, stores water to implement the seven-state Colorado River Compact, and attracts millions of visitors a year for recreation on Lake Powell. Decommissioning the dam would help to restore the natural flow pattern through Marble Canyon and Grand Canyon, probably to the benefit of native endangered species, and would also uncover long-inundated treasures in Glen Canyon. What restoration issues are raised by this proposal, and how should they be decided? We return to those issues at the end of this chapter.

2. *Hazardous waste remediation.* You might think that remediation of contaminated hazardous waste sites, although perhaps technically challenging, poses less difficult philosophical issues than does ecosystem restoration. But does it? If a spill or landfill leachate contaminates a previously unpolluted aquifer, to what cleanup levels should it be remediated? Zero contamination? Natural background levels? Levels dictated by Safe Drinking Water Act standards? Under what principles from earlier chapters should that decision be made?

A Note on Terminology

"Restoration" is a broad term that encompasses all of the material in this chapter, and a range of different strategies to remedy past environmental harm. However, other terminology is used to describe different kinds of restoration efforts, and we retain those distinctions below. For example, the term "remediation" is used extensively to refer to the cleanup of sites contaminated with hazardous materials. The term "reclamation" is used in the Surface Mining Control and Reclamation Act, and applies to the restoration of surface coal mining sites once mining activities are completed. The term "compensatory mitigation" is used to refer to wetlands restoration designed to offset wetland loss or degradation from new developments or other projects. In more comprehensive restoration efforts, however, multiple tools can be used together. For example, remediation of polluted soil, groundwater, or other environmental media might be one important component of a broader ecological restoration effort, but restoration might entail other measures as well. The 1989 *Exxon Valdez* oil spill in Alaska and the 2010 *Deepwater Horizon* offshore platform blowout in the Gulf of Mexico both required extensive remediation efforts to clean up the massive amounts of spilled oil. However, both incidents caused extensive ecological harm that require broader restoration strategies even after as much of the oil is cleaned up as possible. Robust ecological restoration also might include revegetation, reintroduction of animal species whose populations were reduced or eliminated, etc. Likewise, restoration of a damaged aquatic ecosystem might require remediation of contaminated sediments but also restoration of natural stream channels and hydrological flow regimes.

B. REMEDIATION OF CONTAMINATED WASTE SITES

The most straightforward application of environmental restoration is the remediation of sites that are contaminated by leaks, spills, illegal dumping, or even past practices that were lawful (or at least not specifically prohibited) when conducted. Most often, Congress sought to impose this cleanup obligation on the owners of contaminated property or on those responsible in some way for the contamination. Where no such parties can be located, or where they are insolvent, the government often assumes cleanup responsibility itself. We address those liability allocation issues in Chapter 12. The following section focuses on the nature of the remediation and the process for making cleanup decisions.

1. Site Remediation Under CERCLA

In Chapter 10, we focused on the use of CERCLA liability as a means of inducing pollution prevention. However, we also noted there that Congress enacted CERCLA in the wake of Love Canal and other tragic examples of widespread environmental contamination. Another major purpose of CERCLA, therefore, was to provide for the prompt and effective cleanup of contaminated sites. Congress provided EPA with authority under sections 104-106 of CERCLA to either clean up contaminated sites itself and to recoup the costs from potentially responsible parties (PRPs), or to force third parties to conduct cleanups through administrative orders or judicial action. Section 107(a) of CERCLA, in turn, imposes liability for:

> (A) all costs of removal or remedial action incurred by the United States Government or a State or an Indian tribe not inconsistent with the national contingency plan;
> (B) any other necessary costs of response incurred by any other person consistent with the national contingency plan;
> (C) damages for injury to, destruction of, or loss of natural resources, including the reasonable costs of assessing such injury, destruction, or loss resulting from such a release; and
> (D) the costs of any health assessment or health effects study carried out under section 9604(I) of this title.

42 U.S.C. §9607(a). Note first what is *not* included in this list, which is toxic tort-type liability to private parties for damages other than those listed above, although the statute does expressly preserve the availability of common law or other statutory claims for those injuries. *Id*. §9607(j). (The "health assessment or health effects" liability in subsection (D) only covers the costs of the study, conducted by the Agency for Toxic Substances and Disease Registry (ATSDR) within the Centers for Disease Control (CDC), and not actual damages from adverse health effects caused by the release.)

Natural resource damages may be recovered by federal, state, or tribal natural resource trustees, pursuant to a detailed set of regulations promulgated by a group of federal agencies. *See* 42 U.S.C. §9607(f); State of Ohio v. Department of the Interior, 880 F.2d 432 (D.C. Cir. 1989); 59 Fed. Reg. 14265 (March 25, 1994). Unlike the other categories of recoverable damages under CERCLA, however, natural resource damages include a limited exception from the principle of retroactive liability. Damages may not be recovered "where such damages and the release of a hazardous substance from which such damages resulted" occurred "wholly before December 11, 1980." 42 U.S.C. §9607(f)(1). This provision of the statute has been used sparingly. *See* UNITED STATES GENERAL ACCOUNTING OFFICE, STATUS OF SELECTED FEDERAL NATURAL RESOURCE DAMAGE SETTLEMENTS (November 1999); UNITED STATES GENERAL ACCOUNTING OFFICE, SUPERFUND: OUTLOOK AND EXPERIENCE WITH NATURAL RESOURCE SETTLEMENTS (April 1999).

The National Contingency Plan, or NCP, is a lengthy set of EPA regulations outlining "procedures and standards for responding to releases of hazardous substances, pollutants, and contaminants." 42 U.S.C. §9605(a). The NCP is published at 40 C.F.R. §300 (2004). EPA originally developed the NCP to address oil spills and hazardous substance spills under section 311 of the Clean Water Act, 33 U.S.C. §1321, but Congress directed EPA to revise and republish the plan to address the much broader circumstances and responsibilities encompassed in CERCLA. The NCP thus addresses both the handling of emergency spills and leaks, and longer-term responses to the release of hazardous substances at a range of contaminated sites. Compliance with the NCP is particularly important to the CERCLA liability scheme because liability is contingent on the response being "not inconsistent with" the plan in government cost recovery actions, and "consistent with" the plan in private cost recovery actions. *See* Washington State Dep't of Transp. v. Washington Natural Gas Co., 36 E.R.C. 1045 (W.D. Wash. 1992), *aff'd*, 51 F.3d 1489 (9th Cir. 1994), *amended and superseded by* 59 F.3d 793 (9th Cir. 1995) (disallowing recovery due to non-compliance with NCP).

For contaminated sites that are on the National Priorities List (NPL), and that undergo an intensive government cleanup process, a complex "remedy selection" process dictates the nature of the cleanup. The major steps in a government-led process, all of which must be conducted pursuant to the NCP, are outlined in the following table:

Stage	Activity
Site identification	The site is placed on CERCLIS, a national EPA database of contaminated sites. An updated list is available at http://www.epa.gov/superfund/sites.
Preliminary assessment	Agency officials conduct a brief analysis of site conditions based on readily available information.
Site inspection	On-site visit is used, along with the preliminary assessment (jointly known as a "PA/SI") to determine what additional action is needed.

Stage	Activity
Removal action	The federal government is authorized to take immediate action to respond to a release or substantial threat of release of a hazardous substance into the environment, or a release or substantial threat of release of any other pollutant or contaminant into the environment that "may present an imminent and substantial danger to the public health or welfare." Removal actions are designed to reduce or eliminate immediate threats from releases or threatened releases, and may include actions such as the removal of the materials themselves, monitoring, placement of fencing or other containment structures, replacement of contaminated water supply, temporary evacuation and housing of threatened people, and similar emergency assistance.
Hazard ranking/listing	The hazard ranking system is a process by which EPA determines the degree of risk to human health and the environment posed by a site compared to others around the country. While the NPL is used to determine EPA's cleanup priorities and the use of federal cleanup funds, it is not a prerequisite to liability or other statutory abatement authority.
Remedial investigation and feasibility study ("RI/FS") and remedy selection	EPA conducts a more detailed evaluation of the site to determine what contaminants are present and the degree of contamination; and to evaluate feasible alternative remedies based on efficacy, cost, and other factors. Based on this investigation and other considerations discussed below, EPA issues a proposed plan for public comment, followed by a record of decision regarding the appropriate cleanup remedy and methods.

CERCLA section 121 sets forth a confusing and complex set of substantive standards used by EPA to determine the appropriate remedy at particular sites. Section 121(a) requires EPA to select "cost-effective" responses, taking into account both short- and long-term costs and operation and maintenance costs. Presumably, this favors permanent solutions over those that require ongoing treatment or maintenance. Section 121(b) establishes a hierarchy in which "treatment which permanently and significantly reduces the volume, toxicity or mobility of the hazardous substances, pollutants, or contaminants" is preferred over other cleanup methods, and in which off-site transport and disposal of contaminants without treatment is "the least favored alternative remedial action where practicable treatment technologies are available." The provision includes a list of factors EPA should consider in choosing among options, followed by the following:

> The President shall select a remedial action that is protective of human health and the environment, that is cost-effective, and that utilizes permanent solutions and alternative treatment technologies or resource recovery technologies to the maximum extent practicable.

42 U.S.C. §9621(b)(1). Section 121(d) adds to this set of standards a list of requirements under other federal or state environmental laws and regulations that must be met in CERCLA cleanups if they are "legally applicable or relevant and

appropriate" standards (known from this language as "ARARs"). The following case addresses the degree to which EPA complied with those requirements in the NCP, and in turn, the fundamental issue of "how clean is clean" in hazardous waste site remediation:

≡ ***State of Ohio v. U.S. Environmental Protection Agency***
≡ *997 F.2d 1520 (D.C. Cir. 1993)*

PER CURIAM.

These consolidated petitions present a multifarious challenge to Environmental Protection Agency ("EPA") regulations promulgated under the Comprehensive Environmental Response, Compensation, and Liability Act of 1980 ("CERCLA"). . . . The regulations under review are portions of the National Oil and Hazardous Substances Pollution Contingency Plan, 40 C.F.R. Part 300, commonly known as the "NCP."

. . . Of particular importance to this case is the prominent role of the NCP under CERCLA. Section 104(a)(1) of CERCLA authorizes the President "to act, consistent with the national contingency plan, to remove or arrange for the removal of, and provide for remedial action relating to such hazardous substance, pollutant, or contaminant at any time . . . , or take any other response measure consistent with the national contingency plan which the President deems necessary to protect the public health or welfare or the environment." The NCP thus "provide[s] the organizational structure and procedures" for responding to hazardous waste threats. It is the means by which EPA implements CERCLA. . . .

II

The States first challenge several elements of the NCP definition of legally "applicable" or "relevant and appropriate" environmental standards, known as "ARARs." CERCLA does not define ARARs, but the statute does require that remedial actions at Superfund sites result in a level of cleanup or standard of control that at least meets the legally applicable or otherwise relevant and appropriate federal (or stricter state) requirements. 42 U.S.C. §9621(d)(2)(A). The NCP defines "applicable requirements" as follows:

> *Applicable requirements* means those cleanup standards, standards of control, and other substantive requirements, criteria, or limitations promulgated under federal environmental or state environmental or facility siting laws that specifically address a hazardous substance, pollutant, contaminant, remedial action, location, or other circumstance found at a CERCLA site. Only those state standards that are identified by a state in a timely manner and that are more stringent than federal requirements may be applicable.

40 C.F.R. §300.5. "Relevant and appropriate requirements" are those substantive requirements that, while not "applicable," nonetheless "address problems or situations sufficiently similar to those encountered at the CERCLA site that their use is well suited to the particular site." *Id.* . . .

D. Does the NCP Improperly Fail to Apply Zero-Level Maximum Contaminant Level Goals ("MCLGs") as ARARs?

The States challenge EPA's decision that Maximum Contaminant Level Goals ("MCLGs") established under the Safe Drinking Water Act ("SDWA"), 42 U.S.C. §§300f to 300j-26, do not have to be attained for contaminants whose MCLG has been set at a level of zero. The States contend that EPA lacks authority to depart from a statutory requirement to achieve MCLGs, and in the alternative, that even if EPA possesses this authority, it has failed to provide a reasoned basis for its departure.

The SDWA is specifically referenced in section 121(d)(2)(A) of CERCLA as one of the federal laws containing ARARs for Superfund cleanups. The SDWA identifies two standards for exposure to contaminants. The first, Maximum Contaminant Level Goals ("MCLGs"), are generally unenforceable goals that reflect the level for a given contaminant at which "no known or anticipated adverse effects on the health of persons occur and which allows an adequate margin of safety." Many MCLGs for carcinogens are set at zero. The second type of standards, Maximum Contaminant Levels ("MCLs")—the actual maximum permissible concentration levels under the SDWA—must be set as close as "feasible" to their corresponding MCLGs, taking into account available technology and cost.

While MCLGs are unenforceable under the SDWA, section 121 of CERCLA converts them into enforceable goals, providing:

> Such remedial action shall require a level or standard of control which at least attains Maximum Contaminant Level Goals established under the Safe Drinking Water Act . . . where such goals or criteria are relevant and appropriate under the circumstances of the release or threatened release.

42 U.S.C. §9621(d)(2)(A). Consistent with this requirement, the NCP generally requires the attainment of MCLGs. When the MCLG for a contaminant has been set at a level of zero, however, the NCP requires only that the MCL be attained. In essence, EPA has made a categorical determination that MCLGs set at a level of zero are never "relevant and appropriate under the circumstances" of a release.

This determination was based on EPA's conclusion "that it is impossible to detect whether 'true' zero has actually been attained." During rulemaking to promulgate MCLGs under the SDWA, EPA "emphasized that . . . zero is not a measurable level in scientific terms." "Due to limitations in analytical techniques, it will always be impossible to say with certainty that the substance is not present. In theory, RMCLs [Recommended Maximum Contaminant Levels] at zero will always be unachievable (or at least not demonstrable)."

The States contend that EPA's decision concerning zero-level MCLGs is inconsistent with CERCLA's mandate that all remedial actions attain MCLGs. This argument ignores the full language of the section, which imposes the requirement "where such goals . . . are relevant and appropriate under the circumstances of the release or threatened release." This language leaves EPA with discretion to determine when MCLGs are relevant and appropriate. The States contend, though, that such discretion cannot be exercised in a categorical manner, but instead must be based on a case-specific determination at individual sites. Hence, there is no reason for EPA to make an individualized determination of what they have concluded can never be relevant and appropriate.

The States also contend that even if EPA has discretion to conclude that zero-level MCLGs are never relevant and appropriate, it has not justified the decision to do so in this case. But EPA articulated a number of justifications, and we find its reliance on the fact that true zero levels can never be detected to provide adequate support for the Agency's decision. As we understand EPA's scientific analysis, one can never prove a true zero level. If the measuring device indicates zero, this shows only that the device is not sufficiently sensitive to detect the presence of any contaminants. It does not show the total absence of the contaminants. In other words, if one asserts that zero contaminants are present, this can be *falsified* by showing the presence of some detectable level, but it can never be shown to be *true*. EPA chose to set MCLGs for carcinogens at zero under the SDWA because they "are goals which may or may not be practically achievable and the practicality of these goals should be factored into the MCLs," not the MCLGs. In contrast, EPA concluded that "ARARs must be measurable and attainable since their purpose is to set a standard that an actual remedy will attain." . . .

III . . .

C. Does the NCP Cancer Risk Range Improperly Fail to Protect Human Health and the Environment Without Regard to Cost?

The States next challenge EPA's use of a cancer risk range between 10-6 and 10-4 in the NCP, arguing that an exposure level greater than 10-6 is never appropriate. A 10-4 risk subjects the surrounding population to an increased lifetime cancer risk of 1 in 10,000. A 10-6 risk subjects the surrounding population to an increased lifetime cancer risk of 1 in 1,000,000. When EPA develops objectives for a remedial action at a site, it selects a remediation goal that "establish[es] acceptable exposure levels that are protective of human health." EPA attempts to use health-based ARARs to set the goal, but if ARARs are nonexistent or unsuitable for use, EPA establishes the goal based on criteria in the NCP. "For known or suspected carcinogens, acceptable exposure levels are generally concentration levels that represent an excess upper bound lifetime cancer risk to an individual of between 10-6 and 10-4. . . ." The NCP expresses a preference for remedial actions that achieve a level of 10-6 however, the ultimate decision depends on a balancing of nine criteria, including cost.

The States contend that by permitting cost to play a role in determining the level of exposure, the cancer risk range fails to meet the requirement . . . that remedial actions be "protective of human health." The States' argument necessarily depends, though, on the notion that an exposure level greater than 10-6 is not protective of human health. CERCLA requires the selection of remedial actions "that are protective of human health," not as protective as conceivably possible. A "risk range of 10-4 to 10-6 represents EPA's opinion on what are generally acceptable levels." Although cost cannot be used to justify the selection of a remedy that is not protective of human health and the environment, it can be considered in selecting from options that are adequately protective.

The States also argue that the actual risk range selected is not adequately protective. EPA concluded, though, that all levels of exposure within the risk range are protective of human health. *Id.* EPA has used 10-4 as an upper bound for establishing risk levels in the past, and "[m]any ARARs, which Congress specifically intended be used as cleanup standards at Superfund sites, are set at risk levels less stringent than 10-6." The States offer no evidence challenging EPA's position that 10-4 represents a safe level of exposure, and in any event, we give EPA's findings on this point significant deference.

The States also argue that EPA failed to justify the use of a range, instead of a single point. But EPA explained its decision to use a range. While "[t]he use of 10-6 expresses EPA's preference for remedial actions that result in risks at the more protective end of the risk range," the Agency is also required to consider other factors in selecting an appropriate remedy. "Factors related to exposure, uncertainty and technical limitations may justify modifications of initial cleanup levels that are based on the 10-6 risk level." A flexible approach to developing remedial goals is justified by the multiple statutory mandates of CERCLA, so long as EPA meets the statutory requirement of protectiveness. . . .

IV

. . .

A. Does NCP Remedy Selection Guidance Concerning the Use of Engineering and Institutional Controls Violate CERCLA's Remedy Selection Requirements?

The States first argue that one of EPA's "program expectations" violates CERCLA by authorizing the use of institutional controls (such as fences and deed restrictions) as a sole remedy at Superfund sites. The NCP provision regarding selection of an appropriate remedy provides in part as follows:

> (iii) *Expectations.* EPA generally shall consider the following expectations in developing appropriate remedial alternatives:
>
> . . .
>
> (D) EPA expects to use institutional controls such as water use and deed restrictions to supplement engineering controls as appropriate for short- and long-term management to prevent or limit exposure to hazardous substances, pollutants, or contaminants. . . . The use of institutional controls shall not substitute for active response measures (e.g., treatment and/or containment of source material, restoration of ground waters to their beneficial uses) as the sole remedy unless such active measures are determined not to be practicable, based on the balancing of trade-offs among alternatives that is conducted during the selection of remedy.

The States interpret this language to authorize EPA to choose, based on cost considerations, institutional controls as the sole remedy for cleaning up hazardous waste sites. As a result, they believe that this provision may allow EPA to use cost considerations to select a cleanup remedy that may not comply with the minimum human health and environmental protectiveness requirements of CERCLA, and to select a remedy in which there is no treatment or removal of contaminants.

However, EPA explained in the Federal Register that the program expectations are not intended to displace the use of the nine criteria identified [above]:

EPA has placed the expectations in the rule to inform the public of the types of remedies that EPA has achieved, and anticipates achieving, for certain types of sites. These expectations are not, however, binding requirements. Rather, the expectations are intended to share collected experience to guide those developing cleanup options. . . . *However, the fact that a proposed remedy may be consistent with the expectations does not constitute sufficient grounds for the selection of that remedial alternative. All remedy selection decisions must be based on an analysis using the nine criteria.*

Thus, any remedy relying on institutional controls must meet the threshold requirement of protectiveness. . . . [The court did not rule on this issue on the merits, finding that it was not ripe for review prior to actual implementation.]

NOTES AND QUESTIONS ON *OHIO v. EPA*

1. *Cleanup to drinking water standards.* Should groundwater beneath hazardous waste sites always be cleaned up to drinking water standards under the Safe Drinking Water Act regardless of cost? What if no one uses or plans to use the groundwater for water supply purposes? What if it is less expensive to treat only the water that is actually extracted for drinking water, rather than cleaning up the entire aquifer to those standards? But given that Congress decided that drinking water standards are an appropriate remediation goal by identifying them explicitly as an ARAR, is EPA correct in its interpretation of CERCLA section 121(d)(2)(A) (quoted in the opinion) that it is not necessary to always require treatment to MCLGs, which are pure effects-based standards, as opposed to MCLs, which consider feasibility and cost as well?

2. *Permanent remedies.* Why the statutory preference for permanent remedies? Why do you think Congress did not adopt it as a mandatory requirement?

3. *Cancer risk levels and environmental justice.* The court allowed EPA to retain a very large range of appropriate cancer risk levels remaining at sites after remediation, from one in ten thousand to one in a hundred thousand. Does this suggest potential environmental justice or other concerns?

4. *Institutional controls.* The use of so-called institutional controls is controversial, because they suggest that, in some cases, post-cleanup land use can simply be restricted rather than actually cleaning up the site. If the potential land uses at the site are less valuable than the cost of the cleanup, why is such an approach presumptively wrong?

5. *Critiques of CERCLA remedy selection.* Although the details and technical complexities are well beyond the scope of this treatment, remedy selection under CERCLA has been quite controversial on risk assessment and other grounds. The ultimate issue is whether we should spend huge amounts of money to remediate sites such that they are safe for other uses, or simply take steps to eliminate human exposure and other environmental risks from that contamination, at lower cost but usually with the loss of the productive future uses of those sites. *See, e.g.,* Linly Ferris & David Rees, *CERCLA Remedy Selection: Abandoning the Quick Fix Mentality*, 21 ECOLOGY L.Q. 785 (1994); James T. Hamilton & W. Kip Viscusi, *Human Health Risk Assessments for Superfund*, 21 ECOLOGY L.Q. 573 (1994).

6. *RCRA corrective action.* In sections 3004(u) & (v) and 3008(h) of RCRA, 42 U.S.C. §§6924(u), (v), 6928(h), added by the Hazardous and Solid Waste Amendments of 1984, Congress provided similar cleanup remedies for sites subject to RCRA's permitting requirements for hazardous waste treatment, storage, and disposal facilities (TSDFs). EPA expects final corrective action cleanups to be completed at more than 3,500 RCRA sites by 2020.[1] For a good description of the corrective action process, which parallels the CERCLA site remediation process in many respects, see Terry J. Satterlee & Jerry L. Anderson, *RCRA Corrective Action: The Next Wave of Hazardous Substance Cleanup*, 59 UMKC L. Rev. 181, 182 (1991).

7. *Brownfields.* In the Brownfields Revitalization and Environmental Restoration Act of 2001, Pub. L. No. 107-118, Title II, 115 Stat. 2360, Jan. 11, 2002, Congress created an exception from CERCLA liability for developers who purchase property contaminated by prior owners, and who agree to take appropriate steps to stop ongoing releases, mitigate future harm, and remediate the site to appropriate standards. The brownfields program can be viewed as a form of restoration as a condition of future development, a concept discussed further below.

C. COMPENSATORY RESTORATION AS A CONDITION OF FUTURE DEVELOPMENT

Another way to prompt environmental restoration is to impose prospective compensatory restoration requirements on parties who seek to engage in new activities that are likely to cause future environmental harm. In *Riverkeeper*, the Second Circuit held that relying on restoration in lieu of prevention was unlawful under the CWA technology-based provision at issue in that case. In other situations, however, environmental statutes either expressly or implicitly allow future harm with the expectation of some form of compensatory mitigation or restoration. The two key related questions, both suggested in Section A above, are *when* that approach is appropriate, and when it is, what nature and degree of restoration is sufficient to offset the accepted harm? We explore those issues in two separate environmental law contexts.

In some situations we have decided that damaged sites can be restored sufficiently after an activity occurs. A prime example is the Surface Mining Control and Reclamation Act (SMCRA), 30 U.S.C. §§1201 *et seq.*, which requires operators of surface coal mines (so-called strip mines because huge surface areas are mechanically "stripped" away from the earth) to reclaim and revegetate the damaged area after mining activities are completed. However, the Act also calls for threshold judgments about where such an approach is inappropriate through findings that some areas are "unsuitable" for mining.

---

1. U.S. Environmental Protection Agency, Corrective Action, http://www.epa.gov/osw/hazard/correctiveaction/index.htm.

In other cases, a project will cause unavoidable harm to a site that cannot be repaired once the activity ceases, such as a new housing development that will permanently fill or irreparably degrade existing wetlands. In such cases, the permitting agency can require the developer to restore wetlands elsewhere to replace the ecological functions and values that will be lost due to the project. In the Clean Water Act section 404 permitting program, this is known as compensatory mitigation. Under the sequencing process in the section 404 program regulations, however, EPA and the U.S. Army Corps of Engineers are supposed to ensure that wetland damage is prevented or mitigated first, and that restoration is used only when damage is unavoidable. Moreover, as with the unsuitability determination for surface mining, EPA can also determine that damage to some areas will cause "unacceptable adverse effects to the aquatic ecosystem," 33 U.S.C. §1344(c), and thereby prohibit the activity altogether.

1. Reclamation Under the Surface Mining Control and Reclamation Act

Congress adopted the Surface Mining Control and Reclamation Act in 1977 to redress the significant environmental impacts of surface coal mining, including huge swaths of Appalachia and other regions that were left badly scarred by unreclaimed mining sites. In addition to a comprehensive regulatory regime designed to minimize harm during new mining, the statute imposed requirements designed to ensure that operators reclaim sites after the coal is extracted, to a condition suitable for productive post-mining uses. First, however, Congress addressed the issue of *when* it is appropriate to allow future harm in return for the promise of later site reclamation by establishing a process by which both the federal government and individual states can declare areas to be "unsuitable for mining" for two distinct kinds of reasons. First is where the state "determines that reclamation pursuant to the requirements of this chapter is not technologically and economically feasible." 30 U.S.C. §1272(a)(2). Second, the Act requires states to consider petitions to designate land unsuitable for mining where mining will:

> (A) be incompatible with existing State or local land use plans or programs; or
> (B) affect fragile or historic lands in which such operations could result in significant damage to important historic, cultural, scientific, and esthetic values and natural systems; or
> (C) affect renewable resource lands in which such operations could result in a substantial loss or reduction of long-range productivity of water supply or of food or fiber products, and such lands to include aquifers and aquifer recharge areas; or
> (D) affect natural hazard lands in which such operations could substantially endanger life and property, such lands to include areas subject to frequent flooding and areas of unstable geology.

Id. §1272(a)(3). Similar provisions apply to federal lands where mining would adversely affect national parks, wildlife refuges, trails, wilderness areas, wild and scenic rivers, national forests, historic sites, or other important areas. *Id.* §1272(e). For lands that are not designated as unsuitable for mining, however, the statute allows mining to occur so long as adequate reclamation occurs when mining is over. The following is an edited version of the key statutory standards governing the adequacy of post-mining reclamation, and a seminal case interpreting those requirements:

30 U.S.C. §1265 (SMCRA §515). Environmental protection performance standards

(b) General standards. General performance standards shall be applicable to all surface coal mining and reclamation operations and shall require the operation as a minimum to—

(2) restore the land affected to a condition capable of supporting the uses which it was capable of supporting prior to any mining, or higher or better uses of which there is reasonable likelihood. . . .

(3) . . . backfill, compact . . . and grade in order to restore the approximate original contour of the land. . . .

(6) restore the topsoil or the best available subsoil which is best able to support vegetation. . . .

(10) minimize the disturbances to the prevailing hydrologic balance at the mine-site and in associated offsite areas and to the quality and quantity of water in surface and ground water systems both during and after surface coal mining operations and during reclamation. . . .

(19) establish . . . a diverse, effective, and permanent vegetative cover of the same seasonal variety native to the area of land to be affected and capable of self-regeneration and plant succession at least equal in extent of cover to the natural vegetation of the area; except, that introduced species may be used in the revegetation process where desirable and necessary to achieve the approved post-mining land use plan. . . .

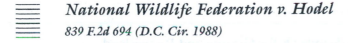

National Wildlife Federation v. Hodel
839 F.2d 694 (D.C. Cir. 1988)

WALD, CHIEF JUDGE, GINSBURG, RUTH BADER, CIRCUIT JUDGE, and SILBERMAN, CIRCUIT JUDGE:

I.   Introduction

The Surface Mining Control and Reclamation Act of 1977, Pub. L. No. 95-87, 91 Stat. 445 (codified as amended at 30 U.S.C. §§1201 *et seq.*) ("the Surface Mining Act," "the Act," or "SMCRA") . . . established "a nationwide program to protect society and the environment from the adverse effects of surface coal mining operations." SMCRA §102(a). Environmental impacts from surface coal mining (and the surface impacts of underground coal mining operations) are regulated through two basic mechanisms: a permit system (§§506-514) and a series of performance standards (§§515-516). The Act's permit provisions require that before engaging in a surface coal mining operation, a mine operator must submit detailed information concerning the environmental consequences of the proposed mining operations and include a plan for reclaiming affected lands as required by the Act. Once the mining operation has begun, the mine operator must adhere to the statutory environmental performance standards, many of which relate to the obligation to restore and reclaim affected lands. *See* SMCRA §§515-516. . . .

III.   Merits

A.   *Prime Farmland and Pastureland Issues . . .*

1.   Revegetation Success Standards for Prime Farmland

In order to show effective reclamation of prime farmland, the Secretary requires, as the measure of soil productivity, and prior to the release of the mine operator's performance bond, the actual growth of crops for at least a three-year period. Industry complains that the Secretary and, on review, the district court failed to consider adequately whether a careful use of soil survey techniques would measure soil productivity in the manner (a) required by the statute, or (b) if not required by the Act, then at least preferable under the relevant section.

The Secretary's regulation calls for a comparison of the reclaimed land's actual crop productivity with the productivity of neighboring, nonmined prime farmland of the same soil type. To promote a valid comparison, similar management techniques must be employed and similar crops must be grown; measurement adjustments may be made, with the concurrence of the U.S. Soil Conservation Service, to account for disease, pest, and weather conditions, or specific management practice variations. Before revegetation will be accepted as successful, resulting in release of all or part of a performance bond or deposit, average yield of the restored soil over a period of three or more crop years must equal or exceed the average yield of the comparison area.

Industry urges initially that the . . . words "until soil productivity for prime farm lands has returned to equivalent levels of yield" are qualified by the further words of the section, "as determined from the soil survey. . . ." Under Industry's reading, a post-mining soil survey, not actual cropping, is the statutory requirement. The district court, however, concluded that the Secretary was entitled to require actual farming and we agree. . . .

2.   Revegetation Success Standards for Grazing and Pastureland

Rejecting NWF's challenge . . . the district court upheld the Secretary's revegetation regulation for land with a post-mining grazing or pastureland use. That regulation aims to ensure reclamation success by requiring, at a minimum, that "the ground cover and production of living plants on the revegetated area shall be at least equal to that of a reference area or such other success standards approved by the regulatory authority."

NWF argues first that soil surveys alone are inadequate to demonstrate the success of grazing land reclamation, and second that actual grazing must be required because it is the only reliable measure of range land revegetation success. The district court agreed that "the use of a soil survey alone is insufficient," but found that the Secretary so recognized. In this court too, the Secretary of the Interior has represented that the regulation does not contemplate reliance on a soil survey "or any other method not based on actual production to establish vegetative success." Thus, there appears to be no contest over the insufficiency of a soil survey. The genuine issue concerns the actual production method necessary or proper to determine vegetation success.

For its second point, NWF relies most heavily on a National Academy of Science Report on mined land reclamation. We comprehend that study, as did the Secretary and the district court, to conclude that evaluation of the productivity of soil reclaimed for grazing must be based on measurements of actual production. But we do not find in the study, any more than the Secretary or the district court did, insistence that grazing is the only acceptable method of establishing range land revegetation success. In sum, we cannot say that the Secretary acted unreasonably in declining to require grazing to test reclamation success on sites designated as post-mining range or pastureland; it was sufficient, we hold, for the Secretary to require the use of a reference area comparison or other approved success standard that measures actual vegetation production. . . .

3. Backfilling and Grading

. . . Unlike the replaced regulations, the revised provisions failed to furnish regulatory authorities with guidance beyond the prescriptions of the Act itself, and on that account the district court remanded the revisions. On appeal, the Secretary and Industry contend that the district court incorrectly read the Act to require, for each statutory prescription, additional regulatory guidance or "fleshing out." We hold, in accord with the Secretary, that the Act does not automatically and inevitably *require* him to "flesh out" the [statute]. . . . [O]nly with respect to terracing did the Secretary adequately explain why guidance beyond the statutory requirements sensibly could not be given to local regulators. . . .

c. Terraces

The direction in §515(b)(3) of the Act to return land to its approximate original contour countenances the substitution of a terraced post-mining landscape for a non-terraced pre-mining landscape. The 1979 regulations required terraces to be constructed with bench widths less than twenty feet and slopes between benches (outslopes) less than fifty percent, unless the regulatory authority approved a wider bench or steeper outslope. As revised, the regulations do not describe a maximum bench width or outslope angle, leaving approval of these and other terrace characteristics to the regulatory authority's judgment. The current regulations do instruct regulators to ensure a reasonable reproduction of the land's original contour. As in the 1979 regulations, the current regulations allow terracing only upon approval of the regulatory authority.

The Secretary has explained on various occasions, both before and after the revisions, that the purpose of the terrace dimension regulations is to ensure the creation of land forms that will support post-mining land uses and provide erosion and water runoff control. The terrace bench and outslope requirements were never intended to fulfill the statutory environmental performance standard of ensuring return to approximate original contour. Instead, these requirements existed to ensure restoration of mined land to a condition capable of supporting its post-mining uses, by affording erosion control and moisture conservation, so that revegetation could be accomplished. . . .

Supporting his elimination of the bench width and outslope angle rules, the Secretary explained that terrace design to control surface erosion and water runoff must be based on local soil characteristics, local soil-management practices, and local climate. This explanation of the inutility of providing national terrace dimension guidelines adequately justifies the Secretary's decision against imposing such guidelines to fill out the statutory approximate original contour standard. We therefore reverse the district court judgment remanding the terrace regulation and uphold the Secretary's action. . . .

NOTES AND QUESTIONS ON *NATIONAL WILDLIFE FEDERATION v. HODEL*

1. *Defining successful restoration.* If a company shows that it restored soils, slopes, hydrology, and other properties of prime farmland to conditions sufficient to support farming, why do the regulations require three years of actual crop growth before declaring reclamation successful? Is the goal to restore soil or to restore productive farms? How are those goals different? Why, then, do the rules not also require three years of successful grazing to demonstrate restoration of grazing or pasture lands? Is the goal to restore grazing vegetation or grazing, and how do those goals differ? If a site is restored to a condition that allows it to be used as or more productively as before mining, why must the operator also restore the site to its "approximate original contour" (AOC)? Why the statutory preference for revegetation with native species?

2. *Reference conditions.* A standard methodology for defining restoration goals is to use a "reference" system, an ecosystem, ecosystem component, or in the case of SMCRA a piece of land with a similar land use, deemed sufficiently similar to the area being restored to serve as a valid basis for comparison. *See* THE HISTORICAL ECOLOGY HANDBOOK: A RESTORATIONIST'S GUIDE TO REFERENCE ECOSYSTEMS (Dave Egan & Evelyn A. Howell eds., 2001). Biological water quality criteria are also defined using reference aquatic ecosystems. What problems do you see with the effort to define restoration by way of reference conditions? For farms, grazing lands, and other economic uses? For ecological uses?

3. *Performance standards or practice standards.* Does SMCRA use performance standards, practice standards, or both to achieve the statutory goal of satisfactory reclamation? How would you characterize the requirement to "restore the land affected to a condition capable of supporting the uses which it was capable of supporting prior to any mining" in section 515(2)? What about the requirement to regrade the site to its "approximate original contour"? Which kind of approach do you think will be more successful in achieving successful restoration?

4. *The debate over "fleshing out."* At one level, this section of the opinion is simply an exercise in statutory construction. Did Congress intend to require more detailed rules for all aspects of the reclamation program, or just those deemed necessary by the Secretary? But this battle can be viewed in two other ways that suggest more significant issues:

    a. *The sufficiency of restoration.* The debate over "fleshing out" relates to the conceptual difficulty of defining successful restoration. Given the substantial variability among individual places and ecosystems, can restoration goals be specified adequately in rules of general applicability, or are they better left to individual site determinations?

b. *Federalism and variable conditions.* The Secretary's decision to eliminate some detailed restoration regulations allowed individual states to determine what level of restoration is sufficient. Given that appropriate restoration requirements are likely to differ around the country, but that Congress enacted SMCRA in part due to the significant perceived ineffectiveness of state surface mining control efforts, was that judgment appropriate?

5. *Bonding and long-term site management and control.* In most environmental programs, we rely on *post hoc* enforcement to redress violations of environmental laws and regulations. The Surface Mining Act and some other statutes, however, require performance bonds or other forms of financial assurance prior to approval of various activities. *See, e.g.*, 42 U.S.C. §6924(t) (financial responsibility requirements for operators of hazardous waste treatment, storage, and disposal facilities). What is it about reclamation requirements under SMCRA (or operation of TSDFs under RCRA) that warrants *post ante* measures to assure compliance?

6. *Abandoned mine reclamation.* SMCRA is designed to ensure appropriate reclamation on existing and future mine sites. What about the thousands of abandoned mine sites that induced Congress to pass this law? Subchapter IV of SMCRA, 30 U.S.C. §§1231 *et seq.*, creates an abandoned mine reclamation program and an abandoned mine reclamation fund fueled by a reclamation fee imposed on all coal mining operators per ton of coal produced. Why should existing mining companies pay for harm caused by past operators, many of which are now out of business?

2. Compensatory Mitigation Under Clean Water Act Section 404

In the surface mining context, surface lands can be restored post-mining. By contrast, where wetlands are permanently destroyed or degraded by development, compensatory restoration can only occur off-site. In other words, the goal is not to restore the original ecological functions and values that were lost, but to *replace* them with similar functions and values elsewhere. What additional problems are suggested by that difference? Does this concept raise the same issues of equivalent currency as posed in the article by Salzman and Ruhl? Does it suggest that it is even more important to avoid wetland losses wherever possible? In 2001, the National Research Council issued a report critiquing the practice and effectiveness of wetlands restoration in several key respects:

> The Corps of Engineers keeps data on the areas of permitted fill and areas of compensatory mitigation required as a condition for permits. From 1993 to 2000, approximately 24,000 acres of wetlands were permitted to be filled, and 42,000 acres were required as compensatory mitigation on an annual basis. Thus, 1.8 acres were supposed to be mitigated (i.e., gained) for every 1 acre permitted (i.e., lost). If the mitigation conditions specified in permits were actually being met, this ratio suggests that the 404 permit program could be described as resulting in a net gain in jurisdictional wetland area and function in the United States. The committee, however, found that the data available from the Corps were not adequate for determining the

status of the required compensation wetlands. In addition, the data do not report the wetland functions that were lost due to the permitted fill. Further, the literature on compensatory mitigation suggests that required mitigation projects often are not undertaken or fail to meet permit conditions. Therefore, the committee is not convinced that the goal of no net loss for permitted wetlands is being met for wetland functions. The magnitude of the shortfall is not precisely known and cannot be determined from current data.

NATIONAL RESEARCH COUNCIL, COMPENSATING FOR WETLAND LOSSES UNDER THE CLEAN WATER ACT (2001).

In part based on this critique, Congress required the Secretary of the Army (through the Army Corps of Engineers) to adopt regulations "establishing performance standards and criteria for the use . . . of on-site, off-site, and in-lieu fee mitigation and mitigation banking as compensation for lost wetlands functions in permits issued by the Secretary of the Army under such section." In 2008, the Army Corps and EPA promulgated new regulations governing the compensatory mitigation process. This is how the agencies explained the concept of compensatory mitigation:

≡ *Compensatory Mitigation for Losses of Aquatic Resources*
≡ *73 Fed. Reg. 19594, 19594-95 (Apr. 10, 2008)*

Compensatory mitigation involves actions taken to offset unavoidable adverse impacts to wetlands, streams and other aquatic resources authorized by Clean Water Act section 404 permits and other Department of the Army (DA) permits. As such, compensatory mitigation is a critical tool in helping the federal government to meet the longstanding national goal of "no net loss" of wetland acreage and function. For impacts authorized under section 404, compensatory mitigation is not considered until after all appropriate and practicable steps have been taken to first avoid and then minimize adverse impacts to the aquatic ecosystem pursuant to 40 CFR part 230 (i.e., the CWA Section 404(b)(1) Guidelines).

Compensatory mitigation can be carried out through four methods: the restoration of a previously-existing wetland or other aquatic site, the enhancement of an existing aquatic site's functions, the establishment (i.e., creation) of a new aquatic site, or the preservation of an existing aquatic site. There are three mechanisms for providing compensatory mitigation: permittee-responsible compensatory mitigation, mitigation banks and in-lieu fee mitigation. Permittee-responsible mitigation is the most traditional form of compensation and continues to represent the majority of compensation acreage provided each year. As its name implies, the permittee retains responsibility for ensuring that required compensation activities are completed and successful. Permittee-responsible mitigation can be located at or adjacent to the impact site (i.e., on-site compensatory mitigation) or at another location generally within the same watershed as the impact site (i.e., off-site compensatory mitigation).

Mitigation banks and in-lieu fee mitigation both involve off-site compensation activities generally conducted by a third party, a mitigation bank sponsor or in-lieu fee program sponsor. When a permittee's compensatory mitigation requirements are satisfied by a mitigation bank or in-lieu fee program, responsibility for ensuring that required compensation is completed and successful shifts from the permittee to the bank or in-lieu fee sponsor. Mitigation banks and in-lieu fee programs both conduct consolidated aquatic resource restoration, enhancement, establishment and preservation projects. . . .

[I]n-lieu fee programs are generally administered by state governments, local governments, or non-profit non-governmental organizations while mitigation banks are usually . . . operated for profit by private entities. [I]n-lieu fee programs rely on fees collected from permittees to initiate compensatory mitigation projects while mitigation banks usually rely on private investment. . . . Most importantly, mitigation banks must achieve certain milestones, including site selection, plan approval, and financial assurances, before they can sell credits, and generally sell a majority of their credits only after the physical development of compensation sites has begun. In contrast, in-lieu fee programs generally initiate compensatory mitigation projects only after collecting fees, and there has often been a substantial time lag between permitted impacts and implementation of compensatory mitigation projects. . . . For all of these reasons, there is greater risk and uncertainty associated with in-lieu fee programs regarding the implementation of the compensatory mitigation project and its adequacy to compensate for lost functions and services.

40 C.F.R. Part 230, Subpart J—Compensatory Mitigation for Losses of Aquatic Resources

§230.93 General compensatory mitigation requirements.

(a) General considerations. (1) The fundamental objective of compensatory mitigation is to offset environmental losses resulting from unavoidable impacts to waters of the United States authorized by [district engineer] DA permits. The district engineer must determine the compensatory mitigation to be required in a DA permit, based on what is practicable and capable of compensating for the aquatic resource functions that will be lost as a result of the permitted activity. . . . Compensatory mitigation requirements must be commensurate with the amount and type of impact that is associated with a particular DA permit. . . .

(2) Compensatory mitigation may be performed using the methods of restoration, enhancement, establishment, and in certain circumstances preservation. Restoration should generally be the first option considered because the likelihood of success is greater and the impacts to potentially ecologically important uplands are reduced compared to establishment, and the potential gains in terms of aquatic resource functions are greater, compared to enhancement and preservation.

(3) Compensatory mitigation projects may be sited on public or private lands. Credits for compensatory mitigation projects on public land must be based solely on aquatic resource functions provided by the compensatory mitigation project, over and above those provided by public programs already planned or in place. . . .

(b) Type and location of compensatory mitigation. (1) When considering options for successfully providing the required compensatory mitigation, the district engineer shall consider the type and location options in the order presented in paragraphs (b)(2) through (b)(6) of this section. In general, the required compensatory mitigation should be located within the same watershed as the impact site, and should be located where it is most likely to successfully replace lost functions and services. . . .

(2) Mitigation bank credits. When permitted impacts are located within the service area of an approved mitigation bank, and the bank has the appropriate number and resource type of credits available, the permittee's compensatory mitigation requirements may be met by securing those credits from the sponsor. . . . Mitigation bank credits are not released for

debiting until specific milestones associated with the mitigation bank site's protection and development are achieved, thus use of mitigation bank credits can also help reduce risk that mitigation will not be fully successful. . . .

(3) In-lieu fee program credits. Where permitted impacts are located within the service area of an approved in-lieu fee program, and the sponsor has the appropriate number and resource type of credits available, the permittee's compensatory mitigation requirements may be met by securing those credits from the sponsor. Where permitted impacts are not located in the service area of an approved mitigation bank, or the approved mitigation bank does not have the appropriate number and resource type of credits available to offset those impacts, in-lieu fee mitigation, if available, is generally preferable to permittee-responsible mitigation. . . .

(4) Permittee-responsible mitigation. . . . Where permitted impacts are not in the service area of an approved mitigation bank or in-lieu fee program that has the appropriate number and resource type of credits available, permittee-responsible mitigation is the only option. . . . [For permittee-responsible mitigation, the rules also establish preferences for mitigation in the watershed, and for on-site mitigation of the same kind of wetlands lost over off-site and out-of-kind mitigation.]

(f) Amount of compensatory mitigation. (1) . . . the amount of required compensatory mitigation must be, to the extent practicable, sufficient to replace lost aquatic resource functions. In cases where appropriate functional or condition assessment methods or other suitable metrics are available, these methods should be used where practicable to determine how much compensatory mitigation is required. If a functional or condition assessment or other suitable metric is not used, a minimum one-to-one acreage or linear foot compensation ratio must be used.

(2) The district engineer must require a mitigation ratio greater than one-to-one where necessary to account for the method of compensatory mitigation (e.g., preservation), the likelihood of success, differences between the functions lost at the impact site and the functions expected to be produced by the compensatory mitigation project, temporal losses of aquatic resource functions, the difficulty of restoring or establishing the desired aquatic resource type and functions, and/or the distance between the affected aquatic resource and the compensation site. . . .

(h) Preservation. (1) Preservation may be used to provide compensatory mitigation for activities authorized by DA permits when all the following criteria are met:

(i) The resources to be preserved provide important physical, chemical, or biological functions for the watershed;

(ii) The resources to be preserved contribute significantly to the ecological sustainability of the watershed. In determining the contribution of those resources to the ecological sustainability of the watershed, the district engineer must use appropriate quantitative assessment tools, where available;

(iii) Preservation is determined by the district engineer to be appropriate and practicable;

(iv) The resources are under threat of destruction or adverse modifications; and

(v) The preserved site will be permanently protected through an appropriate real estate or other legal instrument (e.g., easement, title transfer to state resource agency or land trust). . . .

(m) Timing. Implementation of the compensatory mitigation project shall be, to the maximum extent practicable, in advance of or concurrent with the activity causing the authorized impacts. The district engineer shall require, to the extent appropriate and practicable, additional compensatory mitigation to offset temporal losses of aquatic functions that will result from the permitted activity.

(n) Financial assurances. (1) The district engineer shall require sufficient financial assurances to ensure a high level of confidence that the compensatory mitigation project will be successfully completed, in accordance with applicable performance standards. . . .

§230.95 Ecological performance standards.

(a) The approved mitigation plan must contain performance standards that will be used to assess whether the project is achieving its objectives. Performance standards should relate to the objectives of the compensatory mitigation project, so that the project can be objectively evaluated to determine if it is developing into the desired resource type, providing the expected functions, and attaining any other applicable metrics (e.g., acres).

(b) Performance standards must be based on attributes that are objective and verifiable. . . . Performance standards may be based on variables or measures of functional capacity described in functional assessment methodologies, measurements of hydrology or other aquatic resource characteristics, and/or comparisons to reference aquatic resources of similar type and landscape position. The use of reference aquatic resources to establish performance standards will help ensure that those performance standards are reasonably achievable, by reflecting the range of variability exhibited by the regional class of aquatic resources as a result of natural processes and anthropogenic disturbances. . . .

COMPENSATORY MITIGATION PROBLEM

Answer the following questions using the excerpt from the new compensatory mitigation rules.

1. A developer proposes to build a large new set of condominiums, with an estimated loss of five acres of wetlands. It could avoid all wetlands filling while still reaping a reasonable profit, but it would cost an extra $6 million in design, construction, and other costs. For $3 million, the developer could offset the five acres of wetlands loss by purchasing sufficient mitigation credits from a fully operational and qualified mitigation bank. Can the Corps issue a permit for the less expensive filling option?

2. Section 230.93 provides: "The district engineer must determine the compensatory mitigation to be required . . . based on what is practicable and capable of compensating for the aquatic resource functions that will be lost as a result of the permitted activity." What if there is no practicable alternative to building the condominiums without filling wetlands, and there is insufficient practicable mitigation capable of compensating for the lost wetlands functions. Can the Corps issue a permit?

3. What if the developer can create new wetlands on its property at the end of the construction project? This will be cheaper because it does not have to engage in careful on-site protection efforts for existing wetlands during construction. Is that an acceptable form of mitigation under the regulations?

4. The National Park Service is in the process of restoring riparian wetlands in an adjacent national park, along the same river where the developer proposes to build its project. Can the developer use Park Service efforts as mitigation for its project? What if the developer pays for the Park Service's restoration costs?

5. How many acres of wetland mitigation are required to compensate for the five acres of wetlands expected to be lost?

6. The developer can purchase an adjacent piece of property for less than the $3 million needed to purchase credits from the mitigation bank, because that property is largely undevelopable due to a high groundwater table and other factors. The developer proposes to preserve over ten acres of wetlands on that property by donating the land to a local conservation organization, with an enforceable conservation easement. Under what circumstances might such a scheme work?

7. The developer proposes to restore far more wetlands functions and values than will be destroyed by the project, but it will take almost a decade for those new wetlands to be hydrologically and biologically functional. Can the Corps accept this proposal of "more later" in return for some losses now?

8. What kind of showing must the developer make to prove that the mitigation "worked"? What happens if it does not, and the project is already long built?

NOTES AND QUESTIONS ON COMPENSATORY MITIGATION

1. *Avoidance preference.* If compensatory mitigation is possible, why the preference for avoiding or minimizing wetlands loss?

2. *Restoration preference.* Why the preference for restoration over enhancement, establishment, or preservation (in that order)?

3. *Third party preference.* Why the preference for mitigation by third parties (mitigation banks or in-lieu fee programs) over the permittee?

4. *Type and location preference.* Why the preference for mitigation within the same watershed, and for the same type of wetland the project destroys or degrades?

5. *Performance standards.* Recall the debate about "fleshing out" in the SMCRA regulations, and note that the wetlands regulations rely on permit-specific performance standards based on a very general set of guidelines. Why do you think EPA and the Corps took this approach?

D. LARGE-SCALE ECOSYSTEM RESTORATION

The examples presented above impose specific restoration requirements as either a result or as a condition of particular activities. Some important ecosystems, however, have been so badly degraded that much broader efforts are necessary to restore ecosystem structure and function, because impairment is caused by so many different sources of harm.

At least two of the environmental laws discussed thus far appear to articulate restoration as an affirmative goal. The opening provision of the Clean Water Act (CWA) aspires "to restore and maintain the chemical, physical, and biological integrity of the Nation's waters." 33 U.S.C. §1251(a). Most of the operative provisions of the CWA focus on preventing or mitigating harm from existing and future discharges or other polluting activities rather than restoring the integrity of aquatic ecosystems. However, Congress has established specific restoration programs for a number of large, badly degraded aquatic ecosystems, including the Chesapeake Bay, the Great Lakes, Long Island Sound, and Lake Champlain. *Id.* §§1267-1270. Those programs provide federal funding and support for comprehensive, collaborative watershed management programs designed to identify and redress the most significant sources of aquatic ecosystem impairment. Under the National Estuary Program, individual states can nominate estuaries of "national significance" for similar treatment. *Id.* §1330. The purpose of the Endangered Species Act is "to provide a means whereby the ecosystems upon which endangered species and threatened species depend may be conserved. . . ." 16 U.S.C. §1531(b). The term "conserve" means "all methods and procedures which are necessary to bring any endangered species or threatened species to the point at which the measures provided pursuant to [the Act] are no longer necessary," *id.* §1532(3). Although the term "conserve" seems to refer to the prevention of harm, defining it in terms of "all measures" protecting endangered species also brings "restoration" within the ambit of conservation.

Because large ecosystem restoration typically involves so many different identified or potential sources of harm, however, and seeks to balance a wide range of ecological and societal values, it often presents particularly challenging legal, policy, and scientific problems. "Adaptive management" is an evolving process designed to deal with uncertainties in the law, science, and values of ecosystem restoration. These issues are illustrated by ongoing efforts to restore various components of the Colorado River ecosystem, the background for which is explained in the following excerpt from a report by federal government scientists assembled to study the process (the "SCORE" report). The SCORE report describes the basic attributes of adaptive management.

 The State of the Colorado River Ecosystem in Grand Canyon: A Report of the Grand Canyon Monitoring and Research Center 1991-2004
U.S.G.S. Circular 1282 (2005) 2-6

Administrative History

The Colorado River is the most important water resource in the American West, serving as the main source of drinking water for more than 25 million people. The Colorado River has been extensively engineered to meet the demands placed upon it. There are 22 major storage reservoirs in the Colorado River Basin and eight major out-of-basin diversions. The two largest storage projects—Hoover and Glen Canyon Dams—are located on either end of Grand Canyon National Park. Glen Canyon Dam is located just north of the Grand Canyon National Park boundary, where it creates Lake Powell. . . .

Signed into law by President Dwight D. Eisenhower in 1956, the Colorado River Storage Project Act authorized four mainstem water-storage units, including

Glen Canyon Dam. . . . The CRSP reservoirs allow the upper basin States—Utah, Colorado, Wyoming, and New Mexico—to store water in wet years and release water in times of shortages, thereby enabling the upper basin to meet its obligations under the 1922 Colorado River Compact while also maximizing future water uses. . . . CRSP dams were equipped with hydroelectric generators to produce salable power. Glen Canyon Dam operates eight electric generators, which produce 78% of the total power generated by the CRSP. In 2004, Glen Canyon Dam generated approximately 3.3 million megawatt hours (MWh). The power is sold to approximately 200 wholesale customers—municipal and county utilities, rural electric cooperatives, U.S. Government installations, and other nonprofit organizations—located primarily in six States: Arizona, Colorado, Utah, Wyoming, New Mexico, and Nevada.

Natural History

Before the dam, the Colorado River was a sediment rich river that when swelled with snowmelt from the Rocky Mountains transported large quantities of sediment during spring and early summer and commonly produced flood events. Peak discharge typically reached 85,000 cubic feet per second (cfs) at two-yr intervals and 120,000 cfs at six-yr intervals during these seasonal flood events. By contrast, flows of less than 3,000 cfs were typical during late summer, fall, and winter. Prior to the dam, water temperature also fluctuated seasonally from 32°F to 80°F (0–29°C).

Glen Canyon Dam has changed the seasonal flow, sediment-carrying capacity, and temperature of the Colorado River. Operation of the dam has altered the frequency of floods on the Colorado River and increased median discharge rates at Lees Ferry, whereas managing for hydroelectric power generation has introduced wide-ranging daily fluctuations. [F]rom 1963 to 1991 . . . when the dam was managed primarily to maximize hydroelectric power revenue, it was not uncommon for daily flows to vary from 5,000 to 30,000 cfs. Release patterns of this type caused the river level below the dam to change 7–13 ft (2–4 m) per day, creating public concerns about the quality and safety of fishing and boating and about adverse impacts to natural resources. Because the sediment load of the Colorado River is deposited in Lake Powell, water released from Glen Canyon Dam is essentially clear. Furthermore, because the penstocks of the dam are well below the surface of Lake Powell, the water released from the dam is cold, with an average temperature of 46°F (8°C).

The construction of Glen Canyon Dam also affected a number of aquatic and terrestrial resources downstream in lower Glen and Grand Canyons. Dam-induced changes in the Colorado River's flow, temperature, and sediment-carrying capacity are blamed for narrowing rapids, beach erosion, invasion of nonnative riparian vegetation, and losses of native fishes. These same changes are also associated with an increase in total species richness within Grand Canyon National Park; however, the increases are primarily for species not originally found in Grand Canyon. Some changes to the ecosystem of the Colorado River, such as the introduction of nonnative fish, were already taking place before the construction of Glen Canyon Dam.

It is important to note that Glen Canyon Dam was completed before the enactment of the National Environmental Policy Act of 1969 and the Endangered Species Act of 1973. At the time of Glen Canyon Dam's construction (1956-63), little consideration was given to how dam operations might affect the downstream environment in Grand Canyon National Park. . . .

Federal Efforts to Protect Grand Canyon

The international prominence of Grand Canyon National Park and public concern about the impacts of Glen Canyon Dam caused the Bureau of Reclamation in 1982 to undertake a science program, Glen Canyon Environmental Studies, to examine the effects of dam operations on downstream resources. [A] final report in 1988 concluding that changes in dam operations "could reduce the resource losses occurring under current operations and, in some cases, even improve the status of the resources." In 1989, in response to these findings, Secretary of the Interior Manuel Lujan, Jr., ordered the Bureau of Reclamation to complete an environmental impact statement on the operation of Glen Canyon Dam. To further ensure the protection of downstream resources, Secretary Lujan adopted interim operating criteria for the dam in 1991, which restricted dam operations and remained in effect until the end of the environmental impact statement process.

Congress passed the Grand Canyon Protection Act of 1992 to provide guidance and legal support to the Secretary of the Interior in his efforts to protect Grand Canyon. In addition to directing the Secretary to operate Glen Canyon Dam to protect and improve downstream resources, the act also validated the interim operating criteria, provided a deadline for the completion of the environmental impact statement, required the creation of a long-term monitoring and research program, and allocated program costs. The act clearly stated that it was to be implemented in accordance with existing laws, treaties, and institutional agreements that govern allocation, appropriation, development, and exportation of the waters of the Colorado River Basin. . . .

The Operation of Glen Canyon Dam Final Environmental Impact Statement (hereafter EIS) was filed in March 1995, and the Record of Decision was signed by Bruce Babbitt, Secretary of the Interior, in October 1996. The Record of Decision noted that the goal "was not to maximize benefits for the most resources, but rather to find an alternative dam operating plan that would permit recovery and long-term sustainability of downstream resources while limiting hydropower capacity and flexibility only to the extent necessary to achieve recovery and long-term sustainability." Having established this goal, the Secretary's decision was to implement the modified low fluctuating flow (MLFF) alternative (the preferred alternative in the EIS). . . . The document also formally established the Glen Canyon Dam Adaptive Management Program.

Glen Canyon Dam Adaptive Management Program

The creation of an adaptive management program was a common element for all alternatives considered in the EIS, and its implementation was subsequently mandated by the Record of Decision. Adaptive management was selected to create a process whereby "the effects of dam operations on downstream resources would be assessed and the results of those assessments would form the basis of future modifications of dam operations." . . .

Envisioned as a new paradigm for addressing complex environmental management problems through a dynamic interplay of ecosystem science, management, and policy, adaptive management has gained attention and has been tested in various contexts in the last several decades. Although concepts and methods continue to evolve, adaptive management is generally understood to be a systematic process for continually improving management practices by emphasizing learning through experimentation. Also, adaptive management incorporates collaboration among stakeholders, managers, and scientists as a means of social learning that can prevent policy gridlock. [T]he National Research Council noted that the key components of adaptive management include (1) commitment to ongoing management adjustments based, in part, upon scientific experimentation, (2) shift from "trial and error" to formal experimentation with management actions and alternatives, (3) shift from fragmented scientific investigations to integrated ecosystem science, (4) explicit attention to scientific uncertainties in ecosystem processes and effects of management alternatives, (5) formal experimental design and hypothesis testing to reduce those uncertainties and help guide management adjustments, (6) careful monitoring of ecological and social effects and of responses to management operations, (7) analysis of experimental outcomes in ways that guide future management decisions, and (8) close collaboration among stakeholders, managers, and scientists in all phases of these processes. . . .

_____

The Grand Canyon Adaptive Management Program reflects decades of effort and has documented a significant number of discrete achievements. The SCORE report, however, highlighted significant problems with the effectiveness of the program. The Grand Canyon Trust (an environmental group) challenged the program's compliance with the ESA and the Grand Canyon Protection Act.

 Grand Canyon Trust v. U.S. Bureau of Reclamation
623 F. Supp. 2d 1015 (D. Ariz. 2009)

DAVID G. CAMPBELL, DISTRICT JUDGE.

Plaintiff Grand Canyon Trust (the "Trust") claims that the current operation of Glen Canyon Dam on the Colorado River violates the Endangered Species Act by jeopardizing and taking the endangered humpback chub and by destroying or adversely modifying its critical habitat. The Trust further claims that the Bureau of Reclamation ("Reclamation") and the Fish and Wildlife Service ("FWS")—two federal agencies with environmental responsibilities for the Dam—have failed to comply with relevant statutes. . . .

I. Background

[The court reiterated much of the history in the SCORE report, *supra*.]

The humpback chub is a "big-river fish" that developed three to five million years ago. The species lives in the relatively inaccessible canyons of the Colorado River. Six humpback chub populations have been identified, five upstream of the

Dam and one downstream. Only the downstream population is at issue in this case. The humpback chub was listed as endangered under the statutory predecessor to the Endangered Species Act. In 1973, the chub was formally listed as endangered under the Act. In 1994, some 379 miles of the Colorado River were designated by FWS as "critical habitat" for the chub. "Critical habitat" is habitat essential for the endangered species' survival and therefore in need of special management.

The adult population of humpback chub in the Grand Canyon is estimated to have been 10,000 to 11,000 in 1989, dropping to 4,500 or fewer in 2001. Of some significance for this case are recent studies showing that the chub population has increased in recent years to a total of between 5,300 and 6,700 in 2006. Recent data also show a greater number of young chub in the mainstream of the Colorado River. The reasons for these increases are not presently known, but, as will be seen below, they have influenced agency decisions in this case. . . .

. . . The 1995 FEIS [Final Environmental Impact Statement] evaluated several alternative approaches to operating the Dam and ultimately recommended a system described as "modified low fluctuating flow" or "MLFF." As explained in the FEIS, "this alternative would have the same annual and essentially the same monthly operating plan" as the approach used from 1963 to 1991, but would limit the magnitude of daily and hourly fluctuations in water releases from the Dam. MLFF also included habitat maintenance flows intended "to re-form backwaters and maintain sandbars, which are important for camping beaches and wildlife habitat."

The 1995 FEIS rejected an alternative known as "seasonally adjusted steady flow" or "SASF." SASF did not vary water releases on the basis of electrical power demands, but instead "was developed to enhance the aquatic ecosystem by releasing water at a constant rate within defined seasons and by using habitat maintenance flows. Seasonal variations in minimum flows and habitat maintenance flows were designed with the goal of protecting and enhancing native fish." Water releases under the SASF alternative would be steady throughout any given month, but total monthly releases would be higher in the spring and lower in the summer and fall, more closely tracking the pre-Dam fluctuations of the river.

Secretary of the Interior Bruce Babbitt accepted the recommendation of the 1995 FEIS and, on October 8, 1996, signed a Record of Decision that selected MLFF as the operating system for the Dam (the "1996 ROD"). With the exception of some brief experimental variations that will be mentioned below, MLFF has remained the Dam's method of operation to the present day. . . .

D. *The Law—ESA Consultation and the Effect of a Biological Opinion*

[The court explains the ESA provisions regarding agency consultation under section 7, the preparation of biological opinions describing impacts to listed species, development of "reasonable and prudent alternatives" to avoid jeopardy to listed species, and the issuance of incidental take permits subject to specified conditions.]

E. *The 1994 FWS Opinion, the RPA, and Reclamation's Compliance*

At the heart of this case is a biological opinion issued by FWS in 1994 (the "1994 Opinion"). . . . The opinion concerned Reclamation's selection of MLFF as the operating system for the Dam. FWS concluded that MLFF would jeopardize the humpback chub and adversely modify its habitat. This conclusion was based on the declining chub population and the effect of MLFF on critical chub habitat, particularly the nearshore sandbars and sun-warmed backwaters that were essential for the growth, feeding, and protection of young chub. The 1994 Opinion noted that the fluctuating flows of MLFF reduce the temperatures of backwaters by inundating them with colder water as river levels rise, and reduce food sources in the backwaters. The opinion also noted that fluctuating water levels could force young chub into the more hazardous mainstream of the river.

As required by the ESA, FWS set forth an RPA that would minimize or avoid the adverse effects of MLFF identified in the 1994 Opinion. The RPA included several elements. Although the parties have focused primarily on the steady-flow element, all of the RPA elements are relevant to understanding the actions of the parties in this case.

1. RPA Element 1

RPA element 1 called for Reclamation to develop an "adaptive management program" for the operation of Glen Canyon Dam. The program, referred to as "AMP," was intended to create a forum for all agencies, states, tribes, organizations, and persons with interests in the Dam, the Colorado River, and the Grand Canyon to have a voice in Dam operations. As envisioned by the RPA, the AMP would be used to design studies to determine the effect of river flows on endangered species and to implement actions to increase the likelihood of their survival and recovery. To institute AMP, Reclamation formed the Adaptive Management Working Group ("AMWG"), a 25-member body with representatives from Reclamation, FWS, the National Park Service, other federal and state agencies, the seven Colorado River basin states, environmental groups (including the Trust), electrical power groups, Indian Tribes, and recreation groups. The AMWG makes recommendations to the Secretary of the Interior concerning Dam operations. . . .

2. RPA Element 1A

Element 1A required Reclamation to institute a program of experimental releases from the Dam that included high steady flows in the spring and low steady flows in the summer and fall, and to quantify the effects of such flows on endangered and native fish. . . .

Reclamation used the AMP process to institute high flow tests in 1996 and 2004 and a steady flow test from March to September of 2000, but has not implemented the specific steady flows required by RPA element 1A—high steady flows in the spring and low steady flows in the summer and fall. Nor has Reclamation implemented SASF, the alternative steady-flow regime required by the RPA. As a result, FWS has on several occasions notified Reclamation that element 1A of the RPA "has not seen sufficient progress."

3. RPA Elements 1B . . . and 4

Element 1B called for Reclamation to investigate a system for the "selective withdrawal" of water from Lake Powell. The purpose would be to withdraw warmer water from the lake and thereby increase river temperatures. . . . Reclamation has created preliminary plans for a multi-level water intake structure that could be used to draw warmer water from the lake. . . .

RPA element 4 called for Reclamation to establish a second spawning population of humpback chub downstream of the Dam. The primary spawning colony is located in the lower reaches of the Little Colorado River, near its confluence with the Colorado River. To establish a second spawning population, Reclamation and other agencies, in 2003, relocated 300 young humpback chub to a spot above Chute Falls, a natural barrier on the Little Colorado River. Another 300 chub were moved there in July 2004, followed by another 565 in July 2005. Chub survival and growth rates at this new location have been high. The population above Chute Falls is now reproducing and moving downstream in the Little Colorado, and appears to be a new source for humpback chub in the lower portions of the Little Colorado River and in the mainstem of the Colorado River. . . .

5. Other Conservation Measures

. . . Rainbow trout, a species of fish not native to the Colorado River below the Dam, has thrived in the cold waters created by the Dam. The trout prey on young humpback chub. To address this obstacle to chub survival, the AMP process designed and implemented a program to remove rainbow trout from the key stretch of the Colorado River near the confluence with the Little Colorado. In 2003 and 2004, 16,045 rainbow trout and many other non-native fish were mechanically removed from the river, reducing the population of trout in this stretch by more than 60%. Rainbow and brown trout were also removed from other tributaries such as Bright Angel Creek in anticipation of establishing chub populations in these locations. . . .

F.   The 2008 FWS Opinion

. . . Reclamation created a 2008 Experimental Plan that called for two modifications to MLFF that were designed to benefit the chub—a high water release in March of 2008 to build beach and backwater habitat, and steady flows in September and October of each year from 2008 to 2012 (the "2008 Experimental Plan"). . . . Reclamation performed an Environmental Assessment for this plan and concluded that the environmental impact would not be significant.

Reclamation consulted with FWS concerning the 2008 Experimental Plan and, on February 27, 2008, FWS issued a biological opinion (the "2008 Opinion"). The 2008 Opinion noted recent studies that have shown increases in the humpback chub population, with at least one study concluding that the increases must have started between 1996 and 1999, before Reclamation began conducting experimental flows and removing non-native fish from the river. The 2008 Opinion concluded that "some combination of conditions under MLFF has benefitted the humpback chub, and that more recent conservation actions [such as the removal of rainbow trout] likely have as well[.]" With respect to the two elements of the 2008 Experimental Plan, FWS opined that "implementation of the March 2008 high flow test and the five-year implementation of MLFF with steady releases in September and October, as proposed, is not likely to jeopardize the continued existence of the humpback chub . . . and is not likely to destroy or adversely modify designated critical habitat for the humpback chub."

The 2008 Opinion also noted that Reclamation intended to undertake eight conservation measures to benefit the chub: (1) Reclamation and FWS will reinitiate consultation concerning the chub if the population drops in any single year below 3,500 adult chub; (2) Reclamation, through AMP, will develop a comprehensive plan for the management and conservation of chub in the Grand Canyon; (3) Reclamation will work with the National Park Service to establish spawning populations of the chub in tributaries of the Colorado River such as Havasu, Shinumo, and Bright Angel Creeks; (4) Reclamation, through AMP, will continue to control non-native fish that prey on the chub; (5) Reclamation will takes steps to minimize variations in flow between months—variations that can adversely affect backwater habitat; (6) Reclamation will undertake a nearshore ecology study to examine the effects of flow variations on nearshore habitat; (7) Reclamation and FWS will create a humpback chub refuge in a fish hatchery to protect against catastrophic loss of the chub in the Colorado River; and (8) Reclamation will continue to help other stakeholders in the Little Colorado River watershed develop a plan that protects watershed levels for the chub. FWS found that these conservation measures increase its confidence "that all adverse effects of the proposed action are reduced to the point that the [2008 Experimental Plan] will not jeopardize the species or result in adverse modification of critical habitat."

Significantly for this lawsuit, the 2008 Opinion also stated, in a single sentence and with little explanation, that it "replaces" the 1994 Opinion, the opinion that found MLFF violates the ESA. By replacing the 1994 Opinion, the 2008 Opinion also had the effect of replacing the RPA, including the element 1A requirement that Reclamation implement its own program of steady flows or SASF. Needless to say, the parties have very different views concerning the 2008 Opinion. Reclamation cites the 2008 Opinion as conclusive evidence that it is not violating the ESA by current Dam operations. The Trust argues that the 2008 Opinion is invalid, that it was created as a defense to this lawsuit, that the 1994 Opinion still controls, and that the Dam operations therefore continue to violate the ESA. . . .

III.   Claim 6—Is Reclamation's 2008 Environmental Assessment Valid? . . .

B.   *Did the Environmental Assessment Consider Sufficient Alternatives?*

The Trust contends that Reclamation considered too few alternatives in the 2008 Environmental Assessment. Specifically, the Trust argues that because MLFF constitutes a significant portion of the 2008 Experimental Plan, Reclamation should have considered alternatives to MLFF such as SASF. . . .

The stated purpose of the 2008 Experimental Plan was to engage in Dam releases designed to benefit the humpback chub while complying with federal law and meeting the project purposes of the Dam, including power generation. The releases were to include a spring high flow event during a period of enriched sediment conditions to rebuild sandbars, beaches, and chub habitat, followed by five years of fall steady flows to benefit the chub. Reclamation explained that it sought to preserve recent increases in the humpback chub population while attempting to take further actions to benefit the chub, and therefore proposed a plan that was deliberately conservative. The plan included only two incremental steps—a single spring high flow and five years of fall steady flows—and the only alternative addressed in the Environmental Assessment was a "no action" alternative which would continue operations under MLFF.

The Environmental Assessment evaluated the two steps proposed in the Experimental Plan and found that they would not adversely affect the chub or its habitat. The March 2008 high flow . . . , which was timed to take advantage of increased sediment recently discharged into the Colorado River by the Paria River (a tributary 15 river miles downstream from the Dam), would be an "essential step" in conserving the sediment necessary for chub spawning and in determining the long-term sustainability of sediment resources in the river. The five years of September-October steady flows would be timed to coincide with the emergence of young chub from the Little Colorado River into the mainstem of the Colorado. The steady flows would likely increase the warmth and productivity of backwaters used by young chub to feed and grow. . . .

The Trust argues that the Environmental Assessment's consideration of only two alternatives—the 2008 Experimental Plan and a "no action" alternative fails to satisfy NEPA's requirement that all reasonable and appropriate alternatives be evaluated. . . .

Given the narrowly circumscribed purpose of the 2008 Experimental Plan, the Court concludes that Reclamation's omission of SASF was not unreasonable. In light of recent gains in chub population, the purpose of the project was deliberately conservative: to implement a high flow event during a sediment-rich period in the spring to rebuild beaches and chub habitat, and to implement fall steady flows to aid young chub, all without violating Reclamation's other obligations under the Law of the River or the purposes of the Dam such as power generation. SASF did not fit this narrow objective; it would have worked a much more dramatic change in Dam operations and river conditions. Because SASF was not consistent with the measured approach adopted by Reclamation, NEPA does not require that it be considered. . . .

The Trust argues that Reclamation cannot define the purpose of a project so narrowly as to unreasonably restrict the alternatives considered. This is a correct statement of the law, but the Court does not find the approach taken by Reclamation in the 2008 Experimental Plan to be unreasonable. Not wanting to jeopardize the chub's recent population gains by too dramatic a change, Reclamation opted for a conservative approach. In addition to the unknown effects of dramatic change, Reclamation noted that longer periods of steady flow might cause an increase in warm-water predators and competitors of the chub. Given the deference due the administrative agency charged with managing the Dam, the Court cannot conclude that the purpose of the Experimental Plan was unreasonably narrow. . . .

[B]y arguing that the Environmental Assessment should have . . . considered alternatives such as SASF, the Trust really is arguing that Reclamation should redo the 1995 FEIS. The 1995 FEIS was a NEPA document and was considerably more detailed than the 2008 Environmental Assessment. The 1995 FEIS evaluated MLFF, SASF, and several other alternatives for Dam operations. The FEIS process spanned five years and included wide publication, numerous public meetings, and Reclamation's receipt of more than 17,000 comments. The 1996 ROD, which selected MLFF, committed that "any operational changes will be carried out in compliance with NEPA." The two components of the 2008 Experimental Plan are operational changes from MLFF and were evaluated under NEPA in the Environmental Assessment. . . .

IV.   Claim 7—Does the 2008 FWS Opinion Violate the ESA?

. . . The 2008 Opinion contains a detailed discussion of the Experimental Plan's high flow experiment and concludes that although it might initially have an adverse impact on young chub caught in the high water, it likely will construct more sandbars and backwaters than previous high flow experiments because of the substantial amount of sediment in the river in early 2008. FWS concludes that these formations will be favorable to chub spawning and survival.

The 2008 Opinion also contains a detailed discussion of the Experimental Plan's two-month steady flows in September and October of each year. FWS opines that the effect of these flows "on habitat persistence is most likely to be positive" and that water temperatures are likely to be warmer, benefitting the chub. FWS also determines that the steady flows should increase food sources available for chub in the backwaters. . . .

The key portion of the 2008 Opinion for purposes of this case is the statement that it "replaces" the 1994 Opinion that found MLFF to be a violation of the ESA. As counsel for the Federal Defendants conceded at oral argument, the 2008 Opinion thereby represents FWS's new opinion that MLFF does not violate the ESA. This is a sharp departure from FWS's longstanding opinion.

The 1994 Opinion was clear: "the proposed operation of Glen Canyon Dam according to operating and other criteria of the MLFF . . . is likely to jeopardize the continued existence of the humpback chub . . . and is likely to destroy or adversely modify designated critical habitat." In 1999, FWS stated that Reclamation had not taken sufficient steps to implement the steady flows required by RPA element 1A. Reclamation took the same position in 2002, stating that RPA element 1A "has not seen sufficient progress." FWS reiterated this position in 2006 and noted that "daily fluctuations are detrimental to native fish populations."

In 2007, just one year before it issued the 2008 Opinion, FWS issued a report that confirmed the adverse effects of MLFF on chub habitat. The report observed that "[t]he much hoped for outcome of modest improvement in sandbar resources, as originally proposed and predicted in the [1995 FEIS], has not been realized. . . . Loss of sand habitats in the ecosystem was documented under the No-Action Era (1964-1990), but has continued since dam operations have been altered to mitigate sandbar erosion [through MLFF]." "Although MLFF limitations on the daily allowable peak discharges were intended to reduce sand export and bar erosion, it appears that the annual pattern of monthly volumes released from the dam (with peak daily flows at their highest during the summer sediment input months of July and August) is the greatest factor preventing accumulation of new sand inputs from tributaries over multi-year time scales." Thus, "[t]he [1995

FEIS] assumption that sand would accumulate on the bed of the river over multiple years is now known to be flawed."

The 2008 Opinion changed all of this, but without directly addressing the effect of MLFF on the chub or its habitat. The opinion never explains why FWS's long-held position is incorrect. It never discusses the many studies that seem to confirm that MLFF destroys chub habitat. But in fairness, the 2008 Opinion does contain at least a limited explanation of its departure from the 1994 Opinion. That explanation is set forth here. . . .

> In 1995, in a consultation on the operations of Glen Canyon Dam, specifically on the MLFF, we anticipated that operation of Glen Canyon Dam (the monthly, daily, and hourly operations as defined in the MLFF and the 1996 ROD) would jeopardize the continued existence of the species. Populations in the upper Colorado River basin have declined as of January 2008. The Grand Canyon population, which was the population analyzed in the 1995 biological opinion, appears to have recently improved to around 6,000 adult fish. This is less than the number of adult fish thought to be present in the Grand Canyon in 1995, and indeed the status of the species is reduced overall from what it was in 1995. . . . However, the most recent and best available estimates of humpback chub population trend indicate that there has been increased recruitment into the population from some year classes starting in the mid- to late-1990s, during the period of MLFF operations, causing the decline in humpback chub to stabilize and begin to reverse. This improvement in the population trend has been attributed in part to the results of nonnative fish mechanical removal, increases in temperature due to lower reservoir elevations and inflow events, the 2000 low steady summer flow experiment, and other experimental flows and actions. Considering, though, that the most recent population modeling indicates the increase was due to increased recruitment as early as 1996 but no later than 1999, the increase in recruitment began at least four and as many as nine years prior to implementation of nonnative fish control, incidents of warmer water temperatures, the 2000 low steady summer flow experiment, and the 2004 high flow test. The exact causes of the increase in recruitment, and whether it is attributable to conditions in the mainstem or in the Little Colorado River are unclear. Nevertheless, removal of nonnative fish, increased temperature due to drought, and habitat conditions resulting from natural and experimental actions will likely be beneficial to humpback chub, and further increases in recruitment are likely based on recent catch rates of sub-adult humpback chub. These results indicate that some combination of conditions under MLFF has benefitted humpback chub, and that more recent conservation actions likely have as well, and are likely to continue to.

FWS's rationale seems to progress as follows: (1) the 1994 Opinion predicted the chub would decline under MLFF; (2) although there has been a general decline since 1995, the chub population has stabilized and increased in the last few years; (3) modeling suggests that the increase started under MLFF in the late 1990s, before other helpful conditions and measures had occurred; (4) although the exact cause of the population increase is not known, it appears the increase will continue and even accelerate under MLFF, particularly with the helpful conditions and measures taken to date and the two components of the 2008 Experimental Plan; and (5) therefore, FWS can no longer conclude that MLFF is detrimental to the chub or will cause further declines. [T]he Court finds this logic to be insufficient, even under deferential APA review.

[E]ven if it is conceded that recent science shows a stabilization and increase of the chub population, the 2008 Opinion does not explain why MLFF no longer destroys or adversely modifies the chub's critical habitat, particularly the mainstem sandbars and backwaters considered necessary for the growth and feeding of young chub. The opinion acknowledges that the fluctuating water levels of MLFF erode backwater sandbars and beach habitat, reduce food production, and decrease water temperatures. After conceding these points, the opinion devotes only one paragraph to critical habitat, stating that "[c]ritical habitat . . . along the Colorado River will be affected in the ways described above." This statement would seem to suggest that the critical habitat will continue to be adversely modified by MLFF, and yet the paragraph goes on to assert—without citing any study—that the number of backwaters are likely to increase and that the "quality of nearshore habitats, especially during September and October should also improve, becoming warmer and more productive *relative to current conditions*" (emphasis added). The opinion seems to be saying that the two components of the Experimental Plan will make things better than they would be without the Plan. This might support an opinion that the two components of the Plan will not themselves destroy or adversely modify critical habitat, but it provides no basis for concluding that MLFF does not do so. All of the studies cited in the 2008 Opinion seem to suggest otherwise. . . .

V.   Claim 8—Does the 2008 Environmental Assessment Violate the GCPA?

Claim 8 alleges that the 2008 Experimental Plan violates the GCPA. This claim focuses on MLFF, alleging that it destroys beaches and backwater habitat and impedes recovery of the humpback chub. The Trust claims that these effects of MLFF violate Reclamation's broad obligation under the GCPA "to protect, mitigate adverse impacts to, and improve the values for which Grand Canyon National Park and Glen Canyon National Recreation Area were established, including but not limited to natural and cultural resources and visitor use." . . .

The Trust has . . . failed to show that the 2008 Experimental Plan runs afoul of the complex balancing responsibility imposed on the Secretary of the Interior by the GCPA. Section 1802(a) of the GCPA provides that "[t]he Secretary shall operate Glen Canyon Dam in accordance with [the 1995 FEIS developed under] section 1804 and exercise other authorities under existing law in such a manner as to protect, mitigate adverse impacts to, and improve the values for which Grand Canyon National Park and Glen Canyon National Recreation Area were established, including but not limited to natural and cultural resources and visitor use." Section 1802(b) directs the Secretary to "implement [section 1802] in a manner fully consistent with and subject to . . . the Colorado River Storage Project Act" and other statutes "that govern allocation, appropriation, development, and exportation of the water of the Colorado River basin." The Colorado River Storage Project Act, in turn, requires that the Dam "be operated . . . so as to produce the greatest practicable amount of power and energy that can be sold at firm power and energy rates."

These broadly-worded provisions impose on the Secretary of the Interior an obligation to balance many different interests in the operation of Glen Canyon Dam. Reclamation's Environmental Assessment noted that the 2008 Experimental Plan was designed to do just that—"to determine if prescribed releases can benefit resources located downstream of the dam in Glen, Marble, and Grand Canyons, Glen Canyon National Recreation Area and Grand Canyon National Park, respectively, in accordance with applicable federal law, including the GCPA, while meeting the project purposes of the dam." Reclamation evaluated not only the two components of the Plan, concluding that they would benefit the chub, but also the effect of the Plan on other interests and obligations such as power generation. The Trust has not shown that Reclamation's balancing of these interests violates the broad directives of the GCPA, particularly in light of the "highly deferential" approach the Court must take under the APA.

Moreover, to the extent the Trust asks the Court to enforce the broad, programmatic directives of the GCPA, it asks the Court to undertake a task entrusted by Congress to the Secretary. . . .

NOTES AND QUESTIONS ON *GRAND CANYON TRUST*

1. *Appeal.* On appeal, the Ninth Circuit held that the ESA consultation requirement does not apply to the Bureau of Reclamation's Annual Operating Plans (AOPs), that AOPs are not major federal actions for purposes of NEPA, and that the citizen suit provision of the ESA did not confer federal court jurisdiction to review draft recovery plans for the humpback chub. Grand Canyon Trust v. U.S. Bureau of Reclamation, 691 F.3d 1008 (9th Cir. 2014). How might those holdings affect the ability of outside parties to challenge, and for federal courts to review, the substantive validity and effectiveness of long-term adaptive management programs for large ecosystem restoration?

2. *Breadth of interests at stake.* The court allowed intervention by all seven Colorado River Basin states, three of the largest municipal water providers in the West, one of the most powerful irrigation districts in the country, and one of the largest electric power providers in the Southwest. What does that say about the breadth of interests at stake? Although restoration of the Grand Canyon ecosystem is a laudable goal, against what other societal interests does it compete, who should decide how to strike the appropriate balance between those uses of the resource, and how? Does the Adaptive Management Workgroup (AMWG) formed to advise the Secretary properly account for all of those interests in reaching those decisions? What balance did Congress strike in the Grand Canyon Protection Act, and is it realistic that the Secretary can restore the ecosystem while still complying fully with the "Law of the River" and its multiple water, power, and other economic goals? *See* Robert W. Adler, *Restoring the Environment and Restoring Democracy: Lessons from the Colorado River*, 25 VA. ENVTL. L.J. 55 (2007).

3. *Retroactive nature of restoration.* Unlike the Tellico Dam that was the subject of the snail darter case, Glen Canyon Dam was completed long before enactment of NEPA and the ESA. Why should the ESA affect operation of Glen Canyon Dam? Is that the nature of environmental restoration, and what legal issues does that suggest?

4. *Restoration program components.* The agencies considered a large number of restoration options. Consider the following issues suggested by just some of those options:

    a. *MLFF versus SASF.* The modified low fluctuating flow (MLFF) option was the preferred alternative in the EIS, and was ultimately selected by Secretary Babbitt. The U.S. Fish and Wildlife Service preferred the seasonally adjusted steady flow (SASF) regime because it would more closely mimic the river's natural hydrograph (the natural pattern of large flood flows in the spring and subsiding to very low flows beginning in the mid-late summer). If environmental restoration is the goal, why would the Secretary choose an option that less closely reproduces natural conditions?

b. *Adaptive management and the flow regime.* The MLFF has been in effect for more than 15 years, punctuated by "experimental floods" to move sediment downstream to artificially rebuild beaches, sandbars, and backwater habitats for native fish. Yet the SCORE report concluded that this flow regime has failed to successfully restore many of the river's ecological features. Does the concept of adaptive management suggest that something else should be tried?

c. *Value choices: rainbow trout versus humpback chub.* One perplexing aspect of ecosystem restoration is the target: restoration to *what* when ecosystems frequently evolve, and when the "desired future state" is as much function of values as of science? The prized "tailwater fishery" below the dam draws fly fishers from around the globe who spend considerable amounts of money on guides, equipment, and travel services. The humpback chub is a native fish, was a key component of the natural ecosystem, and is of considerable scientific value, but provides no direct monetary benefits. One conservation measure eliminates rainbow trout to reduce predation on juvenile chub. Why the preference for chub over trout?

5. *Adaptive management, scientific uncertainty, and administrative law.* According to the FWS, there are multiple possible reasons, or combination of reasons, why humpback chub populations declined early in the program but recovered thereafter (although not fully). After decades of study, scientists still do not understand this complex ecosystem fully. What does this suggest for restoration programs? Adaptive management is a process by which, rather than making a decision and sticking to it absent a reason to change, managers make an iterative series of decisions based on carefully designed experiments (not just "trial and error"), often guided by a stakeholder process to address tradeoffs among resource values. *See* C.J. Walters & C.S. Holling, *Large-Scale Management Experiments and Learning by Doing,* 71 ECOLOGY 2060 (1990). How does that change the administrative law process of reaching environmental policy decisions?

6. *NEPA and adaptive management.* The NEPA issue in this case was a garden-variety claim that the agencies failed to consider an adequate range of alternatives. Is NEPA an appropriate tool to use in an adaptive management ecosystem restoration program? First, is the NEPA process unnecessarily duplicative of the adaptive management process? Second, if one attribute of adaptive management is the ability to modify on-the-ground restoration methods flexibly based on the results of earlier restoration experiments, does NEPA do more to delay than to facilitate restoration? The court criticizes FWS for changing its position from the 1994 to the 2008 biological opinion, but doesn't the adaptive management process envision such changes? Does the NEPA "tiering" process used by the Bureau of Reclamation (tiering less detailed environmental assessments off of the 1995 EIS) address this concern?

7. *RPAs as restoration?* In the context of this case, are "reasonable and prudent alternatives" under the ESA mitigation measures or restoration measures?

A Note on Climate Disruption and Restoration

Climate disruption affects environmental restoration in two very different ways. Some scientists suggest that ecological disturbances caused by climate disruption will make restoration more important. *See, e.g.*, Nathaniel E. Seavy et al., *Why Climate Change Makes Riparian Restoration More Important Than Ever: Recommendations for Practice and Research*, 27 ECOL. REST. 330 (2009). But if climate disruption causes dramatic changes in ecosystem characteristics and species ranges, how will that affect restoration program goals? Consider the following excerpt from an analysis by a group of prominent restoration experts, and ask yourself how land managers should address climate disruption in developing and implementing restoration efforts:

Although future climate change scenarios vary in intensity of impact, they share some common features, such as change in mean annual temperatures and changes in patterns of precipitation. . . . Recent work to map changes in biophysical regime in the U.S.A. found that half of the area would have shifts in moisture, temperature, and soil conditions unable to sustain "historic" ecosystems in those areas, that is, those likely to be present pre-settlement. More substantial change is anticipated for high northern latitudes, and evidence of significant change is already being detected. Within the next 100 years, and much sooner in some regions, prescribing restorations using purely historical references will prove increasingly challenging at best and at worst lead to failure.

Ecological restoration programs have a timescale of at least this long, particularly when considering wooded ecosystems and reestablishment of complex food chains. . . . This leads to the question "how appropriate are historical ecosystem types when faced with rapidly changing biophysical conditions?" Is it appropriate to consider a temperate woodland restoration endpoint in an area likely to be flooded by rising sea level? Why establish wetland in an area likely to become semiarid?

As much as rapid climate change makes for difficult scientific and technical issues, there are vexing moral questions, too, that make our thinking and action even more complicated. Threatened species and ecosystems will be increasingly hard to predict, and their recovery more difficult, sometimes practically impossible, to achieve. Whatever means develop for restoring rapidly shifting ecosystems, the translocation of species is a likely technique. This bears the burden of breaking our relations with particular places and upsetting long-duration place-specific evolutionary processes. There is the hazard of becoming more comfortable with serving as active agents in ecosystems to the extent where historical fidelity is almost entirely abandoned. It is one matter to watch change happen in ecosystems and wonder how and how much to intervene, and quite another to become a determining agent in that change. How smart can we be, and how much hubris is there in presuming that we can understand and predict ecological change? Finally, and this is by no means an exhaustive list of moral concerns, there are consequences for the vitality of restoration as a practice in a broader public giving up critical support for ecological integrity when ecosystems are changing rapidly. Why, after all, support the finely honed techniques and ambitions of restoration when mere ecological productivity appears adequate? . . .

The critical question facing us is to elaborate appropriate strategies and tactics for restoration . . . in a world of rapidly changing climate regimes, when in many cases relying on historical references makes less sense. Paradoxically, although specific historical references may be less useful as direct objectives, historical information documenting change may rise in importance in developing models for future ecosystem formations. It is our contention that we need to look outside of simple static species or community metrics to wider consideration of ecosystem functions and processes and that we must be realistic and pragmatic.

There is an increasing interest and application of the use of the concept of ecosystem goods and services, which accrue from the natural capital of the world's combined ecosystems. In effect, these goods and services are the annual interest arising from the composition and structure (stocks) of natural and mostly unmanaged ecological systems that, through their functioning, yield a flow of goods and services useful to people and all other living creatures. . . . These resources are, of course, significantly reduced when ecosystems become degraded by intensive agriculture or pollution, severely reduced when surfaces are sealed by urban and infrastructure development, and permanently lost when species become extinct and ecosystem configurations are shifted into new realms of stability. . . .

There is a way forward, however. The first step is to recognize that without the principal ecosystem functions and processes that characterize natural capital in place, no goods and services will accrue. Second, there are certain goods or services that already have a market value.

So, should we be focusing on past systems as the target for ecological restoration activities—or should we rather be reinstating the space and capacity for ecosystem functions and processes? Presumably in most cases, the matter will not be this stark, but in fact, these two general approaches constitute locations on a continuum from limited human intervention to complete control. Maintaining a commitment to history will remain important in restoration inasmuch that historical change becomes a crucial feature of understanding the range of ecosystems a particular place will support. The extent, pace, and spatial variation of climate-induced change will determine what approach can be taken. Restorationists will almost certainly rely more heavily in the future on the notion of "restoring natural capital" and restoration of delivery of ecosystem goods and services delivered by the ecosystem under consideration and not simply on those metrics based on the numbers and arrangement of the biota.

James A. Harris, Richard J. Hobbs, Eric Higgs & James Aronson, *Ecological Restoration and Global Climate Change*, 14 Restoration Ecology 170, 171-73 (2006).

III ALLOCATION OF RESPONSIBILITY

This part addresses the question of who takes responsibility for environmental issues and problems. Chapter 12 addresses the distribution of private responsibility for cleanup, focusing primarily upon the CERCLA, the statute where these issues arise most often. Chapter 13 discusses the distribution of responsibility and authority for standard setting and enforcement among government units. Chapter 13 emphasizes federalism considerations and explains some of the broad structural decisions found in major statutes.

12

Private Cleanup Responsibility

Generally, statutory regimes and the common law both make private parties responsible for environmental cleanups and other obligations that arise out of their own activities. Governments can also acquire comparable environmental cleanup responsibilities when they pollute while acting in a proprietary capacity. In international environmental law, this concept of responsibility to clean up one's own mess is known as the "polluter pays" principle. *See* Rio Declaration on Environment and Development, U.N. Conference on Environment and Development, U.N. Doc. A/CONF.151/5/Rev.1, 31 I.L.M. 874 (1992), Principle 16. This concept comports with our general sense of fairness, that people should be responsible for their own conduct and the implications of their actions, and should not be allowed to shift environmental or other liabilities to others. The polluter pays principle also makes sense under the basic economic justifications that underlie both common law liability and the rationale for government intervention into the free market. If someone is not required to bear the external costs of her activity, she reaps unfair profits at the expense of those who suffer health problems or live in a degraded environment as a result. In RCRA and CERCLA Congress also intentionally used liability as an incentive to promote waste reduction and site cleanup, respectively.

The statutes we have discussed thus far and the common law both typically address ongoing pollution. In principle, figuring out who has responsibility for cleanup for ongoing pollution under a polluter pays principle is not terribly difficult. If the owner and operator of a facility causes the ongoing pollution, that person or entity bears responsibility for cleanup. *See, e.g.,* 42 U.S.C. §7411(a)(5), (e) (requiring owners and operators of pollution sources to comply with new source performance standards). Not every polluter acquires a cleanup obligation. *See, e.g.,* 42 U.S.C. §§7412(c)(3) (requiring regulation of some, but not all, "area sources" emitting hazardous air pollution), 6921(b)(2)(A) (exempting certain wastes associated with oil and gas production from RCRA). But the polluter pays principle still furnishes a useful general rule explaining many statutory provisions establishing cleanup obligations and a central thrust of the common law.

With respect to hazardous waste dumps, the polluter pays principle does not always get one very far. Often, multiple polluters have contributed to the contamination of a single site. So the polluter pays principle requires some apportionment of liability amongst them. And in many cases, those who dumped hazardous waste have become insolvent or cannot be identified. That scenario raises a question of who should then be responsible for cleanup, or for so-called orphan shares of a cleanup in which some responsible parties are identified and solvent but others are not. The polluter pays principle in this context often does not answer the question of who should be held responsible.

This chapter discusses this question of who has responsibility for environmental harm in the context of the Comprehensive Environmental Response, Compensation, and Liability Act (CERCLA), 42 U.S.C. §§9601-9675, which addresses the difficult problem of who should pay for cleanup of hazardous waste disposal sites. Many of those sites have long, complicated, and obscure histories, making the assignment of responsibility a difficult endeavor. Section A focuses on the assignment of liability for cleanup. Section B discusses cleanup standards for hazardous waste sites, and the process CERCLA establishes for site-specific remedy selection. As a practical matter, both the cost of the remedy and apportionment of responsibility help determine the amount and scope of a party's liability under CERCLA.

A. APPORTIONING STATUTORY LIABILITY FOR ENVIRONMENTAL HARM

A number of federal and state environmental statutes embrace private liability as a principal method of environmental cleanup and protection. In Chapter 10, we discussed the use of liability under CERCLA as an incentive for pollution prevention. A co-equal goal of liability statutes is to promote prompt but effective cleanups of contaminated sites, and to ensure that cleanup costs are borne to the maximum extent possible by responsible private parties, rather than the general public. At the federal level, liability-based statutes include section 311 of the Clean Water Act, 33 U.S.C. §1321, the Oil Pollution Act of 1990, 33 U.S.C. §§2701-2761 (a statute enacted in the aftermath of the *Exxon Valdez* oil spill), and most notably, CERCLA.[1] Simply stating the concept of private liability, however, obscures the difficulty of deciding *who* should be held liable for what kinds of contamination, under what circumstances, and how that liability should be allocated when there are multiple responsible parties. In this section, we explore the manner in which Congress and the courts have allocated liability under CERCLA.

---

1. A number of states have also passed state "Superfund" statutes modeled after CERCLA. *See* AN ANALYSIS OF STATE SUPERFUND PROGRAMS: 50-STATE STUDY, 2001 UPDATE (ENVIRONMENTAL LAW INSTITUTE 2002).

At first blush, some principles and applications of CERCLA liability might seem unfair. Clearly, liability is appropriate for those who actually cause contamination of a site, such as "midnight dumpers" who illegally dispose of hazardous waste under cover of darkness. As you will see, however, CERCLA liability extends to many other private parties as well, including those who arguably "did nothing wrong." As you read the following cases and materials, try to focus on whether the various principles of liability make sense in terms of CERCLA's main goals, and other aspects of public policy.

1. Strict Liability Under CERCLA

≡ *State of New York v. Shore Realty*
759 F.2d 1032 (2d Cir. 1985)

OAKES, CIRCUIT JUDGE.

This case involves several novel questions about the scope of the Comprehensive Environmental Response, Compensation, and Liability Act of 1980 ("CERCLA"). CERCLA . . . was intended to provide means for cleaning up hazardous waste sites and spills, and may generally be known to the public as authorizing the so-called Superfund, the $1.6 billion Hazardous Substances Response Trust Fund.

On February 29, 1984, the State of New York brought suit against Shore Realty Corp. ("Shore") and Donald LeoGrande, its officer and stockholder, to clean up a hazardous waste disposal site at One Shore Road, Glenwood Landing, New York, which Shore had acquired for land development purposes. At the time of the acquisition, LeoGrande knew that hazardous waste was stored on the site and that cleanup would be expensive, though neither Shore nor LeoGrande had participated in the generation or transportation of the nearly 700,000 gallons of hazardous waste now on the premises. On October 15, 1984, the district court granted the State's motion for partial summary judgment. Apparently relying at least in part on CERCLA, it directed by permanent injunction that Shore and LeoGrande remove the hazardous waste stored on the property, subject to monitoring by the State, and held them liable for the State's "response costs."

We affirm, concluding that Shore is liable under CERCLA for the State's response costs. We hold that Shore properly was found to be a covered person under 42 U.S.C. §9607(a); that the nonlisting by the Environmental Protection Agency ("EPA") of the site on the National Priorities List ("NPL"), is irrelevant to Shore's liability; that Shore cannot rely on any of CERCLA's affirmative defenses. Moreover, we hold LeoGrande jointly and severally liable under CERCLA.

Facts

. . . LeoGrande incorporated Shore solely for the purpose of purchasing the Shore Road property. All corporate decisions and actions were made, directed, and controlled by him. By contract dated July 14, 1983, Shore agreed to purchase the 3.2 acre site, a small peninsula surrounded on three sides by the waters of Hempstead Harbor and Mott Cove, for condominium development. Five large tanks in a field in the center of the site hold most of some 700,000 gallons of hazardous chemicals located there, though there are six smaller tanks both above and below ground containing hazardous waste, as well as some empty tanks, on the property. And before June 15, 1984, one of the two dilapidated masonry warehouses on the site contained over 400 drums of chemicals and contaminated solids, many of which were corroded and leaking.[3] It is beyond dispute that the tanks and drums contain "hazardous substances" within the meaning of CERCLA. The substances involved — including benzene, dichlorobenzenes, ethyl benzene, tetrachloroethylene, trichloroethylene, 1,1,1–trichloroethene, chlordane, polychlorinated biphenyls (commonly known as PCBs), and bis (2-ethylhexyl) phthalate — are toxic, in some cases carcinogenic, and dangerous by way of contact, inhalation, or ingestion. These substances are present at the site in various combinations, some of which may cause the toxic effect to be synergistic.

The purchase agreement provided that it could be voided by Shore without penalty if after conducting an environmental study Shore had decided not to proceed. LeoGrande was fully aware that the tenants were then operating — illegally, it may be noted — a hazardous waste storage facility on the site. Shore's environmental consultant, WTM Management Corporation ("WTM"), prepared a detailed report in July, 1983. The report concluded that over the past several decades "the facility ha[d] received little if any preventive maintenance, the tanks (above ground and below ground), pipeline, loading rack, fire extinguishing system, and warehouse have deteriorated." WTM found that there had been several spills of hazardous waste at the site, including at least one large spill in 1978. Though there had been some attempts at cleanup, the WTM testing revealed that hazardous substances, such as benzene, were still leaching into the groundwater and the waters of the bay immediately adjacent to the bulkhead abutting Hempstead Harbor. After a site visit on July 18, 1983, WTM reported firsthand on the sorry state of the facility, observing, among other things, "seepage from the bulkhead," "corrosion" on all the tanks, signs of possible leakage from some of the tanks, deterioration of the pipeline and loading rack, and fifty to one hundred fifty-five gallon drums containing contaminated earth in one of the warehouses. The report concluded that if the current tenants "close up the operation and leave the material at the site," the owners would be left with a "potential time bomb." WTM estimated that the cost of environmental cleanup and monitoring would range from $650,000 to over $1 million before development could begin. After receiving this report Shore sought a waiver from the State Department of Environmental Conservation ("DEC") of liability as landowners for the disposal of the hazardous waste stored at the site. Although the DEC denied the waiver, Shore took title on October 13, 1983, and obtained certain rights over against the tenants, whom it subsequently evicted on January 5, 1984. Nevertheless, between October 13, 1983, and January 5, 1984, nearly 90,000 gallons of hazardous chemicals were added to the tanks. And during a state inspection on January 3, 1984, it became evident that the deteriorating and leaking drums of chemicals referred to above had also been brought onto the site.

3. When these drums concededly were "bursting and leaking," Shore employees asked the State to enter the site, inspect it, and take steps to mitigate the "life-threatening crisis situation." Pursuant to stipulation and order entered on June 15, 1984, Shore began removing the drums. Some may still remain at the site.

Needless to say, the tenants did not clean up the site before they left. Thus, conditions when Shore employees first entered the site were as bad as or worse than those described in the WTM report. As LeoGrande admitted by affidavit, "the various storage tanks, pipe lines and connections between these storage facilities were in a bad state of repair." While Shore claims to have made some improvements, such as sealing all the pipes and valves and continuing the cleanup of the damage from earlier spills, Shore did nothing about the hundreds of thousands of gallons of hazardous waste standing in deteriorating tanks. In addition, although a growing number of drums were leaking hazardous substances, Shore essentially ignored the problem until June, 1984.

On September 19, 1984, a DEC inspector observed one of the large tanks, which held over 300,000 gallons of hazardous materials, with rusting floor plates and tank walls, a pinhole leak, and a four-foot line of corrosion along one of the weld lines. On three other tanks, flakes of corroded metal "up to the size and thickness of a dime" were visible at the floorplate level.

CERCLA

CERCLA was designed "to bring order to the array of partly redundant, partly inadequate federal hazardous substances cleanup and compensation laws."[6] It applies "primarily to the cleanup of leaking inactive or abandoned sites and to emergency responses to spills." And it distinguishes between two kinds of response: remedial actions—generally long-term or permanent containment or disposal programs—and removal efforts—typically short-term cleanup arrangements.

CERCLA authorizes the federal government to respond in several ways. EPA can use Superfund resources to clean up hazardous waste sites and spills. The National Contingency Plan ("NCP"), prepared by EPA pursuant to CERCLA, governs cleanup efforts by "establish[ing] procedures and standards for responding to releases of hazardous substances." At the same time, EPA can sue for reimbursement of cleanup costs from any responsible parties it can locate, allowing the federal government to respond immediately while later trying to shift financial responsibility to others. Thus, Superfund covers cleanup costs if the site has been abandoned, if the responsible parties elude detection, or if private resources are inadequate. In addition, CERCLA authorizes EPA to seek an injunction in federal district court to force a responsible party to clean up any site or spill that presents an imminent and substantial danger to public health or welfare or the environment. In sum, CERCLA is not a regulatory standard-setting statute such as the Clean Air Act. Rather, the government generally undertakes pollution abatement, and polluters pay for such abatement through tax and reimbursement liability.

Congress clearly did not intend, however, to leave cleanup under CERCLA solely in the hands of the federal government. A state or political subdivision may enter into a contract or cooperative agreement with EPA, whereby both may take action on a cost-sharing basis. And states, like EPA, can sue responsible parties

---

6. In defining the term "hazardous substance," CERCLA incorporates by reference the substances designated as hazardous or toxic under the Clean Air Act, the Clean Water Act, the Resource Conservation and Recovery Act of 1976 ("RCRA"), the Toxic Substances Control Act, while authorizing EPA to designate additional substances that "may present substantial danger to the public health or welfare or the environment."

for remedial and removal costs if such efforts are "not inconsistent with" the NCP. While CERCLA expressly does not preempt state law, it precludes "recovering compensation for the same removal costs or damages or claims" under both CERCLA and state or other federal laws, and prohibits states from requiring contributions to any fund "the purpose of which is to pay compensation for claims . . . which may be compensated under" CERCLA. Moreover, "any . . . person" who is acting consistently with the requirements of the NCP may recover "necessary costs of response." Finally, responsible parties are liable for "damages for injury to, destruction of, or loss of natural resources, including the reasonable costs of assessing such injury, destruction, or loss resulting from such a release."

Congress intended that responsible parties be held strictly liable, even though an explicit provision for strict liability was not included in the compromise. Section 9601(32) provides that "liability" under CERCLA "shall be construed to be the standard of liability" under section 311 of the Clean Water Act, which courts have held to be strict liability, and which Congress understood to impose such liability. Strict liability under CERCLA, however, is not absolute; there are defenses for causation solely by an act of God, an act of war, or acts or omissions of a third party other than an employee or agent of the defendant or one whose act or omission occurs in connection with a contractual relationship with the defendant.

Discussion

A. *Liability for Response Costs Under CERCLA*

We hold that the district court properly awarded the State response costs.

1. Covered Persons

CERCLA holds liable four classes of persons:

(1) the owner and operator of a vessel (otherwise subject to the jurisdiction of the United States) or a facility,[15] (2) any person who at the time of disposal of any hazardous substance owned or operated any facility at which such hazardous substances were disposed of, (3) any person who by contract, agreement, or otherwise arranged for disposal or treatment, or arranged with a transporter for transport for disposal or treatment, of hazardous substances owned or possessed by such person, by any other party or entity, at any facility owned or operated by another party or entity and containing such hazardous substances, and (4) any person who accepts or accepted any hazardous substances for transport to disposal or treatment facilities or sites selected by such person.

As noted above, section [107(a)] makes these persons liable, if "there is a release, or a threatened release which causes the incurrence of response costs, of a hazardous substance" from the facility, for, among other things, "all costs of removal or remedial action incurred by the United States Government or a State not inconsistent with the national contingency plan." Shore argues that it is not covered by section 9607(a)(1) because it neither owned the site at the time of

---

15. CERCLA defines the term "facility" broadly to include any property at which hazardous substances have come to be located.

disposal nor caused the presence or the release of the hazardous waste at the facility. While section 9607(a)(1) appears to cover Shore, Shore attempts to infuse ambiguity into the statutory scheme, claiming that section 9607(a)(1) could not have been intended to include all owners, because the word "owned" in section 9607(a)(2) would be unnecessary since an owner "at the time of disposal" would necessarily be included in section 9607(a)(1). Shore claims that Congress intended that the scope of section 9607(a)(1) be no greater than that of section 9607(a)(2) and that both should be limited by the "at the time of disposal" language. By extension, Shore argues that both provisions should be interpreted as requiring a showing of causation. We agree with the State, however, that section 9607(a)(1) unequivocally imposes strict liability on the current owner of a facility from which there is a release or threat of release, without regard to causation.

Shore's claims of ambiguity are illusory; section 9607(a)'s structure is clear. Congress intended to cover different classes of persons differently. Section 9607(a)(1) applies to all current owners and operators, while section 9607(a)(2) primarily covers prior owners and operators. Moreover, section 9607(a)(2)'s scope is more limited than that of section 9607(a)(1). Prior owners and operators are liable only if they owned or operated the facility "at the time of disposal of any hazardous substance"; this limitation does not apply to current owners, like Shore.

Shore's causation argument is also at odds with the structure of the statute. Interpreting section 9607(a)(1) as including a causation requirement makes superfluous the affirmative defenses provided in section 9607(b), each of which carves out from liability an exception based on causation. Without a clear congressional command otherwise, we will not construe a statute in any way that makes some of its provisions surplusage.

Furthermore, as the State points out, accepting Shore's arguments would open a huge loophole in CERCLA's coverage. It is quite clear that if the current owner of a site could avoid liability merely by having purchased the site after chemical dumping had ceased, waste sites certainly would be sold, following the cessation of dumping, to new owners who could avoid the liability otherwise required by CERCLA. Congress had well in mind that persons who dump or store hazardous waste sometimes cannot be located or may be deceased or judgment-proof. We will not interpret section 9607(a) in any way that apparently frustrates the statute's goals, in the absence of a specific congressional intention otherwise. . . .

4. Affirmative Defense

Shore also claims that it can assert an affirmative defense under CERCLA, which provides a limited exception to liability for a release or threat of release caused solely by an act or omission of a third party other than an employee or agent of the defendant, or than one whose act or omission occurs in connection with a contractual relationship, existing directly or indirectly, with the defendant (except where the sole contractual arrangement arises from a published tariff and acceptance for carriage by a common carrier by rail), if the defendant establishes by a preponderance of the evidence that (a) he exercised due care with respect to the hazardous substance concerned, taking into consideration the characteristics of such hazardous substance, in light of all relevant facts and circumstances, and (b) he took precautions against foreseeable acts or omissions of any such third party and the consequences that could foreseeably result from such acts or omissions. 42 U.S.C. §9607(b)(3). We disagree. Shore argues that it had nothing to do with the transportation of the hazardous substances and that it has exercised due care since taking control of the site. Who the "third part(ies)" Shore claims were responsible is difficult to fathom. It is doubtful that a prior owner could be such, especially the prior owner here, since the acts or omissions referred to in the statute are doubtless those occurring during the ownership or operation of the defendant.[23] Similarly, many of the acts and omissions of the prior tenants/operators fall outside the scope of section 9607(b)(3), because they occurred before Shore owned the property. In addition, we find that Shore cannot rely on the affirmative defense even with respect to the tenants' conduct during the period after Shore closed on the property and when Shore evicted the tenants. Shore was aware of the nature of the tenants' activities before the closing and could readily have foreseen that they would continue to dump hazardous waste at the site. In light of this knowledge, we cannot say that the releases and threats of release resulting of these activities were "caused solely" by the tenants or that Shore "took precautions against" these "foreseeable acts or omissions."

D. LeoGrande's Personal Liability

We hold LeoGrande liable as an "operator" under CERCLA for the State's response costs. Under CERCLA "owner or operator" is defined to mean "any person owning or operating" an onshore facility, and "person" includes individuals as well as corporations. More important, the definition of "owner or operator" excludes "a person, who, without participating in the management of a . . . facility, holds indicia of ownership primarily to protect his security interest in the facility." The use of this exception implies that an owning stockholder who manages the corporation, such as LeoGrande, is liable under CERCLA as an "owner or operator." That conclusion is consistent with that of other courts that have addressed the issue. In any event, LeoGrande is in charge of the operation of the facility in question, and as such is an "operator" within the meaning of CERCLA.

NOTES AND QUESTIONS ON *SHORE REALTY*

1. *Who is responsible for cleanup?* Under section 107(a) of CERCLA, a party potentially incurs liability when it falls within one of the four categories identified in section 107(a), *i.e.*, a current owner or operator of a vessel or facility, a past owner or operator at the time of disposal of hazardous substances, an "arranger" for disposal or treatment of hazardous substances, or a transporter of hazardous substances at a facility or site selected by that person. 42 U.S.C. §9607(a). We will discuss the boundaries of these categories of potentially responsible parties (PRPs) in more detail later.

---

23. While we need not reach the issue, Shore appears to have a contractual relationship with the previous owners that also blocks the defense. The purchase agreement includes a provision by which Shore assumed at least some of the environmental liability of the previous owners.

2. *Elements of liability for PRPs.* A party that falls within one of the four categories of PRPs is liable when there is a release or threatened release, from a facility, of a hazardous substance, which causes another person to incur response costs covered by the statute. As noted in the case, Congress defined the terms "facility" and "hazardous substances" very broadly. *Id.* §9601(9), (14). Likewise, the term "release" is defined broadly to include "any spilling, leaking, pumping, pouring, emitting, emptying, discharging, injecting, escaping, leaching, dumping, or disposing into the environment (including the abandonment or discarding of barrels, containers, and other closed receptacles containing any hazardous substance or pollutant or contaminant)," with some relatively narrow exceptions we will address later. *Id.* §9601(22). *See, e.g.*, Vermont v. Staco, Inc., 684 F. Supp. 822 (D. Vt. 1988) (mercury on employee's clothes, washed into local sewer system when laundered at home, constituted a "release" of a hazardous substance).

3. *Strict and retroactive liability.* As noted by the *Shore Realty* court, nothing in section 107(a) or anywhere else in CERCLA uses the words "strict liability." Yet the courts have universally interpreted the law as such, based on the legislative history and other factors. As a result of strict liability, what elements of common law liability are omitted from the CERCLA cause of action? What is the rationale for strict liability, in terms of the law's policy goals?

Strict liability under CERCLA is particularly controversial because it is also retroactive, the constitutionality of which has been challenged unsuccessfully in several cases. *See, e.g.*, United States v. Olin Corp., 107 F.3d 1506 (11th Cir. 1997) (reversing district court finding that retroactive liability under CERCLA is unconstitutional); United States v. Northeastern Pharmaceutical & Chemical Co., 810 F.2d 726, 734-37 (8th Cir. 1986) (citing cases). The statute includes a limited exception to retroactive liability for natural resource damages, discussed *infra*.

4. *Facts.* The court held Shore Realty liable as a current owner even though Shore was not responsible for the disposal or release of hazardous substances on the site. Why did the court deem this fair or appropriate? To what extent does this fulfill CERCLA's twin goals of pollution prevention and expeditious site cleanup?

5. *Past owners and operators, and passive migration.* The second category of potentially responsible parties under CERCLA is "any person who at the time of disposal of any hazardous substance owned or operated any facility at which such hazardous substances were disposed of." 42 U.S.C. §9607(a)(2). The *Shore Realty* court held that current owners or operators are potentially liable regardless of the time of disposal of hazardous substances on the property. Past owners or operators are liable only if hazardous substances were "disposed of" on the site during the period of ownership or operation. Consider the following transactions:

> A owns and operates a PFOA manufacturing facility, which buries drums of waste with PFOA residuals and other hazardous substances out back. A sells the property to B, who merely holds the site for speculation. (No additional waste is added to the site during B's ownership). B sells the property to C, who converts the old manufacturing plant to luxury lofts (and who also does nothing to add to site contamination). During the site conversion, groundwater contamination is discovered.

Under these circumstances, who is potentially liable under the language of CERCLA section 107(a)(1) and (2)? Does this distinction make sense for CERCLA purposes?

The past owner and operator category has generated significant litigation over the meaning of the phrase "at the time of disposal of any hazardous substance." In the above hypothetical, does it matter whether the drums were leaking during the time of B's ownership? Does such a "passive" release, *i.e.*, one in which no affirmative activity leading to the release occurs (such as additional burial of drums), constitute "disposal" for purposes of potential liability? Some courts have found that liability should be imposed even for such "passive" disposal. *See, e.g.*, Nurad, Inc. v. William Hooper & Sons Co., 966 F.2d 837, 846 (4th Cir. 1992) (noting that section 9607 "imposes liability not only for active involvement in the 'dumping' or 'placing' of hazardous waste at the facility, but for ownership of the facility at a time that hazardous wastes were 'spilling' or 'leaking'"); Carson Harbor Village v. Unocal Corp., 270 F.3d 863 (9th Cir. 2001) (en banc) (declining to find passive soil migration to be a "disposal" but holding that other passive migration events can serve as a predicate for CERCLA liability). Does this result make sense in terms of the CERCLA's goals?

Congress did not define "disposal" separately in CERCLA. Rather, the CERCLA definition, 42 U.S.C. §9601(29), adopts by reference the definition of "disposal" in RCRA:

> the discharge, deposit, injection, dumping, spilling, leaking, or placing of any solid waste or hazardous waste into or on any land or water so that such solid waste or hazardous waste or any constituent thereof may enter the environment or be emitted into the air or discharged into any waters, including ground waters.

42 U.S.C. §6903(3). For purposes of RCRA, because of the use of the word "leaking," some courts have found that this definition includes passive as well as active disposal. *E.g.*, United States v. Waste Industries, Inc., 734 F.2d 159 (4th Cir. 1984) (declining to adopt a "strained reading" of disposal under which CERCLA liability does not attach absent "active human conduct"). Some courts, as in the *Nurad* and *Carson Harbor* cases cited above, have followed this reasoning and found CERCLA liability for past owners or operators based on passive migration of wastes. How do you think this interpretation would affect the total number of potentially responsible parties under CERCLA? Other courts, however, have held that the word "leaking" in the RCRA definition takes its meaning from the other surrounding verbs, all of which require some active participation, *e.g.*, United States v. 150 Acres of Land, 204 F.3d 698 (6th Cir. 2000) (disposal under CERCLA cannot occur without "evidence that there was human activity involved in whatever movement of hazardous substances [that] occurred on the property"); United States v. CDMG Realty, 96 F.3d 706 (3d Cir. 1996) (passive migration does not constitute disposal). These courts note the distinction between the list of actions in the RCRA definition, all of which can be read to require active participation, and the CERCLA definition of "release," which includes entirely passive terms such as "escaping" and "leaching." *See* 42 U.S.C. §9601(22).

6. *Affirmative defenses and innocent landowners.* One of the most controversial aspects of strict liability under CERCLA is the notion that a party may be liable for "someone else's mess," without having done anything "wrong" itself. Here, Shore purchased contaminated property, and perhaps allowed contamination to continue

unabated during its ownership, but it dumped no wastes itself at the site. Should an "innocent" purchaser in this situation be held liable for contamination caused by others?

Notwithstanding the background principle of strict liability, section 107(b) of CERCLA does allow potentially responsible parties a series of potential affirmative defenses:

> There shall be no liability for a person otherwise liable who can establish by a preponderance of the evidence that the release or threat of release of a hazardous substance and the damages resulting therefrom were caused solely by—
>
> (1) an act of God;
>
> (2) an act of war;
>
> (3) an act or omission of a third party other than an employee or agent of the defendant, or than one whose act or omission occurs in connection with a contractual relationship, existing directly or indirectly, with the defendant if the defendant establishes by a preponderance of the evidence that (a) he exercised due care with respect to the hazardous substance concerned, taking into consideration the characteristics of such hazardous substances, in light of all relevant facts and circumstances, and (b) he took precautions against foreseeable acts or omissions of any such third party and the consequences that could foreseeably result from such acts or omissions; or
>
> (4) any combination of the foregoing paragraphs.

42 U.S.C. §9607(b). Subsection (3), the act or omission of a third party, is by far the most important of the three statutory affirmative defenses. Why could Shore Realty not establish the elements of this defense?

If Shore had extensive knowledge of the contamination before it purchased the property, how might that have affected the purchase price? Should the result change if Shore knew nothing about the past contamination at the time of purchase? What if Shore made no inquiry whatsoever into the potential presence of site contamination? If it conducted a reasonable inquiry but learned nothing? In the 1986 amendments to CERCLA (known as the Superfund Amendment and Reauthorization Act, or SARA, Pub. L. No. 99-499, Oct. 17, 1986), Congress broadened the third party defense to account for so-called innocent landowners. It did so, however, through a somewhat convoluted definitional back door. Congress added a lengthy definition of the term "contractual relationship," which specifies by exception what a purchaser must do to take advantage of the third party defense:

> The term "contractual relationship" includes, but is not limited to, land contracts, deeds, easements, leases, or other instruments transferring title or possession, unless the real property on which the facility concerned is located was acquired by the defendant after the disposal or placement of the hazardous substance on, in, or at the facility, and one or more of the circumstances described in clause (i), (ii), or (iii) is also established by the defendant by a preponderance of the evidence:
>
> (i) At the time the defendant acquired the facility the defendant did not know and had no reason to know that any hazardous substance which is the subject of the release or threatened release was disposed of on, in, or at the facility.

(ii) The defendant is a government entity which acquired the facility by escheat, or through any other involuntary transfer or acquisition, or through the exercise of eminent domain authority by purchase or condemnation.

(iii) The defendant acquired the facility by inheritance or bequest.

42 U.S.C. §9601(35)(A) (as amended). Subsection (B) provides that, in order to take advantage of the first of these exceptions (lack of knowledge), a purchaser must conduct "all appropriate inquiries" into the condition of the property, and take reasonable actions to mitigate and contain any contamination once it is discovered on the property. *Id.* §9601(35)(B). What is the effect of this statutory amendment on the theory of CERCLA liability? If the purchaser does not "know and had no reason to know" about contamination at the time of purchase, after "all appropriate inquiry," how would this affect the purchase price and other terms of sale in ways that might justify the departure from the CERCLA liability principle? Pursuant to a later statutory amendment, EPA[2] issued regulations further defining the steps a prospective buyer must take in order to meet the "all appropriate inquiries" requirements. 70 Fed. Reg. 66070-01 (Nov. 1, 2005) (Standards and Practices for All Appropriate Inquiries, 40 C.F.R. Part 312).

7. *Brownfields redevelopment and bona fide purchasers.* Another variation on the "innocent landowner" problem is that of prospective developers who want to purchase properties that they *know are contaminated* for purposes of redevelopment. Many former industrial areas are now prime property for urban renewal. In fact, such urban "infill" development is viewed as a potent antidote to the significant environmental problems caused by suburban sprawl, which include air pollution due to increased traffic, loss of open space and wildlife habitat, and storm water runoff pollution. *See* EPA, Smart Growth and Brownfields, Oct. 28, 2003, available at www.epa.gov/smartgrowth/brownfields.htm. Given the prospect of CERCLA liability, however, developers are likely to avoid potentially contaminated properties like the plague, which poses a barrier to redevelopment. Congress addressed this environmental paradox in the Brownfields Revitalization and Environmental Restoration Act of 2001, Pub. L. No. 107-18, Title II, 115 Stat. 2360, Jan. 11, 2002. Congress defined a "brownfield site" as "real property, the expansion, redevelopment, or reuse of which may be complicated by the presence or potential presence of hazardous substance, pollutant, or contaminant." 42 U.S.C. §9601(39)(A). It excludes, however, properties that are already the subject of remediation or enforcement actions under CERCLA or other environmental laws. *Id.* §9601(39)(B). Brownfield status renders a site eligible for federal grants or loans to communities, nonprofit organizations, or developers to assist in site assessment and remediation. *Id.* §9604(k). Federal funding is used as a carrot to encourage the purchase, remediation, and redevelopment of contaminated sites.

Moreover, in the Brownfields Act, Congress created an entirely prospective liability exemption distinct from that already available for innocent purchasers, and tailored to sites that the purchaser knows to be contaminated after making appropriate inquiries. A "bona fide prospective purchaser" is defined as someone who acquires ownership after passage of the brownfields provision, and who can show

---

2. While CERCLA itself requires decisions to be made by "the President," this authority was delegated to EPA shortly after the law was passed. *See* E.O. 12316, 46 Fed. Reg. 42237 (1981); E.O. 12286, 46 Fed. Reg. 9901 (1981). For purposes of simplicity, we will substitute EPA for the statutory references to the President.

that all disposal of hazardous substances occurred prior to acquisition; she made all appropriate inquiries as defined for purposes of the innocent landowner exemption; she took reasonable steps to stop continuing releases, prevent future releases, and mitigate harm from past releases; she cooperates fully with those authorized to take response actions; and she meets other specified requirements. *Id.* §9601(40). Congress then provided that "a bona fide prospective purchaser whose potential liability for a release or threatened release is based solely on the purchaser's being considered to be an owner or operator of a facility shall not be liable so long as the bona fide prospective purchaser does not impede the performance of a response action or natural resource restoration." *Id.* §9607(r)(1). Does the same rationale that justified liability relief for innocent purchasers, who do not know about site contamination at the time of purchase, apply to purchasers who do have such knowledge?

8. *Federally permitted releases.* In spite of the exceptions mentioned so far, CERCLA establishes liability for a wide variety of parties where there is a release or threatened release from a facility or vessel. CERCLA, however, includes the following simple but potentially broad liability exemption: "Recovery by any person (including the United States or any State or Indian tribe) for response costs or damages resulting from a federally permitted release shall be pursuant to existing law in lieu of this section." 42 U.S.C. §9607(j). The statute defines "federally permitted release" to include discharges, emissions, and other releases to the environment covered by a range of federal laws, including the Clean Water Act, the Solid Waste Disposal Act (RCRA), the Ocean Dumping Act, the Safe Drinking Water Act, the Clean Air Act, the Atomic Energy Act, and certain state laws as well. *Id.* §9601(10).

2. Joint and Several Liability Under CERCLA

O'Neil v. Picillo

883 F.2d 176 (1st Cir. 1989)

COFFIN, SENIOR CIRCUIT JUDGE.

In July of 1977, the Picillos agreed to allow part of their pig farm in Coventry, Rhode Island to be used as a disposal site for drummed and bulk waste. That decision proved to be disastrous. Thousands of barrels of hazardous waste were dumped on the farm, culminating later that year in a monstrous fire ripping through the site. In 1979, the state and the Environmental Protection Agency (EPA) jointly undertook to clean up the area. What they found, in the words of the district court, were massive trenches and pits "filled with free-flowing, multi-colored, pungent liquid wastes" and thousands of "dented and corroded drums containing a veritable potpourri of toxic fluids."

This case involves the State of Rhode Island's attempt to recover the cleanup costs it incurred between 1979 and 1982 and to hold responsible parties liable for all future costs associated with the site. The state's complaint originally named thirty-five defendants, all but five of whom eventually entered into settlements totaling $5.8 million, the money to be shared by the state and EPA. After a month-long bench trial, the district court, in a thorough and well reasoned opinion, found three of the remaining five companies jointly and severally liable under section 107 of [CERCLA] for all of the State's past clean-up costs not covered by settlement agreements, as well as for all costs that may become necessary in the future. The other two defendants obtained judgments in their favor, the court concluding that the state had failed to prove that the waste attributed to those companies was "hazardous," as that term is defined under the Act. Two of the three companies held liable at trial, American Cyanamid and Rohm and Haas, have taken this appeal. Both are so-called "generators" of waste, as opposed to transporters or site owners. Neither takes issue with the district court's finding that some of their waste made its way to the Picillo site. Rather, they contend that their contribution to the disaster was insubstantial and that it was, therefore, unfair to hold them jointly and severally liable for all of the state's past expenses not covered by settlements. They further contend that it was error to hold them liable for all future remedial work because the state has not demonstrated that such work ever will be necessary. With far less vigor, they also raise a series of equitable defenses, claiming that their liability should be reduced, either in whole or part, because (1) much of the damage to the site resulted from the government's sloppy handling of barrels; (2) the government's clean-up procedures were not cost-efficient as required by the Act; and (3) their waste ended up at the site through the acts of wholly unrelated third parties. Finally, they argue that the Act should not be applied retroactively and that it was inappropriate for the district court to award the government prejudgment interest in this case. After a careful review of the record, we conclude that none of these arguments suffices to warrant reversal of the judgment below.

Joint and Several Liability

Statutory Background

It is by now well settled that Congress intended that the federal courts develop a uniform approach governing the use of joint and several liability in CERCLA actions. The rule adopted by the majority of courts, and the one we adopt, is based on the Restatement (Second) of Torts: damages should be apportioned only if the *defendant* can demonstrate that the harm is divisible.

The practical effect of placing the burden on defendants has been that responsible parties rarely escape joint and several liability, courts regularly finding that where wastes of varying (and unknown) degrees of toxicity and migratory potential commingle, it simply is impossible to determine the amount of environmental harm caused by each party. It has not gone unnoticed that holding defendants jointly and severally liable in such situations may often result in defendants paying for more than their share of the harm. Nevertheless, courts have continued to impose joint and several liability on a regular basis, reasoning that where all of the contributing causes cannot fairly be traced, Congress intended for those proven at least partially culpable to bear the cost of the uncertainty.

In enacting the Superfund Amendments and Reauthorization Act of 1986 ("SARA"), Congress had occasion to examine this case law. Rather than add a provision dealing explicitly with joint and several liability, it chose to leave the issue with the courts, to be resolved as it had been—on a case by case basis according to the predominant "divisibility" rule. Congress did, however, add two important provisions designed to mitigate the harshness of joint and several liability. First, the 1986 Amendments direct the EPA to offer early settlements to defendants who the Agency believes are responsible for only a small portion of the harm, so-called *de minimis* settlements.[3] Second, the Amendments provide for a statutory cause of action in contribution, codifying what most courts had concluded was implicit in the 1980 Act. Under this section, courts "may allocate response costs among liable parties using such equitable factors as the court determines are appropriate." We note that appellants already have initiated a contribution action against seven parties before the same district court judge who heard this case.

While a right of contribution undoubtedly softens the blow where parties cannot prove that the harm is divisible, it is not a complete panacea since it frequently will be difficult for defendants to locate a sufficient number of additional, solvent parties. Moreover, there are significant transaction costs involved in bringing other responsible parties to court. If it were possible to locate all responsible parties and to do so with little cost, the issue of joint and several liability obviously would be of only marginal significance. We, therefore, must examine carefully appellants' claim that they have met their burden of showing that the harm in this case is divisible.[4]

Even assuming that a strict application of the Restatement rule would allow appellants to escape joint and several liability in a situation such as this—something which is far from clear, appellants having provided us with no common law tort precedents to support their reading of the Restatement formulation—we would nonetheless decline to place this threshold burden on the government in CERCLA actions. As we noted earlier, Congress intended for the federal courts to develop a uniform approach to govern the use of joint and several liability. The Restatement is one source for us to consult. While courts generally have looked to the Restatement for guidance, they have declined to place the burden of showing that defendants are "substantial" contributors on the government, recognizing Congress' concern that cleanup efforts not be held hostage to the time-consuming and almost impossible task of tracing all of the waste found at a dump site. As we also noted earlier, in passing the 1986 Amendments Congress chose not to dismantle the existing approach, but instead, to add provisions dealing with *de minimis* settlements and contribution actions. It is at these stages, then, that the question of "substantiality" should be considered, and not at the point of determining liability to the government.

Divisibility

The district court issued two rulings on joint and several liability. First, the court held appellants jointly and severally liable for all of the state's past costs

---

3. Appellants apparently were offered settlements, but chose instead to try this case.

4. Before we can turn to the divisibility issue, however, we must first resolve a threshold question raised by appellants. Citing the Restatement (Second) of Torts § 433B, appellants contend that before joint and several liability may be imposed, the *government* has the initial burden of showing that the defendants were a "substantial" cause of the harm. If the government cannot prove that the defendants were substantial contributors, then joint and several liability may not be imposed and the defendant's burden of demonstrating that the harm is divisible never arises. We reject this approach.

not covered by settlements, roughly $1.4 million including prejudgment interest. According to appellants, this money was spent exclusively on "removal" costs or "surface cleanup" (e.g., sampling the waste, contacting responsible parties, and ultimately, *removing* the barrels and contaminated soil), and not on remedying the alleged damage to groundwater and other natural resources ("remedial" costs). Second, the district court held appellants jointly and severally liable for all future removal costs to be incurred by the state, as well as for all cost-efficient remedial action the state (and EPA) may deem necessary after conducting further tests. The parties discuss the two holdings separately and we shall do likewise.

Past Costs

Appellants begin by stressing that the state's past costs involved only surface cleanup. They then argue that because it was possible to determine how many barrels of waste they contributed to the site, it is also possible to determine what proportion of the state's removal expenses are attributable to each of them simply by estimating the cost of excavating a single barrel. The EPA advances two reasons why this approach is incorrect. First, it claims that it was not possible to determine how many barrels were traceable to appellants, nor was it possible to determine how much of the contaminated soil removed by the state was attributable to each appellant, and therefore, that it is impossible to apportion the state's removal costs. Second, it argues that even if it were possible to determine what proportion of the state's removal costs are attributable to appellants, joint and several liability still would have been proper because the "harm to be apportioned is not the cost but the environmental contamination that prompts the response action." We shall discuss the EPA's two arguments in reverse order.

We state at the outset that we have some trouble with the EPA's second argument. Assuming the government ultimately undertakes remedial action to clean the groundwater in the area and then seeks to recover the costs of doing so, it will have in effect submitted two separate bills, one for the cost of removing the barrels and soil, and one for cleaning the water. We think it likely that the harm to the water will be indivisible, and therefore, that appellants could properly be held jointly and severally liable for the cost of this remedial action. But simply because the costs associated with cleaning the groundwater cannot be apportioned does not mean that we should decline to apportion the costs of removing the barrels and soil if those costs are in fact divisible. This would seem to follow from the basic common law principle that defendants not be held responsible for those costs traceable to others. We think that the EPA would have to accept as much. Nonetheless, the Agency adheres to the position that it is irrelevant whether or not the costs of *removal* can be apportioned.

The reason the Agency takes this position is not, then, because the environmental harm that *actually occurred* was indivisible, but because the additional environmental harm that the government *averted* would have been indivisible had it occurred. This argument gives us pause because it appears to contravene the basic tort law principle that one pays only for the harm that was, and not for the harm that might have been.

Assume that it costs the government $1 million to remove all of the barrels from a site, but of this million, only $300,000 were spent removing the defendant's barrels. Also assume that had the barrels not been removed, the additional damage to the environment would have been $5 million and that this five million would not have been divisible. The government certainly would not take the position that it could recover $5 million in such a situation. Instead, it would ask only for the $1 million that it actually spent. Yet when it comes to apportioning that million, the Agency argues that we should look to whether the $5 million of averted harm would be divisible.

If we were to accept the EPA's "averted harm" argument, it appears that apportionment would be appropriate only in the highly unlikely event that (1) all of the barrels were empty and no further environmental harm was possible; (2) the individual barrels were sufficiently far apart that even if further spillage occurred, there would be no commingling of wastes and thus no difficulty determining whose waste caused what damage; or (3) every barrel contained precisely the same type of waste so that even if there was further spillage and commingling, the environmental harm could be apportioned according to the volumetric contribution of each defendant. As the EPA undoubtedly recognizes, it rarely, if ever, will be the case that one of these three conditions is present. As a practical matter, then, joint and several liability will be imposed in *every* case.

Because we believe Congress did not intend for joint and several liability to be imposed without exception, we are troubled by the practical implications of the Agency's argument, the more so because it seems to find no support in common law tort principles, which were to be one of our benchmarks in developing a uniform approach to govern the imposition of joint and several liability. At oral argument, the Agency did not claim, however, that its theory fit within the common law framework of joint and several liability, but instead, took the position that these CERCLA cases are not standard tort suits. Although we recognize that Congress deviated from certain tort principles, we had thought that on the issue of joint and several liability we were to take our lead from evolving principles of common law. It would seem incumbent upon the Agency, then, to demonstrate that on this *particular* question of joint and several liability, Congress intended for us to abandon the common law.

Having said all that, we choose not to resolve the issue in this case. Had appellants met their burden of showing that the costs *actually incurred* by the state were capable of apportionment, we would have had no choice but to address the EPA's theory. But because we do not believe appellants have done so, we can, and do, choose to leave the question for another day. We turn now to the EPA's first contention that the state's removal costs are not capable of apportionment.

Removal Costs

The state's removal efforts proceeded in four phases (0-3), each phase corresponding roughly to the cleanup of a different trench. The trenches were located in different areas of the site, but neither party has told us the distance between trenches. Appellants contend that it is possible to apportion the state's removal costs because there was evidence detailing (1) the total number of barrels excavated in each phase, (2) the number of barrels in each phase attributable to them, and (3) the total cost associated with each phase. In support of their argument, they point us to a few portions of the record, but for the most part are content to rest on statements in the district court's opinion. Specifically, appellants point to the following two sentences in the opinion: (1) "I find that [American Cyanamid] is responsible for ten drums of toxic hazardous material found at the site"; and (2) as to Rohm and Haas, "I accept the state's estimate [of 49 drums and 303 five-gallon pails]." Appellants then add, without opposition from the government, that the ten barrels of American Cyanamid waste discussed by the district court were found exclusively in Phase II, and that the 303 pails and 49 drums of Rohm and Haas waste mentioned by the court were found exclusively in Phase III. They conclude, therefore, that American Cyanamid should bear only a minute percentage of the $995,697.30 expended by the state during Phase II in excavating approximately 4,500 barrels and no share of the other phases, and that Rohm and Haas should be accountable for only a small portion of the $58,237 spent during Phase III in removing roughly 3,300 barrels and no share of the other phases. We disagree.

The district court's statements concerning the waste attributable to each appellant were based on the testimony of John Leo, an engineer hired by the state to oversee the cleanup. We have reviewed Mr. Leo's testimony carefully. Having done so, we think it inescapably clear that the district court did not mean to suggest that appellants had contributed only 49 and 10 barrels respectively, but rather, that those amounts were all that could be *positively attributed* to appellants. Mr. Leo testified that out of the approximately 10,000 barrels that were excavated during the four phases, only "three to four hundred of the drums contained markings which could potentially be traced." This is not surprising considering that there had been an enormous fire at the site, that the barrels had been exposed to the elements for a number of years, and that a substantial amount of liquid waste had leaked and eaten away at the outsides of the barrels. Mr. Leo also testified that it was not simply the absence of legible markings that prevented the state from identifying the overwhelming majority of barrels, but also the danger involved in handling the barrels. Ironically, it was appellants themselves who, in an effort to induce Mr. Leo to lower his estimate of the number of barrels attributable to each defendant, elicited much of the testimony concerning the impossibility of accurately identifying all of the waste.

In light of the fact that most of the waste could not be identified, and that the appellants, and not the government, had the burden to account for all of this uncertainty, we think it plain that the district court did not err in holding them jointly and severally liable for the state's past removal costs. Perhaps in this situation the only way appellants could have demonstrated that they were limited contributors would have been to present specific evidence documenting the whereabouts of their waste at all times after it left their facilities. But far from doing so, appellants deny all knowledge of how their waste made its way to the site. Moreover, the government presented evidence that much of Rohm and Haas' waste found at the site came from its laboratory in Spring House, Pennsylvania and that during the relevant years, this lab generated over two thousand drums of waste, all of which were consigned to a single transporter. Under these circumstances, where Rohm and Haas was entrusting substantial amounts of waste to a single transporter who ultimately proved unreliable, we simply cannot conclude, absent evidence to the contrary, that only a handful of the 2,000 or more barrels reached the site.[11]

NOTES AND QUESTIONS ON *O'NEIL v. PICILLO*

1. *Fairness.* Joint and several liability can lead to what can seem to be highly inequitable results. While not likely in practice, a party that contributes a single barrel of waste to a large site contaminated by waste from numerous sources can be held liable for the entire cleanup, especially if other contributors are insolvent or cannot be identified or located. What is the justification for joint and several liability in terms of the pollution prevention and cleanup goals of CERCLA?

2. *Divisibility.* Joint and several liability is not an absolute rule in CERCLA cases. As discussed in the case, the courts leave open the possibility that a *defendant* can prove "divisibility" pursuant to section 433A of the Restatement (Second) of Torts, which provides:

> (1) Damages for harm are to be apportioned among two or more causes where
> (a) there are distinct harms, or
> (b) there is a reasonable basis for determining the contribution of each cause to a single harm.
> (2) Damages for any other harm cannot be apportioned among two or more causes.

In what way does this allocation of the burden of proof serve the statutory goals? What are the inherent difficulties in proving divisibility in hazardous waste cases?

In practice, courts have been very reluctant to find divisibility in cost recovery cases. Defendants must prove divisibility of *harm*, and not just the raw proportion of wastes they contributed to a contaminated site:

> The generator defendants bore the burden of establishing a reasonable basis for apportioning liability among responsible parties. To meet this burden, the generator defendants had to establish that the environmental harm [at Bluff Road] was divisible among responsible parties. They presented no evidence, however, showing a relationship between waste volume, the release of hazardous substances, and the harm at the site. Further, in light of the commingling of hazardous substances, the district court could not have reasonably apportioned liability without some evidence disclosing the individual and interactive qualities of the substances deposited there. Common sense counsels that a million gallons of certain substances could be mixed together without significant consequences, whereas a few pints of others improperly mixed could result in disastrous consequences. Under other circumstances proportionate volumes of hazardous substances may well be probative of contributory harm.

---

11. Even if it were possible to determine how many barrels each appellant contributed to the site, we still would have difficulty concluding that the state's removal costs were capable of apportionment. To apportion the cost of removing the over 10,000 barrels, we would have to know the cost of removing a single barrel. Appellants have proceeded on the assumption that the cost of removing barrels did not vary depending on their content. This assumption appears untenable given the fact that the state had to take added precautions in dealing with certain particularly dangerous substances, including those traceable to Rohm and Haas. Moreover, in addition to excavating barrels the state had to remove large amounts of soil. Because there was substantial commingling of wastes, we think that any attempt to apportion the costs incurred by the state in removing the contaminated soil would necessarily be arbitrary.

United States v. Monsanto Co., 858 F.2d 160, 172 (4th Cir. 1988). Courts have found divisibility in some cases, however, with a limited number of defendants, where the amounts contributed by individual defendants can be quantified easily, and where there are no issues involving the mixture of different wastes. *e.g.*, United States v. Hercules, Inc., 247 F.3d 706 (8th Cir. 2001) (discussing criteria that inform divisibility); In re Bell Petroleum Services, Inc., 3 F.3d 889 (5th Cir. 1993) (finding divisibility where successive owners conducted the same activities, and proportionate activities could be documented).

In Burlington Northern and Santa Fe Railway et al. v. United States, 556 U.S. 599 (2009), other parts of which are excerpted below, the Supreme Court affirmed these basic principles of divisibility under CERCLA, but also affirmed a rare trial court ruling finding that sufficient facts had been proven to support divisibility:

> Although the [district] court found the parties liable, it did not impose joint and several liability on Shell and the Railroads for the entire response cost incurred by the Governments. The court found that the site contamination created a single harm but concluded that the harm was divisible and therefore capable of apportionment. Based on three figures—the percentage of the total area of the facility that was owned by the Railroads, the duration of [one of the PRP's] business divided by the term of the Railroads' lease, and the Court's determination that only two of three polluting chemicals spilled on the leased parcel required remediation and that those two chemicals were responsible for roughly two-thirds of the overall site contamination requiring remediation—the court apportioned the Railroads' liability as 9% of the Governments' total response cost. Based on estimations of chemicals spills of Shell products, the court held Shell liable for 6% of the total site response cost.

Id. at 606.

3. *Incentives to settle.* The combination of strict liability, limited affirmative defenses, and the prospect of joint and several liability provide a huge incentive for defendants to settle for a known, fixed share of the total liability, which can temper the harshness of strict, joint and several liability. Note that 30 of the original 35 defendants entered into settlements with EPA and the state. Why, then, do you think that five of the defendants here chose to litigate and risk joint and several liability rather than accepting a liability-limiting settlement?

In the 1986 SARA amendments, Congress added section 122, which provides a wide range of potential kinds of settlement for various kinds of parties. 42 U.S.C. §9622. Congress added more settlement options and exemptions in the Small Business Liability Relief and Brownfields Revitalization Act of 2002, discussed above in the context of brownfields redevelopment. These include a "de micromis exemption" from response costs for sites on the National Priorities List, for arrangers and transporters (not current or past owners or operators) who can demonstrate that they contributed extremely small quantities of waste to contaminated sites (less than 110 gallons of liquid materials or less than 200 pounds of solid materials), unless those materials "have contributed significantly or could contribute significantly, either individually or in the aggregate, to the cost of the response action or natural resource restoration with respect to the facility." 42 U.S.C. §9607(o). The arranger defendants in *Picillo* probably would not have met these quantity limitations, but if they had, how useful would this exemption have been?

4. *Contribution claims.* A second way liable parties can temper the harshness of joint and several liability, as noted by the court in *Picillo*, is the availability of

contribution actions against other potentially responsible parties. Contribution claims were recognized by courts under the original version of CERCLA, but expressly ratified by Congress in the 1986 Amendments, when it added section 113(f). 42 U.S.C. §9613(f). The court in *Picillo*, however, notes that the right of contribution "is not a panacea since it frequently will be difficult for defendants to locate a sufficient number of additional, solvent parties." In Cooper Industries v. Aviall Services, Inc., 543 U.S. 157 (2004), the Supreme Court held that contribution claims under section 113(f) could be brought only "during or following" a civil action under section 106 or section 107 against the would-be section 113(f) plaintiff. However, *Cooper* expressly left open the question of whether potentially responsible parties (PRPs) nevertheless could bring their own section 107 cost recovery actions directly against other PRPs. This generated a circuit split in which some courts allowed section 107(a) claims by PRPs against other PRPs, while the Third Circuit did not. *Compare* Consolidated Edison Co. of N.Y. v. UGI Utilities, Inc., 423 F.3d 90 (2d Cir. 2005), *and* Metropolitan Water Reclamation District of Greater Chicago v. North American Galvanizing & Coatings, Inc., 473 F.3d 824 (7th Cir. 2007), *with* E.I. DuPont de Nemours & Co. v. United States, 460 F.3d 515 (3d Cir. 2006). The Supreme Court resolved this split and clarified that PRPs may file section 107(a) cost recovery cases against other PRPs for costs incurred in voluntarily cleaning up a site. United States v. Atlantic Research, Inc., 551 U.S. 128 (2007). Taken together, *Cooper* and *Atlantic Research* appear to retain the allocation of responsibility in CERCLA in which all PRPs can be required to contribute to cleanups based on their contribution to a contaminated site. However, unlike section 107(a) claims, section 113(f) contribution claims are not based on joint and several liability, and allocation of liability is based on a set of equitable considerations known as the "Gore factors." As such, does the division of claims and responsibility reflected in these two cases leave any problems with the liability regime?

Unlike cost recovery claims under section 107(a), contribution claims under section 113(f) do not include joint and several liability: "In resolving contribution claims, the court may allocate response costs among liable parties using such equitable factors as the court determines are appropriate." 42 U.S.C. §9613(f)(1). While the statute itself does not identify the factors a court might consider in allocating liability among responsible parties in a contribution claim, some members of Congress identified a list of factors in the legislative process. Known as the "Gore factors" because then-Congressman Al Gore endorsed them, these factors include:

- the ability of the parties to demonstrate that their contribution to releases can be distinguished;
- the degree of toxicity of the hazardous substances involved;
- the amount of hazardous substances involved;
- the parties' degree of involvement in generating, transporting, treating, storing, or disposing of the hazardous substances;
- the degree of care exercised by the parties; and the parties' cooperation with the government to prevent harm to health and the environment.

See, e.g., In re Bell Petroleum Services, Inc., 3 F.3d 889 (5th Cir. 1993) (applying Gore factors). Thus, absent settlements, the process of allocating liability among the various responsible parties is shifted from the initial cost recovery action to any subsequent contribution action. What purpose does this serve in fulfilling the statutory goals? Does it achieve one efficiency goal (expediting the initial cost recovery phase) at the expense of another (requiring a second phase of litigation)?

3. Categories of Responsible Parties

The true significance of strict liability and joint and several liability becomes clear when you focus on the breadth of parties who may fall within the four categories of statutory liability. In *Shore Realty*, the court found the company liable as a current owner of the contaminated property, even though it contributed no waste to the site. Its principal shareholder and official, LeoGrande, was liable not as an owner, but as a current operator of the property, even though he intended to operate a condominium development, not a hazardous waste site. In *Picillo*, American Cyanamid and Rohm & Haas purportedly transferred relatively small amounts of waste to disposal companies, and did not even know where their waste would be shipped. Yet the court found them jointly and severally liable for the entire cleanup at a site that handled wastes from many generators. This gives you a sense of the breadth of parties that might incur extensive CERCLA liability. But it does not even cover all categories of potentially responsible parties.

What acts, omissions, or circumstances justify liability under CERCLA? As you read in *Shore Realty*, to some extent, answers are simply a matter of statutory construction. Courts often construe the statute and answer these questions in light of the major goals of the statute. Some CERCLA liability issues, however, are addressed under principles of common law, in part as a matter of legislative intent, and in part because Congress did not address some issues in the statute. In the case that follows, the Supreme Court provided some guidance on how these issues should be addressed in general, and in the specific context of parent-subsidiary corporate relationships.

≡≡≡ ***United States v. Bestfoods***
≡≡≡ *524 U.S. 51 (1998)*

JUSTICE SOUTER delivered the opinion of the Court.

The United States brought this action for the costs of cleaning up industrial waste generated by a chemical plant. The issue before us, under [CERCLA], is whether a parent corporation that actively participated in, and exercised control over, the operations of a subsidiary may, without more, be held liable as an operator of a polluting facility owned or operated by the subsidiary. We answer no, unless the corporate veil may be pierced. But a corporate parent that actively participated in, and exercised control over, the operations of the facility itself may be held directly liable in its own right as an operator of the facility.

I

. . . [Under CERCLA], those actually "responsible for any damage, environmental harm, or injury from chemical poisons [may be tagged with] the cost of their actions." The term "person" is defined in CERCLA to include corporations and other business organizations, and the term "facility" enjoys a broad and detailed definition as well. The phrase "owner or operator" is defined only by tautology, however, as "any person owning or operating" a facility, and it is this bit of circularity that prompts our review.

II

In 1957, Ott Chemical Co. (Ott I) began manufacturing chemicals at a plant near Muskegon, Michigan, and its intentional and unintentional dumping of hazardous substances significantly polluted the soil and ground water at the site. In 1965, respondent CPC International Inc.[3] incorporated a wholly owned subsidiary to buy Ott I's assets in exchange for CPC stock. The new company, also dubbed Ott Chemical Co. (Ott II), continued chemical manufacturing at the site, and continued to pollute its surroundings. CPC kept the managers of Ott I, including its founder, president, and principal shareholder, Arnold Ott, on board as officers of Ott II. Arnold Ott and several other Ott II officers and directors were also given positions at CPC, and they performed duties for both corporations.

In 1972, CPC sold Ott II to Story Chemical Company, which operated the Muskegon plant until its bankruptcy in 1977. Shortly thereafter, when respondent Michigan Department of Natural Resources (MDNR) examined the site for environmental damage, it found the land littered with thousands of leaking and even exploding drums of waste, and the soil and water saturated with noxious chemicals. MDNR sought a buyer for the property who would be willing to contribute toward its cleanup, and after extensive negotiations, respondent Aerojet-General Corp. arranged for transfer of the site from the Story bankruptcy trustee in 1977. Aerojet created a wholly owned California subsidiary, Cordova Chemical Company (Cordova/California), to purchase the property, and Cordova/California in turn created a wholly owned Michigan subsidiary, Cordova Chemical Company of Michigan (Cordova/Michigan), which manufactured chemicals at the site until 1986.

By 1981, the federal Environmental Protection Agency had undertaken to see the site cleaned up, and its long-term remedial plan called for expenditures well into the tens of millions of dollars. To recover some of that money, the United States filed this action under §107 in 1989, naming five defendants as responsible parties: CPC, Aerojet, Cordova/California, Cordova/Michigan, and Arnold Ott.[6] (By that time, Ott I and Ott II were defunct.) After the parties (and MDNR) had launched a flurry of contribution claims, counterclaims, and cross-claims, the District Court consolidated the cases for trial in three phases: liability, remedy, and

---

3. CPC has recently changed its name to Bestfoods. Consistently with the briefs and the opinions below, we use the name CPC herein.

6. Arnold Ott settled out of court with the Government on the eve of trial.

insurance coverage. So far, only the first phase has been completed; in 1991, the District Court held a 15-day bench trial on the issue of liability. Because the parties stipulated that the Muskegon plant was a "facility" . . . , that hazardous substances had been released at the facility, and that the United States had incurred reimbursable response costs to clean up the site, the trial focused on the issues of whether CPC and Aerojet, as the parent corporations of Ott II and the Cordova companies, had "owned or operated" the facility within the meaning of §107(a)(2).

[The Supreme Court explained the reasoning applied by the district court, which held both parent corporations (CPC and Aerojet) liable as operators. It then quoted the court of appeals' reasoning for reversing the district court in a 7 to 6 en banc opinion:]

> [W]here a parent corporation is sought to be held liable as an operator based upon the extent of its control of its subsidiary which owns the facility, the parent will be liable only when the requirements necessary to pierce the corporate veil [under state law] are met. In other words, whether the parent will be liable as an operator depends upon whether the degree to which it controls its subsidiary and the extent and manner of its involvement with the facility, amount to the abuse of the corporate form that will warrant piercing the corporate veil and disregarding the separate corporate entities of the parent and subsidiary.

Applying Michigan veil-piercing law, the Court of Appeals decided that neither CPC nor Aerojet was liable for controlling the actions of its subsidiaries, since the parent and subsidiary corporations maintained separate personalities and the parents did not utilize the subsidiary corporate form to perpetrate fraud or subvert justice.

We granted certiorari to resolve a conflict among the Circuits over the extent to which parent corporations may be held liable under CERCLA for operating facilities ostensibly under the control of their subsidiaries. We now vacate and remand.

III

It is a general principle of corporate law deeply "ingrained in our economic and legal systems" that a parent corporation (so-called because of control through ownership of another corporation's stock) is not liable for the acts of its subsidiaries. Thus it is hornbook law that "the exercise of the 'control' which stock ownership gives to the stockholders . . . will not create liability beyond the assets of the subsidiary. That 'control' includes the election of directors, the making of by-laws . . . and the doing of all other acts incident to the legal status of stockholders. Nor will a duplication of some or all of the directors or executive officers be fatal." Although this respect for corporate distinctions when the subsidiary is a polluter has been severely criticized in the literature, nothing in CERCLA purports to reject this bedrock principle, and against this venerable common-law backdrop, the congressional silence is audible. The Government has indeed made no claim that a corporate parent is liable as an owner or an operator under §107 simply because its subsidiary is subject to liability for owning or operating a polluting facility.

But there is an equally fundamental principle of corporate law, applicable to the parent-subsidiary relationship as well as generally, that the corporate veil may be pierced and the shareholder held liable for the corporation's conduct when, *inter alia*, the corporate form would otherwise be misused to accomplish certain wrongful purposes, most notably fraud, on the shareholder's behalf. Nothing in CERCLA purports to rewrite this well-settled rule, either. CERCLA is thus like many another congressional enactment in giving no indication that "the entire corpus of state corporation law is to be replaced simply because a plaintiff's cause of action is based upon a federal statute," and the failure of the statute to speak to a matter as fundamental as the liability implications of corporate ownership demands application of the rule that "[i]n order to abrogate a common-law principle, the statute must speak directly to the question addressed by the common law." The Court of Appeals was accordingly correct in holding that when (but only when) the corporate veil may be pierced,[7] may a parent corporation be charged with derivative CERCLA liability for its subsidiary's actions.

IV

A

If the Act rested liability entirely on ownership of a polluting facility, this opinion might end here; but CERCLA liability may turn on operation as well as ownership, and nothing in the statute's terms bars a parent corporation from direct liability for its own actions in operating a facility owned by its subsidiary. The fact that a corporate subsidiary happens to own a polluting facility operated by its parent does nothing, then, to displace the rule that the parent "corporation is [itself] responsible for the wrongs committed by its agents in the course of its business." It is this direct liability that is properly seen as being at issue here.

Under the plain language of the statute, any person who operates a polluting facility is directly liable for the costs of cleaning up the pollution. This is so regardless of whether that person is the facility's owner, the owner's parent corporation or business partner, or even a saboteur who sneaks into the facility at night to discharge its poisons out of malice. If any such act of operating a corporate subsidiary's facility is done on behalf of a parent corporation, the existence of the parent-subsidiary relationship under state corporate law is simply irrelevant to the issue of direct liability.

This much is easy to say: the difficulty comes in defining actions sufficient to constitute direct parental "operation." Here of course we may again rue the uselessness of CERCLA's definition of a facility's "operator" as "any person operating" the facility, which leaves us to do the best we can to give the term its "ordinary or natural meaning." And in the organizational sense more obviously intended by CERCLA, the word ordinarily means "[t]o conduct the affairs of; manage: *operate a business*." So, under CERCLA, an operator is simply someone who directs the workings of, manages, or conducts the affairs of a facility. To sharpen the definition

---

7. There is significant disagreement among courts and commentators over whether, in enforcing CERCLA's indirect liability, courts should borrow state law, or instead apply a federal common law of veil piercing. Since none of the parties challenges the Sixth Circuit's holding that CPC and Aerojet incurred no derivative liability, the question is not presented in this case. . . .

for purposes of CERCLA's concern with environmental contamination, an operator must manage, direct, or conduct operations specifically related to pollution, that is, operations having to do with the leakage or disposal of hazardous waste, or decisions about compliance with environmental regulations.

B

With this understanding, we are satisfied that the Court of Appeals correctly rejected the District Court's analysis of direct liability. But we also think that the appeals court erred in limiting direct liability under the statute to a parent's sole or joint venture operation, so as to eliminate any possible finding that CPC is liable as an operator on the facts of this case.

1

By emphasizing that "CPC is directly liable under section 107(a)(2) as an operator because CPC actively participated in and exerted significant control over Ott II's business and decision-making," the District Court applied the "actual control" test of whether the parent "actually operated the business of its subsidiary," as several Circuits have employed it.

The well-taken objection to the actual control test, however, is its fusion of direct and indirect liability; the test is administered by asking a question about the relationship between the two corporations (an issue going to indirect liability) instead of a question about the parent's interaction with the subsidiary's facility (the source of any direct liability). If, however, direct liability for the parent's operation of the facility is to be kept distinct from derivative liability for the subsidiary's own operation, the focus of the enquiry must necessarily be different under the two tests. "The question is not whether the parent operates the subsidiary, but rather whether it operates the facility, and that operation is evidenced by participation in the activities of the facility, not the subsidiary. Control of the subsidiary, if extensive enough, gives rise to indirect liability under piercing doctrine, not direct liability under the statutory language." The District Court was therefore mistaken to rest its analysis on CPC's relationship with Ott II, premising liability on little more than "CPC's 100-percent ownership of Ott II" and "CPC's active participation in, and at times majority control over, Ott II's board of directors." The analysis should instead have rested on the relationship between CPC and the Muskegon facility itself.

In sum, the District Court's focus on the relationship between parent and subsidiary (rather than parent and facility), combined with its automatic attribution of the actions of dual officers and directors to the corporate parent, erroneously, even if unintentionally, treated CERCLA as though it displaced or fundamentally altered common-law standards of limited liability. Indeed, if the evidence of common corporate personnel acting at management and directorial levels were enough to support a finding of a parent corporation's direct operator liability under CERCLA, then the possibility of resort to veil piercing to establish indirect, derivative liability for the subsidiary's violations would be academic. There would in essence be a relaxed, CERCLA-specific rule of derivative liability that would banish traditional standards and expectations from the law of CERCLA liability. But, as we have said, such a rule does not arise from congressional silence, and CERCLA's silence is dispositive.

2

We accordingly agree with the Court of Appeals that a participation-and-control test looking to the parent's supervision over the subsidiary, especially one that assumes that dual officers always act on behalf of the parent, cannot be used to identify operation of a facility resulting in direct parental liability. Nonetheless, a return to the ordinary meaning of the word "operate" in the organizational sense will indicate why we think that the Sixth Circuit stopped short when it confined its examples of direct parental operation to exclusive or joint ventures, and declined to find at least the possibility of direct operation by CPC in this case.

In our enquiry into the meaning Congress presumably had in mind when it used the verb "to operate," we recognized that the statute obviously meant something more than mere mechanical activation of pumps and valves, and must be read to contemplate "operation" as including the exercise of direction over the facility's activities. The Court of Appeals recognized this by indicating that a parent can be held directly liable when the parent operates the facility in the stead of its subsidiary or alongside the subsidiary in some sort of a joint venture. We anticipated a further possibility above, however, when we observed that a dual officer or director might depart so far from the norms of parental influence exercised through dual officeholding as to serve the parent, even when ostensibly acting on behalf of the subsidiary in operating the facility. Yet another possibility, suggested by the facts of this case, is that an agent of the parent with no hat to wear but the parent's hat might manage or direct activities at the facility.

Identifying such an occurrence calls for line-drawing yet again, since the acts of direct operation that give rise to parental liability must necessarily be distinguished from the interference that stems from the normal relationship between parent and subsidiary. Again norms of corporate behavior (undisturbed by any CERCLA provision) are crucial reference points. Just as we may look to such norms in identifying the limits of the presumption that a dual officeholder acts in his ostensible capacity, so here we may refer to them in distinguishing a parental officer's oversight of a subsidiary from such an officer's control over the operation of the subsidiary's facility. "[A]ctivities that involve the facility but which are consistent with the parent's investor status, such as monitoring of the subsidiary's performance, supervision of the subsidiary's finance and capital budget decisions, and articulation of general policies and procedures, should not give rise to direct liability." The critical question is whether, in degree and detail, actions directed to the facility by an agent of the parent alone are eccentric under accepted norms of parental oversight of a subsidiary's facility.

There is, in fact, some evidence that CPC engaged in just this type and degree of activity at the Muskegon plant. The District Court's opinion speaks of an agent of CPC alone who played a conspicuous part in dealing with the toxic risks emanating from the operation of the plant. G.R.D. Williams worked only for CPC; he was not an employee, officer, or director of Ott II, and thus, his actions were of necessity taken only on behalf of CPC. The District Court found that "CPC became directly involved in environmental and regulatory matters through the work of . . . Williams, CPC's governmental and environmental affairs director. Williams . . . became heavily involved in environmental issues at Ott II." He "actively participated in and exerted control over a variety of Ott II environmental matters," and he "issued directives regarding Ott II's responses to regulatory inquiries."

We think that these findings are enough to raise an issue of CPC's operation of the facility through Williams's actions, though we would draw no ultimate conclusion from these findings at this point.

NOTES AND QUESTIONS ON *BESTFOODS*

1. *Holding.* What is the holding of the case? Are parent corporations ever liable under CERCLA? If so, when? Is Bestfoods liable?

2. *Statute versus common law.* According to the Supreme Court, how should courts decide when to apply common law principles in ruling on issues of CERCLA liability, and when should they ground decisions in the language and policy of the statute? Why shouldn't *all* issues of CERCLA liability be guided, at least in part, by the statutory goals and policies?

3. *Successor corporations.* A similar issue affects the CERCLA liability of successor corporations. Under traditional analysis, there is no liability for successor corporations unless (1) the purchaser expressly or impliedly agrees to assume the liabilities; (2) the transaction is a de facto merger or consolidation; (3) the purchaser is a "mere continuation" of the seller; or (4) the transaction is an effort to fraudulently escape liability. FLETCHER, CYCLOPEDIA OF THE LAW OF PRIVATE CORPORATIONS §7122 (2004). Prior to *Bestfoods*, several circuits had embraced an expansive view of successor liability—the "substantial continuation" theory—that enlarged the "mere continuation" theory of liability beyond the boundaries of traditional federal common law and most states' corporate law. *See, e.g.,* United States v. Mexico Feed and Seed Co., 980 F.2d 478 (8th Cir. 1992) (upholding application of "substantial continuation" theory to effectuate remedial purposes of CERCLA); United States v. Carolina Transformer Co., 978 F.2d 832 (4th Cir. 1992) (same). The justification for such expansion was the broad liability net envisioned by Congress in enacting CERCLA. In *Bestfoods*, however, the Supreme Court found that CERCLA's "failure to speak to a matter as fundamental as the liability implications of corporate ownership demands application of the rule that 'in order to abrogate a common-law principle, the statute must speak directly to the question addressed by the common law.'" 524 U.S. at 64.

Courts addressing successor liability post-*Bestfoods* have ruled that judicially fashioned CERCLA-specific rules—such as the "substantial continuation" theory of successor liability—are not appropriate where an adequate body of applicable common law exists to resolve the issue at hand. *See, e.g.,* New York v. Nat'l Servs. Indus., Inc., 352 F.3d 682, 685 (2d Cir. 2003) ("[W]e take from *Bestfoods* the principle that when determining whether liability under CERCLA passes from one corporation to another, we must apply common law rules and not create CERCLA-specific rules."); United States v. Davis, 261 F.3d 1, 54 (1st Cir. 2001) (observing that after *Bestfoods* there is "little room for the creation of a federal rule of liability under [CERCLA]"); Atchison, Topeka & Santa Fe Ry. Co. v. Brown & Bryant, 159 F.3d 358, 364 (9th Cir. 1998) ("[W]e choose not to extend the 'mere continuation' exception to include the broader notion of a 'substantial continuation' recogniz[ing] that 'the traditional rules of successor liability in most states' should determine the limits of CERCLA liability.").

4. *Owners and operators: reprise.* The *Bestfoods* decision sheds some light on the distinction between the terms "owner" and "operator" under section 107(a)(1) of CERCLA, terms that courts sometimes conflated in earlier decisions. Whether a parent corporation is an "owner" of a facility otherwise held by a subsidiary corporation is, according to the Supreme Court, purely a matter of the preexisting common law of corporate relationships. A parent will be held liable as an "owner" only where the corporate veil is pierced, a rather difficult test to meet. Does this allow a parent corporation to use a poorly capitalized subsidiary to generate profits, but to shelter itself from potential CERCLA liability?

Whether a parent corporation can be held liable as an "operator," however, is a separate inquiry. To meet this test, a parent corporation (or one of its officials) "must manage, direct, or conduct operations specifically related to pollution, that is, operations having to do with the leakage or disposal of hazardous waste, or decisions about compliance with environmental regulations." Thus, officials from a parent corporation can "manage" a subsidiary corporation's fiscal and general business affairs, for purposes of protecting the parent corporation's general investment interests, without incurring CERCLA liability. Once they make decisions that affect environmental compliance and waste management issues, however, the door may be open to liability as an "operator" under CERCLA. What if the parent corporation decides to reduce the environmental compliance budget of the subsidiary to fund more product development work, with a goal of increasing profits?

5. *State or federal common law?* The Supreme Court leaves open the question of whether CERCLA liability should reflect the separate common law (or, where applicable, statutory law) of different states, or a unified body of federal common law. Should concerns about uniformity in application of CERCLA override concerns about uniformity in application of state business law?

6. *Management control.* In *Shore Realty*, recall that the court found LeoGrande liable as an operator. It did not, however, find ownership liability based on the fact that LeoGrande was the sole shareholder of the company. Explain this result using the reasoning of *Bestfoods*. For similar reasons, Congress created statutory exceptions for entities that have ownership interests purely to secure a loan, with a distinction between a pure ownership interest and management participation very similar to that articulated by the Supreme Court in *Bestfoods*:

> The term "owner or operator" does not include a person that is a lender that, without participating in the management of a vessel or facility, holds indicia of ownership primarily to protect the security interest of the person in the vessel or facility.

42 U.S.C. §9601(20)(E)(i). The legislative definition then identifies the kinds of decisions that constitute "participation in management" sufficient to confer liability. *Id.* §9601(20)(F). This includes such actions as exercising decision-making control over environmental compliance, or exercising control over day-to-day facility

management in ways that affect environmental compliance. The definition clarifies, however, that the mere "capacity to influence, or the unexercised right to control" is not sufficient to confer liability, *cf.* United States v. Gurley, 43 F.3d 1188 (8th Cir. 1994) (pre-*Bestfoods* decision finding operator liability based on mere authority to control), and includes a long list of actions that do not constitute "participation in management." 42 U.S.C. §9601(20)(F)(iv). Likewise, in the Asset Conservation Act of 1996, Congress limited the liability of a fiduciary to the value of the assets held, absent evidence of negligence on the part of the fiduciary that gave rise, in whole or in part, to the activities creating CERCLA liability. Asset Conservation, Lender Liability and Deposit Insurance Protection Act of 1996, 110 Stat. 3009 *et seq.*; *see* 42 U.S.C. §9607(n).

The court noted in *Picillo* that the arranger defendants (American Cyanamid and Rohm & Haas) had already filed contribution actions in an effort to avoid the full bite of joint and several liability. The companies brought these claims against various parties along the chain of waste management, including transporters, waste brokers, and others involved in the final disposal site. The continuing saga is reflected in the following decision:

American Cyanamid Co. v. Capuano
381 F.3d 6 (1st Cir. 2004)

TORRUELLA, CIRCUIT JUDGE.

In 1977, Warren Picillo, Sr. and his wife agreed to allow part of their pig farm in Coventry, Rhode Island ("Picillo site") to be used as a disposal site for drummed and bulk waste. Later that year, after thousands of barrels of hazardous waste replaced what pigs at one time called home, a monstrous explosion ripped through the Picillo site. The towering flames, lasting several days, brought the waste site to the attention of the Rhode Island environmental authorities. Rhode Island investigators "discovered large trenches and pits filled with free-flowing, multi-colored, pungent liquid wastes." Recognizing the environmental disaster it had discovered, Rhode Island closed the pig farm and, with the federal government, began the cleanup process.

In a nutshell, this case involves an action under [CERCLA], brought by a company whose hazardous waste was deposited at the Picillo site against a group of people who were involved with the site.

I. Background

A. CERCLA

. . . When the government performs a response action, it can bring "a cost recovery action under §9607 for the costs of the cleanup [against] a party found to be an owner or operator, past operator, transporter, or arranger." "A party found liable under §9607 may in turn bring an action for contribution" against potentially responsible parties ("PRPs") under §9613(f).

B. *The Parties*

Defendants-appellants, Daniel Capuano, Jr.; Jack Capuano; United Sanitation, Inc.; A. Capuano Brothers, Inc.; and Capuano Enterprises, Inc. (hereinafter referred to as "the Capuanos"), were in the business of hauling hazardous waste. Jack Capuano was the president and sole shareholder of Sanitary Landfill, Inc., a landfill operation located in Cranston, Rhode Island. Jack Capuano and Daniel Capuano jointly owned United Sanitation, Inc., a waste hauling company. Jack Capuano was the president of United Sanitation and Daniel was the vice-president. In 1977, the Capuanos reached an agreement with Warren Picillo to dump hazardous waste on his pig farm.

In 1977, plaintiff-appellee, Rohm & Haas Company ("R & H") operated research facilities in Spring House and Bristol, Pennsylvania, which generated hazardous waste. Forty-nine of the 10,000 drums of waste at Picillo were generated by R & H.

These drums ended up at the Picillo site in a round-about way. R & H's Spring House facility contracted with Jonas Waste Removal ("Jonas") to dispose of its waste. Jonas sent the waste to the Chemical Control Corporation, which later contracted with Chemical Waste Removal to dispose of the waste. Chemical Waste Removal disposed of the waste at the Picillo site. R & H's Bristol facility contracted with Scientific Chemical Processing ("SCP") to dispose of its waste. SCP later contracted with Daniel Capuano and United Sanitation to dispose of the waste at the Picillo site.

C. *The Soil Cleanup*

In 1983, Rhode Island brought an enforcement action under CERCLA §107, for cleanup costs at the Picillo site. This initial action was brought against 35 defendants "who were either owner/operators of the site, parties who allegedly transported waste there, parties alleged to have arranged for their waste to be transported to the site, and parties alleged to have produced waste deposited at the site."

Rhode Island settled with twenty of the defendants, including the Capuanos. The Capuanos agreed to pay $500,000. Rhode Island went to trial against five of the remaining defendants, including R & H. After trial, the district court found R & H and two other companies jointly and severally liable for un-reimbursed past response costs of $991,937 and for "all future costs of removal or remedial action incurred by the state includ[ing] any costs associated with the removal of contaminated soil piles." We affirmed . . . [*supra*].

The United States also sought reimbursement for its response costs associated with the soil cleanup at the Picillo site and settled with many parties, including the Capuanos. The Capuanos agreed to pay $1,500,000. The settling parties received contribution protection as part of the settlement agreement. *See* 42 U.S.C. §9613(f)(2) ("A person who has resolved its liability to the United States or a State in an administrative or judicially approved settlement shall not be liable for claims for contribution regarding matters addressed in the settlement."). In 1989, the United States filed a cost recovery action under §9607 against R & H and another company, American Cyanamid.

D. Groundwater Cleanup

In 1987, the United States began developing a Remedial Investigation and Feasibility Study ("RI/FS") with respect to the groundwater at the Picillo site. By September 1993, the United States called for a groundwater cleanup. On March 30, 1994, the United States issued a "special notice letter" to twenty PRPs, including the Capuanos and R & H, demanding they implement a groundwater remedy and reimburse the Environmental Protection Agency ("EPA") for the costs related to the RI/FS and enforcement costs. In response to the United States's letter, two groups of PRPs made settlement offers. The Capuanos joined neither group. R & H joined one of the groups making a settlement offer. As a result, R & H began incurring cleanup costs in late 1994. R & H was expelled from the settlement group, however, in March 1995 because it could not agree with the group regarding R & H's contribution. Without R & H, a group of PRPs settled with the United States and agreed to implement a groundwater remedy.

In 1998, R & H entered a consent decree with the United States to pay $4,350,000 to compensate the United States for direct response costs related to groundwater cleanup, plus $110,000 towards oversight costs, and $69,000 towards natural resource damage. The consent decree was approved in October 1998.

E. R & H's Contribution Action

In April 1995, R & H instituted a contribution action to recover past and future response costs related to groundwater cleanup. The suit named 52 PRPs, including the Capuanos.

II. Part One: Affirmative defenses

C. Contribution Immunity

In 1988, the Capuanos entered settlement agreements with the United States and Rhode Island. In return for contribution immunity, the Capuanos paid $1,500,000 to the United States and $500,000 to Rhode Island. The Capuanos argue that their Consent Decree provides contribution immunity against R & H's contribution claims. The Capuanos' settlement agreement provided immunity for "future liability" for past response costs, but it did not provide immunity for claims related to "groundwater protection or remediation." The Capuanos argue that R & H failed to prove that the money R & H paid to the United States, and for which R & H now seeks contribution, was for groundwater protection or remediation. We disagree. The Capuanos' argument is nothing more than creative word play. According to the Capuanos, R & H settled with the government for "past response costs." R & H's "past response costs" are costs incurred by the United States through October 25, 1995. Thus, R & H's "past response costs" would be "future liability" for past response costs as it pertains to the Capuanos and the Capuanos have contribution protection for future liability for past response costs.

Regardless of how the Capuanos choose to phrase the costs incurred, it is undisputed that the four corners of the Capuanos Consent Decree does not provide contribution immunity for costs relating to groundwater protection or remediation. At trial, R & H introduced documents detailing the work performed by the United States in regard to the groundwater remediation and introduced the testimony of an expert that the cost of the groundwater Remedial Investigation ("RI") and Feasibility Study ("FS") exceeded $4.7 million. The expert testified that the groundwater RI/FS was different from the soil RI/FS and the $4.7 million did not include any costs dealing with the soil remediation. R & H ultimately settled with the United States for $4.35 million and is seeking contribution for a portion of that amount. The evidence showed, therefore, that the costs R & H paid to the United States, for which it now seeks contribution, were for groundwater protection and remediation, and the Capuanos do not have contribution immunity for costs relating to groundwater protection or remediation.

In the alternative, the Capuanos argue that even if there was proof showing that R & H is seeking contribution for the RI/FS relating to the groundwater, a RI/FS is part of a "removal action" and is not "groundwater protection or remediation" and thus it is not a cost that was excluded from the Capuanos' Consent Decree.

The RI/FS is part of the groundwater protection and remediation process. "The purpose of the . . . (RI/FS) is to assess site conditions and evaluate alternatives to the extent necessary to select a remedy. Developing and conducting an RI/FS generally includes the following activities: project scoping, data collection, risk assessment, treatability studies, and analysis of alternatives." Since the RI/FS is the first step in groundwater protection and remediation, the RI/FS is not a cost excluded by this Consent Decree.

III. Issues Relating to the Trial

E. Transporter Liability

The Capuanos appeal the district court's conclusion that the Capuanos transported hazardous waste to the Picillo site. CERCLA imposes transporter liability on "any person who accepts or accepted any hazardous substances for transport to disposal or treatment facilities, incineration vessels or sites selected by such person" from which there is a release of hazardous substances. The district court concluded that United Sanitation and its officers, Jack and Daniel Capuano, were liable as transporters for 7.94% of the waste delivered to the Picillo site since Jack and Daniel selected the Picillo site and United Sanitation transported 960 55-gallon drums of hazardous waste to the site.

The Capuanos argue that the district court's finding was clearly erroneous because (1) United Sanitation did not transport hazardous waste; (2) United Sanitation and the Capuanos had no trucks capable of transporting hazardous waste; and (3) the only Capuano remotely identified with hazardous waste disposal was Anthony Capuano. After examining the record, we find that the district court's conclusion that the Capuanos were "transporters" was not clearly erroneous.

First, Picillo testified that "the Capuanos themselves brought their own waste down [to the Picillo site] on their own trucks" and that some of the barrels "came from Danny Capuano's place." Although this testimony supports the finding that the Capuanos physically transported some of the waste, we have interpreted

CERCLA not to impose liability on a transporter who merely follows the directives of a generator. Rather, for CERCLA liability to attach, a transporter must "actively participate in the selection decision or have substantial input in that decision." In this case, the Capuanos had substantial input in the decision, often making the final determination whether to allow waste to be dumped at their own land fill or to send it on to the Picillo site. Further, the Capuanos arranged for employees of the Scientific Chemical Corporation to visit the Picillo site as a possible waste dumping location. After viewing the site, the visitors concluded "this would be an ideal spot."

Second, according to deposition and trial testimony, trucks carrying hazardous waste would arrive at the Capuanos place of business only to be redirected by the Capuanos, or their employee Louie Falcone, to the Picillo site. Indeed, since the Picillo site was difficult to find, the Capuanos would come to the Picillo site "in a pick-up truck in front of the big trucks and show them where the farm was and show them where the dump was. . . ."

Third, when the drivers arrived at the Picillo site, they would give Picillo, Sr. a bill of lading. At the end of the week, Picillo, Sr. would take the bills of lading to the Capuanos to get paid. The record confirms that Mr. Picillo received United Sanitation checks signed by Jack Capuano and Dan Capuano. Although these payments do not, in and of themselves, prove that the Capuanos transported the waste, the payments do support the inference that the Capuanos were involved with the transportation of waste to the Picillo site.

F. Operator Liability

The Capuanos appeal the district court's conclusion that the Capuanos were liable as operators. . . . [The court summarized the *Bestfoods* standard for operator liability.]

The district court's conclusion that the Capuanos were operators of the site was not clearly erroneous. First, the Capuanos approached Warren Picillo with the idea of dumping on his pig farm. Once Warren agreed, he gave the Capuanos exclusive disposal rights at the site and the Capuanos hired a bulldozer to clear the trees and "dig a big, big hole." The Capuanos walked the operator of the bulldozer to the site and "showed him what to do and how to do it." Such actions are consistent with those of an operator of a facility "who directs the workings of, manages, or conducts the affairs of a facility" [quoting *Bestfoods*].

Second, as discussed earlier, the Capuanos directed the hazardous waste to the Picillo site. If the drivers of the waste did not know how to reach the site, the Capuanos would drive them to the site so they could dump the waste. Further, the Capuanos managed and conducted the affairs of the Picillo site by organizing and implementing its payment structure. The waste generators paid the Capuanos to dispose of their waste and then the Capuanos would give Warren Picillo a share of the money. "[O]perator liability requires an ultimate finding of involvement with operations having to do with the leakage or disposal of hazardous waste." The fact that the Capuanos developed the idea for using the site, prepared the site for dumping, arranged for waste to be dumped at the site, showed transporters where to dump on the site, and collected payment and transmitted a share to Warren

Picillo for dumping at the site demonstrates that the district court's conclusion that the Capuanos were liable as operators of the site was not clearly erroneous.

G. Arranger Liability

The Capuanos appeal the district court's conclusion that the Capuanos were liable as arrangers. The district court concluded that the Capuanos were arrangers because their conduct "constituted active participation as a broker in the disposal of their customer's waste." The Capuanos argue that arranger liability can only be imposed on a party that owned or possessed hazardous materials, not on a party that brokered the disposal of hazardous material.

An arranger is defined as:

> any person who by contract, agreement, or otherwise arranged for disposal or treatment, or arranged with a transporter for transport for disposal or treatment, of hazardous substances owned or possessed by such person, *by any other party or entity,* at any facility owned or operated by another party or entity and containing such hazardous substances.

42 U.S.C. §9607(a)(3) (emphasis added). We begin our inquiry by examining the plain language of the statute. This [language] can be read two ways, depending on which words the clause "by any other party or entity" modifies. First, this clause can be read to modify the preceding words "owned or possessed by such person," which would make liable any person who arranged for the disposal of a hazardous substance "owned or possessed by such person [or] by any other party or entity." Or, second, the clause can be read to modify the words "disposal or treatment," which would make the sentence read "any person who arranged for disposal or treatment by any other party or entity." The sentence structure makes it clear that the latter interpretation is the correct one. The clause "by any other party or entity" clarifies that, for arranger liability to attach, the disposal or treatment must be performed by another party or entity, as was the case here.

Some courts have held parties liable as arrangers even if they did not actually own or physically possess the hazardous waste so long as they had the authority to control the handling and disposal of the hazardous substances. Most of these cases involved a corporate officer of a generator of hazardous waste claiming he could not be liable as an arranger because he did not personally own or possess the waste. Thus, these holdings reflect the idea that a corporate officer can be liable as an arranger if he controls the decision to dispose of the waste on behalf of his company that owns the waste. These cases are distinguishable from the case at hand because this case does not involve corporate officers; rather it involves a party that does not own the waste and that arranges for the disposal of others' waste.

When a broker arranges for the disposal of hazardous waste and it does so by exercising control over the waste, such control can amount to constructive possession of the waste. Were we to interpret CERCLA not to impose liability on a party that constructively possessed hazardous waste and arranged for its illegal disposal, then the statute would be subject to a loophole through which brokers and middlemen could escape liability by arranging to have hazardous waste picked up and deposited at an illegal site. In addition to escaping liability, the broker would also profit by charging a fee for his services. Indeed, the Capuanos earned most of their profits in this manner. The Capuanos found a site, the Picillo pig farm, where hazardous waste could be dumped illegally. They then arranged for the waste to be picked up from various waste generators across New England and dumped on the illegal site. A broker should not be able to profit from such activity, much less escape liability. We therefore hold that a broker can be liable as an arranger if the broker controls the disposal of the waste.

Since the Capuanos, as discussed above, selected, secured, and directed the waste to the Picillo site, all for a fee, it was not clearly erroneous for the district court to conclude that the Capuanos were liable as arrangers given our interpretation of the statute.

NOTES AND QUESTIONS ON *AMERICAN CYANAMID*

1. *Scope of settlements.* Following the *Picillo* case, we discussed the powerful settlement-inducing nature of CERCLA liability, and the resulting frequency and importance of settlements in CERCLA practice. This case underscores the equally important corollary issue of the scope and meaning of CERCLA settlements. Section 113(f)(2) of CERCLA provides:

> A person who has resolved his liability to the United States or a State in an administrative or judicially approved settlement shall not be liable for claims for contribution *regarding matters addressed in the settlement.* Such settlement does not discharge any other potentially liable persons unless its terms so provide, but it reduces the potential liability of the others by the amount of the settlement.

42 U.S.C. §9613(f)(2) (emphasis added). The following subsection preserves the right of the United States or a state to bring cost recovery actions against non-settling parties, as well as the right of settling private parties to bring contribution claims. As between the two kinds of claims, however, contribution claims by private parties remain subordinate to cost recovery claims brought by the governments. *Id.* §9613(f)(3). Section 122 includes more detailed provisions regarding the effect of particular kinds of CERCLA settlements, but embodies the same general principles. *See id.* §9622(c), (f), (g)(5). What was the significance of the language in section 113(f)(2) italicized above in the *Picillo/American Cyanamid* matter?

2. *Other PRP categories.* The *American Cyanamid* case also sheds more light on the breadth of other categories of potentially liable parties:

> a. *Transporters.* The Capuanos were held liable under section 107(a)(4) because they not only physically transported waste to the Picillo pig farm site, but also "had substantial input in the decision" about *where* the waste would go. Why did Congress assign CERCLA liability to transporters who bring wastes to "sites selected by such person," but not to those who simply transport waste to sites selected by the waste generator or someone else? How might the business arrangements differ between waste generators and transporters who select the disposal site and those who do not, and why should that make a difference in terms of CERCLA liability?

Why does the court interpret the statutory words "sites selected by such person" to require only "substantial input into the decision"? *See* United States v. Davis, 261 F.3d 1 (1st Cir. 2001) (discussing the proper interpretation of "sites selected by such person" in determining transporter liability under CERCLA); Tippins, Inc. v. USX Corp., 37 F.3d 87 (3d Cir. 1994) (distinguishing between the propriety of imposing CERCLA liability on a transporter who plays an active role in selecting a disposal site and a transporter who acts as "no more than a conduit of the waste").

b. *Operators.* In *Shore Realty*, the court found LeoGrande liable as an operator because of his direct managerial role in making decisions at the site that affected the ongoing release of hazardous substances. In *Bestfoods*, however, the Supreme Court made clear that general management control is not sufficient to confer operator liability. Rather, "an operator must manage, direct, or conduct operations specifically related to pollution, that is, operations having to do with the leakage or disposal of hazardous waste, or decisions about compliance with environmental regulations." 524 U.S. at 52. Does this standard allow someone to effectively "manage" the environmental result at a site without making decisions "specifically" related to pollution? What did the Capuanos do that led the court to hold that they were "operators" of the disposal site for CERCLA purposes?

c. *Arrangers.* Rohm & Haas and American Cyanamid are the prototypical "arrangers" in the CERCLA liability scheme. The theory of arranger liability contemplates only that the potentially liable party "owned" or "possessed" the relevant hazardous material(s), and that the party arranged for the disposal of such materials, whether by contract, agreement, or otherwise. Raytheon Constructors, Inc. v. Asarco, Inc., 368 F.3d 1214, 1219 (10th Cir. 2003). General intent to dispose of waste is sufficient for liability; specific site or method selection is not necessary. GenCorp, Inc. v. Olin Corp., 390 F.3d 433, 446 (6th Cir. 2004). The Capuanos clearly were not the original generators of the hazardous substances released from the pig farm site. However, the court still found them liable as "arrangers" because of their role as "brokers and middlemen." What purpose does this interpretation serve beyond the liability that already attaches to transporters who choose the disposal site (and for which the Capuanos were already found liable)?

The concept of "arranger" liability has also generated a series of cases in which courts have scrutinized business relationships that led to the generation of hazardous substances in connection with subcontracting of manufacturing processes and product licensing. In United States v. Aceto Agricultural Chemical Corp., 872 F.2d 1373 (8th Cir. 1989), for example, the Eighth Circuit used a "business surrogate" theory to find pesticide manufacturers liable under CERCLA for releases of hazardous substances at the site of a defunct formulator. In the business arrangement at issue in that case, the manufacturers of pesticide active ingredients (PAIs) shipped their products to formulators who mixed the PAIs with inert ingredients and packaged them for sale, with contemporaneous disposal of waste materials. The manufacturers retained ownership of the hazardous products. What is the basis for finding "arranger" liability under these circumstances? Was it the fact that the manufacturers continued to "own" the hazardous substances that led to the release? What if the manufacturer sold the formulator the materials and then bought them back in their reprocessed form? What if a company sells a used product, with hazardous substances that must be disposed of before the remainder can be reused or recycled? *See, e.g.*, Catellus Development Corp. v. United States, 34 F.3d 748 (9th Cir. 1994) (imposing liability for sale of spent auto batteries requiring lead disposal before casings can be reused); Cadillac Fairview v. United States, 41 F.3d 562 (9th Cir. 1999) (imposing liability for sale of contaminated styrene for reprocessing). Ask yourself whether these results would be different under the following subsequent Supreme Court decision:

Burlington Northern and Santa Fe Railway Company v. United States
556 U.S. 559 (2009)

STEVENS, J., delivered the opinion of the Court, in which ROBERTS, C.J., and SCALIA, KENNEDY, SOUTER, THOMAS, BREYER, and ALITO, JJ., joined. GINSBURG, J., filed a dissenting opinion [omitted].

. . . These cases raise the questions whether and to what extent a party associated with a contaminated site may be held responsible for the full costs of remediation.

I

In 1960, Brown & Bryant, Inc. (B & B), began operating an agricultural chemical distribution business, purchasing pesticides and other chemical products from suppliers such as Shell Oil Company (Shell). Using its own equipment, B & B applied its products to customers' farms. B & B opened its business on a 3.8-acre parcel of former farmland in Arvin, California, and in 1975, expanded operations onto an adjacent .9-acre parcel of land owned jointly by the Atchison, Topeka & Santa Fe Railway Company, and the Southern Pacific Transportation Company (now known respectively as the Burlington Northern and Santa Fe Railway Company and Union Pacific Railroad Company) (Railroads). Both parcels of the Arvin facility were graded toward a sump and drainage pond located on the southeast corner of the primary parcel. Neither the sump nor the drainage pond was lined until 1979, allowing waste water and chemical runoff from the facility to seep into the ground water below.

During its years of operation, B & B stored and distributed various hazardous chemicals on its property. Among these were the herbicide dinoseb, sold by Dow Chemicals, and the pesticides D-D and Nemagon, both sold by Shell. Dinoseb was stored in 55-gallon drums and 5-gallon containers on a concrete slab outside B & B's warehouse. Nemagon was stored in 30-gallon drums and 5-gallon containers inside the warehouse. Originally, B & B purchased D-D in 55-gallon drums; beginning in the mid-1960's, however, Shell began requiring its distributors to maintain bulk storage facilities for D-D. From that time onward, B & B purchased D-D in bulk.

When B & B purchased D-D, Shell would arrange for delivery by common carrier. . . . When the product arrived, it was transferred from tanker trucks to a bulk storage tank located on B & B's primary parcel. From there, the chemical was transferred to bobtail trucks, nurse tanks, and pull rigs. During each of these transfers leaks and spills could—and often did—occur. Although the common carrier and B & B used buckets to catch spills from hoses and gaskets connecting the tanker trucks to its bulk storage tank, the buckets sometimes overflowed or were knocked over, causing D-D to spill onto the ground during the transfer process.

. . . Over the course of B & B's 28 years of operation, delivery spills, equipment failures, and the rinsing of tanks and trucks allowed Nemagon, D-D and dinoseb to seep into the soil and upper levels of ground water of the Arvin facility. In 1983, the California Department of Toxic Substances Control (DTSC) began investigating B & B's violation of hazardous waste laws, and the United States Environmental Protection Agency (EPA) soon followed suit, discovering significant contamination of soil and ground water. Of particular concern was a plume of contaminated ground water located under the facility that threatened to leach into an adjacent supply of potential drinking water.

Although B & B undertook some efforts at remediation, by 1989 it had become insolvent and ceased all operations. That same year, the Arvin facility was added to the National Priority List, and subsequently, DTSC and EPA (Governments) exercised their authority under 42 U.S.C. §9604 to undertake cleanup efforts at the site. By 1998, the Governments had spent more than $8 million responding to the site contamination; their costs have continued to accrue.

In 1991, EPA issued an administrative order to the Railroads directing them, as owners of a portion of the property on which the Arvin facility was located, to perform certain remedial tasks in connection with the site. The Railroads did so, incurring expenses of more than $3 million in the process. Seeking to recover at least a portion of their response costs, in 1992 the Railroads brought suit against B & B in the United States District Court for the Eastern District of California. In 1996, that lawsuit was consolidated with two recovery actions brought by DTSC and EPA against Shell and the Railroads.

The District Court conducted a 6-week bench trial in 1999 and four years later entered a judgment in favor of the Governments. In a lengthy order supported by 507 separate findings of fact and conclusions of law, the court held that both the Railroads and Shell were potentially responsible parties (PRPs) under CERCLA—the Railroads because they were owners of a portion of the facility, *see* 42 U.S.C. §§9607(a)(1)-(2), and Shell because it had "arranged for" the disposal of hazardous substances through its sale and delivery of D-D, *see* §9607(a)(3).

[The Court described the factual grounds for divisibility, reproduced *supra*.]

The Governments appealed the District Court's apportionment, and Shell cross-appealed the court's finding of liability. The Court of Appeals acknowledged that Shell did not qualify as a "traditional" arranger under §9607(a)(3), insofar as it had not contracted with B & B to directly dispose of a hazardous waste product. Nevertheless, the court stated that Shell could still be held liable under a "'broader' category of arranger liability" if the "disposal of hazardous wastes [wa]s a foreseeable byproduct of, but not the purpose of, the transaction giving rise to" arranger liability. Relying on CERCLA's definition of "disposal," which covers acts such as "leaking" and "spilling," 42 U.S.C. §6903(3), the Ninth Circuit concluded that an entity could arrange for "disposal" "even if it did not intend to dispose" of a hazardous substance.

Applying that theory of arranger liability to the District Court's findings of fact, the Ninth Circuit held that Shell arranged for the disposal of a hazardous substance through its sale and delivery of D-D:

> "Shell arranged for delivery of the substances to the site by its subcontractors; was aware of, and to some degree dictated, the transfer arrangements; knew that some leakage was likely in the transfer process; and provided advice and supervision concerning safe transfer and storage. Disposal of a hazardous substance was thus a necessary part of the sale and delivery process."

Under such circumstances, the court concluded, arranger liability was not precluded by the fact that the purpose of Shell's action had been to transport a useful and previously unused product to B & B for sale. . . .

. . . We granted certiorari to determine whether Shell was properly held liable as an entity that had "arranged for disposal" of hazardous substances within the meaning of §9607(a)(3). . . .

II

. . . In these cases, it is undisputed that the Railroads qualify as PRPs under both §§9607(a)(1) and 9607(a)(2) because they owned the land leased by B & B at the time of the contamination and continue to own it now. The more difficult question is whether Shell also qualifies as a PRP under §9607(a)(3) by virtue of the circumstances surrounding its sales to B & B.

To determine whether Shell may be held liable as an arranger, we begin with the language of the statute. As relevant here, §9607(a)(3) applies to an entity that "arrange[s] for disposal . . . of hazardous substances." It is plain from the language of the statute that CERCLA liability would attach under §9607(a)(3) if an entity were to enter into a transaction for the sole purpose of discarding a used and no longer useful hazardous substance. It is similarly clear that an entity could not be held liable as an arranger merely for selling a new and useful product if the purchaser of that product later, and unbeknownst to the seller, disposed of the product in a way that led to contamination. Less clear is the liability attaching to the many permutations of "arrangements" that fall between these two extremes—cases in which the seller has some knowledge of the buyers' planned disposal or whose motives for the "sale" of a hazardous substance are less than clear. In such cases, courts have concluded that the determination whether an entity is an arranger requires a fact-intensive inquiry that looks beyond the parties' characterization of the transaction as a "disposal" or a "sale" and seeks to discern whether the arrangement was one Congress intended to fall within the scope of CERCLA's strict-liability provisions.

Although we agree that the question whether §9607(a)(3) liability attaches is fact intensive and case specific, such liability may not extend beyond the limits of the statute itself. Because CERCLA does not specifically define what it means to "arrang[e] for" disposal of a hazardous substance, we give the phrase its ordinary meaning. In common parlance, the word "arrange" implies action directed to a specific purpose. *See* Merriam-Webster's Collegiate Dictionary 64 (10th ed. 1993) (defining "arrange" as "to make preparations for: plan[;] . . . to bring about an agreement or understanding concerning"). . . . Consequently, under the plain language of the statute, an entity may qualify as an arranger under §9607(a)(3) when it takes intentional steps to dispose of a hazardous substance.

The Governments do not deny that the statute requires an entity to "arrang[e] for" disposal; however, they interpret that phrase by reference to the statutory term "disposal," which the Act broadly defines as "the discharge, deposit, injection, dumping, spilling, leaking, or placing of any solid waste or hazardous waste into or on any land or water." 42 U.S.C. §6903(3); *see also* §9601(29) (adopting the definition of "disposal" contained in the Solid Waste Disposal Act). The Governments assert that by including unintentional acts such as "spilling" and "leaking" in the definition of disposal, Congress intended to impose liability on entities not only when they directly dispose of waste products but also when they engage in legitimate sales of hazardous substances knowing that some disposal may occur as a collateral consequence of the sale itself. Applying that reading of the statute, the Governments contend that Shell arranged for the disposal of D-D within the meaning of §9607(a)(3) by shipping D-D to B & B under conditions it knew would result in the spilling of a portion of the hazardous substance by the purchaser or common carrier. Because these spills resulted in wasted D-D, a result Shell anticipated, the Governments insist that Shell was properly found to have arranged for the disposal of D-D.

While it is true that in some instances an entity's knowledge that its product will be leaked, spilled, dumped, or otherwise discarded may provide evidence of the entity's intent to dispose of its hazardous wastes, knowledge alone is insufficient to prove that an entity "planned for" the disposal, particularly when the disposal occurs as a peripheral result of the legitimate sale of an unused, useful product. In order to qualify as an arranger, Shell must have entered into the sale of D-D with the intention that at least a portion of the product be disposed of during the transfer process by one or more of the methods described in §6903(3). Here, the facts found by the District Court do not support such a conclusion.

Although the evidence adduced at trial showed that Shell was aware that minor, accidental spills occurred during the transfer of D-D from the common carrier to B & B's bulk storage tanks after the product had arrived at the Arvin facility and had come under B & B's stewardship, the evidence does not support an inference that Shell intended such spills to occur. To the contrary, the evidence revealed that Shell took numerous steps to encourage its distributors to reduce the likelihood of such spills, providing them with detailed safety manuals, requiring them to maintain adequate storage facilities, and providing discounts for those that took safety precautions. Although Shell's efforts were less than wholly successful, given these facts, Shell's mere knowledge that spills and leaks continued to occur is insufficient grounds for concluding that Shell "arranged for" the disposal of D-D within the meaning of §9607(a)(3). Accordingly, we conclude that Shell was not liable as an arranger for the contamination that occurred at B & B's Arvin facility.

IV

For the foregoing reasons, we conclude that the Court of Appeals erred by holding Shell liable as an arranger under CERCLA for the costs of remediating environmental contamination at the Arvin, California facility. . . .

NOTES AND QUESTIONS ON *BURLINGTON NORTHERN*

1. *Holding.* Did the Supreme Court in *Burlington Northern* significantly change the law on arranger liability as discussed by the First Circuit panel in *American Cyanamid*? After *Burlington Northern*, would the Capuanos still have been found liable as arrangers? If not, what is the distinction?

2. *Impact on business planning.* What kinds of business arrangements might be affected by the Supreme Court's interpretation of arranger liability in *Burlington Northern*, *i.e.*, how might it change responsibility for cleanups in various situations in which parties sell hazardous products to others? After this decision, will businesses like Shell have less incentive to take steps to ensure that their customers handle the materials obtained from Shell properly?

ATRAZINE SUPERFUND LIABILITY AND COUNSELING PROBLEM

For many years, Herbicides, Inc. (HI) manufactured atrazine at one of its facilities. Recently, it decided to discontinue atrazine production. The following additional facts are purely hypothetical. Assume for purposes of this problem that atrazine and wastes created during atrazine production are "hazardous substances" for purposes of CERCLA.

Part 1 — The manufacturing site

After HI discontinues atrazine production, it decides that the remaining chemicals produced at that facility are not profitable enough to justify keeping the plant open. It is also a desirable location for a new high-density housing project for the rapidly growing nearby city, due to its proximity to a new light rail station. Greenbuilder Inc. is interested in purchasing the property for an "eco-friendly" planned community. Greenbuilder proposes to tear down the chemical plant and build a mixed use, transit-oriented development that would allow residents to walk to schools, shopping, and amenities, and commute downtown by train. It would also preserve significant open space on HI's former grounds around the facility.

For decades before HI knew of any dangers from atrazine or related waste products, it disposed of some of its atrazine production wastes on site. Workers dumped large volumes of very dilute wastes on open fields behind the plant. HI was proud of its beautiful grounds, and the wastewater actually irrigated fields of wildflowers while controlling noxious weeds. While this wastewater contained very low concentrations of any particular chemical, over the long

---

period of atrazine production contaminant levels in the soil built up to fairly high levels. When it rains, some of these chemicals leach into nearby drinking water wells and streams. Recently, atrazine has been detected in drinking water from these wells, and in local streams, at levels that exceed the state's drinking water standards and surface water quality standards, respectively.

1. If HI sells the property to Greenbuilders, will HI retain potential CERCLA liability after the sale? Why? Didn't HI do the "right thing" by discontinuing atrazine production? Is it being penalized for making that decision, and then for selling the site to a company that will redevelop it in an environmentally beneficial way?

2. If you were HI's lawyer, what advice would you give it regarding the proposed property sale? Are there any ways in which HI can avoid potentially uncertain CERCLA liability? What steps should it take to avoid or minimize potential liability?

3. What if HI sold the property to a real estate investment trust (REIT), an investment vehicle some people use to defer taxes on retirement income investments. The REIT purchases the property from HI several years before the light rail line is built. It knows about the atrazine contamination and uses that fact to reduce the purchase price, but does nothing to the land, and holds the property until its value skyrockets because of the new rail station. Then it sells the property to Greenbuilders for a significant profit. Is the REIT a PRP under CERCLA after it sells the property? Why or why not?

4. What advice would you give Greenbuilders before it purchases the property? What options does it have to avoid or minimize liability? Assuming that the atrazine contamination has been publicized widely in the local news media, can Greenbuilders take advantage of the "innocent landowner" provisions of CERCLA? What other options does it have under the statute?

Part 2—The landfill

Over the years, HI sent its more concentrated atrazine wastes in barrels to local industrial landfills. In the early years, HI simply contracted with a waste hauling company (Trashco) to collect atrazine wastes along with all of the other waste from the plant (from regular "garbage" to industrial wastes). Trashco decided where it would bring these wastes, choosing from local landfills and other disposal sites depending on costs, capacity, and other factors.

The most frequent destination for HI's atrazine wastes was Ernie's Landfill, Inc., an unlined facility sited on an abandoned gravel mine, with very porous soils. The state environmental agency closed this landfill shortly after enactment of RCRA, and the original company (Ernie's) went bankrupt. The company was wholly owned and managed by Ernie Ernest. Ernie's brother, Bert, owns the property. Bert leased the property to Ernie's Landfill, Inc., but otherwise had no involvement in the operation or management of the landfill.

Later, Waste Disposal Inc. (WDI), a national leader in solid and hazardous waste disposal services, purchased Trashco, along with all of its trucks and other equipment, and took over all of Trashco's existing customers. WDI initially sent HI's atrazine wastes to Ernie's Landfill, Inc., but later discontinued the practice, choosing instead to bring all chemical and other industrial wastes to a new hazardous waste treatment and disposal facility designed, permitted, and operated in full compliance with RCRA and other applicable laws.

Leachate from Ernie's landfill now causes serious groundwater contamination, and an expensive cleanup is needed. Test data shows atrazine and other chemicals related to atrazine production in the contaminated groundwater, along with a chemical soup of other contaminants from many other sources. EPA takes charge of the CERCLA cleanup.

1. After incurring significant costs for the initial removal action, and anticipating significant costs for the later remedial action, EPA wants to initiate a cost recovery action. Which of the following parties are potentially liable for these costs, and why or why not: (1) HI, (2) WDI, (3) Ernie, and (4) Bert?

2. What advice would you give HI regarding the cost recovery action? Should it defend in court, or settle with EPA? If it settles, what issues should it address in the settlement? Assuming that HI incurs significant liability even via settlement, what other steps might it take to recover some of those costs after the settlement?

13

Allocation of Government Responsibility

A. INTRODUCTION

In the last chapter, we discussed allocation of private responsibility for environmental cleanup. Throughout the book, however, you have seen how much responsibility for environmental protection lies in the hands of government. An equally important set of decisions involves where within government various decisions should be made. In Chapter 3, we addressed one aspect of this allocation: which branches of government (legislative, executive, and judicial) make, and review, environmental policy and regulatory decisions. We did not, however, discuss which *level* of government—federal, state, or local—should make various kinds of environmental decisions. We address this choice in this chapter. A range of legal and policy factors, some of constitutional dimensions, influence these allocation decisions. Because our main purpose is to teach environmental law and policy, in this chapter we focus on factors grounded in environmental policy, but explain secondarily how issues of constitutional law may affect or constrain those policy considerations.

B. FEDERAL VERSUS STATE AND LOCAL CONTROL

Where Congress delegates standard setting or other environmental responsibility or authority, it also must choose which level (or levels) of government are appropriate to perform those functions. Some statutes delegate most or all responsibility to federal agencies. In the Toxic Substances Control Act (TSCA) and the Federal Insecticide, Fungicide, and Rodenticide Act (FIFRA), for example, Congress delegated all of the principal implementing authority to the federal EPA. The following chart summarizes some of the key authorities Congress delegated to EPA in these laws. What is it about the regulation of toxic chemicals and pesticides that might explain Congress' judgment that a national approach is appropriate?

Principal Federal Authorities under TSCA and FIFRA

FIFRA		*7 U.S.C. §§136-136y*
	7 U.S.C. §136a(a)	Generally prohibits sale of unregistered pesticides.
	7 U.S.C.§136a(c)(2)	EPA may collect information about pesticides to inform registration decisions.
	7 U.S.C.§136a(c)(5), (6)	EPA may refuse to register pesticides with "unreasonable" environmental effects.[1]
		EPA may refuse to register mislabeled or ineffective pesticides.
	7 U.S.C. §136a	EPA must reregister certain older pesticides.
	7 U.S.C. §136d	EPA may cancel pesticide registrations.
TSCA		*15 U.S.C. §§2601-2692*
	15 U.S.C. §2603	EPA generally must require testing of toxic substances that "may present an unreasonable risk of injury to health or the environment" when needed to fill data gaps.
	15 U.S.C. §2604(a)(2)	EPA may determine which uses of a chemical are significant new uses requiring submission of data.
	15 U.S.C. §2605	EPA must ban or regulate toxic substances that it finds pose an "unreasonable risk of injury to health or the environment."[2]

1. The courts have generally interpreted this requirement as imposing a cost-benefit test on pesticide registration. *See, e.g.,* Envtl. Def. Fund, Inc. v. EPA, 548 F.2d 998, 1012-18 (D.C. Cir. 1976) (proponent of a pesticide must show that its benefits outweigh its risks).

2. The courts have generally interpreted this section as imposing a cost-benefit test on TSCA regulatory decisions. *See* Corrosion Proof Fittings v. EPA, 947 F.2d 1201 (5th Cir. 1991)

In other statutes, including the Clean Air Act, the Clean Water Act, and RCRA, Congress chose a strategy of "cooperative federalism" in which the federal and state governments share responsibility in various ways. Congress delegated some functions to the federal government, and others to the states. In some programs, Congress provided for federal regulation with an option for states to assume program authority, subject to EPA oversight. In the following survey, we explain how Congress allocated various kinds of environmental decisions among different levels of government. This review will also give you a better sense of how each of these statutes operates as a whole.

1. Setting Ambient Effects-Based Standards

Who should be responsible for setting basic environmental standards of the type studied in Part II of this book? Should one set of standards apply nationally, or should individual states adopt different standards to reflect different circumstances?

Recall that EPA sets the National Ambient Air Quality Standards uniformly for the entire country but that states, subject to EPA oversight, establish water quality standards. Why did Congress choose to allocate authority over ambient effects-based standards differently in the two statutes? Does the distinction make any sense?

2. Output Standards and State Planning

Regardless of who establishes ambient standards, significant environmental policy decisions remain even after those standards are in place. Ambient health-based standards do not in themselves dictate which pollution sources must reduce pollution, and by how much, such that the ambient standards will be attained. Congress must choose which levels of government are most appropriate to create output standards either in aid of meeting ambient standards or to reduce pollution not addressed by ambient standards. Congress delegated to EPA the responsibility for setting most of the technology-based standards under the Clean Water Act, *e.g.*, 33 U.S.C. §§1311, 1314 (effluent limitations for existing sources), 1316 (new source performance standards), 1317 (pretreatment standards for indirect dischargers); and some of those under the Clean Air Act, *e.g.*, 42 U.S.C. §§7412(d) (emissions standards for hazardous air pollutants), 7411 (new source performance standards). In the Clean Water Act, states adopt technology-based standards for individual facilities based on "best professional judgment" for those sources for which EPA has not yet issued national standards, and when the state implements the NPDES permit program. *See* 33 U.S.C. §§1342(a)(1)(B), (b). (EPA adopts such standards for individual sources when EPA runs the permit program for a particular state.) What are the arguments for and against setting technology-based standards at a national level? The state level?

a. Attaining Ambient Environmental Standards: SIPs and TMDLs

As you learned in Chapter 4, ambient effects-based environmental standards (most notably, the NAAQS and water quality standards) dictate how clean the air, water, or other environmental media must be where we use them, in the external environment. They do not, however, automatically define the obligations of particular pollution sources to control pollution sufficiently such that, when all reductions are combined, the ambient standards are met. Congress first addressed this difficult allocation task in the 1970 Clean Air Act Amendments. While assigning EPA the job of issuing the NAAQS, Congress delegated to the states the task of developing and implementing output standards in air quality control regions throughout the country in order to meet the ambient standards, subject to minimum statutory requirements and EPA oversight. The Act contemplates substantial state technology-based standard setting in the service of the Act's goal of meeting the NAAQS. The Supreme Court described how this process is designed, and how it compared to the relative federal and state roles under earlier versions of the statute, in an early case:

> Congress initially responded to the problem of air pollution by offering encouragement and assistance to the States. In 1955 the Surgeon General was authorized to study the problem of air pollution, to support research, training, and demonstration projects, and to provide technical assistance to state and local governments attempting to abate pollution. In 1960 Congress directed the Surgeon General to focus his attention on the health hazards resulting from motor vehicle emissions. The Clean Air Act of 1963 authorized federal authorities to expand their research efforts, to make grants to state air pollution control agencies, and also to intervene directly to abate interstate pollution in limited circumstances. Amendments in 1965 broadened federal authority to control motor vehicle emissions and to make grants to state pollution control agencies.
>
> The focus shifted somewhat in the Air Quality Act of 1967. It reiterated the premise of the earlier Clean Air Act "that the prevention and control of air pollution at its source is the primary responsibility of States and local governments." Its provisions, however, increased the federal role in the prevention of air pollution, by according federal authorities certain powers of supervision and enforcement. But the States generally retained wide latitude to determine both the air quality standards which they would meet and the period of time in which they would do so.
>
> The response of the States to these manifestations of increasing congressional concern with air pollution was disappointing. Even by 1970, state planning and implementation under the Air Quality Act of 1967 had made little progress. Congress reacted by taking a stick to the States in the form of the Clean Air Amendments of 1970. These Amendments sharply increased federal authority and responsibility in the continuing effort to combat air pollution. Nonetheless, the Amendments explicitly preserved the principle: "Each State shall have the primary responsibility for assuring air quality within the entire geographic area comprising such State." The difference under the Amendments was that the States were no longer given any choice as to whether they would meet this responsibility. For the first time they were required to attain air quality of specified standards, and to do so within a specified period of time.
>
> The Amendments directed that within 30 days of their enactment the Environmental Protection Agency should publish proposed regulations describing national quality standards for the "ambient air," which is the statute's term for the outdoor air used by the general public. After allowing 90 days for comments on the proposed standards, the Agency was then obliged to promulgate such standards. The standards were to be of two general types: "primary" standards, which in the judgment of the Agency were "requisite to protect the public health," and "secondary" standards, those that in the judgment of the Agency were "requisite to protect the public welfare from any known or anticipated adverse effects associated with the presence of such air pollutant in the ambient air."
>
> Within nine months after the Agency's promulgation of primary and secondary air quality standards, each of the 50 States was required to submit to the Agency a plan designed to implement and maintain such standards within its boundaries. The Agency was in turn required to approve each State's plan within four months of the deadline for submission, if it had been adopted after public hearings and if it satisfied eight general conditions set forth in §110(a)(2).[2] Probably the principal of these conditions, and the heart of the 1970 Amendments, is that the plan provide for the attainment of the national primary ambient air quality standards

___

2. Section 110(a)(2), 42 U.S.C. §1857c–(a)(2), reads as follows:

"The Administrator shall, within four months after the date required for submission of a plan under paragraph (1), approve or disapprove such plan, or each portion thereof. The Administrator shall approve such plan, or any portion thereof, if he determines that it was adopted after reasonable notice and hearing and that—

in the particular State "as expeditiously as practicable but . . . in no case later than three years from the date of approval of such plan." In providing for such attainment, a State's plan must include "emission limitations, schedules, and timetables for compliance with such limitations"; it must also contain such other measures as may be necessary to insure both timely attainment and subsequent maintenance of national ambient air standards.

Train v. Natural Resources Defense Council 421 U.S. 60, 63-67 (1975).

A year later, the Court addressed the degree of flexibility states have in deciding how to attain the NAAQS in air quality control regions within their states:

≡≡≡ *Union Electric Co. v. Environmental Protection Agency*
≡≡≡ *427 U.S. 246 (1976)*

JUSTICE MARSHALL delivered the opinion of the Court.

After the Administrator of the Environmental Protection Agency (EPA) approves a state implementation plan under the Clean Air Act, the plan may be challenged in a court of appeals within 30 days, or after 30 days have run if newly discovered or available information justifies subsequent review. We must decide whether the operator of a regulated emission source, in a petition for review of an

---

"(A) (i) in the case of a plan implementing a national primary ambient air quality standard, it provides for the attainment of such primary standard as expeditiously as practicable but (subject to subsection (e) of this Section) in no case later than three years from the date of approval of such plan (or any revision thereof to take account of a revised primary standard); and (ii) in the case of a plan implementing a national secondary ambient air quality standard, it specifies a reasonable time at which such secondary standard will be attained;

"(B) it includes emission limitations, schedules, and timetables for compliance with such limitations, and such other measures as may be necessary to insure attainment and maintenance of such primary or secondary standard, including, but not limited to, land-use and transportation controls;

"(C) it includes provision for establishment and operation of appropriate devices, methods, systems, and procedures necessary to (i) monitor, compile, and analyze data on ambient air quality and, (ii) upon request, make such data available to the Administrator;

"(D) It includes a procedure, meeting the requirements of paragraph (4), for review (prior to construction or modification) of the location of new sources to which a standard of performance will apply;

"(E) it contains adequate provisions for intergovernmental cooperation, including measures necessary to insure that emissions of air pollutants from sources located in any air quality control region will not interfere with the attainment or maintenance of such primary or secondary standard in any portion of such region outside of such State or in any other air quality control region;

"(F) it provides (i) necessary assurances that the State will have adequate personnel, funding, and authority to carry out such implementation plan, (ii) requirements for installation of equipment by owners or operators of stationary sources to monitor emissions from such sources, (iii) for periodic reports on the nature and amounts of such emissions; (iv) that such reports shall be correlated by the State agency with any emission limitations or standards established pursuant to this Act, which reports shall be available at reasonable times for public inspection; and (v) for authority comparable to that in section 303, and adequate contingency plans to implement such authority;

"(G) it provides, to the extent necessary and practicable, for periodic inspection and testing of motor vehicles to enforce compliance with applicable emission standards; and

"(H) it provides for revision, after public hearings, of such plan (i) from time to time as may be necessary to take account of revisions of such national primary or secondary ambient air quality standard or the availability of improved or more expeditious methods of achieving such primary or secondary standard; or (ii) whenever the Administrator finds on the basis of information available to him that the plan is substantially inadequate to achieve the national ambient air quality primary or secondary standard which it implements."

EPA-approved state plan filed after the original 30-day appeal period, can raise the claim that it is economically or technologically infeasible to comply with the plan.

I

[The Court summarized the history and explanation of the 1970 Amendments provided in *Train*, set forth above.]

On April 30, 1971, the Administrator promulgated national primary and secondary standards for six air pollutants he found to have an adverse effect on the public health and welfare. Included among them was sulfur dioxide, at issue here. After the promulgation of the national standards, the State of Missouri formulated its implementation plan and submitted it for approval. Since sulfur dioxide levels exceeded national primary standards in only one of the State's five air quality regions the Metropolitan St. Louis Interstate region, the Missouri plan concentrated on a control strategy and regulations to lower emissions in that area. The plan's emission limitations were effective at once, but the State retained authority to grant variances to particular sources that could not immediately comply. The Administrator approved the plan on May 31, 1972.

Petitioner is an electric utility company servicing the St. Louis metropolitan area, large portions of Missouri, and parts of Illinois and Iowa. Its three coal-fired generating plants in the metropolitan St. Louis area are subject to the sulfur dioxide restrictions in the Missouri implementation plan. Petitioner did not seek review of the Administrator's approval of the plan within 30 days, as it was entitled to do under §307(b)(1) of the Act, but rather applied to the appropriate state and county agencies for variances from the emission limitations affecting its three plants. Petitioner received one-year variances, which could be extended upon reapplication. The variances on two of petitioner's three plants had expired and petitioner was applying for extensions when, on May 31, 1974, the Administrator notified petitioner that sulfur dioxide emissions from its plants violated the emission limitations contained in the Missouri plan. Shortly thereafter petitioner filed a petition in the Court of Appeals for the Eighth Circuit for review of the Administrator's 1972 approval of the Missouri implementation plan. . . .

Since a reviewing court regardless of when the petition for review is filed may consider claims of economic and technological infeasibility only if the Administrator may consider such claims in approving or rejecting a state implementation plan, we must address ourselves to the scope of the Administrator's responsibility. The Administrator's position is that he has no power whatsoever to reject a state implementation plan on the ground that it is economically or technologically infeasible, and we have previously accorded great deference to the Administrator's construction of the Clean Air Act. After surveying the relevant provisions of the Clean Air Amendments of 1970 and their legislative history, we agree that Congress intended claims of economic and technological infeasibility to be wholly foreign to the Administrator's consideration of a state implementation plan.

As we have previously recognized, the 1970 Amendments to the Clean Air Act were a drastic remedy to what was perceived as a serious and otherwise uncheckable problem of air pollution. The Amendments place the primary responsibility for formulating pollution control strategies on the States, but nonetheless subject the States to strict minimum compliance requirements. These requirements are of a "technology-forcing character," and are expressly designed to force regulated sources to develop pollution control devices that might at the time appear to be economically or technologically infeasible.

This approach is apparent on the face of 110(a)(2). The provision sets out eight criteria that an implementation plan must satisfy, and provides that if these criteria are met and if the plan was adopted after reasonable notice and hearing, the Administrator "shall approve" the proposed state plan. The mandatory "shall" makes it quite clear that the Administrator is not to be concerned with factors other than those specified, and none of the eight factors appears to permit consideration of technological or economic infeasibility. Nonetheless, if a basis is to be found for allowing the Administrator to consider such claims, it must be among the eight criteria, and so it is here that the argument is focused.

It is suggested that consideration of claims of technological and economic infeasibility is required by the first criterion that the primary air quality standards be met "as expeditiously as practicable but in no case later than three years," and that the secondary air quality standards be met within a "reasonable time." The argument is that what is "practicable" or "reasonable" cannot be determined without assessing whether what is proposed is possible. This argument does not survive analysis.

Section 110(a)(2)(A)'s three-year deadline for achieving primary air quality standards is central to the Amendments' regulatory scheme and, as both the language and the legislative history of the requirement make clear, it leaves no room for claims of technological or economic infeasibility. The 1970 congressional debate on the Amendments centered on whether technology forcing was necessary and desirable in framing and attaining air quality standards sufficient to protect the public health, standards later termed primary standards. . . .

It is argued that when such a state plan calls for proceeding more rapidly than economics and the available technology appear to allow, the plan must be rejected as not "practicable." Whether this is a correct reading of §110(a)(2)(A) depends on how that section's "as expeditiously as practicable" phrase is characterized. The Administrator's position is that §110(a)(2)(A) sets only a minimum standard that the States may exceed in their discretion, so that he has no power to reject an infeasible state plan that surpasses the minimum federal requirements—a plan that reflects a state decision to engage in technology forcing on its own and to proceed more expeditiously than is practicable. On the other hand, petitioner and Amici supporting its position argue that §110(a)(2)(A) sets a mandatory standard that the States must meet precisely and conclude that the Administrator may reject a plan for being too strict as well as for being too lax.

We read the "as may be necessary" requirement of §110(a)(2)(B) to demand only that the implementation plan submitted by the State meet the "minimum conditions" of the Amendments.[13] Beyond that, if a State makes the legislative determination that it desires a particular air quality by a certain date

---

13. Economic and technological factors may be relevant in determining whether the minimum conditions are met. Thus, the Administrator may consider whether it is economically or technologically possible for the state plan to require more rapid progress than it does. If he determines that it is, he may reject the plan as not meeting the requirement that primary standards be achieved "as expeditiously as practicable" or as failing to provide for attaining secondary standards within "a reasonable time."

and that it is willing to force technology to attain it — or lose a certain industry if attainment is not possible — such a determination is fully consistent with the structure and purpose of the Amendments, and §110(a)(2)(B) provides no basis for the EPA Administrator to object to the determination on the ground of infeasibility.

In sum, we have concluded that claims of economic or technological infeasibility may not be considered by the Administrator in evaluating a state requirement that primary ambient air quality standards be met in the mandatory three years. And, since we further conclude that the States may submit implementation plans more stringent than federal law requires and that the Administrator must approve such plans if they meet the minimum requirements of §110(a)(2), it follows that the language of §110(a)(2)(B) provides no basis for the Administrator ever to reject a state implementation plan on the ground that it is economically or technologically infeasible. Accordingly, a court of appeals reviewing an approved plan under §307(b)(1) cannot set it aside on those grounds, no matter when they are raised.

III

Our conclusion is bolstered by recognition that the Amendments do allow claims of technological and economic infeasibility to be raised in situations where consideration of such claims will not substantially interfere with the primary congressional purpose of prompt attainment of the national air quality standards. Thus, we do not hold that claims of infeasibility are never of relevance in the formulation of an implementation plan or that sources unable to comply with emission limitations must inevitably be shut down.

Perhaps the most important forum for consideration of claims of economic and technological infeasibility is before the state agency formulating the implementation plan. So long as the national standards are met, the State may select whatever mix of control devices it desires, and industries with particular economic or technological problems may seek special treatment in the plan itself. Moreover, if the industry is not exempted from, or accommodated by, the original plan, it may obtain a variance, as petitioner did in this case; and the variance, if granted after notice and a hearing, may be submitted to the EPA as a revision of the plan. Lastly, an industry denied an exemption from the implementation plan, or denied a subsequent variance, may be able to take its claims of economic or technological infeasibility to the state courts.

NOTES AND QUESTIONS ON *UNION ELECTRIC* AND SIPs

1. *Holding.* According to this decision, how much flexibility do states have in implementing the NAAQS? Can they be stricter than the statute demands to achieve the NAAQS more quickly, or with a higher degree of confidence? Does it matter whether a state chooses to shut down a particular facility in order to meet the standards? Conversely, can a state adopt a weaker SIP to keep a particular facility open, for example to save jobs, if it decides that preventing unemployment is more important than meeting the standards quickly?

2. *Zero sum game.* If a state weakens air pollution controls for a particular source or category of sources in a SIP or a SIP amendment, to save jobs or otherwise, what must it then do to compensate for the resulting increase in emissions? Assume that serious air pollution in a city results partly from the local steel industry, which employs a large percentage of the workforce and provides significant secondary economic stimulus. A large portion of the air pollution, however, comes from automobiles. The state could tighten controls on the steel mills, at the risk of plant closures and economic dislocation. Or, it could try to reduce the amount people drive through devices such as land use controls, higher parking fees, increased mass transit, and public education. How should it decide which approach to take?

3. *The federalism rationale.* Congress assigned EPA the task of promulgating the NAAQS, while requiring the states to adopt the necessary implementing plans, with EPA oversight of that process. Does this strike the proper balance between federal and state needs and interests?

4. *EPA oversight and SIP enforceability.* Under what circumstances can EPA disapprove a SIP? Should EPA approve a SIP in which a state decides that it can obtain adequate emissions reductions to meet the NAAQS through largely voluntary efforts, such as "no drive days" encouraged through public education, rather than enforceable emissions limits on stationary sources?

5. *EPA and state and local land use.* If EPA believes that more transit, denser land use patterns, and higher parking fees are the keys to reducing automotive pollution sufficiently to meet the standards, can it impose those solutions on a state? In 1990, Congress eliminated much of EPA's authority to address such issues as parking fees, tolls, or certain other aspects of land use and transportation planning. *See* 42 U.S.C. §7410(c); Penny Mintz, *Transportation Alternatives Within the Clean Air Act: A History of Congressional Failure to Effectuate and Recommendations for the Future*, 3 N.Y.U. ENVTL. L.J. 156 (1994). Why is federal control over such issues so controversial?

6. *Federal Implementation Plans (FIPs).* Ultimately, if EPA disapproves a SIP or a SIP revision and the state fails to adopt adequate changes, EPA is required, at least in theory, to adopt a federal implementation plan (FIP) to replace the defective SIP. What are the federalism implications of such an action? How likely is it politically to occur? (In practice, EPA has drafted but never imposed a FIP.) Would EPA adoption of a FIP violate states' rights under the Tenth Amendment? *See* Commonwealth of Virginia v. Browner, 80 F.3d 869, 882-83 (4th Cir. 1996) (holding that CAA's highway sanction, offset sanction, and requirement for federal implementation plan (FIP) in absence of adequate SIP did not violate spending power or Tenth Amendment).

7. *Process and uncertainty.* To get some sense of what is involved in developing, tracking, and, if necessary, revising a SIP, think through what minimum steps states must go through to comply with section 110. You begin with EPA's NAAQS, which themselves can be stated in quite simple terms. The standard for sulfur dioxide at issue in *Union Electric*, for example, was .03 parts per million (p.p.m.) (annual level) and 0.14 p.p.m. (maximum 24-hour concentration not to be exceeded more than once a year). 40 C.F.R. §§50.4-50.5 (1975). After that, however, the process can get rather complicated and infused with uncertainty. What must a state do to ascertain with adequate certainty whether the air in a

particular region violates the NAAQS, and if so, by how much? What real-world variables might affect whether particular levels of emissions will cause NAAQS violations in a given region? Assuming there is a violation, how then does the state determine the source of all emissions of the pollutant in question, or at least a high enough percentage of those emissions to develop a workable plan? Next, how does the state decide what emissions reductions are possible, from which sources, and with what costs and other considerations that may be relevant to its decision? Only then is the state prepared to make the difficult decision of "whose ox gets gored," *i.e.*, which sources must reduce emissions by how much, such that the standard is likely to be met in a timely way. Finally, once the state establishes (and EPA approves) pollution control obligations in the SIP, what must the state do to assure compliance with those obligations and attainment of the NAAQS?

8. *Complexity*. The above discussion gives only a sketch of the SIP process. Already complex in the 1970 statute, Congress added many layers of detail in the 1990 Clean Air Act Amendments, in part in response to persistent nonattainment problems around the country nearly two decades after the initial round of SIPs. Different statutory requirements now apply to different pollutants. *See, e.g.*, 42 U.S.C. §§7511 *et seq.* (ozone); 7512 *et seq.* (carbon monoxide); 7513 *et seq.* (particulate matter); 7514 *et seq.* (sulfur oxides, nitrogen dioxide, and lead). Requirements also vary between attainment areas, nonattainment areas, and "maintenance" areas that formerly violated but now meet the NAAQS. *See, e.g., id.* §§7502 (general nonattainment plan provisions); 7507 (motor vehicle emission standards in nonattainment areas); 7511-7511f (additional provisions for ozone nonattainment areas); 7512-7512a (additional provisions for carbon monoxide nonattainment areas); 7513-7513b (additional provisions for particulate matter nonattainment areas); 7514-7514a (additional provisions for nonattainment areas for sulfur oxides, nitrogen dioxide, and lead); 7505a (provisions for maintenance areas). In general, the 1990 requirements are far more prescriptive than those included in the 1970 law, and leave states with less flexibility in planning and implementing SIPs. Is this trend toward increased congressional prescription consistent with the general philosophy of the Act described in the above cases regarding allocation of authority between the federal and state governments? Do you think it will help or hurt attainment of the statutory goals? We leave most of the details to your own study or practice, or to upper level courses in air pollution law.

9. *Implementation*. Under section 110 of the Clean Air Act, SIPs must include enforceable emissions limitations and other requirements sufficient to ensure that targeted emissions reductions are achieved. That task is relatively easy for small numbers of stationary sources that can be identified and regulated individually. What happens, however, when a significant portion of air pollution responsible for NAAQS violations comes from a large number of very diffuse sources? In heavily polluted urban areas in Southern California, for example, violation of the ozone NAAQS cannot be met without reductions in emissions from such sources as lawn-mowers, lighter fluid from barbeque grills, and spray paints. How can states prove to EPA that control requirements for those sources are sufficiently "enforceable" to pass muster?

b. Assessment of the SIP Process

The following table provides a highly simplified summary of the relative federal and state roles under the CAA, and how they fit together:

Principal Federal and State Clean Air Act Roles

Federal Roles	*State Roles*
Issue National Ambient Air Quality Standards	Designate Air Quality Control Regions
Approve SIPs and SIP Amendments or issue Federal Implementation Plans (FIPs)	Adopt State Implementation Plans (SIPs) and SIP Amendments (different requirements for attainment, nonattainment, and maintenance areas)
Adopt national technology-based standards (*e.g.*, new sources, hazardous air pollutants)	Adopt technology-based standards for individual sources
Adopt national mobile source standards	Adopt land use and transportation controls
Enforce SIP provisions	Enforce SIP provisions

The SIP process has a checkered history of successes and failures. While some regions have come into compliance with the NAAQS, there has also been a significant history of delays, missed deadlines, litigation, SIP revisions, political haggling between EPA and the states, congressional fine-tuning or mass overhauls, and yet more revisions to respond to statutory changes and judicial remands. After describing the history and complexity of the SIP process in overwhelming detail, Professor Arnold Reitze, who has been one of the leading students of CAA law and policy for many years, writes his sobering assessment of the SIP program's failure, and why he thinks it has failed, with equally notable brevity:

Arnold W. Reitze, Jr., Air Quality Protection Using State Implementation Plans— Thirty-Seven Years of Increasing Complexity

15 Vill. Envtl. L.J. 209 (2004)

§7. The Failure of the SIP Approach

The Air Quality Act of 1967 began an air pollution control program based on reaching ambient air quality goals through an implementation plan that imposed specific requirements on air pollution sources. The 1970 CAA Amendments greatly expanded federal authority. National Ambient Air Quality Standards (NAAQS) would be established by EPA to be reached pursuant to a state implementation plan. An attainment date of 1975 was specified, with a few exceptions. The pervasive failure to achieve these goals led to the 1977 CAA Amendments, which extended the compliance date to 1982, or 1987 for areas that could not meet ozone or carbon monoxide NAAQS due to transportation related emissions. This effort also failed, although substantial progress was made in reducing the air pollution emissions from stationary sources per unit of production and from motor vehicles based on an emission per vehicle mile traveled. When the 1990 CAA Amendments were enacted, 100 areas exceeded the ozone standard, fifty-one exceeded the SO_2 standard and twelve exceeded the lead standard. The 1990 Amendments provided more time for meeting NAAQS. For ozone, the most difficult pollutant to control, extensions as late as November 15, 2010 were provided for the most polluted areas. For the areas with marginal violations, compliance was to be achieved by November 15, 1993. Other areas compliance dates ranged between 1993 and 2010, but milestones are specified that must be met. Carbon monoxide nonattainment areas had an attainment date as late as December 31, 2000, for seriously polluted areas.

Despite the twenty-five percent reduction in aggregate emissions of the six criteria pollutants since 1970, approximately 133 million people in 2001 lived in counties that violated one or more NAAQS. This number would be considerably lower if the PM2.5 and eight-hour ozone standards had not been promulgated July 18, 1997. Under the pre-1997 regulations, 40.2 million people live in counties that have ozone NAAQS violations and 11.1 million people live in counties with PM10 NAAQS violations. About 3.4 million people live in areas violating any of the other four NAAQS. In 1990 there were 230 nonattainment areas; in 2001 there were 130 nonattainment areas. In 2002, forty-one states and the District of Columbia exceeded the ozone standard nearly 9,000 times, a ninety percent increase from 2001. Solving the nation's air pollution problem turned out to be more difficult than expected in 1967, but progress is being made. Some of the reasons for the failure of many SIPs to meet the NAAQS are listed, and briefly discussed below.

(1) The air quality problems the CAA has been attempting to correct are exacerbated by increases in population and consumption. The 1970 U.S. resident population of 203.984 million grew to 249.464 million by 1990, and grew to 275.130 million in 2000. U.S. energy use, which is responsible for most air pollution, went from 66.43 quadrillion Btus in 1970 to 84.2 quads in 1990. Electric power generation, the most significant stationary source of air pollution, grew from 1532 billion kilowatt hours (KWh) in 1970 to 2795 billion KWh in 1990. Energy consumed by the highway transportation sector grew from 15.32 quads in 1970 to 21.66 quads in 1990 to 26.52 quads in 2000. The size of the motor vehicle fleet in the U.S. grew from 108 million vehicles in 1970 to 189 million vehicles in 1980 and to 220.5 million vehicles in 2000. The effect of this growth was to nullify much of the progress made under the Clean Air Act.

The ability of the SIP program to comply with the NAAQS will continue to be challenged by growth in the population and in energy use. President Bush's National Energy Policy Development Group estimates that in the next twenty years U.S. oil consumption will increase thirty-three percent and electricity demand will increase forty-five percent. The Bush Administration projects a need for an additional 393,000 MW of generating capacity in the next twenty years, which will require between 1,300 and 1,900 new power plants to be constructed or about sixty to ninety plants per year. This projection is unlikely to occur, but the use of energy is expected to grow substantially. Much of the increase in electric power baseload generation capacity will be fueled by coal with the attendant air pollutant emissions. Petroleum consumption is expected to rise from 19.5 million barrels per day in 2000 to 25.8 million barrels per day in 2020, primarily because of the demand for fuel for transportation. Thus, SIPs can be expected to be periodically revised to continue the trend of increased stringency and higher costs.

(2) Although Congress passed the CAA Amendments and the President signed them into law, those concerned with the costs of air pollution control are working to control the costs of implementing the CAA. Some sources are seriously burdened because the CAA imposes its costs unevenly. Economic growth in some areas of the nation is restricted more than in other areas. Some industries faced huge compliance costs while dealing with stiff foreign competition. This leads to political opposition to new air pollution controls. The various administrations, acting through the Office of Management and Budget have slowed or stopped regulations or required that they be rewritten to lower costs to the private sector. The appropriation process is used by Congress to limit the money needed to implement the CAA. The Congressional oversight process has sometimes been used to limit EPA's aggressive pursuit of the CAA goals.

(3) The 1970 CAA demanded a ninety percent reduction in motor vehicle emissions. This anticipated reduction from motor vehicles was programmed into SIPs through the modeling assumptions that states used to develop an air program and led to under-predicting of overall emissions. The mobile source air pollution program is very successful when compared to other pollution control programs, but achieving a ninety percent reduction in emissions has been difficult. Further, both vehicle miles traveled (VMT) and the energy consumed by transportation were increasing more rapidly than projected by the emission inventories used to implement the 1970 CAA. This helped create nonattainment status for much of the urbanized United States. Moreover, the mix of vehicles changed dramatically as the number of trucks grew from 18.8 million in 1970 to 54.47 in 1990, to 87.1 million in 2000, which increased fuel consumption. The shift in the mix of vehicles resulted in a greater portion of VMT in an area is driven by light truck and SUVs, which usually have higher emissions. Heavy duty trucks are an even more serious problem. In the Metropolitan Washington D.C. area, for example, heavy-duty diesel vehicles account for less than three percent of the VMT, but produce about thirty percent of the NOx emissions. Diesel engines are not subject to more stringent regulations until 2007.

(4) From 1982 to 1997, developed land increased by forty-seven percent, but the population increased by only seventeen percent. This dispersion of the population contributed to VMT growth that for the last thirty years has increased roughly at a rate four times faster than the population.

Most air quality planning occurs with little concern for the impact of land use. Transportation air quality plans are based on projections of growth in VMTs with little concern for utilizing land use planning that will be more protective of air quality. Sprawl is more strongly correlated to peaks levels of ozone than is per capita income or employment levels.

(5) The mathematical models used to develop the SIPs projected overly optimistic reductions because:

(a) incorrect data was used as inputs in many models;

(b) linear rollback models that initially were used did not work well, especially for ozone because its atmospheric formation is complex, and more sophisticated models subsequently used also had significant limitations; and

(c) unjustified assumptions concerning the effectiveness of various control strategies were used in SIPs.

A report of EPA's Inspector General reported that air pollution control strategies are threatened by unreliable emission factors used to estimate releases from stationary sources. Emission factors are used to estimate air releases when more reliable data is unavailable. In 1985, EPA used 2073 emission factors; in 1996 it used more than 16,000. Almost half were not rated for reliability, and thousands were considered to have below average or poor reliability. The problem, according to EPA's Inspector General, was the result of EPA alliance with industry in developing emission factors. While the validity of models continues to improve, their costs have become significant. In 2002, the Washington D.C. region spent over $400,000 in four months to model and test the air quality conformity of its proposed long-range transportation plan and its transportation improvement plan. Maintaining and applying the models in this region requires about thirty-six percent of the transportation planning budget, or about $2.9 million per year.

(6) The CAA regulated new sources much more stringently than existing sources. The expectation was that over time air quality would improve as existing sources were replaced. The costs of complying with the CAA, however, led industry to maintain existing facilities beyond their expected useful life. Thus, the imposition of new source standards moved more slowly than originally expected. The New Source Review (NSR) program has been very controversial, and the adverse impact on air quality of old electric power plants is an ongoing controversy.

(7) Control measures were not implemented because:

(a) technology was not available or was too costly to use; or

(b) local opposition prevented the quick and effective implementation of strategies such as I/M and Stage II vapor recovery.

(8) Gasoline volatility was increased by the refiners, in part to compensate for the effects of not using lead additives in gasoline because more "light ends such as butane, benzene and zylene were in the fuel." This resulted in increases in VOC emissions in the 1980s that led to new provisions in

the CAA to control Reed Vapor Pressure (RVP), which is the measure of gasoline volatility.

(9) Control measures and other requirements of the CAA were not always adequately enforced. EPA's civil judicial settlements numbered 215 in FY 1999, 219 in FY 2000, 221 in FY 2001 and 216 in FY 2002. In FY 2002, EPA issued about 1,300 administrative orders, and 250 criminal cases were referred to the Department of Justice.

(10) Ozone transport from upwind states has not been effectively controlled by the CAA's programs. This means that downwind areas are held hostage to regulatory and enforcement efforts made by upwind states. Moreover, EPA has been willing to grant extensions due to ozone transport to areas that have not implemented the applicable rate of progress requirements.

(11) There is no punishment imposed on a state or its elected officials for a failure to achieve the goals of the SIP. The development and implementation of a stringent SIP-based program, however, could lead to the subsequent defeat of an elected official. Thus, there is little incentive for an elected official to aggressively pursue CAA compliance. Moreover, the probability that EPA will promulgate a FIP is small.

(12) EPA threatens to impose sanctions, but it virtually never imposes them. In 1997, the Congressional Research Service reported that the only area in the nation that was subject to an EPA-imposed sanction was a small area in East Helena, Montana.

(13) In 1990, Congress in section 182(g) provided for milestones to be used to measure progress in meeting the NAAQS for ozone. If appropriate progress is not made, EPA can force the state to have the area reclassified or require implementing additional measures. EPA, however, has been criticized for the collapse of the milestone program, which prevents state failures from being identified and remedied.

§8. Conclusion

The SIP program may have largely outlived its usefulness, but after more than thirty years of evolution, drastic change may be more harmful than beneficial. Most likely, SIPs will continue to become both more complex and irrelevant. The weakness of the SIP process is not due to a failure to accomplish its goals. Since 1970 the gross domestic product has increased by 164 percent and energy consumption [is] up forty-two percent, yet the aggregate emissions of the six criteria pollutants [are] down forty-eight percent.

The SIP's failure is related to the premise that air pollution is a localized phenomenon that is best handled as a state program with minimum federal involvement. That changed over the years as federal mandated measures became an increasing portion of the emission reduction demanded by the SIP. The CAA's subchapter II program for mobile sources and their fuels have, since 1970, played an important role in determining the effectiveness of the SIP program. The inspection and maintenance program for in-use motor vehicles, the use of reformulated gasoline and conformity planning that are discussed in the body of this article are examples of the SIP process being federalized in order to obtain the reductions necessary to have a SIP that projects attainment. The sulfur dioxide control program under CAA subchapter IV has become the most important program for sulfur emissions control, yet it operates largely outside of the SIP program. In the future, federally mandated measures will be the major cause of the additional emissions reductions that are needed if progress is to be made. The heavy-duty diesel rule and the associated sulfur reduction from diesel fuel will provide significant air quality improvement. Additional control on nonroad vehicles and more stringent Tier 2 requirements for motor vehicles also will be important. The eight-hour ozone standard and the PM2.5 standard will require more effort to be made to control interstate transport of pollution if these air quality standards are to be met. The pending Clear Skies legislation, or some variant, will add additional federal limitations on emissions. Finally, the continued promulgation and implementation of MACT standards to control air toxics impose federally-based limitations on emissions from major sources. The effect of these legislative and regulatory requirements will be to continue the trend of reducing the importance of state SIP implementation.

NOTES AND QUESTIONS ON REITZE CRITIQUE

1. *Reasons for nonattainment.* Which of Professor Reitze's suggested reasons for continued nonattainment do you think are most significant? Which do you think are easiest and hardest to fix, and why?

2. *Drastic change.* Despite his detailed critique of SIPs, Professor Reitze concludes that "drastic change may be more harmful than beneficial." Do you agree? Why or why not?

c. The Clean Water Act (CWA) Planning Process

The CWA includes planning provisions that similarly assign states the job of ensuring that aggregate pollution controls on numerous and diverse sources suffice to attain state water quality standards. However, while EPA implemented the SIP process as the centerpiece of the CAA program shortly after the 1970 amendments, it relegated the water quality planning provisions to the back seat for many years. Since the early 1990s, however, in the face of significant pressure from citizen suits, EPA began to take the CWA planning requirements more seriously, with increased focus on the "total maximum daily load" (TMDL) process that serves as the functional analogy to SIPs. *See generally* OLIVER HOUCK, THE CLEAN WATER ACT TMDL PROGRAM: LAW, POLICY, AND IMPLEMENTATION (2d ed. 2002).

The SIP process is complicated by the fact that so much air pollution comes from large numbers of automobiles, and from dispersed "area sources," as well as smaller numbers of stationary sources. Similarly, TMDLs and other aspects of comprehensive water pollution planning are complicated by potentially large numbers of pollution sources and types of sources, and the fact that Congress tackled two categories of water pollution in very different ways. *See* Robert W. Adler, *Integrated Approaches to Water Pollution: Lessons from the Clean Air Act*, 23 HARV. ENVTL. L. REV. 203 (1999). "Point sources," defined as "any discernable, confined, and discrete conveyance," 33 U.S.C. §1362(14), may not discharge pollutants into "waters of the United States" without a permit that imposes enforceable effluent limitations dictated by EPA, the states, or both. *See id.* §§1311, 1313, 1314, 1341, 1342, 1344. Congress left control of so-called nonpoint source pollution, however, largely to the states. *See id.* §§1288 (comprehensive state water quality planning program included in the 1972 statute), 1329 (specific nonpoint source pollution planning program added in 1987). Nonpoint sources include a somewhat nebulous category of activities that might best be characterized as "anything but point sources," and can include dispersed pollution from farms, logging operations, and any other land disturbance or other activities that contaminate runoff, as well as structures such as dams that alter the "chemical, physical, or biological, and radiological integrity of water." *See id.* §1362(19) (definition of "pollution"). To the extent that this distinction was not clear in the 1972 law, in 1977, Congress added the following exception to the statutory definition of point source: "This term does not include agricultural stormwater discharges and return flows from irrigated agriculture." 33 U.S.C. §1362(14).

Pronsolino v. Nastri
291 F.3d 1123 (9th Cir. 2002)

BERZON, CIRCUIT JUDGE.

The United States Environmental Protection Agency ("EPA") required California to identify the Garcia River as a water body with insufficient pollution controls and, as required for waters so identified, to set so-called "total maximum daily loads" ("TMDLs") . . . for pollution entering the river. Appellants challenge the EPA's authority under the Clean Water Act ("CWA" or the "Act") §303(d), to apply the pertinent identification and TMDL requirements to the Garcia River. The district court rejected this challenge, and we do as well.

CWA §303(d) requires the states to identify and compile a list of waters for which certain "effluent limitations" "are not stringent enough" to implement the applicable water quality standards for such waters. Effluent limitations pertain only to point sources of pollution; point sources of pollution are those from a discrete conveyance, such as a pipe or tunnel. Nonpoint sources of pollution are nondiscrete sources; sediment run-off from timber harvesting, for example, derives from a nonpoint source. The Garcia River is polluted only by nonpoint sources. Therefore, neither the effluent limitations referenced in §303(d) nor any other effluent limitations apply to the pollutants entering the Garcia River.

The precise statutory question before us is whether the phrase "are not stringent enough" triggers the identification requirement both for waters as to which effluent limitations apply but do not suffice to attain water quality standards and for waters as to which effluent limitations do not apply at all to the pollution sources impairing the water. We answer this question in the affirmative, a conclusion which triggers the application of the statutory TMDL requirement to waters such as the Garcia River.

Congress enacted the CWA in 1972, amending earlier federal water pollution laws that had proven ineffective. Prior to 1972, federal water pollution laws relied on "water quality standards specifying the acceptable levels of pollution in a State's interstate navigable waters as the primary mechanism for the control of water pollution." The pre-1972 laws did not, however, provide concrete direction concerning how those standards were to be met in the foreseeable future.

In enacting sweeping revisions to the nation's water pollution laws in 1972, Congress began from the premise that the focus "on the tolerable effects rather than the preventable causes of pollution" constituted a major shortcoming in the pre-1972 laws. The 1972 Act therefore sought to target primarily "the preventable causes of pollution," by emphasizing the use of technological controls.

At the same time, Congress decidedly did not in 1972 give up on the broader goal of attaining acceptable water quality. Rather, the new statute recognized that even with the application of the mandated technological controls on point source discharges, water bodies still might not meet state-set water quality standards. The 1972 statute therefore put in place mechanisms other than direct federal regulation of point sources, designed to "restore and maintain the chemical, physical, and biological integrity of the Nation's waters." §101(a).

In so doing, the CWA uses distinctly different methods to control pollution released from point sources and that traceable to nonpoint sources. The Act directly mandates technological controls to limit the pollution point sources may discharge into a body of water. On the other hand, the Act "provides no direct mechanism to control nonpoint source pollution but rather uses the 'threat and promise' of federal grants to the states to accomplish this task," thereby "recogniz[ing], preserv[ing], and protect[ing] the primary responsibilities and rights of States to prevent, reduce, and eliminate pollution, [and] to plan the development and use of land and water resources" §101(b).

Section 303 is central to the Act's carrot-and-stick approach to attaining acceptable water quality without direct federal regulation of nonpoint sources of pollution. Entitled "Water Quality Standards and Implementation Plans," the provision begins by spelling out the statutory requirements for water quality standards: "Water quality standards" specify a water body's "designated uses" and "water quality criteria," taking into account the water's "use and value for public water supplies, propagation of fish and wildlife, recreational purposes, and agricultural, industrial, and other purposes." §303(c)(2). The states are required to set water quality standards for all waters within their boundaries regardless of the sources of the pollution entering the waters. If a state does not set water quality standards, or if the EPA determines that the state's standards do not meet the requirements of the Act, the EPA promulgates standards for the state. §§303(b), (c)(3)–(4).

2. Section 303(d): "Identification of Areas with Insufficient Controls; Maximum Daily Load"[1]

Section 303(d)(1)(A) requires each state to identify as "areas with insufficient controls" "those waters within its boundaries for which the effluent limitations

---

1. The complete text of sections 303(d)(1)(A) and (C) reads:

   (A) Each State shall identify those waters within its boundaries for which the effluent limitations required by section 1311(b)(1)(A) and section 1311(b)(1)(B) of this title are not stringent enough to required by section [301(b)(1)(A)] and section [301(b)(1)(B)] of this title are not stringent enough to implement any water quality standard applicable to such waters." The CWA defines "effluent limitations" as restrictions on pollutants "discharged from point sources." CWA §502(11). Section 301(b)(1)(A) mandates application of the "best practicable control technology" effluent limitations for most point source discharges, while §301(b)(1)(B) mandates application of effluent limitations adopted specifically for secondary treatment at publicly owned treatment works.

For waters identified pursuant to §303(d)(1)(A) (the "§303(d)(1) list"), the states must establish the "total maximum daily load" ("TMDL") for pollutants identified by the EPA as suitable for TMDL calculation.[2] "A TMDL defines the specified maximum amount of a pollutant which can be discharged or 'loaded' into the waters at issue from all combined sources." The TMDL "shall be established at a level necessary to implement the applicable water quality standards. . . ." §303(d)(1)(c).

Section 303(d)(2), in turn, requires each state to submit its §303(d)(1) list and TMDLs to the EPA for its approval or disapproval. If the EPA approves the list and TMDLs, the state must incorporate the list and TMDLs into its "continuing planning process," the requirements for which are set forth in §303(e). If the EPA disapproves either the §303(d)(1) list or any TMDLs, the EPA must itself put together the missing document or documents. The state then incorporates any EPA-set list or TMDL into the state's continuing planning process.

Each state must also identify all waters not placed on its §303(d)(1) list (the "§303(d)(3) list") and "estimate" TMDLs for pollutants in those waters. §303(d)(3). There is no requirement that the EPA approve the §303(d)(3) lists or . . . TMDLs . . . for those waters.

The EPA in regulations has made more concrete the statutory requirements. Those regulations, in summary, define "water quality limited segment[s]" — those waters that must be included on the §303(d)(1) list—as "[a]ny segment where it is known that water quality does not meet applicable water quality standards, and/or is not expected to meet applicable water quality standards, even after the application of the technology-based effluent limitations required by sections 301(b) and 306." 40 C.F.R. §130.2(j) (2000). The regulations then divide TMDLs into two types: "load allocations," for nonpoint source pollution, and "wasteload allocations," for point source pollution. Under the regulations, states must identify those waters on the §303(d)(1) lists as "still requiring TMDLs" if any required effluent limitation

implement any water quality standard applicable to such waters. The State shall establish a priority ranking for such waters, taking into account the severity of the pollution and the uses to be made of such waters.

(C) Each State shall establish for the waters identified in paragraph (1)(A) of this subsection, and in accordance with the priority ranking, the total maximum daily load, for those pollutants which the Administrator identifies under section 1314(a)(2) of this title as suitable for such calculation. Such load shall be established at a level necessary to implement the applicable water quality standards with seasonal variations and a margin of safety which takes into account any lack of knowledge concerning the relationship between effluent limitations and water quality.

2. The EPA has identified all pollutants, under proper technical conditions, as suitable for TMDL calculation. 43 Fed. Reg. 60662 (Dec. 28, 1978).

or other pollution control requirement (including those for nonpoint source pollution) will not bring the water into compliance with water quality standards.

Continuing Planning Process

The final pertinent section of §303, §303(e), requiring each state to have a "continuing planning process," gives some operational force to the prior information-gathering provisions. The EPA may approve a state's continuing planning process only if it "will result in plans for all navigable waters within such State" that include, inter alia, effluent limitations, TMDLs, areawide waste management plans for nonpoint sources of pollution, and plans for "adequate implementation, including schedules of compliance, for revised or new water quality standards." The upshot of this intricate scheme is that the CWA leaves to the states the responsibility of developing plans to achieve water quality standards if the statutorily-mandated point source controls will not alone suffice, while providing federal funding to aid in the implementation of the state plans. TMDLs are primarily informational tools that allow the states to proceed from the identification of waters requiring additional planning to the required plans. As such, TMDLs serve as a link in an implementation chain that includes federally-regulated point source controls, state or local plans for point and nonpoint source pollution reduction, and assessment of the impact of such measures on water quality, all to the end of attaining water quality goals for the nation's waters. . . .

The Statutory Scheme as a Whole

The Pronsolinos' objection is, in essence, that the CWA as a whole distinguishes between the regulatory schemes applicable to point and nonpoint sources, so we must assume such a distinction in applying §§303(d)(1)(A) and (c). We would hesitate in any case to read into a discrete statutory provision something that is not there because it is contained elsewhere in the statute. But here, the premise is wrong. . . .

Point sources are treated differently from nonpoint sources for many purposes under the statute, but not all. In particular, there is no such distinction with regard to the basic purpose for which the §303(d) list and TMDLs are compiled, the eventual attainment of state-defined water quality standards. Water quality standards reflect a state's designated uses for a water body and do not depend in any way upon the source of pollution.

Nor is there any other basis for inferring from the structure of the Act an implicit limitation in §§303(d)(1)(A) and (C). The statutory subsection requiring water quality segment identification and TMDLs appears in the section entitled "Water Quality Standards and Implementation Plans," not in the immediately preceding section, entitled "Water Quality Related Effluent Limitations." So the section heading does not suggest any limitation to waters subject to effluent limitations.

Additionally, §303(d) follows the subsections setting forth the requirements for water quality standards, §303(a)–(c)—which, as noted above, apply without regard to the source of pollution—and precedes the "continuing planning process" subsection, §303(e), which applies broadly as well. Thus, §303(d) is structurally part of a set of provisions governing an interrelated goal-setting, information-gathering, and planning process that, unlike many other aspects of the CWA, applies without regard to the source of pollution.

True, there are, as the Pronsolinos point out, two sections of the statute as amended, §208 and §319, that set requirements exclusively for nonpoint sources of pollution. But the structural inference we are asked to draw from those specialized sections—that no other provisions of the Act set requirements for waters polluted by nonpoint sources—simply does not follow. Absent some irreconcilable contradiction between the requirements contained in §§208 and 319, on the one hand, and the listing and TMDL requirements of §303(d), on the other, both apply.

There is no such contradiction. Section 208 provides for federal grants to encourage the development of state "areawide waste treatment management plans" for areas with substantial water quality problems, and requires that those plans include a process for identifying and controlling nonpoint source pollution "to the extent feasible." Section 319, added to the CWA in 1987, directs states to adopt "nonpoint source management programs"; provides grants for nonpoint source pollution reduction; and requires states to submit a report to the EPA that "identifies those navigable waters within the State which, without additional action to control nonpoint sources of pollution, cannot reasonably be expected to attain or maintain applicable water quality standards or the goals and requirements of this chapter." This report must also describe state programs for reducing nonpoint source pollution and the process "to reduce, to the maximum extent practicable, the level of pollution" resulting from particular categories of nonpoint source pollution. §319(a)(1)(C), (D).

The CWA is replete with multiple listing and planning requirements applicable to the same waterways (quite confusingly so, indeed), so no inference can be drawn from the overlap alone.

Nor are we willing to draw the more discrete inference that the §303(d) listing and TMDL requirements cannot apply to nonpoint source pollutants because the planning requirements imposed by §208 and §319 are qualified ones—"to the extent feasible" and "to the maximum extent practicable"—while the §303(d) requirements are unbending. For one thing, the water quality standards set under §303 are functional and may permit more pollution than it is "feasible" or "practicable" to eliminate, depending upon the intended use of a particular waterway. For another, with or without TMDLs, the §303(e) plans for attaining water quality standards must, without qualification, account for elimination of nonpoint source pollution to the extent necessary to meet those standards. . . .

Essentially, §319 encourages the states to institute an approach to the elimination of nonpoint source pollution similar to the federally-mandated effluent controls contained in the CWA, while §303 encompasses a water quality-based approach applicable to all sources of water pollution. As various sections of the Act encourage different, and complementary, state schemes for cleaning up nonpoint source pollution in the nation's waterways, there is no basis for reading any of those sections—including §303(d)—out of the statute.

There is one final aspect of the Act's structure that bears consideration because it supports the EPA's interpretation of §303(d): The list required by §303(d)(1)(A) requires that waters be listed if they are impaired by a combination of point sources and nonpoint sources; the language admits of no other reading. Section 303(d)(1)(C), in turn, directs that TMDLs "shall be established at a level necessary to implement the applicable water quality standards. . . ." So, at least in blended waters, TMDLs must be calculated with regard to nonpoint sources of pollution; otherwise, it would be impossible "to implement the applicable water quality standards," which do not differentiate sources of pollution. . . .

Nothing in the statutory structure—or purpose—suggests that Congress meant to distinguish, as to §303(d)(1) lists and TMDLs, between waters with one insignificant point source and substantial nonpoint source pollution and waters with only nonpoint source pollution. Such a distinction would, for no apparent reason, require the states or the EPA to monitor waters to determine whether a point source had been added or removed, and to adjust the §303(d)(1) list and establish TMDLs accordingly. . . .

Federalism Concerns

The Pronsolinos finally contend that, by establishing TMDLs for waters impaired only by nonpoint source pollution, the EPA has upset the balance of federal-state control established in the CWA by intruding into the states' traditional control over land use. That is not the case.

The Garcia River TMDL identifies the maximum load of pollutants that can enter the Garcia River from certain broad categories of nonpoint sources if the river is to attain water quality standards. It does not specify the load of pollutants that may be received from particular parcels of land or describe what measures the state should take to implement the TMDL. Instead, the TMDL expressly recognizes that "implementation and monitoring" "are state responsibilities" and notes that, for this reason, the EPA did not include implementation or monitoring plans within the TMDL.

Moreover, §303(e) requires—separately from the §303(d)(1) listing and TMDL requirements—that each state include in its continuing planning process "adequate implementation, including schedules of compliance, for revised or new water quality standards" "for all navigable waters within such State." The Garcia River TMDL thus serves as an informational tool for the creation of the state's implementation plan, independently—and explicitly—required by Congress.

California chose both if and how it would implement the Garcia River TMDL. States must implement TMDLs only to the extent that they seek to avoid losing federal grant money; there is no pertinent statutory provision otherwise requiring implementation of §303 plans or providing for their enforcement. . . .

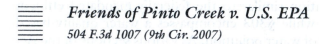

Friends of Pinto Creek v. U.S. EPA
504 F.3d 1007 (9th Cir. 2007)

HUG, CIRCUIT JUDGE.

I. Factual Background

Pinto Creek is a desert river located near Miami, Arizona, approximately 60 miles east of Phoenix. It has been listed by the American Rivers Organization as one of the country's most endangered rivers due to threats from proposed mining operations. Pinto Creek and its riparian environs are home to a variety of fish, birds, and other wildlife, some of which are specially protected. Due to excessive copper contamination from historical mining activities in the region, Pinto Creek is included on Arizona's list of impaired waters under §303(d) of the Clean Water Act, 33 U.S.C. §1313(d), as a water quality limited stream due to non-attainment of water quality standards for dissolved copper.

Carlota proposed to construct and operate an open-pit copper mine and processing facility approximately six miles west of Miami, Arizona, covering over 3000 acres while extracting about 100 million tons of ore. Part of the operation plan includes constructing diversion channels for Pinto Creek to route the stream around the mine, as well as groundwater cut-off walls to block the flow of groundwater into the mine.

. . . Because the proposed action would involve the discharge of pollutants into Pinto Creek, Carlota applied to the EPA for an NPDES permit under §402 of the Clean Water Act in 1996. The EPA ultimately issued the permit, and the Environmental Appeals Board ("Appeals Board"), the internal appellate board of the EPA, denied review.

II. Issues

A. Whether the issuance of the permit to discharge a pollutant, dissolved copper, into Pinto Creek, which already exceeded the amount of dissolved copper allowed under the Section 303(d) Water Quality Standard, is in violation of the Clean Water Act and . . . regulations. . . .

IV. Analysis

. . . In this case, the state had prepared the §303(d)(1) list, but it had not prepared a TMDL. Therefore, in response to the Petitioners' objection, the EPA prepared the TMDL utilized in its awarding of the permit.

B. Carlota's Discharge into an Impaired Waterway

The Petitioners contend that as a "new discharger" Carlota's discharge of dissolved copper into a waterway that is already impaired by an excess of the copper pollutant violates the intent and purpose of the Clean Water Act. . . . 40 C.F.R. §122.4(i) addresses the situation where a new source seeks to permit a discharge of pollutants into a stream already exceeding its water quality standards for that pollutant. Section 122.4 states in relevant part:

No permit may be issued:

. . .

(i) To a new source or a new discharger if the discharge from its construction or operation will cause or contribute to the violation of water quality standards. The owner or operator of a new source or new discharger proposing to discharge into a water segment which does not meet applicable water quality standards or is not expected to meet those standards . . . and for which the State or interstate agency has performed a pollutants load allocation for the pollutant to be discharged, must demonstrate, before the close of the public comment period, that:

(1) There are sufficient remaining pollutant load allocations to allow for the discharge; and

(2) The existing dischargers into that segment are subject to compliance schedules designed to bring the segment into compliance with applicable water quality standards.

The plain language of the first sentence of the regulation is very clear that no permit may be issued to a new discharger if the discharge will contribute to the violation of water quality standards. . . .

The EPA contends that the partial remediation of the discharge from the Gibson Mine will offset the pollution. However, there is nothing in the Clean Water Act or the regulation that provides an exception for an offset when the waters remain impaired and the new source is discharging pollution into that impaired water.

The regulation does provide for an exception where a TMDL has been performed and the owner or operator demonstrates that *before the close of the comment period* two conditions are met, which will assure that the impaired waters will be brought into compliance with the applicable water quality standards. The plain language of this exception to the prohibited discharge by a new source provides that the exception does not apply unless the new source can demonstrate that, under the TMDL, the plan is designed to bring the waters into compliance with applicable water quality standards.

The EPA argues that under the requirements of clause (1), there are sufficient remaining load allocations to allow for the discharge because the TMDL provides a method by which the allocations could be established to allow for the discharge. There is no contention, however, that these load allocations represent the amount of pollution that is currently discharged from the point sources and nonpoint sources, and there is no indication of any plan that will effectuate these load allocations so as to bring Pinto Creek within the water quality standards. The TMDL merely provides for the manner in which Pinto Creek *could* meet the water quality standards if all of the load allocations in the TMDL were met, not that there are sufficient remaining pollutant load allocations under existing circumstances.

With regard to the requirements of clause (2), the EPA argues that the requirement of "compliance schedules" pertains only to point sources for which there is a permit. This does not correspond to the plain language of clause (2), which provides "the existing discharges into that segment [of Pinto Creek] are subject to compliance schedules designed to bring the segment into compliance with applicable water quality standards." 40 C.F.R. §122.4(i)(2) (2000).

. . . The term "discharge" is defined to mean "the discharge of a pollutant." 40 C.F.R. §122.2 (2000). The term "discharge of a pollutant," is defined as any addition of any "pollutant" or combination of pollutants to "waters of the United States" from "*any point source.*" *Id.* at §122.2(a) (emphasis added). Thus, under the plain language of the regulation, compliance schedules are not confined only to "permitted" point source discharges, but are applicable to "any" point source.

The EPA contends that this would amount to a complete ban of the discharge of pollution to impaired waters. This is based on its misreading of the plain language of the regulation to state that the remediation has to be *completed* before Carlota's discharge. The plain language of clause (2) of the regulation, instead, provides that existing discharges into that segment (of the waters) are "subject to *compliance schedules* designed to bring the segment into compliance with applicable water quality standards." 40 C.F.R. §122.4(i)(2) (2000) (emphasis added). This is not a complete ban but a requirement of schedules to meet the objective of the Clean Water Act.

Here the existing discharges from point sources are not subject to compliance schedules designed to bring Pinto Creek into compliance with water quality standards. Thus, Carlota has not demonstrated that clause (2) of 40 C.F.R. §122.4(i) has been met. This is the regulation upon which Carlota and the EPA rely for issuance of the permit. . . .

The Respondents and Carlota rely on Arkansas v. Oklahoma, 503 U.S. 91 (1992), in support of their contentions. That case involved the issuance of a permit for a city in Arkansas to discharge effluent into a stream in Arkansas that entered a river that eventually flowed into Oklahoma. Oklahoma challenged the permit before the EPA, alleging that the discharge violated Oklahoma Water Quality Standards. In that case, the EPA found that the discharge would not lead to a "detectable change in water quality," which the Supreme Court held was supported by substantial evidence. In the opinion, the Court stated that "the parties have pointed to nothing that mandates a complete ban on discharges into a waterway that is in violation of those standards. The statute does, however, contain provisions designed to remedy existing water quality violations and to allocate the burden of reducing undesirable discharges between existing sources and new sources. *See, e.g.*, §1313(d)." Section 1313(d) of the Clean Water Act, referred to by the Court, is the one that provides for the establishment of water quality standards and TMDLs.

The Supreme Court in *Arkansas v. Oklahoma* also referred to §1288(b)(2), which provides for the development of area-wide programs to eliminate existing pollution in the context of area-wide waste treatment management. *Id.* That section provides details required of any plan to eliminate the pollution, including schedules, time lines, identification of agencies, and identification of measures necessary to carry out the plan. . . .

In this case, the Petitioners do not argue for an absolute ban on discharges into a waterway that is in violation of the water quality standards. Rather, the Petitioners point to the §122.4(i) exception by which a new discharger can comply with the Clean Water Act requirements. Those requirements simply were not met. Thus, no conflict exists with the Supreme Court's opinion in *Arkansas v. Oklahoma*. . . .

NOTES AND QUESTIONS ON *PRONSOLINO* AND *PINTO CREEK*

1. *Point versus nonpoint sources.* Why do you think Congress imposed strict, mandatory federal obligations on point sources, but relegated the control of nonpoint source pollution to individual state discretion? Is it explained by the policy articulated by Congress in section 101(b) of the Act, "to recognize, preserve, and protect the primary responsibilities and rights of States to prevent, reduce, and eliminate pollution [and] *to plan the development and use of land and water resources,*" *id.* §1251(b) (emphasis added)?

2. *TMDLs versus SIPs.* What similarities are there between TMDLs and SIPs? What differences? There seemed to be no question that SIPs should account for all

kinds of sources of air pollution, from stationary sources to the ubiquitous auto-mobile. Why would Congress, as the *Pronsolino* plaintiffs argued, exclude nonpoint sources from the TMDL process?

3. *The stakes.* The court seems clear that even where EPA writes a TMDL, the states are in charge of implementation under the continuing planning process in section 303(e), including decisions about whether, and how, to regulate non-point sources. If so, why did the plaintiffs care whether TMDLs apply to nonpoint sources? The Ass'n of Metropolitan Sewerage Agencies (AMSA), which represents point source public dischargers from the largest cities in the country, intervened on EPA's side of this case. Why did this representative of large point source dischargers care about the results of this case?

4. *Complexity and uncertainty.* As is true for SIPs, what may seem like a simple process in concept can get complicated very quickly. The same general sequence of analysis is needed for TMDLs as for SIPs. States first must monitor waters to deter-mine where water quality standards are violated, and by how much. Then, they must identify and quantify the sources of the pertinent kind of pollution, ascer-tain what controls are potentially achievable, allocate pollution reduction obliga-tions among those sources, decide on implementing methods, and then continue to monitor to determine whether standards are attained. Consider, however, the following examples of the kinds of complexities and uncertainties inherent in this process:

    a. *Nonpoint sources.* Some uncertainty exists for any kind of environmental monitoring. For point sources, discharges may vary over time in volume, concentration of pollutants, and other factors. However, at least we know where the outlet source is, and can sample effluent directly. It is consid-erably more difficult to measure pollution from nonpoint sources such as thousands of acres of farm fields within a watershed.

    b. *Pollutant fate and transport.* Measuring and predicting water quality would be much easier in a "closed system," in which everything we put into the water remains and everything we take out is gone. What variables in real water bodies affect concentrations of pollutants in the water, and, hence, the degree to which water quality standards are attained or violated? In what ways might concentrations of different kinds of pollutants change once they enter a real waterway, and how would those factors affect the degree to which water quality standards are met?

    c. *Different forms of water quality criteria.* Unlike the NAAQS, which are expressed entirely in numerical terms, water quality criteria come in differ-ent forms: narrative, numeric, toxicity-based, and biological. TMDLs are required for all violations of water quality criteria, whatever the format. How would you write TMDLs for narrative water quality criteria, such as waters free from noxious odors? Toxicity-based criteria, such as no more than 1 percent mortality of test organisms exposed to a given level of water quality? Biocriteria, such as 75 percent of species diversity compared to an unimpaired reference stream? What would implementation plans for those kinds of TMDLs look like?

5. *Implementation.* Section 301(b)(1)(C) of the Clean Water Act (in conjunction with the section 402 permitting requirement and other provisions) requires that point sources achieve effluent limitations sufficient to ensure the attainment of water quality standards, if those limits are stricter than imposed by applicable technology-based requirements. No such firm requirement exists for nonpoint sources. In the face of litigation and political pressure, EPA withdrew the proposed regulations identified by the court, which would have required implementation plans for all TMDLs. How much does this detract from the significance of the requirement to prepare TMDLs for all water bodies?

6. *New pollution in impaired areas.* Does the *Pinto Creek* decision, as EPA argued, effectively impose a ban on new point source discharges to impaired water segments? What about nonpoint sources, and why should they be treated differently? How does the CWA approach differ from that used for new emissions in nonattainment areas under the CAA?

7. *Assessment.* As noted above, EPA began to implement the SIP program immediately after Congress adopted the 1970 CAA Amendments. As Professor Houck explains in detail, however, EPA focused primarily on implementing the technology-based requirements of the CWA as implemented through the NPDES permitting program, largely to the exclusion of the TMDL process, until forced to implement TMDLs by a rash of citizen suits. Therefore, EPA did not begin to implement the TMDL program seriously until more than two decades after the 1972 amendments. *See* OLIVER HOUCK, THE CLEAN WATER ACT TMDL PROGRAM: LAW, POLICY, AND IMPLEMENTATION (2d ed. 2002). The following is a simplified depiction of the major federal and state roles under the CWA:

Principal Federal and State Clean Water Act Roles

Federal Roles	*State Roles*
Issue national technology-based effluent limitations standards	
Review state-issued point source permits; authority to veto inadequate permits	Apply technology-based standards in individual point source permits
Issue water quality criteria guidance; review and approve state water quality standards, or issue federal water quality standards	Adopt water quality standards (WQS)
Review and approve state TMDLs, or issue federal TMDLs	Adopt "total maximum daily loads" (TMDLs) for water bodies that do not meet WQS; revise point source permits as necessary to implement TMDLs
No authority to issue federal nonpoint source control plans or water quality implementation plans (remedies limited to withholding grants)	Adopt nonpoint source control plans and water quality implementation plans

Whether for this or for other reasons, one of us has noted that the nation faces failures in achieving water quality standards similar to the CAA nonattainment problems identified by Professor Reitze: "More than a third of the nation's rivers and almost half of its lakes do not meet designated water quality uses in whole or in part—trends that have not changed significantly over the past decade—because of a combination of chemical pollution and other factors." Robert W. Adler, *The Two Lost Books in the Water Quality Trilogy: The Elusive Objectives of Physical and Biological Integrity*, 33 ENVTL. L. 29, 49-50 (2003). Do you think the TMDL program has any better chance of success than the SIP process? Why or why not? What are the major impediments to the TMDL program, and how might they be fixed?

PROBLEM: AN ATRAZINE TMDL

Where a water body is impaired by numerous and diverse sources, TMDLs (like SIPs) can become extremely complex. Among the many thorny implementation problems are uncertainties in measurement, modeling, environmental variability, and other factors similar to those identified by Professor Reitze in the SIP process. Consider the following relatively simple hypothetical scenario for atrazine. (Actual TMDLs can be considerably more complex.)

One of the factories that produces atrazine is located on the banks of the Maizey River. In the past, the factory dumped atrazine wastes onto adjacent fields, and atrazine has now seeped into the groundwater beneath those fields. Some of that atrazine regularly leaches from the groundwater into the adjacent river. Current atrazine wastes from the factory are treated as part of the facility's overall waste stream, but some atrazine residuals remain in the wastewater released into the river. Some highly concentrated atrazine wastes were also sent in barrels to a nearby industrial waste landfill. Due to improper handling and storage of those barrels, some atrazine has leaked into the ground beneath the landfill. However, the landfill has a leachate collection and treatment system, through which some atrazine residuals are discharged into the Maizey River. Finally, atrazine runs off into the river from farms that spray atrazine products on their fields.

Thus, there are at least four existing sources of atrazine discharge into the Maizey River (the groundwater, the factory discharge, the landfill discharge, and farm runoff). The state department of environmental quality (DEQ) determines that atrazine levels in the river exceed the state water quality criterion, and that total atrazine releases into the river (from all sources combined) must be reduced by 100 micrograms of atrazine per day in order to meet the standards.

1. On what basis should the state "allocate" the required load reductions among the three existing sources? What principles can you think of that a state might use in deciding how to allocate pollution reduction allocations among various parties in a TMDL process?

2. Once the state makes that determination, how will it implement and enforce those required reductions? How will it enforce reductions for the factory and landfill discharges? What about the groundwater seepage and the farm runoff? Are those point or nonpoint sources? Should they be included

in the TMDL under the *Pronsolino* case? If so, how can any reductions be implemented and enforced? How can compliance with any required reduction be monitored?

3. Now, assume that the flow of the Maizey River varies over time. During the spring, heavy rains cause the river to swell to high levels, but by the end of September, the river is a fraction of what it is in May. Why does this matter in writing a TMDL? What flow assumption should the state use in writing the TMDL?

4. What if experts predict that the flow of the Maizey River will decline over the next decade due to climate disruption? How should that be taken into account in writing the TMDL?

5. A new herbicide formulator wants to locate on the Blue River upstream of existing discharges, to take advantage of increasing demand for atrazine products due to climate disruption. Despite the use of best practices, the facility will generate additional atrazine releases to the Maizey River. The Governor supports the new facility because it will create new jobs and stimulate the economy, and because it will reduce herbicide costs to the state's farmers compared to out-of-state sources. Can the state allow the new discharge, even when the atrazine water quality standard is already violated? If so, what must the state do to allow the new discharge?

A Note on the Scope and Coverage of Federal Regulation

Federal environmental regulation can extend to activities that otherwise might seem quite local in scope and impact. Under section 404 of the Clean Water Act, for example, the Army Corps of Engineers regulates construction of new homes or shopping centers if construction involves the discharge of dredge or fill material into wetlands or other waters of the United States. *See, e.g.*, Bersani v. EPA, 850 F.2d 36 (1st Cir. 1988) (shopping mall); Buttrey v. United States, 690 F.2d 1170 (5th Cir. 1982) (housing development). Similarly, section 7 of the ESA requires the Fish and Wildlife Service to determine whether otherwise local projects might jeopardize the continued existence of a threatened or endangered species, and whether the project may proceed or must implement reasonable and prudent alternatives. *See, e.g.*, Rancho Viejo v. Norton, 323 F.3d 1062 (D.C. Cir. 2003) (upholding ESA applicability to toad species limited to small habitats entirely within Southern California); National Ass'n of Homebuilders v. Babbitt, 130 F.3d 1041 (D.C. Cir. 1997) (upholding ESA application to fly restricted to eight-mile radius in two California counties).

The reach of federal environmental laws theoretically might be limited by the scope of federal power under the Commerce Clause, especially under the Supreme Court's rulings in United States v. Lopez, 514 U.S. 549 (1995), and United States v. Morrison, 529 U.S. 598 (2000), which invalidated, as beyond the scope of federal commerce power, aspects of federal gun control legislation and the civil remedy provisions of legislation designed to protect women against violent crimes, respectively. To date, however, courts have either rejected or avoided Commerce Clause challenges to a range of federal environmental statutes. *See, e.g.*, United States v. Olin Corp., 107 F.3d 1506 (11th Cir. 1997) (CERCLA); Gibbs v. Babbitt, 214 F.3d 483 (4th Cir. 2000) (ESA); State of Nebraska v. EPA, 331 F.3d 995 (D.C. Cir. 2003) (Safe Drinking Water Act); Solid Waste Agency of Northern Cook County v. U.S. Army Corps of Engineers, 531 U.S. 159 (2001) (Clean Water Act; Commerce Clause issue avoided).

As a matter of policy, however, Congress might find that states and localities should regulate activities of some kinds, in some places, or with impacts that fall below a certain threshold, rather than the federal government. Those line-drawing exercises, in turn, might affect the manner in which comprehensive statutory schemes work, as suggested by the problems of controlling air pollution from diffuse sources and water pollution from nonpoint sources.

You have seen that courts can interpret the manner in which Congress allocated water pollution control authority under the CWA in light of stated statutory goals or policies regarding states' rights. In *PUD No. 1 of Jefferson County*, for example, the Supreme Court considered the proper scope of state authority to use its water quality standards to control water flows through a federally licensed dam in light of Congress' stated policy that "the authority of each State to allocate quantities of water within its jurisdiction shall not be superseded, abrogated or otherwise impaired" by the CWA. 33 U.S.C. §1251(g). Similarly, the court in *Mississippi Commission on Natural Resources*, interpreted state power to determine the appropriate designated uses of water bodies in light of Congress' policy to recognize and preserve state authority over land and water uses. *See* 33 U.S.C. §1251(b).

Several key issues remain hotly disputed regarding the relative scope of federal and state regulation under the CWA, governed by specific statutory text and definitions but guided by policy factors and constitutional overtones. In section 301 of the CWA, Congress prohibited "the discharge of any pollutant by any person," 33 U.S.C. §1311(a), absent a valid permit under section 402 of the Act. *Id.* §1342 (providing for NPDES permits). "Discharge of a pollutant" is defined as "any addition of any pollutant to navigable waters from any point source." *Id.* §1362(12). Parties continue to litigate the meaning of all three of the key terms included in this definition—"addition," "navigable waters," and "point source"—to determine which activities are governed by federal law and which are left to the states:

1. *Addition.* In National Wildlife Federation v. Gorsuch, 693 F.2d 156 (D.C. Cir. 1982), the D.C. Circuit upheld EPA's decision not to require NPDES permits for discharges of water through dams, because those discharges move pollutants from one part of a river to another, and thus do not constitute an "addition" of pollutants to navigable waters. While the court based its decision in part on the statutory text, it was also influenced by indications in the statute and in the legislative history that Congress "did not want to interfere any more than necessary with state water management." *Id.* at 178-79. *See also* National Wildlife Federation

v. Consumers Power Co., 862 F.2d 580 (6th Cir. 1988) (upholding EPA decision that NPDES permit was not required for discharges of dead fish through pumped storage hydropower facility). More recently, three circuits found that an NPDES permit is required for discharges that transfer pollutants from one water body to another. Catskill Mountains Chapter of Trout Unlimited v. City of New York, 273 F.3d 481 (2d Cir. 2001) (holding that water pumped from a reservoir, through a tunnel, into a creek required a permit); Dubois v. U.S. Department of Agriculture, 102 F.3d 1273 (1st Cir. 1996) (requiring permit for water pumped from a river to a mountain pond for snowmaking at ski resort); Miccosukee Tribe v. South Florida Water Management District, 280 F.3d 1364 (11th Cir. 2002) (requiring permit for stormwater runoff from canal pumped through levee into undeveloped water conservation area).

The Supreme Court reviewed the Eleventh Circuit's decision in *Miccosukee*, remanding to the district court for a determination of whether the pumping source and the discharge location were "meaningfully distinct water bodies." South Florida Water Management District v. Miccosukee Tribe of Indians, 541 U.S. 95, 112 (2005). While not reaching the issue of whether Congress excluded these activities from the NPDES program as a matter of federalism, Justice O'Connor explained the competing federalism implications of the issue:

> If we read the Act to require an NPDES permit for every engineered diversion of one navigable water into another, thousands of new permits might have to be issued, particularly by western States, whose water supply networks often rely on engineered transfers among various natural water bodies. Many of those diversions might also require expensive treatment to meet water quality criteria. It may be that construing the NPDES program to cover such transfers would therefore raise the costs of water distribution prohibitively, and violate Congress' specific instruction that "the authority of each State to allocate quantities of water within its jurisdiction shall not be superseded, abrogated or otherwise impaired" by the Act. §1251(g). On the other hand, it may be that such permitting authority is necessary to protect water quality, and that the States or EPA could control regulatory costs by issuing general permits to point sources associated with water distribution programs.

Id. at 108. Should the decision in this case be governed by the congressional policy of preserving state authority over water allocation, or by the statutory objective of controlling water pollution? EPA later adopted a "water transfer rule" exempting discharges needed only to move water supplies among water bodies, so long as the water is "conveyed without being subjected to an intervening industrial, municipal, or commercial use." 73 Fed. Reg. 33699 (June 13, 2008) (to be codified at 40 C.F.R. Part 122).

In S.D. Warren v. Maine Board of Environmental Protection, 547 U.S. 370 (2006), the Supreme Court distinguished section 401 of the CWA from section 402, and held that an addition of a pollutant was not required to meet the definition of discharge (triggering the need for state water quality certification under section 401, *see PUD No. 1 of Jefferson County*), as it is to constitute the "discharge of a pollutant" for purposes of section 402 (triggering the need for an NPDES permit). Ironically, however, by establishing a broader definition of discharge for purposes of section 401, the Supreme Court expanded state authority to control water pollution from federally licensed facilities.

2. *Navigable waters.* The term "navigable waters" is defined in the Act as "waters of the United States, including the territorial seas," and has been the subject of much dispute regarding the geographic scope of federal regulation of water pollution. In United States v. Riverside Bayview Homes, 474 U.S. 121 (1985), the Supreme Court upheld the Corps of Engineers' interpretation of "navigable waters" as including wetlands that are "adjacent to" navigable bodies of water, relying on the CWA's broad water quality goals. However, the Court left open the question of whether the statute applied to so-called isolated waters that are not adjacent to traditionally navigable waters. In *Solid Waste Agency of Northern Cook County (SWANCC)*, the Court rejected Clean Water Act jurisdiction based on use of an isolated series of ponds by migratory birds, and implicitly found that discharges to isolated waters cannot be regulated under the Act. Rather than focusing primarily on the statutory goal of restoring the integrity of the Nation's waters, Chief Justice Rehnquist argued that the statutory language must be read narrowly to avoid an unnecessary constitutional decision, especially where federalism concerns are at stake:

> Where an administrative interpretation of a statute invokes the outer limits of Congress' power, we expect a clear indication that Congress intended that result. This requirement stems from our prudential desire not to needlessly reach constitutional issues and our assumption that Congress does not casually authorize administrative agencies to interpret a statute to push the limit of congressional authority. *This concern is heightened where the administrative interpretation alters the federal-state framework by permitting federal encroachment upon a traditional state power.*

531 U.S. at 172-73 (emphasis added).

Following *SWANCC*, lower courts decided numerous cases trying to draw the line between "adjacent" waters governed by the Act under *Riverside Bayview Homes*, and "isolated" waters excluded from that coverage under *SWANCC. See, e.g.*, United States v. Rapanos, 339 F.3d 447 (6th Cir. 2003) (concluding that *SWANCC* was relevant only to jurisdiction asserted under the Migratory Bird Rule and did not preclude jurisdiction under the CWA over a roadside ditch and the adjacent wetlands); United States v. Deaton, 332 F.3d 698 (4th Cir. 2003) (reading *SWANCC* narrowly and determining that the CWA provides for jurisdiction over inland waters, provided that those waters have a hydrological connection to navigable waters); Headwaters, Inc. v. Talent Irrigation District, 243 F.3d 526 (9th Cir. 2001) (concluding that polluted irrigation canals that received water from natural streams and lakes were not isolated waters and were properly subject to jurisdiction under the CWA); *but see* In re Needham, 354 F.3d 340 (5th Cir. 2003) (deciding that *SWANCC* limits jurisdiction under the CWA to navigable waters and water bodies directly abutting navigable waters).

The Supreme Court revisited this issue in 2006 in two cases involving wetlands connected to navigable waters by ditches or other man-made conveyances. Rapanos v. United States, 547 U.S. 715 (2006). Writing for a four-member plurality, Justice Scalia would impose two limiting conditions to the exercise of CWA jurisdiction. His first proposed condition relates to the nature of the water body:

> In sum, on its only plausible interpretation, the phrase "the waters of the United States" include only those relatively permanent, standing or continuously flowing bodies of water "forming geographic features" that are described in ordinary parlance as "streams[,] . . . ocean, rivers, [and] lakes." *See* Webster's Second 2882. The phrase does not include channels through which water flows intermittently or ephemerally, or channels that periodically provide drainage for rainfall.

Id. at 739. Justice Scalia's second suggested condition relates to the degree of connection between the water body to be regulated and a traditional navigable water:

> Therefore, *only* those wetlands with a continuous surface water connection to bodies that are "waters of the United States" in their own right, so that there is no clear demarcation between "waters" and wetlands, are "adjacent to" such waters and covered by the Act. Wetlands with only an intermittent, physically remote hydrologic connection to "waters of the United States" do not implicate the boundary-drawing problem in *Riverside Bayview*, and thus lack the necessary connection to covered waters that we described as a "significant nexus" in *SWANCC*.

Id. at 742 (emphasis in original). A prominent theme in Justice Scalia's opinion was that a broader interpretation of the Act's scope was not consistent with Congress' expressed goal, in section 101(b) of the Act, to recognize the primary role of the states in water pollution control. *See id.* at 722, 737-38.

Justice Kennedy, concurring in the judgment, would require only an adequate showing, on the record, that the water or wetland to be regulated has a " 'significant nexus' to waters that are or were navigable in fact or that could reasonably be so made." *Id.* at 759. Justices Stevens, Souter, Ginsburg, and Breyer dissented, and would have upheld the agencies' exercise of jurisdiction based on the principles articulated in *Riverside Bayview Homes. Id.* at 787 *et seq.* Those opinions focused more heavily on Congress' intent to control water pollution and to protect aquatic ecosystems on a national scale, without as much attention to states' rights. Given the fractured nature of the opinions, lower courts have differed on what rules to apply to cases involving various bodies of water.

3. *Point sources.* In *Pronsolino*, you saw that Congress included point sources within the federal regulatory scheme while leaving nonpoint source controls largely to individual states, in large part because of a concern about the degree to which federal regulation of nonpoint sources would intrude on state authority over land and water use. The stakes here are very high. Point sources require NPDES permits that may bring hefty permit application and compliance costs, and subject the discharger to significant potential enforcement liability for any violations. State nonpoint source controls typically are weak to nonexistent. As a result, parties have litigated intensively whether various activities are covered by the definition of point source. *See, e.g.*, Concerned Area Residents for the Environment v. Southview Farm, 34 F.3d 114 (2d Cir. 1994) (manure spreading and spraying); Natural Resources Defense Council v. Train, 510 F.2d 692 (D.C. Cir. 1974) (stormwater); The Avoyelles Sportsmen's League, Inc. v. Marsh, 715 F.2d 897 (5th Cir. 1983) (construction equipment); United States v. Earth Sciences, Inc., 599 F.2d 368 (10th Cir. 1979) (mining ponds); Dague v. City of Burlington, 935 F.2d 1343 (2d Cir. 1991) (landfill). The statute defines a "point source" as:

[A]ny discernible, confined and discrete conveyance, including but not limited to any pipe, ditch, channel, tunnel, conduit, well, discrete fissure, container, rolling stock, concentrated animal feeding operation, or vessel or other floating craft, from which pollutants are or may be discharged. This term does not include agricultural stormwater discharges and return flows from irrigated agriculture.

33 U.S.C. §1362(14). In deciding where the point/nonpoint source line should be drawn, should courts focus more on the functional issues suggested in the definition, *i.e.*, whether the discharge is amenable to regulation in a permit because it is "discernible, confined and discrete," or federalism concerns of whether the *activity* to be regulated affects state authority over land and water use?

3. Delegating Federal Programs to States

In some cases, rather than delegating responsibility either to the federal government or to states, Congress took a middle ground in which programs are implemented by federal agencies unless they are delegated to willing states and subject to federal approval and oversight. Key examples include 33 U.S.C. §1342 (CWA NPDES permits); *id.* §1344 (CWA dredge and fill permits); 42 U.S.C. §7661 (CAA permits); 42 U.S.C. §6926 (RCRA hazardous waste planning); *id.* §6933 (RCRA hazardous waste management); 30 U.S.C. §§1253-1254 (Surface Mining Conservation and Reclamation Act (SMCRA) program). This form of cooperative federalism, however, raises additional issues regarding the degree to which the federal government should oversee delegated state programs. Consider the following case, which explains the balance Congress struck in allowing EPA to delegate the NPDES program to states, but with significant ongoing EPA oversight:

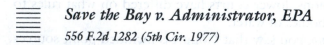

Save the Bay v. Administrator, EPA
556 F.2d 1282 (5th Cir. 1977)

GOLDBERG, CIRCUIT JUDGE.

The 1972 amendments to the Federal Water Pollution Control Act joined the Environmental Protection Agency and the fifty states in a delicate partnership charged with controlling and eventually eliminating water pollution throughout the United States. . . .

The Mississippi Air and Water Pollution Control Commission is a member of this pollution battling alliance. In 1975 the Commission granted to E. I. DuPont de Nemours & Co. a permit to operate a titanium dioxide plant at St. Louis Bay, Mississippi. EPA acquiesced in this action by its partner; petitioner here challenges that acquiescence. Petitioner specifically claims, first, that the Commission so mishandled DuPont's permit application that the EPA should have revoked the Commission's authority to grant such permits. Second, petitioner would have this court review EPA's failure to block the DuPont permit.

EPA strenuously urges that this court is without jurisdiction to consider either of petitioner's contentions. We conclude that this court has both the authority and obligation to review EPA decisions to withdraw or not to withdraw a state's delegated permit authority. Certain preconditions to that review are here missing, however, and preclude our determination of the merits of petitioner's first claim. Second, we conclude that this court lacks jurisdiction to review EPA's failure to veto the permit. To the extent EPA's action in this regard is reviewable, original jurisdiction must lie in the district courts.

I. Legislative and Factual Background

The Federal Water Pollution Control Act Amendments of 1972 (hereinafter "Amendments") substantially overhauled the nation's system of water quality control, declaring "the national goal that the discharge of pollutants into the navigable waters be eliminated by 1985." Toward that end the Amendments introduced a system of "effluent limitations" on "point sources" of pollutants. Formerly federal water pollution control efforts centered on standards of water quality specifying acceptable levels of pollution in interstate navigable waters. Through the shift in the 1972 Amendments to strict limitations applicable to each individual point of discharge, Congress intended to "facilitate enforcement by making it unnecessary to work backward from an overpolluted body of water to determine which point sources are responsible and which must be abated."

To enforce the effluent limitations, the Amendments created the National Pollution Discharge Elimination System (NPDES), a scheme for issuing permits to individual dischargers of pollutants. Without an NPDES permit, one may not lawfully discharge a pollutant. Discharge in compliance with the terms of an NPDES permit, on the other hand, is with few exceptions deemed compliance with the Amendments for enforcement purposes. Thus the terms of individual NPDES permits provide the chief means of implementing the strict national standards mandated by the Amendments.

Congress vested this all-important permit issuing authority in EPA as an original matter. In keeping with congressional desire "to recognize, preserve, and protect the primary responsibilities and rights of States to prevent, reduce, and eliminate pollution," the 1972 legislation also offered states the opportunity to obtain permit issuing authority. Under §402(b), a state may submit to EPA a proposed permit program governing discharges into navigable waters within its borders. The state must demonstrate that it will apply the effluent limitations and the Amendments' other requirements in the permits it grants and that it will monitor and enforce the terms of those permits.[3] Unless the Administrator of EPA determines that the proposed state program does not meet these requirements, he must approve the proposal.

Upon approval of a state program, EPA must suspend its own issuance of permits covering those navigable waters subject to the program. Although its role as issuer of NPDES permits thereupon ceases, the federal agency retains review authority and responsibility over an approved state program. The two aspects of this supervisory role form the subjects of the case at bar.

---

3. The Amendments set out the full list of requirements a state program must meet at §402(b). Under §304(h)(2), EPA sets procedural, monitoring, and enforcement guidelines to which state proposals must conform.

First, EPA may withdraw its approval of a state program upon determining, after notice and an opportunity to respond, that the program is not being administered in compliance with the requirements of §402. *See* §402(c)(3). Second, EPA may veto individual permits issued under approved state programs. Section 402(d)(1) requires a state to send EPA a copy of each permit application it receives and to notify EPA of every action related to the application, including any proposed permit. Section 402(d)(2)(B) provides that no permit shall issue

> if the Administrator within ninety days of the date of transmittal of the proposed permit by the State objects in writing to the issuance of such permit as being outside the guidelines and requirements of this chapter.

The Administrator may waive his right to object to any individual permit application. §402(d)(3). Additionally, at the time he approves a state program the administrator may waive as to any category of point sources the requirement that the state transmit proposed permit applications and related action as well as his veto power over permits within the category. §402(e). The Administrator may also promulgate regulations, applicable to every approved state program, designating categories of point sources within which the transmittal requirements and veto power will not apply. §402(f). . . .

Mississippi submitted a proposed NPDES program for EPA approval in August 1973. The federal agency gave its approval on May 1, 1974, transferring authority to issue NPDES permits for dischargers in Mississippi to the Mississippi Air and Water Pollution Control Commission (hereinafter "Commission").

On August 28, 1974, the Commission sent EPA a copy of DuPont's application for a permit to discharge from a proposed titanium dioxide manufacturing plant to be located on St. Louis Bay. The company proposed one discharge point into the Bay and two into a deep well injection system. EPA did not waive its authority to review the DuPont proposal. Rather the agency undertook consideration of the matter in consultation with the Commission's staff. EPA suggested certain changes in the Commission's proposed permit, including increased monitoring requirements of the deep well discharges and a requirement that DuPont conduct a study to determine the present levels of various elements in the Bay.

On January 17, 1975, the Commission sent EPA a final draft permit, incorporating the requested changes. EPA informed the Commission it would not veto the permit as drafted, but requested further changes. On February 3, 1975, the Commission issued the DuPont permit, which again incorporated all EPA's requests.

Save the Bay, Inc., an incorporated association concerned with environmental protection, filed its petition in this court on March 11, 1975. Petitioner presses two claims. First, it asserts that the Commission so violated federal guidelines in handling the DuPont permit that EPA should have revoked the state's NPDES authority pursuant to §402(c)(3). Second, petitioner claims EPA should have vetoed the permit as "outside the guidelines and other requirements" of the Amendments. EPA vigorously responds that this court lacks jurisdiction over either of petitioner's claims.

[The court concluded it lacked jurisdiction over the claims as presented. It held that EPA had not yet taken a final agency action on the request to withdraw Mississippi's NPDES program, and that EPA decisions on whether to veto individual permits could not be reviewed by the court of appeals under CWA section 509. It did find that the district courts could review EPA's decisions regarding individual permit vetoes under a very limited standards, as explained below:]

The Administrator may veto proposed permits on the grounds that they are "outside the guidelines and requirements" of the Amendments. §402(d)(2). The reference to guidelines and requirements includes at least the effluent limitation regulations promulgated under §301, the more general effluent limitations guidelines issued under §304(b), and the guidelines governing the procedure for issuing NPDES permits, promulgated under §304(h).

While these guidelines and regulations could provide "law to apply" in reviewing a decision not to veto a permit, the legislative history makes very clear that Congress intended EPA to retain discretion to decline to veto a permit even after the agency found some violation of applicable guidelines. That legislative history, more explicit and unequivocal than generally found, leans in almost every expression toward a minimal federal intervention when a state plan has been approved. First, there was a significant shift in the language of the veto provision during the legislative process. The original Senate version provided that, unless the Administrator affirmatively waived his review of a specific permit, it could not issue "until the Administrator is satisfied that the conditions meet the requirements of this Act." The conference compromise, in addition to retaining the waiver provisions, allows the state permit to issue unless the Administrator affirmatively objects, which the statute authorizes, but does not expressly require, upon a finding of departure from the guidelines. While the use of permissive language is of little persuasive effect itself, the shift from the original Senate version does suggest that not every permit out of compliance with the guidelines need be vetoed.

The post-conference floor debates also disclose intent to confer such discretion. The House had originally rejected any permit-by-permit veto power. The floor managers set out to mollify opponents of that power by explaining the nature of the veto prerogative inserted at conference. Representative Jones emphasized that the Administrator was not intended to veto a permit except upon a "clear showing" of noncompliance with the guidelines. Congressman Wright noted that the Administrator "may stop" the issuance of an unlawful permit and further explained:

> I must give added emphasis to this point. The managers expect the Administrator to use this authority judiciously; it is their intent that the Act be administered in such a manner that the abilities of the States to control their permit programs will be developed and strengthened.

The primacy of state and local enforcement of water pollution controls is a theme that resounds throughout the legislative history of the Amendments. In light of the pervasiveness of this theme, the specific references to the veto power above, and the conferral of broad discretion to waive review of individual permits, we conclude that Congress intended to allow the Administrator to consider the significance of any guideline violations in terms of the overall goal of the Amendments, the elimination of all discharge of pollutants into the nation's navigable waters by 1985. Federal refractions are to be very limited, and 20/20 vision by the states is not to be expected or exacted. To conclude otherwise would contravene the spirit of the federal-state partnership created by the Amendments and establish an undue incentive for the EPA to waive review of proposed permits.

Given discretion to weigh the substantiality of any violations of the guidelines and requirements of the Amendments as well as a mandate to determine the presence of such violations, EPA's decision not to veto a particular permit takes on a breadth that in our judgment renders the bottom line of that decision unreviewable in the federal courts. Once the relevant factors are before the agency, it can weigh them within this broad mandate with an expertise to which the restraining powers of judicial review could add little. Given such a mandate, a judge's judgment on the significance in terms of water quality of the provisions of a permit is not likely to be sounder or fairer to the challenger, whether environmentalist or industrialist, than that of the EPA.

Accordingly, we hold that the Administrator's conclusion not to veto an individual permit is itself immune to judicial review. However, this observation does not mean that the Administrator is completely beyond the scrutiny of the federal courts in performing the supervisory role over state permits that Congress, after exhaustive debate on the specific subject, saw fit to establish.

While Congress in considering the Amendments articulated a definite commitment to a hands-off policy toward the states, equally clearly it did not intend the hands of the federal government completely to be tied. In light of the precedent for partial review of administrative action, we must be loathe totally to eradicate judicial review from a legislative framework in which the federal government has not wholly abdicated its role. From that perspective we find that judicial review may appropriately confine EPA's discretion along two very narrow lines. First, nothing in the statute or its history suggest any basis for allowing EPA in reviewing the merits of a permit totally to omit consideration of a particular violation of the guidelines and requirements of the Amendments. When all the relevant factors are before the agency, there is such insufficient likelihood of improving the decision that the presumption for judicial review falls. Judicial review, however, can quite easily be effective to assure that all those factors receive the agency's attention. Accordingly, an aggrieved person must be able to present a claim in district court that a proposed permit contains a violation of applicable federal guidelines that the agency has failed to consider. Upon sufficient showing of a violation, the agency, if it claims to have attended to the factor during its review, will have to explain in a manner that cannot be labeled arbitrary how it concluded the violation did not warrant veto. Failing that, it will have to reconsider its decision in light of the new factor.

The other available avenue of review runs in precisely the opposite direction. There is no suggestion anywhere in the Amendments' history that EPA may base a decision not to veto on factors other than a specific permit's consistency with the guidelines or the insignificance of any departures. There must accordingly be room for claims that unlawful factors have tainted the agency's exercise of its discretion. For example, there is no room for consideration of the political popularity of a decision to veto a permit and, thereby, some local project. Nor could EPA let pass a permit it would otherwise veto on acknowledgment of the fact that the state agency involved had generally drawn up lawful permits. Once EPA explained or removed the alleged illegitimate factor, of course, the final decision not to veto would be within its unreviewable discretion.

With only that minimal intrusion, the partial review outlined will help assure that potentially serious violations of law in proposed permits that threaten individuals or businesses will not go unattended as EPA carries out the supervisory responsibility Congress unequivocally placed within its walls. The limited scope of the reviewable issues and the nonreviewability of EPA's final determination offer sufficient sanctuary from any imagined onslaught of frivolous petitions. The courts may easily supply this limited review. To do less would be to ignore the limited but important federal side of the partnership created by the Amendments; moreover, it would be unnecessarily to denigrate the role of private citizens of all persuasions in the administrative process and to abrogate the strong presumption in favor of judicial review of administrative action.

V. Conclusion

We have been called upon to examine a statutory scheme that has the potential for the optimum of federalism. The legislation contains problems of accommodation that will require additional interstitial interpretation and environmental exploration as the partners pirouette. The success of their federalist venture will depend not only upon the grace, but also the substance of movement by both partners in the ballet. We have endeavored to ink a most self-effacing role for the federal judiciary, one which should foster a harmonious background to the dance and necessitate intervention only when a point of unmelodious discord seriously threatens the contrapuntal balance.

NOTES AND QUESTIONS ON *SAVE THE BAY*

1. *Holding.* Because the court never reached the merits of Save the Bay's claims, it does not tell us how much discretion EPA has in reviewing state permit decisions and broader requests to review state program implementation. How much deference does the court *suggest* EPA should afford state permit decisions? How much deference does the court suggest a reviewing court (the district court) should afford EPA's decisions in reviewing state permits or programs? What message does this send to states about how much scrutiny their programs will receive? Is it justified by the federalism rationale of state program delegation?

2. *Clean Air Act.* Congress used a similar approach to federalism in the Clean Air Act and the Clean Water Act. In the 1990 Amendments to the Clean Air Act, Congress adopted Title V, which embodies a similar permitting program to the NPDES, and a similar relationship between EPA and the states. Under section 502, EPA adopted regulations specifying the minimum requirements for CAA permitting programs. Congress directed the states to submit to EPA programs complying with those rules. After a state misses several opportunities to correct any deficiencies, EPA is required to adopt and implement a program for the deficient state.

When presented with citizen suits challenging the stringency of EPA oversight of Title V programs, courts have taken an approach similar to that adopted in *Save the Bay*, finding EPA's decisions subject to wide discretion and therefore not subject to meaningful judicial review. *See* Ohio Public Interest Research Group, Inc. v. Whitman, 386 F.3d 792 (6th Cir. 2004) (holding that EPA non-enforcement decision under CAA Title V was a matter of agency discretion and thus left no avenue for judicial review); Public Citizen, Inc. v. U.S. E.P.A., 343 F.3d 449 (5th Cir. 2003) (upholding EPA's approval of Texas' Title V program despite ongoing resolution of program deficiencies because EPA's action was entitled to substantial deference and holding that related EPA non-enforcement decisions were immune from judicial review). EPA may also use other statutory "sanctions" against states, as discussed in the last section of this chapter.

With respect to individual permit decisions, however, the Supreme Court upheld an EPA action disapproving a state permit that EPA believed did not properly implement one of the technology-based provisions of the statute ("best available control technology" (BACT) for new or modified sources in attainment areas subject to the "prevention of significant deterioration" (PSD) provisions of the Act). While upholding EPA's action, however, the Court was mindful of the balance to be struck between flexibility to account for variations in local conditions and circumstances, and the need to uphold the basic statutory requirements:

> Understandably, Congress entrusted state permitting authorities with initial responsibility to make BACT determinations "case-by-case." A state agency, no doubt, is best positioned to adjust for local differences in raw materials or plant configurations, differences that might make a technology "unavailable" in a particular area. But the fact that the relevant statutory guides—"maximum" pollution reduction, considerations of energy, environmental, and economic impacts—may not yield a "single, objectively 'correct' BACT determination," surely does not signify that there can be no *unreasonable* determinations. Nor does Congress' sensitivity to site-specific factors necessarily imply a design to preclude in this context meaningful EPA oversight. EPA claims no prerogative to designate the correct BACT; the Agency asserts only the authority to guard against unreasonable designations.

Alaska Dep't of Envtl. Conservation v. EPA, 540 U.S. 461, 488-89 (2004).

3. *RCRA*. In RCRA, Congress adopted a somewhat similar program of cooperative federalism, but with an interesting twist. Congress divided the universe of solid waste into two broad categories: hazardous solid waste and non-hazardous solid waste (although certain specified categories of wastes may fall somewhere in between, *see* 42 U.S.C. §3001(b)(3)). Generally speaking, hazardous wastes are subject to more federal control than non-hazardous wastes. EPA promulgates regulations governing which materials are deemed hazardous, *id.* §3001; and standards applicable to hazardous waste generators, transporters, and "treatment, storage and disposal facilities" (TSDFs), including detailed treatment standards for particular kinds of wastes, *id.* §§3002-3004. EPA also issues permit requirements for TSDFs. *Id.* §6925. However, Congress authorized states to adopt hazardous waste management programs pursuant to EPA guidelines, in which case the state may assume hazardous waste permitting responsibility. *Id.* §6926. Congress also established provisions for state non-hazardous waste plans subject to EPA guidelines, review, and approval, as well as federal funding assistance. 42 U.S.C.

§§6942-6948. Federal requirements for approval of non-hazardous solid waste programs, however, are far less prescriptive than those for hazardous waste. In essence, states must commit to two main substantive requirements: (1) existing open dumps in the state must be closed or upgraded to sanitary landfills meeting federal guidelines, and new open dumps must be prohibited; and (2) solid waste in the state either must be used for resource recovery (reused or recycled) or disposed of in approved sanitary landfills. *Id.* §6943(a).

4. *One-tiered preemption and the motor vehicle exception.* A common theme in the environmental statutes with optional delegated programs is that states may adopt and enforce pollution standards that are stricter, but not weaker, than those specified in the federal statute or regulations. One example is in the hazardous waste title of RCRA, which provides:

> Upon the effective date of regulations under this subchapter no State or political subdivision may impose any requirements less stringent than those authorized under this subchapter respecting the same matter as governed by such regulations. . . . Nothing in this chapter shall be construed to prohibit any State or political subdivision thereof from imposing any requirements, including those for site selection, which are more stringent than those imposed by such regulations.

42 U.S.C. §6929. *See also id.* §7416 (CAA); 33 U.S.C. §1370 (CWA). What is the justification for allowing states the authority to strengthen, but not to weaken, federal environmental requirements?

One notable exception to the one-tiered preemption principle is that, with limited exceptions, section 209 of the CAA prohibits states from adopting emissions requirements for motor vehicles that are stricter *or* weaker than those set by Congress and EPA pursuant to Title II of the CAA. *See* 42 U.S.C. §7543. *See also id.* §§7574(c)(4) (motor vehicle fuels), 7573 (airplane emissions). Why do you think Congress generally preempted state regulation of motor vehicle emissions and fuels (aside from the exceptions discussed below), regardless of how much vehicle emissions may contribute to nonattainment in any given state or region within a state, and despite the fact that states are free to adopt standards stricter than required by federal law for other major sources of pollution that contribute to nonattainment? *See* Motor Vehicle Mfrs. Ass'n of U.S. v. New York State Dep't of Environmental Conservation, 810 F. Supp. 1331 (N.D.N.Y. 1993), *modified on reconsideration*, 831 F. Supp. 57, *affirmed in part, reversed in part on other grounds*, 17 F.3d 521 (2d Cir. 1994).

Congress, however, provided a limited exception for California, which faces particularly difficult vehicle-related emissions problems, to adopt and maintain vehicle emissions standards stricter than those required by federal law. *See* 42 U.S.C. §7543(b); Ford Motor Co. v. Environmental Protection Agency, 606 F.2d 1293 (D.C. Cir. 1979). Moreover, other states may adopt vehicle emissions standards identical to (*i.e.*, no stricter than) those adopted by California, in order to control emissions in nonattainment areas. *See* 42 U.S.C. §7507. Some states have tested the breadth of this set of preemption requirements, for example, by requiring auto manufacturers to produce and offer for sale in the state a particular number of "zero emission vehicles" (ZEVs), or that ZEVs comprise a certain percentage of vehicle sales in a particular state. Do such requirements constitute a

"standard relating to the control of emissions from any new motor vehicle" prohibited by section 209 of the CAA? *See, e.g.*, Ass'n of Int'l Auto. Mfrs., Inc. v.
Commissioner, Mass. Dep't of Environmental Protection, 208 F.3d 1 (1st Cir.
2000) (finding Massachusetts' ZEV sales mandates to be standards, and thus pre-
empted by CAA section 209); American Auto. Mfrs. Ass'n v. Cahill, 152 F.3d 196
(2d Cir. 1998) (holding New York ZEV requirement to be "standard relating to
the control of emissions" that was preempted by CAA section 209).

C. ENFORCING STATE OBLIGATIONS

The above survey identified a number of ways in which Congress — based on
various policy considerations — allocates environmental authority and responsibility among the federal and state governments. As you know from your study of
constitutional law, however, Congress is not simply free to assume any possible
authority for the federal government, or to delegate obligations to states and localities without limit. The Constitution, as interpreted by the courts, identifies those
areas in which Congress may act, and the methods by which it may permissibly
assign responsibilities to the states. As you read the following case, think about
how the principles articulated by the Supreme Court would apply to the various
allocations of environmental authority described above:

New York v. United States
505 U.S. 144 (1992)

JUSTICE O'CONNOR delivered the opinion of the Court.

These cases implicate one of our Nation's newest problems of public policy and
perhaps our oldest question of constitutional law. The public policy issue involves
the disposal of radioactive waste: In these cases, we address the constitutionality of three provisions of the Low-Level Radioactive Waste Policy Amendments
Act of 1985. The constitutional question is as old as the Constitution: It consists
of discerning the proper division of authority between the Federal Government
and the States. We conclude that while Congress has substantial power under the
Constitution to encourage the States to provide for the disposal of the radioactive waste generated within their borders, the Constitution does not confer upon
Congress the ability simply to compel the States to do so. We therefore find that
only two of the Act's three provisions at issue are consistent with the Constitution's
allocation of power to the Federal Government.

I

We live in a world full of low level radioactive waste. Radioactive material is
present in luminous watch dials, smoke alarms, measurement devices, medical fluids, research materials, and the protective gear and construction materials used by
workers at nuclear power plants. Low level radioactive waste is generated by the

Government, by hospitals, by research institutions, and by various industries. The waste must be isolated from humans for long periods of time, often for hundreds of years. Millions of cubic feet of low level radioactive waste must be disposed of each year.

[The Court described the sequential closure of low-level waste disposal sites.]

Faced with the possibility that the Nation would be left with no disposal sites for low level radioactive waste, Congress responded by enacting the Low-Level Radioactive Waste Policy Act. Relying largely on a report submitted by the National Governors' Ass'n, Congress declared a federal policy of holding each State "responsible for providing for the availability of capacity either within or outside the State for the disposal of low-level radioactive waste generated within its borders," and found that such waste could be disposed of "most safely and efficiently . . . on a regional basis." The 1980 Act authorized States to enter into regional compacts that, once ratified by Congress, would have the authority beginning in 1986 to restrict the use of their disposal facilities to waste generated within member States. The 1980 Act included no penalties for States that failed to participate in this plan.

By 1985, only three approved regional compacts had operational disposal facilities; not surprisingly, these were the compacts formed around South Carolina, Nevada, and Washington, the three sited States. The following year, the 1980 Act would have given these three compacts the ability to exclude waste from nonmembers, and the remaining 31 States would have had no assured outlet for their low level radioactive waste. With this prospect looming, Congress once again took up the issue of waste disposal. The result was the legislation challenged here, the Low-Level Radioactive Waste Policy Amendments Act of 1985.

The 1985 Act was again based largely on a proposal submitted by the National Governors' Ass'n. In broad outline, the Act embodies a compromise among the sited and unsited States. The sited States agreed to extend for seven years the period in which they would accept low level radioactive waste from other States. In exchange, the unsited States agreed to end their reliance on the sited States by 1992.

The mechanics of this compromise are intricate. The Act directs: "Each State shall be responsible for providing, either by itself or in cooperation with other States, for the disposal of . . . low-level radioactive waste generated within the State," with the exception of certain waste generated by the Federal Government. The Act authorizes States to "enter into such [interstate] compacts as may be necessary to provide for the establishment and operation of regional disposal facilities for low-level radioactive waste." For an additional seven years beyond the period contemplated by the 1980 Act, from the beginning of 1986 through the end of 1992, the three existing disposal sites "shall make disposal capacity available for low-level radioactive waste generated by any source," with certain exceptions not relevant here. But the three States in which the disposal sites are located are permitted to exact a graduated surcharge for waste arriving from outside the regional compact in 1986–1987, $10 per cubic foot; in 1988–1989, $20 per cubic foot; and in 1990–1992, $40 per cubic foot. After the 7-year transition period expires, approved regional compacts may exclude radioactive waste generated outside the region. The Act provides three types of incentives to encourage the States to comply with their statutory obligation to provide for the disposal of waste generated within their borders.

1. *Monetary incentives.* One quarter of the surcharges collected by the sited States must be transferred to an escrow account held by the Secretary of Energy. The Secretary then makes payments from this account to each State that has complied with a series of deadlines. By July 1, 1986, each State was to have ratified legislation either joining a regional compact or indicating an intent to develop a disposal facility within the State. By January 1, 1988, each unsited compact was to have identified the State in which its facility would be located, and each compact or stand-alone State was to have developed a siting plan and taken other identified steps. By January 1, 1990, each State or compact was to have filed a complete application for a license to operate a disposal facility, or the Governor of any State that had not filed an application was to have certified that the State would be capable of disposing of all waste generated in the State after 1992. The rest of the account is to be paid out to those States or compacts able to dispose of all low level radioactive waste generated within their borders by January 1, 1993. Each State that has not met the 1993 deadline must either take title to the waste generated within its borders or forfeit to the waste generators the incentive payments it has received.

2. *Access incentives.* The second type of incentive involves the denial of access to disposal sites. States that fail to meet the July 1986 deadline may be charged twice the ordinary surcharge for the remainder of 1986 and may be denied access to disposal facilities thereafter. States that fail to meet the 1988 deadline may be charged double surcharges for the first half of 1988 and quadruple surcharges for the second half of 1988, and may be denied access thereafter. States that fail to meet the 1990 deadline may be denied access. Finally, States that have not filed complete applications by January 1, 1992, for a license to operate a disposal facility, or States belonging to compacts that have not filed such applications, may be charged triple surcharges.

3. *The take-title provision.* The third type of incentive is the most severe. The Act provides: "If a State (or, where applicable, a compact region) in which low-level radioactive waste is generated is unable to provide for the disposal of all such waste generated within such State or compact region by January 1, 1996, each State in which such waste is generated, upon the request of the generator or owner of the waste, shall take title to the waste, be obligated to take possession of the waste, and shall be liable for all damages directly or indirectly incurred by such generator or owner as a consequence of the failure of the State to take possession of the waste as soon after January 1, 1996, as the generator or owner notifies the State that the waste is available for shipment."

These three incentives are the focus of petitioners' constitutional challenge.

In the seven years since the Act took effect, Congress has approved nine regional compacts, encompassing 42 of the States. All six unsited compacts and four of the unaffiliated States have met the first three statutory milestones. New York, a State whose residents generate a relatively large share of the Nation's low level radioactive waste, did not join a regional compact. Instead, the State complied with the Act's requirements by enacting legislation providing for the siting and financing of a disposal facility in New York. The State has identified five potential sites, three in Allegany County and two in Cortland County. Residents of the two counties oppose the State's choice of location.

Petitioners—the State of New York and the two counties—filed this suit against the United States in 1990. They sought a declaratory judgment that the Act is inconsistent with the Tenth and Eleventh Amendments to the Constitution, with the Due Process Clause of the Fifth Amendment, and with the Guarantee Clause of Article IV of the Constitution. The States of Washington, Nevada, and South Carolina intervened as defendants. The District Court dismissed the complaint. The Court of Appeals affirmed. Petitioners have abandoned their due process and Eleventh Amendment claims on their way up the appellate ladder; as the cases stand before us, petitioners claim only that the Act is inconsistent with the Tenth Amendment and the Guarantee Clause.

II

A

While no one disputes the proposition that "[t]he Constitution created a Federal Government of limited powers;" and while the Tenth Amendment makes explicit that "[t]he powers not delegated to the United States by the Constitution, nor prohibited by it to the States, are reserved to the States respectively, or to the people"; the task of ascertaining the constitutional line between federal and state power has given rise to many of the Court's most difficult and celebrated cases.

These questions can be viewed in either of two ways. In some cases the Court has inquired whether an Act of Congress is authorized by one of the powers delegated to Congress in Article I of the Constitution. In other cases the Court has sought to determine whether an Act of Congress invades the province of state sovereignty reserved by the Tenth Amendment. In a case like these, involving the division of authority between federal and state governments, the two inquiries are mirror images of each other. If a power is delegated to Congress in the Constitution, the Tenth Amendment expressly disclaims any reservation of that power to the States; if a power is an attribute of state sovereignty reserved by the Tenth Amendment, it is necessarily a power the Constitution has not conferred on Congress.

It is in this sense that the Tenth Amendment "states but a truism that all is retained which has not been surrendered." This has been the Court's consistent understanding: "The States unquestionably do retai[n] a significant measure of sovereign authority to the extent that the Constitution has not divested them of their original powers and transferred those powers to the Federal Government."

Congress exercises its conferred powers subject to the limitations contained in the Constitution. Thus, for example, under the Commerce Clause Congress may regulate publishers engaged in interstate commerce, but Congress is constrained in the exercise of that power by the First Amendment. The Tenth Amendment likewise restrains the power of Congress, but this limit is not derived from the text of the Tenth Amendment itself, which, as we have discussed, is essentially a tautology. Instead, the Tenth Amendment confirms that the power of the Federal Government is subject to limits that may, in a given instance, reserve power to the States. The Tenth Amendment thus directs us to determine, as in this case, whether an incident of state sovereignty is protected by a limitation on an Article I power.

This framework has been sufficiently flexible over the past two centuries to allow for enormous changes in the nature of government. The Federal Government undertakes activities today that would have been unimaginable to the Framers in two senses; first, because the Framers would not have conceived that *any* government would conduct such activities; and second, because the Framers would not have believed that the *Federal* Government, rather than the States, would assume such responsibilities. Yet the powers conferred upon the Federal Government by the Constitution were phrased in language broad enough to allow for the expansion of the Federal Government's role. Among the provisions of the Constitution that have been particularly important in this regard, three concern us here.

First, the Constitution allocates to Congress the power "[t]o regulate Commerce among the several States." Art. I, §8, cl. 3. Interstate commerce was an established feature of life in the late 18th century. The volume of interstate commerce and the range of commonly accepted objects of government regulation have, however, expanded considerably in the last 200 years, and the regulatory authority of Congress has expanded along with them. As interstate commerce has become ubiquitous, activities once considered purely local have come to have effects on the national economy, and have accordingly come within the scope of Congress' commerce power.

Second, the Constitution authorizes Congress "to pay the Debts and provide for the general Welfare of the United States." Art. I, §8, cl. 1. As conventional notions of the proper objects of government spending have changed over the years, so has the ability of Congress to "fix the terms on which it shall disburse federal money to the States." While the spending power is "subject to several general restrictions articulated in our cases," these restrictions have not been so severe as to prevent the regulatory authority of Congress from generally keeping up with the growth of the federal budget.

The Court's broad construction of Congress' power under the Commerce and Spending Clauses has of course been guided, as it has with respect to Congress' power generally, by the Constitution's Necessary and Proper Clause, which authorizes Congress "[t]o make all Laws which shall be necessary and proper for carrying into Execution the foregoing Powers."

Finally, the Constitution provides that "the Laws of the United States shall be the supreme Law of the Land any Thing in the Constitution or Laws of any State to the Contrary notwithstanding." U.S. Const., Art. VI, cl. 2. As the Federal Government's willingness to exercise power within the confines of the Constitution has grown, the authority of the States has correspondingly diminished to the extent that federal and state policies have conflicted. We have observed that the Supremacy Clause gives the Federal Government "a decided advantage in th[e] delicate balance" the Constitution strikes between state and federal power.

The actual scope of the Federal Government's authority with respect to the States has changed over the years, therefore, but the constitutional structure underlying and limiting that authority has not. In the end, just as a cup may be half empty or half full, it makes no difference whether one views the question at issue in these cases as one of ascertaining the limits of the power delegated to the Federal Government under the affirmative provisions of the Constitution or one of discerning the core of sovereignty retained by the States under the Tenth Amendment. Either way, we must determine whether any of the three challenged provisions oversteps the boundary between federal and state authority.

B

Petitioners do not contend that Congress lacks the power to regulate the disposal of low level radioactive waste. Space in radioactive waste disposal sites is frequently sold by residents of one State to residents of another. Regulation of the resulting interstate market in waste disposal is therefore well within Congress' authority under the Commerce Clause. Petitioners likewise do not dispute that under the Supremacy Clause Congress could, if it wished, pre-empt state radioactive waste regulation. Petitioners contend only that the Tenth Amendment limits the power of Congress to regulate in the way it has chosen. Rather than addressing the problem of waste disposal by directly regulating the generators and disposers of waste, petitioners argue, Congress has impermissibly directed the States to regulate in this field.

Most of our recent cases interpreting the Tenth Amendment have concerned the authority of Congress to subject state governments to generally applicable laws.

This litigation instead concerns the circumstances under which Congress may use the States as implements of regulation; that is, whether Congress may direct or otherwise motivate the States to regulate in a particular field or a particular way. Our cases have established a few principles that guide our resolution of the issue.

1

As an initial matter, Congress may not simply "commandee[r] the legislative processes of the States by directly compelling them to enact and enforce a federal regulatory program." Hodel v. Virginia Surface Mining & Reclamation Assn., Inc. In *Hodel*, the Court upheld the Surface Mining Control and Reclamation Act of 1977 precisely because it did *not* "commandeer" the States into regulating mining. The Court found that "the States are not compelled to enforce the steep-slope standards, to expend any state funds, or to participate in the federal regulatory program in any manner whatsoever. If a State does not wish to submit a proposed permanent program that complies with the Act and implementing regulations, the full regulatory burden will be borne by the Federal Government."

The Court reached the same conclusion the following year in *FERC v. Mississippi*. At issue in *FERC* was the Public Utility Regulatory Policies Act of 1978, a federal statute encouraging the States in various ways to develop programs to combat the Nation's energy crisis. We observed that "this Court never has sanctioned explicitly a federal command to the States to promulgate and enforce laws and regulations." As in *Hodel,* the Court upheld the statute at issue because it did not view the statute as such a command.

These statements in *FERC* and *Hodel* were not innovations. While Congress has substantial powers to govern the Nation directly, including in areas of intimate concern to the States, the Constitution has never been understood to confer upon Congress the ability to require the States to govern according to Congress' instructions.

In providing for a stronger central government, therefore, the Framers explicitly chose a Constitution that confers upon Congress the power to regulate individuals, not States. As we have seen, the Court has consistently respected this choice. We have always understood that even where Congress has the authority under the Constitution to pass laws requiring or prohibiting certain acts, it lacks the power directly to compel the States to require or prohibit those acts. The allocation of power contained in the Commerce Clause, for example, authorizes Congress to regulate interstate commerce directly; it does not authorize Congress to regulate state governments' regulation of interstate commerce.

2

This is not to say that Congress lacks the ability to encourage a State to regulate in a particular way, or that Congress may not hold out incentives to the States as a method of influencing a State's policy choices. Our cases have identified a variety of methods, short of outright coercion, by which Congress may urge a State to adopt a legislative program consistent with federal interests. Two of these methods are of particular relevance here.

First, under Congress' spending power, "Congress may attach conditions on the receipt of federal funds." Such conditions must (among other requirements) bear some relationship to the purpose of the federal spending; otherwise, of course, the spending power could render academic the Constitution's other grants and limits of federal authority. Where the recipient of federal funds is a State, as is not unusual today, the conditions attached to the funds by Congress may influence a State's legislative choices. . . .

Second, where Congress has the authority to regulate private activity under the Commerce Clause, we have recognized Congress' power to offer States the choice of regulating that activity according to federal standards or having state law pre-empted by federal regulation. This arrangement, which has been termed "a program of cooperative federalism," is replicated in numerous federal statutory schemes. These include the Clean Water Act, the Occupational Safety and Health Act of 1970, the Resource Conservation and Recovery Act of 1976, and the Alaska National Interest Lands Conservation Act.

By either of these methods, as by any other permissible method of encouraging a State to conform to federal policy choices, the residents of the State retain the ultimate decision as to whether or not the State will comply. If a State's citizens view federal policy as sufficiently contrary to local interests, they may elect to decline a federal grant. If state residents would prefer their government to devote its attention and resources to problems other than those deemed important by Congress, they may choose to have the Federal Government rather than the State bear the expense of a federally mandated regulatory program, and they may continue to supplement that program to the extent state law is not pre-empted. Where Congress encourages state regulation rather than compelling it, state governments remain responsive to the local electorate's preferences; state officials remain accountable to the people.

By contrast, where the Federal Government compels States to regulate, the accountability of both state and federal officials is diminished. If the citizens of New York, for example, do not consider that making provision for the disposal of radioactive waste is in their best interest, they may elect state officials who share their view. That view can always be pre-empted under the Supremacy Clause if it is contrary to the national view, but in such a case it is the Federal Government that makes the decision in full view of the public, and it will be federal officials that suffer the consequences if the decision turns out to be detrimental or unpopular. But where the Federal Government directs the States to regulate, it may be state officials who will bear the brunt of public disapproval, while the federal officials who devised the regulatory program may remain insulated from the electoral ramifications of their decision. Accountability is thus diminished when, due to federal coercion, elected state officials cannot regulate in accordance with the views of the local electorate in matters not pre-empted by federal regulation. . . .

III

The parties in these cases advance two quite different views of the Act. As petitioners see it, the Act imposes a requirement directly upon the States that they regulate in the field of radioactive waste disposal in order to meet Congress' mandate that "[e]ach State shall be responsible for providing for the disposal of low-level radioactive waste." Petitioners understand this provision as a direct command from Congress, enforceable independent of the three sets of incentives provided by the Act. Respondents, on the other hand, read this provision together with the incentives, and see the Act as affording the States three sets of choices. According to respondents, the Act permits a State to choose first between regulating pursuant to federal standards and losing the right to a share of the Secretary of Energy's escrow account; to choose second between regulating pursuant to federal standards and progressively losing access to disposal sites in other States; and to choose third between regulating pursuant to federal standards and taking title to the waste generated within the State.

The Act could plausibly be understood either as a mandate to regulate or as a series of incentives. Under petitioners' view, however the Act would clearly "commandee[r] the legislative processes of the States by directly compelling them to enact and enforce a federal regulatory program." We must reject this interpretation of the provision for two reasons. First, such an outcome would, to say the least, "upset the usual constitutional balance of federal and state powers." "[I]t is incumbent upon the federal courts to be certain of Congress' intent before finding that federal law overrides this balance," but the Act's amenability to an equally plausible alternative construction prevents us from possessing such certainty. Second, "where an otherwise acceptable construction of a statute would raise serious constitutional problems, the Court will construe the statute to avoid such problems unless such construction is plainly contrary to the intent of Congress. This rule of statutory construction pushes us away from petitioners' understanding of the Act, under which it compels the States to regulate according to Congress' instructions.

Construed as a whole, the Act comprises three sets of "incentives" for the States to provide for the disposal of low level radioactive waste generated within their borders. We consider each in turn.

A

The first set of incentives works in three steps. First, Congress has authorized States with disposal sites to impose a surcharge on radioactive waste received from other States. Second, the Secretary of Energy collects a portion of this surcharge and places the money in an escrow account. Third, States achieving a series of milestones receive portions of this fund.

The first of these steps is an unexceptionable exercise of Congress' power to authorize the States to burden interstate commerce. While the Commerce Clause has long been understood to limit the States' ability to discriminate against interstate commerce, that limit may be lifted, as it has been here, by an expression of the "unambiguous intent" of Congress. Whether or not the States would be permitted to burden the interstate transport of low level radioactive waste in the absence of Congress' approval, the States can clearly do so *with* Congress' approval, which is what the Act gives them.

The second step, the Secretary's collection of a percentage of the surcharge, is no more than a federal tax on interstate commerce, which petitioners do not claim to be an invalid exercise of either Congress' commerce or taxing power. The third step is a conditional exercise of Congress' authority under the Spending Clause: Congress has placed conditions—the achievement of the milestones—on the receipt of federal funds. Petitioners do not contend that Congress has exceeded its authority in any of the four respects our cases have identified. The expenditure is for the general welfare; the States are required to use the money they receive for the purpose of assuring the safe disposal of radioactive waste. The conditions imposed are unambiguous; the Act informs the States exactly what they must do and by when they must do it in order to obtain a share of the escrow account. The conditions imposed are reasonably related to the purpose of the expenditure; both the conditions and the payments embody Congress' efforts to address the pressing problem of radioactive waste disposal. Finally, petitioners do not claim that the conditions imposed by the Act violate any independent constitutional prohibition.

Petitioners contend nevertheless that the *form* of these expenditures removes them from the scope of Congress' spending power. Petitioners emphasize the Act's instruction to the Secretary of Energy to "deposit all funds received in a special escrow account. The funds so deposited shall not be the property of the United States." Petitioners argue that because the money collected and redisbursed to the States is kept in an account separate from the general treasury, because the Secretary holds the funds only as a trustee, and because the States themselves are largely able to control whether they will pay into the escrow account or receive a share, the Act "in no manner calls for the spending of federal funds."

The Constitution's grant to Congress of the authority to "pay the Debts and provide for the general Welfare" has never, however, been thought to mandate a particular form of accounting. That the States are able to choose whether they will receive federal funds does not make the resulting expenditures any less federal; indeed, the location of such choice in the States is an inherent element in any conditional exercise of Congress' spending power.

The Act's first set of incentives, in which Congress has conditioned grants to the States upon the States' attainment of a series of milestones, is thus well within the authority of Congress under the Commerce and Spending Clauses. Because the first set of incentives is supported by affirmative constitutional grants of power to Congress, it is not inconsistent with the Tenth Amendment.

B

In the second set of incentives, Congress has authorized States and regional compacts with disposal sites gradually to increase the cost of access to the sites, and then to deny access altogether, to radioactive waste generated in States that do not meet federal deadlines. As a simple regulation, this provision would be within the power of Congress to authorize the States to discriminate against interstate commerce. Where federal regulation of private activity is within the scope of the Commerce Clause, we have recognized the ability of Congress to offer States the choice of regulating that activity according to federal standards or having state law pre-empted by federal regulation.

This is the choice presented to nonsited States by the Act's second set of incentives: States may either regulate the disposal of radioactive waste according to federal standards by attaining local or regional self-sufficiency, or their residents who produce radioactive waste will be subject to federal regulation authorizing sited States and regions to deny access to their disposal sites. The affected States are not compelled by Congress to regulate, because any burden caused by a State's refusal to regulate will fall on those who generate waste and find no outlet for its disposal, rather than on the State as a sovereign. A State whose citizens do not wish it to attain the Act's milestones may devote its attention and its resources to issues its citizens deem more worthy; the choice remains at all times with the residents of the State, not with Congress. The State need not expend any funds, or participate in any federal program, if local residents do not view such expenditures or participation as worthwhile. Nor must the State abandon the field if it does not accede to federal direction; the State may continue to regulate the generation and disposal of radioactive waste in any manner its citizens see fit.

The Act's second set of incentives thus represents a conditional exercise of Congress' commerce power, along the lines of those we have held to be within Congress' authority. As a result, the second set of incentives does not intrude on the sovereignty reserved to the States by the Tenth Amendment.

C

The take title provision is of a different character. This third so-called "incentive" offers States, as an alternative to regulating pursuant to Congress' direction, the option of taking title to and possession of the low level radioactive waste generated within their borders and becoming liable for all damages waste generators suffer as a result of the States' failure to do so promptly. In this provision, Congress has crossed the line distinguishing encouragement from coercion.

The take title provision offers state governments a "choice" of either accepting ownership of waste or regulating according to the instructions of Congress. Respondents do not claim that the Constitution would authorize Congress to impose either option as a freestanding requirement. On one hand, the Constitution would not permit Congress simply to transfer radioactive waste from generators to state governments. Such a forced transfer, standing alone, would in principle be no different than a congressionally compelled subsidy from state governments to radioactive waste producers. The same is true of the provision requiring the States to become liable for the generators' damages. Standing alone, this provision would be indistinguishable from an Act of Congress directing the States to assume the liabilities of certain state residents. Either type of federal action would "commandeer" state governments into the service of federal regulatory purposes, and would for this reason be inconsistent with the Constitution's division of authority between federal and state governments. On the other hand, the second alternative held out to state governments—regulating pursuant to Congress' direction—would, standing alone, present a simple command to state governments to implement legislation enacted by Congress. As we have seen, the Constitution does not empower Congress to subject state governments to this type of instruction.

Because an instruction to state governments to take title to waste, standing alone, would be beyond the authority of Congress, and because a direct order to regulate, standing alone, would also be beyond the authority of Congress, it follows that Congress lacks the power to offer the States a choice between the two. Unlike the first two sets of incentives, the take title incentive does not represent the conditional exercise of any congressional power enumerated in the Constitution. In this provision, Congress has not held out the threat of exercising its spending power or its commerce power; it has instead held out the threat, should the States not regulate according to one federal instruction, of simply forcing the States to submit to another federal instruction. A choice between two unconstitutionally coercive regulatory techniques is no choice at all. Either way, "the Act commandeers the legislative processes of the States by directly compelling them to enact and enforce a federal regulatory program," an outcome that has never been understood to lie within the authority conferred upon Congress by the Constitution.

Respondents emphasize the latitude given to the States to implement Congress' plan. The Act enables the States to regulate pursuant to Congress' instructions in any number of different ways. States may avoid taking title by contracting with sited regional compacts, by building a disposal site alone or as part of a compact, or by permitting private parties to build a disposal site. States that host sites may employ a wide range of designs and disposal methods, subject only to broad federal regulatory limits. This line of reasoning, however, only underscores the critical alternative a State lacks: A State may not decline to administer the federal program. No matter which path the State chooses, it must follow the direction of Congress.

The take title provision appears to be unique. No other federal statute has been cited which offers a state government no option other than that of implementing legislation enacted by Congress. Whether one views the take title provision as lying outside Congress' enumerated powers, or as infringing upon the core of state sovereignty reserved by the Tenth Amendment, the provision is inconsistent with the federal structure of our Government established by the Constitution.

NOTES AND QUESTIONS ON *NEW YORK*

1. *Holding.* How would you characterize the dividing line the Court established between permissible congressional incentives to states and impermissible coercion? What is fundamentally different about the "take title" provisions of the Low Level Radioactive Waste Act and the provisions upheld by the Court?

2. *Direct preemption.* Why did the state plaintiffs in *New York* concede that the federal government has the power to regulate low level radioactive waste directly? As we noted at the beginning of this chapter, to date, most federal environmental statutes have survived challenges based on Commerce Clause and other constitutional limits. In *SWANCC*, however, the majority indicated that the Clean Water Act, as applied to the facts of that case, at least approaches the limits of the Commerce Clause, but declined to rule on those grounds in favor of a more limiting interpretation of the statute.

3. *Conditional preemption.* Congress uses conditional preemption when it regulates a field directly but provides an option for states to assume program responsibility. In essence, Congress gives each state the choice of regulating a particular activity itself, or allowing the federal government to regulate the state's economic or other resources directly, something states often fear. How much less coercive do you think that is than the "take title" provisions the Court found unconstitutional in *New York*? What factors would you expect states to consider in deciding whether to assume program responsibility?

4. *Spending power.* The Court explains that Congress can use federal tax dollars as an incentive to state action, so long as the spending promotes the general welfare and any strings attached are reasonably related to the purpose of the spending. Congress provides significant amounts of funding to states and localities to implement environmental programs.

5. *Sanctions.* Congress armed EPA with a set of particularly onerous *potential* sanctions to redress state violations of the SIP obligations of the CAA, including the ability to prevent the Secretary of Transportation from awarding grants for state highway projects. 42 U.S.C. §7509(b). *See* William J. Klein, *Pressure or Compulsion? Federal Highway Fund Sanctions of the Clean Air Act Amendments of 1990*, 26 RUTGERS L.J. 855 (1995). Is this a legitimate use of Congress' spending power authority? *See* Commonwealth of Virginia v. Browner, 80 F.3d 869 (4th Cir. 1996) (upholding highway sanctions and offset sanctions under the CAA as legitimate exercise of congressional spending power). For political reasons, EPA has been quite reluctant to exercise its sanction authority.

In its first Affordable Care Act (ACA) decision, the Supreme Court held that withholding all existing Medicaid funding from states that failed to expand Medicaid under the new Act constituted unconstitutional "coercion" of states under the Spending Clause. *See* National Fed'n of Indep. Bus. v. Sebelius, 132 S. Ct. 2566, 2603-05 (2012). The Court relied on the fact that the threatened withdrawal of existing Medicaid funding threatened the "loss of over 10 percent of a State's overall budget." *Id.* at 2005. At the same time, the Court indicated that withholding new federal financing of Medicaid Expansion from states that failed to fully implement the ACA's Medicaid Expansion program would pass constitutional muster. *Id.* at 2606. Does this change your answer to the question about the validity of withholding funding for state highway projects from states that fail to complete SIPs?

6. *Federal regulation of states and localities.* State and local governments often are regulated directly under various environmental statutes. Local sewage treatment plants that discharge to waters of the United States, for example, must obtain NPDES permits and comply with applicable treatment and discharge standards. Municipal solid waste incinerators must comply with regulations under both the Clean Air Act and RCRA. Governments can be liable for hazardous substance releases under CERCLA. Why can Congress "mandate" that states and localities act under those provisions, but not under the kinds of provisions that the Court invalidated in *New York*?

7. *Unfunded federal mandates.* Does it matter how much money it costs cities to comply with federal mandates, or whether the federal government provides any financial assistance? The Supreme Court has rejected constitutional challenges to such "unfunded federal mandates" so long as the underlying statute is otherwise lawful. *See* Printz v. United States, 521 U.S. 898 (1997) (invalidating aspects of federal handgun control because they "commandeered" the local regulatory apparatus, but not because they were unfunded federal mandates). However, Congress provided some relief to states and localities in the Unfunded Mandates Reform Act. While the Act does not prohibit unfunded mandates, it requires analysis of the impacts of new mandates imposed by Congress or federal agencies. For a critique of the statute and the unfunded mandates issue generally, see Robert W. Adler, *Unfunded Mandates and Fiscal Federalism: A Critique*, 50 VAND. L. REV. 1137 (1997).

FEDERALISM AND CLIMATE DISRUPTION

1. Could Congress pass a law requiring each state to allow, condition, or prohibit the sale of consumer appliances based upon the state's own assessment of the degree to which such appliances are energy efficient?

2. Is there any question that Congress could regulate the emission of greenhouse gases directly? From electric generating facilities? From cars? From agricultural practices?

3. Could Congress direct EPA to regulate greenhouse gas emissions, but provide each state with a choice to do so itself? How?

4. Could Congress provide direct, unconditional grants to states to address the health and environmental effects of climate disruption? Could it condition those grants on state regulation of some aspect of greenhouse

> gas emissions? Could it condition those grants on a requirement that the state "take title" to carbon sequestered from electric generating plants within their borders?
>
> 5. Municipalities generate greenhouse gas emissions through a myriad of facilities they operate, from bus lines to sewage treatment plants. Can Congress hold the city liable for violation of applicable federal regulatory standards with respect to such emissions?

D. RECAPITULATION: THE RESIDUAL ROLE OF THE COMMON LAW IN A STATUTORY WORLD

While Congress and state legislatures augmented the common law with comprehensive statutory schemes, in most cases they did not replace common law solutions. Rather, common law remedies remain to fulfill their original purposes, and to fill in gaps in the modern regulatory regime. Modern statutes may regulate activities prospectively, require cleanup of environmental hazards caused by past activities, and provide for restoration of public resources, but they do not provide for compensation to injured private parties. The Superfund statute, for example, allows public trustees to collect natural resource damages from past releases of hazardous substances, but does not allow pollution victims to obtain compensation. *See* 42 U.S.C. §9607(a). Pollution victims may, however, bring private damage actions, as in the Woburn, Massachusetts toxic tort case studied in Chapter 2.

Whether a particular statute allows preexisting common law claims to continue is governed by the law of preemption. Under the Supremacy Clause in Article VI of the U.S. Constitution, the preemption doctrine governs whether a provision of federal law supersedes or overrides state or local law. Because the result depends on the specific language and legislative history of each statute, however, be careful not to assume that the results of the following cases will be the same under other statutes. In Chapter 12, for example, you learned that in Superfund, Congress deliberately embraced existing principles of common law liability within the statutory system in a way that leaves particular applications subject to the common law of individual states. The U.S. Supreme Court ruled that the Federal Insecticide, Fungicide, and Rodenticide Act (FIFRA) does not preempt common law and state statutory claims by farmers against herbicide manufacturers. Bates v. Dow Agrosciences LLC, 544 U.S. 431 (2005). *See generally* Robert L. Glicksman, *Federal Preemption and Private Legal Remedies for Pollution*, 134 U. PA. L. REV. 121 (1985) (surveying cases and evaluating the legal and policy arguments for and against preserving common law remedies).

In this section, we use the Clean Water Act (CWA) as an example of the relationship between the new statutory regime and the common law. The CWA is a good case study of the statutory-common law intersection because the Supreme Court has decided several major cases that define this relationship. In the first case in this saga, the Court, in a decision by Justice Douglas, rejected the City of

Milwaukee's argument that the then-existing Federal Water Pollution Control Act preempted Illinois' action for the abatement of Milwaukee's sewage discharges into Lake Michigan under the federal common law of nuisance, relying in part on statutory language that stated that federal enforcement action "shall not" displace state actions "to abate pollution." Illinois v. Milwaukee, 406 U.S. 91 (1972) (*Milwaukee I*). This first decision, however, was decided under an early version of the Federal Water Pollution Control Act (commonly referred to as the Clean Water Act) that left most enforcement authority in the hands of the states. Following Congress' comprehensive amendment to the Act in 1972, Milwaukee renewed its attempt to dismiss Illinois' common law suit, with the result set forth in the case below, often referred to as the *Milwaukee II* decision.

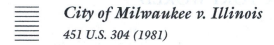

City of Milwaukee v. Illinois
451 U.S. 304 (1981)

Justice Rehnquist delivered the opinion of the Court.

When this litigation was first before us we recognized the existence of a federal "common law" which could give rise to a claim for abatement of a nuisance caused by interstate water pollution. Subsequent to our decision, Congress enacted the Federal Water Pollution Control Act Amendments of 1972. We granted certiorari to consider the effect of this legislation on the previously recognized cause of action. . . .

I

[The Court reiterated, in somewhat more detail, the sewage pollution problems for which the plaintiffs sought redress, along with the Supreme Court's prior decision and the relief granted by the district court.]

Five months [after the new complaint was filed in district court] Congress, recognizing that "the Federal water pollution control program . . . has been inadequate in every vital aspect," passed the Federal Water Pollution Control Act Amendments of 1972. The Amendments established a new system of regulation under which it is illegal for anyone to discharge pollutants into the Nation's waters except pursuant to a permit. To the extent that the Environmental Protection Agency, charged with administering the Act, has promulgated regulations establishing specific effluent limitations, those limitations are incorporated as conditions of the permit. Permits are issued either by the EPA or a qualifying state agency. Petitioners operated their sewer systems and discharged effluent under permits issued by the Wisconsin Department of Natural Resources (DNR). . . . Petitioners did not fully comply with the requirements of the permits and, as contemplated by the Act, the state agency brought an enforcement action in state court. On May 25, 1977, the state court entered a judgment requiring discharges from the treatment plants to meet the effluent limitations set forth in the permits and establishing a detailed timetable for the completion of planning and additional construction to control sewage overflows.

Trial on Illinois' claim commenced on January 11, 1977. On July 29 the District Court rendered a decision finding that respondents had proved the existence of a nuisance under federal common law, both in the discharge of inadequately treated sewage from petitioners' plants and in the discharge of untreated sewage from sewer overflows. The court ordered petitioners to eliminate all overflows and to achieve specified effluent limitations on treated sewage. A judgment order entered on November 15 specified a construction timetable for the completion of detention facilities to eliminate overflows. Separated sewer overflows are to be completely eliminated by 1986; combined sewer overflows by 1989. The detention facilities to be constructed must be large enough to permit full treatment of water from any storm up to the largest storm on record for the Milwaukee area. Both the aspects of the decision concerning overflows and concerning effluent limitations . . . went considerably beyond the terms of petitioners' previously issued permits and the enforcement order of the state court.

On appeal, the Court of Appeals for the Seventh Circuit affirmed in part and reversed in part. The court ruled that the 1972 Amendments had not pre-empted the federal common law of nuisance, but that "[i]n applying the federal common law of nuisance in a water pollution case, a court should not ignore the Act but should look to its policies and principles for guidance." The court reversed the District Court insofar as the effluent limitations it imposed on treated sewage were more stringent than those in the permits and applicable EPA regulations. The order to eliminate all overflows, however, and the construction schedule designed to achieve this goal, were upheld.

II

Federal courts, unlike state courts, are not general common-law courts and do not possess a general power to develop and apply their own rules of decision. *Erie R. Co. v. Tompkins.* . . . The enactment of a federal rule in an area of national concern, and the decision whether to displace state law in doing so, is generally made not by the federal judiciary, purposefully insulated from democratic pressures, but by the people through their elected representatives in Congress. *Erie* recognized as much in ruling that a federal court could not generally apply a federal rule of decision, despite the existence of jurisdiction, in the absence of an applicable Act of Congress. When Congress has not spoken to a particular issue, however, and when there exists a "significant conflict between some federal policy or interest and the use of state law," the Court has found it necessary, in a "few and restricted" instances, to develop federal common law. Nothing in this process suggests that courts are better suited to develop national policy in areas governed by federal common law than they are in other areas, or that the usual and important concerns of an appropriate division of functions between the Congress and the federal judiciary are inapplicable. We have always recognized that federal common law is "subject to the paramount authority of Congress." It is resorted to "[i]n absence of an applicable Act of Congress." . . . Federal common law is a "necessary expedient," and when Congress addresses a question previously governed by a decision rested on federal common law the need for such an unusual exercise of lawmaking by federal courts disappears. . . .

III

We conclude that, at least so far as concerns the claims of respondents, Congress has not left the formulation of appropriate federal standards to the courts through application of often vague and indeterminate nuisance concepts and maxims of equity jurisprudence, but rather has occupied the field through the establishment of a comprehensive regulatory program supervised by an expert administrative agency. The 1972 Amendments to the Federal Water Pollution Control Act were not merely another law "touching interstate waters." . . . Rather, the Amendments were viewed by Congress as a "total restructuring" and "complete rewriting" of the existing water pollution legislation considered in that case. Congress' intent in enacting the Amendments was clearly to establish an all-encompassing program of water pollution regulation. Every point source discharge is prohibited unless covered by a permit, which directly subjects the discharger to the administrative apparatus established by Congress to achieve its goals. The "major purpose" of the Amendments was "to establish a comprehensive long-range policy for the elimination of water pollution." No Congressman's remarks on the legislation were complete without reference to the "comprehensive" nature of the Amendments. . . . The establishment of such a self-consciously comprehensive program by Congress, which certainly did not exist when *Illinois v. Milwaukee* was decided, strongly suggests that there is no room for courts to attempt to improve on that program with federal common law.[14]

Turning to the particular claims involved in this case, the action of Congress in supplanting the federal common law is perhaps clearest when the question of effluent limitations for discharges from the two treatment plants is considered. The duly issued permits under which the city Commission discharges treated sewage . . . incorporate, as required by the Act, the specific effluent limitations established by EPA regulations. . . . There is thus no question that the problem of effluent limitations has been thoroughly addressed through the administrative scheme established by Congress, as contemplated by Congress. This being so there is no basis for a federal court to impose more stringent limitations than those imposed under the regulatory regime by reference to federal common law, as the District Court did in this case. . . . Federal courts lack authority to impose more stringent effluent limitations under federal common law than those imposed by the agency charged by Congress with administering this comprehensive scheme. . . .

The invocation of federal common law by the District Court and the Court of Appeals in the face of congressional legislation supplanting it is peculiarly inappropriate in areas as complex as water pollution control. . . . Not only are the technical

14. This conclusion is not undermined by Congress' decision to permit States to establish more stringent standards. While Congress recognized a role for the States, the comprehensive nature of its action suggests that it was the exclusive source of federal law. Cases recognizing that the comprehensive character of a federal program is an insufficient basis to find pre-emption of state law are not in point, since we are considering which branch of the Federal Government is the source of federal law, not whether that law pre-empts state law. Since federal courts create federal common law only as a necessary expedient when problems requiring federal answers are not addressed by federal statutory law, the comprehensive character of a federal statute is quite relevant to the present question, while it would not be were the question whether state law, which of course does not depend upon the absence of an applicable Act of Congress, still applied.

problems difficult—doubtless the reason Congress vested authority to administer the Act in administrative agencies possessing the necessary expertise—but the general area is particularly unsuited to the approach inevitable under a regime of federal common law. Congress criticized past approaches to water pollution control as being "sporadic" and "ad hoc," characterizations of any judicial approach applying federal common law.

It is also significant that Congress addressed in the 1972 Amendments one of the major concerns underlying the recognition of federal common law in *Illinois v. Milwaukee.* We were concerned in that case that Illinois did not have any forum in which to protect its interests unless federal common law were created. In the 1972 Amendments Congress provided ample opportunity for a State affected by decisions of a neighboring State's permit-granting agency to seek redress. [The Court described the statutory mechanism by which a downstream state may ask EPA to reject or modify a permit issued by an upstream state, noting that the plaintiffs did not avail themselves of these statutory mechanisms.] The statutory scheme established by Congress provides a forum for the pursuit of such claims before expert agencies by means of the permit-granting process. It would be quite inconsistent with this scheme if federal courts were in effect to "write their own ticket" under the guise of federal common law after permits have already been issued and permittees have been planning and operating in reliance on them.

Respondents argue that congressional intent to preserve the federal common-law remedy recognized in *Illinois v. Milwaukee* is evident in §§510 and 505(e) of the statute. Section 510 provides that nothing in the Act shall preclude States from adopting and enforcing limitations on the discharge of pollutants more stringent than those adopted under the Act.[20] It is one thing, however, to say that States may adopt more stringent limitations through state administrative processes, or even that States may establish such limitations through state nuisance law, and apply them to in-state discharges. It is quite another to say that the States may call upon federal courts to employ federal common law to establish more stringent standards applicable to out-of-state dischargers. Any standards established under federal common law are federal standards, and so the authority of States to impose more stringent standards under §510 would not seem relevant. Section 510 clearly contemplates state authority to establish more stringent pollution limitations; nothing in it, however, suggests that this was to be done by federal-court actions premised on federal common law.

---

20. In full, §510 provides:

"Except as expressly provided in this chapter, nothing in this chapter shall (1) preclude or deny the right of any State or political subdivision thereof or interstate agency to adopt or enforce (A) any standard or limitation respecting discharges of pollutants, or (B) any requirement respecting control or abatement of pollution; except that if any effluent limitation, or other limitation, effluent standard, prohibition, pretreatment standard, or standard of performance is in effect under this chapter, such State or political subdivision or interstate agency may not adopt or enforce any effluent limitation, or other limitation, effluent standard, prohibition, pretreatment standard, or standard of performance which is less stringent than the effluent limitation, or other limitation, effluent standard, prohibition, pretreatment standard, or standard of performance under this chapter; or (2) be construed as impairing or in any manner affecting any right or jurisdiction of the States with respect to the waters (including boundary waters) of such States."

Subsection 505(e) provides:

"Nothing *in this section* shall restrict any right which any person (or class of persons) may have under any statute or common law to seek enforcement of any effluent standard or limitation or to seek any other relief (including relief against the Administrator or a State agency)" (emphasis supplied).

Respondents argue that this evinces an intent to preserve the federal common law of nuisance. We, however, are inclined to view the quoted provision as meaning what it says: that nothing in §505, the citizen-suit provision, should be read as limiting any other remedies which might exist. Subsection 505(e) is virtually identical to subsections in the citizen-suit provisions of several environmental statutes. The subsection is common language accompanying citizen-suit provisions and we think that it means only that the provision of such suit does not revoke other remedies. It most assuredly cannot be read to mean that the Act as a whole does not supplant formerly available federal common-law actions but only that the particular section authorizing citizen suits does not do so. No one, however, maintains that the citizen-suit provision pre-empts federal common law. We are thus not persuaded that §505(e) aids respondents in this case, even indulging the unlikely assumption that the reference to "common law" in §505(e) includes the limited federal common law as opposed to the more routine state common law. . . .[22]

We therefore conclude that no federal common-law remedy was available to respondents in this case. The judgment of the Court of Appeals is therefore vacated, and the case is remanded for proceedings consistent with this opinion.

It is so ordered.

JUSTICE BLACKMUN, with whom JUSTICE MARSHALL and JUSTICE STEVENS join, dissenting. . . .

It is well settled that a body of federal common law has survived the decision in Erie R. Co. v. Tompkins. *Erie* made clear that federal courts, as courts of limited jurisdiction, lack general power to formulate and impose their own rules of decision. The Court, however, did not there upset, nor has it since disturbed, a deeply rooted, more specialized federal common law that has arisen to effectuate federal interests embodied either in the Constitution or an Act of Congress. Chief among the federal interests served by this common law are the resolution of interstate disputes and the implementation of national statutory or regulatory policies.

Both before and after *Erie*, the Court has fashioned federal law where the interstate nature of a controversy renders inappropriate the law of either State.

---

22. The dissent's criticism of our reading of §505(e), post, at 1805, is misplaced. There is nothing unusual about Congress enacting a particular provision, and taking care that this enactment by itself not disturb other remedies, without considering whether the rest of the Act does so or what other remedies may be available. The fact that the language of §505(e) is repeated *in haec verba* in the citizen-suit provisions of a vast array of environmental legislation, indicates that it does not reflect any considered judgment about what other remedies were previously available or continue to be available under any particular statute. The dissent refers to our reading as "extremely strained," but the dissent, in relying on §505(e) as evidence of Congress' intent to preserve the federal common-law nuisance remedy, must read "nothing in this section" to mean "nothing in this Act." We prefer to read the statute as written. Congress knows how to say "nothing in this Act" when it means to.

When such disputes arise, it is clear under our federal system that laws of one State cannot impose upon the sovereign rights and interests of another. . . .

II

In my view, the language and structure of the Clean Water Act leaves no doubt that Congress intended to preserve the federal common law of nuisance. Section 505(e) of the Act reads: "Nothing in this section shall restrict any right which any person (or class of persons) may have under any statute or common law to seek enforcement of any effluent standard or limitation or to seek any other relief (including relief against the Administrator or a State agency)."

The Act specifically defines "person" to include States, and thus embraces respondents Illinois and Michigan. It preserves their right to bring an action against the governmental entities who are charged with enforcing the statute. Most important, as succinctly stated by the Court of Appeals in this case: "There is nothing in the phrase 'any statute or common law' that suggests that this provision is limited to state common law." To the best of my knowledge, every federal court that has considered the issue has concluded that, in enacting §505(e), Congress meant to preserve federal as well as state common law.

Other sections of the Clean Water Act also support the conclusion that Congress in 1972 had no intention of extinguishing the federal common law of nuisance. Although the Act established a detailed and comprehensive regulatory system aimed at eliminating the discharge of pollutants into all navigable waters, it did not purport to impose a unitary enforcement structure for abating water pollution. In particular, Congress expressly provided that the effluent limitations promulgated under the Act do not preclude any State from establishing more stringent limitations. It also made clear that federal officers or agencies are not foreclosed from adopting or enforcing stricter pollution controls and standards than those required by the Act.

Thus, under the statutory scheme, any permit issued by the EPA or a qualifying state agency does not insulate a discharger from liability under other federal or state law. To the contrary, the permit granted pursuant to §402(k) confers assurances with respect to certain specified sections of the Act, but the requirements under other provisions as well as separate legal obligations remain unaffected. Congress plainly anticipated that dischargers might be required to meet standards more stringent than the minimum effluent levels approved by the EPA. Those more stringent standards would necessarily be established by other statutes or by common law. Because the Act contemplates a shared authority between the Federal Government and the individual States, it is entirely understandable that Congress thought it neither imperative nor desirable to insist upon an exclusive approach to the improvement of water quality. . . .

NOTES AND QUESTIONS ON *MILWAUKEE II*

1. *Arbitrary about-face or reasoned distinction of prior precedent?* What seems to explain the different outcome in *Milwaukee II* from *Milwaukee I*? What did the

Court find to be the critical elements of the 1972 Amendments to the CWA that justified supplanting the federal common law of nuisance?

2. *Holding and aftermath.* Does the Court hold that the CWA preempts *all* common law claims, or simply those based on *federal* common law? On remand in *Milwaukee III*, 519 F. Supp. 292 (N.D. Ill. 1981), the district court interpreted *Milwaukee II* to permit state common law claims for liability resulting from interstate water pollution and allowed Illinois to proceed against the City of Milwaukee under the Illinois law of nuisance. The Seventh Circuit reversed, 731 F.2d 403 (7th Cir. 1984) holding that the CWA precluded a state claiming injury from asserting its own laws, whether statutory or common law, as a basis for imposing liability on a discharging sister state. The Seventh Circuit reasoned that the CWA "may well preserve a right under statutes or the common law of the state within which a discharge occurs (State I) to obtain enforcement of prescribed standards or limitations, and we see no reason why such a right could not be asserted by an out-of-state plaintiff injured as a result of the violation. However, it seems implausible that Congress meant to preserve or confer any right of the state claiming injury (State II) or its citizens to seek enforcement of limitations on discharges in State I by applying the statutes or common law of State II." *Id.* at 414. The Supreme Court agreed with this result six years later, holding that the law of the discharging state controls in order to preserve the comprehensive regulatory regime envisioned by the CWA, thus precluding suits based on the common law of the receiving state, but not those based on the common law of the source state. International Paper v. Ouellette, 479 U.S. 481 (1987).

3. *Role of comprehensive scheme.* If this decision merely bars federal common law claims, how relevant to the holding is the fact that Congress adopted a comprehensive statutory scheme? Should that not also bar state common law claims as well? And if so, what did Congress intend to accomplish in the section 505(e) savings clause?

4. *Institutional factors.* In some ways, the majority opinion echoes the reluctance of the *Boomer* court to address complex environmental issues, in favor of an approach that relies on legislative action and the expertise of administrative agencies rather than judicial discretion. If the major purpose of statutory schemes was to replace the unpredictable, uncertain nature of case-by-case decisions as a means of environmental protection, isn't the Court correct here to reject that approach once a comprehensive administrative regime is in place? Should the residual role of the common law be limited to damages, as opposed to corrective action?

5. Sea Clammers. In the same term, the Supreme Court decided in Middlesex County Sewerage Authority v. National Sea Clammers Ass'n, 453 U.S. 1 (1981), that the Clean Water Act similarly preempted any federal common law claims regarding ocean pollution. The *Sea Clammers* decision also held that neither the CWA nor the Marine Protection, Research, and Sanctuaries Act (MPRSA, or Ocean Dumping Act) included an implied right of action other than the specific citizen suit and other remedies expressly provided in those laws.

6. *State of the law.* Reading all of the opinions together (*Milwaukee I* and *II*, along with *International Paper* and *Sea Clammers*), the result is that the Supreme Court has held that Congress intended to preempt the federal common law of nuisance and the common law of states that may receive pollution from other states,

but not the common law of the discharging state. How does this view of the residual role of the common law fit with the regulatory programs in the statute, and how might a broader common law role interfere with those programs?

7. Milwaukee*'s expansion?* As we discussed in Chapter 2, eight states brought claims against six electric power corporations for their contributions to the "public nuisance of global warming." In American Electric Power v. Connecticut, 131 S. Ct. 2527 (2011), the Supreme Court held that the Clean Air Act displaced federal common law nuisance actions. At the time, EPA had commenced a rule-making process to establish greenhouse gas emission standards for power plants, but had yet to finalize and apply such regulations. The Court rejected the defendant's argument that the federal common law of nuisance is not displaced until EPA actually exercises its regulatory authority with respect to the defendant plants, holding that "[t]he critical point is that Congress delegated to EPA the decision whether and how to regulate carbon-dioxide emissions from power plants; the delegation is what displaces federal common law." *Id.* at 2538. In doing so, did the *American Electric Power* Court follow *Milwaukee II* or move beyond it? Does the decision mean that the common law can be preempted even where EPA declines or flat out refuses to regulate under a congressional delegation? The Court said it did. *Id.* at 2538-39 ("Indeed, were EPA to decline to regulate carbon-dioxide emissions altogether at the conclusion of its ongoing §7411 rulemaking, the federal courts would have no warrant to employ the federal common law of nuisance to upset the agency's expert determination."). Is this good policy?

8. Milwaukee *and state common law actions.* The *American Electric Power* Court left open the issue of whether the Clean Air Act preempted state common law, stating that the plaintiffs' state-law claims had not been briefed by the parties. If you had a chance to brief this issue, what would you argue on behalf of the plaintiffs? On behalf of the defendants? Consider your answer in view of this language currently contained in section 116 of the Clean Air Act:

> . . . nothing in this Act shall preclude or deny the right of any State or political subdivision thereof to adopt or enforce (1) any standard or limitation respecting emissions of air pollutants . . . ; except that . . . such State or political subdivision may not adopt or enforce any emission standard or limitation which is less stringent than [a standard or limitation adopted or approved by the federal government].

42 U.S.C. §7416.

IV

COMPLIANCE AND ENFORCEMENT

Standard-setting decisions appear in the Federal Register (or sometimes in statutes themselves) as mere pieces of paper. These papers only reduce pollution if polluters comply with the standards that government officials create. Accordingly, company efforts to understand and comply with standards and, if need be, enforcement actions play a critical role in government efforts to address environmental problems.

Chapter 14 discusses the problem of detecting non-compliance by describing mechanisms to enable polluting companies and enforcers to discover violations. Chapter 15 provides an overview of government enforcement, focusing primarily upon policies governing the use of civil and criminal penalties to encourage compliance. Chapter 16 focuses upon citizen enforcement.

Traditionally, environmental law has relied upon a deterrence model of enforcement, *i.e.*, on the idea that threats of substantial penalties should deter would-be violators. Understanding that concept will prove crucial to making sense of the materials presented in this part. In recent years, however, government has placed increasing reliance on a model that relies more on cooperative relationships between government and the parties it regulates in order to encourage compliance. As you learn the particulars of how environmental law is enforced, you should think about how they fit in with the deterrence model and about emerging critiques of that model. Accordingly, we provide below a presentation and critique of these models, which will serve as an introduction to these chapters on detection of violations, government enforcement, and citizen enforcement.

Clifford Rechtschaffen, Deterrence vs. Cooperation and the
Evolving Theory of Environmental Enforcement
71 S. Cal. L. Rev. 1181 (1997-1998)

* * *

II.   The Current System

The traditional practice of environmental enforcement is grounded in theory on a deterrence-based model of enforcement. It assumes that most regulated entities are rational economic actors that act to maximize profits. As such, decisions regarding compliance are based on self-interest. In short, businesses comply where the costs of noncompliance outweigh the benefits of noncompliance. The benefits of noncompliance consist of money saved by not purchasing pollution control equipment or taking other required measures. The costs of noncompliance include the costs of implementing control measures once a violation is detected, plus any additional penalties imposed for being found in violation, multiplied (discounted) by the probability that the violations will be detected. The task for enforcement agencies is to make penalties high enough and the probability of detection great enough that it becomes economically irrational for facilities to violate environmental requirements. The speed and the certainty with which sanctions are imposed are also important factors in obtaining compliance.

Deterrence may be achieved through civil or criminal sanctions. Criminal sanctions may be more appropriate where the amount of civil penalties needed to constitute an economic deterrent is unrealistic. Many also believe that the unique moral stigma and threat of jail time from criminal enforcement constitute the most powerful incentives to obey the law. But whether the penalty is civil or criminal, the essential inquiry turns on the same pleasure-pain calculus: Make the penalty sufficiently painful so that rational actors will be deterred despite the benefits of noncompliance. . . .

. . .

By contrast, a "compliance" or cooperative system emphasizes securing compliance rather than sanctioning wrongdoing. Penalties are seen as threats rather than sanctions, and sanctions are typically withdrawn if compliance is achieved. Levying penalties is seen as a mark of the system's failure (to otherwise obtain compliance); compliance systems rely far more on rewards and incentives than penalties. Enforcement is primarily prospective, oriented toward inducing conditions that lead to conformity. The system focuses more on the underlying conditions or violations than on the violator.

Deterrence-based enforcement is the prevailing societal approach for controlling unlawful individual and corporate conduct. This theory underlies the EPA's current enforcement system. The agency's enforcement approach is legalistic, and its extensive enforcement policies stress the use of formal enforcement actions. Since the mid-1980s, one of its guiding principles has been ensuring "timely and appropriate responses" to observed violations, which involves applying a series of escalating actions once noncompliance is detected. The agency has traditionally measured the success of its program by the number of inspections conducted, the number of enforcement actions initiated, and the number and size of penalties assessed—all indicators that some type of formal enforcement action has been taken. . . .

Although the theoretical underpinning of the current enforcement system relies largely on deterrence, in practice the process is much more flexible. Most enforcers use a hybrid strategy that includes elements of both coercion and cooperation; few rely on a strictly legalistic model. Most enforcement activity, particularly state enforcement, is aimed at bringing violators back into compliance rather than punishing or deterring. . . .

III.   The Push for Reform . . .

A.   Changed Corporate Attitudes and Practices

One of the most vigorously asserted arguments is that the current enforcement system is based on an outdated model of corporate attitudes and behavior. The argument has several related components: (1) Most businesses try to comply with environmental laws because of a sense of social responsibility, and adherence to social and moral norms; (2) businesses are highly motivated to comply voluntarily because of external factors such as market forces, potential reputational harm, and third-party liability claims; and (3) many businesses have implemented sophisticated internal regulatory systems that parallel or exceed governmental requirements. As a result, a punitive enforcement approach is largely unnecessary. . . .

B.   The Complexity of Environmental Regulation

Another motivation underlying current reform efforts is the complexity of environmental law. . . .

. . . One local prosecutor's guide candidly acknowledges that "[n]o facility of moderate complexity which handles hazardous materials or wastes . . . can be expected to be in full compliance at all times." Likewise, a survey of general corporate counsel at major firms found that two-thirds believed their businesses had operated, at least some time in the prior year, in violation of environmental laws. Nearly seventy percent indicated that they did not believe absolute compliance was achievable because of the law's complexity, varying interpretations by regulators, the role of human error, and cost considerations. Numerous other observers have likewise noted the difficulty of maintaining perfect, continuous compliance with all environmental rules. Small businesses face particularly great challenges in dealing with complicated environmental regulations. . . .

The complexity of environmental law suggests a number of things. It points out the need for agencies to spend considerably more resources on education and compliance promotion, particularly with smaller businesses. It highlights the need for agencies to be flexible and pragmatic in their enforcement of many requirements, which is how most environmental agencies operate in practice. It also indicates the need to re-examine the very liberal *mens rea* requirements of criminal environmental statutes. . . . But the law's complexity is not a justification for a wholesale dismantling of the enforcement system. . . .

C. The Deterrence-Is-Counterproductive Argument

Critics charge that a cooperative approach to enforcement is the best way to achieve compliance and that sanction-oriented enforcement is counterproductive. The basic argument proceeds from the assumption that corporations have a generalized commitment to abiding by the law. Under this mind-set, persuasion works better than punishment; essentially, carrots are superior to sticks. . . .

On the other hand, a host of studies, most notably a series of reports by the General Accounting Office and EPA's Inspector General, demonstrate considerable levels of noncompliance by regulated entities. In one recent report, for instance, the GAO found that one in six major facilities was in "significant noncompliance" of the discharge limits in their NPDES permits, and that the actual number could be twice as high. Moreover, during fiscal year 1994, fifty percent of major dischargers violated their permits at some time during the year (including both lesser infractions and significant violations). Other observers have reached similar conclusions. These latter studies do not tell us, however, whether noncompliance resulted from flaws in the deterrence-based model, or, as others argue, from a *lack of* meaningful deterrence-based enforcement.

The limited empirical data actually comparing deterrence and cooperative-oriented strategies is mixed. . . .

D. The Inefficiency Argument Against Deterrence

. . . Many critics note that government agencies lack the resources necessary to enforce environmental law according to the traditional model. The traditional model requires agencies to monitor and detect violations, inspect facilities, and timely and appropriately respond to each observed violation. Responses range from informal warnings to civil or administrative penalty actions. This is a highly resource-intensive approach. By contrast, a system that places greater reliance on self-policing and self-enforcement would allow a government to concentrate its limited resources on the most serious instances of noncompliance. It would also allow increased government spending on outreach and education efforts that commentators suggest can reach a larger audience and educate regulated entities at a lower cost to enforcement agencies. . . .

A cooperative approach, however, may or may not save agencies money, depending on its structure. Agencies will be spared some of the costs of monitoring, detecting, and proving violations, which will shift to private corporations. On the other hand, agencies will have to devote considerably more resources to providing technical advice and cooperative assistance to regulated facilities. In addition, the government oversight of regulated firms in a cooperative scheme may be just as costly as the traditional inspection model it is replacing. For example, inspectors in Cal/OSHA's Cooperative Compliance Program stopped most routine compliance inspections and were assigned to assist the joint labor-management safety committee in improving safety at construction sites. This new role for OSHA staff was expensive as inspectors spent up to ten times more time inspecting these sites than they did at other facilities. Likewise, as the General Accounting Office recently reported, measuring the results of cooperative enforcement strategies can be quite expensive. . . .

IV.   The Benefits of Deterrence-Based Enforcement

While the rush to dismantle traditional environmental enforcement may seem a welcome shift in some sectors, a heavy axe approach is short-sighted and detrimental to the country's long-term interest in effective environmental enforcement. A deterrence-based system contains many positive attributes that are essential to an effective system of enforcement. . . .

A.   *The Expressive Function of Environmental Enforcement*

Environmental regulation, like other areas of law, serves important expressive functions. . . .

. . . . Deterrence-based enforcement, with its reliance on sanctions and enforcement orders, conveys a set of meanings about environmental violations that is very different from that communicated by a cooperative-oriented approach, with its emphasis on negotiation and conciliation. The message imparted by deterrence reaffirms for the public that environmental statutes are important and that transgressions are to be taken very seriously. This message is consistent with the public's expressed strong disapproval of noncompliance with environmental requirements—a desire evidenced by the harsh sweeping penalties for noncompliance and the potent enforcement tools contained in all of the major environmental statutes.

B.   *The Dangers of Agency Capture and Inconsistent Treatment*

1.   Agency Capture

A fundamental tenet of a cooperative-based system is that regulators work closely and in alliance with regulated facilities; they act more as educators and consultants than inspectors or punishers, seeking to solve problems jointly and bring facilities into compliance. While this approach can be highly beneficial, it raises an important countervailing concern: Regulators who become so cozy and closely identified with regulated entities will overlook important violations and bend over too far in the direction of lenient treatment. In short, the agency staff will be captured by those they are ostensibly regulating. . . .

2.   Inconsistent Treatment

One of the most desired features of any enforcement system is consistency—similarly situated enterprises should be treated consistently. Such consistency is essential to ensuring the credibility of an enforcement program and widespread voluntary compliance. An oft-quoted and sagacious maxim of enforcement practice coined by Chester Bowles, a member of the 1941 wartime Office of Price Administration, holds that "20 percent of the regulated population will automatically comply with any regulation, 5 percent will attempt to evade it, and the remaining 75 percent will comply as long as they think that the 5 percent will be caught and punished." . . .

C.   A Strong, Credible Threat of Enforcement

Environmental enforcement, like other areas of regulatory enforcement, is highly "leveraged." Because regulators lack the resources to systematically inspect and monitor every entity, their enforcement actions must provide a big bang for their buck. The actions must send a credible signal to other regulated entities that their noncompliance will also result in meaningful and certain penalties, including recovery of any economic gain realized from noncompliance. Without this general deterrent effect, widespread voluntary compliance is unlikely.

The perception of enforcement consequences is as important as the reality in achieving compliance. . . .

A fundamental problem with relying primarily on cooperative enforcement is that it threatens to significantly weaken the general deterrent effect of individual enforcement actions. Punitive enforcement may remain as a backstop for non-compliance, but it is likely to be used far less frequently, which regulated entities will understand. The public message will be that noncompliance is far more likely to be met with conciliation than sanctions, at least for most first-time violations. Experience has demonstrated that efforts to promote compliance are often ineffective alone. Moreover, having the opportunity to remedy noncompliance without the threat of penalty greatly reduces the incentive to comply. As one analyst explains:

> [I]t is now generally recognized that if the polluter expects no consequence from noncompliance (except having to meet with government officials to agree to do what was required in the first place), he has little incentive to undertake any costs of compliance before getting caught. This has proven to be true even when it is broadly understood that clean-up costs will increase substantially if violations are not corrected early and where actual cost savings from compliance activities has been realized.

Likewise, the General Accounting Office has concluded that penalties

> play a key role in environmental enforcement by deterring violators and by ensuring that regulated entities are treated fairly and consistently so that no one gains a competitive advantage. . . . [T]he Clean Water Act and other environmental statutes have been violated repeatedly when penalties have not been applied.

. . .

D.   A Strong System of Citizen Enforcement

Currently, citizen enforcement is a feature in all the major federal environmental statutes. As a general matter, these statutes allow citizens to sue companies for violations when the government fails to do so and various, often strict, procedural conditions are met. Traditionally, Congress has viewed citizen enforcement as an important supplement to agency enforcement and an important prod to agency regulators. Congress therefore has repeatedly sought to strengthen it.

. . .

Citizen enforcement has played an extremely valuable role in achieving compliance with environmental law, including spurring EPA and state agency enforcement efforts. . . . Citizen action thus provides an important deterrent to noncompliance when government agencies fail to act either because of lack of resources or political will. . . .

V. How to Reform Environmental Enforcement

As discussed in Part III, the evidence is mixed about the best way to achieve compliance with environmental laws; it does not decidedly show the superiority of either deterrence or cooperative-oriented enforcement. Each approach has its strengths and weaknesses, and elements of both systems are desirable. . . .

A. *Agencies Should Provide More Consultation and Cooperative Assistance*

Enforcement agencies have always considered compliance promotion and education necessary to enforcement programs. Until recently, these efforts have often been overlooked and underfunded. One positive element in current reforms has been a push to expand cooperative assistance efforts significantly, particularly those directed at small businesses. . . .

B. *Policies Automatically Precluding Sanctions and Eliminating Enforcement Discretion Are Undesirable*

One very popular strand of current reform efforts seeks to preclude or greatly mitigate penalties for certain classes of violations or against small businesses. While in many circumstances this type of enforcement response is entirely appropriate, it is unwise public policy to negate agency discretion totally and mandate that sanctions are impermissible.

The most notable example of this type of initiative is the [Small Business Regulatory Enforcement Fairness Act] . . . , enacted by Congress in 1996. The statute requires federal agencies to develop policies that provide for the reduction *and waiver* of minor violations by small businesses in certain instances, such as when the violation is corrected within a reasonable period or is discovered in a compliance-assistance program. . . .

On the one hand, the notion of excusing first-time minor violations seems quite reasonable, particularly if limited in scope and tied to proactive measures by regulated facilities, such as requesting agency assistance or making good-faith efforts to comply. This allows agencies to devote their resources to serious cases and minimizes resentment by businesses when they are penalized for insignificant violations.

On the other hand, it is poor policy either to *mandate* that all minor violations be forgiven, or that they be forgiven simply because they are corrected. Such a policy is unnecessary since repeated empirical studies show that environmental requirements are enforced in a pragmatic way, with little likelihood of penalties being imposed rigidly or arbitrarily. More importantly, this approach removes *any* incentive for entities to comply before they are found in violation, since being caught has essentially no consequence other than perhaps a warning. . . . [T]his approach "often signals to the regulated community that it need not comply until enforcement begins." . . .

C. Greater Self-Regulation Should Be Encouraged to Supplement, Not Replace Enforcement

The environmental enforcement reforms advanced with the greatest vigor and currently attracting the most intense controversy concern internal environmental audits and environmental management systems. Businesses and other reformers aggressively have pushed to substitute these self-regulatory systems for traditional enforcement activities. Twenty-three states have adopted environmental audit privilege or immunity laws that provide qualified immunity from penalties for violations disclosed and corrected as a result of voluntary internal audits. Reformers propose to afford similar treatment to the self-policing efforts of management systems.

The expansion of internal regulatory systems is a positive development that should be encouraged. In fact, audits should be made mandatory for publicly traded corporations. Non-publicly traded firms that implement audits or management systems should receive enforcement benefits such as reduced penalties and inspections. But audit privilege and immunity laws, promoted by some businesses as a strategy to curtail government enforcement, should be resisted. These laws undermine incentives for preventative compliance measures and conceal important environmental information. More generally, self-policing systems should supplement, but not replace, traditional enforcement activities. . . .

[P]rivilege/immunity measures . . . seriously undermine the incentives for facilities to take preventative steps to achieve compliance. To varying degrees, they permit firms to sit back and wait until an audit is conducted before coming into compliance. . . . Second, privilege laws are highly objectionable because, as described above, they keep a category of public environmental information pertaining to the facility's compliance with environmental requirements secret and out of the public's reach. . . .

VI. Conclusion

The movement to transform environmental enforcement is being advanced with exceptional ardor. Before the old system is discarded however, it is critical for policymakers to engage in a careful and sober assessment of the calls for reform. If the system is flawed, will the proposed changes improve it? In particular, is there a sufficient basis on which to conclude that the new approaches will be superior to the ones being reformed?

The materials that follow will show how the deterrence-based model has influenced particular legal rules on enforcement, and present some information about the cooperative model reforms Professor Rechtschaffen mentions. As you read these materials, think about which model makes sense and what policy measures would best serve the goals of securing compliance.

14
Detecting Violations: Permitting, Monitoring, Record Keeping, and Reporting

A. PERMITTING

Counsel for facilities that release a variety of pollutants may need to read and interpret numerous regulations and statutory provisions to understand the owners' legal obligations. In order to make sure that each facility's operator knows and understands its legal obligations and to facilitate enforcement, the environmental statutes often require facility-specific permits. These permits are media-specific. Thus, a facility that releases pollution into both the air and water may need both an air and water permit. The air permit will collect the legal obligations restricting its air emissions and the water permit will collect the legal obligations limiting its effluent discharges. *Cf.* EPA OFFICE OF THE INSPECTOR GENERAL, SUBSTANTIAL CHANGES NEEDED IN IMPLEMENTATION AND OVERSIGHT OF TITLE V PERMITS IF PROGRAM GOALS ARE TO BE FULLY REALIZED, Report No. 2005-P-00010, at 5 (2005), available at http://www.epa.gov/oig/reports/2005/20050309-2005-P-00010.pdf (discussing failures to clearly state the obligations of sources in permits).

Generally, government officials and citizens can only enforce specifically defined legal obligations. This raises a fundamental question of the relationship between pollution control standards and compliance. Should the basic rule be that firms cannot release pollutants without explicit government permission? Or, instead, should the rule be that firms may pollute freely except to the extent government has adopted specific requirements limiting releases of particular pollutants?

≡ *Atlantic States Legal Found. v. Eastman Kodak Co.*

≡ *12 F.3d 353 (2d Cir. 1993)*

WINTER, CIRCUIT JUDGE.

This appeal raises the issue of whether private groups may bring a citizen suit pursuant to Section 505 of the Federal Water Pollution Control Act (commonly known as the Clean Water Act), to stop the discharge of pollutants not listed in a valid permit issued pursuant to the Clean Water Act ("CWA" or "The Act"). We hold that the discharge of unlisted pollutants is not unlawful under the CWA. We also hold that private groups may not bring such a suit to enforce New York State environmental regulations.

Background

Appellee Eastman Kodak Company ("Kodak") operates an industrial facility in Rochester, New York that discharges wastewater into the Genesee River and Paddy Hill Creek under a State Pollutant Discharge Elimination System ("SPDES") permit issued pursuant to 33 U.S.C. §1342. Appellant Atlantic States Legal Foundation, Inc. ("Atlantic States") is a not-for-profit environmental group based in Syracuse, New York. . . .

On November 14, 1991, Atlantic States filed the complaint in the instant matter. The complaint alleged that Kodak had violated Sections 301 and 402 of the Clean Water Act, by discharging large quantities of pollutants not listed in its SPDES permit. . . .

Discussion

. . .

Atlantic States brought the present action under the citizen suit provision of Section 505, which permits private suits to enforce a CWA "effluent standard or limitation." Section 505 defines such an enforceable standard or limitation as, inter alia, "an unlawful act under section 1311," [section 301] and "a permit or condition thereof issued under . . . section 1342 of this title, which is in effect under this chapter." The question then is whether Atlantic States' action seeks to enforce an "effluent standard or limitation" imposed by the Act or by Kodak's SPDES permit issued by the DEC [New York State Department of Environmental Conservation].

A. *"Standards and Limitations" of the Clean Water Act*

Atlantic States argues first that the plain language of Section 301 of the CWA prohibits the discharge of any pollutants not expressly permitted. With regard to this claim, therefore, Atlantic States' standing to bring this action turns on the merits of the action itself.

Section 301(a) reads: "Except as in compliance with this section and sections 1312, 1316, 1317, 1328, 1342, and 1344 of this title, the discharge of any pollutant by any person shall be unlawful." This prohibition is tempered, however, by a self-referential host of exceptions that allow the discharge of many pollutants once a polluter has complied with the regulatory program of the CWA. The exception relevant to the instant matter is contained in Section 402, which outlines the NPDES, and specifies the requirements for suspending the national system with the submission of an approved state program. Section 402(k) contains the so-called "shield provision," which defines compliance with a NPDES or SPDES permit as compliance with Section 301 for the purposes of the CWA's enforcement provisions. The Supreme Court has noted that "The purpose of [Section 402(k)] seems to be . . . to relieve [permit holders] of having to litigate in an enforcement action the question whether their permits are sufficiently strict."

Atlantic States' view of the regulatory framework stands that scheme on its head. Atlantic States treats permits as establishing limited permission for the discharge of identified pollutants and a prohibition on the discharge of unidentified pollutants. Viewing the regulatory scheme as a whole, however, it is clear that the permit is intended to identify and limit the most harmful pollutants while leaving the control of the vast number of other pollutants to disclosure requirements. Once within the NPDES or SPDES scheme, therefore, polluters may discharge pollutants not specifically listed in their permits so long as they comply with the appropriate reporting requirements and abide by any new limitations when imposed on such pollutants.

The EPA lists tens of thousands of different chemical substances in the Toxic Substances Control Act Chemical Substance Inventory. . . . However, the EPA does not demand even information regarding each of the many thousand chemical substances potentially present in a manufacturer's wastewater because "it is impossible to identify and rationally limit every chemical or compound present in a discharge of pollutants." "Compliance with such a permit would be impossible and anybody seeking to harass a permittee need only analyze that permittee's discharge until determining the presence of a substance not identified in the permit." Indeed, Atlantic States could provide no principled reason why water itself, which is conceded to be a chemical, would not be considered a "pollutant" under its view of the Act.

The EPA has never acted in any way to suggest that Atlantic States' absolutist and wholly impractical view of the legal effect of a permit is valid. In fact, the EPA's actions and policy statements have frequently contemplated discharges of pollutants not listed under a NPDES or SPDES permit. It has addressed such discharges by amending the permit to list and limit a pollutant when necessary to safeguard the environment without considering pre-amendment discharges to be violations calling for enforcement under the CWA. . . .

The EPA is the federal agency entrusted with administration and enforcement of the CWA. As such, EPA's reasonable interpretations of the Act are due deferential treatment in the courts. . . . Because the EPA's implementation of the CWA is entirely reasonable, we defer to it.

B. New York Environmental "Standards and Limitations"

Atlantic States argues alternatively that the permit itself provides grounds for enforcement of New York State's regulations. States may enact stricter standards for wastewater effluents than mandated by the CWA and federal EPA regulations. These states' standards may be enforced under the CWA by the states or the EPA, but private citizens have no standing to do so. New York chose to implement its own environmental policies through its DEC's issuance of SPDES permits pursuant to N.Y. Envtl. Conserv. Law §17-0815 (McKinney 1984). However, state regulations, including the provisions of SPDES permits, which mandate "a greater scope of coverage than that required" by the federal CWA and its implementing regulations are not enforceable through a citizen suit under 33 U.S.C. §1365.

Atlantic States relies heavily on General Provision 1(b) of the SPDES permit to show a violation of the CWA. In particular, Atlantic States points to the final clause of that provision that requires, pursuant to N.Y. Envtl. Conserv. Law §17-0815(3), that

> [T]he discharge of any pollutant not identified and authorized or the discharge of any pollutant more frequently than or at a level in excess of that identified and authorized by this permit shall constitute a violation of the terms and conditions of this permit.

However, General Provision 1(b) itself contemplates "new, increased or decreased discharges" that do not "violate the effluent limitations specified in this permit."[10] Moreover, Special Reporting Requirement 2(a) of the SPDES permit specifically contemplates discharges of pollutants not identified by the permit. It states, in relevant part:

> All existing manufacturing . . . dischargers must notify the [DEC] as soon as they know or have reason to believe . . . [t]hat they have begun or expect to begin to use or manufacture as an intermediate or final product or byproduct any toxic pollutant which was not reported in the permit application. . . .

Like the SPDES permit, the DEC itself contemplates the discharge of unlisted pollutants. In September 1988, DEC notified Kodak that it was aware of 45 substances "reported to have releases to the Genesee River" out of which only 23 were "specifically limited or monitored by the SPDES permit." DEC advised Kodak that although the bulk of these 23 substances either did not appear to be a major concern, or at least did not "appear to be acutely toxic to aquatic life at the levels of discharge indicated," the remaining four should receive "additional attention."

It thus appears that the DEC's view of the SPDES permit is the same as the EPA's. If so, Atlantic States' action fails for reasons stated in Point A above. We need not resolve the issue, however, for, even if Atlantic States is right about New York law, the action would fail because New York would be implementing a regulatory scheme broader than the CWA, and such broader state schemes are

---

10. General Provision 1(b) reads:

> b. All discharges authorized by this permit shall be consistent with the terms and conditions of this permit; facility expansions, production increases, decreases, or process modifications which result in new, increased or decreased discharges of pollutants must be reported by submission of a new SPDES application or, if such new, increased, or decreased discharge does not violate the effluent limitations specified in this permit, by submission to the permit issuing authority of notice of such new or increased discharges of pollutants (in which case the permit may be modified to specify effluent limitations or any pollutants not identified and limited herein); the discharge of any pollutant not identified and authorized or the discharge of any pollutant more frequently than or at a level in excess of that identified and authorized by this permit shall constitute a violation of the terms and conditions of this permit.

unenforceable through Section 505 citizen suits. A citizen's suit under Section 505 is thus barred either because Section 17-0815(3) and the final clause of General Provision 1(b) implement a program with broader scope than that promulgated under the CWA and EPA regulations or because the permit more narrowly interpreted shields Kodak from such an action.

Conclusion

For the reasons stated above, we affirm the order of the district court granting summary judgment to Kodak.

NOTES AND QUESTIONS ON *ATLANTIC STATES*

1. *Rationale.* Section 301(a) prohibits "the discharge of any pollutant" except as in compliance with various sections of the Act. So why exactly does the court not allow Atlantic States to enforce the restriction on discharge of pollutants not listed in its permit? Do you agree with the court's rationale? In thinking about this, study sections 301 and 402(k) carefully. Could New York State prosecute Eastman Kodak for discharging a non-listed pollutant? The Eleventh Circuit disagreed with the *Atlantic States* court's holding that citizens may not enforce state law provisions in an NPDES permit in Parker v. Scrap Metal Processors, Inc., 386 F.3d 993, 1006 n.15 (11th Cir. 2004). Could Atlantic States enforce an identical permit in the Eleventh Circuit?

2. *What is a pollutant?* Atlantic States argued that plain water might be a pollutant. Could Atlantic States have taken a narrower view of the definition of a pollutant without compromising its case against Eastman Kodak? Should it have? Suppose that New York State seeks to prosecute a manufacturer for discharging a pollutant listed in the Clean Water Act, but not listed in the relevant permit. Could a district court within the Second Circuit hold that the discharger has violated section 301?

3. *Policy.* Should the law proceed on the premise that pollution is prohibited unless authorized or the premise that it is authorized unless prohibited? If you were the lawyer for a polluting company and the law prohibits discharges unless authorized, would you seek to delay the promulgation of effluent limitations? What if the law allows discharges until prohibited?

4. *Permit shields.* The permit shield provision mentioned in *Atlantic States* is one of several requirements in environmental statutes that seek to ensure, at a minimum, that uncertainty about the legality and interpretation of regulations is resolved prior to an enforcement proceeding whenever possible. This early clarification also serves goals of encouraging proper compliance to obviate the needs for enforcement. As noted in Adamo Wrecking Co. v. United States, 434 U.S. 275, 285 (1978), the Clean Air Act contains a provision, 42 U.S.C. §7607(b)(2), forbidding litigation about the validity of a regulation in an enforcement proceeding. Similar requirements exist in other statutes. Often, however, the precise implications of a regulation for a facility require some interpretation of the regulation. Because regulatory requirements often are imprecise and permit a variety of compliance alternatives, specific requirements in permits can vary, even when the

underlying regulation is the same nationwide. The permitting provisions of the statutes aim to resolve these questions in the permitting proceeding, rather than in the enforcement proceeding. Permit shield provisions like that set out in section 402(k) of the Clean Water Act protect operators, at a minimum, from government departures from interpretations of regulations arrived at in permitting proceedings. *See, e.g.*, 33 U.S.C. §1342(k), 42 U.S.C. §7661c(f).

5. *Information disclosure.* In answering the question of whether polluters should be liable for discharges not expressly limited in a permit, should it matter whether the discharger disclosed the presence (or potential presence) of the pollutant in its permit application?

As you read the following case, think about whether it's consistent with *Atlantic States.*

Northwest Envtl. Advocates v. City of Portland
56 F.3d 979 (9th Cir. 1995)

Pregerson, Circuit Judge.

Northwest Environmental Advocates and Nina Bell ("NWEA") appeal the district court's judgment in favor of Portland on their claims that the City is violating the Clean Water Act ("CWA"). On April 16, 1991, NWEA filed suit in the district court alleging that Portland's practice of discharging raw sewage during times of precipitation from 54 outfall points was not covered by a permit and that the practice had caused and was continuing to cause violations of Oregon's water quality standards. After a trial on the written record, the district court held that (1) the contested discharge points were covered by Portland's pollution permit, and (2) the court lacked jurisdiction to consider NWEA's water quality violation claims.

In *Northwest Environmental Advocates v. City of Portland* (*Northwest*), we affirmed. We held that the contested discharge points were covered by Portland's pollution permit and we held that *Northwest Environmental Advocates* lacked standing to bring a citizen suit under §505(a)(1) of the Clean Water Act to enforce water quality standards contained in Portland's permit. On December 28, 1993, NWEA filed a petition for rehearing with suggestion for rehearing en banc. While this petition was still pending, the Supreme Court decided PUD No. 1 of Jefferson County v. Washington Department of Ecology, [511] U.S. [700] (1994) (*Jefferson County*).

Jefferson County cast into considerable doubt our holding in *Northwest* that citizens do not have standing under the Clean Water Act to enforce water quality standards unless they have been translated into end-of-pipe effluent limitations. In light of *Jefferson County* and upon reconsideration of our prior opinion in *Northwest*, we now vacate that opinion and issue the following opinion.

II. . . .

B. *Does NWEA Have a Cause of Action for Water Quality Violations?*

NWEA argues that the district court erred in finding that it did not have jurisdiction over a citizen suit for the enforcement of the water quality maintenance provision of the NPDES permit.

. . . Specifically, NWEA alleged that Portland's CSO [combined sewer overflow] events violated a permit condition prohibiting any discharges that would violate Oregon water quality standards. The 1984 permit held, as a condition in Schedule A, that "notwithstanding the effluent limitations established by this permit, no wastes shall be discharged and no activities shall be conducted which will violate Water Quality Standards.["] . . .

The district court never reached the question of Portland's liability for violations of this permit condition. Instead, the district court held that §505 of the Clean Water Act did not grant federal jurisdiction for the citizen enforcement of water quality violations, "because water quality standards do not equal 'effluent standards or limitations under this chapter.'" The court concluded that violations of water quality standards may be actionable "only if they are incorporated into an NPDES permit through effluent limitations." Because the plain language of CWA §505, the legislative history, and case law support a finding of citizen suit jurisdiction in this case, we reverse on this issue.

The plain language of CWA §505 authorizes citizens to enforce *all* permit conditions. That section provides: "[A]ny citizen may commence a civil action . . . (1) against any person . . . who is alleged to be in violation of (A) an effluent standard or limitation under [the Clean Water Act]." . . . An effluent standard or limitation includes "(2) an effluent limitation or other limitation under section 1311 . . . *or* (6) a permit or condition thereof. . . ." This language clearly contemplates citizen suits to enforce "a permit or condition thereof." Portland holds a National Pollutant Discharge Elimination System (NPDES) permit. . . .

Portland argues that §505 allows citizens to enforce only those water quality standards that are translated into effluent limitations. To support this argument, Portland reasons that the effluent limitations, which were imposed by the 1972 amendments to the CWA, effectively displaced water quality standards as the primary means of regulating pollution. Portland explains that Congress retained water quality standards as the ultimate goal of pollution control, but sought to achieve this goal through end-of-the-pipe limitations. . . .

By introducing effluent limitations into the CWA scheme, Congress intended to improve enforcement, not to supplant the old system.

Ample case law supports our view that Congress intended to confer citizens standing to enforce water quality standards. Most notably, in *Jefferson County*, the Supreme Court held that the Clean Water Act allows States to enforce the broad narrative criteria contained in water quality standards. In *Jefferson County*, a county which proposed to build an electricity-generating facility on a river challenged a minimum stream flow condition established by the State. Although the county did not contest the State's authority to set limitations designed to ensure compliance with state water quality standards adopted under CWA §303, the county argued that §303 requires the State to protect water quality standards solely through implementation of "specific numerical criteria." The county contended that the State may not require it to operate the dam in a manner consistent with a "designated use," which is a *qualitative* requirement of the §303 water quality standards.

The Court rejected the county's argument, and held that the State may require a permit applicant to comply with the qualitative designated uses requirement. The Court explained that under the literal terms of CWA §303(c)(2), a water quality standard must "consist of the designated uses of the navigable waters involved *and* the water quality criteria for such waters based upon such uses." Thus, the Court concluded that a project that does not comply with a designated use of the water does not comply with the applicable water quality standards. The Court also explained that CWA §401(d), which provides for State certification of projects, explicitly authorizes "any . . . Limitations . . . necessary to assure that [the applicant] will comply with any . . . limitations under . . . [CWA §303] . . . and any other appropriate requirement of state law."

By its holding, the Court expressly rejected the county's argument that designated use requirements are "too open-ended" to be enforceable and that the Clean Water Act only contemplates enforcement of the more "specific and objective" numerical criteria. . . .

The county's losing argument in *Jefferson County* is very similar to the argument advanced by Portland in the instant case. Portland argues that citizens may not enforce the broad narrative conditions of state water quality standards, but may enforce *only* those conditions that have been translated into numeric effluent limitations.

We disagree with Portland's contention that *Jefferson County* is inapposite to the issue before us. Even though *Jefferson County* involved a state's authority to impose conditions under CWA §401, whereas the present litigation involves citizen suit enforcement of CWA §402 conditions, both the §401 certification process and the §402 permit process require applicants to comply with CWA §301. As noted above, §301 incorporates by reference the water quality requirements of §303.

Moreover, although *Jefferson County* addressed the authority of States, not citizens, to enforce the narrative conditions of CWA §303 water quality standards, nothing in the language of the Clean Water Act, the legislative history, or the implementing regulations restricts citizens from enforcing the same conditions of a certificate or permit that a State may enforce. To the contrary, as demonstrated above, these sources uniformly support broad citizen enforcement authority, including the authority to enforce water quality standards. . . .

By interpreting §505 to exclude citizen suit enforcement of water quality standards that are not translated into quantitative limitations, Portland would have us immunize the entire body of qualitative regulations from an important enforcement tool. Such a result would be especially troubling in this case, because no effluent limitations cover the discharges from Portland's combined . . . CSOs. . . .

III. Conclusion

For the foregoing reasons, we AFFIRM the district court's holding that the 1984 permit covered the CSOs, and we REVERSE the district court's holding that CWA §505(a) does not confer jurisdiction for citizen suits to enforce water quality standards when they are conditions of a CWA permit. . . .

KLEINFELD, CIRCUIT JUDGE, dissenting:

I respectfully dissent from Part II-B of the opinion. . . .

. . . The majority opinion suggests that *Jefferson County* has changed the law. . . . [I]t does not.

The question before us is whether citizens' suits may be brought to enforce water quality standards, as opposed to effluent limitations. *Jefferson County* says nothing about that. . . .

Nevertheless, we previously concluded on the basis of analysis of several additional provisions of the statute that it is not the permittee who must comply with the water quality standards, but rather the issuing authority, which has a "duty . . . to include in the permit end-of-pipe effluent limitations that will ensure that water quality standards are met." That makes sense in light of what the Supreme Court said in *Jefferson County*. Congress meant for the issuing authority to decide upon end-of-pipe effluent standards for the permit, which it could derive from water quality standards, when Congress allowed citizens' suits to enforce permit limitations. It did not mean for citizens' suits to proceed on the basis of permit violations, where the permittee complied with end-of-pipe discharge limitations but the water still wound up being too polluted. A water quality standard should be deemed to be not among those authorized by the statute for purposes of citizen suit enforcement. . . .

The majority argues that as a matter of policy, Congress meant to prevent pollution, and citizens' suits add power to anti-pollution enforcement mechanisms, so there is no reason to deny citizens' suits enforcement. The first two propositions do not imply the third. There can be too much of a good thing. There is too much of a good thing when its value is exceeded by the value of other good things available for the same or less cost.

Water quality standards are a useful device for government enforcement authorities (who decided not to prosecute this case against the City of Portland), because they provide standards for effluent limitations and goals toward which enforcement should be aimed. They are too uncertain and amorphous, however, for use against specific polluters. Suppose, hypothetically, that a water quality standard allows for 100 units of a pollutant, upstream and non-point source polluters discharge 50 units, and the downstream discharger is permitted to discharge 50 units. If the upstream and non-point source polluters increase their discharge to 80 units, it does not automatically follow that the downstream discharger should be limited to 20. The burdens of so severe a limitation may exceed the burdens of the extra pollution, or enforcement efforts might more appropriately be directed at the other polluters. In the case at bar, the majority concedes that the social costs of filling the streets and basements of Portland with sewage, or spending between a half billion and $1.2 billion dollars on renovation, are the practical alternatives to tolerating violations of the water quality standards. A public authority might rationally decide that filling the streets and basements with sewage is worse than polluting the river with it, and that the citizens of Portland need several years to raise and spend the money necessary to avoid running the sewage into the streets, the basements, and the river. . . .

NOTES AND QUESTIONS ON *NORTHWEST ENVIRONMENTAL ADVOCATES*

1. *Consistency.* Is this case consistent with *Atlantic States*?

2. *Ease of compliance and enforcement.* Which is easier to comply with and enforce, a prohibition on interference with water quality standards or a general prohibition of discharges of pollutants not listed in a permit?

3. *The dissent.* Under the dissent's view of the law, would the government be able to collect civil penalties for a plant's failure to meet water quality standards?

4. *A permit's function.* At a minimum, a permit should collect the requirements applicable to a pollution source and spell out how that source will comply with the requirements. This collection function matters, because, often, several different regulations will apply to a pollution source. By collecting the requirements in one place and spelling out how the requirements apply to a particular polluter, a permit clarifies the precise compliance obligations of a facility operator. This should aid the operator, making it clearer what she should be doing in order to comply. The permit can aid the public in understanding the scope of requirements applicable to a facility. The permit also can facilitate enforcement, allowing both citizen and government enforcers to compare a facility's environmental performance to its legal obligations. But monitoring compliance requires the collection of information about a facility's performance.

B. MONITORING, RECORD KEEPING, AND REPORTING

Both effective voluntary compliance and, if necessary, enforcement, require some means of allowing companies and potential enforcers to detect non-compliance. You might think that government inspectors should simply monitor each plant to determine if violations have occurred. And the environmental statutes do authorize government agencies to inspect polluting facilities. Inspectors often detect some environmental violations. But inspections provide a very incomplete deterrent. Government could never hire a sufficient number of inspectors to regularly inspect each of the thousands of facilities regulated under the various pollution control laws. Furthermore, an inspector frequently cannot tell whether a polluter has violated a permit condition by just looking at the facility. Often one needs some way of measuring or estimating the amount of pollution being released.

For these reasons, regulatory enforcement relies heavily upon voluntary compliance and a self-monitoring system, where polluters themselves monitor their compliance status and have obligations to report violations to government officials. *See* generally Arnold W. Reitze, Jr. & Steven D. Schell, *Self-Monitoring and Self-Reporting of Routine Air Pollution Releases*, 24 COLUM. J. ENVTL. L. 63 (1999). These obligations include monitoring, record keeping, and reporting (MRR) obligations. Why are all three essential?

The acid rain program experience suggests that stringent MRR obligations have the capacity to greatly encourage compliance. The law governing this program requires continuous monitoring of emissions and frequent electronic reporting of emissions data to the government. The deterrent effect of these strict MRR obligations may explain the lack of violations of the acid rain regulations. Most regulatory programs, though, have much weaker MRR requirements and much weaker compliance records.

1.   Monitoring

The key issue in monitoring is often what monitoring technology is feasible and how often monitoring is conducted. Generally, more frequent and stringent monitoring produces more reliable information about compliance status, but may impose higher cost than less frequent and stringent monitoring. We examine these issues, first through a rare example of a case actually discussing policy considerations that influence monitoring decisions, and then through a note on the Enhanced Monitoring Provisions in the 1990 Clean Air Act Amendments.

United States Steel Corp. v. Train
556 F.2d 822, 850-51 (7th Cir. 1977)

TONE, CIRCUIT JUDGE.

. . . U.S. Steel has two basic complaints regarding the monitoring required by the permit: it is to be done too often and at too many places.

The initial monitoring requirements contained in the permit correspond closely to U.S. Steel's present monitoring practices, as required by the Indiana Stream Pollution Control Board. The final requirements increase the monitoring at all process-water outfalls, requiring daily monitoring for several pollutants as well as temperature and continuous monitoring for flow and pH at several outfalls. Both the remaining process-water and all cooling-water outfalls will be monitored once a week for several pollutants and once a month for others. All the monitoring requirements exceed those proposed by U.S. Steel and present levels, both in the frequency of measurement and in the number of pollutants for which measurements must be taken.

Section 308 of the [Clean Water] Act grants the Administrator broad authority to require NPDES permittees to monitor "at such locations [and] at such intervals" as he shall prescribe, "whenever [it is] required to carry out the objective of [the Act]." Similarly, §402 vests him with authority to "prescribe conditions for [NPDES] permits . . . , including conditions on data and information collection. . . ." We conclude that the monitoring requirements set forth in the permit are within this broad authority.

EPA considered four factors in determining the monitoring requirements, and set the requirements separately for each outfall. These factors were: the nature of the discharges and their impact on the receiving stream; the variability of the discharges; the volume of water discharged; and the present monitoring practices of U.S. Steel. These factors are proper, and the record establishes that they were given appropriate weight by EPA. For example, because of the higher concentrations and greater variety of pollutants present in process water, the permit appropriately requires more frequent monitoring of process-water discharges than of cooling-water discharges. Similarly, more frequent monitoring was required at those outfalls which tended to fluctuate in the amount and quality of their discharges.

The monitoring requirements—similar to or less stringent than those imposed in the approximately 50 other steel-plant permits issued in Region Five—will not work an unjustified economic hardship on U.S. Steel. The chief difference between

U.S. Steel's present monitoring practices and the initial requirements is that compliance at nine of the outfalls will be based on a 24-hour composite sample rather than the 8-hour composite sample presently prepared. The use of the 24-hour composite sample is extended to all outfalls by the final monitoring requirements. These changes will more than triple the number of samples taken. The use of a 24-hour composite sample will doubtless be more expensive than present monitoring practices, but it will present a more complete picture of the discharges from the Gary Works, reflecting fluctuations over the course of an entire day of production. At the outfalls monitored on a daily basis, it will allow an almost continuous check on the performance of the treatment facilities at Gary Works.

By comparison, U.S. Steel's permit proposals call for monitoring only once a week, even at the seven outfalls now sampled five times in eight days, and would replace the monitoring for several pollutants now conducted at each outfall with monitoring at the Pennsylvania Railroad Bridge, four-and-one-half miles downstream. Monitoring at each outfall enables the permittee and EPA to pinpoint the source of any discharges that exceed the plant-wide limitations on particular pollutants. Furthermore, the U.S. Steel proposal would, in effect, allow it to use the four-and-one-half mile stretch of the river as an extended treatment facility, something hardly contemplated by either the Indiana water quality standards or the FWPCA.

We cannot say that EPA exceeded its authority or acted unreasonably when it determined that regular and frequent monitoring at each outfall is necessary to insure prompt detection and rectification of permit violations. Therefore, we affirm the initial and final monitoring requirements set forth in the permit.

NOTES AND QUESTIONS ON *U.S. STEEL*

1. *Variability.* EPA states that it takes the "variability" of discharges into account in writing monitoring requirements. Do highly variable discharges suggest the need for more frequent monitoring or less frequent monitoring than very constant discharges? Why?

2. *Discharge's nature.* EPA also takes into account the "nature of the discharges and their impact on the receiving streams." This suggests that EPA would require more frequent monitoring of pollutants it considers especially damaging. Should the stringency of monitoring vary with the impact of the pollution?

3. *Consistency.* The court cites the consistency of EPA's monitoring requirements for U.S. Steel with the monitoring regime imposed on other steel plants in the region as evidence that the requirements impose no "unjustified economic hardship" on U.S. Steel. Does consistency prevent economic hardship or provide a justification for it? Suppose that U.S. Steel was losing money and that the additional monitoring would add $1 million a year to its compliance costs. Would the monitoring impose an economic hardship? Why would consistency justify the hardship? Is taking into account the impact of discharges on receiving waters (as EPA does) an approach likely to lead to consistent monitoring requirements?

4. *Sources of monitoring requirements.* In this case, monitoring requirements seem to come from discretionary decisions in a permit proceeding. EPA generally writes monitoring, record keeping, and reporting requirements into its regulations. But the

regulations sometimes provide requirements too vague to determine precisely what monitoring an individual source will perform, often because EPA gives polluters a menu of monitoring options, instead of mandating a specific set of requirements.

Sometimes, agencies have failed to impose specific monitoring requirements on sources even in a permit proceeding. *See, e.g., Office of the EPA Inspector General*, at 19. For nonpoint source pollution and fugitive air pollution, monitoring is frequently impossible, and agencies and corporate environmental staff must rely instead on emission estimates. As you read section 308 of the Clean Water Act below (which is also cited in *U.S. Steel*), ask yourself whether EPA may decline to require monitoring when monitoring is possible, as it frequently is for point sources of water pollution:

> Whenever required to carry out the objective of this chapter, including but not limited to
>
> > (1) developing or assisting in the development of any effluent limitation, or other limitation, prohibition, or effluent standard, pretreatment standard, or standard of performance under this chapter;
> > (2) determining whether any person is in violation of any such effluent limitation, or other limitation, prohibition or effluent standard, pretreatment standard, or standard of performance;
> > (3) any requirement established under this section; or
> > (4) carrying out sections 1315, 1321, 1342, 1344 (relating to State permit programs), 1345, and 1364 of this title —
> > > (A) the Administrator shall require the owner or operator of any point source to
> > > > (i) establish and maintain such records,
> > > > (ii) make such reports,
> > > > (iii) install, use, and maintain such monitoring equipment or methods (including where appropriate, biological monitoring methods),
> > > > (iv) sample such effluents (in accordance with such methods, at such locations, at such intervals, and in such manner as the Administrator shall prescribe), and
> > > > (v) provide such other information as he may reasonably require.

33 U.S.C. §1318(a). *See* Environmental Defense Fund v. Costle, 439 F. Supp. 980, 1003-04 (E.D.N.Y. 1977) (stating that EPA has a mandatory duty to require monitoring and reporting, but rejecting a claim that EPA violated this section by funding sewage treatment plants while requiring some monitoring by regulation).

A Note on the 1990 Clean Air Act Amendments

While discharge monitoring reports under the Clean Water Act have often facilitated government and citizen enforcement, air pollution monitoring has often been limited to occasional stack tests, and has sometimes been absent altogether. These lax monitoring requirements, together with the lack of a general permit program, may have made enforcement far more complex and often ineffectual under the Clean Air Act than under the Clean Water Act. The 1990 Clean Air Act Amendments introduced a general operating permit program into the Clean Air Act for the first time. Section 114, introduced into the Act in 1990, also contains the following enhanced monitoring provision:

> (3) The Administrator shall in the case of any person which is the owner or operator of a major stationary source, and may, in the case of any other person, require enhanced monitoring and submission of compliance certifications. Compliance certifications shall include
>> (A) identification of the applicable requirement that is the basis of the certification,
>> (B) the method used for determining the compliance status of the source,
>> (C) the compliance status,
>> (D) whether compliance is continuous or intermittent,
>> (E) such other facts as the Administrator may require.

42 U.S.C. §7414(c)(3). Does this subsection require improvement of monitoring for any group of sources? Does it require the use of continuous monitoring? *See* Natural Resources Defense Council v. EPA, 194 F.3d 130, 138 (D.C. Cir. 1999) (holding that EPA's enhanced monitoring rule violated requirement to certify "whether compliance is 'continuous or intermittent,'" but upholding "compliance assurance monitoring"). Consider section 504(b) of the Act, which authorizes EPA to prescribe monitoring requirements, but states that "continuous emissions monitoring need not be required if alternative methods . . . provide sufficiently reliable . . . information for determining compliance." 42 U.S.C. §7661c(b). Does section 114, read together with this section, require continuous emissions monitoring for highly variable sources?

2. Reporting

In *U.S. Steel*, the monitoring seemed primarily aimed at enabling corporate compliance officials and EPA to detect non-compliance with effluent limits. In such cases, the reporting requirements inform enforcers about violations and facilitate enforcement. Obviously, honest reporting can aid in the detection of violations. But a system requiring self-reporting can fail if it does not provide adequate incentives to keep reporting honest.

Section 114(a)(3) of the Clean Air Act requires the owner or operator of major stationary sources to submit "compliance certifications," which "shall include the compliance status." 42 U.S.C. §7414(a)(3). Section 504(c) then requires "a responsible corporate official" to sign and "certify" the "accuracy" of any report "required . . . by a permit." 42 U.S.C. §7661c(c). Section 113(c)(1) of the Act makes knowing violation of this certification requirement a criminal offense. 42 U.S.C. §7413(c)(1). If an operator of a source signs a document certifying that the facility is in compliance when it is not in compliance, do criminal penalties apply? Under the Clean Water Act, a person who "knowingly makes any false material statement, representation, or certification" may receive fines of up to $10,000 and/or up to two years in prison. 33 U.S.C. §1319(c)(4). *Cf.* United States v. Kuhn, 345 F.3d 431, 433 (6th Cir. 2003) (reviewing criminal sentence for falsifying monitoring results in report submitted to the government); United States v. Sinskey, 119 F.3d 712, 718-20 (8th Cir. 1997) (upholding criminal conviction for falsifying reported monitoring results). Should the government require operators to certify whether or not the facility is in compliance and then punish false statements criminally? If you were a manager required to file the certification, would you simply rely on the reports submitted to you by your engineers, or would you take additional steps to assure the accuracy of the data? What additional steps would you take? If you were given numbers showing a violation, would you certify non-compliance with the Act's requirements? Requirements for operators to certify the compliance status of water dischargers and the possibility of severe penalties for false reporting led many operators to report discharges in excess of permit levels during the 1980s. This made enforcement relatively simple, since the reports themselves documented violations of discharge levels. *Cf.* United States v. Allegheny Ludlum Corp., 366 F.3d 164, 170-76 (3d Cir. 2004) (allowing a "laboratory error" defense, but noting a split of authority on the issue of whether a company should ever escape liability when its own reports document a violation).

EPA has required manufacturers to provide EPA with a list of "any toxic pollutant which the applicant currently uses or manufactures as an intermediate or final product or byproduct." Does such a requirement facilitate the enforcement of effluent standards? In justifying this reporting requirement, EPA claimed that this requirement would enable it to see if it needed to impose additional discharge limitations in a permit, provide guidance about what substances EPA should test for when it does inspections, and assist EPA in recommending best management practices to prevent spills. Are these purposes permissible justifications for reporting requirements under section 308? *See* Natural Resources Defense Council v. EPA, 822 F.2d 104, 117-19 (D.C. Cir. 1987).

CERCLA requires the person in charge of a facility to report "any release" of a hazardous substance that exceeds quantity thresholds EPA establishes to the National Response Center. *See* 42 U.S.C. §§9602, 9603. An overlapping provision in the Emergency Planning and Community Right to Know Act (EPCRA) requires immediate notification of state and local emergency coordinators after release of an "extremely hazardous substance." 42 U.S.C. §11004(a)-(b). Why the discrepancy in who gets the reports? What purposes do you suppose these provisions serve? What do you expect the agencies getting the reports to do with this information?

Here's how one district court described the purposes of these reporting requirements:

> The purpose of [sic] CERCLA notice requirement is to provide the EPA and other regulatory agencies with the information they need to assess hazards and mitigate potential injury from releases. Similarly, EPCRA establishes a framework of agencies designed to inform the public about the presence of hazardous and toxic chemicals, and to provide emergency response in the event of health-threatening releases. Without the required notices of alleged releases, regulatory agencies are without knowledge of the releases; and are consequently impeded from adequately mitigating the releases.

Sierra Club, Inc. v. Tyson Foods, Inc. 299 F. Supp. 2d 693, 705 (W.D. Ky. 2003). Under CERCLA, liability can attach for releases at levels below the reportable quantities. *See* United States v. Alcan Aluminum Corp., 990 F.2d 711, 720-21 (2d Cir. 1993) (holding that liability attaches regardless of the quantity of pollution released). Notice that the Clean Water Act reporting requirements envision reporting use of toxic pollutants that would probably not violate the Act. In any case, many environmental statutes have reporting requirements that allow the agency to calibrate a regulatory response or cope with an emergency, rather than solely to enforce existing pollution control obligations. *See generally* Roger M. Klein, *The Continuing Nature of Notification Violations Under Environmental Statutes*, 26 ENVTL. L. 565, 567 (1996) (stating that reporting allows EPA to minimize the effects of releases of toxic substances).

A Note on Audit Privileges

Since the 1970s, firms have set up systems to audit themselves in order to make themselves aware of possible violations of environmental laws, to improve environmental management, and/or to evaluate potential risks that could affect the firm. *See* William L. Thomas, Bertram C. Frey & Fern Fleischer Daves, *Using Auditing, Pollution Prevention, and Management Systems to Craft Superior Environmental Enforcement Solutions*, 30 ENVTL. L. REP. (ENVTL. L. INST.) 10299, 10300 (2000). These audits can go beyond specific monitoring duties established by specific regulation. EPA has generally encouraged these audits.

Questions have arisen about what role these audits should play in enforcement. On the one hand, audits might reveal useful information that could aid enforcement of environmental laws. On the other hand, if regulators routinely sought discovery of audits for enforcement purposes, this might discourage useful efforts by firms to self-police.

Consider the range of policies adopted respecting audits over time and in different jurisdictions. How do these policies differ? Which policy do you think is best?

EPA's 1986 audit policy. EPA generally refrained from requesting audits routinely as a method for detecting possible violations. But EPA reserved the right to request audit reports once a facility became a target for an investigation of a possible violation. EPA did not promise any particular relief to parties conducting audits, but retained the discretion to reduce penalties for parties that promptly disclosed violations of environmental laws and took appropriate remedial action.

EPA's 1995 self-policing policy. EPA may eliminate "gravity-based" penalties (*i.e.*, those that go beyond recouping the economic benefit realized through noncompliance) when facility operators find, promptly disclose, and correct violations found through an audit.

State audit shield laws. Several states have enacted statutes that shield companies from prosecution for violations uncovered through an audit.

Of course, the question of which policy one prefers directly implicates the debate between cooperative and deterrence-based approaches to compliance and enforcement. Should EPA require audits instead of providing incentives to get voluntary audits?

A National Conference of State Legislatures study concluded that "state audit privilege and immunity laws do not encourage facilities to begin auditing, to increase the number of audits they perform, or to disclose more violations to regulators." *See* Nancy K. Stoner & Wendy J. Miller, *National Conference of State Legislatures Study Finds That State Environmental Audit Laws Have No Impact on Company Self-Auditing and Disclosure of Violations*, 29 ENVTL. L. REP. (ENVTL. L. INST.) 10265, 10265 (1999). The same study found that "inspector presence" strongly motivates companies to audit. *Id.* If this study's conclusions are correct, what implications do these conclusions have for the choice of policy toward audits?

15

Government Enforcement

This chapter addresses what government does once it detects violations. It contains a section on civil penalties and one on criminal penalties. The deterrence/ cooperative enforcement debate influences the sanctions imposed for violations of environmental law. As you learn about the civil and criminal penalty provisions in the statutes, think about how they serve (or fail to serve) the deterrence goal. And think about how some of the reforms in enforcement policy in recent years reflect an increased reliance on a cooperative enforcement model.

A. CIVIL PENALTIES

The Clean Water Act contains the following civil penalty provision:

33 U.S.C. §1319. Enforcement

(d) Civil penalties; factors considered in determining amount

Any person who violates [certain Federal Water Pollution Control Act requirements] shall be subject to a civil penalty not to exceed $25,000 per day for each violation. In determining the amount of a civil penalty the court shall consider the seriousness of the violation or violations, the economic benefit (if any) resulting from the violation, any history of such violations, any good-faith efforts to comply with the applicable requirements, the economic impact of the penalty on the violator, and such other matters as justice may require. For purposes of this subsection, a single operational upset which leads to simultaneous violations of more than one pollutant parameter shall be treated as a single violation.

1. Maximum Penalty

This provision is similar to comparable provisions in other environmental statutes. *See, e.g.,* 42 U.S.C. §7413(e). Suppose that a discharger violates effluent limits for biological oxygen demand and for nutrient loadings for one day. What is the maximum penalty? Suppose that she violates one effluent limit for 40 days. What is the maximum penalty? Does EPA have discretion to ask for less than the maximum penalty?

The Clean Air Act also provides a maximum penalty of $25,000 per day of violation. 42 U.S.C. §7413(b). In 2003, a federal district court concluded that Ohio Edison Company failed to install state-of-the-art pollution control devices when it modified its facility on several occasions between 1984 and 1998, as required by the new source review provisions of the Clean Air Act. *See* United States v. Ohio Edison Co., 276 F. Supp. 2d 829 (S.D. Ohio 2003). Ohio Edison subsequently agreed to spend $1.1 billion on pollution control, $25 million for supplemental environmental projects (cleanup projects going beyond the polluters' existing legal obligations), and pay a civil penalty of $8.5 million. Why do you think Ohio Edison agreed to such an expensive settlement? Three oil refiners also settled new source review enforcement actions by agreeing to spend $1 billion on pollution control. *See Three Oil Refiners to Spend $1 Billion to Reduce Air Emissions, Pay Penalties*, 36 ENVTL. RPTR. (BNA) 1279 (June 24, 2005). *Cf. Trial to Begin July 6 in Enforcement Case Against American Electric Power in Ohio*, 36 ENVTL. RPTR. (BNA) 1281 (June 24, 2005).

2. Gravity-Based Penalty

Notice that section 309 (and other similar provisions as well) requires courts to take into account the seriousness of the violation. EPA refers to penalties based on the seriousness of violations as gravity-based penalties. Do you think that gravity-based penalties advance deterrence? Or would deterrence be better served by having uniform penalties, regardless of the seriousness of the violation? Should courts assume that harm is very serious when releases greatly exceed permit limits, or only when concrete harms to human health from the release are proven in court?

3. Economic Benefit

The Clean Water Act requires consideration of the economic benefits of non-compliance in assessing a civil penalty. In the following case, a district court explained how the economic benefit factor is taken into account, in part through a reference to a model known as "BEN" that EPA uses to calculate economic benefit:

> The Defendant, as a holder of an NPDES discharge permit, should not profit from noncompliance with that permit. If [the South Carolina Department of Health and Environmental Control] DHEC assessed a penalty that was below the Defendant's economic benefit of noncompliance, DHEC would not have penalized the Defendant at all; instead, the Defendant would have been rewarded for noncompliance with its permit. Economic benefit is the after-tax present value of avoided or delayed expenditures on necessary pollution control measures. Economic benefit represents the opportunity a polluter had to earn a return on funds that should have been spent to purchase, operate, and maintain appropriate pollution control devices. To determine a company's economic benefit from noncompliance with its permit, one must compare the company's cash flows associated with the delayed permit compliance measures to

what those cash flows would have been if the company had obtained the necessary pollution control equipment on time.

EPA describes the nature of the economic benefit enjoyed by a firm that delays compliance with pollution control laws as follows:

> An organization's decision to comply with environmental regulations usually implies a commitment of financial resources; both initially, in the form of a capital investment or one-time expenditure, and over time, in the form of annual, continuing expenses. These expenditures might result in better protection of public health or environmental quality; however, they are unlikely to yield any direct economic benefit (i.e., net gain) to the organization. If these financial resources were not used for compliance, they presumably would be invested in projects with an expected direct economic benefit to the organization. This concept of alternative investment; that is, the amount the violator would normally expect to make by not investing in pollution control, is the basis for calculating the economic benefit of noncompliance.
>
> As part of the Civil Penalty Policy, EPA uses the Agency's penalty authority to remove or neutralize the economic incentive to violate environmental regulations. In the absence of enforcement and appropriate penalties, it is usually in the organization's best economic interest to delay the commitment of funds for compliance with environmental regulations and to avoid certain other associated costs, such as operating and maintenance expenses.

Friends of the Earth v. Laidlaw Environmental Services, Inc., 890 F. Supp. 470, 481 (D.S.C. 1995), *vacated on other grounds*, 149 F.3d 303 (4th Cir. 1998), *reversed*, 528 U.S. 167 (2000) (quoting EPA, *BEN User's Manual* I-6 (July 1990)). Because DHEC had not recouped the economic benefit Laidlaw had realized for its non-compliance when it filed a collusive lawsuit, the *Laidlaw* court found that the state had not diligently prosecuted Laidlaw and allowed a citizen suit to proceed. *Id.* at 499. The court later resolved a battle of economic expert witnesses and concluded that Laidlaw's non-compliance saved it $1,092,581. Friends of the Earth v. Laidlaw Environmental Services, 956 F. Supp. 588, 603 (D.S.C. 1997). *See generally* United States v. Municipal Auth. of Union Township, 150 F.3d 259, 264-65 (3d Cir. 1998) (district court judgments of economic benefit need not be precise because of the difficulty of determining economic benefit). Nevertheless, the district court awarded a penalty of only $405,800, because Laidlaw had incurred substantial legal expenses and would have to pay the attorneys' fees of its opponents. *Laidlaw*, 956 F. Supp. at 610-11. Was that appropriate? Which do you think is more difficult: proving a violation of a discharge limitation when monitoring data is accurate and reasonably frequent, or proving the economic benefit realized by non-compliance? More generally, a deterrence model seems to require confiscation of economic benefits derived from avoiding pollution control requirements.

4. Collection

Surprisingly often, the government fails to collect all, or even a substantial portion of the fine assessed in an enforcement action. *See* Martha Mendoza & Christopher Sullivan, *Billions Uncollected in Penalties for Wrongdoing: How Does It Happen?: The System Punishes Symbolically, Imposing Massive Fines*, SALT LAKE

TRIBUNE, Mar. 19, 2006, available at http://www.sltrib.com/nationworld/ci_3618149; *see also* EPA OFFICE OF INSPECTOR GENERAL, EPA NEEDS TO IMPROVE ITS REPORTING OF FINES AND PENALTIES (2010) (noting that EPA often fails to track or disclose actual collection of penalties). Government officials defended the frequent practice of drastically reducing penalties, sometimes even after announcing them to the public, by explaining that the agency's goal is "compliance," not the collection of penalties. Does reduction of assessed penalties serve the compliance goal?

A Note on Supplemental Environmental Projects

Most cases, of course, produce settlements, not trials. The settlements usually involve some combination of penalties and an agreement to take specific steps to remedy the violations. Increasingly, however, EPA has become interested in including requirements for supplemental environmental projects (SEPs), projects that go beyond merely correcting violations to provide affirmative, but not legally required, environmental benefits. *See* Final EPA Supplemental Environmental Projects Policy Issued, 63 Fed. Reg. 24796 (May 5, 1998) [hereinafter *SEP Policy*]. Commentators have praised the inclusion of these projects as mechanisms to benefit communities damaged by pollution. *See, e.g.*, Kathleen Boergers, *The EPA's Supplemental Environmental Projects Policy*, 26 ECOLOGY L.Q. 777 (1999); Jeff Ganguly, *Environmental Remediation Through Supplemental Environmental Projects and Creative Negotiation: Renewed Community Involvement in Federal Enforcement*, 26 B.C. ENVTL. AFF. L. REV. 189 (1998-1999).

In order to obtain the benefit of a SEP, EPA will sometimes agree to decrease a gravity-based penalty. This poses a significant legal issue, since both the environmental statutes and the Miscellaneous Receipts Act generally require that civil penalties go to the United States Treasury. 31 U.S.C. §3302(b) (2000); Gwaltney of Smithfield, Ltd. v. Chesapeake Bay Foundation, 484 U.S. 49, 53 (1987) (stating that if a citizen prevails in a citizen suit, the court may impose a civil penalty "payable to the U.S. Treasury"). *Cf.* 42 U.S.C. §7604(g)(2) (2000) (authorizing use of a portion of a civil penalty to fund certain "beneficial mitigation projects"). If violators of environmental statutes spend money that would otherwise have gone to the Treasury to fund a SEP, this raises a question of whether civil penalties have been illegally diverted. *See* Sierra Club v. Elec. Controls Design, 909 F.2d 1350, 1352-56 (9th Cir. 1990) (allowing payment to an environmental organization "for their efforts to . . . protect" Oregon water quality, because no liability has been found, so no civil penalty has been diverted); Public Interest Research Group of New Jersey v. Powell Duffryn Terminals, Inc., 913 F.2d 64, 81-82 (3d Cir. 1990) (stating that "once the court labeled the money as civil penalties it could only be paid to the Treasury").

Accordingly, EPA's 1998 policy on SEPs requires that the minimum penalty assessed must remain greater than the economic benefit the polluter realized by not complying with the law. *See SEP Policy*, 63 Fed. Reg. at 24801. Should EPA reduce gravity-based penalties in exchange for SEPs? Should EPA collect less of a monetary penalty than required to deprive the violator of any economic benefit from the violation? EPA has suggested that it may reconsider the requirement of making penalties adequate to confiscate any economic benefit, while noting that the 1998 guidance "is based upon the premise that collection of at least economic benefit ensures that violators are not allowed to obtain an economic advantage over their competitors who complied with the law." Memorandum from John Peter Suarez, Assistant Adm'r, EPA, to Various Administrators and Staff, Expanding the Use of Supplemental Environmental Projects 3 (July 11, 2003), available at http://www.epa.gov/compliance/resources/policies/civil/seps/seps-expandinguse.pdf. Does this premise hold up? Is this the best rationale for the policy? Should EPA approve profitable SEPs? Would more liberal SEP policies better serve deterrence? Would they create a more cooperative atmosphere? Which is more important?

In Public Interest Research Group of New Jersey v. Powell Duffryn Terminals, Inc., 913 F.2d 64, 82 (3d Cir. 1990), the Third Circuit stated that payments to an environmental benefit fund could qualify as injunctive relief if there is a "nexus" between the harm and the remedy. To the extent SEP payments are regarded as injunctive relief, the monies spent upon them do not fall into the category of civil penalties, which must go the Treasury, rather than to community or industry environmental projects. In 1993, EPA settled a case involving mobile source emission reductions by accepting public relations expenditures in exchange for a reduction in civil penalties. The Comptroller General questioned the legality of this settlement under the Miscellaneous Receipts Act because of the lack of nexus between the public relation expenditures and the harm from violating pollution control requirements, notwithstanding language in the relevant section of the Clean Air Act, 42 U.S.C. §7524, authorizing EPA to "compromise" civil penalties "with conditions." Opinion of the Comptroller General of the United States, GAO No. B-247155.2, available at 1993 WL 798227 (Mar. 1, 1993). *See also* Opinion of the Comptroller General of the United States, GAO No. B-247155.2, available at 1992 WL 726317 (July 7, 1992). Suppose that the public relations campaign touted the benefits of low emission vehicles for the environment. Do you think that expenditures for this purpose have an adequate nexus to the harms done by violating mobile source pollution control requirements to qualify as appropriate injunctive relief?

Should problems of potential sweetheart deals lead to the abandonment of the possible environmental gains from SEPs? Should EPA allow companies to "promote" compliance in their industry by holding seminars as a SEP? *See SEP Policy*, 63 Fed. Reg. at 24800. What about environmental audits? *Id.* at 24799-800. Funding of university environmental research? *Id.* at 24801.

The pollution control statutes generally authorize courts to award any "appropriate relief." *See, e.g.*, 42 U.S.C. §7413(b). Why not just ask the court to order a SEP in addition to penalties, rather than induce one through penalty reduction?

In any case, civil remedies include fines and injunctions. The SEPs provide, in principle, a means of trading off some of the fines for agreement to a broad form of injunctive relief. But, these are not the only potential consequences of violations of pollution control statutes.

B. CRIMINAL PENALTIES

Several statutes now supplement civil penalties with criminal penalties for certain kinds of violations. These penalties certainly have galvanized the attention of the regulated community and serve deterrence. But they have raised fairness concerns. The cases that follow focus on the problem of defining the sorts of violations that trigger criminal penalties. Generally, criminal penalties properly apply to only a subset of all violations.

United States v. Weitzenhoff

35 F.3d 1275 (9th Cir. 1993) (en banc)

FLETCHER, CIRCUIT JUDGE.

Michael H. Weitzenhoff and Thomas W. Mariani, who managed the East Honolulu Community Services Sewage Treatment Plant, appeal their convictions for violations of the Clean Water Act ("CWA"), contending that the district court misconstrued the word "knowingly" under section 1319(c)(2) of the CWA.

We affirm the convictions.

B. Facts and Procedural History

In 1988 and 1989 Weitzenhoff was the manager and Mariani the assistant manager of the East Honolulu Community Services Sewage Treatment Plant ("the plant"), located not far from Sandy Beach, a popular swimming and surfing beach on Oahu. The plant is designed to treat some 4 million gallons of residential wastewater each day by removing the solids and other harmful pollutants from the sewage so that the resulting effluent can be safely discharged into the ocean. The plant operates under a permit issued pursuant to the National Pollution Discharge Elimination System ("NPDES"), which established the limits on the Total Suspended Solids ("TSS") and Biochemical Oxygen Demand ("BOD") indicators of the solid and organic matter, respectively, in the effluent discharged at Sandy Beach. During the period in question, the permit limited the discharge of both the TSS and BOD to an average of 976 pounds per day over a 30-day period. It also imposed monitoring and sampling requirements on the plant's management.

. . . [W]aste activated sludge ("WAS") was pumped to WAS holding tanks. From the holding tanks, the WAS could either be returned to other phases of the treatment process or hauled away to a different sewage treatment facility.

From March 1987 through March 1988, the excess WAS generated by the plant was hauled away to another treatment plant. . . . In March 1988, certain improvements were made to the East Honolulu plant and the hauling was discontinued. Within a few weeks, however, the plant began experiencing a buildup of excess WAS. Rather than have the excess WAS hauled away as before, however, Weitzenhoff and Mariani instructed two employees at the plant to dispose of it on a regular basis by pumping it from the storage tanks directly into the outfall, that is, directly into the ocean. The WAS thereby bypassed the plant's effluent sampler so that the samples taken and reported to Hawaii's Department of Health ("DOH") and the EPA did not reflect its discharge.

The evidence produced by the government at trial showed that WAS was discharged directly into the ocean from the plant on about 40 separate occasions from April 1988 to June 1989, resulting in some 436,000 pounds of pollutant solids being discharged into the ocean, and that the discharges violated the plant's 30-day average effluent limit under the permit for most of the months during which they occurred. Most of the WAS discharges occurred during the night, and none was reported to the DOH or EPA. DOH inspectors contacted the plant on several occasions in 1988 in response to complaints by lifeguards at Sandy Beach that sewage was being emitted from the outfall, but Weitzenhoff and Mariani repeatedly denied that there was any problem at the plant. In one letter responding to a DOH inquiry in October 1988, Mariani stated that "the debris that was reported could not have been from the East Honolulu Wastewater Treatment facility, as our records of effluent quality up to this time will substantiate." One of the plant employees who participated in the dumping operation testified that Weitzenhoff instructed him not to say anything about the discharges, because if they all stuck together and did not reveal anything, "they [couldn't] do anything to us."

Following an FBI investigation, Weitzenhoff and Mariani were charged in a thirty-one-count indictment with conspiracy and substantive violations of the Clean Water Act ("CWA"). At trial, Weitzenhoff and Mariani admitted having authorized the discharges, but claimed that their actions were justified under their interpretation of the NPDES permit. The jury found them guilty of six of the thirty-one counts.

Weitzenhoff was sentenced to twenty-one months and Mariani thirty-three months imprisonment. Each filed a timely notice of appeal.

Discussion

A. Intent Requirement

Section 1311(a) of the CWA prohibits the discharge of pollutants into navigable waters without an NPDES permit. 33 U.S.C. §1311(a). Section 1319(c)(2) makes it a felony offense to "knowingly violate section 1311, 1312, 1316, 1317, 1318, 1321(b)(3), 1328, or 1345, or any permit condition or limitation implementing any of such sections in a permit issued under section 1342."

Prior to trial, the district court construed "knowingly" in section 1319(c)(2) as requiring only that Weitzenhoff and Mariani were aware that they were discharging the pollutants in question, not that they knew they were violating the terms of the statute or permit. According to appellants, the district court erred in its interpretation of the CWA and in instructing the jury that "the government is not required to prove that the defendant knew that his act or omissions were unlawful," as well as in rejecting their proposed instruction based on the defense that they mistakenly believed their conduct was authorized by the permit. Apparently, no court of appeals has confronted the issue raised by appellants.

As with certain other criminal statutes that employ the term "knowingly," it is not apparent from the face of the statute whether "knowingly" means a knowing violation of the law or simply knowing conduct that is violative of the law. We turn, then, to the legislative history of the provision at issue to ascertain what Congress intended.

In 1987, Congress substantially amended the CWA, elevating the penalties for violations of the Act. Increased penalties were considered necessary to deter would-be polluters. With the 1987 amendments, Congress substituted "knowingly" for the earlier intent requirement of "willfully" that appeared in the predecessor to section 1319(c)(2). The Senate report accompanying the legislation explains that the changes in the penalty provisions were to ensure that "criminal liability shall attach to any person who is not in compliance with all applicable Federal, State and local requirements and permits *and causes* a POTW [publicly owned treatment works] to violate any effluent limitation or condition in any permit issued to the treatment works." Similarly, the report accompanying the House version of the bill, which contained parallel provisions for enhancement of penalties, states that the proposed amendments were to "provide penalties for dischargers or individuals who knowingly or negligently violate *or cause the violation of* certain of the Act's requirements." Because they speak in terms of "causing" a violation, the congressional explanations of the new penalty provisions strongly suggest that criminal sanctions are to be imposed on an individual who knowingly engages in conduct that results in a permit violation, regardless of whether the polluter is cognizant of the requirements or even the existence of the permit.

Our conclusion that "knowingly" does not refer to the legal violation is fortified by decisions interpreting analogous public welfare statutes. The leading case in this area is United States v. International Minerals & Chem. Corp., 402 U.S. 558 (1971). In *International Minerals*, the Supreme Court construed a statute which made it a crime to "knowingly violate any regulation" promulgated by the [Interstate Commerce Commission] pursuant to 18 U.S.C. §834(a), a provision authorizing the agency to formulate regulations for the safe transport of corrosive liquids. The Court held that the term "knowingly" referred to the acts made criminal rather than a violation of the regulation, and that "regulation" was a shorthand designation for the specific acts or omissions contemplated by the act. "Where . . . dangerous or deleterious devices or products or obnoxious waste materials are involved, the probability of regulation is so great that anyone who is aware that he is in possession of them or dealing with them must be presumed to be aware of the regulation."

[The court discusses its own precedent and cases in other jurisdictions following *International Minerals* in various cases, including several environmental cases.]

Subsequent to the filing of the original opinion in this case, the Supreme Court decided two cases which Weitzenhoff contends call our analysis into question. *See* Ratzlaf v. United States, 510 U.S. 135 (1994); Staples v. United States, 511 U.S. 600 (1994). We disagree.

The statute in *Ratzlaf* does not deal with a public welfare offense, but rather with violations of the banking statutes. . . . In contrast, parties such as Weitzenhoff are closely regulated and are discharging waste materials that affect public health. The *International Minerals* rationale requires that we impute to these parties knowledge of their operating permit. This was recognized by the Court in *Staples*.

The specific holding in *Staples* was that the government is required to prove that a defendant charged with possession of a machine gun knew that the weapon he possessed had the characteristics that brought it within the statutory definition of a machine gun. But the Court took pains to contrast the gun laws to other regulatory regimes, specifically those regulations that govern the handling of "obnoxious waste materials." It noted that the mere innocent ownership of guns is not a public welfare offense. The Court focused on the long tradition of widespread gun ownership in this country and, recognizing that approximately 50% of American homes contain a firearm, acknowledged that mere ownership of a gun is not sufficient to place people on notice that the act of owning an unregistered firearm is not innocent under the law.

Staples thus explicitly contrasted the mere possession of guns to public welfare offenses, which include statutes that regulate ["]dangerous or deleterious devices or products or obnoxious waste materials["], and confirmed the continued vitality of statutes covering public welfare offenses, which "regulate potentially harmful or injurious items" and place a defendant on notice that he is dealing with a device or a substance "that places him in 'responsible relation to a public danger.'" . . . "In such cases Congress intended to place the burden on the defendant to ascertain at his peril whether [his conduct] comes within the inhibition of the statute."

Unlike "[g]uns [which] in general are not 'deleterious devices or products or obnoxious waste materials,' that put their owners on notice that they stand 'in responsible relation to a public danger[,']" the dumping of sewage and other pollutants into our nation's waters is precisely the type of activity that puts the discharger on notice that his acts may pose a public danger. Like other public welfare offenses that regulate the discharge of pollutants into the air, the disposal of hazardous wastes, the undocumented shipping of acids, and the use of pesticides on our food, the improper and excessive discharge of sewage causes cholera, hepatitis, and other serious illnesses, and can have serious repercussions for public health and welfare.

The criminal provisions of the CWA are clearly designed to protect the public at large from the potentially dire consequences of water pollution and as such fall within the category of public welfare legislation. *International Minerals* . . . controls the case at hand. The government did not need to prove that Weitzenhoff and Mariani knew that their acts violated the permit or the CWA. . . .

We *AFFIRM* both the convictions.

KLEINFELD, CIRCUIT JUDGE, with whom CIRCUIT JUDGES REINHARDT, KOZINSKI, TROTT, and THOMAS G. NELSON join, dissenting from the order rejecting the suggestion for rehearing en banc.

I respectfully dissent from our decision to reject the suggestion for rehearing en banc.

. . . In my view, this is a case of exceptional importance, for two reasons. First, it impairs a fundamental purpose of criminal justice, sorting out the innocent from the guilty before imposing punishment. Second, it does so in the context of the Clean Water Act. This statute has tremendous sweep. Most statutes permit anything except what is prohibited, but this one prohibits all regulated conduct involving waters and wetlands except what is permitted. Much more ordinary, innocent, productive activity is regulated by this law than people not versed in environmental law might imagine.

. . . If we use prison to achieve social goals regardless of the moral innocence of those we incarcerate, then imprisonment loses its moral opprobrium and our criminal law becomes morally arbitrary.

We have now made felons of a large number of innocent people doing socially valuable work. They are innocent, because the one thing which makes their conduct felonious is something they do not know. It is we, and not Congress, who have made them felons. The statute, read in an ordinary way, does not. If we are fortunate, sewer plant workers around the circuit will continue to perform their vitally important work despite our decision. If they knew they risk three years in prison, some might decide that their pay, though sufficient inducement for processing the public's wastes, is not enough to risk prison for doing their jobs. We have decided that they should go to prison if, unbeknownst to them, their plant discharges exceed permit limits. Likewise for power plant operators who discharge warm water into rivers near their plants, and for all sorts of other dischargers in public and private life. If they know they are discharging into water, have a permit for the discharges, think they are conforming to their permits, but unknowingly violate their permit conditions, into prison they go with the violent criminals.

The statute does not say that. The statute at issue makes it a felony, subject to three years of imprisonment, to "knowingly violate[] . . . any permit condition or limitation." 33 U.S.C. §1319(c)(2)(A). . . .

In this case, the defendants, sewage plant operators, had a permit to discharge sewage into the ocean, but exceeded the permit limitations. The legal issue for the panel was what knowledge would turn innocently or negligently violating a permit into "knowingly" violating a permit. Were the plant operators felons if they knew they were discharging sewage, but did not know that they were violating their permit? Or did they also have to know they were violating their permit? Ordinary English grammar, common sense, and precedent, all compel the latter construction.

. . . NPDES permits are often difficult to understand and obey. The EPA had licensed the defendants' plant to discharge 976 pounds of waste per day, or about 409,920 pounds over the fourteen months covered by the indictment, into the ocean. The wrongful conduct was not discharging waste into the ocean. That was socially desirable conduct by which the defendants protected the people of their city from sewage-borne disease and earned their pay. The wrongful conduct was violating the NPDES permit by discharging 26,000 more pounds of waste than the permit authorized during the fourteen months. Whether these defendants were innocent or not, in the sense of knowing that they were exceeding their permit limitation, the panel's holding will make innocence irrelevant in other permit violation cases where the defendants had no idea that they were exceeding permit limits. The only thing they have to know to be guilty is that they were dumping sewage into the ocean, yet that was a lawful activity expressly authorized by their federal permit.

The statute says "knowingly violates . . . any permit condition or limitation." "Knowingly" is an adverb. It modifies the verb "violates." The object of the verb is "any permit condition or limitation." The word "knowingly" is placed before "violates" to "explain its meaning in the case at hand more clearly." Congress has distinguished those who knowingly violate permit conditions, and are thereby felons, from those who unknowingly violate permit conditions, so are not. The panel reads the statute as though it says "knowingly discharges pollutants." It does not. If we read the statute on the assumption that Congress used the English language in an ordinary way, the state of mind required is knowledge that one is violating a permit condition.

This approach has the virtue of attributing common sense and a rational purpose to Congress. It is one thing to defy a permit limitation, but quite another to violate it without realizing that one is violating it. Congress promulgated a parallel statute making it a misdemeanor "negligently" to violate a permit condition or limitation. 33 U.S.C. §1319(c)(1)(A). If negligent violation is a misdemeanor, why would Congress want to make it a felony to violate the permit without negligence and without even knowing that the discharge exceeded the permit limit? . . .

. . . [F]or the sake of discussion, suppose that the statute is ambiguous, as the panel says. Then the rule of lenity requires that the construction allowing the defendant more liberty rather than less be applied by the courts. "Lenity principles demand resolution of ambiguities in criminal statutes in favor of the defendant." The reason is the need for "fair warning."

The panel . . . tries to bolster its construction by categorizing the offense as a "public welfare offense," as though that justified more aggressive criminalization without a plain statutory command. This category is a modernized version of "malum prohibitum." Traditionally the criminal law distinguishes between *malum in se*, conduct wrong upon principles of natural moral law, and *malum prohibitum*, conduct not inherently immoral but wrong because prohibited by law. To put this in plain, modern terms, any normal person knows murder, rape and robbery are wrong, and they would be wrong even in a place with no sovereign and no law. Discharging 6% more pollutants than one's permit allows is wrong only because the law says so. Substitution of the modern term "public welfare offense" for the traditional one, *malum prohibitum*, allows for confusion by rhetorical suggestion. The new term suggests that other offenses might merely be private in their impact, and therefore less serious. The older set of terms made it clear that murder was more vile than violating a federal regulation. The category of *malum prohibitum*, or public welfare offenses, makes the rule of lenity especially important, most particularly for felonies, because persons of good conscience may not recognize the wrongfulness of the conduct when they engage in it.

Staples v. United States reminds us that "offenses that require no *mens rea* generally are disfavored." *Mens rea* may be dispensed with in public welfare offenses, but the penalty is a "significant consideration in determining whether the statute should be construed as dispensing with *mens rea*."

The potentially harsh penalty attached to violation of §5861(d)—up to 10 years' imprisonment—confirms our reading of the Act. Historically, the penalty imposed under a statute has been a significant consideration in determining whether the statute should be construed as dispensing with *mens rea*. Certainly, the cases that first defined the concept of the public welfare offense almost uniformly involved statutes that provided for only light penalties such as fines or short jail sentences, not imprisonment in the state penitentiary. . . .

Precedent cuts strongly against the panel's decision. Two Supreme Court decisions came down this term which should have caused us to rehear the case.

Ratzlaf v. United States, reversing a decision of ours, holds that to commit the crime of "willfully violating" the law against structuring cash transactions to evade currency transaction reporting requirements, the defendant has to know that his conduct is unlawful. It is not enough that he is engaging in the cash transactions with a purpose of evading currency transaction reporting requirements. Ignorance of the law generally is no excuse, but "Congress may decree otherwise." The Court was concerned that a narrower reading of the mental element of the crime would criminalize conduct committed without the criminal motive with which Congress was concerned.

At issue in *Staples v. United States* was a statute which made it a felony to possess an unregistered "firearm." The statute defined "firearm" to include a fully automatic gun, which would fire more than one bullet on a single pull of the trigger, but not a semiautomatic. The defendant possessed a fully automatic gun, but testified that he did not know it would fire more than one bullet with a single trigger pull. The trial judge had instructed the jury that his ignorance did not matter, so long as the government proved he possessed "a dangerous device of a type as would alert one to the likelihood of regulation." The Supreme Court again rejected dilution of the mental element of the crime. The Court explained that unlike the hand grenades in United States v. Freed, 401 U.S. 601 (1971), semiautomatics are innocently possessed by many people. Nor was knowledge that guns are regulated enough to require the owner to ascertain compliance with the regulations at his peril. That might do for a misdemeanor, but the felony status of the offense suggested a more plainly criminal mental state. Nor would the dangerousness of guns suffice to weaken the *mens rea* requirement:

> If we were to accept as a general rule the Government's suggestion that dangerous and regulated items place their owners under an obligation to inquire at their peril into compliance with regulations, we would undoubtedly reach some untoward results. Automobiles, for example, might also be termed "dangerous" devices and are highly regulated at both the state and federal levels. Congress might see fit to criminalize the violation of certain regulations concerning automobiles, and thus might make it a crime to operate a vehicle without a properly functioning emission control system. But we probably would hesitate to conclude on the basis of silence that Congress intended a prison term to apply to a car owner whose vehicle's emissions levels, wholly unbeknownst to him, began to exceed legal limits between regular inspection dates.

Staples, 511 U.S. [at 614].

The panel cites *United States v. International Minerals & Chem. Corp.*, 402 U.S. 558 (1971), in support of its reading. *International Minerals* was a pre-*Ratzlaf* misdemeanor case. Because of the syntactically similar statute at issue in that case, it is the strongest authority for the panel's decision and raises the most serious question for my own analysis. It held that a shipper of sulfuric acid could be convicted of violating a statute applying to those who "knowingly violate[ ]" regulations governing shipments of corrosive liquids, regardless of whether he had knowledge of the regulations. *International Minerals* expressly limits its holding to "dangerous or deleterious devices or products or obnoxious waste materials." The Court distinguished materials not obviously subject to regulation:

> Pencils, dental floss, paper clips may also be regulated. But they may be the type of products which might raise substantial due process questions if Congress did not require "*mens rea*" as

to each ingredient of the offense. But where, as here, dangerous or deleterious devices or products or obnoxious waste materials are involved, the probability of regulation is so great that anyone who is aware that he is in possession of them or dealing with them must be presumed to be aware of the regulation.

Id. at 564-65.

International Minerals would have much persuasive force for Weitzenhoff, because of the grammatical similarity of the statute, if (1) the Clean Water Act limited pollutants to "dangerous or deleterious devices or products or obnoxious waste materials"; (2) the crime was only a misdemeanor; and (3) *Staples* had not come down this term. But all three of these conditions are contrary to fact. The pollutants to which the Clean Water Act felony statute applies include many in the "pencils, dental floss, paper clips" category. Hot water, rock, and sand are classified as "pollutants" by the Clean Water Act. *See* 33 U.S.C. §1362(6). Discharging silt from a stream back into the same stream may amount to discharge of a pollutant. For that matter, so may skipping a stone into a lake. So may a cafeteria worker's pouring hot, stale coffee down the drain. Making these acts a misdemeanor is one thing, but a felony is quite another, as *Staples* teaches.

Congress made it a serious felony "knowingly" to violate permit limitations on discharge of pollutants. The harsh penalty for this serious crime must be reserved for those who know they are, in fact, violating permit limitations.

NOTES AND QUESTIONS ON KNOWING VIOLATIONS

1. *Majority versus dissent.* Do you agree with the majority or the dissent in *Weitzenhoff*? Why?

2. *Fairness.* Is it fair to hold defendants liable for discharges if they do not know that they violate a permit? The permit at issue in *Weitzenhoff* authorized operators to bypass treatment and discharge effluent directly into the ocean for "essential maintenance to assure efficient operation." *Weitzenhoff*, 35 F.3d at 1287. Consider the following hypothetical variant on the *Weitzenhoff* problem. Suppose that Weitzenhoff can prove that accumulating sludge threatened to impede efficient operation of the plant. He consults with legal counsel who affirms, in good faith, that Weitzenhoff may legally discharge directly into the ocean, which he then does openly without trying to deceive anybody. EPA, however, ultimately disagrees with Weitzenhoff's interpretation of the permit condition authorizing bypass. EPA does not consider the bypass "essential" maintenance, because Weitzenhoff could have stored the waste or treated it off-site. EPA charges Weitzenhoff with "knowingly" violating his plant's NPDES permit. The court agrees with EPA's interpretation of the permit condition, reasoning that EPA could reasonably interpret the permit to deem bypass unessential when any plausible alternative existed. Should Weitzenhoff be held criminally liable for the violation?

What if the bypass only violated the bypass provision of the permit, but the discharge did not exceed effluent limitations? This would still be a violation of the permit, because permits forbid bypass unless one falls within the authorizing clause. But should it be a criminal violation? If not, should the law prohibit criminal prosecution under these circumstances, or should prosecutors employ discretion to eschew legally authorized criminal charges in this situation? Do you think that EPA would charge Weitzenhoff criminally under these facts?

3. *The limits of a knowing violation.* Suppose that Weitzenhoff had dumped the sludge into a pipe that he thought conducted the sludge into the treatment system. In fact, however, unknown to him, maintenance workers had rerouted the pipe to discharge directly into the ocean. If the effluent so discharged exceeded permit limits would there be a violation of the Act? Would the violation trigger criminal sanctions?

4. *Similar provisions.* Similar provisions exist in many other environmental statutes. *See, e.g.,* 15 U.S.C. §2615(b) (criminalizing knowing or willful violations of several TSCA provisions); 42 U.S.C. §7413(c) (criminal penalties for knowing violations of the Clean Air Act); §9603(b)(3), (c) (CERCLA); §11045(b)(4) (criminal penalties for knowing violations of one Emergency Planning and Community Right to Know Act provision); §6928(d) (criminal penalties for knowing violations of RCRA). Notice that the courts frequently consider interpretation of enforcement provisions in other statutes in interpreting a particular statutory provision. *See generally* William W. Buzbee, *The One Congress Fiction in Statutory Interpretation,* 149 U. Pa. L. Rev. 171 (2000).

5. *Knowing endangerment.* RCRA authorizes prison sentences of up to 15 years if a person illegally and "knowingly transports, treats, stores, disposes of, or exports" hazardous waste if he "knows . . . that he thereby places another person in imminent danger of death or serious bodily injury." 42 U.S.C. §6928(e). RCRA also authorizes criminal sanctions for knowing violations of RCRA if the violator does not endanger anybody or does not know that she does. *See* 42 U.S.C. §6928(d). But the maximum prison terms for first-time violations not involving knowing endangerment are two years of imprisonment for most violations and five years for some of them. *See id.* Should any criminal penalty apply if the violator does not know that the acts put another in imminent danger?

In United States v. Hansen, 262 F.3d 1217 (11th Cir. 2001), the Court of Appeals for the Eleventh Circuit upheld the conviction of two CEOs and a plant manager for conspiracy to violate a number of environmental statutes and for knowing endangerment under RCRA. The knowing endangerment conviction arose out of the storage of highly caustic wastewater in a basement. Employees coming into contact with this wastewater testified that they suffered serious skin and respiratory conditions as a result. *Id.* at 1243. Suppose that nobody had suffered any serious bodily harm, but that the wastewater had the capacity to cause serious bodily harm. Should the court uphold a conviction for knowing endangerment?

≡ **United States v. Ahmad**
≡ *101 F.3d 386 (5th Cir. 1996)*

Smith, Circuit Judge.

Attique Ahmad appeals his conviction of, and sentence for, criminal violations of the Clean Water Act ("CWA"). Concluding that the district court erred in its instructions to the jury, we reverse and remand.

I

This case arises from the discharge of a large quantity of gasoline into the sewers of Conroe, Texas, in January 1994. In 1992, Ahmad purchased the "Spin-N-Market No. 12," a combination convenience store and gas station. . . . Some time after Ahmad bought the station, he discovered that one of the tanks, which held high-octane gasoline, was leaking. This did not pose an immediate hazard, because the leak was at the top of the tank; gasoline could not seep out. The leak did, however, allow water to enter into the tank and contaminate the gas. . . .

In October 1993, Ahmad hired CTT Environmental Services ("CTT"), a tank testing company, to examine the tank. CTT determined that it contained approximately 800 gallons of water, and the rest [7,200 gallons] mostly gasoline. Jewel McCoy, a CTT employee, testified that she told Ahmad that the leak could not be repaired until the tank was completely emptied, which CTT offered to do for 65 cents per gallon plus $65 per hour of labor. After McCoy gave Ahmad this estimate, he inquired whether he could empty the tank himself. She replied that it would be dangerous and illegal to do so. On her testimony, he responded, "Well, if I don't get caught, what then?"

On January 25, 1994, Ahmad rented a hand-held motorized water pump from a local hardware store, telling a hardware store employee that he was planning to use it to remove water from his backyard. [Ahmad pumped gasoline and water from his tank, whence it flowed into Possum Creek and into the city sewer system. As a result, city officials had to use several vacuum trucks to decontaminate the creek, a sewage treatment plant supervisor evacuated the plant and called a hazardous materials crew to the scene, and firefighters evacuated two schools because of a "tremendous explosion hazard."] . . .

Ahmad was indicted for three violations of the CWA: knowingly discharging a pollutant from a point source into a navigable water of the United States without a permit . . . , knowingly operating a source in violation of a pretreatment standard . . . , and knowingly placing another person in imminent danger of death or serious bodily injury by discharging a pollutant. . . . At trial, Ahmad did not dispute that he had discharged gasoline from the tank or that eventually it had found its way to Possum Creek and the sewage treatment plant. Instead, he contended that his discharge of the gasoline was not "knowing," because he had believed he was discharging water.

[Ahmad attempted unsuccessfully to introduce evidence to] show that Ahmad did not knowingly discharge gasoline himself, but rather only negligently left the pump in the hands of his employees. . . . The jury found Ahmad guilty on counts one and two and deadlocked on count three.

II

Ahmad argues that the district court improperly instructed the jury on the *mens rea* required for count[] one. . . . The instruction on count one stated in relevant part:

> For you to find Mr. Ahmad guilty of this crime, you must be convinced that the government has proved each of the following beyond a reasonable doubt:

(1)   That on or about the date set forth in the indictment,
(2)   the defendant knowingly discharged
(3)   a pollutant
(4)   from a point source
(5)   into the navigable waters of the United States
(6)   without a permit to do so.

Ahmad contends that the jury should have been instructed that the statutory *mens rea*—knowledge—was required as to each element of the offenses, rather than only with regard to discharge or the operation of a source. . . .

The language of the CWA is less than pellucid. Title 33 U.S.C. §1319(c)(2)(A) says that "any person who knowingly violates" any of a number of other sections of the CWA commits a felony. One of the provisions that §1319(c)(2)(A) makes it unlawful to violate is §1311(a), which, when read together with a series of definitions in §1362, prohibits the addition of any pollutant to navigable waters from a "point source." That was the crime charged in count one. . . .

The principal issue is to which elements of the offense the modifier "knowingly" applies. . . . Ahmad argues that . . . "knowingly violates" should be read to require him knowingly to have acted with regard to each element of the offenses. The government, in contrast, contends that "knowingly violates" requires it to prove only that Ahmad knew the nature of his acts and that he performed them intentionally. Particularly at issue is whether "knowingly" applies to the element of the discharge's being a pollutant, for Ahmad's main theory at trial was that he thought he was discharging water, not gasoline.

The Supreme Court has spoken to this issue in broad terms. In United States v. X-Citement Video, Inc., 513 U.S. 64 (1994), the Court read "knowingly" to apply to each element of a child pornography offense, notwithstanding its conclusion that under the "most natural grammatical reading" of the statute it should apply only to the element of having transported, shipped, received, distributed, or reproduced the material at issue. The Court also reaffirmed the long-held view that "the presumption in favor of a scienter requirement should apply to each of the statutory elements which criminalize otherwise innocent conduct."

. . .

Our own precedents are in the same vein. In United States v. Baytank (Houston), Inc., 934 F.2d 599, 613 (5th Cir. 1991), we concluded that a conviction for knowing and improper storage of hazardous wastes under 42 U.S.C. §6928(d)(2)(A) requires "that the defendant know[] factually what he is doing—storing, what is being stored, and that what is being stored factually has the potential for harm to others or the environment, and that he has no permit. . . ." This is directly analogous to the interpretation of the CWA that Ahmad urges upon us. Indeed, we find it eminently sensible that the phrase "knowingly violates" in §1319(c)(2)(A), when referring to other provisions that define the elements of the offenses §1319 creates, should uniformly require knowledge as to each of those elements rather than only one or two. . . .

In support of its interpretation of the CWA, the government cites cases from other circuits. We find these decisions both inapposite and unpersuasive on the point for which they are cited. In United States v. Hopkins, 53 F.3d 533, 537-41 (2d Cir. 1995), the court held that the government need not demonstrate that a §1319(c)(2)(A) defendant knew his acts were illegal. The illegality of the defendant's actions is not an element of the offense, however. In United States v. Weitzenhoff, 35 F.3d 1275 (9th Cir. 1994), the court similarly was concerned almost exclusively with whether the language of the CWA creates a mistake-of-law defense. Both cases are easily distinguishable, for neither directly addresses mistake-of-fact or the statutory construction issues raised by Ahmad.

The government also protests that CWA violations fall into the judicially-created exception for "public welfare offenses," under which some regulatory crimes have been held not to require a showing of *mens rea*. On its face, the CWA certainly does appear to implicate public welfare.

As recent cases have emphasized, however, the public welfare offense exception is narrow. The *Staples* Court, for example, held that the statute prohibiting the possession of machine guns fell outside the exception, notwithstanding the fact that "[t]ypically, our cases recognizing such offenses involve statutes that regulate potentially harmful or injurious items."

Though gasoline is a "potentially harmful or injurious item," it is certainly no more so than are machine guns. Rather, *Staples* held, the key to the public welfare offense analysis is whether "dispensing with *mens rea* would require the defendant to have knowledge only of traditionally lawful conduct." The CWA offenses of which Ahmad was convicted have precisely this characteristic, for if knowledge is not required as to the nature of the substance discharged, one who honestly and reasonably believes he is discharging water may find himself guilty of a felony if the substance turns out to be something else.

The fact that violations of §1319(c)(2)(A) are felonies punishable by years in federal prison confirms our view that they do not fall within the public welfare offense exception. As the *Staples* Court noted, public welfare offenses have virtually always been crimes punishable by relatively light penalties such as fines or short jail sentences, rather than substantial terms of imprisonment. Serious felonies, in contrast, should not fall within the exception "absent a clear statement from Congress that *mens rea* is not required." Following *Staples*, we hold that the offenses charged in counts one and two are not public welfare offenses and that the usual presumption of a *mens rea* requirement applies. With the exception of purely jurisdictional elements, the *mens rea* of knowledge applies to each element of the crimes.

. . .

IV

Because we reverse Ahmad's convictions, we need not address his sentencing claims. The convictions are REVERSED and the case REMANDED.

ADDITIONAL NOTES AND QUESTIONS ON THE "KNOWINGLY VIOLATED" STANDARD

1. *Consistency with* Weitzenhoff. Is *Ahmad* consistent with *Weitzenhoff*?

2. *Public welfare offense.* The *Ahmad* court held that Ahmad's Clean Water Act violation did not amount to a public welfare offense. What is the consequence

of that holding? The *Ahmad* holding on that point seems to be a minority view. *See* United States v. Kelley Technical Coatings, Inc., 157 F.3d 432, 439 n.4 (6th Cir. 1998) (expressing the Sixth Circuit's agreement with the Second and Ninth Circuits that CWA violations constitute public welfare offenses). On the other hand, the Supreme Court has held (as both cases noted) that illegal possession of a machine gun does not constitute a public welfare offense. Should violations of the Clean Water Act be deemed a public welfare offense if violations of regulations of machine guns are not?

3. *When is criminal enforcement appropriate?* An EPA working group concluded that criminal enforcement should apply to the "most serious forms of environmental misconduct." Consensus Work Group, EPA, Management Review of EPA's Criminal Enforcement Program 2 (1986). *Cf.* Susan F. Mandiberg, *Environmental Criminal Protection: Essential Tool or Government Overreaching?*, 2009 Utah L. Rev. 1177 (2008) (discussing the tension between federal sentencing guidelines' emphasis on severity of harm and environmental statutes' emphasis on intent). The working group established three goals: (1) deterring intentional violations, (2) severely punishing egregious violators, and (3) assuring the integrity of all EPA regulatory programs. Do you think that jailing Ahmad is consistent with the philosophy? What about Weitzenhoff?

4. *The BP Gulf oil spill.* On April 20, 2010, an explosion occurred on an oil rig producing oil for British Petroleum (BP) in the Gulf of Mexico that set the rig on fire, killed 11 men, and released huge amounts of oil. According to the CEOs of several oil companies, BP had violated industry norms in several respects. BP chose a single string casing design for the well that was less safe and expensive than the "liner" and "tieback" design often used, used 6 "centralizers" when pouring cement rather than the 21 engineers that the contractor it had hired recommended, failed to adequately check the cement casing, and did not circulate weighted mud throughout the well to check for abnormalities. *See* Letter from Henry A. Waxman, Chairman, House of Representatives Committee on Energy and Commerce and Bart Stupak, Chairman, House of Representatives Subcommittee on Oversight and Investigations to Tony Hayward, BP CEO (June 14, 2010). Did BP commit a knowing violation of the Clean Water Act, which generally prohibits discharges of oil? *See* 33 U.S.C. §§1319(c)(2), 1321(b)(3). Did BP negligently violate the Clean Water Act, 33 U.S.C. §1319(c)(1)? The Clean Water Act authorizes up to a year of imprisonment for negligent violations. Should prosecutors charge the CEO criminally, even though he was not directly involved in making these particular decisions? *Cf.* Rena Steinzor, Why Not Jail?: Industrial Catastrophes, Corporate Malfeasance, and Government Inaction (2014) (discussing this incident and others and suggesting that criminal liability is often appropriate for top management when those managers send strong signals to cut costs even at the expense of safety); Robert W. Adler & Charles Lord, *Environmental Crimes: Raising the Stakes*, 59 Geo. Wash. L. Rev. 781, 782, 822 (1990-1991) (discussing negligence in the *Exxon Valdez* spill).

5. *Willful violations.* The Safe Drinking Water Act and the Emergency Planning and Community Right to Know Act only apply criminal penalties for willful violations. *See* 42 U.S.C. §§300h-2(b)(2), 11045(b)(4). Should courts require knowledge that the acts deliberately undertaken violate the law when this language is

employed? *Cf.* United States v. Wilson, 133 F.3d 251, 262 (4th Cir. 1997) (suggesting that when Congress changed the Clean Water Act's "willful" violation language to establish a "knowing" violation trigger for criminal penalties, it rejected requirement of knowledge of an act's illegality). While only the government can seek criminal penalties under the environmental statutes, citizens can sometimes seek civil penalties on their own. We turn to this use of citizen suits in the next chapter.

CLIMATE DISRUPTION ENFORCEMENT PROBLEM

The following are provisions from the Clean Air Act:

> 42 U.S.C. §7522. Prohibited acts
> (a) Enumerated prohibitions
> The following acts and the causing thereof are prohibited—
> (3)(A) for any person to remove or render inoperative any device or element of design installed on or in a motor vehicle or motor vehicle engine in compliance with regulations under this subchapter prior to its sale and delivery to the ultimate purchaser, or for any person knowingly to remove or render inoperative any such device or element of design after such sale and delivery to the ultimate purchaser; or
> (B) for any person to manufacture or sell, or offer to sell, or install, any part or component intended for use with, or as part of, any motor vehicle or motor vehicle engine, where a principal effect of the part or component is to bypass, defeat, or render inoperative any device or element of design installed on or in a motor vehicle or motor vehicle engine in compliance with regulations under this subchapter, and where the person knows or should know that such part or component is being offered for sale or installed for such use or put to such use.
> §7524. Civil penalties
> (a) Violations
> [A]ny manufacturer or dealer who violates section 7522(a)(3)(A) of this title shall be subject to a civil penalty of not more than $25,000. [A]ny person who violates section 7522(a)(3)(B) of this title shall be subject to a civil penalty of not more than $2,500. . . . Any such violation with respect to paragraph . . . (3)(A) . . . of section 7522(a) of this title shall constitute a separate offense with respect to each motor vehicle or motor vehicle engine. Any such violation with respect to section 7522(a)(3)(B) of this title shall constitute a separate offense with respect to each part or component.

Suppose EPA receives an anonymous tip that North American Automobile Manufacturers (NAAM) is selling a version of its popular four-door sedan, the "Sizzler," that is out of compliance with EPA's new motor vehicle emissions standards for greenhouse gases. Suppose, hypothetically, that these standards require that all motor vehicles sold are equipped with an engine misfire monitoring system. Misfiring decreases the fuel economy of a vehicle and hence leads to greater emissions of greenhouse gases. To encourage owners to repair misfiring vehicles, the system causes a red light on the dashboard to flash on and off for five seconds whenever a misfire occurs.

Upon further investigation, EPA learns that NAAM is supplying several of its dealerships with Sizzlers that are equipped with a manual "misfire notification override switch." Once flicked, a transmitter in the switch sends a signal to the engine misfiring monitoring system that disables the blinking red dashboard light whenever the engine misfires. EPA determines that, to date, NAAM has sold one thousand vehicles equipped with the manual override switch.

1. *Calculating civil penalties.* What is the maximum penalty that EPA could assess against NAAM with respect to this incident? Support your figure with references to the statutory text. What do you anticipate to be NAAM's best arguments for a smaller penalty?

2. *SEPs.* Suppose NAAM proposes that, in exchange for a reduction in the penalty it owes, it will fund public service announcements on major media outlets across the nation touting the carbon sequestration benefits of tree-planting. Can EPA agree to this? Should it? Suppose instead NAAM agrees to pay to plant whatever number of trees is required to sequester the amount of carbon dioxide that could have been emitted as a result of the manual misfire override switches.

3. *Criminal penalties.* Suppose that criminal penalties attach to violations of §7522(a)(3)(A) and (3)(B) where the defendant "knowingly violated" the statute. Suppose EPA seeks criminal penalties from the owners of independent car dealerships who sold vehicles manufactured by NAAM that contained the manual misfiring override switch but who did not know the cars were equipped with the switch. Are the dealers liable for criminal penalties under *United States v. Weitzenhoff*? Under *United States v. Ahmad*?

16

Citizen Enforcement

Congress included citizen enforcement provisions in numerous environmental statutes. *See, e.g.*, 42 U.S.C. §§6972 (RCRA), 7604 (Clean Air Act); 33 U.S.C. §1365 (Clean Water Act). It did so in order to supplement government enforcement resources. These provisions also serve as a check on lax government enforcement. During the Reagan Administration, for example, citizen suit enforcement assumed a leading role when federal enforcement dwindled.

This chapter first discusses the relationship between citizen enforcement and government enforcement. It then presents materials governing statutory and constitutional standing to sue, which are heavily influenced by ideas about the legitimacy of citizen suits. It addresses a matter of great practical importance, attorneys' fees. The chapter closes with a very brief review of enforcement's record and a final climate disruption problem that challenges you to work out an enforcement strategy, taking into account some of what you've learned from previous chapters.

A. RELATIONSHIP TO GOVERNMENT ENFORCEMENT

Allowing citizens to sue may invigorate enforcement, but it means that government cannot shield violators from penalties by simply declining to enforce. This may enhance the deterrent effect of enforcement, because polluters cannot rely on political power to limit enforcement. But it raises issues for those who believe that enforcement should be subject to political constraints and reasonably direct democratic controls.

A typical citizen suit provision (from the Clean Water Act) follows. As you read it, try to think about how it addresses the relationship between government and citizen enforcement:

33 U.S.C. §1365. Citizen suits

(a) Authorization; jurisdiction

. . . [A]ny citizen[1] [having an interest which may be adversely affected] may commence a civil action on his own behalf—

(1) against any person . . . who is alleged to be in violation of (A) an effluent standard or limitation under this chapter or (B) an order issued by the Administrator or a State with respect to such a standard or limitation. . . .

The district courts shall have jurisdiction to enforce such an effluent standard or limitation, or such an order . . . and to apply any appropriate civil penalties under section 1319(d) of this title.

(b) Notice

No action may be commenced—

(1) under subsection (a)(1) of this section—

(A) prior to sixty days after the plaintiff has given notice of the alleged violation (i) to the Administrator, (ii) to the State in which the alleged violation occurs, and (iii) to any alleged violator of the standard, limitation, or order, or

(B) if the Administrator or State has commenced and is diligently prosecuting a civil or criminal action in a court of the United States, or a State to require compliance with the standard, limitation, or order, but in any such action in a court of the United States any citizen may intervene as a matter of right. . . .

(c) Venue; intervention by Administrator; United States interests protected

(1) Any action respecting a violation by a discharge source of an effluent standard or limitation or an order respecting such standard or limitation may be brought under this section only in the judicial district in which such source is located.

(2) In such action under this section, the Administrator, if not a party, may intervene as a matter of right.

(3) PROTECTION OF INTERESTS OF UNITED STATES—Whenever any action is brought under this section in a court of the United States, the plaintiff shall serve a copy of the complaint on the Attorney General and the Administrator. No consent judgment shall be entered in an action in which the United States is not a party prior to 45 days following the receipt of a copy of the proposed consent judgment by the Attorney General and the Administrator.

Which subsections of this citizen suit provision set out above seek to preserve government discretion? How do they do this? Do they strike an appropriate balance between the desire for political control of enforcement and the desire to have citizen suits as an effective deterrent?

Notice that the Clean Water Act's citizen suit provision (and similar provisions in other statutes) bars citizen suits when the state or federal government

---

1. Another subsection of this section defines citizen as "a person . . . having an interest which is or may be adversely affected." 42 U.S.C. §1365(g).

has commenced and is "diligently prosecuting" a violation. Should citizen suits be barred in this instance? Should citizen suits be barred only for "diligent" prosecution or for any prosecution? Why do you suppose Congress allowed citizen suits when a non-diligent prosecution is underway? What constitutes diligent prosecution?

≡ **Jones v. City of Lakeland**
≡ *224 F.3d 518 (6th Cir. 2000) (en banc)*

KRUPANSKY, CIRCUIT JUDGE.

. . . Plaintiffs seek redress against the City for its ongoing practice of discharging contaminated sewage, sludge, and other toxic, noxious, and hazardous substances into Oliver Creek, in amounts exceeding those permitted by [its] National Pollutant Discharge Elimination System Permit (NPDES permit). . . .

The City responded by asserting that federal court jurisdiction over citizen enforcement actions is denied by the Clean Water Act if the Administrator of the Environmental Protection Agency, or a state, had already commenced and was diligently prosecuting an action to require compliance with a standard, limitation, or order of the Agency or the state. The plaintiffs countered by stating that their complaint facially impugned the [State's] action of issuing, but not effectively enforcing, a series of compliance orders while concurrently permitting the City to continue to discharge increasing amounts of impermissible toxic, noxious, hazardous, and health-threatening sewage and other raw waste into Oliver Creek during the ten years preceding their legal action; and that the [State's] demonstrated lax enforcement did not constitute "diligent prosecution" mandated by the Clean Water Act that would preclude their suit. . . .[2]

. . . TDEC's [the Tennessee Department of Environment and Conservation's] administrative enforcement action over a ten-year period was inadequate to address plaintiffs' concerns. During this inordinately long period of administrative enforcement, TDEC: (1) permitted the City to discharge impermissible volumes of contaminated raw human sewage, sludge, and other toxic, noxious substances into Oliver Creek on an ongoing basis thereby creating significant risks to human health and wildlife in, about, and along the water course; (2) permitted the City . . . to increase the impermissible volume of contaminated raw waste water discharging into the stabilizing lagoon that feeds Oliver Creek by allowing the City to continue to make connections and/or line extensions to its wastewater collection system; (3) waived countless NPDES violation notices; (4) extended and waived the compliance deadlines of three, possibly four, of its sweetheart consent orders with the City; and (5) imposed nominal token penalties in lieu of punitive compliance incentive penalties of $10,000.00 per day authorized by the Clean Water Act, all of which conduct contradicted a level of "diligent prosecution" demanded by 33 U.S.C. §1365(b), especially in light of the City's ongoing impermissible

---

2. The original case refers to the "City's" action of issuing compliance orders and lax enforcement. The rest of the case makes clear that the State, not the City, was the enforcer whose diligence is at issue here.

pollution of Oliver Creek as late as September 30, 1996, the date this action was commenced. The trial court's resolution to the contrary is not convincing and clearly erroneous, and is REVERSED. . . .

NORRIS, CIRCUIT JUDGE, dissenting.

   . . . I respectfully dissent. . . .

   In their complaint, plaintiffs alleged that the "TDEC failed to undertake any action to prevent or abate the continuing current discharge by [the city] into Oliver Creek from the existing stabilization lagoon and thereby allowed the wrongful discharge to increase." Plaintiffs' primary contention appears to be not that the TDEC is doing nothing but, rather, that its prosecution cannot be diligent if it continues to allow the city to dump impermissible amounts of waste into Oliver Creek and if its attempts to remedy the problem are limited to entering a series of ineffective administrative orders.

   I cannot agree with plaintiffs' view of the record. In concluding that the state was in fact diligently prosecuting an action against the city, the district court noted that four orders had been entered between the city (or its predecessor in interest) and the TDEC, the last of which was on August 26, 1996, one month prior to plaintiffs' filing of this action. This latest order required that the city be in full compliance with its National Pollutant Discharge Elimination System ("NPDES") permit by July 1, 1997. The court cited this fourth order as an example of the state's diligent prosecution of its action against the city. The record before this court further reflects that the city attempted to comply with the orders and that the TDEC extended deadlines in response to practical difficulties the city encountered in reaching full compliance. The fourth order required the city to pay a fine and provided for additional fines should the city fail to meet the full requirements of the order. The district court recognized that an enforcing agency must be accorded the latitude to respond to circumstances that delay remedial projects and warrant reassessment of compliance target dates. In using the term "diligently prosecuting," Congress did not contemplate the rigidity plaintiffs would have us visit upon the Clean Water Act's enforcement scheme. It is clear that the TDEC is attempting to remedy the specific problems plaintiffs cite in their complaint. Accordingly, I am unable to say that the district court erred when it concluded that the TDEC's continued enforcement represents diligent prosecution as contemplated by the statute. . . .

NOTES AND QUESTIONS ON *JONES*

   1. *What is diligent prosecution?* Should the court find diligent prosecution under the facts of this case? *Cf.* Friends of Milwaukee's Rivers v. Milwaukee Metropolitan Sewerage District, 556 F.3d 603, 610 (7th Cir. 2009) (inquiry into whether prosecution was diligent should focus on whether the settlement was "calculated to eliminate the causes of the violations"). Does a citizen suit in this context usefully supplement the state action or improperly interfere with state efforts to correct the violations? Assume that the state could intervene in the citizen suit (*i.e.*, secure a status where it has a right to participate in the court proceedings). Would the court

tend to defer to the state when questions arose about what remedial orders and penalties were appropriate?

2. *Diligent administrative enforcement.* A number of courts have held that the diligent prosecution bar in section 505 only applies when a governmental entity has brought an action in state or federal court. *See* 33 U.S.C. §1365(b)(1)(B). Yet many states, like the federal government, often use administrative rather than judicial proceedings as enforcement mechanisms. Section 309(g)(6)(A) establishes a diligent prosecution bar for federal administrative enforcement actions and for actions under state administrative enforcement provisions that are "comparable" to the federal administrative enforcement provisions. *See* 33 U.S.C. §1319(g)(6)(A)(i), (ii). *Cf.* Black Warrior Riverkeeper v. Cherokee Mining, 548 F.3d 986 (11th Cir. 2008) (no diligent prosecution bar attaches when citizens give notice of suit before a state administrative enforcement action commences). Should courts hold state provisions comparable when they provide for smaller penalties than the federal statute? *Compare* North and South Rivers Watershed Ass'n v. Town of Scituate, 949 F.2d 552, 556 (1st Cir. 1991) (holding that a state statutory scheme authorizing the state to levy similar penalties to those provided by federal law is "comparable" even if the particular provision the state invoked does not authorize penalties), *with* Citizens for a Better Environment, California v. Union Oil Co. of California, 83 F.3d 1111, 1117-18 (9th Cir. 1996) (finding no comparability when California relied on a provision that did not authorize comparable civil penalties). What if a state statute provides identical penalties, but fails to offer citizens a right to participate in the crafting of a remedy, a right available in federal administrative proceedings? *Compare Jones*, 224 F.3d at 523-24 (holding that such state statutory provisions are not comparable to the federal provision); McAbee v. City of Fort Payne, 318 F.3d 1248, 1256-57 (11th Cir. 2003) (state law providing for only after-the-fact participation without adequate notice found not comparable to federal provision), *with* Arkansas Wildlife Federation v. ICI Americas, Inc., 29 F.3d 376, 381-82 (8th Cir. 1994) (finding comparability even though the state law only provided for after-the-fact citizen participation); Lockett v. EPA, 319 F.3d 678, 684-87 (5th Cir. 2003) (holding that state statute providing for public participation as of right for orders contested by the polluter and administrative discretion to offer the public an after-the-fact hearing for uncontested orders is comparable to federal provision).

B. STANDING AND THE *GWALTNEY* PROBLEM

The original citizen suit provisions in many statutes authorized "any person" to bring suit. *See, e.g.,* 42 U.S.C. §7604(a). *Cf.* 33 U.S.C. §1365(g) (defining a citizen who can bring suit as a person "having an interest which is or may be adversely affected"). This reflects an intention to allow an individual citizen to function as a private attorney general enforcing the law. Attitudes toward the legitimacy of such a role have influenced both the interpretation of the statutory citizen suit provisions and the judicial doctrine of standing, which limits who may sue.

In an early case in which the Sierra Club sought to challenge a United States Forest Service proposal to authorize a ski resort in the Mineral King Valley in California, the Supreme Court held:

> The injury alleged by the Sierra Club will be incurred entirely by reason of the change in the uses to which Mineral King will be put, and the attendant change in the aesthetics and ecology of the area. Thus, in referring to the road to be built through Sequoia National Park, the complaint alleged that the development "would destroy or otherwise adversely affect the scenery, natural and historic objects and wildlife of the park and would impair the enjoyment of the park for future generations." We do not question that this type of harm may amount to an "injury in fact" sufficient to lay the basis for standing under §10 of the [Administrative Procedure Act]. Aesthetic and environmental well-being, like economic well-being, are important ingredients of the quality of life in our society, and the fact that particular environmental interests are shared by the many rather than the few does not make them less deserving of legal protection through the judicial process. But the "injury in fact" test requires more than an injury to a cognizable interest. It requires that the party seeking review be himself among the injured.

Sierra Club v. Morton, 405 U.S. 727, 734-35 (1972). Thus, the Court accepted the idea that non-economic injury could create standing to sue. At the same time, it rejected a pure private attorney general theory that "any person" could be considered an aggrieved party entitled to judicial review under the Administrative Procedure Act (APA), the statute the Sierra Club relied upon to justify judicial review. The Court required the Sierra Club to show that it or some of its members would experience some of the environmental harms that the Mineral King development might bring. The early citizen suit provisions authorizing "any person" to sue thus offered broader statutory standing than that afforded by the APA.

In the following case, the court interpreted the Clean Water Act's citizen suit provision narrowly, thus denying an environmental group the right to litigate some kinds of violations:

Gwaltney of Smithfield, Ltd. v. Chesapeake Bay Foundation, Inc.
484 U.S. 49 (1987)

JUSTICE MARSHALL delivered the opinion of the Court.

In this case, we must decide whether §505(a) of the Clean Water Act, also known as the Federal Water Pollution Control Act . . . confers federal jurisdiction over citizen suits for wholly past violations.

I

. . . Between 1981 and 1984, petitioner repeatedly violated the conditions of [its] permit by exceeding effluent limitations on five of the seven pollutants covered. These violations are chronicled in the Discharge Monitoring Reports that the permit required petitioner to maintain. . . . Petitioner installed new equipment to improve its chlorination system in March 1982, and its last reported chlorine violation occurred in October 1982. The new chlorination system also helped to control the discharge of fecal coliform, and the last recorded fecal coliform violation occurred in February 1984. Petitioner installed an upgraded wastewater treatment system in October 1983, and its last reported TKN violation occurred on May 15, 1984.

Respondents Chesapeake Bay Foundation and Natural Resources Defense Council, two nonprofit corporations dedicated to the protection of natural resources, sent notice in February 1984 to Gwaltney, the Administrator of EPA, and the Virginia State Water Control Board, indicating respondents' intention to commence a citizen suit under the Act based on petitioner's violations of its permit conditions. Respondents proceeded to file this suit in June 1984, alleging that petitioner "has violated . . . [and] will continue to violate its NPDES permit." . . .

Before the District Court reached a decision, Gwaltney moved in May 1985 for dismissal of the action for want of subject-matter jurisdiction under the Act. Gwaltney argued that the language of §505(a), which permits private citizens to bring suit against any person "alleged to be in violation" of the Act,[3] requires that a defendant be violating the Act at the time of suit. . . .

We granted certiorari to resolve [a] three-way conflict in the Circuits. We now vacate the Fourth Circuit's opinion and remand the case.

II

A

. . . The most natural reading of "to be in violation" is a requirement that citizen-plaintiffs allege a state of either continuous or intermittent violation[,] that is, a reasonable likelihood that a past polluter will continue to pollute in the future. Congress could have phrased its requirement in language that looked to the past ("to have violated"), but it did not choose this readily available option.

Respondents urge that the choice of the phrase "to be in violation," rather than phrasing more clearly directed to the past, is a "careless accident," the result of a "debatable lapse of syntactical precision." But the prospective orientation of that phrase could not have escaped Congress' attention. Congress used identical language in the citizen suit provisions of several other environmental statutes that authorize only prospective relief. *See, e.g.*, Clean Air Act, 42 U.S.C. §7604; Resource Conservation and Recovery Act of 1976, 42 U.S.C. §6972 (1982 ed. and Supp. III); Toxic Substances Control Act, 15 U.S.C. §2619 (1982 ed. and

---

3. In its entirety, §505(a), as codified, 33 U.S.C. §1365(a), provides:

"Except as provided in subsection (b) of this section, any citizen may commence a civil action on his own behalf—

"(1) against any person (including (i) the United States, and (ii) any other governmental instrumentality or agency to the extent permitted by the eleventh amendment to the Constitution) who is alleged to be in violation of (A) an effluent standard or limitation under this chapter or (B) an order issued by the Administrator or a State with respect to such a standard or limitation, or

"(2) against the Administrator where there is alleged a failure of the Administrator to perform any act or duty under this chapter which is not discretionary with the Administrator.

"The district courts shall have jurisdiction, without regard to the amount in controversy or the citizenship of the parties, to enforce such an effluent standard or limitation, or such an order, or to order the Administrator to perform such act or duty, as the case may be, and to apply any appropriate civil penalties under section 1319(d) of this title."

Supp. IV). Moreover, Congress has demonstrated in yet other statutory provisions that it knows how to avoid this prospective implication by using language that explicitly targets wholly past violations.

. . .

B

Any other conclusion would render incomprehensible §505's notice provision, which requires citizens to give 60 days' notice of their intent to sue to the alleged violator as well as to the Administrator and the State. If the Administrator or the State commences enforcement action within that 60-day period, the citizen suit is barred, presumably because governmental action has rendered it unnecessary. It follows logically that the purpose of notice to the alleged violator is to give it an opportunity to bring itself into complete compliance with the Act and thus likewise render unnecessary a citizen suit. If we assume, as respondents urge, that citizen suits may target wholly past violations, the requirement of notice to the alleged violator becomes gratuitous. Indeed, respondents, in propounding their interpretation of the Act, can think of no reason for Congress to require such notice other than that "it seemed right" to inform an alleged violator that it was about to be sued.

Adopting respondents' interpretation of §505's jurisdictional grant would create a second and even more disturbing anomaly. The bar on citizen suits when governmental enforcement action is under way suggests that the citizen suit is meant to supplement rather than to supplant governmental action. The legislative history of the Act reinforces this view of the role of the citizen suit. The Senate Report noted that "[t]he Committee intends the great volume of enforcement actions [to] be brought by the State," and that citizen suits are proper only "if the Federal, State, and local agencies fail to exercise their enforcement responsibility." Permitting citizen suits for wholly past violations of the Act could undermine the supplementary role envisioned for the citizen suit. This danger is best illustrated by an example. Suppose that the Administrator identified a violator of the Act and issued a compliance order under §309(a). Suppose further that the Administrator agreed not to assess or otherwise seek civil penalties on the condition that the violator take some extreme corrective action, such as to install particularly effective but expensive machinery, that it otherwise would not be obliged to take. If citizens could file suit, months or years later, in order to seek the civil penalties that the Administrator chose to forgo, then the Administrator's discretion to enforce the Act in the public interest would be curtailed considerably. The same might be said of the discretion of state enforcement authorities. Respondents' interpretation of the scope of the citizen suit would change the nature of the citizens' role from interstitial to potentially intrusive. We cannot agree that Congress intended such a result.

. . .

III

Our conclusion that §505 does not permit citizen suits for wholly past violations does not necessarily dispose of this lawsuit, as both lower courts recognized.

The District Court found persuasive the fact that "[respondents'] allegation in the complaint, that Gwaltney was continuing to violate its NPDES permit when plaintiffs filed suit[,] appears to have been made fully in good faith." On this basis, the District Court explicitly held, albeit in a footnote, that "even if Gwaltney were correct that a district court has no jurisdiction over citizen suits based entirely on unlawful conduct that occurred entirely in the past, the Court would still have jurisdiction here." The Court of Appeals acknowledged, also in a footnote, that "[a] very sound argument can be made that [respondents'] allegations of continuing violations were made in good faith," but expressly declined to rule on this alternative holding. Because we agree that §505 confers jurisdiction over citizen suits when the citizen-plaintiffs make a good-faith allegation of continuous or intermittent violation, we remand the case to the Court of Appeals for further consideration.

Petitioner argues that citizen-plaintiffs must prove their allegations of ongoing noncompliance before jurisdiction attaches under §505. We cannot agree. The statute does not require that a defendant "be in violation" of the Act at the commencement of suit; rather, the statute requires that a defendant be *"alleged* to be in violation." Petitioner's construction of the Act reads the word "alleged" out of §505. . . . Our acknowledgment that Congress intended a good-faith allegation to suffice for jurisdictional purpose, however, does not give litigants license to flood the courts with suits premised on baseless allegations. Rule 11 of the Federal Rules of Civil Procedure, which requires pleadings to be based on a good-faith belief, formed after reasonable inquiry, that they are "well grounded in fact," adequately protects defendants from frivolous allegations.

. . .

Because the court below erroneously concluded that respondents could maintain an action based on wholly past violations of the Act, it declined to decide whether respondents' complaint contained a good-faith allegation of ongoing violation by petitioner. We therefore remand the case for consideration of this question. The judgment of the Court of Appeals is vacated, and the case is remanded for further proceedings consistent with this opinion.

NOTES AND QUESTIONS ON *GWALTNEY*

1. *The verb tense.* Do you agree that the verb tense employed in the citizen suit provision justifies the holding that suits do not lie for "wholly past" violations?

2. *Notice.* The Court also supports its holding by positing that the 60-day-notice provision's purpose is to give the alleged violator "an opportunity to bring itself into complete compliance and therefore render" the suit unnecessary. Suppose that the Court (or Congress through a change of verb tense) authorizes citizen suits for wholly past violations. Does this wholly deprive the 60-day notice to violators of any purpose?

3. *Relationship to government enforcement.* Notice that the Court also relies on the diligent prosecution bar to support its holding, citing it as evidence that Congress intended the citizen suit "to supplement rather than to supplant government[]" enforcement. In light of the diligent prosecution bar, is there any need for

a blanket prohibition on suits for past violations? Consider the Court's example. Suppose that the Administrator does not seek civil penalties but imposes "extreme corrective action" requirements. Would that constitute diligent enforcement barring the citizen suit? If not, would government intervention in the citizen suit (which is, remember, available as of right) prevent citizens from interfering with a fairly satisfactory remedy? After *Gwaltney*, suppose that the Administrator demands extremely lax corrective action in exchange for no penalties? Can the citizen sue? What if the Administrator demands that the violation be cured, but collects no penalties? Can the citizen sue? What if government does nothing, but the company cures the violation before filing? Can the citizen sue? Should the law authorize a citizen suit in any or all of these situations?

4. *Complication of citizen enforcement. Gwaltney* has greatly complicated citizen enforcement. Recall that the Clean Water Act requires polluters to report their discharges and violations to state environmental agencies enforcing the Act. Prior to *Gwaltney*, a citizen could simply rely on the reported violations as an adequate basis for seeking and obtaining at least some relief in court. Suppose that a polluter claims that it has cured the violation under *Gwaltney*. What must citizens do to evaluate whether this claim is correct? Could a polluter shut down the particular unit causing a violation when the suit is filed (thus reducing effluent from that unit to zero), and just start up again after securing dismissal under *Gwaltney*?

5. *Pleading and ethics.* Notice that the Court does not order dismissal of the suit, because the environmental plaintiffs had alleged a continuing violation. Can environmental plaintiffs routinely avoid dismissal under *Gwaltney* by simply alleging continuing violations? *Cf.* Jones v. Dow Chemical Co., 885 F. Supp. 905, 910-11 (M.D. La. 1994) (dismissing citizen suit under Safe Drinking Water Act when citizens failed to allege a continuing violation). Suppose that the only information that the plaintiffs have at the time of filing are discharge reports showing frequent past violations. Would an allegation of a continuing violation be appropriate if the last discharge report was a month old at the time of filing? Recall that under Federal Rule of Civil Procedure 11, lawyers presenting pleadings to a federal court certify that "the factual contentions have evidentiary support or, if specifically so identified, are likely to have evidentiary support after a reasonable opportunity for further investigation or discovery. . . ." FRCP 11(b)(3). *Cf.* Ohio Public Interest Research Group v. Laidlaw Environmental Services, 963 F. Supp. 635, 640-41 (S.D. Ohio 1996) (finding compliance with rule 11 when plaintiffs submit evidence of discharges after the complaint was filed).

6. *Deterrence.* Does the *Gwaltney* holding advance the statutory goal of deterrence?

7. *Implications for other statutes.* Notice that the Court's ruling rests on an interpretation of the Clean Water Act, not upon constitutional grounds. On the other hand, the Court stated that other citizen suit provisions had similar language.

Suppose that a chemical company has on several occasions in the past emitted more air pollution than its permit allows. A citizen group looks over the state records and discovers that the company has exceeded its permit limits again. The group sues under this citizen suit provision from the Clean Air Act:

. . . Any person may commence a civil action . . . against any person . . . who constructs any new or modified major emitting facility without a permit. . . .

42 U.S.C. §7604(a)(3). This permit must impose a host of permanent pollution control obligations on the permit holder under the Act. The violator modified the facility a decade ago. Should the case be dismissed? *See* New York v. Niagara Mohawk Power Corp., 263 F. Supp. 2d 650, 658-60 (W.D.N.Y. 2003) (rejecting motion to dismiss claims alleging past violations of requirements for modified facilities).

At the time of Sierra Club v. Morton, the Court's standing jurisprudence represented primarily an interpretation of the APA. In subsequent years, however, the Court frequently stated that Article III of the United States Constitution, which authorizes the judiciary to adjudicate "cases or controversies," requires that litigants satisfy much of the Court's standing doctrine. The case below invalidating a citizen suit provision (at least in some applications), however, represented the first case where the Court actually invalidated an express statutory grant of standing as unconstitutional:

Lujan v. Defenders of Wildlife
504 U.S. 555 (1992)

JUSTICE SCALIA delivered the opinion of the Court with respect to Parts I, II, III-A, and IV, and an opinion with respect to Part III-B in which THE CHIEF JUSTICE, JUSTICE WHITE, and JUSTICE THOMAS join.

This case involves a challenge to a rule promulgated by the Secretary of the Interior interpreting §7 of the Endangered Species Act of 1973 in such fashion as to render it applicable only to actions within the United States or on the high seas. The preliminary issue, and the only one we reach, is whether the respondents here, plaintiffs below, have standing to seek judicial review of the rule.

I

The ESA seeks to protect species of animals against threats to their continuing existence caused by man. The ESA instructs the Secretary of the Interior to promulgate by regulation a list of those species which are either endangered or threatened under enumerated criteria, and to define the critical habitat of these species. Section 7(a)(2) of the Act then provides, in pertinent part:

> Each Federal agency shall, in consultation with and with the assistance of the Secretary [of the Interior], insure that any action authorized, funded, or carried out by such agency is not likely to jeopardize the continued existence of any endangered species or threatened species or result in the destruction or adverse modification of habitat of such species which is determined by the Secretary, after consultation as appropriate with affected States, to be critical. 16 U.S.C. §1536(a)(2).

In 1978, the Fish and Wildlife Service (FWS) and the National Marine Fisheries Service (NMFS), on behalf of the Secretary of the Interior and the Secretary of Commerce respectively, promulgated a joint regulation stating that the obligations imposed by §7(a)(2) extend to actions taken in foreign nations. The next year, however, the Interior Department began to reexamine its position. A revised joint regulation, reinterpreting §7(a)(2) to require consultation only for actions taken in the United States or on the high seas, was . . . promulgated in 1986.

Shortly thereafter, respondents, organizations dedicated to wildlife conservation and other environmental causes, filed this action against the Secretary of the Interior, seeking a declaratory judgment that the new regulation is in error as to the geographic scope of §7(a)(2), and an injunction requiring the Secretary to promulgate a new regulation restoring the initial interpretation. The District Court granted the Secretary's motion to dismiss for lack of standing. The Court of Appeals for the Eighth Circuit reversed by a divided vote. On remand, the Secretary moved for summary judgment on the standing issue, and respondents moved for summary judgment on the merits. The District Court denied the Secretary's motion, on the ground that the Eighth Circuit had already determined the standing question in this case; it granted respondents' merits motion, and ordered the Secretary to publish a revised regulation. The Eighth Circuit affirmed. We granted certiorari.

II

While the Constitution of the United States divides all power conferred upon the Federal Government into "legislative Powers," Art. I, §1, "[t]he executive Power," Art. II, §1, and "[t]he judicial Power," Art. III, §1, it does not attempt to define those terms. To be sure, it limits the jurisdiction of federal courts to "Cases and Controversies," but an executive inquiry can bear the name "case" (the Hoffa case) and a legislative dispute can bear the name "controversy" (the Smoot-Hawley controversy). Obviously, then, the Constitution's central mechanism of separation of powers depends largely upon common understanding of what activities are appropriate to legislatures, to executives, and to courts. . . . [A] landmark[] setting apart the "Cases" and "Controversies" that are of the justiciable sort referred to in Article III—"serv[ing] to identify those disputes which are appropriately resolved through the judicial process,"—is the doctrine of standing. Though some of its elements express merely prudential considerations that are part of judicial self-government, the core component of standing is an essential and unchanging part of the case-or-controversy requirement of Article III.

Over the years, our cases have established that the irreducible constitutional minimum of standing contains three elements: First, the plaintiff must have suffered an "injury in fact"—an invasion of a legally-protected interest which is (a) concrete and particularized,[4] and (b) "actual or imminent, not 'conjectural' or 'hypothetical.'" Second, there must be a causal connection between the injury and the conduct complained of—the injury has to be "fairly . . . trace[able] to the challenged action of the defendant, and not . . . th[e] result [of] the independent action of some third party not before the court." Third, it must be "likely," as opposed to merely "speculative," that the injury will be "redressed by a favorable decision."

The party invoking federal jurisdiction bears the burden of establishing these elements. . . .

---

4. By particularized, we mean that the injury must affect the plaintiff in a personal and individual way.

When the suit is one challenging the legality of government action or inaction, the nature and extent of facts that must be averred (at the summary judgment stage) or proved (at the trial stage) in order to establish standing depends considerably upon whether the plaintiff is himself an object of the action (or forgone action) at issue. If he is, there is ordinarily little question that the action or inaction has caused him injury, and that a judgment preventing or requiring the action will redress it. When, however, as in this case, a plaintiff's asserted injury arises from the government's allegedly unlawful regulation (or lack of regulation) of *someone else*, much more is needed. In that circumstance, causation and redressability ordinarily hinge on the response of the regulated (or regulable) third party to the government action or inaction—and perhaps on the response of others as well. The existence of one or more of the essential elements of standing "depends on the unfettered choices made by independent actors not before the courts and whose exercise of broad and legitimate discretion the courts cannot presume either to control or to predict," and it becomes the burden of the plaintiff to adduce facts showing that those choices have been or will be made in such manner as to produce causation and permit redressability of injury. Thus, when the plaintiff is not himself the object of the government action or inaction he challenges, standing is not precluded, but it is ordinarily "substantially more difficult" to establish.

III

We think the Court of Appeals failed to apply the foregoing principles in denying the Secretary's motion for summary judgment. Respondents had not made the requisite demonstration of (at least) injury and redressability.

A

Respondents' claim to injury is that the lack of consultation with respect to certain funded activities abroad "increas[es] the rate of extinction of endangered and threatened species." Of course, the desire to use or observe an animal species, even for purely esthetic purposes, is undeniably a cognizable interest for purpose of standing. *See, e.g.*, Sierra Club v. Morton, 405 U.S., at 734. "But the 'injury in fact' test requires more than an injury to a cognizable interest. It requires that the party seeking review be himself among the injured." *Id.* at 734-735. To survive the Secretary's summary judgment motion, respondents had to submit affidavits or other evidence showing, through specific facts, not only that listed species were in fact being threatened by funded activities abroad, but also that one or more of respondents' members would thereby be "directly" affected apart from their "'special interest' in th[e] subject."

With respect to this aspect of the case, the Court of Appeals focused on the affidavits of two Defenders' members—Joyce Kelly and Amy Skilbred. Ms. Kelly stated that she traveled to Egypt in 1986 and "observed the traditional habitat of the endangered nile crocodile there and intend[s] to do so again, and hope[s] to observe the crocodile directly," and that she "will suffer harm in fact as a result of [the] American . . . role . . . in overseeing the rehabilitation of the Aswan High Dam on the Nile . . . and [in] develop[ing] . . . Egypt's . . . Master Water Plan." Ms. Skilbred averred that she traveled to Sri Lanka in 1981 and "observed th[e] habitat" of "endangered species such as the Asian elephant and the leopard" at what is now the site of the Mahaweli project funded by the Agency for International Development (AID), although she "was unable to see any of the endangered species"; "this development project," she continued, "will seriously reduce endangered, threatened, and endemic species habitat including areas that I visited . . . [, which] may severely shorten the future of these species" ; that threat, she concluded, harmed her because she "intend[s] to return to Sri Lanka in the future and hope[s] to be more fortunate in spotting at least the endangered elephant and leopard." When Ms. Skilbred was asked at a subsequent deposition if and when she had any plans to return to Sri Lanka, she reiterated that "I intend to go back to Sri Lanka," but confessed that she had no current plans: "I don't know [when]. There is a civil war going on right now. I don't know. Not next year, I will say. In the future."

We shall assume for the sake of argument that these affidavits contain facts showing that certain agency-funded projects threaten listed species—though that is questionable. They plainly contain no facts, however, showing how damage to the species will produce "imminent" injury to Mses. Kelly and Skilbred. That the women "had visited" the areas of the projects before the projects commenced proves nothing. As we have said in a related context, " 'Past exposure to illegal conduct does not in itself show a present case or controversy regarding injunctive relief . . . if unaccompanied by any continuing, present adverse effects.' " And the affiants' profession of an "inten[t]" to return to the places they had visited before—where they will presumably, this time, be deprived of the opportunity to observe animals of the endangered species—is simply not enough. Such "some day" intentions—without any description of concrete plans, or indeed even any specification of *when* the some day will be—do not support a finding of the "actual or imminent" injury that our cases require.[5]

---

5. The dissent acknowledges the settled requirement that the injury complained of be, if not actual, then at least *imminent*, but it contends that respondents could get past summary judgment because "a reasonable finder of fact could conclude . . . that . . . Kelly or Skilbred will soon return to the project sites." This analysis suffers either from a factual or from a legal defect, depending on what the "soon" is supposed to mean. If "soon" refers to the standard mandated by our precedents—that the injury be "imminent"—we are at a loss to see how, as a factual matter, the standard can be met by respondents' mere profession of an intent, some day, to return. But if, as we suspect, "soon" means nothing more than "in this lifetime," then the dissent has undertaken quite a departure from our precedents. Although "imminence" is concededly a somewhat elastic concept, it cannot be stretched beyond its purpose, which is to insure that the alleged injury is not too speculative for Article III purposes—that the injury is "*certainly* impending." It has been stretched beyond the breaking point when, as here, the plaintiff alleges only an injury at some indefinite future time, and the acts necessary to make the injury happen are at least partly within the plaintiff's own control. In such circumstances we have insisted that the injury proceed with a high degree of immediacy, so as to reduce the possibility of deciding a case in which no injury would have occurred at all. There is no substance to the dissent's suggestion that imminence is demanded only when the alleged harm depends upon "the affirmative actions of third parties beyond a plaintiff's control." Our cases *mention* third-party-caused contingency, naturally enough; but they also mention the plaintiff's failure to show that he will soon expose *himself* to the injury. And there is certainly no reason in principle to demand evidence that third persons will take the action exposing the plaintiff to harm, while *presuming* that the plaintiff himself will do so. Our insistence upon these established requirements of standing does not mean that we would, as the dissent contends, "demand . . . detailed descriptions" of damages, such as a "nightly schedule of attempted activities" from plaintiffs alleging loss of consortium. That case and the others posited by the dissent all involve *actual* harm; the existence of standing is clear, though the precise extent of harm remains to be determined at trial. Where there is no actual harm, however, its imminence (though not its precise extent) must be established.

Besides relying upon the Kelly and Skilbred affidavits, respondents propose a series of novel standing theories. The first, inelegantly styled "ecosystem nexus," proposes that any person who uses *any part* of a "contiguous ecosystem" adversely affected by a funded activity has standing even if the activity is located a great distance away. This approach, as the Court of Appeals correctly observed, is inconsistent with our opinion in *National Wildlife Federation*, which held that a plaintiff claiming injury from environmental damage must use the area affected by the challenged activity and not an area roughly "in the vicinity" of it. . . .

Respondents' other theories are called, alas, the "animal nexus" approach, whereby anyone who has an interest in studying or seeing the endangered animals anywhere on the globe has standing; and the "vocational nexus" approach, under which anyone with a professional interest in such animals can sue. Under these theories, anyone who goes to see Asian elephants in the Bronx Zoo, and anyone who is a keeper of Asian elephants in the Bronx Zoo, has standing to sue because the Director of . . . AID did not consult with the Secretary regarding the AID-funded project in Sri Lanka. This is beyond all reason. Standing is not "an ingenious academic exercise in the conceivable," but as we have said requires, at the summary judgment stage, a factual showing of perceptible harm. It is clear that the person who observes or works with a particular animal threatened by a federal decision is facing perceptible harm, since the very subject of his interest will no longer exist. It is even plausible—though it goes to the outermost limit of plausibility—to think that a person who observes or works with animals of a particular species in the very area of the world where that species is threatened by a federal decision is facing such harm, since some animals that might have been the subject of his interest will no longer exist. It goes beyond the limit, however, and into pure speculation and fantasy, to say that anyone who observes or works with an endangered species, anywhere in the world, is appreciably harmed by a single project affecting some portion of that species with which he has no more specific connection.

B

Besides failing to show injury, respondents failed to demonstrate redressability. Instead of attacking the separate decisions to fund particular projects allegedly causing them harm, the respondents chose to challenge a more generalized level of Government action (rules regarding consultation), the invalidation of which would affect all overseas projects. This programmatic approach has obvious practical advantages, but also obvious difficulties insofar as proof of causation or redressability is concerned. As we have said in another context, "suits challenging, not specifically identifiable Government violations of law, but the particular programs agencies establish to carry out their legal obligations . . . [are], even when premised on allegations of several instances of violations of law, . . . rarely if ever appropriate for federal-court adjudication."

The most obvious problem in the present case is redressability. Since the agencies funding the projects were not parties to the case, the District Court could accord relief only against the Secretary: He could be ordered to revise his regulation to require consultation for foreign projects. But this would not remedy respondents' alleged injury unless the funding agencies were bound by the Secretary's regulation, which is very much an open question. Whereas in other contexts the ESA is quite explicit as to the Secretary's controlling authority with respect to consultation the initiative, and hence arguably the initial responsibility for determining statutory necessity, lies with the agencies. When the Secretary promulgated the regulation at issue here, he thought it was binding on the agencies. The Solicitor General, however, has repudiated that position here, and the agencies themselves apparently deny the Secretary's authority. (During the period when the Secretary took the view that §7(a)(2) did apply abroad, AID and FWS engaged in a running controversy over whether consultation was required with respect to the Mahaweli project, AID insisting that consultation applied only to domestic actions.)

Respondents assert that this legal uncertainty did not affect redressability (and hence standing) because the District Court itself could resolve the issue of the Secretary's authority as a necessary part of its standing inquiry. Assuming that it is appropriate to resolve an issue of law such as this in connection with a threshold standing inquiry, resolution by the District Court would not have remedied respondents' alleged injury anyway, because it would not have been binding upon the agencies. They were not parties to the suit, and there is no reason they should be obliged to honor an incidental legal determination the suit produced. The Court of Appeals tried to finesse this problem by simply proclaiming that "[w]e are satisfied that an injunction requiring the Secretary to publish [respondents' desired] regulatio[n] . . . would result in consultation." We do not know what would justify that confidence, particularly when the Justice Department (presumably after consultation with the agencies) has taken the position that the regulation is not binding. The short of the matter is that redress of the only injury-in-fact respondents complain of requires action (termination of funding until consultation) by the individual funding agencies; and any relief the District Court could have provided in this suit against the Secretary was not likely to produce that action.

A further impediment to redressability is the fact that the agencies generally supply only a fraction of the funding for a foreign project. AID, for example, has provided less than 10% of the funding for the Mahaweli project. Respondents have produced nothing to indicate that the projects they have named will either be suspended, or do less harm to listed species, if that fraction is eliminated. As in *Simon*, it is entirely conjectural whether the nonagency activity that affects respondents will be altered or affected by the agency activity they seek to achieve. There is no standing.

IV

The Court of Appeals found that respondents had standing for an additional reason: because they had suffered a "procedural injury." The so-called "citizen-suit" provision of the ESA provides, in pertinent part, that "any person may commence a civil suit on his own behalf (A) to enjoin any person, including the United States and any other governmental instrumentality or agency . . . who is alleged to be in violation of any provision of this chapter." 16 U.S.C. §1540(g). The court held that, because §7(a)(2) requires interagency consultation, the citizen-suit provision creates a "procedural righ[t]" to consultation in all "persons" — so that *anyone* can file suit in federal court to challenge the Secretary's (or presumably any other official's) failure to follow the assertedly correct consultative procedure, notwithstanding his or her inability to allege any discrete injury flowing from that failure. To understand the remarkable nature of this holding one must be clear about what it does *not* rest upon: This is not a case where plaintiffs are seeking to enforce a procedural requirement the disregard of which could impair a separate concrete interest of theirs (*e.g.*, the procedural requirement for a hearing prior to denial of their license application, or the procedural requirement for an environmental impact statement before a federal facility is constructed next door to them).[6] Nor is it simply a case where concrete injury has been suffered by many persons, as in mass fraud or mass tort situations. Nor, finally, is it the unusual case in which Congress has created a concrete private interest in the outcome of a suit against a private party for the government's benefit, by providing a cash bounty for the victorious plaintiff. Rather, the court held that the injury-in-fact requirement had been satisfied by congressional conferral upon *all* persons of an abstract, self-contained, noninstrumental "right" to have the Executive observe the procedures required by law. We reject this view.[7]

We have consistently held that a plaintiff raising only a generally available grievance about government—claiming only harm to his and every citizen's interest in proper application of the Constitution and laws, and seeking relief that no more directly and tangibly benefits him than it does the public at large—does not state an Article III case or controversy. . . .

We hold that respondents lack standing to bring this action and that the Court of Appeals erred in denying the summary judgment motion filed by the United States. The opinion of the Court of Appeals is hereby reversed, and the cause remanded for proceedings consistent with this opinion.

It is so ordered.

JUSTICE KENNEDY, with whom JUSTICE SOUTER joins, concurring in part and concurring in the judgment.

. . .

---

6. There is this much truth to the assertion that "procedural rights" are special: The person who has been accorded a procedural right to protect his concrete interests can assert that right without meeting all the normal standards for redressability and immediacy. Thus, under our case-law, one living adjacent to the site for proposed construction of a federally licensed dam has standing to challenge the licensing agency's failure to prepare an Environmental Impact Statement, even though he cannot establish with any certainty that the Statement will cause the license to be withheld or altered, and even though the dam will not be completed for many years. (That is why we do not rely, in the present case, upon the Government's argument that, *even if* the other agencies were obliged to consult with the Secretary, they might not have followed his advice.) What respondents' "procedural rights" argument seeks, however, is quite different from this: standing for persons who have no concrete interests affected—persons who live (and propose to live) at the other end of the country from the dam.

7. The dissent's discussion of this aspect of the case distorts our opinion. We do *not* hold that an individual cannot enforce procedural rights; he assuredly can, so long as the procedures in question are designed to protect some threatened concrete interest of his that is the ultimate basis of his standing. The dissent, however, asserts that there exist "classes of procedural duties . . . so enmeshed with the prevention of a substantive, concrete harm that an individual plaintiff may be able to demonstrate a sufficient likelihood of injury just through the breach of that procedural duty." If we understand this correctly, it means that the Government's violation of a certain (undescribed) class of procedural duty satisfies the concrete-injury requirement by itself, without any showing that the procedural violation endangers a concrete interest of the plaintiff (apart from his interest in having the procedure observed). We cannot agree. . . .

I agree with the Court's conclusion in Part III-A that, on the record before us, respondents have failed to demonstrate that they themselves are "among the injured." . . .

While it may seem trivial to require that Mss. Kelly and Skilbred acquire airline tickets to the project sites or announce a date certain upon which they will return, this is not a case where it is reasonable to assume that the affiants will be using the sites on a regular basis, nor do the affiants claim to have visited the sites since the projects commenced. With respect to the Court's discussion of respondents' "ecosystem nexus," "animal nexus," and "vocational nexus" theories, I agree that on this record respondents' showing is insufficient to establish standing on any of these bases. I am not willing to foreclose the possibility, however, that in different circumstances a nexus theory similar to those proffered here might support a claim to standing.

In light of the conclusion that respondents have not demonstrated a concrete injury here sufficient to support standing under our precedents, I would not reach the issue of redressability that is discussed by the plurality in Part III-B.

I also join Part IV of the Court's opinion with the following observations. As government programs and policies become more complex and far-reaching, we must be sensitive to the articulation of new rights of action that do not have clear analogs in our common-law tradition. Modern litigation has progressed far from the paradigm of Marbury suing Madison to get his commission or Ogden seeking an injunction to halt Gibbons' steamboat operations. In my view, Congress has the power to define injuries and articulate chains of causation that will give rise to a case or controversy where none existed before, and I do not read the Court's opinion to suggest a contrary view. In exercising this power, however, Congress must at the very least identify the injury it seeks to vindicate and relate the injury to the class of persons entitled to bring suit. The citizen-suit provision of the Endangered Species Act does not meet these minimal requirements, because while the statute purports to confer a right on "any person . . . to enjoin the United States and any other governmental instrumentality or agency . . . who is alleged to be in violation of any provision of this chapter," it does not of its own force establish that there is an injury in "any person" by virtue of any "violation." 16 U.S.C. §1540(g)(1)(A).

The Court's holding that there is an outer limit to the power of Congress to confer rights of action is a direct and necessary consequence of the case and controversy limitations found in Article III. I agree that it would exceed those limitations if, at the behest of Congress and in the absence of any showing of concrete injury, we were to entertain citizen-suits to vindicate the public's nonconcrete interest in the proper administration of the laws. While it does not matter how many persons have been injured by the challenged action, the party bringing suit must show that the action injures him in a concrete and personal way. This requirement is not just an empty formality. It preserves the vitality of the adversarial process by assuring both that the parties before the court have an actual, as opposed to professed, stake in the outcome, and that "the legal questions presented . . . will be resolved, not in the rarefied atmosphere of a debating society, but in a concrete factual context conducive to a realistic appreciation of the consequences of judicial action."

In addition, the requirement of concrete injury confines the Judicial Branch to its proper, limited role in the constitutional framework of Government.

An independent judiciary is held to account through its open proceedings and its reasoned judgments. In this process it is essential for the public to know what persons or groups are invoking the judicial power, the reasons that they have brought suit, and whether their claims are vindicated or denied. The concrete injury requirement helps assure that there can be an answer to these questions; and, as the Court's opinion is careful to show, that is part of the constitutional design.

With these observations, I concur in Parts I, II, III-A, and IV of the Court's opinion and in the judgment of the Court.

JUSTICE STEVENS, concurring in the judgment.

Because I am not persuaded that Congress intended the consultation requirement in §7(a)(2) of the Endangered Species Act of 1973 (ESA), 16 U.S.C. §1536(a)(2), to apply to activities in foreign countries, I concur in the judgment of reversal. I do not, however, agree with the Court's conclusion that respondents lack standing because the threatened injury to their interest in protecting the environment and studying endangered species is not "imminent." Nor do I agree with the plurality's additional conclusion that respondents' injury is not "redressable" in this litigation.

I

In my opinion a person who has visited the critical habitat of an endangered species has a professional interest in preserving the species and its habitat, and intends to revisit them in the future has standing to challenge agency action that threatens their destruction.

. . . [T]he "imminence" of such an injury should be measured by the timing and likelihood of the threatened environmental harm, rather than—as the Court seems to suggest—by the time that might elapse between the present and the time when the individuals would visit the area if no such injury should occur. . . .

The plurality also concludes that respondents' injuries are not redressable in this litigation. . . .

[But] [w]e must presume that if this Court holds that §7(a)(2) requires consultation, all affected agencies would abide by that interpretation and engage in the requisite consultations. Certainly the Executive Branch cannot be heard to argue that an authoritative construction of the governing statute by this Court may simply be ignored by any agency head. Moreover, if Congress has required consultation between agencies, we must presume that such consultation will have a serious purpose that is likely to produce tangible results. . . .

II

Although I believe that respondents have standing, I nevertheless concur in the judgment of reversal because I am persuaded that the Government is correct in its submission that §7(a)(2) does not apply to activities in foreign countries.

JUSTICE BLACKMUN, with whom JUSTICE O'CONNOR joins, dissenting.

I part company with the Court in this case in two respects. First, I believe that respondents have raised genuine issues of fact—sufficient to survive summary judgment—both as to injury and as to redressability. Second, I question the Court's breadth of language in rejecting standing for "procedural" injuries. I fear the Court seeks to impose fresh limitations on the constitutional authority of Congress to allow citizen-suits in the federal courts for injuries deemed "procedural" in nature. I dissent.

I

. . . To survive petitioner's motion for summary judgment on standing, respondents need not prove that they are actually or imminently harmed. They need show only a "genuine issue" of material fact as to standing. This is not a heavy burden. . . .

1

Were the Court to apply the proper standard for summary judgment, I believe it would conclude that the sworn affidavits and deposition testimony of Joyce Kelly and Amy Skilbred advance sufficient facts to create a genuine issue for trial concerning whether one or both would be imminently harmed by the Aswan and Mahaweli projects. . . .

. . . [A] reasonable finder of fact could conclude from the information in the affidavits and deposition testimony that either Kelly or Skilbred will soon return to the project sites, thereby satisfying the "actual or imminent" injury standard. . . .

By requiring a "description of concrete plans" or "specification of *when* the some day [for a return visit] will be" the Court, in my view, demands what is likely an empty formality. No substantial barriers prevent Kelly or Skilbred from simply purchasing plane tickets to return to the Aswan and Mahaweli projects. . . .

I fear the Court's demand for detailed descriptions of future conduct will do little to weed out those who are genuinely harmed from those who are not. More likely, it will resurrect a code-pleading formalism in federal court summary judgment practice, as federal courts, newly doubting their jurisdiction, will demand more and more particularized showings of future harm. . . .

2

The Court . . . rejects respondents' claim of vocational or professional injury. The Court says that it is "beyond all reason" that a zoo "keeper" of Asian elephants would have standing to contest his government's participation in the eradication of all the Asian elephants in another part of the world. I am unable to see how the distant location of the destruction *necessarily* (for purposes of ruling at summary judgment) mitigates the harm to the elephant keeper. If there is no more access to a future supply of the animal that sustains a keeper's livelihood, surely there is harm.

I have difficulty imagining this Court applying its rigid principles of geographic formalism anywhere outside the context of environmental claims. . . .

B

A plurality of the Court suggests that respondents have not demonstrated redressability: a likelihood that a court ruling in their favor would remedy their injury. The plurality identifies two obstacles. The first is that the "action agencies" (*e.g.*, AID) cannot be required to undertake consultation with petitioner Secretary, because they are not directly bound as parties to the suit and are otherwise not indirectly bound by being subject to petitioner Secretary's regulation. Petitioner, however, officially and publicly has taken the position that his regulations regarding consultation under §7 of the Act are binding on action agencies. . . .

. . . I am not as willing as the plurality is to assume that agencies at least will not try to follow the law. . . . I believe respondents' injury would likely be redressed by a favorable decision.

The second redressability obstacle relied on by the plurality is that "the [action] agencies generally supply only a fraction of the funding for a foreign project." What this Court might "generally" take to be true does not eliminate the existence of a genuine issue of fact to withstand summary judgment. Even if the action agencies supply only a fraction of the funding for a particular foreign project, it remains at least a question for the finder of fact whether threatened withdrawal of that fraction would affect foreign government conduct sufficiently to avoid harm to listed species.

The plurality states that "AID, for example, has provided less than 10% of the funding for the Mahaweli project." The plurality neglects to mention that this "fraction" amounts to $170 million, not so paltry a sum for a country of only 16 million people with a gross national product of less than $6 billion in 1986 when respondents filed the complaint in this action.

. . .

. . . The plurality overlooks an Interior Department memorandum listing eight endangered or threatened species in the Mahaweli project area and recounting that "[t]he Sri Lankan government has requested the assistance of AID in mitigating the negative impacts to the wildlife involved." . . .

I do not share the plurality's astonishing confidence that, on the record here, a factfinder could only conclude that AID was powerless to ensure the protection of listed species at the Mahaweli project. . . .

I find myself unable to agree with the plurality's analysis of redressability, based as it is on its invitation of executive lawlessness . . . , unfounded assumptions about causation, and erroneous conclusions about what the record does not say. In my view, respondents have satisfactorily shown a genuine issue of fact as to whether their injury would likely be redressed by a decision in their favor.

II

The Court concludes that any "procedural injury" suffered by respondents is insufficient to confer standing. . . .

Most governmental conduct can be classified as "procedural." . . .

The Court expresses concern that allowing judicial enforcement of "agencies' observance of a particular, statutorily prescribed procedure" would "transfer from the President to the courts the Chief Executive's most important constitutional duty, to 'take Care that the Laws be faithfully executed,' Art. II, sec. 3." In fact, the principal effect of foreclosing judicial enforcement of such procedures is to transfer power into the hands of the Executive at the expense — not of the courts — but of Congress, from which that power originates and emanates.

Under the Court's anachronistically formal view of the separation of powers, Congress legislates pure, substantive mandates and has no business structuring the procedural manner in which the Executive implements these mandates. . . .

Congress legislates in procedural shades of gray not to aggrandize its own power but to allow maximum Executive discretion in the attainment of Congress' legislative goals. . . . It is to be hoped that over time the Court will acknowledge that some classes of procedural duties are so enmeshed with the prevention of a substantive, concrete harm that an individual plaintiff may be able to demonstrate a sufficient likelihood of injury just through the breach of that procedural duty. For example, in the context of the NEPA requirement of environmental-impact statements, this Court has acknowledged "it is now well settled that NEPA itself does not mandate particular results [and] simply prescribes the necessary process," but "*these procedures are almost certain to affect the agency's substantive decision.*" Robertson v. Methow Valley Citizens Council, 490 U.S. 332, 350 (1989) (emphasis added). This acknowledgment of an inextricable link between procedural and substantive harm does not reflect improper appellate factfinding. It reflects nothing more than the proper deference owed to the judgment of a coordinate branch — Congress — that certain procedures are directly tied to protection against a substantive harm.

In short, determining "injury" for Article III standing purposes is a fact-specific inquiry. . . . There may be factual circumstances in which a congressionally imposed procedural requirement is so insubstantially connected to the prevention of a substantive harm that it cannot be said to work any conceivable injury to an individual litigant. But, as a general matter, the courts owe substantial deference to Congress' substantive purpose in imposing a certain procedural requirement. . . . There is no room for a *per se* rule or presumption excluding injuries labeled "procedural" in nature.

In conclusion, I cannot join the Court on what amounts to a slash-and-burn expedition through the law of environmental standing. In my view, "[t]he very essence of civil liberty certainly consists in the right of every individual to claim the protection of the laws, whenever he receives an injury." Marbury v. Madison, 1 Cranch 137, 163 (1803).

I dissent.

NOTES AND QUESTIONS ON *DEFENDERS OF WILDLIFE*

1. *Injury-in-fact. Defenders* requires that the injury be "imminent." Suppose that Defenders submitted affidavits showing that one of their members planned to go to Sri Lanka in five years. Would that be sufficiently imminent? Do you agree that the member must go to the place whence the species may vanish to be harmed by the loss of a species? Is the dissent correct to assert that this decision

demands more of a showing than is appropriate on a summary judgment motion with respect to injury? The concurrence supports the idea that Congress may create standing by defining injury and articulating chains of causation. Suppose that Congress passes a law granting any person the right to sue when an administrative action threatens a species they have observed in the wild or studied. Should the Court find that the Defenders of Wildlife affiants have standing?

2. *Procedural rights.* This case concerns the right to invoke a particular procedure, a consultation process for projects potentially affecting endangered species. Since procedures do not, by their nature, dictate outcomes, does it follow that claims of injuries from government failures to follow prescribed procedures cannot provide a sufficient basis for standing? *Cf.* Federal Election Commission v. Akins, 524 U.S. 11 (1998) (standing granted to seek information required to be disclosed); Summers v. Earth Island Institute, 555 U.S. 488 (2009) (denying citizens standing to challenge exemption of salvage timber sales from notice and comment and administrative appeal procedures).

3. *Causation.* Suppose that Defenders produced an affidavit showing a plan to go to the location of vanishing elephants within one year. Should the Court find that the causation requirement is met?

4. *Redressability.* Do Justice Scalia's views on redressability command a majority? Do you agree with him?

5. *Is standing for environmental plaintiffs different?* Justice Scalia suggests that environmental plaintiffs should have more difficulty establishing standing than regulated parties. How does he justify this conclusion? Is it fair that standing doctrine not place both sides of a controversy on an equal footing? Is it appropriate under Article III? *Cf.* Massachusetts v. EPA, 549 U.S. 497, 520-21 (2007) (suggesting that states as environmental plaintiffs enjoy some latitude in seeking standing).

6. *Implications.* Do you think that this case will seriously impair the ability of environmental groups to bring citizen suits? What effect do you expect it to have? *See Massachusetts*, 549 U.S. at 542 (dissenting opinion) (refusing to accept modeling predictions about global warming's impact in 2100 as a basis for imminent injury). What are the "obvious practical advantages" of challenging a rule, rather than individual applications of the rule? Do you expect citizens to eschew programmatic challenges in favor of challenging specific projects in light of the *Defenders* holding?

Defenders dealt with standing to try to avoid a potential future injury. The next two cases address standing to seek remedies for past violations of environmental statutes. As you read these cases, ask yourself if the Court converted the *Gwaltney* rule against citizen suits addressing wholly past violations from a statutory interpretation into a constitutional principle.

Steel Company v. Citizens for a Better Environment
523 U.S. 83 (1998)

JUSTICE SCALIA delivered the opinion of the Court.

This is a private enforcement action under the citizen-suit provision of the Emergency Planning and Community Right-To-Know Act of 1986 (EPCRA). . . .

I

Respondent, an association of individuals interested in environmental protection, sued petitioner, a small manufacturing company in Chicago, for past violations of EPCRA. EPCRA establishes a framework of state, regional and local agencies designed to inform the public about the presence of hazardous and toxic chemicals, and to provide for emergency response in the event of health-threatening release. Central to its operation are reporting requirements compelling users of specified toxic and hazardous chemicals to file annual "emergency and hazardous chemical inventory forms" and "toxic chemical release forms," which contain, *inter alia*, the name and location of the facility, the name and quantity of the chemical on hand, and, in the case of toxic chemicals, the waste-disposal method employed and the annual quantity released into each environmental medium. . . .

In 1995 respondent sent a notice to petitioner, the Administrator, and the relevant Illinois authorities, alleging—accurately, as it turns out—that petitioner had failed since 1988, the first year of EPCRA's filing deadlines, to complete and to submit the requisite hazardous-chemical inventory and toxic-chemical release forms. . . . Upon receiving the notice, petitioner filed all of the overdue forms with the relevant agencies. . . .

IV

. . .

The "irreducible constitutional minimum of standing" contains three requirements. First and foremost, there must be alleged (and ultimately proved) an "injury in fact"—a harm suffered by the plaintiff that is "concrete" and "actual or imminent, not 'conjectural' or 'hypothetical.'" Second, there must be causation—a fairly traceable connection between the plaintiff's injury and the complained-of conduct of the defendant. And third, there must be redressability—a likelihood that the requested relief will redress the alleged injury. This triad of injury in fact, causation, and redressability constitutes the core of Article III's case-or-controversy requirement, and the party invoking federal jurisdiction bears the burden of establishing its existence.

. . . The complaint contains claims "on behalf of both [respondent] itself and its members." It describes respondent as an organization that seeks, uses, and acquires data reported under EPCRA. It says that respondent "reports to its members and the public about storage and releases of toxic chemicals into the environment, advocates changes in environmental regulations and statutes, prepares reports for its members and the public, seeks the reduction of toxic chemicals and further seeks to promote the effective enforcement of environmental laws." The complaint asserts that respondent's "right to know about [toxic-chemical] releases and its interests in protecting and improving the environment and the health of its members have been, are being, and will be adversely affected by [petitioner's] actions in failing to provide timely and required information under EPCRA." The complaint also alleges that respondent's members, who live in or frequent the area near petitioner's facility, use the EPRCA-reported information "to learn about toxic chemical releases, the use of hazardous substances in their communities, to plan emergency preparedness in the event of accidents, and to attempt to reduce the toxic chemicals in areas in which they live, work and visit." The members' "safety, health, recreational, economic, aesthetic and environmental interests" in the information, it is claimed, "have been, are being, and will be adversely affected by [petitioner's] actions in failing to file timely and required reports under EPCRA."

As appears from the above, respondent asserts petitioner's failure to provide EPCRA information in a timely fashion, and the lingering effects of that failure, as the injury in fact to itself and its members. We have not had occasion to decide whether being deprived of information that is supposed to be disclosed under EPCRA—or at least being deprived of it when one has a particular plan for its use—is a concrete injury in fact that satisfies Article III. And we need not reach that question in the present case because, assuming injury in fact, the complaint fails the third test of standing, redressability.

The complaint asks for (1) a declaratory judgment that petitioner violated EPCRA; (2) authorization to inspect periodically petitioner's facility and records (with costs borne by petitioner); (3) an order requiring petitioner to provide respondent copies of all compliance reports submitted to the EPA; (4) an order requiring petitioner to pay civil penalties of $25,000 per day for each violation of §§11022 and 11023; (5) an award of all respondent's "costs, in connection with the investigation and prosecution of this matter, including reasonable attorney and expert witness fees, as authorized by Section 326(f) of [EPCRA]"; and (6) any such further relief as the court deems appropriate. None of the specific items of relief sought, and none that we can envision as "appropriate" under the general request, would serve to reimburse respondent for losses caused by the late reporting, or to eliminate any effects of that late reporting upon respondent.

The first item, the request for a declaratory judgment that petitioner violated EPCRA, can be disposed of summarily. There being no controversy over whether petitioner failed to file reports, or over whether such a failure constitutes a violation, the declaratory judgment is not only worthless to respondent, it is seemingly worthless to all the world.

Item (4), the civil penalties authorized by the statute might be viewed as a sort of compensation or redress to respondent if they were payable to respondent. But they are not. These penalties—the only damages authorized by EPCRA—are payable to the United States Treasury. In requesting them, therefore, respondent seeks not remediation of its own injury—reimbursement for the costs it incurred as a result of the late filing—but vindication of the rule of law—the "undifferentiated public interest" in faithful execution of EPCRA. This does not suffice. Justice Stevens thinks it is enough that respondent will be gratified by seeing petitioner punished for its infractions and that the punishment will deter the risk of future harm. . . . By the mere bringing of his suit, *every* plaintiff demonstrates his belief that a favorable judgment will make him happier. But although a suitor may derive great comfort and joy from the fact that the United States Treasury is not cheated, that a wrongdoer gets his just deserts, or that the Nation's laws are faithfully enforced, that psychic satisfaction is not an acceptable Article III remedy because it does not redress a cognizable Article III injury. Relief that does not remedy the injury suffered cannot bootstrap a plaintiff into federal court; that is the very essence of the redressability requirement.

[Justice Scalia states that the reimbursement for the cost of suing cannot constitute redressability for standing purposes.]

The remaining relief respondent seeks (item (2), giving respondent authority to inspect petitioner's facility and records, and item (3), compelling petitioner to provide respondent copies of EPA compliance reports) is injunctive in nature. It cannot conceivably remedy any past wrong but is aimed at deterring petitioner from violating EPCRA in the future. The latter objective can of course be "remedial" for Article III purposes, when threatened injury is one of the gravamens of the complaint. If respondent had alleged a continuing violation or the imminence of a future violation, the injunctive relief requested would remedy that alleged harm. But there is no such allegation here—and on the facts of the case, there seems no basis for it. Nothing supports the requested injunctive relief except respondent's generalized interest in deterrence, which is insufficient for purposes of Article III.

The United States, as *amicus curiae*, argues that the injunctive relief does constitute remediation because "there is a presumption of [future] injury when the defendant has voluntarily ceased its illegal activity in response to litigation," even if that occurs before a complaint is filed. This makes a sword out of a shield. The "presumption" the Government refers to has been applied to refute the assertion of mootness by a defendant who, when sued in a complaint that alleges present or threatened injury, ceases the complained-of activity. It is an immense and unacceptable stretch to call the presumption into service as a substitute for the allegation of present or threatened injury upon which initial standing must be based. To accept the Government's view would be to overrule our clear precedent requiring that the allegations of future injury be particular and concrete. "Past exposure to illegal conduct does not in itself show a present case or controversy regarding injunctive relief . . . if unaccompanied by any continuing, present adverse effects." Because respondent alleges only past infractions of EPRCA, and not a continuing violation or the likelihood of a future violation, injunctive relief will not redress its injury.

Having found that none of the relief sought by respondent would likely remedy its alleged injury in fact, we must conclude that respondent lacks standing to maintain this suit, and that we and the lower courts lack jurisdiction to entertain it. However desirable prompt resolution of the merits EPCRA question may be, it is not as important as observing the constitutional limits set upon courts in our system of separated powers. EPCRA will have to await another day.

The judgment is vacated and the case remanded with instructions to direct that the complaint be dismissed.

It is so ordered.

JUSTICE STEVENS, with whom JUSTICE SOUTER joins as to Parts I, III, and IV, and with whom JUSTICE GINSBURG joins as to Part III, concurring in the judgment.

* * *

II

. . .

. . . The Court's conclusion that respondent does not have standing comes from a mechanistic application of the "redressability" aspect of our standing doctrine. "Redressability," of course, does not appear anywhere in the text of the Constitution. Instead, it is a judicial creation of the past 25 years. . . .

[T]he Court has never held—until today—that a plaintiff who is *directly injured* by a defendant lacks standing to sue because of a lack of redressability.

The Court acknowledges that respondent would have had standing if Congress had authorized some payment to respondent. Yet the Court fails to specify why payment to respondent—even if only a peppercorn—would redress respondent's injuries, while payment to the Treasury does not. Respondent clearly believes that the punishment of the Steel Company, along with future deterrence of the Steel Company and others, redresses its injury, and there is no basis in our previous standing holdings to suggest otherwise.

When one private party is injured by another, the injury can be redressed in at least two ways: by awarding compensatory damages or by imposing a sanction on the wrongdoer that will minimize the risk that the harm-causing conduct will be repeated. Thus, in some cases a tort is redressed by an award of punitive damages; even when such damages are payable to the sovereign, they provide a form of redress for the individual as well.

History supports the proposition that punishment or deterrence can redress an injury. In past centuries in England, in the American colonies, and in the United States, private persons regularly prosecuted criminal cases. The interest in punishing the defendant and deterring violations of law by the defendant and others was sufficient to support the "standing" of the private prosecutor even if the only remedy was the sentencing of the defendant to jail or to the gallows. Given this history, the Framers of Article III surely would have considered such proceedings to be "Cases" that would "redress" an injury even though the party bringing suit did not receive any monetary compensation.

The Court's expanded interpretation of the redressability requirement has another consequence. Under EPCRA, Congress gave enforcement power to state and local governments. Under the Court's reasoning, however, state and local governments would not have standing to sue for past violations, as a payment to the Treasury would no more "redress" the injury of these governments than it would redress respondent's injury. This would be true *even if Congress explicitly granted state and local governments this power.* Such a conclusion is unprecedented.

[The concurring Justices, however, would hold that the citizen suit provision does not authorize suits for wholly past violations.]

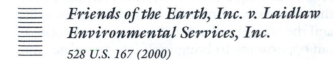

Friends of the Earth, Inc. v. Laidlaw Environmental Services, Inc.

528 U.S. 167 (2000)

Justice Ginsburg delivered the opinion of the Court.

This case presents an important question concerning the operation of the citizen-suit provisions of the Clean Water Act. Congress authorized the federal district courts to entertain Clean Water Act suits initiated by "a person or persons having an interest which is or may be adversely affected." To impel future compliance with the Act, a district court may prescribe injunctive relief in such a suit; additionally or alternatively, the court may impose civil penalties payable to the United States Treasury. In the Clean Water Act citizen suit now before us, the District Court determined that injunctive relief was inappropriate because the defendant, after the institution of the litigation, achieved substantial compliance with the terms of its discharge permit. The court did, however, assess a civil penalty of $405,800. The "total deterrent effect" of the penalty would be adequate to forestall future violations, the court reasoned, taking into account that the defendant "will be required to reimburse plaintiffs for a significant amount of legal fees and has, itself, incurred significant legal expenses."

The Court of Appeals vacated the District Court's order. The case became moot, the appellate court declared, once the defendant fully complied with the terms of its permit and the plaintiff failed to appeal the denial of equitable relief. "Civil penalties payable to the government," the Court of Appeals stated, "would not redress any injury Plaintiffs have suffered." Nor were attorneys' fees in order, the Court of Appeals noted, because absent relief on the merits, plaintiffs could not qualify as prevailing parties.

We reverse the judgment of the Court of Appeals. The appellate court erred in concluding that a citizen suitor's claim for civil penalties must be dismissed as moot when the defendant, albeit after commencement of the litigation, has come into compliance. In directing dismissal of the suit on grounds of mootness, the Court of Appeals incorrectly conflated our case law on initial standing to bring suit with our case law on post-commencement mootness. A defendant's voluntary cessation of allegedly unlawful conduct ordinarily does not suffice to moot a case. The Court of Appeals also misperceived the remedial potential of civil penalties. Such penalties may serve, as an alternative to an injunction, to deter future violations and thereby redress the injuries that prompted a citizen suitor to commence litigation.

I

A

. . .

Under §505(a) of the Act, a suit to enforce any limitation in an NPDES [National Pollutant Discharge Elimination System] permit may be brought by any "citizen," defined as "a person or persons having an interest which is or may be adversely affected." Sixty days before initiating a citizen suit, however, the would-be plaintiff must give notice of the alleged violation to the EPA, the State in which the alleged violation occurred, and the alleged violator. "The purpose of notice to the alleged violator is to give it an opportunity to bring itself into complete compliance with the Act and thus render unnecessary a citizen suit." Accordingly, we have held that citizens lack statutory standing under §505(a) to sue for violations that have ceased by the time the complaint is filed. The Act also bars a citizen from suing if the EPA or the State has already commenced, and is "diligently prosecuting," an enforcement action.

. . .

B

In 1986, defendant-respondent Laidlaw Environmental Services (TOC), Inc., bought a hazardous waste incinerator facility in Roebuck, South Carolina, that included a wastewater treatment plant. . . .

. . . [Laidlaw] received [an NPDES] permit, [and] began to discharge various pollutants into the waterway; repeatedly, Laidlaw's discharges exceeded the limits set by the permit. . . .

On April 10, 1992, plaintiff-petitioner Friends of the Earth (FOE) . . . sent a letter to Laidlaw notifying the company of their intention to file a citizen suit against it under §505(a) of the Act after the expiration of the requisite 60-day notice period. . . . Laidlaw's lawyer then contacted DHEC [the South Carolina Department of Health and Environmental Control] to ask whether DHEC would consider filing a lawsuit against Laidlaw. The District Court later found that Laidlaw's reason for requesting that DHEC file a lawsuit against it was to bar FOE's proposed citizen suit through the [statutory diligent prosecution bar]. DHEC agreed to file a lawsuit against Laidlaw; the company's lawyer then drafted the complaint for DHEC and paid the filing fee. On June 9, 1992, the last day before FOE's 60-day notice period expired, DHEC and Laidlaw reached a settlement requiring Laidlaw to pay $100,000 in civil penalties and to make " 'every effort' " to comply with its permit obligations.

On June 12, 1992, FOE filed this citizen suit against Laidlaw under §505(a) of the Act, alleging noncompliance with the NPDES permit and seeking declaratory and injunctive relief and an award of civil penalties. Laidlaw moved for summary judgment on the ground that FOE had failed to present evidence demonstrating injury in fact, and therefore lacked Article III standing to bring the lawsuit. . . . [T]he District Court denied Laidlaw's summary judgment motion, finding that FOE had standing to bring the suit.

Laidlaw also moved to dismiss the action on the ground that the citizen suit was barred . . . by DHEC's prior action against the company. The . . . District Court held that DHEC's action against Laidlaw had not been "diligently prosecuted"; consequently, the court allowed FOE's citizen suit to proceed. The record indicates that after FOE initiated the suit, but before the District Court rendered judgment, Laidlaw violated the mercury discharge limitation in its permit 13 times. The District Court also found that Laidlaw had committed 13 monitoring and 10 reporting violations during this period. The last recorded mercury discharge violation occurred in January 1995, long after the complaint was filed but about two years before judgment was rendered.

On January 22, 1997, the District Court issued its judgment, . . . [awarding civil penalties, but declining injunctive relief on the ground that] "Laidlaw has been in substantial compliance with all parameters in its NPDES permit since at least August 1992."

FOE appealed the District Court's civil penalty judgment, arguing that the penalty was inadequate, but did not appeal the denial of declaratory or injunctive relief. Laidlaw cross-appealed, arguing, among other things, that FOE lacked standing to bring the suit. . . .

On July 16, 1998, the Court of Appeals for the Fourth Circuit issued its judgment. The Court of Appeals assumed without deciding that FOE initially had standing to bring the action, but went on to hold that the case had become moot. The appellate court stated, first, that the elements of Article III standing—injury, causation, and redressability—must persist at every stage of review, or else the action becomes moot. Citing our decision in *Steel Co.*, the Court of Appeals reasoned that the case had become moot because "the only remedy currently available to [FOE]—civil penalties payable to the government—would not redress any injury [FOE has] suffered." The court therefore vacated the District Court's order and remanded with instructions to dismiss the action. In a footnote, the Court of Appeals added that FOE's "failure to obtain relief on the merits of [its] claims precludes any recovery of attorneys' fees or other litigation costs because such an award is available only to a 'prevailing or substantially prevailing party.'"

According to Laidlaw, after the Court of Appeals issued its decision but before this Court granted certiorari, the entire incinerator facility in Roebuck was permanently closed, dismantled, and put up for sale, and all discharges from the facility permanently ceased.

We granted certiorari to resolve the inconsistency between the Fourth Circuit's decision in this case and the decisions of several other Courts of Appeals, which have held that a defendant's compliance with its permit after the commencement of litigation does not moot claims for civil penalties under the Act.

II

A...

   ...

In *Lujan v. Defenders of Wildlife*, we held that, to satisfy Article III's standing requirements, a plaintiff must show (1) it has suffered an "injury in fact" that is (a) concrete and particularized and (b) actual or imminent, not conjectural or hypothetical; (2) the injury is fairly traceable to the challenged action of the defendant; and (3) it is likely, as opposed to merely speculative, that the injury will be redressed by a favorable decision....

Laidlaw contends first that FOE lacked standing from the outset even to seek injunctive relief, because the plaintiff organizations failed to show that any of their members had sustained or faced the threat of any "injury in fact" from Laidlaw's activities. In support of this contention Laidlaw points to the District Court's finding, made in the course of setting the penalty amount, that there had been "no demonstrated proof of harm to the environment" from Laidlaw's mercury discharge violations.

The relevant showing for purposes of Article III standing, however, is not injury to the environment but injury to the plaintiff. To insist upon the former rather than the latter as part of the standing inquiry ... is to raise the standing hurdle higher than the necessary showing for success on the merits in an action alleging noncompliance with an NPDES permit. Focusing properly on injury to the plaintiff, the District Court found that FOE had demonstrated sufficient injury to establish standing. For example, FOE member Kenneth Lee Curtis averred in affidavits that he lived a half-mile from Laidlaw's facility; that he occasionally drove over the North Tyger River, and that it looked and smelled polluted; and that he would like to fish, camp, swim, and picnic in and near the river between 3 and 15 miles downstream from the facility, as he did when he was a teenager, but would not do so because he was concerned that the water was polluted by Laidlaw's discharges. . . .

These sworn statements, as the District Court determined, adequately documented injury in fact. We have held that environmental plaintiffs adequately allege injury in fact when they aver that they use the affected area and are persons "for whom the aesthetic and recreational values of the area will be lessened" by the challenged activity.

. . .

Laidlaw argues next that even if FOE had standing to seek injunctive relief, it lacked standing to seek civil penalties. Here the asserted defect is not injury but redressability. Civil penalties offer no redress to private plaintiffs, Laidlaw argues, because they are paid to the government, and therefore a citizen plaintiff can never have standing to seek them.

. . .

We have recognized on numerous occasions that "all civil penalties have some deterrent effect." More specifically, Congress has found that civil penalties in Clean Water Act cases do more than promote immediate compliance by limiting the defendant's economic incentive to delay its attainment of permit limits; they also deter future violations. This congressional determination warrants judicial attention and respect. "The legislative history of the Act reveals that Congress wanted the district court to consider the need for retribution and deterrence, in addition to restitution, when it imposed civil penalties. . . . [The district court may] seek to deter future violations by basing the penalty on its economic impact."

It can scarcely be doubted that, for a plaintiff who is injured or faces the threat of future injury due to illegal conduct ongoing at the time of suit, a sanction that effectively abates that conduct and prevents its recurrence provides a form of redress. Civil penalties can fit that description. To the extent that they encourage defendants to discontinue current violations and deter them from committing future ones, they afford redress to citizen plaintiffs who are injured or threatened with injury as a consequence of ongoing unlawful conduct.

The dissent argues that it is the *availability* rather than the *imposition* of civil penalties that deters any particular polluter from continuing to pollute. This argument misses the mark in two ways. First, it overlooks the interdependence of the availability and the imposition; a threat has no deterrent value unless it is credible that it will be carried out. Second, it is reasonable for Congress to conclude that an actual award of civil penalties does in fact bring with it a significant quantum of deterrence over and above what is achieved by the mere prospect of such penalties. A would-be polluter may or may not be dissuaded by the existence of a remedy on the books, but a defendant once hit in its pocketbook will surely think twice before polluting again.

. . .

Laidlaw contends that the reasoning of our decision in *Steel Co.* directs the conclusion that citizen plaintiffs have no standing to seek civil penalties under the

Act. We disagree. *Steel Co.* established that citizen suitors lack standing to seek civil penalties for violations that have abated by the time of suit. We specifically noted in that case that there was no allegation in the complaint of any continuing or imminent violation, and that no basis for such an allegation appeared to exist. In short, *Steel Co.* held that private plaintiffs, unlike the Federal Government, may not sue to assess penalties for wholly past violations, but our decision in that case did not reach the issue of standing to seek penalties for violations that are ongoing at the time of the complaint and that could continue into the future if undeterred.[8]

B

Satisfied that FOE had standing under Article III to bring this action, we turn to the question of mootness.

The only conceivable basis for a finding of mootness in this case is Laidlaw's voluntary conduct—either its achievement by August 1992 of substantial compliance with its NPDES permit or its more recent shutdown of the Roebuck facility. It is well settled that "a defendant's voluntary cessation of a challenged practice does not deprive a federal court of its power to determine the legality of the practice." . . . In accordance with this principle, the standard we have announced for determining whether a case has been mooted by the defendant's voluntary conduct is stringent: "A case might become moot if subsequent events made it absolutely clear that the allegedly wrongful behavior could not reasonably be expected to recur." The "heavy burden of persuading" the court that the challenged conduct cannot reasonably be expected to start up again lies with the party asserting mootness.

The Court of Appeals justified its mootness disposition by reference to *Steel Co.*, which held that citizen plaintiffs lack standing to seek civil penalties for wholly past violations. In relying on *Steel Co.*, the Court of Appeals confused mootness with standing. The confusion is understandable, given this Court's repeated statements that the doctrine of mootness can be described as "the doctrine of standing set in a time frame: The requisite personal interest that must exist at the commencement of the litigation (standing) must continue throughout its existence (mootness)."

. . .

Standing doctrine functions to ensure, among other things, that the scarce resources of the federal courts are devoted to those disputes in which the parties have a concrete stake. In contrast, by the time mootness is an issue, the case has been brought and litigated, often (as here) for years. To abandon the case at an advanced stage may prove more wasteful than frugal. . . .

Laidlaw . . . asserts . . . that the closure of its Roebuck facility, which took place after the Court of Appeals issued its decision, mooted the case. The facility

---

8. . . . [T]he dissent's broader charge that citizen suits for civil penalties under the Act carry "grave implications for democratic governance" seems to us overdrawn. Certainly the Federal Executive Branch does not share the dissent's view that such suits dissipate its authority to enforce the law. In fact, the Department of Justice has endorsed this citizen suit from the outset, submitting *amicus* briefs in support of FOE in the District Court, the Court of Appeals, and this Court. As we have already noted, the Federal Government retains the power to foreclose a citizen suit by undertaking its own action. And if the Executive Branch opposes a particular citizen suit, the statute allows the Administrator of the EPA to "intervene as a matter of right" and bring the Government's views to the attention of the court.

closure, like Laidlaw's earlier achievement of substantial compliance with its permit requirements, might moot the case, but—we once more reiterate—only if one or the other of these events made it absolutely clear that Laidlaw's permit violations could not reasonably be expected to recur. The effect of both Laidlaw's compliance and the facility closure on the prospect of future violations is a disputed factual matter. FOE points out, for example and Laidlaw does not appear to contest—that Laidlaw retains its NPDES permit. These issues have not been aired in the lower courts; they remain open for consideration on remand.

. . .

For the reasons stated, the judgment of the United States Court of Appeals for the Fourth Circuit is reversed, and the case is remanded for further proceedings consistent with this opinion.

It is so ordered.

JUSTICE SCALIA, with whom JUSTICE THOMAS joins, dissenting.

The Court begins its analysis by finding injury in fact on the basis of vague affidavits that are undermined by the District Court's express finding that Laidlaw's discharges caused no demonstrable harm to the environment. It then proceeds to marry private wrong with public remedy in a union that violates traditional principles of federal standing—thereby permitting law enforcement to be placed in the hands of private individuals. Finally, the Court suggests that to avoid mootness one needs even less of a stake in the outcome than the Court's watered-down requirements for initial standing. I dissent from all of this.

I

Plaintiffs, as the parties invoking federal jurisdiction, have the burden of proof and persuasion as to the existence of standing. The plaintiffs in this case fell far short of carrying their burden of demonstrating injury in fact. . . .

Typically, an environmental plaintiff claiming injury due to discharges in violation of the Clean Water Act argues that the discharges harm the environment, and that the harm to the environment injures him. This route to injury is barred in the present case, however, since the District Court concluded after considering all the evidence that there had been "no demonstrated proof of harm to the environment," that the "permit violations at issue in this citizen suit did not result in any health risk or environmental harm," that "all available data . . . fail to show that Laidlaw's *actual* discharges have resulted in harm to the North Tyger River," and that "the overall quality of the river exceeds levels necessary to support . . . recreation in and on the water."

The Court finds these conclusions unproblematic for standing, because "the relevant showing for purposes of Article III standing . . . is not injury to the environment but injury to the plaintiff." This statement is correct, as far as it goes. We have certainly held that a demonstration of harm to the environment is not *enough* to satisfy the injury-in-fact requirement unless the plaintiff can demonstrate how he personally was harmed. In the normal course, however, a lack of demonstrable harm to the environment will translate, as it plainly does here, into a lack of demonstrable harm to citizen plaintiffs. . . .

. . . By accepting plaintiffs' vague, contradictory, and unsubstantiated allegations of "concern" about the environment as adequate to prove injury in fact, and accepting them even in the face of a finding that the environment was not demonstrably harmed, the Court makes the injury-in-fact requirement a sham. If there are permit violations, and a member of a plaintiff environmental organization lives near the offending plant, it would be difficult not to satisfy today's lenient standard.

II

The Court's treatment of the redressability requirement—which would have been unnecessary if it resolved the injury-in-fact question correctly—is equally cavalier. . . . Only last Term, we held that penalties [paid to the United States Treasury] do not redress any injury a citizen plaintiff has suffered from past violations. The Court nonetheless finds the redressability requirement satisfied here, distinguishing *Steel Co.* on the ground that in this case the petitioners allege ongoing violations; payment of the penalties, it says, will remedy petitioners' injury by deterring future violations by Laidlaw. It holds that a penalty payable to the public "remedies" a threatened private harm, and suffices to sustain a private suit.

That holding has no precedent in our jurisprudence, and takes this Court beyond the "cases and controversies" that Article III of the Constitution has entrusted to its resolution. Even if it were appropriate, moreover, to allow Article III's remediation requirement to be satisfied by the indirect private consequences of a public penalty, those consequences are entirely too speculative in the present case. The new standing law that the Court makes—like all expansions of standing beyond the traditional constitutional limits—has grave implications for democratic governance. . . .

A . . .

. . . [R]elief against prospective harm is traditionally afforded by way of an injunction, the scope of which is limited by the scope of the threatened injury. In seeking to overturn that tradition by giving an individual plaintiff the power to invoke a public remedy, Congress has done precisely what we have said it cannot do: convert an "undifferentiated public interest" into an "individual right" vindicable in the courts. The sort of scattershot redress approved today makes nonsense of our statement . . . that the requirement of injury in fact "insures the framing of relief no broader than required by the precise facts." A claim of particularized future injury has today been made the vehicle for pursuing generalized penalties for past violations, and a threshold showing of injury in fact has become a lever that will move the world.

B

As I have just discussed, it is my view that a plaintiff's desire to benefit from the deterrent effect of a public penalty for past conduct can never suffice to establish a case or controversy of the sort known to our law. Such deterrent effect is, so to speak, "speculative as a matter of law." Even if that were not so, however, the deterrent effect in the present case would surely be speculative as a matter of fact.

The Court recognizes, of course, that to satisfy Article III, it must be "likely," as opposed to "merely speculative," that a favorable decision will redress plaintiffs' injury. Further, the Court recognizes that not *all* deterrent effects of *all* civil penalties will meet this standard—though it declines to "explore the outer limits" of adequate deterrence. It concludes, however, that in the present case "the civil penalties sought by FOE carried with them a deterrent effect" that satisfied the "likely [rather than] speculative" standard. There is little in the Court's opinion to explain why it believes this is so.

The Court cites the District Court's conclusion that the penalties imposed, along with anticipated fee awards, provided "adequate deterrence." There is absolutely no reason to believe, however, that this meant "deterrence adequate to prevent an injury to these plaintiffs that would otherwise occur."

. . .

If the Court had undertaken the necessary inquiry into whether significant deterrence of the plaintiffs' feared injury was "likely," it would have had to reason something like this: Strictly speaking, no polluter is deterred by a penalty for past pollution; he is deterred by the *fear* of a penalty for *future* pollution. That fear will be virtually nonexistent if the prospective polluter knows that all emissions violators are given a free pass; it will be substantial under an emissions program such as the federal scheme here, which is regularly and notoriously enforced; it will be even higher when a prospective polluter subject to such a regularly enforced program has, as here, been the object of public charges of pollution and a suit for injunction; and it will surely be near the top of the graph when, as here, the prospective polluter has already been subjected to *state* penalties for the past pollution. The deterrence on which the plaintiffs must rely for standing in the present case is the marginal increase in Laidlaw's fear of future penalties that will be achieved by adding federal penalties for Laidlaw's past conduct.

I cannot say for certain that this marginal increase is zero; but I can say for certain that it is entirely speculative whether it will make the difference between these plaintiffs' suffering injury in the future and these plaintiffs' going unharmed. In fact, the assertion that it will "likely" do so is entirely far-fetched. . . .

In sum, if this case is, as the Court suggests, within the central core of "deterrence" standing, it is impossible to imagine what the "outer limits" could possibly be. The Court's expressed reluctance to define those "outer limits" serves only to disguise the fact that it has promulgated a revolutionary new doctrine of standing that will permit the entire body of public civil penalties to be handed over to enforcement by private interests.

C

Article II of the Constitution commits it to the President to "take Care that the Laws be faithfully executed," Art. II, §3, and provides specific methods by which all persons exercising significant executive power are to be appointed, Art. II, §2. As Justice Kennedy's concurrence correctly observes, the question of the conformity of this legislation with Article II has not been argued—and I, like the

Court, do not address it. But Article III, no less than Article II, has consequences for the structure of our government, and it is worth noting the changes in that structure which today's decision allows.

By permitting citizens to pursue civil penalties payable to the Federal Treasury, the Act does not provide a mechanism for individual relief in any traditional sense, but turns over to private citizens the function of enforcing the law. A Clean Water Act plaintiff pursuing civil penalties acts as a self-appointed mini-EPA. Where, as is often the case, the plaintiff is a national association, it has significant discretion in choosing enforcement targets. Once the association is aware of a reported violation, it need not look long for an injured member, at least under the theory of injury the Court applies today. And once the target is chosen, the suit goes forward without meaningful public control. The availability of civil penalties vastly disproportionate to the individual injury gives citizen plaintiffs massive bargaining power—which is often used to achieve settlements requiring the defendant to support environmental projects of the plaintiffs' choosing. Thus is a public fine diverted to a private interest.

To be sure, the EPA may foreclose the citizen suit by itself bringing suit. This allows public authorities to avoid private enforcement only by accepting private direction as to when enforcement should be undertaken—which is no less constitutionally bizarre. Elected officials are entirely deprived of their discretion to decide that a given violation should not be the object of suit at all, or that the enforcement decision should be postponed. This is the predictable and inevitable consequence of the Court's allowing the use of public remedies for private wrongs.

III

. . .

By uncritically accepting vague claims of injury, the Court has turned the Article III requirement of injury in fact into a "mere pleading requirement"; and by approving the novel theory that public penalties can redress anticipated private wrongs, it has come close to "making the redressability requirement vanish." The undesirable and unconstitutional consequence of today's decision is to place the immense power of suing to enforce the public laws in private hands. I respectfully dissent.

NOTES AND QUESTIONS ON *LAIDLAW* AND *STEEL COMPANY*

1. *Consistency.* Are *Laidlaw* and *Steel Co.* consistent? How does the *Laidlaw* Court seek to distinguish *Steel Co.*? Do you find the distinction drawn persuasive? Do penalties redress an injury or not? Would an injury alleged in the *Steel Co.* case be redressable if Congress allowed plaintiffs to keep some or all of the penalties, instead of directing that they go the federal treasury?

2. *Injury-in-fact.* The *Laidlaw* majority relies upon injury to the plaintiff as opposed to injury to the environment. This distinction helps justify the Court's acceptance of Friends of the Earth's (FOE) allegations that the discharges at issue here limit its members' use of the North Tyger River. Justice Scalia, however,

would require citizen enforcers to prove that the particular discharge prompting the citizen suit damaged the environment the plaintiffs would like to use. Suppose that Justice Scalia's approach had become the law. Would this greatly damage the capacity of citizen suits to serve as an effective deterrent? Why does the majority claim that requiring proof of environmental harm "raises the standing bar higher than necessary for success on the merits"? What must plaintiffs prove to show an NPDES violation?

On the other hand, does acceptance of plaintiffs' allegations without proof of environmental harm mean that the Court has accepted purely psychological harms as the basis for an injury-in-fact allegation? If so, is that appropriate?

3. *The legitimacy of citizen suits.* Justice Scalia expresses grave doubts about the legitimacy of citizen suits in his *Laidlaw* dissent:

> By permitting citizens to pursue civil penalties payable to the Federal Treasury, the Act does not provide a mechanism for individual relief in any traditional sense, but turns over to private citizens the function of enforcing the law. A Clean Water Act plaintiff pursuing civil penalties acts as a self-appointed mini-EPA. Where, as is often the case, the plaintiff is a national association, it has significant discretion in choosing enforcement targets. Once the association is aware of a reported violation, it need not look long for an injured member, at least under the theory of injury the Court applies today. And once the target is chosen, the suit goes forward without meaningful public control. The availability of civil penalties vastly disproportionate to the individual injury gives citizen plaintiffs massive bargaining power which is often used to achieve settlements requiring the defendant to support environmental projects of the plaintiffs' choosing. Thus is a public fine diverted to a private interest.

Laidlaw, 528 U.S. at 209-10. Do you agree that a settlement creating an environmental project chosen by an environmental organization diverts "a public fine to a private interest"? Does the lack of public control over an environmental organization's choice of enforcement targets interfere with the Executive Branch's duty to "take care the law is faithfully executed"? *See* William W. Buzbee, *Standing and the Statutory Universe*, 11 Duke Envtl. L. & Pol'y Forum 247, 276 (2001) (arguing that citizen suits vindicate several layers of political judgment employed in setting standards).

C. ATTORNEYS' FEES

While citizen enforcement may supplement government enforcement of environmental law, few attorneys can afford to bring citizen suits frequently, unless there is some prospect of reimbursement for the costs involved in bringing suit, including attorneys' fees. In Alyeska Pipeline Service Co. v. Wilderness Society, 421 U.S. 240 (1975), the Supreme Court reversed a decision employing a court's equitable discretion to award attorneys' fees to an environmental group suing to force the Department of the Interior to comply with the Mineral Leasing Act of 1920 and the National Environmental Policy Act of 1969. The Supreme Court held that the use of attorneys' fees to reward successful private attorneys general conflicted with the traditional "American rule," which generally requires each side to bear its own costs.

In order to encourage citizen enforcement, Congress ordered a departure from the American rule in several environmental statutes. But the Court construed these departures narrowly. In Ruckelshaus v. Sierra Club, 463 U.S. 680 (1983), the Court interpreted a Clean Air Act provision authorizing attorneys' fees "whenever [the court] determines that such award is appropriate." Although the provision on its face seemed to offer district courts wide latitude in deciding whether to award a fee, the Court, in a 5-4 decision, reversed a ruling awarding a fee to an environmental group that had, in the Court's judgment, helped EPA ward off some industry challenges, but had not prevailed on any of its own claims. The Court insisted that fee awards were only appropriate if the citizen suing was a prevailing party.

The courts have generally defined a "prevailing party" as one that succeeds on any significant issue in litigation that achieves some of the benefits the party sought in bringing suit. See Hensley v. Eckerhart, 461 U.S. 424, 433 (1983). An issue often arises as to whether citizens can collect attorneys' fees when the government (or other defendant) voluntarily complies with the law to avoid suit. The courts have generally allowed plaintiffs to collect fees on a "catalyst" theory, when its suit seemed to cause the defendant to conform its conduct to the law. See, e.g., Environmental Defense Fund v. EPA, 716 F.2d 916, 919 (D.C. Cir. 1983) (allowing fees in a RCRA case on a catalyst theory). In Buckhannon Board and Care Home, Inc. v. West Virginia Dep't of Health and Human Resources, 532 U.S. 598, 605 (2001), however, the Supreme Court interpreted provisions in federal civil rights statutes awarding fees to prevailing parties as not embracing a catalyst theory. The lower courts, however, have continued to adhere to the catalyst theory in citizen suits under provisions offering fees where "appropriate," see, e.g., Ass'n of California Water Agencies v. Evans, 386 F.3d 879, 885 (9th Cir. 2004) (Endangered Species Act); Sierra Club v. EPA, 322 F.3d 718, 721-26 (D.C. Cir. 2003) (Clean Air Act); Loggerhead Turtle v. County Council of Volusia County, 307 F.3d 1318, 1325-27 (11th Cir. 2002) (Endangered Species Act); Center for Biological Diversity v. Norton, 262 F.3d 1077, 1080 n.2 (10th Cir. 2001) (assuming that a catalyst theory applies), but not under provisions offering fees to "substantially prevailing parties," see Sierra Club v. City of Little Rock, 351 F.3d 840, 845-46 (8th Cir. 2004) (reversing an attorneys' fee award predicated upon a catalyst theory under the Clean Water Act). The courts continuing to grant fees in catalyst cases relied on the citizen suit provisions' language authorizing an award of fees "whenever appropriate" and upon legislative history suggesting congressional support for liberal granting of fees to encourage citizen suits.

Often, plaintiffs prevail on some of their claims, but not others. The courts often award a full fee award in such cases, because it is difficult to apportion fees between interrelated claims. See Hensley, 461 U.S. at 435-38 (declining to divide up a fee award in a civil rights case, but suggesting that division may sometimes be appropriate).

The Court trimmed fees in City of Burlington v. Dague, 505 U.S. 557 (1992). Generally, courts calculate a "lodestar" attorneys' fee by multiplying the reasonable hours invested in litigation by a "reasonable" hourly rate, typically determined by the prevailing rates for attorneys with comparable experience in the relevant community. In *Dague*, however, the lower court had increased the fee to reflect the risk that the plaintiff might get no fees at all, since he had accepted the case on a contingency basis (*i.e.*, no victory, no payment). The Court held that trial courts should not augment attorneys' fees in citizen suits to reflect the difficulty of the case and the risks involved. Justice Scalia, writing for the majority, expressed a concern that providing a risk premium would "provide attorneys with the same incentive to bring relatively meritless claims as relatively meritorious ones." Do you think that providing a risk premium (raising fee awards for especially complex or risky cases) would have this effect? *See* DAVID M. DRIESEN, THE ECONOMIC DYNAMICS OF ENVIRONMENTAL LAW 143 (2003). How much does the attorney collect if he loses his client's case?

Does the current approach to attorneys' fees provide an adequate incentive to bring citizen suits? Does it provide an incentive for too much litigation? *See* Michael S. Greve, *The Private Enforcement of Environmental Law*, 65 TUL. L. REV. 339 (1990) (arguing that the citizen suit provisions create too much deterrence). What, if any, reforms should Congress enact to improve the incentives provided for citizen suits?

D. ENFORCEMENT: A GENERAL ASSESSMENT

In spite of the array of statutory provisions aimed at enforcement, noncompliance remains widespread. *See, e.g.*, Robert W. Adler & Charles Lord, *Environmental Crimes: Raising the Stakes*, 59 GEO. WASH. L. REV. 781, 789 (1990-1991) (discussing reports by the General Accounting Office and various environmental organizations). Although data gaps make it difficult to draw clear lessons about whether a deterrence strategy or a cooperative enforcement strategy works best, a correlation exists between increased state per capita spending on environmental protection and compliance. *See* Victor B. Flatt & Paul M. Collins, Jr., *Environmental Enforcement in Dire Straits: There Is No Protection for Nothing and No Data for Free*, 85 NOTRE DAME L. REV. 55 (2009). Reports show a significant decline in civil penalty assessment, but an increase in the reported value of injunctive relief over the decade preceding the Obama Administration. *See* UNITED STATES GENERAL ACCOUNTING OFFICE, CLEAN WATER ACT: LONGSTANDING ISSUES IMPACT EPA'S AND STATE'S ENFORCEMENT EFFORTS (2009); UNITED STATES GENERAL ACCOUNTING OFFICE, ENVIRONMENTAL ENFORCEMENT: EPA NEEDS TO IMPROVE THE ACCURACY AND TRANSPARENCY OF MEASURES USED TO REPORT PROGRAM EFFECTIVENESS 3 (2008) (finding a decline in penalty assessment from $240.6 million in 1998 to $137.7 in 2007, but an increase in the estimated value of injunctive relief from $4.4 billion to $10.9 billion over a similar period). EPA, however, only reports the fines it assesses, not the amounts collected, and recent reports emphasize a failure to consistently track and collect assessed penalties. The estimates of the value of injunctive relief constitute projections, sometimes relying on the violator's information, and do not necessarily reflect completed cleanups. EPA has increased its reliance on state enforcement in recent years, but state and federal enforcement resources have not nearly kept up with inflation or the increasing scope of regulatory programs.

CLIMATE DISRUPTION CITIZEN SUIT PROBLEM

The Clean Air Act includes the following provisions:

§7604. Citizen suits
(a) Authority to bring civil action; jurisdiction
Except as provided in subsection (b) of this section, any person may commence a civil action on his own behalf—

(1) against any person . . . who is alleged to have violated (if there is evidence that the alleged violation has been repeated) or to be in violation of (A) an emission standard or limitation under this chapter or (B) an order issued by the Administrator or a State with respect to such a standard or limitation. . . .

(b) Notice
No action may be commenced—

(1) under subsection (a)(1) of this section—

(A) prior to 60 days after the plaintiff has given notice of the violation . . . or

(B) if the Administrator or State has commenced and is diligently prosecuting a civil action in a court of the United States or a State to require compliance with the standard, limitation, or order, but in any such action in a court of the United States any person may intervene as a matter of right.

1. *Diligent prosecution.* Suppose that EPA has just agreed to settle its enforcement case against North American Automobile Manufacturers (NAAM) for the conduct discussed previously—selling Sizzler sedans that are equipped with the manual misfiring override switch. According to the terms of the draft consent decree, in exchange for EPA dropping the case, NAAM agrees to plant 200 acres of trees. Citizens Against Climate Disruption is outraged. Can the organization file a citizen suit against NAAM seeking civil penalties for the same alleged violations that form the basis of EPA's enforcement action?

2. *Standing.* Does Citizens Against Climate Disruption have standing to sue NAAM for violations of the Clean Air Act? Consider the following facts: Members of Citizens Against Climate Disruption enjoy hiking and birdwatching on Long Beach Island, a barrier island off the New Jersey coast. The group has scheduled several outings on Long Beach Island for the upcoming year. The group estimates that NAAM's installation of misfire override switches in 1,000 vehicles could result in the addition of 50,000 metric tons of carbon dioxide. In 2007, the total global contribution of carbon dioxide emissions from the burning of fossil fuels was approximately 29 gigatons, or 29 billion metric tons, of which the United States' portion was approximately 6 gigatons, or 6 billion metric tons. Motor vehicles are responsible for approximately a quarter of carbon dioxide emissions in the United States.

Table of Cases

Principal cases appear in italics.

Index